CORRECTION CHART

The following abbreviations and symbols may be used by your instructor when marking your papers. Refer to the page numbers in parentheses for discussions of each topic.

agr	faulty agreement (347–348, 378–380, 381–384)
cap	capitalize (461–463)
cf	comma fault (411–415)
cs	comma splice (350, 371–373)
dangler	dangling modifier (356–357, 385–386)
det	add specific details
div	improper word division (423–426)
ex	give an example
frag	sentence fragment (363, 368–371)
fs	fused sentence (354, 373–374)
lc	change to lower case letter (461–463)
logic	faulty logic or reasoning
p	incorrect punctuation (411–443)
red	redundant (403)
ref	incorrect or remote pronoun referent (381–385)
run-on	run-on sentence (374–375)
sp	misspelling (448–456)
squint	squinting modifier (356)
t	improper tense (314–316, 381)
trans	transition needed
ww	wrong word (397–400, Chapter 16)
ℯ	omit material indicated
∧	something is omitted
∼	reverse the order
¶	begin a new paragraph (Chapter 4)
no ¶	do not begin a new paragraph here (Chapter 4)
//	faulty parallel construction (104–105, 387–388)
⊙ ⊙ ⊙	any punctuation that is circled is incorrect
⚇ ⚇ ⚇	insert this punctuation mark where indicated

Writing Today

A Rhetoric and Handbook

Writing Today

A Rhetoric and Handbook

Patricia A. Moody

Syracuse University

Prentice-Hall, Inc./Englewood Cliffs, N.J.

To My Wonderful Family and Friends

Library of Congress Cataloging in Publication Data

Moody, Patricia A
  Writing today.

  Includes index.
  1. English language—Rhetoric. 2. English language—
Grammar—1950–   I. Title.
PE1408.M596   808'.042   80-29523
ISBN 0-13-971556-8

Printed in the United States of America.

10 9 8 7 6 5 4 3 2 1

Prentice-Hall International, Inc., *London*
Prentice-Hall of Australia, Pty. Ltd., *Sydney*
Prentice-Hall of Canada, Ltd., *Toronto*
Prentice-Hall of India Private Limited, *New Delhi*
Prentice-Hall of Japan, Inc., *Tokyo*
Prentice-Hall of Southeast Asia (Pte.) Ltd., *Singapore*
Whitehall Books Limited, *Wellington, New Zealand*

Art Director: Florence Dara Silverman
Production Editor: Anne G. Pietropinto
Book Designer: Natasha Sylvester
Cover Photo: A. Wasinski/The Image Bank
Cover Designer: Natasha Sylvester
Line Art: Danmark & Michaels, Inc.
Photo Researcher: Anita Duncan
Manufacturing Buyer: Ray Keating

Credits for chapter-opening photos: Ch. 1: Mimi Forsyth/Monkmeyer. Ch. 2: Ellis
Herwig/Stock, Boston. Ch. 3: Sam Falk/Monkmeyer. Ch. 4: Mimi Forsyth/Monk-
meyer. Ch. 5: Sam Falk/Monkmeyer. Ch. 6: Irene Springer. Ch. 7: Irene Springer.
Ch. 8: UPI. Ch. 9: Mimi Forsyth/Monkmeyer. Ch. 10: Springer/Bettmann Film Ar-
chive. Ch. 11: Marc Anderson. Ch. 12: Mimi Forsyth/Monkmeyer.

Acknowledgments for quoted works begin on page 505.

Contents

I   The Composing Process   1

1   Invention: Discovering What to Say   3

Why Write? 4   Writing for Ourselves 4   Writing for Ourselves and Others 6   Writing for Others 7   **The Composing Process** 8   Four Stages of Writing 9   **Getting Started—Prewriting** 11   Note Taking 11   Brainstorming 12   Keeping a Journal 12   **Probing** 13   Probing Yourself 14   Probing the Subject 14   Probing the Audience 15   **Using Prewriting Techniques and Probes** 15
Exercises 21

2   Evidence: Thinking About What to Say   27

Appeals and Evidence 28   Emotional Appeals 28   Ethical Appeals 29   Rational Appeals 29   **The Nature of Evidence** 30   External Testimony 31   Statistics 31   Facts, Inferences, and Opinions 32   **Problems with Rational Appeals** 34   Not Enough Facts 34   Confusing the Issue 37   Mixing the Appeals 39   **Evaluating Appeals** 40
Exercises 41

3 Organization: Shaping Your Material

Deciding on Organization 50 **Producing a Thesis** 50 Supporting the Thesis 51 Placing the Thesis 53 **Organizing with a Formal Outline** 54 **Discerning Order in the Subject Matter** 56 Chronology 56 Process 58 Spatial Organization 59 **Internal Patterns of Organization** 60 **Other Patterns of Organization** 62 Classical Rhetoric 62 Innovative Patterns 64 **Coherence in the Essay** 65 **Exercises** 67

4 Paragraphs

Patterns of Development 72 Induction and Deduction 73 Definition 74 Illustration 74 **Analogy** 75 Classification 76 Analysis 76 Comparison and Contrast 77 Description 78 Cause and Effect 80 **Mixing Patterns of Development** 81 **Special Paragraphs** 83 The Introductory Paragraph 83 The Transitional Paragraph 86 The Concluding Paragraph 87 **Paragraph Checklist** 88 **Exercises** 89

5 Sentences

Pitfalls in Sentence Writing 94 Nouns Modifying Nouns 94 Preposition Piling 95 Sentence Modifiers 95 Passive Construction 95 Delayed Subject 96 Deadwood 97 **Sentence Variations** 97 Intentions 97 Structure 98 Length 99 **Sentence Style: Training Eye and Ear** 100 Positioning 101 Positive Wording 101 Periodic Sentences 102 Balanced Sentences 103 Antithesis 104 Parallelism 104 Parenthesis 105 Rhythm 106 **A Checklist for Sentences** 107 **Exercises** 107

6 Words

The Dictionary and the Thesaurus 112 **Inflated Language** 115 Jargon 115 Buzz Words 115 Fad Words 116 Reshaping Sexist Language 117 **General versus Specific Language** 118 **Guides to Sharpening Your Language** 120 Use Strong Verbs 120 Avoid Weasel Words 120 Be Careful of "Sound-alike" Words 121   Avoid Fillers 121   **Denotation and Connotation** 121   **Metaphors, Mixed Metaphors, and Clichés** 123 **Exercises** 124

7 Revision: Reseeing and Rewriting   129

Distancing Yourself 130   Time as Distancer 131   Outside Commentary as Distancer 131   Role-playing as Distancer 132 Anything Can Be Changed 134   **Revision Strategies** 134   Use the Probes 135   Examine the Title and Lead-in 135   Examine the Thesis 136   Examine Opening Paragraphs 137   Examine the Body Paragraphs Closely 140   Examine Your Strategy 141   Examine the Closing Paragraphs 143   Examine the Sentences 143   Examine the Words 144   Check the Mechanics and Proofread 145   **Writing and Rewriting an Essay: A Walkthrough** 146   **Revising Under Pressure** 150 **Exercises** 151

II Applications   157

8 Writing Description, Narration, and Exposition   159

The Forms of Discourse 160   **Applying the Forms of Discourse** 162   **Writing Description** 165   Objective and Subjective Description 165   Sensory Appeals 167   **Writing Narration** 168   Objective and Subjective Narration 169   Order in Narration 171   **Writing Exposition** 172   Classification and Division 173   Definition 175   Process Description 177 Analysis 178   Comparison and Contrast 178 **Exercises** 179

9 Argument and Persuasion   185

The Nature of Argument and Persuasion 186   Stating the Purpose 187   Determining the Audience 189   Analyzing the Subject 191   **The "Why" of Argument/Persuasion** 192   **Beginning the Argument** 193   Defining Terms 193   Hidden Value Judgments 194   Cultural Conditioning 195   **Patterns of Argument** 196   Formal Argument 197   Informal Argument 197 **Exercises** 200

10   Writing About Literature   209

The Literary Essay 210   **Probing** 211   **Approaches to the Literary Essay** 212   Plot 213   Characterization 213 Setting 214   Point of View 215   Theme 215 Comparison/Contrast 215   **Structure of the Literary Essay** 216 A Note on Evidence 217   Choosing a Title 218   The Opening Paragraph 219   Sticking to the Thesis 219   The Body of the Essay 222   The Conclusion 227   **Documenting the Essay** 228   Footnotes 228   Quotations in the Text 229 **Writing About Film** 231   Guidelines for Film Analysis 232 **Exercises** 233

11   The Library Research Paper   239

Paper Required: The Nature of the Quest 240   What a Research Paper Is 240   Ideas for the Paper 241   Brainstorming for Ideas 241   **The Library** 242   Coming Prepared 243 Using the Card Catalog 244   Making Bibliography Cards 246 On the Trail: One Thing Leads to Another 247   **Taking Notes: The Raw Material of Your Paper** 248   Integrity 248   Note Cards 249   Culling the Sources 249   Types of Notes 250 **Crediting Your Sources** 253   MLA Footnote Style 254 Sample Footnotes 255   MLA Bibliography Style 256   Crediting Sources in the Social and Natural Sciences 257   **Building the Paper** 258   **Writing and Revising the Paper** 261   **Sample Library Research Paper** 262   **Reference Sources** 271   General Reference Sources 271   Specialized Reference Books, Encyclopedias, Indexes 272 **Exercises** 275

12   Writing Today: For School and Work   279

The Exam Essay 280   Read the Question 280   Watch the Clock 281   Make Your Answer's Structure Evident 282 Compare and Contrast 283   Analysis 284   Analysis and Evaluation 286   **The Resume** 286   Format and Appearance 287 Types of Resumes—Functional and Chronological 288   **Writing for Business** 290   Business Letters 293   Memos and Reports 294   **Writing for School and Work** 297   The Brief 297 The Précis or Abstract 298   The Report 299   **Technical or Scientific Writing** 299   **The Oral Report** 303 **Exercises** 304

III Handbook of Grammar and Usage 307

13 A Review of Grammar 309

Subjects and Predicates 310   Exercises 311   **Nouns and Pronouns** 311   Exercises 312   **Verbs** 313   Tense 314   Mood 316   Exercises 318   **Modification** 319   Attributive Adjectives 319   Determiners 319   Adverbs 320   Comparison of Modifying Words 320   Exercises 321   **Phrases** 322   Prepositional Phrases 322   Verbals 323   Exercises 324   **Clauses** 324   Exercises 326   **Basic Patterns for Subjects** 327   Exercises 329   **Basic Patterns for Predicates** 330   Exercises 332   **Variations in Basic Sentence Patterns** 333   Questions 333   *There/It* as Expletives 335   Indirect Objects 335   Passives 336   Interrupters 337   Exercises 337   **Compounding** 338   Linking Ideas at Clause Level 341   Exercises 343   **Conclusion** 344

14 Glossary of Grammatical Terms 345

15 The Conventions of Writing 367

Principle 1: Conventional Sentences 368   Sentence Fragments 368   Comma Splices 371   Fused Sentences 373   Run-ons 374   Exercises 375   **Principle 2: Matched Parts** 377   Subject-Verb Agreement 378   Shifts in Verb Tense 381   Pronoun-Reference and Pronoun-Antecedent Agreement 381   Pronoun Case 384   Misplaced or "Dangling" Modifiers 385   Parallelism 387   Incomplete or Misconstructed Comparisons 388   Passive Voice 389   Exercises 390   **Principle 3: The Right Word** 393   Wrong Part of Speech for the Purpose 393   Incorrect Choice of Transitive and Intransitive Verbs 394   Faulty Predication 395   Improper Idiom 396   Misuse of Words 397   Invented Words 399   Inappropriate Level of Usage 400   Deadwood 401   Redundancy 403   Vagueness 404   Euphemisms 405   Clichés 405   Inappropriate and "Mixed" Metaphors 406   Exercises 407   **Principle 4: Conventional Punctuation** 411   Commas 411   Semicolons 416   Colons 418   Dashes 421   Hyphens 423   Question Marks 426   Exclamation Points 427

x   **Contents**

Parentheses and Brackets   428   Apostrophes   432   Quotation
Marks   435   Italics   439   Ellipses   441   Slashes   443
Exercises   443   **Principle 5: Mechanics**   448   Spelling: General
Problems   448   Formation of Plurals   453   Syllabication   456
Abbreviations   458   Numbers   459   Capitalization   461
Manuscript Format   463   Exercises   468

16   **Glossary of Usage**   471

Introduction to Glossary of Usage   472   Uses of the Language   472   **Glossary of Usage**   473

Acknowledgments   505

Index   511

Preface

Writing Today has been carefully prepared to combine new ideas about the teaching of writing with the body of knowledge traditionally understood as rhetoric. My aim has been to make the craft of writing as accessible to students as possible and to place in the hands of teachers a text that lends itself to a variety of course formats. Above all, however, my objective has been to present a text that is *teachable.*

Students who use this book will gain, I think, an understanding of the process of writing and of the components of written expression. They will acquire a set of skills that should help them to approach *any* writing task with greater confidence because they have come to understand how a writer's intention, the audience's needs, and the subject's (or context's) limitations affect how we shape written discourse. I hope that the book will promote positive attitudes toward the process of writing, so that students will continue to develop and polish their writing skills long after the freshman course has been completed. To that end, I have suggested applications of writing beyond the limits of any one composition course.

I have tried throughout to emphasize the positive, to build confidence as I introduce concrete "attack skills" for writing, to present the craft of writing as an infinite set of choices. I have tried not to be dogmatic but to present as honestly as possible the conventions of the written language that we all must use.

ORGANIZATION

There are many ways of organizing the material of an introductory writing text (and as this book has evolved, I have tried several different strategies—to my editor's chagrin!). I have decided to organize this text as simply as possible so that it might be the more useful to a variety of course formats. Thus, I move from the larger issues in the process of writing—such as gathering material, evaluating evidence and appeals, shaping the content—to the particular parts of written discourse—the paragraph, the sentence, the word—and then to the applications for particular purposes or audiences.

The last four chapters of the textbook constitute a handbook of grammar and usage. The handbook contains an extensive review of grammar that has been created for the student who must write English; it is not grammar for grammar's sake. A glossary of grammatical terms is also included as a reference aid.

The heart of the handbook is a chapter called "The Conventions of Writing." It is a comprehensive presentation of the principles of usage and is based on a survey that was made of errors committed by students in their papers. Its approach is diagnostic. The final chapter of the handbook is a glossary of usage devoted to those knotty usage problems encountered by every writer.

EXAMPLES AND EXERCISES

The text provides numerous examples of good writing—examples that illustrate the point at hand and that are, themselves, interesting to read. I have also used student writing wherever I could in the belief that students need to see other students being successful at assignments they themselves might encounter. Detailed questions and a wealth of exercises for class use appear at the end of each chapter in the rhetoric and throughout two chapters of the handbook. The suggestions for themes have been carefully worked out and relate to students' own experiences as well as to the content of the text.

SUPPLEMENTS

Writing Today brings with it a full list of supplements for the student and the teacher. A useful instructor's manual has been written that contains an overview of each chapter that appears in the text. The manual also contains an annotated bibliography to guide the instructor in further reading, a handsome array of transparency masters for classroom use, and a diagnostic test that may be administered at the instructor's discretion.

Another supplementary item is the student workbook. The workbook stands completely independent of the text but has been designed in such a way as to be used in conjunction with it, if so desired.

ACKNOWLEDGMENTS

I have had a long apprenticeship in learning how to teach writing, and I am indebted to many people. I wish to thank those whose books have inspired or irritated me (or both) but from whom I have learned. Their names make up a Who's Who of rhetoricians and linguists, critics and writers. May I be forgiven for not reciting their names here.

I also must acknowledge my colleagues and friends at Syracuse University who have contributed to my intellectual life: in particular John Hagaman and Peter De Blois. And I happily express my gratitude to Pamela Miller, a friend from graduate school days, who has shared her ideas and experiences with me and from whose friendship and editorial help I have benefited more than once.

A number of teachers of English from around the country have reviewed the manuscript of this text in all its manifestations. I thank them for their comments, criticisms, and encouragement: Barbara Agonia, Las Vegas Community College; Mary Jane Dickerson, University of Vermont; Janis Forman, Goucher College; John K. Hanes, Duquesne University; Lynne Kellermann, Livingston College, Rutgers University; Dallas Lacy, University of Texas at Arlington; David B. Merrell, Abilene Christian University; Lawrence Schwartz, Director of Freshman English, Montclair State College; Ronald Strahl, Indiana University/Purdue University, Indianapolis; Laura M. Zaidman, South Georgia College.

I wish also to acknowledge my indebtedness to all of the people who have contributed quite specifically and substantially to the creation of this book: Kathy Baum, Jyotsna Singh, Annette Muir, Harry L. Wagner, Peter Morris, Susan C. Joseph, and David Weir. In particular I want to thank Marie Sprayberry and Karen Szymanski—two whose loyalty and hard work have been inspiring.

I wish also to extend my thanks to the members of the Prentice-Hall staff—some of whom I know and many of whom I do not—for the vital roles they played in the development of *Writing Today*. The excellent market research of Jean Lyons kept me on target and always aware of my audience. My editor, David Conti, provided encouragement when it was needed and was at all times a model of patience with a book whose content and form must at times have seemed like quicksilver in the hands of an author who kept wanting to try another way or change something one more time. In addition, I wish to thank Cecil Yarbrough for his expert guidance and diligence in the book's final stages of development and production.

The final and largest debt is owed to my family, who had to put up with a book project that began in my head, spread to and consumed my study, and, before it was done, had usurped our home and our lives. I thank them here publicly for their endurance and support.

—Patricia A. Moody

I

The Composing Process

1 Invention: Discovering What to Say   3

2 Evidence: Thinking About What to Say   27

3 Organization: Shaping Your Material   49

4 Paragraphs   71

5 Sentences   93

6 Words   111

7 Revision: Reseeing and Rewriting   129

Invention: Discovering What to Say

Why Write?
Writing for Ourselves
Writing for Ourselves and Others
Writing for Others

The Composing Process
Four Stages of Writing

Getting Started—Prewriting
Note Taking
Brainstorming
Keeping a Journal

Probing
Probing Yourself
Probing the Subject
Probing the Audience

Using Prewriting Techniques and Probes

Exercises

About 4000 years ago, a ruler in the land of Ur, in what is now Syria, sent this message:

The characters stand for the words *"Maru shipria la takallam,"* which means: "Do not detain my ambassador." The written characters are in the ancient Sumarian script, the oldest known form of true writing.

Even then, people found it necessary to send clear written messages. Today, the need is even greater, despite—or perhaps because of—the many advances in the ways we transmit information. The possibilities for confusion as well as for communication have become so much greater in the last two or three decades that clear writing with a clear purpose has become more important than ever before.

The ruler in Ur had a purpose in writing and a good idea of what he wanted to say. You, however, may find yourself at a complete loss when faced with the latest writing assignment from your history teacher. If that is the case, read the rest of this chapter carefully. You have more resources as a writer than you think, and this chapter will help you to discover them. The techniques it offers will not only help you put your ideas together and get your creative juices flowing, but will give you the confidence to shape and reshape your material as you work.

WHY WRITE?

Generally, we can break down the situations for writing into three main categories: writing only for ourselves; writing for ourselves but also for others; and writing primarily for others.

Writing for Ourselves

Often we write *for* ourselves by writing *to* ourselves. We want to remember something, so we make up a shopping list or note down an item we have read or heard. We can also write for ourselves to explore our experiences—to observe and to record what we have done, what has happened to us, and to reflect upon and analyze events. On the simplest level, we can keep notes, as the White King does, in Lewis Carroll's *Through the Looking Glass:*

The King was saying, "I assure you, my dear, I turned cold to the very ends of my whiskers!"

To which the Queen replied, "You haven't got any whiskers."

"The horror of that moment," the King went on, "I shall never, *never* forget!"

"You will, though," the Queen said, "if you don't make a memorandum of it."

Alice looked on with great interest as the King took an enormous memorandum-book out of his pocket, and began writing.

Few people, of course, write for themselves simply to aid a bad memory. Sometimes, we record events that have greatly affected us soon after they have occurred in order to give vent to our emotions and perhaps find a moment or two of peace. The author of the following passage had lived through a momentous thirty-six hours during which her city was taken by Union forces during the Civil War. She found it necessary to write down what she had done and seen.

Richmond, Virginia

April 3—Agitated and nervous, I turn to my diary tonight as the means of soothing my feelings. We have passed through a fatal thirty-six hours. Yesterday morning we went, as usual, to St. James's Church . . . the services being over, we left the church, and our children joined us, on their way to the usual family gathering in our room on Sunday. . . .

John remarked to his father, that he had just returned from the War Department, and that there was sad news—General Lee's lines had been broken, and the city would probably be evacuated within twenty-four hours. . . .

Oh, who shall tell the horror of the past night! Union men began to show themselves; treason walked abroad. About two o'clock in the morning we were startled by a loud sound like thunder; the house shook and the windows rattled. . . . It was soon understood to be the blowing up of a magazine below the city. In a few hours another exploded on the outskirts of the city . . . it was then daylight, and we were standing out upon the pavement. The lower part of the city was burning.

—Judith Brockenbrough McGuire
Heroines of Dixie: Winter of Desperation

Another writer, a young Jewish girl named Anne Frank, who spent two years with her family hiding from the Nazis during World War II, realized that writing was a kind of lifeline—a means of expressing thoughts and feelings for which she had no sympathetic listener:

I haven't written for a few days, because I wanted first of all to think about my diary. It's an odd idea for someone like me to keep a diary; not only because I have never done so before, but because it seems to me that neither I—nor for that matter anyone else—will be interested in the unbosomings of a thirteen-year-old schoolgirl. Still, what does that matter? I want to write, but more than that, I want to bring out all kinds of things that lie buried deep in my heart.

There is a saying that "paper is more patient than man"; it came back to me on one of my slightly melancholy days. . . . Yes, there is no doubt that paper is patient and as I don't intend to show this cardboard-covered notebook . . . to anyone, unless I find a real friend, boy or girl, probably nobody cares. And now I come to the root of the matter, the reason for my diary: it is that I have no such real friend.

We can also write for ourselves as a means of thinking. Putting our thoughts into words helps us when we want to analyze, explain, or interpret something. If we can explain a process or a phenomenon in our own words, we come closer to an understanding of it.

The authors of these passages did not particularly concern themselves with correctness of form or usage. In writing for ourselves, such neglect is permissible and even advisable, for the point of this kind of writing is simply to express ourselves as freely as possible. When writing involves others, however, some concerns besides self-expression become important.

Writing for Ourselves and Others

A student seeking any college degree will have to write required papers and reports, regardless of her field of study. She will probably have to write letters to business firms to apply for a job. Term papers and business letters are examples of writing for ourselves with motivation from outside ourselves.

When writing involves others, it requires more conscious planning, organizing, and shaping. Others will read this writing, and they will judge it—and the writer—by it. In many cases, they will know the writer *only* by what she writes. They will judge the writing on the basis of clarity, completeness, accuracy, simplicity, effectiveness, and persuasiveness. Moreover, they will expect it to conform to community standards of grammatical usage, spelling, and punctuation. For many, these concerns seem more trivial and troublesome than useful. But if you received a letter that was full of grammatical errors and misspellings from a company you were considering doing business with, you might have second thoughts. The writer's carelessness might rightly indicate his carelessness in business as well.

Which of the firms represented in the following business letters would you prefer to deal with?

FOREIGN CAR REPAIR SERVICE
1369 Warren Avenue, Anytown, Ohio 45505

January 11, 1981

Arthur r. Smith
111 Elm Street
Anytown, Ohio 45505

We are sory you are still having problems with your automobile. As you indicated in your letter dated January 7 1981 that you would be in the area on or about the end of March. We will certainly make necessary repairs to the carburetor if indeed thier the falt lies and at no cost to you.

B. Jones, Svc. Manager F.C.R.S.

113 Hudson Park Dr.
Troy, N.Y. 13445
9 March 1981

Mr. Mike Ferris
15 Blaine Ave.
Troy, N.Y. 13446

Dear Mike,

If you are planning to paint your house in the spring and if you do not plan to have the same fellows who did your roof do the job, now would be a good time to schedule the work.

As you know, I am experienced and insured, and the quality of my work is well known in the neighborhood—see for yourself next door at 13 Blaine, at 631 Selby Springs around the corner, at 104 and 106 Greenview, at 311 Jackson Road.

I can give you a firm price—not an estimate—in advance, and, if you care to shop around a bit, I can beat any *bona fide* professional bid. Best of all, if you contract with me to do the job early in the spring, you can have your house looking its best as soon as the weather breaks.

I look forward to hearing from you at 314-9002.

Your satisfaction with any work that I do for you is guaranteed, of course.

Sincerely,
Henry C. Bowman

Writing for Others

In some things we write, we may move away entirely from writing for ourselves. We may write solely to influence our readers or to provide information.

An example of writing to inform is the essay or book that tells some-one how to do something—anything from keeping score in tennis to building a house. In the passage that follows, the author gives instructions on how to exercise effectively through stationary running.

> To avoid foot and ankle trouble, wear cushioned-soled shoes and run on a soft surface, preferably on a thick rug. Pick your knees up in front lifting your feet at least 8 inches off the floor and run at the rate of 80–90 steps per minute. If that seems too fast for you, try 70–80 steps.
>
> To check your speed, count every time your left foot hits the floor. Do this for 15 seconds, then multiply by 4. This gives you your step-per-minute figure.
>
> Some women like to do their stationary running in time to music. It helps keep the rhythm steady and reduces boredom. The trick is finding a record with the proper beat and one that maintains a steady rhythm for a long enough period. There are some jogging records on the market that can be used very effectively in a stationary running program.
>
> —Kenneth H. Cooper, *The New Aerobics*

Other forms of writing for others seek to change an audience's behavior or thinking in some way. Advertisements, pamphlets for political candidates, editorials and letters to the editor, the Declaration of Independence, and the *Communist Manifesto* all fall into this category.

THE COMPOSING PROCESS

Written communication is made up of three essential and interrelating components: the writer, the topic the writer wants to write about, and the audience who will read what the writer has written. The act of writing involves satisfying the demands of these three components. No matter what prompts the need to write, the attempt to satisfy these demands will determine the tone and style of what you write. You must fit your style of writing to the circumstances. For example, you might write this note to your girlfriend:

> Tiger—no can do Sat. afternoon. Heavy paper due. Will call in p.m. Love and XXX, Paul

In declining an invitation from your biology professor, however, a completely different kind of note becomes necessary. You are addressing a different audience and must take on a different role as a writer with a different style to match.

Dear Professor Clark,
Thank you for your invitation to the science symposium and reception on Saturday afternoon. Unfortunately, some pressing deadlines will keep me from attending. I am sorry to have to miss it.

Sincerely yours,
Paul Stuart

When you sit down to write the "heavy paper" itself, you must allow for the fact that you are not only addressing a different audience this time, but writing about a different kind of subject. Your method of treatment, as well as your style, must be altered. You might begin the paper this way:

> Russia in 1905 was a nation in chaos. The Communist Party was gaining strength, and workers' strikes were closing factories all over the country. The nation was also in the midst of a disastrous war with Japan, a war begun by Nicholas II at the urging of his cousin the Kaiser. Revolution seemed almost inevitable—and yet the rebellions of that year did not succeed in toppling the Tsarist regime. In this paper, I will examine the factors that prevented revolution in Russia in 1905 and kept Nicholas on his throne for another twelve years.

You know—as well as sense naturally—that the components of written communication will make different demands every time you put pen to paper. The more conscious your adjustment to the demands of each writing assignment, the more successful the result is likely to be.

Four Stages of Writing

The oyster creates a pearl because it is irritated. A bit of sand gets inside an oyster's shell, and to ease the discomfort, the oyster secretes a liquid around the offending speck. This liquid hardens and eventually becomes a pearl. Something like this happens in the mind of a writer. At first there is an itch, a problem that requires an answer, a discrepancy that needs to be resolved. The writer wants to scratch the itch, answer the problem, resolve the discrepancy.

The process involved in scratching that itch—writing—advances in four stages. First, the writer probes, asking questions about himself, the subject, and the audience (not always strictly in this order, of course). Second, the writer develops strategies for dealing with the subject matter. Third, the writer shapes the materials he has assembled in accordance with the answers he has given to the probes plus the strategies he has developed. Finally, the writer edits the material, selecting those points he wants to make and eliminating those that do not contribute to his purposes. This whole process, which may seem alien and complicated to you at first, actually progresses quite naturally from one stage to the next. It constitutes a whole, even if we have to take it apart to examine its stages.

Sherlock Holmes once remarked to his ever-faithful but slow-witted Watson, "You see, but you don't observe." The probing, developing, shaping, and editing that go into a piece of writing are all devices for helping the writer convert passive seeing to active observing both for himself and the reader. Throughout the writing process, the stages help the writer to focus on what is important to the work in progress.

Focus is as important to a writer as it is to a photographer. It is the factor that helps each to decide what will be up front and what will be kept in the background, what will be "panned over" briefly and what will be examined in "stop-action." Neither a piece of writing nor a photograph can present all details with equal clarity. Neither the camera nor the pen could render them, and the mind of the observer or reader could not comprehend such absolute objectivity. The writer, no less than the photographer, must "see" selectively. He must observe actively and, in observing, select from a world of detail to focus on what is most important. Like the photographer, too, the writer must develop the technical ability to make the most of his focus and must be prepared to refocus and reshoot as often as need be.

The following excerpt from Robert Pirsig's *Zen and the Art of Motorcycle Maintenance* will give you an idea of the importance of focus in good writing. A student has been unable to complete an assigned 500-word essay on her hometown of Bozeman, Montana; twice she has explained to her teacher that she just couldn't think of anything to say.

He was furious. "You're not looking!" he said. A memory came back of his own dismissal from the University for having too much to say. For every fact there is an infinity of hypotheses. The more you look the more you see. She really wasn't looking and yet somehow didn't understand this.

He told her angrily, "Narrow it down to the front of one building on the main street of Bozeman. The Opera House. Start with the upper left-hand brick."

Her eyes, behind the thick-lensed glasses, opened wide.

She came in the next class with a puzzled look and handed him a five-thousand-word essay on the front of the Opera House on the main street of Bozeman, Montana. "I sat in the hamburger stand across the street," she said, "and started writing about the first brick, and the second brick, and then by the third brick it all started to come and I couldn't stop. They thought I was crazy, and they kept kidding me, but here it all is. I don't understand it."

Neither did he, but on long walks through the streets of town he thought about it and concluded she was evidently stopped with the same kind of blockage that had paralyzed him on his first day of teaching. She was blocked because she was trying to repeat, in her writing, things she had already heard, just as on the first day he had tried to repeat things he had already decided to say. She couldn't think of anything to write about Bozeman because she couldn't recall anything she had heard worth repeating. She was strangely unaware that she could look and see freshly for herself, as she wrote, without primary regard for what had been said before. The narrowing down to one brick destroyed the blockage because it was so obvious she had to do some original and direct seeing.

Some of you, like her, may be trying to take in too much of a fairly large subject instead of focusing on some aspect of it that you *can* handle.

GETTING STARTED—PREWRITING

The beginning of writing is *writing*—getting something down on paper.

One takes a piece of paper, anything, the flat of a shingle, slate, cardboard and with anything handy to the purpose begins to put down the words after the desired expression in mind. The blankness of the writing surface may cause the mind to shy, it may be impossible to release the faculties. Write, write anything; it is in all probability worthless anyhow, it is never hard to destroy written characters. But it is absolutely essential to the writing of anything worthwhile that the mind be fluid and release itself to the task.

—William Carlos Williams, "How To Write"

Prewriting involves those techniques of writing that are for yourself only; others are not expected to read it at this stage. As William Carlos Williams urges in the passage quoted above, you should set down the words without worrying about form or correctness; just try to put together ideas and relationships that may prove valuable to you later. You should get into the habit of writing things down. Such techniques as jotting down notes, free-associating or brainstorming, and keeping a journal are all forms of prewriting.

Note Taking

A note need be nothing more than jotting down a few words or even drawing on a piece of scrap paper to help remember a topic, an idea, or a clever line you have heard or read. More significantly, note taking can be a way of putting something you have learned into your own words. And, most importantly, it can be a means of preserving the beginnings of ideas you may wish to use now or later in your writing. For example, here are excerpts from a page of Nathaniel Hawthorne's *American Notebooks*. These entries, written in 1840, are ideas for possible stories, two of which Hawthorne later turned into published works—"The Great Stone Face" and "The Birthmark."

> Some moderns to build a fire on Ararat with the remnants of the ark.
> Two little boats of cork, with a magnet in one and steel in the other.
> To make a story of all strange and impossible things as the Salamander, the Phoenix.
> The semblance of a human face to be formed on the side of a mountain, or in the fracture of a small stone, by a *lusus naturae*. The face is an object of curiosity for years or centuries, and by and by a boy is born, whose features gradually assume the aspect of that portrait. At some critical juncture, the resemblance is found to be perfect. A prophesy may be connected.
> A person to be the death of his beloved in trying to raise her to more than mortal perfection; yet this should be a comfort to him for having aimed so highly and holily.

Brainstorming

Similar to note taking is the prewriting technique of free-associating or brainstorming. This involves putting down ideas about a certain topic just as they come to you. In the center of a sheet of paper write down a topic you want to write on. Let your mind associate freely on ideas prompted by the topic, and write down whatever you come up with. Some of these ideas may run far afield, but since you will not know which are useful and which are not, you should put down all the ideas that come to you. Relate them to one another by drawing lines connecting them to the topic or to one another. Later, the shaping process can begin and the irrelevant material can be eliminated, the dead ends abandoned. Brainstorming is just one way of exploring what there is to write about. But do it in writing! Daydreams fade quickly.

Keeping a Journal

In a journal, diary, or daybook, you can keep a record of what happens to you, what you do, and what occurs to you; it need not be a strict day-by-day account, but it should be kept fairly regularly. A journal gives you a place to write down words, ideas, and events that you may want to remember or reflect on. Best of all, it is a private affair, allowing you to meditate in an uninhibited manner on all the things that interest you. Nearly all the examples of "writing for ourselves" that we have seen in this chapter have been excerpts from journals; as you can tell from rereading these, a writer can discuss almost anything in a journal, in any way he or she pleases. If you have never tried keeping a journal, you might do so. It will give you excellent practice in the skill of rendering often half-formed thoughts and impressions into concrete terms that you can refer to in the future. The British novelist Virginia Woolf, who kept a diary for many years, described its value for her:

> I have just re-read my year's diary and am much struck by the rapid haphazard gallop at which it swings along, sometimes indeed jerking almost intolerably over the cobbles. Still if it were not written rather faster than the fastest typewriting, if I stopped and took thought, it would never be written at all; and the advantage of the method is that it sweeps up accidentally several stray matters which I should exclude if I hesitated, but which are the diamonds of the dustheap.

You might not find any "diamonds" in your own "dustheap," but the chances are good that you will turn up a few uncultured pearls for use in future papers.

PROBING

Before you actually begin outlining and developing a paper, you should get in the habit of asking yourself questions—probing. The questions you will read here are not the only ones you should ask—they are only models. You should not simply run through all the questions at one time and then consider yourself finished. You should first pause to identify the questions that need to be answered concerning the topic you will be writing on. You should then decide *how* to answer the questions before starting in on them. Some may need to be answered in detail, others less fully. After you have answered the questions, you should return to them as often as necessary while you continue your work. Feel free to ask questions you did not use before or to use previously answered questions in different ways. If you find some of the answers changing as you learn new facts or ask questions differently, do not panic or pretend it is not happening. Your final product will be stronger if it takes the changed circumstances into account than if it ignores them. Probing entails asking questions about yourself as the writer, about the subject, and about the audience.

Probing Yourself

The point of the first set of probes—those concerning yourself as the writer—is to discover who you are in relation to the topic you are going to write about. You will want to begin by asking questions like these about yourself:

Who am I? What roles can I play as writer? What are my attitudes? What stand do I want to take? What is important to me? What do I want to accomplish?

At first, these may seem to be large and general questions. But if you remember to respond to them *in connection with the topic you plan to write about* and then sort them out accordingly, a pattern will emerge. You may not need every question on this list; you may need a few that are not on the list. Remember to *focus*.

You will also want to ask questions about what you know. Begin by asking questions about the people who have been important to you and then ask about the places you have been.

Who are the people most important to me? Why have they influenced me? Is the influence positive or negative? Where have I been—literally? What countries have I visited? Where have I been figuratively? What places have I been interested in?

Answers to these questions give you an insight into the influences that have shaped your thinking and your interests. This insight, in turn, may provide you with further clues to the stand you wish to take toward your topic.

Finally, you will want to ask questions about your experiences.

What have I done? What has happened to me? Where have I been in the past? What am I doing currently? What do I want to do in the future?

Again, setting down on paper the answers to some of these questions may help you to establish the particular "self" you wish to be when you write.

Probing the Subject

The second set of questions you will want to ask concerns the subject you want to write about. Not all the questions will be relevant for all topics, however. If you read through them beforehand, you should be able to establish which ones you can use in any particular case.

What is the subject? What is it like? Unlike? What are its parts? Which of these parts are most important? What have others said about it?

What examples are there of it? What exceptions do I have to make to it? What qualifications does it have? What purpose does it have? What are its implications? What are its consequences? Is it logically related to something else? What advantages does it have? What disadvantages?

You will discover that probing the subject provides you with materials to examine and consider and ideas to express—the raw material of the essay you will write.

Probing the Audience

For the third set of questions—questions about your audience—you can repeat some of the questions you asked about yourself. Make a study of the audience in relation to the topic, just as you studied yourself in relation to it.

Who is the audience? What are its prejudices? What is its educational level? How much does it know? Where has it been? Where does it want to go? What is the audience ready to hear?

The answers to these questions will help you to determine the tone and style you will adopt for the final draft of the paper. Will you be formal or casual? Serious or humorous? Will you present a series of facts or make an emotional appeal? These categories, naturally, are not mutually exclusive. For many audiences, you may choose to combine approaches.

Once you have asked many of these questions, you will discover that you have a great deal more to say than you can really use. Far from having nothing to write, you will have to begin the process of selecting and organizing material from an overabundant supply.

USING PREWRITING TECHNIQUES AND PROBES

To understand more clearly just how the prewriting techniques and the probes we have discussed might work for you, you may find it helpful to imagine yourself in the situation of a real student faced with a real paper topic. Pretend, for example, that you are a freshman in the School of Management of a large university, and that your English teacher has just assigned you a 750-word essay on the topic of your school's proposal to make a liberal arts "core curriculum" a requirement. What do you do?

Your first reaction to the assignment is probably to assume that you have nothing to say and that you do not care about it. Your roommate, an engineering student, takes a different view of the matter. "If I were you," he says, "I could get pretty worked up about that. What if they pass that for all the professional schools—Management, Engineering, Forestry, Agriculture, everything? We'll all be stuck with a lot of courses that none of us wants to take."

You agree with your roommate's opinion and sit down at your desk to write your paper, but nothing happens. You gaze out the window and chew on your pen. You glare at the blank paper. Finally, in desperation, you take out your notes from English class and look them over. Brainstorming, free association, probing—would any of this work? Well, why not? Nothing else seems to.

You write the term "liberal arts" in the middle of your page and try to think about the term itself. Gradually you write the following after it:

Liberal arts: courses like literature, philosophy, history, art.
> *What else? Can't think of anything. Try words separately.*
Liberal: attitude—broad, openminded. Politics, reform. Generous
> My father is *liberal* when he gives me my allowance.
> My folks are *liberal* in treating me like an adult.
> My father is *liberal* about changes taking place in society.
> My mother is *conservative*—wants things to stay the way they are.
Traditional? Liberal-nontraditional?
> Liberate, liberation: Women's Lib, Gay Lib. Freedom? Change for what was before? Revolution?
Arts: classical music, "great" books, art museums, operas, ballet, all that old stuff. *Wait a minute. How can I have old stuff with revolution and freedom and change at the same time? Think about this.*
> Art. Frivolous, impractical, beautiful (I guess), can't use it, boring (my opinion).
> What my folks tell me: Refining, civilizing, creative, separates us from the animals.
> *OK, what to do with all this? Especially the old-stuff vs. freedom bit? Try defining terms again.*
Liberal arts—an openminded study of the arts? What about philosophy and history? A broad study of the arts and things connected with the arts. What about the nonconservative problem?
> *Come back to this later. Maybe I need to talk to somebody about it.*

You realize that you have reached an impasse in the brainstorming, so you decide to put it aside for the moment and try the probes. Perhaps you can establish more about the subject if you know more about yourself as the writer and about the audience.

Me as writer: Who am I?—A freshman in the School of Management at Upstate U.

Why am I in School of M? What do I want to be? Easy. I want to be a businessman when I get out of here. Make lots of money. Power. But if I have to waste my time taking a lot of irrelevant courses, I won't learn the important things and I might not reach my goal.

What roles can I play?—I guess I'm someone who's really down on the whole idea of a liberal arts curriculum. Negative. Have to watch out, though—I could get carried away, look like I'm too subjective, like all I want is my own way. Look objective. How?—Do I have to try to show both sides of the issue? I guess it wouldn't really be convincing if I didn't—I *know* I'm right but I can't expect some people to take it just on my say-so. If I were doing this like a senator introducing a bill or somebody writing a letter to the editor, they'd want reasons, not just arguments. Wait a minute—who are "they"? What's the audience? Maybe I can think better about the image I have to present if I know the audience.

Audience: People who agree with me: Students like me who want to prepare for *real* jobs. Teachers in the professional schools. (Check this. Better make sure.)

People who disagree with me: Arts & Sciences professors (don't want to lose their jobs). Arts & Sciences students (don't want to admit they're wasting their money).

A mixed group. Maybe I could pretend I've been asked to be the student representative to present the anti–core-curriculum side to the Faculty Senate or some group like that. An important group, and a good mix of opinions in it, most likely. And they'd be the ones making the final decision—so I (singlehandedly, of course) have to convince all of them that things should stay as they are. OK. If I did that I'd go in dressed in my business blues—so in my writing I should sound serious, earnest, in the know. On top of the situation. I can see it now.

What does the audience want to hear? What kind of argument? A *persuasive* essay, but one that has an argument in it. That should do it—don't try to knock them off their chairs, just convince them. What to say, though. I'll have to work out my reasons and show that they're not just mine or that they don't just represent the views of lazy, beer-drinking students. I think I'm back to what I got stuck on before, the whole "liberal arts" thing. The subject.

Your roommate comes back in and announces that it is time for dinner. "How are you doing?" he asks.

"Stalled out at the moment," you reply.

He looks at your notes. "You call that stalled out? You have more than 750 words already. I didn't know you were such a whiz in English. Let's go have dinner."

You look down at what you have. It is not an essay, but it is a lot closer to one than the blank page you had an hour ago. You allow yourself to be taken to dinner.

When you return, you reread your notes. You now have a sense of yourself as speaker, of the audience, and of the "scene" for the writing. But the contradiction that seems to exist within the term "liberal arts"— "liberal" versus "arts"—still puzzles you, and you are unable to think of any way to consider the other side of the issue. In fact, you are not convinced that there *is* another side. To try to solve the problems, you decide to look up "liberal arts" in the dictionary. You write the following:

Webster's New World Dictionary:
    liberal arts, n. [arts befitting a freeman: so named in contrast to *artes servile*, lower . . . arts, and because open to study only by freemen; in later use understood as "arts becoming a gentleman"] the subjects of an academic college course, including literature, philosophy, languages, history, and, usually survey courses of the sciences, as distinguished from professional or technical subjects.
OK, this kind of ties in with what I've thought—all those courses that spread me all over the place and keep me from getting down to the stuff I need to know to be successful once I get out of here. Anyway, who wants to be a *gentleman?* I want to be a *businessman.*
Here is another entry on "liberal education"—that might tie in with all this, too.
    liberal education, n. an education mainly in the liberal arts, providing the student with a broad cultural background rather than any specific professional training.
There it is again—no "specific professional training." If it doesn't prepare you for something specific and professional, what good is it? And, it still doesn't take care of the "liberal" business, either. If it's not specific and professional, how can it be nontraditional or free or openminded or generous or any of the things that liberal can mean? All I can figure is that we're going to get a liberal dose of the arts—that sure seems to be what they're planning for us. I think I better go see Professor Slowburn.

The next day, you walk into Professor Slowburn's office and place your notes on her desk. Taking a deep breath, you begin, "I've been thinking about that assignment you gave us yesterday, and I've started working on it. I used your suggestions about brainstorming and probing. They really helped—I've got a lot of material. But I'm having some problems in dealing with the subject. Can you help me?"

She reaches for your papers. "Give me a few minutes to look these over and figure out where you need to go from here. Have a seat."

She reads for the next ten minutes or so; she smiles at a few things, and you hope that she is smiling *with* you and not *at* you. Finally, she says, "I'm impressed with what you have done so far. For a first effort, you pushed hard and got a lot down on paper. The work on your own voice and on the audience is good. You can't do much more with that until you start putting the paper together. Your decision to write a persuasive paper is good, given the nature of the material. You also have some focus—some idea of what you want to accomplish. This will help you narrow the topic and then analyze the material and find a thesis. What you need to do now is to go after information on the subject more aggressively than you've been doing."

"How?" you ask. "I've done about as much as I can already."

"Not necessarily. Aside from the dictionary definitions and so forth, you examine the subject of 'liberal arts' only from a *very* limited perspective. You say yourself in your probing that you need to present your case as though it is more than just your personal gripe. What comes out in your notes, though, is that it is very much your personal gripe. You *do* need a strong sense of yourself as the writer, yes. But you need to go beyond yourself in your examination of the subject, or you won't convince many people."

"Sure," you say, slightly chastened. "But how *do* I get beyond myself?"

"Research. Investigation."

"Yecch!"

She laughs outright this time. "I never said learning was easy, did I? The thing is, though, you might find yourself getting interested. You can find things you didn't know before. You might even change your mind."

"No way!"

" 'No way' is right. If you don't keep an open mind, there *isn't* any way. If you go about researching a subject with your mind already made up, you'll be trying to fit your information into a scheme that may not even be workable. You'll miss things. You won't *see*. I'm not saying you *will* change your mind. But, no matter what you decide, you will have a greater sense of the complexity of the issue. Very few things are absolutely right or wrong, and not many of the decisions we make in our lives are cut and dried."

"I guess so," you say. "But how do I go about checking out my subject?"

"Well, you're in luck. The 'core curriculum' is a pretty hot topic because so many colleges and universities are considering instituting similar requirements. A lot of articles have recently been written on the subject, but reading them and taking notes of them goes a little beyond the scope of a 750-word paper. If you ever did make a presentation to the Faculty Senate, a working knowledge of that material would be impressive and effective. For a classroom assignment like this, though, it is more than you need. How about a few interviews with well-chosen people? Start with a couple of people involved in the 'liberal arts'—a teacher or two and maybe a student. Then you could talk to students and teachers in the professional schools. You'll need to go to at least one other school besides Management, because what might work in one school might not work in another."

"Yikes!"

"Relax. I can recommend at least a few professors to you."

Two days later, you are looking over the notes you have made of several brief interviews with some of the teachers Professor Slowburn has suggested, plus a few students. Professor Slowburn was right; you *have* found out a great deal you did not know before.

Prof. Riley, English: cleared up problem with liberal/arts—liberal arts are related to human, the study of men and women as individuals and in relation to others. The *liberal* part has to do with opening up the student's mind to different ways of looking at himself and the world, to realizing that ideas and opinions can be more complex than assumed. (Sounds like he and Slowburn are trying to tell me something.)

Prof. Rosel, Philosophy: Can develop skills that can be used in any profession—analysis, research, inquiry.

Prof. Gamble, School of Management: All that liberal arts stuff is drivel. We prepare our students for real jobs in the real world. Inflation is skyrocketing, good jobs aren't easy to come by, college tuition is expensive.

Prof. Woods, School of Communication: The core plan isn't a bad idea. Specializing is important, but too much and too soon can be limiting. It can leave you with only one or two ways of looking at things. You need range, breadth, even imagination, and liberal arts can develop these. Why not ask the Placement Office about liberal arts majors in the job market these days?

Manuel Forella, Placement Office: The situation is changing. Businesses have begun to complain about graduates who can't write or think, who have no sense of the world. Medical schools are getting more and more interested in English and philosophy majors—students trained to think about and reflect upon what they're doing, the possible consequences of their actions.

Hank Goldberg, freshman in Engineering: A liberal arts core curriculum? Are you kidding? I'll be lucky if I pass calculus as it is—I'll flunk for sure if I have to take all that philosophy and English stuff!

Leslie Thomas, sophomore in Spanish: I'd be glad to see it, if only because I never met anybody from Management or Engineering who could talk about anything else. It might improve the quality of social life around here.

You are still not sure how you are going to approach the subject in the paper. In fact, you are a good deal less certain that your earlier "negative" attitude toward the core curriculum proposal will hold up throughout a whole essay. What you *do* know, however, is that you now have a considerably broad range of ideas and opinions to draw from in shaping your argument. So you sit down at your desk and start making notes again. You are not, this time, searching for something to say; you are busy trying to say it effectively.

EXERCISES

1. You probably write much more than you realize. The writing you do may reveal to you a sense of yourself as a writer, of your subject, and of your audience. Sit down with a pen and some paper and take a few minutes to check off the categories that apply to you on the list (a.) below. Then choose three of the categories you have checked and answer the questions that follow (b.) in relation to your choices.

a). Kinds of Writing I Do:
1. Letters to parents _____
2. Letters to brothers and sisters _____
3. Letters to relatives (grandparents, aunts, uncles, etc.) _____
4. Letters to friends _____ ; brief notes to friends _____
5. Letters of application (for part-time jobs, scholarships, financial aid, etc.) _____
6. Notes to myself _____
7. Scribbles while on the phone, in a class, etc. _____
8. Journal or diary _____
9. Notes to teachers _____
10. Research notes _____
11. Lecture notes _____
12. Informal class papers _____
13. Research papers _____
14. Term papers _____
15. Essay exams _____

b). Questions to Ask Yourself:
1. When do I write? Why do particular situations or feelings make me want to write or force me to write?
2. What are the differences among the types of writing I have chosen in situation, audience, content, and tone?
3. What are the factors that cause or influence these differences?
4. Do I ever use the same content with two different audiences? If so, how and why does the change in audience affect the way I write?
5. Do these changes affect the way I shape the content or the way I decide to include or exclude material?

c). Writing Assignment:
The next time you write a letter, a note, a diary entry, or a paper, keep a short journal in which you record everything you do and feel as you go through the process of writing it. What is the content of the writing you are doing? Who is the audience of it? What role do you adopt as the writer of it? Using this journal as the source, write a paper in which you describe or analyze the writing process.

2. Brainstorming
a). Choose one of the words listed below. For ten minutes, brainstorm the word. That is, associate it with as many other words as you can think of and write them down. If any of the words lead, in turn, to other ideas, write them down as well. Work fairly quickly and do not worry—for the moment—about anything that seems farfetched or absurd. When your time is up, go over what you have. Do any words, phrases, or images particularly attract your attention? How? Why? Do connections emerge among any of them? If so, what is the nature of these connections? Make brief notes of your answers to these questions.

> macho
> holiday
> marijuana
> conservative
> examination
> polyester

b). Writing Exercises:
1. Write a paragraph in which you explain how and why you are attracted to one particular word, phrase, or image you have produced while brainstorming.
2. Write a paragraph in which you describe, as accurately as possible, the process by which you arrived at this word, phrase, or image from the original word.
3. Write a brief essay in which you develop more fully the connection between the original word and the word, phrase, or image of your choice.
4. Write a brief essay in which you develop the connections (if any) that have emerged between this word, phrase, or image and others in your material.

3. Probing an Object
a). Pick an object—a tombstone, an orange, a tennis racket, or anything else you choose—that you think you could discuss or write about using a number of different approaches. Before your next class period, copy the following form and fill it in with observations on the subject.
Object _____
1. What class of objects does it belong to?
2. What does it look, sound, feel, taste, and smell like? How can I describe it?
3. In what ways can I use it?
4. What classes of objects might it belong to if I stretched my imagination a bit?

5. What attitudes can I have toward it? What roles as observer/writer can I play in relation to it?
6. What different audiences can I talk to about it?
7. In what different ways can I talk to the audience about it? What different approaches can I make?
8. What situations could arise in which I would want to talk about it?

b). In class, discuss the various objects you have chosen and the forms that have been filled out about them. Which objects lend themselves most readily to this kind of treatment? Why? Which responses to the questions are the most effective? Why? How does the nature of "effectiveness" vary with the nature of the objects discussed?

c). Writing Exercise:

Imagine that you are a Martian explorer who has been sent to Earth on a fact-finding mission. While there, you come across one of the objects listed below. In your observation book, you explore your subject as thoroughly as you can. After you finish your note taking and figuring, write a report for Mars Mission Control in which you describe the object and its possible uses.

a paper clip   a yo-yo
a pair of pliers   a dollar bill
a well-used gym sneaker

4. Probing a Photograph

According to Russell Lee, the photographer who took this picture, the hands of this woman tell the story of her whole life. As a photographer, Lee

(RUSSELL LEE: Iowa Homesteader's Wife, 1936)

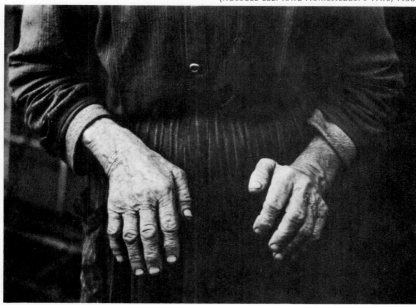

tried to convey this story through the visual image; in a writing class, we try to do the same thing in words.

a). Begin by analyzing the photograph. Remember, the objects themselves, their placement (the places in which they appear in the picture and the ways in which they relate to other objects), light and shadow, and textures, all make up the photographer's medium of expression or language, just as images, sentence patterns, sounds, and the like make up the written language. Ask yourself the following questions about the picture and make notes of your answers.

1. Name the objects in the photograph. Describe them as specifically and concretely as possible. Try not just to see them, but to hear, feel, touch, taste, and smell them as well. For example, look at the woman's skirt. Does it look new or old? Practical or frivolous? If you could touch it, how would it feel? Coarse, soft, slippery, rough, smooth? All of these or combinations? Can you think of other questions?

2. Once you have named the objects, identify their locations. What is the layout of the photograph? What draws our attention in it? Why? How does the photographer draw our attention? What stays in the background? Why? Would the total effect of the picture be different without the background, with a different one, with a blacked-out background? Why? What objects are omitted from the picture altogether? Why? Would the picture be different if these objects were included? How?

3. Once you have gathered all of this information, think about the photographer's assertion that the woman's story is in her hands. What *is* her story, especially as Lee is trying to convey it? What is he trying to say about the nature and quality of this woman's life? Could he have said it differently? How? Why do you suppose he has chosen to do it in this way? Use the observations you have gathered to support your answers to these questions.

b). Writing Assignment:
Write a brief descriptive essay. Use as your main idea a statement about this woman's life—how her life can be understood when we really see and comprehend what her hands tell us. In the body of the paper, rely on description—of the hands and the rest of the photograph—to support your assertion.

c). Writing Assignment:
Take the above essay and rewrite it using a specific point of view. You can play the role of the woman in the picture telling her own story. You can be a son, daughter, husband, or friend of the woman. You can be a speaker who knows the facts but who is detached from them. You can be a speaker who can be distant and "objective," but who can also get into the mind of one of the important people of the story in order to see and understand things from his or her perspective.

d). Writing Assignment:
Would the essays you have written be effective for any audience? Why do you think so? Can you think of any audience for whom this story would be boring, sentimental, incomprehensible? Do you think an audience of col-

lege students would respond to and identify with the same parts of the story as would a middle-aged audience or an audience close to the age of the woman in the photograph? If you were writing for these different audiences, would you need to rearrange or completely reconceive the story so that the audience could understand and respond to it? Rewrite the essay again, but do it as if you were writing to one of the following audiences:

1. You are writing the essay for a school magazine. Your audience is made up of college students.
2. You are writing for the *Reader's Digest*; your audience is primarily middle-aged and middle-class.
3. You are writing for an audience over the age of sixty.

5. Probing a Broad Subject with Subcategories

As you know, you will not always be assigned paper topics such as a paper clip, an orange, or a photograph. The next step up in complexity from these is the broad and general subject that must be divided into subcategories and then examined. In other words, you must probe this kind of subject on two levels instead of one. You might, for instance, be assigned an essay on "Campus Characters." Instead of simply profiling yourself and your buddies, you should try to identify some unusual character *types* on campus: the Hare Krishnas, the punk-rockers, the Ultimate Frisbee players, and so on. Better still, you might group the various types according to the patterns they follow or the purpose that they serve: the members of religious or psychic groups, the musicians, the devotees of unusual sports. You then settle down to the work of probing each type for its essential characteristics, as you have been doing up to this point with individual objects. Do not forget to establish your audience and your role as writer, either; these are, if anything, more important in dealing with more complicated subjects than in treating fairly simple ones.

   a). Writing Assignment:
Pick one subject from the following list:

   spectators at athletic events
   pets and the people who own them
   shoes (or T-shirts, hats, etc.) and their wearers
   places where people go for vacations

Answer the following questions, making brief notes on your responses:

1. First, probe your subject. How can you break it down into specific categories? Is there more than one way of doing so? If so, what are the different ways?
2. Probe a typical member or element of each category, using the guidelines you have been given in this chapter and in the other exercises. (See the form in Exercise **3,** for example.)
3. Probe your audience. For whom are you writing this? Why? What approaches will you need? and so on.
4. Probe yourself as speaker or writer. From what point of view do you yourself approach this material? What attitude do you take toward it?
   Using the notes you have accumulated, write a brief essay classifying the significant types or categories within the subject you have chosen.

Evidence:
Thinking About
What to Say

Appeals and Evidence
Emotional Appeals
Ethical Appeals
Rational Appeals

The Nature of Evidence
External Testimony
Statistics
Facts, Inferences, and Opinions

Problems with Rational Appeals
Not Enough Facts
Confusing the Issue
Mixing the Appeals

Evaluating Appeals

Exercises

Chapter 1 presented various ways of determining what you want to say in an essay and ways of generating material for it. This chapter will examine more closely the possible uses of the material you have generated. In particular, it will show the ways in which the material may be used to form appeals to an audience and to supply evidence and support for such appeals.

Imagine again that you are that School of Management student from Chapter 1 who is doing a paper on the liberal arts "core curriculum." You want to be taken seriously, and so you must state your case to your audience, the faculty senate, as effectively and in as many ways as possible. Or imagine that you are living near a large and pleasant park. Suddenly, the city announces plans to sell the park to a corporation that wants to build a shopping center on it. If you want to save the park, you and your neighbors must persuade the city not to sell it. To do this, you must use every kind of appeal you can command.

APPEALS AND EVIDENCE

Because no two human situations are exactly alike, you will find that no foolproof formula exists for bringing a reader over to your point of view. Of the three types of appeals—emotional, ethical, and rational—you can rarely rely on one to the exclusion of the others. And the combinations you employ will vary from one case to the next. You can develop, however, an instinct for knowing "the rules of the game"—that is, for knowing which appeals can be used successfully in some situations and which in others. If, for example, your position calls for a great deal of detailed factual support, you will not want to launch into an appeal so emotional that it might be accompanied by swelling violin music. On the other hand, if you can best accomplish your purpose by swaying emotions, you should probably refrain from simply presenting a list of cold statistics. Let us begin by looking at the three types of appeals and examining their capabilities and limits.

Emotional Appeals

Emotional appeals stem from feelings, and their aim is to stir an audience's feelings about something. Young children arguing with their parents may provide the purest examples of emotional appeals. When a parent tells a child to finish his lima beans, and the child replies, "Aw, please, Daddy, I *hate* lima beans!", the child is relying on his dislike for lima beans and the possibility of getting his father to sympathize with this dislike. Needless to say, you can seldom carry an argument on the basis of an emotional appeal alone. The child, for example, will probably have to finish his lima beans whether he wants to or not. Likewise, arguing against the "core curriculum" in the faculty senate by reciting the hardships the new requirements will cause in the professional schools will not necessarily impress the professors, no matter how touching your speech sounds. In some situations, however, the emotional appeal can be the crowning touch to an argument. If you are attempting to persuade the city to spare your park, you can wind up your plea far more effectively with a description of what the park means to the community than you could with an unimpassioned cost–benefit analysis.

Ethical Appeals

Ethical appeals seek to draw the audience to the personality of the speaker or writer. In essence, an ethical appeal says, "You should believe me because I am a good person," or "You should believe me because I am an authority and know a great deal about the subject." As that management student arguing your case in the faculty senate, for example, you would present yourself as a serious, responsible student who has studied the issue in order to arrive at a well-informed position. Likewise, in presenting your defense of the park to the city council, you would want to make clear your status as a resident of the community and your specific knowledge of the problems a shopping center would create. It is virtually impossible, however, to put together a convincing ethical appeal without other types of appeals to back it up: you cannot convince people that you are a person to be believed without presenting evidence of one kind or another to prove it.

Abuses of ethical appeals—ethical appeals outside a person's real field of knowledge or experience—are common, especially in advertisements. Why, after all, should we believe a former television doctor's warnings about caffeine jitters or a hockey player's advice about mutual funds? You should not underestimate the power of ethical appeals, but you should use them only when you can claim some kind of "expertise" on the subject as well.

Rational Appeals

Rational appeals are so named because they spring from a speaker's or writer's sense of reason and logic, and they appeal to that same sense in an audience. Instead of playing on the audience's emotions or calling attention to her own personality, the pleader of a cause making a rational appeal will either examine the internal relationships among elements in the situation she is discussing or call in external testimony to support her position.

"Reason" and "logic," of course, do not mean the same things to all people in all places at all times. Another culture's concept of "reason" and "reasonable behavior" can be quite different from our own. Still, within our own culture, we observe certain conventions for the use of reason in convincing an audience; the writer who wishes to bring a Western audience over to her point of view must learn these conventions.

In a rational appeal you can examine the elements within a situation in many ways, although the particular methods you use will vary in each case. You can, for example, consider *causes and effects*. If you want to persuade the city not to put a shopping center in the park, for example, you can list the bad effects that shopping centers can cause—increases in traffic and vandalism; heavier use of such public facilities as roads and sewers; air pollution; drops in residential property values; noise problems; and the like. Some of these, in fact, may cause further effects: increased traffic means increased danger for children in the area; increased use of public facilities may lead to increased taxes. If you are arguing against the "core curriculum," you might point out that the increase in liberal arts requirements may force students in the professional schools to take fewer professional courses, thereby discouraging many potential employers from hiring them.

In a rational appeal you can also *compare* elements in the situation you are examining to corresponding elements in a similar situation. For example, if the effects of converting another city park to a shopping center have been bad, you can compare these bad effects to the possible effects on your own community. You can also *contrast* corresponding elements. If another university has required a liberal arts "core curriculum" in its professional schools and the job placement rate for graduates has dropped significantly, you could contrast this fact with your own university's *present* placement rate. You must not, of course, frame a comparison or a contrast when you lack legitimate grounds for doing so. If another university's job placement rate has *not* been affected by its change in curriculum, a comparison will not advance your position.

THE NATURE OF EVIDENCE

No matter what appeal you use to examine a situation, your position will not be convincing without some sort of evidence to support it. The testimony of others on the subject at hand, statistics that relate to your subject, scientific studies, legal opinions, and even the letter of the law itself can be cited by you to advance your position. (Chapter 11, "The Library Research Paper," will direct you further in searching for and using various sorts of evidence.)

External Testimony

External testimony can take several forms. You can cite the words of experts or informed individuals on the topic in question. For example, you might quote an urban planner's assessment of the situation in your effort to save the park. Or you might present the views of your school's Placement Office and various professors to support your opposition to the "core curriculum." You can also cite testimony given by laypeople involved in the situation at hand—the statements of your neighbors about the park question or those of your fellow students about the "core curriculum." When citing external testimony you must be careful to consider your sources' degree of expertise on the given subject, their possible motives for giving testimony (Is your roommate genuinely opposed to the core curriculum, or is he simply afraid of taking English classes?), and the strength of other forces that could affect their statements. You must also be careful not to misrepresent testimony or to alter it to suit your own purposes. If the Placement Office's statement gives your position only partial support, you should not ignore parts of its statement that do not support your position. Finally, you should carefully consider what kind of testimony your audience will respond to. If the park you are trying to save is notorious for late-night fraternity parties, the testimony of fraternity members will not sway city council members who may be interested in maintaining peace and quiet.

Statistics

Another form of evidence available to you is statistics. If, for example, you are asserting that the "core curriculum" requirement will ultimately harm professional school students' chances in the job market, you had better have some facts and figures to back you up. Likewise, statistical proof of the bad effects you claim shopping centers have on residential neighborhoods—figures to show *how much* taxes, traffic, and vandalism have increased in that community across town, for example—will help to convince the city council that you may be right.

You cannot, however, simply accept all statistics as fact. Statistics may reflect only a limited set of conditions or may conflict with other statistics; they may be affected by the motives and biases of those who compile them.

In order to be able to determine which of the pieces of information you encounter can be used legitimately in various situations, you need to know the difference between a fact, an inference drawn from a fact, and a judgment or opinion based on a fact. None of these is bad or good in itself, but mistaking one for another can seriously damage your position.

	1975	1976	1977	1978	1979
TOTAL MONTHLY PRECIPITATION IN SYRACUSE, NEW YORK					
January	2.54	2.79	1.84	5.77	4.70
February	3.05	2.71	1.62	.80	2.54
March	2.67	4.62	3.47	3.08	2.73
April	2.01	8.12	3.04	1.87	3.89
May	2.74	7.41	.75	1.90	3.07
June	4.08	7.42	3.30	3.58	2.33
July	9.32	5.24	4.76	2.78	2.33
August	5.35	6.73	4.93	3.31	3.69
September	8.81	3.27	6.54	3.93	5.25
October	3.69	6.53	4.75	2.68	2.91
November	3.54	1.53	5.31	1.25	3.25
December	4.10	1.80	4.33	4.12	1.84
ANNUAL	51.90	58.17	44.64	35.07	38.53

The statistics for January 1975 through October 1979 are from the official publication of the National Oceanic and Atmospheric Administration, Environmental Data Service, National Climatic Center, Asheville, NC, Vols. 82–91.
The information for November and December 1979 was obtained directly from the United States Weather Service at Hancock Field.
The measurements were taken at the Weather Service Station at Hancock Field.

Facts, Inferences, and Opinions

One good way to learn about facts, inferences, and opinions is to examine the different statements you can make about a set of statistics. In this instance we will use the monthly figures for precipitation in Syracuse, New York. (See the chart on p. 00). We generally agree to call *facts* those statements that answer questions regarding "what something is" or "whether something is." The statement, "Syracuse received 6.54 inches of precipitation in September 1977" is, by general consent, a factual statement. You should bear in mind, however, that some facts may not be absolutely reliable or accurate because the circumstances in which they are gathered may vary considerably. You might, for example, ask yourself these questions about the precipitation statistics:

1. For what parts of Syracuse are the figures representative? All of Syracuse? Or simply one patch of cement at the airport (Hancock Field) where the weather bureau set up its equipment?
2. Who gathered the data? How can we be sure that the gatherer was telling the truth? How recently had his eyes been checked? Was he sober?

3. Were the instruments accurate? How recently had *they* been checked? Were there any mechanical problems with them?
4. Was any method used to cross-check or double-check the data?

If all these questions can be answered to your satisfaction, you can consider "Syracuse received 6.54 inches of precipitation in September 1977" a fact—a valid declaration based on proven data. What you *cannot* do, however, is to mistake statements you make on the basis of this declaration or others like it for facts. When you figure up the average precipitation for September in Syracuse and estimate the precipitation for next September, you are not stating facts, but making *inferences.* Just as it is possible to have an incorrect statement of a fact because of some irregularity in its gathering, so it is also possible to draw an inference that is invalid because it is based on insufficient facts.

If you examined the precipitation figures for September and said, "Syracuse has gray skies for much of the month of September," this would be a valid inference; "Syracuse sure gets a lot of rain in the fall," however, would *not* be a valid inference, because it would not be based on all the fall figures. You cannot hope to establish a position on a subject, let alone persuade others to agree with your position, without making inferences from facts. But you must take care not to confuse inferences with facts and not to draw inferences from inadequate data.

Opinions are statements that attempt to answer questions regarding "what kind something is" or "what quality something is." Opinions can be damaging when they are confused with facts. Opinion, unlike inference, is purely a matter of personal taste and judgment. For example, if a sun-worshiper and a rain-lover looked at the September figures and said, "Syracuse has lousy weather in September!" and "Syracuse has wonderful weather in September!", there would be no way of contradicting either of them. Both are statements of personal taste. You would not, however, want to present either statement as a fact. Opinions, like inferences, can be based on insufficient data, and such opinions can be dangerous when presented as fact. The sun-worshiper, for instance, could say, "Syracuse has lousy weather in September, and it should therefore be wiped off the map." This example may seem farfetched, but several groups of people in the twentieth century have produced equally farfetched opinions and acted on them as facts. This is not to say, of course, that you can or should omit everything resembling an opinion from your attempts to bring readers to your point of view. Opinion, in truth, is the very heart and soul of emotional appeal—and it enters inevitably into the other types of appeals as well. You must, however, be able to discriminate between fact and opinion in supporting a rational appeal, and you must guard against the use of opinions based on too few facts even in making an emotional appeal. The inability to distinguish between facts and opinions—and sometimes between facts and inferences as well—causes most of the commonly recognized problems in making rational appeals.

PROBLEMS WITH RATIONAL APPEALS

Not Enough Facts

One problem with attempts at making a rational appeal is that the appeal is simply not supported with enough facts. Intentionally or unintentionally, the framers of such appeals fail to mention important facts about a situation or to report them correctly, thereby making the situations seem a good deal simpler (and the writers' positions more unequivocally "right") than they really are.

LACK OF OBJECTIVITY. The inability or unwillingness to see that there may be more than one side to an issue is called *lack of objectivity*. People sometimes have such an emotional investment in a certain viewpoint that their singleminded loyalty to that viewpoint blinds them to the possible validity of other positions on the issue. Thus, one of the first techniques law students learn is to argue a case from all sides, if only to make sure that no vital point escapes them.

Knowing an issue thoroughly requires familiarity with *all* of its aspects. Notice the writer's lack of objectivity in the following letter to the editor of a metropolitan newspaper:

> I just read the article by Colonel Tucker re: these "Hell no—I won't go" jerks, especially these college clowns. I ask a question, to these college boys or anyone else. Just what have these people done for their country that they believe they have the right to march, protest and other stupid actions? I believe an American should stand up for his country, but, if they insist on this "hell no" business, they should be taken out of college and taught a few things about patriotism.
>
> If one has contributed to his country and the world in general, I say they are entitled to voice an opinion, 90 percent of these college heroes are in school thanks to parents or government grants, the ones on government grants seem to have the loudest mouths against the draft and who incidentally don't even pay back the money they were given by the taxpayers.

Aside from the wild-eyed quality of the letter, the writer's omissions and distortions of fact make it difficult for a reader to take him seriously. The premise on which he bases his entire argument is that no one is "entitled to voice an opinion" in this country unless he has "contributed to his country and the world in general." The fact is, however, that the Constitution guarantees the rights of free speech and peaceful assembly to every citizen, regardless of the degree of his "contribution" to the country; controversy does exist as to how far "free speech" should extend, but certainly "contribution"—whatever that may mean—has never been a criterion for it.

The writer also states that "90 percent of these college heroes are in school thanks to parents or government grants," that "the ones on government grants seem to have the loudest mouths against the draft," and that these students "don't even pay back the money they were given by the taxpayers." This series of statements overlooks or misrepresents a whole group of facts. The "90 percent" figure is not authenticated in any way, and the context in which it is mentioned suggests that it is a disgrace for college students to accept any form of financial assistance, which is not necessarily true. The statements about students on government grants are particularly flawed: no evidence is given to suggest that such students are more deeply involved in protest than other students, that they have less right to protest than other students, or that every one of them makes a practice of defaulting on his loans. The writer of this letter is certainly entitled to defend his position. But did his strong feelings about the issue lead him to omit some facts and alter others?

EITHER/OR THINKING.   Either/or thinking is another problem that can damage a rational appeal. Many people find it a real temptation, in a society whose every issue seems to consist of ifs, ands, and buts, to try to simplify matters with "either/or"—that is, to think about things as if there were only two sides to every issue and as if only one of these were the correct one. Few matters today are this simple, however. We must remember that issues can have more than two sides and that simple solutions to complex issues are often not possible.

Consider the following passage from an article by economist Milton Friedman on the conflict between economic controls and personal freedom, in which he takes the Food and Drug Administration to task:

> The drug industry is an example of an industry that has been seriously hampered by government intervention and regulation, especially since the days of Estes Kefauver in 1962. I believe that the Food and Drug Administration has, on the whole, done a great deal more harm than good. The reason is very simple—no Food and Drug administrator has ever been pilloried for *not* approving a drug which was potentially capable of saving lives. Any Food and Drug administrator is bound to be pilloried for making the other mistake, namely, approving a drug which turned out to be harmful. As a result, the Food and Drug people have a bias in favor of holding up good drugs in order to avoid the possibility of a mistake in approving a bad one. The result is that there are many effective drugs which are available in Canada, in Britain, and elsewhere which cannot be purchased by people in the United States, but which might very well save their lives.
>
> —Milton Friedman, "Economic Controls vs. Personal Freedom"

What Friedman calls the FDA's "bias in favor of holding up good drugs" may well have prevented some helpful new drugs from reaching the American market as quickly as they might have become available in other countries. But the issue is by no means as simple and clear-cut as Friedman makes it appear. Is it fair or correct, for example, to call the FDA's policy of caution a "bias"? Is it possible to prove that a drug really *is* a "good" drug without extensive testing? (Few American mothers in the late 1950s, for example, would have called the FDA's policy on thalidomide a "bias." The sedative was found to cause deformities in the children of expectant mothers who took it, but far fewer babies were affected in the U.S. than in Europe because the drug was still being tested in this country.) Some people might argue that a few drugs currently available in America should have been tested even *more* thoroughly. As you can see, statements as sweeping as Friedman's on an issue of any real complexity are risky at best. Those who make them should at least be prepared to define and qualify them appropriately and to provide facts and examples to back them up.

STEREOTYPING.   *Stereotyping* is an example of a writer's inability or unwillingness to consider all the facts of a situation. Many people—too many—find that it is easier to view entire groups of people in terms of a few members of these groups. We still encounter unfounded assumptions about "thrifty" Scots, "absent-minded" professors, "stupid" jocks, and "dumb" blondes from those who ought to know better. The truth is, of course, that not all Scots are thrifty, not all professors are absent-minded, not all athletes are stupid, and not all blondes are dumb. The stereotypes persist, however, either because they present an easy alternative to analyzing the precise nature of particular individuals and groups or because they have become so ingrained in a society that no one questions them. If a writer finds herself using stereotypes to analyze situations, she should ask herself what it is about the position she is taking that requires this kind of oversimplification.

CULTURAL CONDITIONING.   Stereotypes are often a part of *cultural conditioning*—the system of values learned and reinforced within a culture. You do not, of course, have to try to avoid making use of any aspect of this conditioning as a writer. Indeed, you could not hope to establish effective contact with an audience within your own culture if you did so. You must not, however, allow it to influence your judgments of people and things outside your own culture. It is not really fair to pass judgment on a culture or subculture by the standards of your own group. For example, would you be within your rights to dismiss the Amish as "backward" simply because they do not accept modern technology the way most Americans do? Is owning an all-electric home and driving a fancy car valuable in itself, or has our society simply assigned a positive value to this style of living? Hasty judgments based on the standards of your own group contribute to misunderstandings between neighbors as well as nations.

Cultural conditioning also contributes to many of the opinions you may form about the nature of your own society. For example, in the past women were portrayed in subservient roles on television and radio, in books, and even in children's primers. As a result, many people have been conditioned to *think* of women only in subservient roles. Now, in the wake of the feminist movement of the 1960s and 1970s, we are being reconditioned. Current TV commercials portray husbands popping spinach casseroles into microwave ovens all by themselves, while their wives exchange lawyerly quips with judges while drinking cups of decaffeinated coffee. Such portrayals, of course, do not reflect reality for all American couples, either.

As the fabric of our society changes, so does the way in which we are conditioned to perceive it. When you write, try to be aware that conditioning may prevent you from doing justice to the facts as they exist.

Confusing the Issue

Sometimes writers fail to frame a rational appeal, whether deliberately or unconsciously, by not presenting enough facts. At other times writers simply confuse an issue through their perception of it. These problems can be unintentional or intentional—that is, they can stem from fuzzy thinking on an issue, or they can originate in a deliberate desire to mislead an audience. You should learn to avoid confusing an issue both in the writing of others and in your own.

BEGGING THE QUESTION.   *Begging the question* in an appeal means asserting as valid or correct the very point you are trying to prove. It is a common way of confusing an issue. The problem is usually one of circular reasoning, and many young writers are unaware that it is a problem. They may write, "Murder is wrong because it is not morally right," or "Students should be allowed to drink beer on campus because it would not be fair to forbid them to do it," without realizing that the thing they are trying to prove and the means by which they are trying to prove it are actually one and the same. Questions can be begged more subtly than this. If a lawyer were to say, "This murderer should be found guilty of the charges against him," he has in effect just *found* him guilty by labeling him a murderer. If your attempt to bring an audience to your point of view is only a matter of statement and restatement, there probably is not much *to* your argument.

EQUIVOCATION.   The use of a word or a phrase in two or more different meanings is known as *equivocation* and is another means of confusing an issue. A humorous example of equivocation is the statement,

"A good steak is rare these days, so be sure not to order yours well done." The word "rare" is used in two different senses: as a judgmental adjective meaning "hard to find" or "unusual" and as a cooking designation. In more serious circumstances, forcing an important point to depend solely upon an equivocation is like begging the question—an indication that your position may be shaky to begin with.

FALSE ANALOGY.   A *false analogy* is yet another way of confusing an issue. False analogies compare two things, persons, or actions that are alike in some respects but not in others. Comparison, as you learned earlier, can be a very effective means of making a rational appeal. If, however, you ignore significant differences when making analogies, you can confuse your readers and undermine your position.

Examine this letter to the editor of a college newspaper for examples of false analogies, as well as a few examples of equivocation:

> With a great show of moral indignation, it was recently revealed that 47 percent of Monroe College students "cheated" on examinations. Since then, readers of the *Bulletin* have been deluged with pious commentaries. Isn't it about time someone asked whether our modern Puritans aren't being overly righteous in this matter?
>
> On the contrary, copying or the use of crib notes seems quite pardonable in many cases. In a course which requires remembering a lot of facts, why not use crib notes? It's only a difference of degree between using them and using some elaborate system for memorizing facts. Both are artificial means to help you remember.
>
> If we view the problem from another angle, we can see that what is so smugly denounced as "dishonesty" may actually reveal foresight—which is certainly a praiseworthy trait. If you were going into an unknown wilderness, you would take along the things you knew were needed for survival, wouldn't you? Taking crib notes into the unknown territory of an examination shows the same foresight. Now suppose also that one of your companions desperately needed water or food or help of some sort. You'd do what you could for him, wouldn't you? Helping someone on an examination isn't any different.
>
> To put the matter another way, suppose we define charity as "giving to a person in need." Isn't one therefore performing an act of charity during an exam when one gives some "needy" person the desired information? The fact that one isn't giving money or food doesn't make the act any less charitable.

The first analogy in the letter—the comparison of crib notes and "some elaborate system for memorizing facts"—breaks down immediately when it is examined. Any "system" a person uses to remember facts at least guarantees that he will *do* the remembering; crib notes release a test taker from the necessity of having to remember anything at all. The second comparison, the one between taking a survival kit into "unknown territory" and taking notes into an exam, is equally flimsy.

The material covered in an examination should not be "unknown territory" unless the student taking the exam has been playing pinball all semester. The analogy between helping a starving person in the wilderness and helping a fellow student on an examination is also dubious. A person in trouble in the wilderness is less personally responsible for the troublesome circumstances and more in need of the actual necessities of life than any floundering exam taker. The final analogy—the comparison between extending charity to a person in need and helping someone on a test—breaks down for much the same reasons as the third one does: the more questionable motives and lesser actual "need" of the student accepting assistance on an exam must be considered.

Equivocation accompanies false analogy more often than not. Notice the way in which the writer of this letter alters the meanings of "artificial means to help you remember," "unknown territory," and "charity," to make something negative seem positive.

Mixing the Appeals

A third problem in framing a rational appeal can be the temptation to mix other kinds of appeals—emotional or ethical—with the rational appeal, or to present an emotional or ethical appeal as a rational appeal. There is nothing wrong with an emotional appeal or an ethical appeal as long as you present it plainly for what it is. In fact, a properly placed and worded emotional appeal can help you carry the day in many situations. When you present one of these appeals as a purely rational appeal, however—that is, when you treat an emotion or an opinion as a matter of simple fact and use it as the rationale for whatever follows in stating your position—you are, in effect, hitting your reader below the belt.

AGAINST THE MAN. The *argument against the man* (known in Latin as *argumentum ad hominem*) is one example of an emotional appeal masquerading as a rational one. The framer of such an argument attacks his opponent personally instead of addressing the substance of his opponent's argument. At a political debate, for example, if a candidate were to respond to another candidate's remarks with "Hawkins makes some surprisingly good points for a former Communist sympathizer," or "Even if he didn't have a drinking problem and three ex-wives, I still wouldn't agree with Hawkins about the nuclear reactor," she would be demonstrating the "argument against the man" in its purest form. It is a manifestly unfair way of defending a position, but examples of it continue to make the front pages every day.

APPEAL TO NUMBERS. The *appeal to numbers* (*argumentum ad populem*) is another common mixture of the appeals. It is also known as the "bandwagon" technique: a speaker or writer tries to bring people to his point of view—to "get them on the bandwagon"—by using numbers or statistics as the *sole* means of persuasion. Admirers of the late Elvis Presley, for example, used to say, "Fifty million Elvis fans can't be wrong!". The implicit suggestion was that still more people should be moved to add themselves to the number. The problem with this appeal is that if one does not like or has no particular interest in Elvis's music, it simply does not matter how many others do. The "appeal to numbers" is also often used to justify far more dubious matters. The student who wrote the letter on cheating at Monroe College, for instance, might have contended, "Forty-seven percent of Monroe College students cheat. Therefore, it can't be wrong." The other fifty-three percent might well object to this statement—and with justification.

APPEAL TO PITY.   Still another emotional appeal disguised as a rational appeal is the *appeal to pity* (*argumentum ad misericordiam*). It asks the reader to feel sorry for the writer or for the central figure in an issue instead of evaluating the genuine worth of the case. The student who writes at the end of an essay, "I hope you like this paper. I stayed up all night and skipped breakfast this morning to finish it," is appealing to her teacher's pity. The chances are good that her teacher will not be impressed.

The Monroe College student, through the analogies he sets up in his letter on cheating, is also making an "appeal to pity" on behalf of that forty-seven percent of his classmates. As you have seen, though, that appeal does not succeed. The objects of an "appeal to pity" may truly deserve the reader's pity, but the case for it must be based on more convincing evidence than simply the appeal itself.

EVALUATING APPEALS

Using what you have learned about the different types of appeals, the kinds of evidence that can be used with these appeals, and the problems possible in the framing of these appeals, you may find it instructive and helpful to sit down and analyze some of the hundreds of appeals that are beamed at us in the course of a day. Radios and televisions blare, billboards vie for our attention, unsolicited mail arrives—how many of these appeals appeal to us honestly? Take this one, based on typical advertisements you see on television and in magazines. "More doctors recommend Stop Throb than any other pain reliever." What does "more" mean here? (Two out of three? Six out of ten?) What kinds of doctors are doing the recommending? (Ph.D.s? Veterinarians? Chiropractors?) In what sense is the word "recommend" being used? (Remember that the principal ingredient in Stop Throb is plain aspirin; do the doctors actually recommend Stop Throb by name, or do they say, "Go home, put your foot in a bucket of hot water, and take two aspirins"?) And, finally, "More doctors recommend Stop Throb"—than *what kind* of pain reliever? (An ice pack to the head? Heroin?)

Such analyses will give you excellent practice for evaluating the positions you take in your own papers. You yourself may have been framing statements as slippery as "More doctors recommend Stop Throb" and expecting them to be accepted as absolute truth. Careful examinations of both your own and others' appeals should bring you to a much fuller understanding of what does and does not constitute an effective presentation of a point of view by the standards of our culture.

Effective presentation depends not only on the strength of what you have to say, but on the way in which you shape and organize your material. Chapter 3 will introduce you to the possibilities available to you in shaping your essays.

EXERCISES

1. Appeals

a). In the passages and advertisement below, identify the words, phrases, or aspects of the photograph that signal appeals to emotions, authority, and reason. Answer the following questions in relation to the materials presented:

1. Do any of the examples use only one of the appeals or a combination of the various appeals? Why? Do some kinds of appeals dominate others? Why?
2. How does the audience dictate the nature of the appeal? The speaker? The purpose or content of the material?

The whole process of spraying seems caught up in an endless spiral. Since DDT was released for civilian use, the process of escalation has been going on in which ever more toxic materials must be found. This has happened because insects, in a triumphant vindication of Darwin's principle of the survival of the fittest, have evolved super races immune to the particular insecticide used, hence a deadlier one has always to be developed—and then a deadlier one than that. It has happened also because, for reasons to be described later, destructive insects tend to undergo a "flareback," or resurgence, after spraying, in numbers greater than before. Thus the chemical war is never won, and all life is caught in its violent crossfire.

—Rachel Carson, *Silent Spring*

The unabridged Second Edition of Webster's Dictionary—a volume of no small repute—gives the following as the second definition of the word *plant*: "Any living thing that cannot move voluntarily, has no sense organs and generally makes its own food. . . ." I have chosen the second definition in favor of the first because it better serves my purpose, which is to prove once and for all that, except in extremely rare instances, a plant is really not the sort of thing that one ought to have around the house. That this might be accomplished in an orderly manner, I have elected to consider each aspect of the above definition individually. Let us begin at the beginning.

—Fran Lebowitz, *Metropolitan Life*

What does a woman want?
—SIGMUND FREUD

Nothing else feels like real gold

Giving real gold means giving Karat Gold. Personal, beautiful —anytime, anywhere. Karat Gold Jewelry.

(Courtesy of Intergold)

The biggest problem, however, is that the faith of the American people in the experts has been badly shaken. People have learned, for one thing, that certified technical gospel is far from immortal. Medicine changes its mind about tonsillectomies that used to be routinely performed. Those dazzling phosphate detergents turn out to be anathema to the environment. Scarcely a week goes by without the credibility of one expert or another falling afoul of some spike of fresh news. (Just last week an array of nonprescription sedatives used by millions was linked, through the ingredient methapyrilene, to cancer.) Moreover, experts are constantly challenging experts, debating the benefits and hazards of virtually every technical thrust. Who knows anything for sure? Could supersonic aircraft truly damage the ozone? The technical sages disagree.

> —Frank Trippett, "A New Distrust of the Experts"

b). Write paragraphs, draw cartoons, or make up advertisements that do the following:

1. Use only one kind of appeal.
2. Mix the appeals in an attempt to win the audience with openness.
3. Mix the appeals in a subtle way to mislead and manipulate the audience.
4. Mix the appeals but clearly let one kind dominate.

c). Take your examples for numbers 1. and 4. in the last exercise and rework:

1. Use the same material but make a different appeal.
2. Use the same material but let a different appeal dominate the combination.

d). Bring visual and written examples of the three different appeals to class. Choose two or three and use them for class analysis. Then, write a brief analysis of one of your examples. Trade with another student and analyze his or hers. Compare the two analyses of each piece.

e). Find three samples (essays, letters to the editor, fiction, newspaper advertisements) illustrating appropriate use of appeals. Write a brief essay discussing what makes them appropriate. Do the same for three examples that use the appeals unfairly or inappropriately.

f). What kinds of appeals can be used in the following situations and how can they be made? Think of as many different approaches as possible.

1. You want to share a special moment—first with a friend, and then, with a new acquaintance.
2. You are the inventory control manager in a small company, and you must tell your dependable assistant that she is going to lose her job because the budget is being cut, and executives in the company think she is too aggressive.
3. You are a professor of English who teaches freshman composition.

Try to get your students to understand why clear, well-organized writing is important.

4. You are a lawyer involved in a divorce and custody case. You and your client want the judge to approve a joint custody decision. Your client's spouse and lawyer want sole custody. No solid evidence of the unfitness of either parent has been presented in the case.
5. Persuade someone you have met in this class to go out with you.
6. Submit a report to your boss in which you recommend the purchase of a very expensive piece of equipment for your company.

2. Facts, Inferences, Judgments

a). Analyze the following entries and identify the facts, inferences, and judgments in each.

According to McCombe, attendance at Chapel services, including the Protestant one criticized as too "conservative" by Eggers, has risen since 1970. This fact, assuming that it is true, points out two things about McCombe: once again, that he is popular among students, and his brand of Christianity is not discouraging students from attending Sunday services.

I don't think that anyone can deny that Church attendance, for all denominations, is down considerably nationwide over the last decade. In his report to the Board of Trustees last month even Eggers pointed out that he could remember a time "when the Chapel was filled to overflowing with students and elders participating in the services." Obviously, McCombe's popularity among students has succeeded in overcoming a nationwide phenomenon of decreasing attendance.

—A student paper

Lord Peter Wimsey stretched himself luxuriously between the sheets provided by the Hotel Meurice. After his exertions in the unravelling of the Battersea Mystery, he had followed Sir Julian Freke's advice and taken a holiday. He had felt suddenly weary of breakfasting every morning before his view over Green Park; he had realised [sic] that the picking up of first editions at sales afforded insufficient exercise for a man of thirty-three; the very crimes of London were over-sophisticated. He had abandoned his flat and his friends and fled to the wilds of Corsica. For the last three months he had forsworn letters, newspapers, and telegrams. He had tramped about the mountains, admiring from a cautious distance the wild beauty of Corsican peasant-women, and studying the vendetta in its natural haunt. In such conditions murder seemed not only reasonable, but lovable. Bunter, his confidential man and assistant sleuth, had nobly sacrificed his civilized habits, had let his master go dirty and even unshaven, and had turned his faithful camera from the recording of finger-prints to that of craggy scenery. It had been very refreshing.

Now, however, the call of blood was upon Lord Peter. They had returned late last night in a vile train to Paris, and had picked up their luggage. . . .

—Dorothy Sayers, *Clouds of Witness*

b). Analyze this advertisement. What are the facts of it? What do the advertisers want us to infer? How are the facts and inferences presented to help us arrive at a definition of classic? Write a brief essay that begins with the following phrase: According to the MG advertisement, *classic* can be defined as . . .

3. Barriers to Logical Thinking
Read each of the following passages. Identify the barrier(s) to logical thinking in each. Explain how and why each barrier obstructs the logical pattern of thought.

Our colleges were bulging at the seams with enrollment because momma and daddy did not want sonny to go to war, so whether he was college material or not, if momma and daddy had to hock their souls they sent sonny to college. Are these individuals who shirked their duty during World War II and the Korean War the parents of these protestors at our universities and colleges now? I wouldn't be the least surprised to find out that this is why these protestors show no love for this country. Or are these the younger brothers and sisters of the ones who sought havens in other countries to escape the conflict in Vietnam? Take your pick.

—Letter to the Editor

A century ago, every half-educated person knew who the great poets were. Who are the great poets now? Indeed, who reads contemporary poetry at all?

This, of course, is a different world, and the cognoscenti who over 25 centuries from Pindar to Housman eagerly discussed the poet of the hour now have other diversions.

—Jenkin Lloyd Jones, "A Good Case for Miniver Cheevy"

There is a basic need for most men to play the role of a good provider, even a hero. Most men still need to go out and do, literally and figuratively, and gain some measure of honor, respect and approval in the world.

The whole point, it seems to me, of being a hero or heroine, of winning the prize is to have someone to win for.

If a man seeks approval only for himself, he ends up isolated and alone. In spite of his achievements, life remains empty. Achievement is not enough. In all cases, it is a woman who must ultimately appear in a man's life. She must appear to give his achievements a deeper sense of meaning and completion.

In a good marriage, it is the woman too for whom the man is doing battle. She is the person who humanizes his life and makes it worthwhile. She has the capacity to balance his thoughts with feeling, his coldness with warmth, his ambition with compassion.

Personally, for men and women alike, I think that one finding love, warmth and approval—without and within—is what truly gives ultimate meaning to our lives.

—Dr. Pierre Mornell, *Passive Men, Wild Women*

"If you're not with the one you love, love the one you're with." "Why don't we do it in the road." "And let it out and let it in, Hey Jude, begin . . ." These lyrics are by now almost cliches. But at the time that they landed on top of the music charts they were shocking to most Americans. This is not to suggest that Rock and Roll initiated "free love," but rather that it propelled the idea into the realm of public acceptance for the first time in the history of our country. This same cause-effect relationship between Rock and the sexual revolution can be adeptly applied to Rock and Roll and public attitudes about drug use and abuse. The heroes of Rock were unquestionably not pioneers in the field of alteration of body chemistry states and subsequent altered states of consciousness. They were, however, the first group of artists to gain national recognition on the subject. In this way Rock and Roll, to a considerable degree, closed the communication gap between youth's social and drug-related actions, and their parents' understanding of these activities.

Indeed Rock and Roll has changed America. Although music, of any kind, is not normally considered to have a profound effect on the minds of the listener, Rock and Roll is the exception to the rule. It *is* the exception because during the sixties and seventies there existed a unique supply-demand situation. The demand was for people to say and feel what their minds and bodies told them; to say it bravely, without hesitation or inhibition; and to say it with the determination that can only be the voice of a proud people. Rock and Roll said it.

—A student paper

4. Formal Papers

a). Write a paper in which you argue for a particular judgment of the Mornell essay. Your audience is the person who must make a decision about accepting or rejecting it for publication.

b). Make up a new product. Write an essay (include visual material, if you like) that tries to sell the product to a test audience that has no need for the product.

c). You are defending a company whose recently marketed product has caused blindness in a number of consumers. Write your closing speech to the judge and jury.

d). Write an essay proving the validity and truth of one of the following judgments (or its opposite).

1. English courses are stupid, unnecessary, and a waste of time.
2. Students should receive professional training throughout their four years in college; they should not waste time on liberal arts requirements.
3. The legal age for drinking should remain at the age of eighteen.
4. Students should not be allowed in college until they have proved they can read and write at the level of high school seniors.

Organization: Shaping Your Material

Deciding on Organization

Producing a Thesis
Supporting the Thesis
Placing the Thesis

Organizing with a Formal Outline

Discerning Order in the Subject Matter
Chronology
Process
Spatial Organization

Internal Patterns of Organization

Other Patterns of Organization
Classical Rhetoric
Innovative Patterns

Coherence in the Essay

Exercises

In Chapter 1, you learned how to discover *what* you can say in an essay. In Chapter 2, you learned the ways you can appeal to an audience and the types of evidence you can use in these appeals. In this chapter, you will learn how to use the material you have generated and your knowledge of appeals and evidence in the *shaping* of an essay. You will learn how to organize and pattern an essay in ways that will best suit the material, your purpose in presenting the material, and the audience for which you intend it.

The mind wanders, but a good essay must not if it is to succeed. The selection, development, and arrangement of your ideas is as important to the success of your essay as the ideas themselves. There is, however, no one correct way of organizing your material. Organization must depend upon your particular subject, audience, and purpose. The discussion that follows will provide you with suggestions for organizing your essay and will describe and illustrate some of the common forms.

DECIDING ON ORGANIZATION

If you have pursued the prewriting techniques conscientiously, you know how to search for a topic for your essay. Once you have decided on the best approach to your topic—decided how your material is best suited to your purpose and audience—you still may not know how to shape your essay. This problem can be most easily solved by preparing a *thesis*—a clear and precise statement of the position you will take on your topic. The work that will go into pinpointing your exact intentions in one or two sentences will actually do much of your organizing for you.

PRODUCING A THESIS

Why should you bother with a thesis? Most readers are not mind readers, and they do not have the time to figure out what your intentions are. If you cannot state early in your essay exactly what you are trying to demonstrate or prove, your readers may decide—perhaps correctly—that you do not know either. Consider the following introduction to an essay:

> Some people say that human beings cannot be held responsible for their actions. They claim that every form of human behavior may only be a response to the environment. These people say there's a little good in everybody, regardless of the way they act. Even the most hardened criminal may be basically good.

The writer plainly has no idea of what he wants to prove. Is he trying to say that human beings cannot be held responsible for their actions, or that human beings are essentially good? Who are "some people"? Which forms of "behavior" and which "environment" does the writer have in mind? Not all essays that lack clear theses are vague and puzzling, of course, but an essay that has a clear thesis will certainly save the reader the kind of guessing game that this introduction makes necessary.

A good thesis should be a clear statement, not just of your *topic*, but of your exact stand on the topic. Recall the illustration in Chapter 2 concerning an attempt to save a city park. If you are presenting your case for the park to the city council, you should not simply say that "Building a shopping center on the park site will have many effects on the neighborhood." This statement is far too simple. "Building a shopping center on the park site will have many *bad* effects on the neighborhood," is better, because it presents a position. But you should take the statement a step further and make it absolutely clear that you do not want the shopping center to be built. You must also make it clear that you wish the park to remain a park. Nothing in the statement indicates that you are opposed to the city selling the park for another project. Make the thesis reflect your real point in full: "The city should maintain Ellesmere Park as a park. The shopping center proposed for the site by Peabody Development Corporation would have many bad effects on the neighborhood. The park, in contrast, provides much pleasure to the residents of the area."

A thesis as precise as this one lets the reader know your exact position and, in part, helps to determine the structure of your essay. This thesis commits you to a two-part structure. In the first part, you must state what the effects of the shopping center will be and why they will be bad. In the second part, you must point out the ways in which the park provides pleasure to the residents of the area. Such a thesis aids the reader as well as the writer. The reader receives a clear idea both of the essay's intentions and of its organization, even before he comes to grips with the actual body of the essay.

Supporting the Thesis

Once a thesis is established you can begin to decide how to develop it so that the reader will accept your position. As you learned in Chapter 2, you should never assume that a reader will automatically agree with your position in an essay; you must provide evidence, illustrations, examples. One way of reviewing the options open to you in supporting your thesis is to reconsider the "brainstorming" of a topic you may have done in prewriting, or to brainstorm further if need be. A brainstorm of the park controversy might look like the figure on p. 52.

Why?
_____

City short of money to maintain it;
   needs to raise money for
   treasury
   (How much of a gain will this
   be in long run?)

   (Needs zone change: can city
   do this?)

Personal Reactions
_____

No!!
I go there to play frisbee almost
   every afternoon
Had a picnic for my family there
   when they came up to see me
Park one of ways I meet my
   neighbors
Don't want some smelly, noisy,
   crowded shopping center
   across the street!

ELLESMERE PARK AS SHOPPING CENTER?

Effects
_____

Noise
Increase in traffic
More roads will have to be built,
   existing ones widened
Increased burden on sewers, etc.
More people in area: possible
   increase in crime, vandalism?
Further zone changes; increased
   development possible once this
   begins

Neighborhood reaction
_____

Neighbors against it—
   —Their kids have a place to
    play now; increased traffic
    means danger for kids
   —Burden on roads and sewers;
    increases in taxes
   —Don't want crowds; worried
    about vandalism
Some might actually move to
   suburbs if shopping center
   built

In deciding which of these points to use in supporting your thesis, you must first determine which will be most effective in convincing your audience—the city council. You must then decide which points will work best in each of the two parts of your essay. For the first part, which is concerned with the "bad effects on the neighborhood," you can construct a cause-and-effect argument using almost all the points in the "Effects" column of the brainstorming. Make sure to trace the effects of these effects as well; city officials are generally as anxious as most neighborhood residents to avoid endangering children and increasing vandalism. Reminding the council members of these possibilities decreases the chance that they might overlook or make light of some of your points. In the second part of your essay, which concerns the pleasure the park provides the residents of the area, you can select those details from the "Personal Reactions" and "Neighborhood Reaction" columns that will be most likely to impress the council members:

the importance of the park as a playground for children, as a gathering place for families, and as a spot where neighbors can become better acquainted.

The brainstorm can also help you to recall important points that you may have forgotten or overlooked in the initial formulation of your thesis. For example, one of the points covered in the "Why?" column of the brainstorm—the city's reasons for wanting to sell the park—is an objection to your position that must be met in your essay. The thesis does not acknowledge it. A paragraph in your essay, therefore, should concede that the city's shortage of money is a genuine problem. But the objection should be overcome by pointing out that a measure likely to alienate voters and drive people from the city to the suburbs will not be worth the money it provides. You must also adjust your thesis to cover this new point.

One common way of including in a thesis objections that you intend to overcome in your essay is to add a statement beginning with "although" that identifies the objection: "Although selling Ellesmere Park to Peabody Development Corporation would provide the city with needed funds for a short time, the city should maintain Ellesmere Park as a park. The shopping center proposed by Peabody for the site would have more bad effects on the neighborhood than the amount of money to be gained by the sale would justify. In addition, the park provides much pleasure to the residents of the area." Remember, in planning your essay, that your thesis must indicate to the reader the major points you are to make, as well as the nature of your position on a topic. If you decide to include some points that your original thesis does not cover, change or add to your thesis accordingly.

Placing the Thesis

When you begin to write the first draft of your essay, you might make your thesis the first sentence of the draft. Getting it down on paper at once, and having it before you for easy reference, ensures that you will not lose sight of your points or be tempted to stray off into some other topic. In later drafts, however, opening with the thesis is not such a good idea. In many instances—as in the present one, for example—you need to prepare your audience for a thesis that it may not find attractive.

THE FUNNEL.   One pattern for such an introduction is the *funnel*, in which you begin with a general statement or a statement of general interest and narrow this down in the introductory paragraph to the actual thesis in the next-to-last or last sentence. For example:

City parks are an important part of a city's environment, and Ellesmere Park is no exception. The park provides city dwellers such as myself with a place to relax and unwind, meet my neighbors, have a cookout, and commune with nature. This park is now being threatened by a proposed shopping center. The sale of the park to the shopping center developers would have a damaging effect on my neighborhood and the entire city.

Depending on the length and nature of your material, the "narrowing" process may require more than one paragraph. Whether you place your thesis at the end of your introduction in your final draft or place it at the beginning, you should always formulate a thesis before beginning an essay. No other procedure can do as much to help you plan and organize a paper.

ORGANIZING WITH A FORMAL OUTLINE

Someone hands you a grocery list and off you go to the supermarket. The list reads as follows:

bacon
dog food
link sausage
gravy mix
laundry detergent
oregano

You find the bacon almost immediately and begin your aisle-to-aisle search for dog food. Six aisles over, you locate the dog food, only to discover that you must now backtrack to the bacon aisle for the sausage. You veer your cart back to the bacon aisle and look at the next thing on the list: gravy mix. After another three aisles of searching, you find the gravy mix and set off on the trail of the laundry detergent. As you toss a box of it into your cart, you begin to feel that all your troubles are over—until you realize that you will have to backtrack yet again to find the oregano.

Grocery lists are seldom as efficient as they could be, and that is why a writer's ideal "grocery list" is much more organized than the one described above. Before beginning the formal task of composing an essay, the writer attempts to organize the material within some kind of logical framework. The formal outline is one of the most practical ways to accomplish such organization.

Making an outline is simply a formal version of something all of us do naturally: putting things into groups. We keep our socks in one drawer, underwear in another; soup on this shelf, cereal on that one.

When we see some logical relationship between two or more things, we group them. When we group things, the logical relationship we see is usually some characteristic common to all the items in the group— similar things go together. When we outline ideas, we often go through exactly the same process of matching similarities—or we may see some other relationship.

To illustrate the way a formal outline works, let us take the grocery list above and organize the items into logical groups. The list might be arranged to cover your needs aisle by aisle, like this:

bacon
link sausage

gravy mix
oregano

dog food

laundry detergent

In a formal outline, the list would be written this way:

Items to Purchase
  I. Meats
    A. bacon
    B. link sausage
 II. Condiments
    A. gravy mix
    B. oregano
III. Miscellaneous
    A. dog food
    B. laundry detergent

As you can see, the items are grouped by category. Roman numeral headings for each category make the organization clear. One rule to re- member when you make an outline is that you must have at least two items in each category. For instance, because we have two separate meats on our grocery list, there is a separate category for meats:

I. Meats
  A. bacon
  B. link sausage

If the list mentioned only one meat, however, it would be listed under "Miscellaneous" with other unpaired items. Now suppose that our gro- cery list called for the purchase of three different kinds of link sausage. This is how we would outline it:

  I. Meats
    A. bacon
    B. link sausage
      1. Farmer John's Deluxe Link Sausage
      2. Mrs. Smith's Country Fresh Link Sausage
      3. Peter's Brown 'n' Serve Link Sausage

The original heading of "Meats" could be subdivided even further if the grocery list called for two kinds of Peter's Brown 'n' Serve Link Sausage:

  I. Meats
    A. bacon
    B. link sausage
      1. Farmer John's Deluxe Link Sausage
      2. Mrs. Smith's Country Fresh Link Sausage
      3. Peter's Brown 'n' Serve Link Sausage
        a. lightly seasoned
        b. highly seasoned

The ideas you may want to examine in an essay will not always conform to such easy groupings. You may find it necessary to categorize them under slightly more complex headings. Remember, too, that things can be organized in a variety of ways. One person might use the categories headed "Meats" and "Condiments," while a diet-conscious shopper might group such items as either "Fattening" or "Non-Fattening." Someone else might do away with the headings "Meats" and "Condiments" altogether and replace them with "Aisle One," "Aisle Two," and so on, organizing the items according to their position in the store. Methods of organization, in other words, are as varied as the organizers themselves. You should avoid methods that are obviously unsuited to your material, your own role as writer, or your audience. It would not help the average shopper, for example, to arrange the items on our grocery list alphabetically. If you find yourself stuck at any point in the organizational process, remember that you can use the probing techniques that you learned in Chapter 1 to help yourself out of the difficulty. Remember, too, that your thesis will help you to determine how the outline and the essay will proceed.

DISCERNING ORDER IN THE SUBJECT MATTER

Chronology

Some subjects have a pattern of order already built into them. In these passages from his book *Broca's Brain*, for example, Carl Sagan uses *chronology*—the ordering of events in time—to organize his account of his

coins to satisfy a crusading clergyman who thought it imperative. Next, from the disappearance of the motto in 1907 and its absence for a year, our foreign scholar would correctly conclude that the choice lay within the discretion of the Secretary of the Treasury. As for our present paper money, he would see that it is too richly decorated with signatures and serial numbers to leave room for the creed.

No sooner would he be confident that the motto had no official standing than he would read in the leading American newspapers about the decision of Congress—ninety-two years after Chase's—to make the words official and inscribe them on all our currency, both metal and paper [Bill signed by Eisenhower July 30, 1956] . . . .
—Jacques Barzun and Henry F. Graff, *The Modern Researcher*

So far, we have discussed two general types of self-ordering patterns: the chronological and the process. Since the writer cannot change the time of events or alter the steps in a process, he has few decisions to make about the organization of such essays. He can move an event or a step out of order to emphasize it if he wishes, but the essential order remains the same.

Spatial Organization

But what happens when the writer is faced with the problem of describing people, rooms, people in rooms, objects surrounding the people in rooms, and so on? Obviously everything cannot be described at once. The writer must choose one point in space and move from right to left, from left to right, from near to far, or in some other pattern; the pattern does not exist, however, until the writer imposes it. *Spatial organization* can be as natural as chronological organization, but it places greater demands on the writer. Consider its usefulness as a device in the following passage:

When he opened his "Dental Parlors," he felt that his life was a success, that he could hope for nothing better. In spite of the name, there was but one room. It was a corner room on the second floor over the branch post-office, and faced the street. McTeague made it do for a bedroom as well, sleeping on the big bed-lounge against the wall opposite the window. There was a washstand behind the screen in the corner where he manufactured his moulds. In the round bay window were his operating chair, his dental engine, and the movable rack on which he laid out his instruments. Three chairs, a bargain at the second hand store, ranged themselves against the wall with military precision underneath a steel engraving of the court of Lorenzo d'Medici . . . a small marble-topped center table covered with back numbers of "The American System of Dentistry," a stone pug dog sitting before the little stove, and a ther-

Paragraphs

Patterns of Development
Induction and Deduction
Definition
Illustration
Analogy
Classification
Analysis
Comparison and Contrast
Description
Cause and Effect

Mixing Patterns of Development

Special Paragraphs
The Introductory Paragraph
The Transitional Paragraph
The Concluding Paragraph

Paragraph Checklist

Exercises

The paragraph is the basic building block of your writing. Paragraphs are like building blocks used in construction in that they come in different shapes and sizes and serve different purposes, so paragraphs vary in size and purpose. Knowing how to write paragraphs is a little like knowing how to use the right kind of building blocks. In each case, knowing what kind of blocks to use is determined partly by the material and partly by the purpose. In Chapter 1, you learned how to generate material for your writing. In this chapter, you will learn how to build paragraphs from that material.

We might compare the skills needed to shape a paragraph with the skills of playing tennis. The good tennis player has a number of different strokes to call upon in an actual game. The player has practiced hours on end to perfect each particular stroke. In the game, the player must be able to serve, volley, or smash—whichever stroke is needed. The player must be able to perform each part of the game of tennis well and quickly. In the same way, the writer of the paragraph needs a repertory of paragraph-building skills to call upon when writing an essay. The more skillfully you can write paragraphs, the simpler writing essays becomes. Just as the game of tennis bewilders the beginner, the idea of the paragraph may overwhelm the beginning writer. Since isolating the ingredients of the paragraph will help build the skills you need, this chapter will first treat the basic patterns for the material of paragraphs, and then examine the basic paragraph patterns in various combinations.

Paragraphs vary in lengths, proportions, and patterns. Not all paragraphs are, or should be, the same. You may find it convenient to think of a typical one as having 100 words or so, but many will run longer or shorter. Similarly, all paragraphs do not use the same methods of organization. A paragraph describing Christmas shoppers jammed into a bargain basement might want to assume a crowded look, whereas a more relaxed organizational scheme might work better for a description of an Arizona commune. Whatever the look of the paragraph, however, a few basic rules apply to all good paragraphs.

PATTERNS OF DEVELOPMENT

Readers expect a paragraph to proceed in an orderly, linear fashion, so you might think of paragraphs as beginning with a topic sentence. The topic sentence establishes the "territory" of the paragraph, and lets the reader sense the writer's concerns.

The topic sentence does not have to be the first sentence of the paragraph. Remember, though, that the most emphatic spots of the paragraph are the beginning and the end. Sometimes the topic sentence can also appear to good effect in the middle of the paragraph, particularly when the paragraph employs a mixed pattern of development. Wherever you decide to put the topic sentence, make sure that the material in the paragraph supports that sentence. Generally, the supporting material will follow one or more of the following patterns of development.

Induction and Deduction

The two most general patterns of development are those called inductive and deductive. We use deduction when we verify our assumptions about the way things are by noting the specifics that we observe. Induction, on the other hand, presents the specific evidence that allows a general conclusion to be put at the end of the presentation. When writing paragraphs, we follow deductive order when we present the generalization first and follow the generalization with the details that support it. Inductive order, on the other hand, presents specific details and then the general conclusion suggested by the details.

Suppose you are writing a paragraph describing how, during exam week, one of your friends will eat only bananas and chocolate; another insists upon wearing a strange, floppy hat; still another develops a skin infection. An inductive final statement could be that exam-week tension generates bizarre behavior and symptoms of illness in some freshmen. If you turned your approach around and presented the general statement first and then went on to back it up with various examples, you would be employing the deductive pattern.

What are the relative merits of inductive and deductive patterning? Induction, by offering evidence first, invites the reader to arrive at conclusions along with the writer. Deduction gives the reader a general overview before proceeding to give specifics. Either deductive or inductive paragraphs can be developed by one or more of the basic patterns. The following paragraph opens with a generalization, and then supplies supporting materials for the generalization; this is the deductive pattern:

> Greeks themselves, of course, in their compartmentalized city-state existence, had never been uncritical of other Greeks. A Rhodian, representative of a state which in less troubled times was the object of widespread admiration, had said in the Senate in 167 BC, 'Some people are irascible, some headstrong, others pusillanimous. Some drink too much and some are over-sexed. The Athenians are traditionally impetuous and indulge in bold enterprises which are beyond their power; Spartans procrastinate. Nor can I deny that, as a whole, Greeks living in western Asia Minor are empty-headed and that we open our mouths far too wide.'
> —J.P.V.D. Balsdon, *Romans and Aliens*

The Rhodian's speech offers particular details in support of Balsdon's general statement that the Greeks were highly critical of one another.

An example of the inductive pattern, in which details are presented first and followed by a general conclusion, can be seen in the following paragraph:

> Nevertheless, my old friends' shrewd eyes would take in much that is new and sharply different from the classical factories they knew. They would notice, for example, that instead of all the H–P employees arriving at once, punching the clock, and racing to their work stations, they are able, within limits, to choose their own individual working hours. Instead of being forced to stay in one work location, they are able to move about as they wish. My old friends would marvel at the freedom of the H–P employees, again within limits, to set their own work pace. To talk to managers or engineers without worrying about status or hierarchy. To dress as they wish. In short, to be individuals. In fact, my old companions in their heavy steel-tipped shoes, dirty overalls, and workingmen's caps would find it hard, I believe, to think of the place as a factory at all.
> —Alvin Toffler, *The Third Wave*

The opening sentence of this paragraph prepares us for the specific details that follow, all leading to a definition of a different kind of factory, the last sentence of the paragraph.

Definition

In Chapter 1, we considered how to use a series of questions about a subject to discover material for an essay. One of the first and most important questions was, "What is it?" When you say what something is, or what it means, you may be *defining*. In your paragraphs you can sometimes define a term quickly—with a synonym, with examples, or with a concise definition—to make sure that your reader knows the meaning of the term. You can then go on to discuss a particular aspect of the term. At other times, your paragraph alone will develop the definition. This approach is necessary if you are exploring the significance of a term that many people use, but whose real meaning or implications are generally misunderstood.

Formal definition places the term to be defined in a category and then explains how the term differs from other items in the category.

Illustration

Illustration helps the reader understand an idea by giving one or more examples. In the following paragraph, the writer discusses the key role that chance plays in our lives. To support his claim that contemporary people are just as awed and ruled by chance as people from "less sophisticated" societies, the writer provides a series of "for instances":

> Chance, its proverbs and instruments, makes up an astonishingly large part of the furnishings of our mind. We laugh at the supposedly primitive man who believes the spirit of the tiger can inhabit a tree, but we ourselves are often sure an equally malign force may inhabit our bed, so that getting out on the wrong side may ruin a day. . . . On occasion we fly like birds to temples of chance in Nevada or the Caribbean islands or Monte Carlo, there to indulge in the delicious thrill of invoking the blind forces which normally we keep away from our lives by touching lampposts and not stepping on cracks in the sidewalk. . . .
> —Samuel Grafton, "Choice and Chance in Human Affairs"

The writer does not simply assert that chance is a major force in our lives. He proves his claim by giving specific examples of human behavior concerning superstitions. Thus, the reader may accept the truth of the topic sentence.

Analogy

Such illustrations give the reader a better idea of what you mean. Analogy can also, by suggesting that two things are alike. Sometimes a writer uses analogy to explain the function of one thing in the language of another. In other instances, analogy is a more concrete way to explain something. It can also draw attention to the similar qualities of two things that seem different. If your subject is abstract or difficult to visualize, you might want to use an analogy to bring it to life:

> Imagine God as tailor. His shelves are lined with rolls of skin, each with its subtleties of texture and hue. Six days a week He cuts lengths with which to wrap those small piles of flesh and bone into the clever parcels we call babies. Now engage the irreverence to consider that, either out of the tedium born of infinity, or out of mere sly parsimony, He uses for the occasional handicraft a remnant of yard goods, the last of an otherwise perfect bolt, dusty, soiled, perhaps a bit too small or large. . . . I have received many such people in my examination rooms. Like imperfect postage stamps, they are the collectors' items of the human race.
> —Richard Selzer, *Mortal Lessons: Notes on the Art of Surgery*

The analogy embraces only one aspect of the God/tailor comparison—that of a God creating babies the way a tailor might cut out a coat. It does not attempt to equate God and the tailor in any other way. A successful analogy, such as this one, should be as specific as possible.

Classification

If you were to discuss the various types of physical exercise students might undertake, you could conceivably group the exercises according to whether they help people lose weight, increase endurance, or develop muscles. Or, if you wanted to explain to doubtful readers that house-plant care is easy if approached logically, you might group a half-dozen plants according to their needs for sunlight and watering. Your aim in both cases would be to make a subject clearer and more accessible. You would, in both cases, be classifying your subject.

When we classify, we attempt to break a topic down by a consistent and useful standard. It is important to consider the needs of your reader when you classify something, just as you consider the subject itself and the purpose of the classification. It probably would not help an indoor gardener to group plants according to the shape of their leaves, although such a classification would be routine for a botanist. And while it would be informative to group certain foods according to their nutritional value, it would be less helpful to group them according to the geographic region in which they were produced.

In the following paragraph, lamb to be bought and cooked is classified according to the age of the lamb before it is slaughtered. The passage begins with the authors' explanation of why one classification no longer exists. The last part of the passage discusses similarities and differences among the now-established classifications as they pertain to cooking procedures.

> Since lamb is shipped from different climates it is no longer referred to as spring lamb. When it is from 3 to 5 months old, lamb is now called baby or milk-finished lamb. From 5 months to a year and half, it is simply called lamb, and from there out—mutton. Mutton may be substituted for lamb, but the cooking time is usually increased from 5 to 10 minutes to the pound. Both lamb and mutton are covered with a whitish brittle fat, called the fell, which is usually removed before cooking, as it tends to make the flavor of the meat strong.
> —Irma S. Rombauer and Marion Rombauer Becker, *Joy of Cooking*

Note how each new sentence makes a further classification based on the previous one.

Analysis

Another method of paragraph development is analysis. When using analysis, an author probes a specific subject from several angles by breaking down the subject into its component parts.

As might be expected, he was a mass of eccentricities. He refused to have a telephone, kept his books stacked along the wall in their original packing cases, and saw no sense in daily making up the beds; they were thrown back in the morning and pulled up again at night. Lazy, he allowed the dishes to accumulate until the cupboard was bare and then washed the whole messy heap by turning the hose on them. Taciturn, he would sit for hours in silence when all his visitors were eager to hear his pronouncements. A flouter of convention, he gave all his students the same grade, regardless of their work, but when one student needed a higher mark to qualify for scholarship, Veblen gladly changed a C into an A. . . . And perhaps strangest of all, this sardonic and unprepossessing man had that indefinable quality of being attractive to women. He was always engaged in one liaison or another, and not always of his own doing. "What are you to do if the woman moves in on you?" he once inquired of a friend.

—Robert L. Heilbruner, *The Worldly Philosophers*

In this example, the author examines the eccentric personality of the great economist Thorsten Veblen by analyzing or breaking down into describable parts some of his behavior.

Comparison and Contrast

This method of development allows the writer to probe similarities and/or differences between two things. (Similarities are compared; differences are contrasted.) Just as in the essay that compares or contrasts, the paragraph developed by comparison and contrast needs to have an order. You might describe one person or object and then describe the second person or object in the same order, but emphasize the differences. Or, you might compare the two persons or objects with respect to particular categories. Here human language is compared both with communication among bees and the use of American sign language by chimpanzees:

The distinctive feature of human communication is the ability to use symbols, to remove language from direct experience. Some people argue that the language of the bees is similar to man's, since bees can communicate very precise and complicated information about faraway pollen sources through their "dances." But the language of the bees is limited to just that—description of the location of food sources. There is no indication that bees can communicate more complex thoughts. "Gee, I saw a wonderful-looking batch of pollen yesterday, but there were men with spray guns not far away, darn it!" is beyond a bee's capacity. So is, "I think the queen is getting rather fat, don't you?" The language of bees cannot compare with the range and sophistication of man's symbols. Nor can the American sign language used by chimpanzees (the result of a re-markable series of experiments begun by R. A. and Beatrice Gardner in 1966). While chimpanzees have been shown to be capable of mastering word-symbols and even of combining them in creative new ways (one chimp, seeing a duck for the first time, called it a "water bird"), this abil-ity remains limited. Even after intensive training and reward, not one chimp has ever attained the language skills a four-year-old human child masters without any formal training or instruction at all.

—Donna Woolfolk Cross, *Word Abuse*

Bees and chimpanzees have communication systems that are quite dif-ferent from that of man, and the author illustrates the differences with specific examples.

The student who wrote the following opening paragraph for a com-parison/contrast essay, points out similarities between two characters and their feelings of confinement.

Upon returning from the movies, Tom, in Scene 4 of *The Glass Me-nagerie,* emphasizes his desire to escape his present situation by talking about the magician who was nailed in a coffin and got out. He then com-pares the coffin to the apartment and his situation in life. Just as Tom feels confined within the walls of a "coffin," Joe, in *The Long Goodbye,* feels trapped within his past and his childhood and desires to escape into the adult world. By leaving home, each character searches for free-dom from the past. At the end of *The Long Goodbye,* Joe gives a sym-bolic mock salute "goodbye" to his apartment and his past. Joe is freed from his past by leaving home, whereas Tom isn't quite fortunate enough to find the sense of independence that Joe finds.

Though this paragraph compares two elements, rather than three as in the preceding example, it is harder to follow. The previous example states the generalization, discusses bees in relation to it, discusses chim-panzees in relation to that, and draws a conclusion. The student ex-ample compares Tom to Joe, draws a conclusion, and then compares Joe to Tom.

Comparison/contrast is a useful strategy for paragraph development and it is a favorite form for essay exam questions. Just remember to con-trol the comparisons and contrasts within *some* pattern, so that you do not jump back and forth randomly and confuse the reader.

Description

If you were describing your dormitory room, you would not find it log-ical to present its features (walls, furniture, rug, windows, and so on) in random order. You would want to consider the items according to their location in the room. You might go from floor to ceiling, describing first the rug, then the walls, and finally the ceiling itself. Or you could reverse the order and go from ceiling to floor. If you preferred yet another *space order*, you could take an imaginary walk clockwise (or counterclockwise) around the room, depicting each item as you encountered it.

Space order is particularly appropriate when you describe a scene or an object. Depending on what you are describing, other types of space order may be suitable: east to west, near to far. See if you can follow the movement in the description below.

> A little later I was wandering out along the one good roadway of the island, looking over low walls on either side into small flat fields of naked rock. I have seen nothing so desolate. Grey floods of water were sweeping everywhere upon the limestone, making at times a wild torrent of the road, which twined continually over low hills and cavities in the rock or passed between a few small fields of potatoes or grass hidden away in corners that had shelter. Whenever a cloud lifted I could see the edge of the sea below me on the right, and the naked ridge of the island above me on the other side. Occasionally I passed a lonely chapel or schoolhouse, or a line of stone pillars with crosses above them and inscriptions asking a prayer for the soul of the person they commemorated.
> —J. M. Synge, *The Aran Islands*

Time order, also called chronological order, may move either forward or backward in time. The Synge paragraph above, you will notice, follows a time order as well as a space order. Because it moves in time, chronological ordering is also appropriate to a description of *process*.

As a method of development, process description can be as straightforward as a recipe ("first mix the oil and sugar in a large bowl, then add yogurt") or as intricate as the step-by-step instructions that accompany a build-it-yourself radio transmitter. A process description can also describe a natural event—how a plant grows from a seed, for instance, or how a piece of machinery operates. Its purpose is largely informational, and it should be used when process is central to understanding.

In preparing a process description, you may want to distinguish between a repeated process and a singular one. A repeated process is *objective*; you might simply describe the stages, one by one, of an event or operation (how to obtain a driver's license, for example). Your readers could assume that the procedure at the motor vehicle bureau would be the same for them as it was for you when you applied.

The analysis of a singular process, on the other hand, is *subjective*. It stresses your particular experience. In trying to obtain a driver's license, you might explain how rude or polite the staff was to you, or how frustrated you felt when you flunked the eye test. In the paragraph that follows, the novelist Samuel Beckett has the main character Molloy describe his search for some form of security by describing how he collects "sucking stones":

I took advantage of being at the seaside to lay in a store of sucking stones. They were pebbles but I call them stones. . . . I distributed them equally between my four pockets, and sucked them turn and turn about. This raised a problem which I first solved in the following way. I had say sixteen stones, four in each of my four pockets, these being the two pockets of my trousers and the two pockets of my greatcoat. Taking a stone from the right pocket of my greatcoat, and putting it in my mouth, I replaced it in the right pocket of my greatcoat by a stone from the right pocket of my trousers, which I replaced by a stone from the left pocket of my trousers, which I replaced by a stone from the left pocket of my greatcoat, which I replaced by the stone which was in my mouth, as soon as I had finished sucking it. Thus there were still four stones in each of my four pockets, but not quite the same stones. . . . But this solution did not satisfy me fully. For it did not escape me that, by an extraordinary hazard, the four stones circulating thus might always be the same four. In which case, far from sucking the sixteen stones turn and turn about, I was really only sucking four, always the same, turn and turn about.

—Samuel Beckett, *Molloy*

Whether you write using the objective or the subjective process, be sure that you describe events according to their occurrence in time, just as Beckett does in the paragraph above.

Cause and Effect

Suppose you observe an increase in attendance at student activities such as lectures, church groups, and square dances that up until now had not been popular with students. You might wonder what caused the change. Conversations with student leaders might bring out the reason: the high cost of other forms of entertainment and the cost of the gas needed to attend certain events have prompted students to seek out inexpensive, on-campus diversions.

In asking your original question, and then in finding the answer to it, you have pinpointed a cause-and-effect relationship. You have established that an event—rising prices—has led to another event—a change in the way that many students are spending their leisure time.

Developing a paragraph by cause and effect is a way of probing the connections between events, and making those connections clearer for readers. When using cause and effect, remember to examine the implications of a cause-and-effect relationship. The fact that students must increasingly rely on campus-sponsored, low-cost recreational activities may mean that the college will have to step up its recreational programs to accommodate growing numbers of students. Will the high cost of gas prompt the school to provide group transportation for commuters? Should it?

Vance Packard uses cause and effect here to trace the rise of hedonism in contemporary America:

> Puritanical traits were esteemed as necessary for survival by the settlers struggling to convert the forest and prairie into a national homeland. By the nineteenth century, however, a flamboyant streak was beginning to emerge clearly in the American character. . . . As more and more Americans found themselves living in metropolitan areas, hedonism as a guiding philosophy of life gained more and more disciples. People sought possessions more than formerly in emulation of, or competition with, their neighbors. Quite possibly, the environment of thickly settled areas brought a lessening of serenity and a feeling of being swallowed up that impelled the people to strive for distinctive emblems and gratification through consumption. The growing availability of manufactured goods undoubtedly had a great deal to do with the rise in hedonism. The upheaval of wars and the uncertainty of life in an atomic era also contributed to the live-for-the-moment spirit.
>
> —Vance Packard, *The Waste Makers*

MIXING PATTERNS OF DEVELOPMENT

So far, we have been discussing various patterns of development for simple paragraphs. With practice, you will be able to use several of these patterns in a single paragraph. You will be able to mix them to create paragraphs that amplify, analyze, describe, and interpret. Although it is useful to practice these methods separately, remember that paragraphs that most accurately reflect the sophisticated nature of ideas and thought usually incorporate several methods simultaneously.

We will now look at how some writers have used various methods of development to shape the material of a paragraph.

> I live by a creek, Tinker Creek, in a valley in Virginia's Blue Ridge. An anchorite's hermitage is called an anchor-hold; some anchor-holds were simple sheds clamped to the side of a church like a barnacle to a rock. I think of this house clamped to the side of Tinker Creek as an anchor-hold. It holds me at anchor to the rock bottom of the creek itself and it keeps me steadied in the current, as a sea anchor does, facing the stream of light pouring down. It's a good place to live; there's a lot to think about. The creeks—Tinker and Carvin's—are an active mystery, fresh every minute. Theirs is the mystery of the continuous creation and all that providence implies: the uncertainty of vision, the horror of the fixed, the dissolution of the present, the pressure of fecundity, the elusiveness of the free, and the flawed nature of perfection. The mountains—Tinker and Brushy, McAffe's Knob and Dead Man—are a passive mystery, the oldest of all. Theirs is the one simple mystery of creation from nothing, of matter itself, anything at all, the given. Mountains are giant, restful, ab-

sorbent. You can heave your spirit into a mountain and the mountain will keep it, folded, and not throw it back as some creeks will. The creeks are the world with all its stimulus and beauty; I live there. But the mountains are home.

—Annie Dillard, *Pilgrim at Tinker Creek*

The creek is compared to a hermitage, and living by the creek is compared with the larger issue of "living." The paragraph narrates, describes, and interprets.

Here is another example of a paragraph in which the writer uses a variety of basic development patterns:

Contemporary Christianity, diverse and complex as we find it, actually may show more unanimity than the Christian churches of the first and second centuries. For nearly all Christians since that time, Catholics, Protestants, or Orthodox, have shared three basic premises. First, they accept the canon of the New Testament; second, they confess the apostolic creed; and third, they affirm specific forms of church institution. But every one of these—the canon of Scripture, the creed, and the institutional structure—emerged in its present form only toward the end of the second century. Before that time, as Irenaeus and others attest, numerous gospels circulated among various Christian groups, ranging from those of the New Testament, Matthew, Mark, Luke, and John, to such writings as the *Gospel of Thomas,* the *Gospel of Philip,* and the *Gospel of Truth,* as well as many other secret teachings, myths, and poems attributed to Jesus or his disciples. Some of these, apparently, were discovered at Nag Hammadi; many others are lost to us. Those who identified themselves as Christians entertained many—and radically differing—religious beliefs and practices. And the communities scattered throughout the known world organized themselves in ways that differed widely from one group to another.

—Elaine Pagels, *The Gnostic Gospels*

First the author states the general principle that the paragraph will support through deduction. Then she explains how Christians today are more nearly unified because of their sharing three common denominators. By contrast, early Christians had no such common denominators, an idea the author presents by means of various examples.

Here is another example:

The glass collection can be seen as representative of the play as a whole. In the first speech of the play, Tom lets the audience know that the play is a memory. And in the description of Scene I, Williams explains that memory may leave out or add events and feelings according to what a person wants to remember. In other words, a memory is arranged, in accordance with the emotions surrounding that memory, into an acceptable form and is then kept in that structure. The collection of glass is similar because it too is arranged in a pleasing fashion and is then displayed in that pattern.

In this paragraph from a student paper, the writer analyzes *The Glass Menagerie* by comparing the collection of glass animals with the way memory works. A different "mix" of basic patterns can be seen.

SPECIAL PARAGRAPHS

Up to now we have been examining paragraphs in isolation, even though we began the chapter by comparing paragraphs to building blocks—the parts of a larger structure. We will now examine three special kinds of paragraphs for different parts of an essay. These paragraphs are *introductory, transitional,* and *concluding* paragraphs. Each will, in turn, bring your reader into your essay, move the essay from one part to another, and end the essay.

The Introductory Paragraph

The *introductory* paragraph, writers almost unanimously agree, is the hardest part of an essay to write. It is hard because it *is* the beginning, the committing of ideas to paper, and that means putting a shape to those ideas.

Why not do it last? What you really need in order to begin writing is a clear statement of your whole main point. Write that much down. After you have roughed out the body of your essay, you can go back and think about ways to begin it.

An introductory paragraph serves four functions: it introduces the topic; it sets the boundaries of the topic; it suggests the organization the essay will follow; and it gets the reader's attention.

Introducing the topic can be a straightforward statement of purpose. For an example of this, look at the first paragraph of this chapter. Sometimes, however, the subject will be so complex or difficult that its limitation will need to be stated negatively, rather than positively. Thus Robert A. Fothergill introduces his study of English diaries, *Private Chronicles*, by saying:

The following study does not claim to be an exercise in literary history. No attempt is made to lay out a comprehensive picture of English diary-writing, or to devote space to . . . every diarist of any note since Edward VI. Not only would such a book be a monster of indigestibility, but the limited function that it could serve has been very largely served already.

Setting the boundaries of the topic is important both for the reader and for you. If you read an article whose first sentence was "I will discuss the entire history of mankind through the ages ..." would you continue reading? Probably not. An introductory paragraph should provide a clear focus for readers and should limit the topic so it is manageable. Do not take on more than you can handle. Define your boundaries immediately. Once again, as with statements of introduction, boundary statements can be explicit or implicit.

Robert Winks, the editor of *The Historian as Detective*, begins his introduction this way:

> I have compiled this book of essays for fun, and I claim no high purpose for it. . . . What I have tried to explore in this anthology is the relationship between the colorful world of fictional intrigue, then, and the good gray world of professional scholarship, and to show how much of the excitement, the joy, and even the color properly belongs to the latter.

Use such explicit statements of purpose only when the material may be tough going for the reader. If you introduce very simple material with an explicit statement of purpose, you call attention to the simplicity of the material. You may even lead the reader to assume that *you* find it complicated!

Since implicit statements of purpose arise from the material itself, they are far more varied in form than statements of the kind "my purpose is. . . ." Thus Marjorie Rowling begins a chapter on "Charlemagne and Society" with a paragraph beginning with the death of Charlemagne, and ending with this sentence, an implicit limitation of subject:

> There he is shown as laying foundations which—although some of the edifices reared upon them may have been temporarily destroyed—remained as the solid basis for much that became part of the very fabric of medieval Europe.

The reader knows from this statement that the essay will spell out Charlemagne's contributions to "the fabric of medieval Europe."

Suggesting the organization of the essay is often as simple as the sentence that sets the boundaries. If you want to consider several categories, you can write a sentence with a list in it. This sentence (the first of the second paragraph) from the Rowling book on *Life in Medieval Times* clearly suggests the organization the writer will employ in her book.

> In every facet of life—territorial, economic, educational, political, cultural, ecclesiastical and social—something at least of Charles' acts and ideals lived on.

Clearly, Rowling intends to go on to examine the ways in which her subject left his mark on many aspects of medieval times. Suggesting the organization of an argumentative essay in a single sentence can be done by using a concessive clause:

> Although they are more difficult to right when tipped over, catamarans are so much more fun than single-hulled sailboats that their advantages far outweigh their hazards.

The reader expects that this writer's argument will employ comparison and contrast.

Getting the reader's attention is probably the most important function of the introductory paragraph. No one is obliged to read a piece of writing. Given the choice, readers will be more likely to continue reading something that catches their attention right away. But this does not mean that you should hit the reader over the head with the topic. Essays that begin with a flat statement of topic—"In this essay I will discuss X"—may strike the reader as stilted, stiff, or uninventive and dull.

Try to involve the reader directly, but gradually. Involve him in what you are going to say. How do you anticipate the interests of a particular audience? Probe them. Ask yourself what type of approach would interest the people you are writing for, or what approach is best suited to the material you want to present.

Here are some ways you can build introductory paragraphs:

1. Start with a general statement—more general than your thesis statement will be—and particularly one the reader can identify as being true or correct. Be careful not to use clichés, such as: "In today's world of modern times, technology is becoming quite complicated."
2. Begin with a definition. In general it is best to avoid dictionary definitions, as they have become something of a cliché in student writing. But you might find it useful to experiment with informal definitions—the kind that rely on humor, wit, irony, or idiom. The following introductory paragraph includes an informal definition.:

> Juggling, the continuous tossing and catching of objects in the air, is an excellent example of man's extraordinary capacity for play. Some other animals, such as the seal, have been trained to balance objects, but true juggling seems beyond the abilities of even the other higher primates (despite occasional circus posters that falsely picture chimpanzees juggling). That juggling is unique to man should not be surprising, as it involves not only remarkable use of the hands but also complex spatial perception and cognitive skills.
> —Marcello Truzzi, "On Keeping Things up in the Air."

3. Begin with a question, especially one that involves the reader. (The probes in Chapter 1 may give you some idea of appropriate questions to ask.) But be careful about asking rhetorical questions that the reader can answer in a way that you do not want, with a "who cares?" back for you!

4. Begin with a provocative statement. Joan Didion begins *The White Album,* "We tell ourselves stories in order to live." The provocative statement might be put in question form, of course: Thurber asks, "Is sex necessary?"

5. Begin with a striking simile or metaphor. "Marriage is like a traffic light; you have to follow the signals. . . ." Avoid obvious absurdities, however: "Love is like a baseball game—three strikes and you're out."

6. Begin with a witty remark or a paradox. "The past was real, yet truth is relative" is the way Robin Collingwood introduced an essay called "The Problem of Testimony," while Eudora Welty began a review of *Charlotte's Web:* "If I had the qualifications (a set of spinnerets and the know-how), I'd put in tonight writing 'Adorable' across my web, to be visible Sunday morning hung with dewdrops for my review of *Charlotte's Web.*"

You might find that using the probes will help you with some final considerations concerning introductory paragraphs. You should decide how you are going to approach your topic. You might mention in your introduction what prompted you to write on your topic. You might try to define yourself as the writer in relation to your topic and choose whether or not to write as "I." Deciding on your role as the writer of your piece will determine the strategies your essay will employ.

The Transitional Paragraph

As its name suggests, the *transitional paragraph* directs the discussion from one major point to the next. It accomplishes its task by reminding the reader of the element from the previous paragraph, indicating the connection between that element and the next one coming, and then introducing the new paragraph. Transitional paragraphs are most useful in longer pieces, or in especially complex ones. Learn to become economical in employing transitional paragraphs, for they are not always needed. To decide whether two paragraphs do, in fact, require a "bridge," imagine that you are the reader. Is the mental leap between the two paragraphs too wide to make on your own? If you think it is, then a transitional paragraph may be necessary.

Here is how Lewis Thomas gets us from the first paragraph of an essay "On Warts," in which he compares warts to fortresses, to the third paragraph, in which he explains that warts are viruses:

> In a certain sense, warts are both useful and essential, but not for us. As it turns out, the exuberant cells of a wart are the elaborate reproductive apparatus of a virus.

You might find that, rather than a transitional paragraph, you need only a careful transitional word or phrase to get yourself from one paragraph to the next. Below is a list of transitional words and phrases, grouped according to the logical relationships they suggest. They are useful, also, for linking sentence to sentence.

1. *Addition* signals: first, in the first place, first of all, one, for one thing, second, secondly, third, the third reason, last of all, finally, a final reason, also, too, in addition, moreover, likewise, furthermore, next, another, again, and.
2. *Change of direction* signals: but, however, yet, in contrast, instead, even though, otherwise, still, on the contrary, on the other hand.
3. *Conclusion* signals: therefore, then, consequently, thus, as a result, to conclude, in summary, last of all, finally, a final reason.
4. *Illustration* signals: for example, for instance, specifically, as an illustration, once.
5. *Emphasis* signals: most importantly, the most important reason, the basic cause, the biggest advantage, the best thing, the chief factor, principally, most of all, especially significant, valuable to note, special attention should be paid, remember that, a major concern, a key feature, the most notable aspect.

The Concluding Paragraph

In writing an introductory paragraph, your goal is to announce your topic in a way that invites your readers to join you in exploring it. By the same token, if you end your essay too abruptly, your readers may feel that you have abandoned them or left them hanging on a limb.

A concluding paragraph should give your readers a feeling of completion. You may want to restate your thesis and some of your chief supporting points, but avoid a word-for-word restatement of the thesis in the conclusion. Try to vary your phrasing.

You can also use your concluding paragraph to evaluate in some way the material you have discussed, or you can make a final appeal, in which you urge your readers to consider the implications of your ideas and take appropriate action. Many newspaper editorials end this way. Do not be afraid to rely on straightforward rhetorical signals like "in conclusion" or "finally."

Sometimes you may even want to rely on the natural climax of the topic itself. If you are explaining, for instance, how to make a holiday wreath from nuts, cones, and other materials, you might conclude your writing quite smoothly by describing where the wreath can be hung once it is finished.

As another means of signaling your conclusion, you might want to change sentence length and pattern. Read the end of the essay aloud. Try to listen to its sound—have you structured the sentences so that it *sounds* like the end?

Still another device for concluding the essay is to return to a key term or idea you used at the beginning. Remember the beginning of Eudora Welty's review of *Charlotte's Web*? Here is the end of that review: " 'At-at-at, at the risk of repeating myself,' as the goose says, I will say *Charlotte's Web* is an adorable book."

Whatever kind of conclusion you use, be sure that you use the conclusion to conclude. It is certainly not the place to bring up *new* points, or to swerve off in an entirely different direction.

PARAGRAPH CHECKLIST

This chapter concludes with a checklist for the paragraphs in your essay.

1. Does every paragraph have a topic sentence, either stated or implied?
2. Is the paragraph unified? Does every sentence relate to the topic sentence?
3. Have you provided supporting evidence sufficient to back up the topic sentence for the audience you are addressing? What possible questions or objections could the audience make to the point of the paragraph?
4. Have you presented the material in a logical plan or in some perceptible order?
5. Is the paragraph coherent? Does each sentence advance the idea of the topic sentence and move naturally to the following sentence? Does the paragraph flow?
6. Is the relationship of each paragraph to the one before it and the one following it clear? Have transitional elements or connective devices made the relationship of the paragraphs clear? Have you provided transitional paragraphs where necessary?

EXERCISES

1. Topic Sentences

a). Underline the topic sentence in the following paragraph.

The earth has become, just in the last decade, too small a place. We have the feeling of being confined—shut in; it is something like outgrowing a small town in a small county. The views of the dark, pocked surface of Mars, still lifeless to judge from the latest photographs, do not seem to have extended our reach; instead, they bring closer, too close, another unsatisfactory feature of our local environment. The blue noonday sky, cloudless, has lost its old look of immensity. The word is out that the sky is not limitless; it is finite. It is, in truth, only a kind of local roof, a membrane under which we live, luminous but confusingly refractile when suffused with sunlight; we can sense its concave surface a few miles over our heads. We know that it is tough and thick enough so that when hard objects strike it from the outside they burst into flames. The color photographs of the earth are more amazing than anything outside: we live inside a blue chamber, a bubble of air blown by ourselves. The other sky beyond, absolutely black and appalling, is wide-open country, irresistible for exploration.

—Lewis Thomas, "Ceti"

b). Using each of the topic sentences listed below, write three paragraphs. Vary the placement of the topic sentence in each paragraph you write, placing it in the beginning, middle, or end of the paragraph.

1. It was apparent that he had run out of ideas.
2. These new experiences illustrate the fact that the value of college life extends far beyond the confines of the classroom.
3. A doorman is always on duty to help the residents of the building.

2. Paragraph Development: Single Line of Development

a). Choose one of the topics listed below. Compose a chart with headings for the patterns of development discussed in this chapter: definition, illustration, analogy, classification, analysis, comparison and contrast, description, and cause and effect. The items you list under each heading represent a line of development that can be used for writing a paragraph or an essay. It will be helpful to use the brainstorming techniques discussed in Chapter 1.

fingernails	cars
grasshoppers	friends
chocolate	types of professors
comic books	types of people on campus

b). Use the material from the chart you have composed and write a paragraph for each line of development. That is, write a paragraph that employs analogy, or comparison and contrast, etc.

3. Paragraphs: Mixed Development

a). Select an essay you have written for another class. Type it with triple-spacing between lines. Exchange this for a paper written by another student. Analyze the paragraphs, identifying the different kinds of development used in each paragraph.

b). Using the material in the previous exercise, write a paragraph using a combination of patterns of development.

4. Introductory Paragraphs

a). Read the following opening paragraphs. Identify which of the four functions of introductions are being used in each.

> Catherine Morland is the main character and the heroine of Jane Austen's novel, *Northanger Abbey*. Catherine is not a typical heroine. She is a normal, ordinary person, unlike the beautiful, solitary, introverted heroines of the romantic novels. Catherine is plain and not exceptionally bright, but she can be educated—and is by the end of the book. Catherine is at first naive and innocent but she begins to mature when she starts believing in her own judgments. In her refusal to stand up a second time when she is pressed by Isabella, James, and John to go on a day trip, Catherine is asserting herself, is sticking to her beliefs, and is well on her way to maturity.
>
> —A student paper

> Men smarter than myself have said that everything can be replaced. I'd like to differ with that theory. Although it is time that the horse and buggy was very ably replaced by the automobile, and the light bulb has, in recent days, lit more homes than the candle, certain things cannot be replaced. One of the most irreplaceable items on the face of the earth, at least in my opinion, is the fool.
>
> —A student paper

> The day was clear and bright, and the sun baked the red brick sidewalk. The brownstone buildings simmered in the blazing heat. The humid summer air was heavy and thick. Sounds of gaiety penetrated the stillness. Children in small, doll-like, white outfits were running everywhere. Women in bright print dresses hovered about the yard sipping wine. Men in leisure suits drank beer. The quartet struck up another tune, and the colorful mass mobilized into groups of dancers.
>
> —A student paper

> "Little Red Riding Hood was my first love. I felt that if I could have married Little Red Riding Hood, I should have known perfect bliss." This statement by Charles Dickens indicates that he, like untold millions of children all over the world throughout the ages, was en-

chanted by fairy tales. Even when world-famous, Dickens acknowledged the deep formative impact that the wondrous figures and
events of fairy tales had had on him and his creative genius. He repeatedly expressed scorn for those who, motivated by an uninformed
and petty rationality, insisted on rationalizing, bowdlerizing, or out-
lawing these stories, and thus robbed children of the important contributions fairy tales could make to their lives. Dickens understood
that the imagery of fairy tales helps children better than anything else
in their most difficult and yet most important and satisfying task:
achieving a more mature consciousness to civilize the chaotic pres-
sures of their unconscious.

—Bruno Bettelheim, *The Uses of Enchantment*

b.) How would you introduce the topics listed below? List as many possibilities as you can.

life with rats   my favorite spot
changing your image   finding an off-campus apartment
vacationing in Maine   women should be drafted
where I live   housebreaking a puppy

c). Choose one of the possibilities for each of the topics that you listed
in the previous exercise. Write introductory paragraphs for each.

5. Concluding Paragraphs

a). Analyze the following paragraphs. Isolate the concluding techniques
used in each.

At this point, you have accomplished two, and possibly three,
things. You have increased your knowledge of sports considerably; so
not only will you impress your sports enthusiast, you will impress others. More importantly, however, you have attained your goal: you are
able to live with the sports enthusiast. Furthermore, you may have
even developed a love for sports yourself!

—A student paper

Now, sitting in the funeral home, John thought about the gift his
grandmother gave him. It was the understanding of how true love
shapes someone's life. And even with her gone, thinking about his
grandmother would bring a warm feeling. She gave him something
precious. She gave him love.

—A student paper

b). Write concluding paragraphs to match the introductory paragraphs
from exercise 4a.

Sentences

Pitfalls in Sentence Writing
Nouns Modifying Nouns
Preposition Piling
Sentence Modifiers
Passive Construction
Delayed Subjects
Deadwood

Sentence Variations
Intentions
Structure
Length

Sentence Style: Training Eye and Ear
Positioning
Positive Wording
Periodic Sentences
Balanced Sentences
Antithesis
Parallelism
Parenthesis
Rhythm

A Checklist for Sentences

Exercises

Behind every style is a decisive individual. Perhaps it is a person who decides to dress a certain way, or a writer who decides to write a certain way. Style is a conscious decision, a distinctive way of presenting yourself to someone else. In everyday life we are attracted to those unique and self-assured people who have style. In writing, style can be the source of a similar attraction if we learn to work with the basic rhetorical tool: the sentence.

Just as we determine a person's "style" from the way he or she dresses, speaks, and behaves, we get a feel for a writer from the way the writer's sentences look and sound. As Kenneth Burke notes in *Permanence and Change*, "Speech in its essence is not neutral—it is full of feeling, attitude, and emotion." The trick is to shape our "speech"—our sentences—to project the self we want to project, a self that can be shared with, and appreciated by, readers. Consider the passage below. What kind of self does it present? Did a person or a computer write it? What does it mean? Does the style make you care what it means?

> An Academic Planning Model must involve a futures planning component. Goals should be set for some time in the future. These goals should be translated into shorter-term objectives for which the degree of detail and concreteness varies inversely with the lead time. There should also be reasonable suspense dates for implementation of plans and a definitive methodology for evaluation and feedback. The interfacing of long-term . . . and short-term planning should result.
> —as quoted in *The Underground Grammarian*

Such prose is unnecessarily difficult to understand. Sentence style and word choice both contribute to the problems. Word choice will be examined in the next chapter. In this chapter, we will look at words as they work together in sentences. First we will examine some pitfalls in writing sentences. When you have learned to avoid these pitfalls, you will be able to develop a strong, controlled prose style, which is the emphasis of the second half of the chapter. If you have trouble with any of the terms used in these discussions, consult Chapter 14, "Glossary of Grammatical Terms."

PITFALLS IN SENTENCE WRITING

Nouns Modifying Nouns

As much as possible, avoid making nouns modify other nouns. A string of nouns is difficult to read. In the first sentence of the prose passage above, for example, "a futures planning component" is harder to understand than "a component to plan for the future." "Do not discriminate on religion or race grounds" could be better written as "Do not discriminate on religious or racial grounds." Wherever possible, turn the nouns into adjectives, as in the last sentence. Where this is not possible, you may need to use prepositional phrases. The object is to make the sentence read better, but be careful with prepositional phrases, since piling up prepositions is another sure way to add flab to the sentence.

Preposition Piling

Avoid piling up prepositions and prepositional phrases. The overuse of this construction can make your prose jerky. Consider the violation of this rule in the following "sentence."

> An upsurge in the last five years of this decade in the use of computers as engineering aids in the control of patterns of traffic flow has made us marvel at, though not necessarily feel confidence in, the vast, technological environment we are all the products of.

The writer simply means "The use of computers to control traffic patterns has made us ponder the entire technological system."

Sentence Modifiers

Avoid sentence modifiers; they can obscure your meaning. The adverb *hopefully*, when used to modify a whole sentence, is the most notorious, and probably the most familiar, example.

> Hopefully, the problem will go away when the fiscal year ends.

The position of "hopefully" at the beginning of the sentence suggests that it modifies *the problem*. However, it cannot modify *the problem*, because problems cannot *hope*. What it is really meant to modify does not appear in the sentence: the writer or some other person. An appropriate revision of the sentence is:

> *We hope* that the problem will go away when the fiscal year ends.

Passive Construction

Avoid the weak passive. The passive voice delays a sentence and keeps the reader from knowing who performs the action of the sentence until the end (if even then). Passives turn the actual object of a verb into the apparent subject, and the actual subject into an apparent object. Compare the following:

> I threw the book across the room.
> The book was thrown by me across the room.

The first sentence uses fewer words and makes its point more directly; it is therefore much stronger than the second. Much of present-day writing, particularly in government, business, and education, relies heavily on the passive. Perhaps bureaucrats and executives feel that the impersonal sound of the passive somehow lends "authority" to their writing. What the passive really does, however, is make writing stilted and wordy. Use the active voice whenever possible. Sometimes, of course, you do not know who or what the subject is, and in such cases the passive is appropriate:

> The young woman down the street was mugged last night as she walked in Walnut Park.

Since you do not know who did the mugging, you cannot avoid the passive in this case.

Look carefully, and decide whether you really need to use the passive construction. If your sentence is less wordy and more direct with the active voice, then use it, and save the passive voice for those few times when you really need to suppress the "doer" of the action.

Delayed Subject

Avoid beginning sentences with *it is* or *there are*. If you do, you throw away one of the sentence's most emphatic spots—the beginning.

> There are basically four types of comic strips.

Better to say:

> Four types of comic strips are popular today.

Instead of delaying the impact of a sentence, such as:

> It is the case that Christopher is slow-witted.

Why not just say it?

> Christopher is slow-witted.

Deadwood

Avoid deadwood. Deadwood—unnecessary words or phrases—makes the sentence less clear. The person who writes, "Children can watch objectionable TV programs at home when they are there in an unsupervised capacity," could make his point just as effectively and less pompously by writing "Children can watch objectionable TV programs when they are alone at home." The educator who wrote for public consumption,

> Thus, in conclusion, let it be said plainly, that in the perception of this observer, . . . for what the thought of any one individual may be worth, our conceptual foundations have deteriorated to the point that action is now occurring in a virtual void of theory. . . .
> —as quoted in *The Underground Grammarian*

might have kept more of his audience awake if he had said simply

> Our concepts have deteriorated so far that we now act with almost no theories to back us up.

In writing, as in other endeavors, less can sometimes be more.

SENTENCE VARIATIONS

Avoid the pitfalls, and you will write cleaner, clearer prose. Good style, however, is not simply a matter of avoidance. Since style is making choices, writing that makes no choices has no style. We defined style as an impression you create, a *self* you project by arranging sentence patterns to fit your own patterns of thought. Readers expect more than a single-minded adherence to limited patterns—they expect range and variety. The proficient writer does not simply follow pat formulas or cling slavishly to specified frameworks of development.

You do not want to make *every* sentence completely different in sound and structure. Nor will you want to make every sentence echo every other sentence in form, rhythm, and arrangement. The best writing is always a mixture.

Intentions

Vary your sentences according to your intentions. Sentences can be classified into four main groups according to the writer's intention: those that state, those that ask, those that request or command politely, and those that express emotion strongly.

Declarative statements predominate in essays where the primary objective is to provide information and ideas. You can vary your writing, however, by occasionally phrasing a fact as a question, a request, or a command.

In the following passage, a surgeon–writer relates his impressions of an ex-patient who washed his cancerous forehead with water from Lourdes, a site of miraculous cures. Note how the author effectively uses questions in the midst of descriptive and declarative sentences. (We have italicized the questions in this excerpt.)

> I see Joe now and then at the diner. He looks anything but a fleshly garden of miracles. Rather, he has taken on a terrible ordinariness—Eden after the fall, and minus its most beautiful features. There is a certain slovenliness, a dishevelment of the tissues. *Did the disease ennoble him, and now that it is gone, is he somehow diminished?* Perhaps I am wrong. Perhaps the only change is the sly wink with which he greets me, as though to signal that we have shared something furtive. *Could such a man have felt the brush of [angels'] wings?* How often it seems that the glory leaves as soon as the wound is healed. But then it is only saints who bloom in martyrdom, becoming less and less the flesh that pains, more and more ghost-colored weightlessness.
>
> —Richard Selzer, *Mortal Lessons*

Why are these two italicized sentences worded as questions? Selzer is sharing with his readers his own uncertainty upon beholding a patient who is apparently the beneficiary of a miraculous cure. Such sharing of oneself with the reader is a mark of a writer with style.

Structure

Vary your sentences according to structure. A passage containing only simple sentences (those with no dependent clauses) may become boringly repetitive. The reader may wish for some coordination and subordination to enlarge and clarify the relationships among the ideas the writer is presenting.

By the same token, a paragraph composed almost entirely of complex sentences can be burdensome and overly intricate. The *ideal* paragraph, if there is such a thing, contains a healthy mixture of sentence structures.

As an example of writing that not only contains variation, but uses variation to make a point about character, look at the following paragraph from Mark Twain's *Life on the Mississippi.* The character is a riverboat pilot who has an infinite memory and an unstoppable tongue:

> And so on, by the hour, the man's tongue would go. He could *not* forget anything. It was simply impossible. The most trivial details remained

as distinct and luminous in his head, after they had lain there for years, as the most memorable events. His was not simply a pilot's memory; its grasp was universal. If he were talking about a trifling letter he had received seven years before, he was pretty sure to deliver you the entire screed from memory. And then, without observing that he was departing from the true line of his talk, he was more than likely to hurl in a long-drawn parenthetical biography of the writer of that letter, and you were lucky indeed if he did not take up that writer's relatives, one by one, and give you their biographies.

As Twain's description of the pilot's loquaciousness becomes more specific, his sentences become more intricate, unstoppable.

Length

Vary the length of your sentences. Three or four medium-to-long *building* sentences followed by a climactic statement consisting of three or four words can be extremely effective in a long or medium-length paragraph. See how Pirsig breaks the flow of the following paragraph by varying sentence length. Notice particularly where the shorter sentences are, and how they work:

> The ideas began with what seemed to be a minor difference of opinion between John and me on a matter of small importance: how much one should maintain one's own motorcycle. It seems natural and normal to me to make use of the small tool kits and instruction booklets supplied with each machine, and keep it tuned and adjusted myself. John demurs. He prefers to let a competent mechanic take care of these things so that they are done right. Neither viewpoint is unusual, and this minor difference would never have become magnified if we didn't spend so much time riding together and sitting in country roadhouses drinking beer and talking about whatever comes to mind. What comes to mind, usually, is whatever we've been thinking about in the half hour or forty-five minutes since we last talked to each other. When it's roads or weather or people or old memories or what's in the newspapers, the conversation just naturally builds pleasantly. But whenever the performance of the machine has been on my mind and gets into the conversation, the building stops. The conversation no longer moves forward. There is a silence and a break in the continuity. It is as though two old friends, a Catholic and Protestant, were sitting drinking beer, enjoying life, and the subject of birth control somehow came up. Big freeze-out.
> —Robert Pirsig, *Zen and the Art of Motorcycle Maintenance*

Notice that the first variation in sentence length occurs about one-third of the way into the paragraph, and that it punctuates a turn in the paragraph's development: "John demurs." The second short sentence in the paragraph comes at the very end, in the form of an effective sentence fragment. It represents the writer's evaluation of the imaginary conversation and the awkward pause that would result.

A student writer, writing to persuade her audience that people in America really do live with rats, and should not have to, varies sentence length quite effectively in this sentence near the end of her essay:

> I buried another rat yesterday. Sometimes we find those rats that have consumed the poison dead in our driveway, in our yard, under our porch. It is no triumph. There are his cousins, his brothers, his sisters, his children. Even burying them brings no satisfaction and is only an additional repulsive chore.

The simple statement, "It is no triumph," makes the paragraph stop and draws attention to itself, coming as it does right in the middle of two catalogs that demonstrate that the rats are everywhere.

Such matching of sentence's length to its content is one of the skillful writer's hallmarks. With practice you can look for appropriate spots in the development of your essay to vary sentence length and improve your prose. In addition to considering sentence length, structure, and intention, however, you can use additional stylistic devices to sharpen your prose and to develop that self you share with your reader. To learn these devices, you will need to use your ears as well as your eyes.

SENTENCE STYLE: TRAINING EYE AND EAR

From time to time, you have probably read a poem aloud. Poetry lends itself to recitation because its rhyme, rhythm, and repetition of sound have a musical quality that enchants the ear as well as the eye. But have you ever thought of reading a passage of prose aloud?

Well-written prose can appeal to our ears as well as our eyes, and give us a better feel for the language we use. Read the following sentences aloud and listen.

> The cadaver has dignity and reserve; it is distanced by death.
> —Richard Selzer, *Mortal Lessons*

Notice the repeated "d" and "r" sounds. They give the sentence a solid yet lilting quality, and add to the effectiveness of the sentence by their patterned arrangement.

> And for ordinary people, the war in Europe ended—not when they heard the hoarse voice of the radio, nor when they saw the paper blizzards falling between skyscrapers, nor even when they ate their first food in freedom—but slowly and silently, by degrees, somewhere in each man's heart.
> —*Time* magazine, as quoted in Joseph Satin,
> *Reading Literature*, p. 107

Do key words in the sentence above ring clearly? Do their sounds in any way suggest their meanings? Do you notice any repetition of sounds, especially of consonants at the beginnings of words? Do you find yourself pronouncing some words deliberately and slowly, while skipping over other words and phrases?

Reading prose aloud, aside from developing your ability to read, is a good way to develop your own writing style. There are other ways, too, which we will be examining in this section. We will now look at some structural devices that demonstrate how form can contribute to a sentence's content.

Positioning

Put the most important part of the sentence in an emphatic position. Every sentence has two spots where you have the opportunity to grab the reader's attention: the very beginning and the end. Pay attention to where you put the important words of each sentence. Remember the caution against using the *it is* and *there are* patterns in your sentences. These patterns throw away the possible strength of the beginning of the sentence. To be sure, you can sometimes accomplish a good effect by holding the important idea of the sentence to the very end. In the paragraph above, on living with rats, the attention-getting short sentence begins with *it* and works very well; the reader's attention is drawn to the end of that short sentence and the words "no triumph."

Writers who ignore the emphatic positions, however, fall into the habit of not committing themselves to saying what they mean by using *it is* and *there are* sentence patterns. See the following example:

> There is truth to the fact that no method of voting is completely sound, insuring a selection free of bias all the time.

A more careful and committed writer can make a clearer and stronger statement:

> Any voting method will have some bias in selection.

Positive Wording

Put ideas positively rather than negatively. Most of the time a sentence put positively will be shorter and more emphatic than its negative version.

I do not have many tomatoes.

is longer than

I have few tomatoes.

Here is another example:

Do not retain excess words in your sentences

is longer and less emphatic than

Eliminate excess words in your sentences.

Use the negative statement only on the rare occasion when it yields ironic understatement. Thus,

He was not incapable of floating.

is longer and less emphatic than

He could float.

But if you wanted to turn such a sentence to witty effect, you might say

He was not incapable of floating, though his considerable bulk might lead one to assume he would sink to the bottom.

Paying attention to the emphatic positions in the sentence—the beginning and ending—can result in interesting sentences. The greatest stylistic effect can occur when you build a sentence toward its ending, as in cumulative sentences.

Periodic Sentences

Periodic sentences can add variety to paragraphs. In periodic sentences, the essential information is withheld until the end. This device keeps the reader in suspense, waiting to find out the writer's point.

The noted Yiddish writer, Sholom Aleichem, beginning a chapter of *Adventures of Mottel, The Cantor's Son* with a periodic sentence, gives the reader a sense of how endless a journey to the New World must have seemed:

If you've never travelled on the sea, if you've never been imprisoned on Ellis Island, if you've never seen with your own eyes all the troubles and tribulations, all the sorrows and miseries of the immigrants, if you've never floundered in a flood of tears, and if you've never yearned impatiently for your friends and relatives to deliver you from bondage—if you've never experienced any of these things, you cannot possibly understand how one feels—how we felt—when our feet were finally on American soil.

Aleichem uses a long series of "if" subordinate clauses to convey what it must feel like to travel the ocean in steerage class (the cheapest), to arrive at Ellis Island and be subjected to further crowded rooms, endless medical examinations, rudeness from the immigration officials, and so on. Each "if" clause delays the reader one more time, just as the book's title character was delayed time and time again before touching American soil.

Here is another periodic sentence that describes a writer and his companions coming upon an unmapped lake in the caribou-hunting regions of northern Canada:

> Once on the high bank of the shore, and raised from the downward-sloping surface of the river, we saw stretching to the horizon on the west the clear, livid blue of open water under a blazing sun.
> —Farley Mowat, *People of the Deer*

In this sentence Mowat makes the reader wait twice: once for the subject, *we*, which does not appear until mid-sentence; then again for the direct object, *blue*, and its accompanying modifiers.

Why might the author have delayed both subject and direct object? Perhaps he wanted his readers to experience his own sense of vastness and remoteness when coming upon the uncharted waters.

Effective as this technique is, it should be used only when a particular experience calls for it. If *every* sentence is written as a periodic sentence, the reader will not feel any sense of wonder or surprise.

Balanced Sentences

Use balanced sentences occasionally. Balance gives equal weight to two ideas. We might, for example, set up two independent clauses on either side of a coordinating conjunction or semicolon. The example that follows is from Lytton Strachey's biographical essay on Florence Nightingale, which contrasts the "real" Nightingale with the legendary one:

> And so it happens that in the real Miss Nightingale there was more that was interesting than in the legendary one; there was also less that was agreeable.
> —Lytton Strachey, *Eminent Victorians*

Balancing the clauses "more that was interesting" and "less that was agreeable" allows Strachey to sum up his view of Nightingale in one striking, provocative sentence. The contrast of the two clauses reinforces their effective balance.

Antithesis

When one part of the sentence plays against another, a kind of war of words—antithesis—results. It can be highly effective. Dorothea Dix, for example, uses antithesis wittily in her pithy appraisal of sacrifice as it relates to the sexes:

> A woman sacrifices herself in a thousand needless little ways which do no one any good, but when a man makes a sacrifice it is big with heroism, and counts.
>
> —Dorothea Dix, "Are Women Growing Selfish?"

The first part of the sentence establishes the subject in a seemingly "final" way, while the second contrasts the structures of the first for ironic effect: "a thousand needless little ways" versus "a sacrifice big with heroism," and "do no one any good" versus "counts." Antithesis can be used between clauses, or within a single clause. Note how it works in the following sentence:

> Kindled by summer though cool by nature, she was a beauty.
>
> —Elizabeth Bowen, *A World of Love*

Balance and antithesis depend upon similar grammatical structures similarly arranged for their effectiveness.

Parallelism

Use parallelism for effective style. Elements similar in function should be structured similarly. Parallel structure can arrange material and make clear that the material is to be considered as a whole. You can also use parallel structure to create balance and emphasis in the sentence. And you can use parallel structure to help create rhythm, which is, after all, the expectation of pattern. Here is another example from Elizabeth Bowen's *A World of Love*, in which she uses parallel structure to create a fine rhythmic effect:

> Revulsion had driven the elder sister out from the valley; shame drove her far from the river or very thought of it. Humiliation caused her to pluck Guy's letter like an asp from her breast: blindly she scrambled uphill with it to entomb it under the flat stone under the stifling elder.

Here the clauses' parallel structure in the first sentence yokes and balances the two clauses. But Bowen continues the parallelism, and creates the pattern of expectation with the first clause of the next sentence that begins "humiliation caused her. . . ."

Some of the finest, most rhythmical passages in the language may be found in the King James translation of the Bible, and in the Book of Common Prayer, both products of a time when people spoke what is described lovingly as "the King's English." Here is just one such passage. Notice how the parallel sentence structure creates the rhythm:

> We have erred, and strayed from thy ways like lost sheep. We have followed too much the devices and desires of our own hearts. We have offended against thy holy laws. We have left undone those things which we ought to have done; and we have done those things which we ought not to have done; and there is no health in us.
> —"General Confession for Morning and Evening Prayer,"
> *The Book of Common Prayer*

Parenthesis

Sometimes you may want to interrupt the movement of a sentence to make a point. You can include *parenthetical remarks* in sentences without distracting from rhythm or content. And sometimes useful, even necessary, information can be included parenthetically. Remember, however, to use this device to emphasize the really important ideas of a sentence. Overuse of parenthetical remarks can create choppy prose. Parenthetical remarks can give the writer a chance to change the focus of a sentence to bring attention to the writer and away from the content for effect.

Parenthesis (the singular form is used for the rhetorical device) can be achieved by using parentheses or dashes. In the sentence below, parenthetical information is important to the sentence's effect and idea. In his account of the creation of the first United States atomic weapon in 1945, Robert Jungk writes:

> The main topic of conversation among the atomic scientists working at Los Alamos naturally turned to the question, "Will the 'gadget'—the word 'bomb' was discreetly avoided—go off or not?"
> —Robert Jungk, *Brighter than a Thousand Suns*

In this passage parenthesis works well, calling attention to the scientist's reticence about using the word *bomb*. But be very careful about using parenthesis. Too many jolting interruptions can annoy readers until they are conscious only of them, not of the passage's overall content. Unless you want to create a particular effect through multiplying parenthesis, use the device sparingly.

Rhythm

As we indicated earlier in talking about balance and parallelism, rhythm in prose or poetry is the expectation of fulfillment of a pattern. In a sentence that lacks rhythm, the reader trudges through deep snow in heavy boots because the writer has not provided natural, easy movement from one word or phrase to the next. Words, phrases, repeated sounds, pronouns, sentence patterns—patterns of stress—any repetition of these may create rhythm. Skillful writers use a variety of devices, in fact, to create a rhythmic effect that does not call attention to itself. Consider the following passage from Jane Austen as an example, and see if you can pinpoint why it sounds rhythmical:

> Seldom, very seldom, does complete truth belong to any human disclosure; seldom can it happen that something is not a little disguised or a little mistaken; but where, as in this case, though the conduct is mistaken, the feelings are not, it may not be very material.
>
> —*Emma*

Each of the stylistic devices discussed in this chapter can be overused; indeed, they are most effective when least obtrusive. When they are too heavy-handed, they may make the reader cringe—or laugh.

> Lashed to her lovelorn listlessness, Letitia lay sprawled on her gigantic, four-poster—she'd wanted a queen-size but the store didn't have any—bed, half-heartedly nibbling an artichoke heart which didn't seem half as broken, frayed though it was, as hers.

Why does this sentence make us roll our eyeballs? It repeats the "l" sounds too much and therefore calls attention to the "l" sound. It uses parenthesis ineffectively, for no good reason. And it forces the sentence into a sledgehammer rhythm. It is too much. In contrast, here is a passage from Eudora Welty's lyrical novel, *Losing Battles*. Notice its unobtrusive use of the stylistic devices we have examined in this chapter:

> The car took the only way left open and charged up Banner Top in a bombardment of pink clods like thrown roses. Aycock appeared in its train of dust. He was running after it, waving his guitar. He caught hold and was borne on up as if by some large, not local bird. The car never stopped. The dogs streaked with it, barking it further off the road. Dust solid as a waterfall poured over the bank along whose roof the car rolled on, tossing a fence post, mowing down plum bushes. There was a shriek out of Etoyle, a blow, a scraping sound, a crack, then silence, even from the dogs.

When Pope wrote that the "sound must seem an echo to the sense," he spoke truth. The good writer's prose has *euphony*—it sounds good because the *way* the idea is expressed not only matches the content, but creates it.

A CHECKLIST FOR SENTENCES

1. Do I have any nouns modifying other nouns?
2. Have I piled up prepositions or prepositional phrases unnecessarily?
3. Have I begun the sentence with a vague sentence modifier?
4. Have I used the weak passive?
5. Does the sentence begin with an inappropriate *it is* or *there are* pattern?
6. Is there any deadwood? Have I said what I have to say as economically as possible?
7. Have I put important material in an emphatic position?
8. Have I put the idea positively?
9. Have I varied sentence type?
10. Have I varied sentence length?
11. Have I varied sentence structure?
12. Have I used stylistic devices more than once? Appropriately? Effectively?

EXERCISES

1. Sentence Pitfalls

  a). Rewrite each of the following sentences. Remove all elements that are pitfalls of good sentence writing. Identify the pitfalls in each one.

1. Today's youth is classified as a radical and revolutionary generation.
2. It is a good thing today is Saturday since this headache is going to take time to cure.
3. Decontrolling gas prices is the only way to go with the energy crisis.
4. There are a row of trees along each side of the stairs, which blocks the sun, thus shading the area and giving it an eerie, almost spooky, feeling.
5. There are huge, stained glass windows on each side of the door and a long corridor in front in which there is a statue on the right side.
6. There are five points that need to be prioritized.
7. The record company must also assist in molding the image-conscious artist.
8. An interesting trend that has developed is that even when people are not crazy about the artist, if the people attend the concert, they may enjoy the artist in concert more than on record.
9. We computerized the information according to the systematization we had previously worked out.
10. It has been some years since Papa died.
11. She enjoys her church work and does it just about everyday.
12. Qualification is one of the key variables which intensifies the lack of skill barrier.

13. Also, firms are afraid to train those with an above-average tendency to quit because of retraining costs.
14. It was at this moment that one of the three other players on the scene decided to intervene by tackling the guard.

b). Revise a draft of an old paper (no longer than three pages) to eliminate sentence pitfalls.

2. Parallel Structure

a). Correct the faulty parallelism in each of the following student sentences:

1. Many long days were spent on repairs, rebuilding, and the planting of the crop.
2. She was a good wife and mother: hard working, level headed, and knew how to keep Andrew happy.
3. Antonio helped her so gently through the birth of her son, and she comforting him when Joey became eighteen and left home.
4. More people are staying in school longer and trying to get the necessary experience for the jobs they desire.
5. The audience is assessed according to their level of education, economic status, class ranking, demographic grouping, and size.
6. The design of the text involves the layout of the page print; determining the page size; positioning and insertion of chapter titles, running heads, and page number; the spacing of text print; and blocking of margins.
7. Since money is important, recording costs must be kept down in relation to how important the artist is.

b). Write a sentence for each group of words listed below. Make sure to revise to avoid faulty parallelism.

1. neighbors, dressed, black, to join, wailing, follow, procession
2. nineteenth century, mentally ill, not distinguished, alcoholics, the aged, anyone who exhibited antisocial behavior.
3. students and faculty, accuse, station, poor audience attraction, that programming is poor, equipment broken, operation is disorganized

3. Sentence Length and Variety

a). Analyze and discuss the following paragraphs. Consider the length and variety of the sentences. How do they contribute to the effectiveness of the paragraph? Choose one example and imitate its patterns.

"For years I have had a recurrent dream. I take a road that runs toward the west. It is summer; I pass by a strange summer forest, in which there are mysterious beings, though I know that, on the whole, they are shy and benign. If I am fortunate and find the way, I arrive at a wonderful river, which runs among boulders, with rapids, between alders and high-spread trees, through a countryside fresh, green and wide. We go swimming; it is miles away from anywhere. We plunge in the smooth flowing pools. We make our way to the middle of the stream and climb up on the pale round gray stones and sit naked in the sun and the air, while the river glides away below us."
—Edmund Wilson, *The Old Stone House*

Bert Hale, the world-famous inventor, walked into Kensington Gardens with his latest invention under his arm. It was the afternoon of Sunday, August 1st. High overhead, in a fitful easterly wind, kites were dancing, like spots before liverish eyes. From the bandstand, as if a door were being intermittently opened and closed on the music, the strains of a Gilbert and Sullivan medley blared out, then receded to a pianissimo, rose and were shut off: the scarlet and brass of the bandsmen twinkled between the low trees, as the leaves stirred nervously. A newspaper sheet wrapped itself round Bert's leg. He rubbed his eyes, into which the wind had puffed some dust, and stamping the newspaper flat, read the headlines:

Soviet Delegation Here Tomorrow. Is It Peace?

Bert's mind registered the headline as part of something that was in the air, something talked about all round him, tuning with the gay, vague, yet exasperated atmosphere of the summer afternoon, the high-flying kites, the strolling crowds, the children and dogs weaving among them—an atmosphere of suspense. But he was not concerned with it: his own private suspense was concentrated upon a single point—would the invention work?
—Nicholas Blake [C. Day Lewis], *The Whisper in the Gloom*

b). Choose one of the following topics. Write a paragraph using different kinds and lengths of sentences.
the bookstore on the first day of class
registration
a rock concert
a crowded beach
getting to class right as the teacher begins a lecture

4. Sentence Cutting
Rewrite the following sentences in as few words as possible.

1. The purpose of the chapel on campus is to promote the spirit and welfare of the community.
2. Though I am not an expert on the subject of mental health, and in considering the facts that this subject is a sensitive one and most authorities' views are subjective, the case in point may seem to be weak.
3. There are many factors that must be considered.
4. The trouble was that it was the only job an immigrant could get.
5. There are many difficulties that must be confronted when making the big transition from high school to college.
6. It becomes readily apparent that if each man does his part, the tasks assigned to them are more easily accomplished.
7. The concepts of unity and humiliation as part of the fraternity pledging process are still misunderstood by most parents.
8. At first glance, Anna would appear to an onlooker as a conventional grandmother: small, gray, and stooped, without distinctive features.
9. Another problem confronting the homeowner could be mildew on the siding.
10. There are two balconies on each side of the auditorium that are also filled with rows of chairs facing the stage.

Words

The Dictionary and the Thesaurus

Inflated Language
Jargon
Buzz Words
Fad Words
Reshaping Sexist Language

General versus Specific Language

Guides to Sharpening Your Language
Use Strong Verbs
Avoid Weasel Words
Be Careful of "Sound-alike" Words
Avoid Fillers

Denotation and Connotation

Metaphors, Mixed Metaphors, and Clichés

Exercises

In his book, *Strictly Speaking*, Edwin Newman states,

> Those for whom words have lost their value are likely to find that ideas have also lost their value.

The value of an idea is often directly related to the words used to express it. Express an idea poorly, and you might as well have no idea; express it precisely, and it will be able to live in a world beyond the confines of your own mind. Our purpose in this chapter is to examine the capabilities of vocabulary and language in expressing ideas, and to discuss some of the ways in which a careful writer can use words to his advantage in an essay.

THE DICTIONARY AND THE THESAURUS

Where does a writer find words? "The dictionary, of course," you might think, "or perhaps the thesaurus." You would be right—but not altogether right. The dictionary and the thesaurus, used with care, are invaluable aids to the writer. Nevertheless, they are not infallible guides to correct word choice.

To determine what the dictionary can and cannot tell us, we should look at the complete entry for a deceptively simple word:

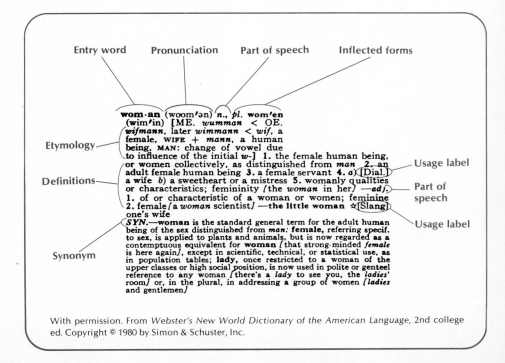

With permission. From *Webster's New World Dictionary of the American Language,* 2nd college ed. Copyright © 1980 by Simon & Schuster, Inc.

This entry tells us a great deal about the word *woman*.

SPELLING, SYLLABICATION, PRONUNCIATION. The entry word appears in bold or dark type, divided into syllables. The word's pronunciation appears next, usually within parentheses. An accent mark indicates which syllable or syllables are stressed. A guide to the pronunciation symbols used by your dictionary will usually be found at the bottom of the page.

PART OF SPEECH AND INFLECTED FORMS. An abbreviation appears next, indicating the word's part of speech. In this example, *n.* stands for *noun* and *adj.* stands for *adjective*. Inflected forms of the word follow. Irregularly formed plurals of nouns, principal parts of verbs, and comparatives and superlatives of adjectives and adverbs are given.

ETYMOLOGY. Within the brackets you will find a brief summary of the origins of the entry word. You are shown its root words and the changes it has undergone over the centuries. The symbol > means *derived from;* ME is an abbreviation for *Middle English* and OE for *Old English.* You should consult the introduction to your dictionary for more information on how to read this part of the entry.

DEFINITIONS. The definitions of the entry word appear next, grouped under the part of speech. In our sample entry, you can see six numbered definitions under the noun label and two under the adjective label. Consult your dictionary on the reasons for the order in which the definitions appear. The ordering principles vary in dictionaries.

USAGE LABELS. Usage labels indicate the circumstances in which a word is usually used. In the example, you can see that one of the meanings of the word *woman* is considered dialect and another slang.

SYNONYMS. The entry ends with a listing of several synonyms and examples of the contexts in which they are used.

This entry seems, in fact, to be a complete guide to the word *woman;* and it is a very good dictionary entry. However, you must know more about the word *woman* if you are to use it carefully and correctly. The dictionary is not a complete guide. It does not inform the word hunter that a letter to a women's rights group beginning "Ladies ..." would probably be thrown into the wastebasket, while an incautious reference to Miss America or the Queen of England as a *woman* might be considered an insult in some circles. The English language changes continuously to reflect changes in society, but the dictionary, by its very nature, is a fixed form. The dictionary only "knows" definitions and pronunciations that already exist in the language (and may already be passing out of the language).

The thesaurus provides even less specific guidance to the use of a word than the dictionary does. It simply lists the synonyms for words, with occasional hints in brackets as to the nationality, age, or intentions of some synonyms. Here is a brief excerpt from the list of synonyms for *woman* in *Roget's International Thesaurus:*

matron, dame, dowager	mother, grandmother, etc.
gammer [dial. Eng.]	wife, etc.
good woman, goodwife	bachelor girl, spinster, etc.
[arch.], goody	mollycoddle, etc.
girl, etc.	(effeminate person)
old woman, etc. (elder)	adult, etc.

As you can see, the writer who takes synonyms from a list like this without regard for their differing shades of meaning is likely to run into trouble. If he refers to his mother as a *dame* and his girlfriend as a *bachelor girl* in an essay on women he has known, for example, his readers will snicker and his mother and girlfriend may make it difficult for him to return to his home town. If you know the exact shade of meaning you want a word to convey, the thesaurus can be invaluable in helping you find the word. Like the dictionary, however, it is a fixed form, and it too should be used with care.

The dictionary and the thesaurus are guides to the language primarily as it is used by the most influential groups in our society and as it is used in formal writing. What these sources do not reflect is the full *range* of word use in America, from street talk to the language of legal documents. And because they do not reflect this range in its entirety, they also do not accurately reflect the process of change in our language. Many words and phrases that were acceptable only as "slang" some years ago have moved through persistent use—first in informal speech and then in informal writing—to respectability in formal speech and writing. The phrase "tell it like it is," for example, originated in the speech of black Americans in the 1960s and was picked up as a slogan by black leaders of that time; it now appears in contexts as far from its origins as *Time Magazine* articles and university commencement addresses. Changes in the spoken language precede changes in the written one. They occur so rapidly that dictionaries and thesauruses do not usually reflect the spoken language. They are not, therefore, absolutely accurate guides to the proper use of a word or a phrase.

In other ways, too, the dictionary and the thesaurus fall short of being complete guides to word usage. While some meanings of a word remain constant, some may fade as new ones evolve, and the dictionary and thesaurus do not always discriminate accurately among these. The situation becomes even more confusing when some of these "faded" meanings linger on in a word's connotations or implied meanings. The word *woman*, for example, is rarely used today in the senses suggested by the third and fifth definitions of the sample dictionary entry ("a fe-male servant" and "a man with qualities conventionally regarded as feminine . . ."). For some people, however, *woman* still has overtones of both these definitions, and a writer still might hesitate about using the word when one of these shades of meaning is likely to obscure his own. Neither the dictionary nor the thesaurus, moreover, is a completely re-liable guide to idioms—patterns of language peculiar to one language only. If a native of France, for example, wants to know why "How do you do?" is a standard greeting in English (the French equivalent is, liter-ally, "How do you go?"), most English dictionaries cannot tell her. In short, this chapter must do more than simply demonstrate how to use the dictionary and the thesaurus; correct word choice in writing re-quires more than this.

INFLATED LANGUAGE

The evolution of a language is not a simple and straightforward process. Nor is every new word added to the language an improvement. Special occupations and areas of interest—the armed services, the professions (e.g., medicine, law, and teaching), and many sports and hobbies, to name a few—are major sources of new words and phrases.

Jargon

The particular language of any of these fields is called its *jargon.* Jargon is fine as long as it is either used within its original context or used in such a way that the uninitiated reader does not have to guess at what is being said. Too often, however, the speakers or writers of a particular kind of jargon will use it in a context where it does *not* belong, and trouble begins.

Buzz Words

Buzz words are terms that have escaped from a particular jargon to play a larger—and generally unfortunate—role in the language. They sound sharp and professional, yet they do not mean a great deal out of context (some do not even mean much *in* context). Obviously, people without a great deal to say find them useful. Unfortunately, as specialized areas of knowledge and their corresponding jargons flourish, so do buzz words. Thus a newspaper columnist writing for a general audience can borrow the language of the social scientist to say,

> [The American father], too, is tempted by mobility and affluence and by plain logistical feasibility to indulge his whims.
> —Mario Ross, *The Syracuse Herald-American*

when what he really means is, "It is easier for a father to dodge his responsibilities these days." And a Secretary of the Treasury can refuse to abandon economic jargon even in a pamphlet intended to help corporations "do a better job of speaking out":

> At the same time, high inflation inevitably drags down the rate of growth in real incomes, for it depresses investment and productivity growth, diverting economic activity into unprofitable channels.
> —Michael C. Blumenthal,
> "Liberalism in the 1980s Must Face Basic Economic Realities"

This can be translated as, "Inflation slows economic growth."

Some buzz words, in fact, have become so popular, so common, and so meaningless that they lend themselves readily to a game of mix-and-match. Consider this list, for example, that first appeared in *Newsweek:*

prioritize	projectionable	coordinates
methodize	multifaceted	input
systematize	practicable	modules
merge	synchronizable	variants

One sure-fire way to turn any word into a buzz word, you may notice, is to add *-able* or *-ize* to it. Try putting these words together in random combinations. You will find that you too can sound like an expert as you "merge projectionable coordinates" or "methodize multifaceted modules." Inflated prose makes very simple ideas appear far more serious or elaborate than they are.

Fad Words

Some words in inflated prose are used so frequently that they can be called *fad words*. They, too, suggest far more, in a vague and grand way, than their plainer equivalents. As this book is being written, *system* is one such word. It can make almost anything sound bigger and more complex. People listen to "home entertainment systems," not stereos; they shave with "shaving systems," not razors; and they go in and out of their homes through "entry systems," not doors. (The real extremists eat with "culinary consumption systems" instead of knives, forks, and spoons.) *Impact, viable, experience, classic*—the list could go on and on—are all current fad words.

Columnists have noted the tendency toward inflated language by using such language to humorous effect. Russell Baker, one such watchdog of the language, turned a familiar fairy tale into "bureaucratese":

> In an effort to make the classics accessible to contemporary readers, I am translating them into the modern American language. Here is the translation of "Little Red Riding Hood." Once upon a point in time, a small person named Little Red Riding Hood initiated plans for the preparation, delivery, and transportation of foodstuffs to her grandmother, a senior citizen resident at a place of residence in a forest of indeterminate dimension. In the process of implementing this program, her incursion into the forest was in mid-transportation process when it attained interface with an alleged perpetrator. This individual, a wolf, made inquiry as to the whereabouts of Little Red Riding Hood's goal, as well as inferring that he was desirous of ascertaining the contents of Little Red Riding Hood's foodstuffs basket, and all that. . . .
>
> —"Little Red Riding Hood Revisited,"
> *The New York Times,* January 13, 1980

Fad words, such as *implement* and *interface*, and buzz words, such as *point in time, initiate plans*, and *alleged perpetrator*, as well as other examples of inflated diction are turned to humor by Baker in this passage.

In defense of some of these buzz words and fad words, we should make it clear that many of them have crept into the language from the best of motives. Anyone who has read carefully the language of the warranty for a product must realize how simple conditions can be made complex.

Reshaping Sexist Language

In the same way, concern for the labels of language and the values they carry with them prompts us to make women as visible in the language as they are in reality. The nineteenth-century grammarians who are primarily responsible for the rules of grammar that have been taught in the schools were men. They were ministers and statesmen, merchants and mathematicians. They held attitudes about their culture—and woman's place in it—that are reflected in many of the rules that they made up. The rule that when the gender of the noun is unknown, the masculine form of the pronoun should be used, is an example of men's control of the language. Today, however, the drive for equality in language, as in life, has caused some linguistic problems. Stewards and stewardesses have become *flight attendants;* chairmen are now *chairpersons* or *chairs.* And what a mess we have made with pronouns! The unnatural, unfortunate forms s/he and she/he have been coined to indicate the possibility of either gender.

What are the solutions to the tangle? Use of the plural wherever possible is one solution—but that has its own trap, namely turning the indefinite pronouns (singular) into plural forms. For example, *"Everyone* turned in *their* books yesterday,"* in place of *"Everyone* turned in *his* book yesterday."* Another solution is simply to be careful about assuming masculinity or femininity. This book has "mixed up" genders so that sometimes a student is he and sometimes she; sometimes a teacher is she and sometimes he. Such careful attention to the assumptions being reflected in the language is more important and more consonant with the idea of equality of gender than distortions of the language. In our efforts to reshape sexist language—as in our efforts to deal with other complexities of modern life—we should not lose sight of the need for language that is accurate, specific, and capable of being translated from one specialized field to another without losing its meaning in the process.

GENERAL VERSUS SPECIFIC LANGUAGE

As a rule, general words give the reader vague impressions. To describe a summer vacation to a school friend as "good" or "terrific" does not give the friend a very clear idea of it, not if you were thinking of pale blue twilights, sailboat races, and fireworks on the Fourth of July. Nor does describing a roommate in a letter home as "gross" give an accurate idea of a person who brushes her teeth twice a semester, picks her nose, and waits to do her laundry until it begins growing fungus.

On the other hand, using a general vocabulary is sometimes the best strategy. If, for instance, sensitive negotiations between countries have ground to a halt, an intelligent diplomat would hardly tell the press corps, "Country X is refusing to remove its troops from the border, and Country Y will not allow them to remain there." Rather, he would use language general enough to preserve optimism and to protect the negotiations: "Country X and Country Y have reached an impasse over the question of maintaining troops on the border. The commitment of both countries to the cause of peace, however, remains unshaken."

As you learned in Chapter 1, you must consider your subject, your audience, and your own stance as a writer throughout the process of writing. The same considerations must apply even to your choice of words. If a situation demands a general vocabulary, you must use a general vocabulary; if it allows you to be more specific, you may be so.

To some extent, too, the culture we live in dictates our choice of general or specific words. These rules are built right into the language. In Eskimo dialects, for instance, there is no *general* word for snow—only words for specific *kinds* of snow. Usually, cultures lack general words for concepts that they do not recognize or that otherwise do not mean much to them. Also, they do not have specific words for concepts that have little practical application or are embarrassing. The writer attempting to deal with sex or death, for example, is going to be hard-pressed to find many terms for those concepts that are neither overly scientific nor vulgar. If the English language backs you into a corner, you have little choice but to make the best of the situation.

Actually, though, the resources of the English language are such that you will seldom find yourself strapped for words. And in your student writing, you seldom find yourself in situations that demand general language exclusively. Readers need specifics, particularly when something is being described, explained, or evaluated:

> Looking out a window over an orange grove, one researcher remarked, "We are growing chemicals now, not oranges." Dried juice vesicles, powdered and mixed with water, produce a thick and foamy solution which is used to fight forest fires. Albedecone, a pharmaceutical which stops leaks in blood vessels, is made from hespiridin, a substance in the peels of oranges. But the main use of the leftover rinds is cattle feed, either as molasses made from the peel sugars or as dried shredded meal. Citrus pulp and chopped rinds are dried for dairy feed much in the same way that clothes are dried in a home dryer—in a drum within a drum, whirling. The exhaust vapors perfume the countryside . . . people often assume that they are smelling the making of orange juice when they are actually smelling cattle feed.
>
> —John McPhee, *Oranges*

Notice how the author uses specific words and phrases to change the reader's perceptions of the fruit: the orange is analyzed for its specific uses, not extolled for its "naturalness." Note, too, that McPhee's *intention* is plainly to change the reader's perceptions of the orange, and that the specific language contributes to this end. Even the slightly sinister impression created by the details is part of the "debunking" effect: Though McPhee is certainly not openly opposed to the idea of oranges as chemicals, he does want to counteract the image of the orange most of us have. No description, after all, can ever be completely objective, and as long as a writer is aware of the impression his words create and can use this impression to his advantage, it creates no problem.

Compare the McPhee paragraph with this one:

> When you peel off the wrinkled skin, a trinkle of juice sprays out and a pleasant aroma fills the air. As your mouth begins to water, you taste a section of the orange and satisfy your taste buds. Section after section, each bite is filled with vitamins and nourishment that make it even more enticing. The orange—an irresistible taste that is great for dessert or snack.

Except for the opening visual image of the "trinkle" of juice—and it has an absurd effect, of which the writer seems unaware—this paragraph frustrates the reader by offering no specific details to back up its assertions about the taste of the orange. What *is* it that satisfies the taste buds? Why *is* the taste "irresistible"? We are never told. The writer is retreating to the safe and general language of a television commercial instead of giving us specific information in specific terms.

In most cases, specific language that is properly controlled and directed will be far more effective than timid generalities. No magic formula exists that will enable you to write sparkling specifics immediately, of course. The advice that follows, however, should help you a great deal.

GUIDES TO SHARPENING YOUR LANGUAGE

Use Strong Verbs

Always try to replace an adverb plus a verb with a stronger verb. This rule is simple, but it is all too often neglected. Adding an adverb, after all, is the easiest way to liven up a sentence, and many writers would rather not take the trouble to hunt for a stronger verb. The verb, however, is the focal point of the sentence, and a series of sentences with slack verbs plus assorted adverbs can seem weak and stringy. Specific and colorful verbs can tighten up such sentences in a hurry. For instance, change a sentence like "The baby *moved slowly* toward the door," to "The baby *crawled* toward the door." Instead of "The students *rudely forced* the Dean out of his office," try "The students *catapulted* the Dean out of his office." Using a stronger verb can help you to be concise and forceful.

Avoid Weasel Words

Try not to overqualify or undersay what you have to say. *Weasel words* are those adverbs that seem to take the hard edge off some sentences: *quite, rather, certainly, possibly, perhaps, maybe,* are some examples. Weasel words can often make what you say look as though you have not really said what you just said: "It's certainly possible that Reggie was rather angry at Laura." "Perhaps you should consider saving that quotation for the last paragraph. It might possibly be more effective there." The use of such words make sentences less emphatic, less forceful. By overqualifying your statements, you can undersay what you need to say. The examples above can be tightened as follows: "Reggie could have been angry at Laura." "Why not save that quotation for the last paragraph? It might be more effective there." You should not be rude, but you should not weasel your way out of a direct statement, either.

Be Careful of "Sound-alike" Words

Make sure you have the right word for your purpose. A statement can be robbed of much of its precision if it includes words that sound right, but are not. For example, in the sentence "A person in our society who cannot read is often considered mentally *efficient*," the writer means that such a person is considered mentally *deficient*—lacking in something essential. The use of "efficient" where "deficient" is intended suggests that such a person is actually considered to be functioning well. This, of course, is rarely the case. Sometimes such incorrect use of words can call down not only objections but laughter from readers. The student who writes "I disliked *Tom Jones* because I felt that it was too *sedimental*" distracts his readers from anything he might have to say about *Tom Jones* by his confusion of "sentimental" (here, "showing tender, gentle, or delicate feelings in an excessive, superficial, or maudlin way") with "sedimental" ("pertaining to matter that settles to the bottom of a liquid"). Many confusing pairs of words are listed in the "Glossary of Usage." If you are in doubt about a word and cannot find it in the "Glossary," consult a dictionary.

Avoid Fillers

In informal speech, we often feel compelled to fill up nervous little gaps or to emphasize points with "filler" words and phrases—"like, man, you know what I mean?" Avoid these in writing—you should have no nervous little gaps in an essay. You can emphasize points with specific language and well-chosen examples more effectively than you can with "you know?"

DENOTATION AND CONNOTATION

In your attempts to use language as precisely as possible, you must consider not only the *denotations*—the literal dictionary definitions—of words, but also their *connotations*—the meanings implied in them, the feelings they can convey to the reader. Virtually every word has several connotations that go beyond its denotation; the language of feeling exists alongside and can sometimes take precedence over the language of meaning.

A writer can easily get into trouble with a word if he is not aware of its connotation in a specific context. Many words, for example, undergo changes in connotation over the years, and the writer who fails to take these changes into account may find that he has opened a real breach between himself and his audience. The thesaurus-scanner who casually describes his mother as a "dame" and his girlfriend as a "bachelor girl," for example, will find himself in this kind of difficulty. When you begin searching for words to lend variety to your writing, you must have an ear for what is current in the language and a sense of what will work best with your audience.

Many words may have two or more different connotations in current usage, depending on the contexts in which they appear. An *exclusive* country club may be one that denies membership to certain ethnic minorities, or it may simply be one that has twelve tennis courts and a marble-inlaid sauna. A *fair* performance by an actor could mean anything from "passably good" to "downright mediocre." An individual who is *eccentric* may live in a tumble-down house with thirty cats and perform strange rites in the attic, or she may merely wear white socks on Thursdays. A *prejudiced* person may be an out-and-out bigot or may just have strong opinions. If the exact connotation of one of these words or another like it is not immediately evident from the rest of the sentence in which you place it, you run the risk of confusing—or, with words like *prejudiced*, possibly angering—your audience. In such cases, you should find a synonym for the word or describe more fully the situation you mean it to define.

Making use of the connotations of words, however, is not just a matter of avoiding their misuse. You can consciously choose words that will help you to reinforce your point of view and to satisfy the expectations of your audience. Examine, for example, these two accounts of an imaginary senator's activities. One could have been released by the senator's own public relations staff, and the other could have been published by his detractors:

> Senator Homer Pellagra introduced an important new bill on the Senate floor yesterday that would increase the defense budget by a much-needed ten billion dollars. The Senator is acting in the best interests of the American people in these troubled times and in the best traditions of American patriotism. Our weak defense budget needs this increase if we are to resume our rightful place among the nations of the world. Please give the Senator your support in the November general elections.

> Senator Homer Pellagra introduced not only an unnecessary, but a dangerous new bill on the Senate floor yesterday. The measure, if passed, would increase the defense budget by another ten billion dollars. The Senator is exhibiting a hawkishness bordering on paranoia. His trigger-happy proposal will only cut further into the programs we need here and now in America. Please support Gary Ricketts in the November general elections.

Leaving the actual merits of the supporters' and detractors' arguments out of the question, look at the cumulative effects of the words used in these accounts: *important* versus *unnecessary* and *dangerous*; *much-needed* versus *another*; *best, American,* and *patriotism* versus *hawkishness, paranoia,* and *trigger-happy.* Neither account, strictly speaking, is fair, but both are certainly effective for their different purposes.

METAPHORS, MIXED METAPHORS, AND CLICHÉS

When used properly, metaphors can give language a heightened precision and intensity. By definition, a metaphor is a figure of speech containing an implied comparison, in which a word or phrase ordinarily used to mean one thing is applied to another. In other words, a comparison is drawn in the words used. The phrase "the white-winged ship," for example, is not meant to suggest that a ship has white wings, but to make a comparison between the sails of a ship and the wings of a bird. Writers use metaphors to make an image, feeling, or idea more concrete or easier for the reader to grasp.

Problems arise, however, when metaphors are mixed or begin to run amok. In the following paragraph, a whole group of conflicting metaphors compete for the reader's attention:

> Everything was coming up roses for a young west suburban married couple as long as two paychecks, his and hers, were rolling in. Then came the first of five children and the cozy little two-paycheck dream world of Donald B. and his wife Phyllis collapsed into a rat race, slowly at first, then the vicious circle of debt accumulation began to close in. When its grip was total, it embraced the young couple in $5,000 worth of debt.
> —Arn and Charlene Tibbets, *What's Happening to American English?*

Roses come up, paychecks roll in, a dream world collapses into a rat race, and a vicious circle of debt closes in, gripping and embracing; small wonder Donald and Phyllis are in trouble. Not content to sustain any one of these metaphors through the paragraph, the writer grabs at one after another, and the result is chaos.

Another problem with the use of metaphors is the temptation to lapse into clichés—tired or hackneyed figures of speech that were once fresh images but have become stale through overuse. The writer of the paragraph just examined uses a few clichés—"coming up roses" and "vicious circle". You will find it easy to think of more: "clean as a whistle," "bored to tears," "white as snow," "between the devil and the deep blue sea." Defenders of clichés like to argue, "A cliché is a cliché because it is true!" True clichés may well be, but it is also true that your readers will wonder just how fresh your ideas are if you require stale figures of speech to express them. You can sometimes get a little more mileage out of a cliché by altering it slightly for humorous effect, as Dorothy Parker did in writing of Katharine Hepburn that Miss Hepburn "ran the gamut of emotions from A to B." Clichés almost never contribute to effective writing in any other circumstances. You should strive for fresh expressions of your own instead of using worn-out ones.

Bearing these warnings in mind, you should nevertheless remember that an original metaphor, effectively sustained as long as it proves useful, can do more than the windiest definition to define an idea for a reader. Consider this paragraph:

> Some characters appear to triumph with history; others to be overwhelmed by it. The boiling torrent of events throws up one foam-capped wave which seems to sweep everything before it, and the spectators cry "A genius!" and name a whole stretch of the river "the age of so and so." Here and there, for a moment, a rock resists; then the flood sweeps over it, and the spectators note only an individual tragedy, unconscious of the solid base cleaving the current below. But the integrity of granite, not less than the theory of rushing water, shapes the final course of the stream. This is the story of a life which shaped history by not moving with its flow.
>
> —Garrett Mattingly, *Catherine of Aragon*

This paragraph sustains the image of the river as a metaphor for human events, and the image of the rock for those persons (in this case, Catherine of Aragon) who attempt to resist that flow. The language and style of the paragraph make it effective as well. Notice that the rhythm of the paragraph changes from smooth and flowing, when the flood is being described, to hesitant, when the rock is resisting: the paragraph sounds like what it is describing.

If you find the whole idea of using metaphors intimidating, remember that they can serve a very useful function, helping us to perceive objects and communicate our feelings about them in concrete, human terms.

The creation of metaphors is not simply for poets. It is going on every day. With due imagination and due restraint, you can contribute as effectively as anyone.

EXERCISES

1. Dictionary Definitions

a). Identify five words with more than one definition. List the possible informal and formal meanings.

b). Choose two of the words that have more than one definition. Write sentences for each of those definitions.

c). Choose one of the following words and copy the entry for it from a good dictionary. Explain how the definition is limited. How would you build upon the dictionary definition in order to use the word effectively in your writing?

Revision: Reseeing and Rewriting

Distancing Yourself
Time as Distancer
Outside Commentary as Distancer
Role-playing as Distancer
Anything Can Be Changed

Revision Strategies
Use the Probes
Examine the Title and Lead-ins
Examine the Thesis
Examine Opening Paragraphs
Examine the Body Paragraphs Closely
Examine Your Strategy
Examine the Closing Paragraphs
Examine the Sentences
Examine the Words
Check the Mechanics and Proofread

Writing and Rewriting an Essay: A Walk-through

Revising Under Pressure

Exercises

anything—that would be cheating. The individual should simply offer advice as to where you have gone wrong and what you can do about it. After your teacher returns the paper to you, either for revision or "for keeps," do not hesitate to ask for further help and advice. Even if this paper has already received a final grade, it is never too late to improve on the next one—or on your writing for another course, for that matter.

You have been up late finishing the first draft of an assigned paper. The next day you glance over it yourself, feel vaguely dissatisfied but cannot say why, and hand it to a senior on your floor who is an English major. She reads it and announces that your essay jumps from one topic to another, that your time frames are mixed up, that your references are unclear, that the main point is obscure, that your examples digress, and

Role-playing as Distancer

When it is not possible to use time *or* another person as a distancing agent, you can use other devices to force yourself to look at what you have written with a fresh and objective eye. Pretend, for example, that you are a member of that audience for which the piece of writing is intended. Imagine some of the attitudes and biases of such a person, and then read your work as that person might. Is it still persuasive, interesting, coherent? Better still, pretend you are someone quite different from the audience you have in mind—someone who comes on the piece by accident. Does the writing make sense to that kind of person? Is it informative, complete? Would such a person be able to follow the train of your thought?

Take still another role—that of the most skeptical critic of what you are trying to say. Question every statement you make, or as you read, turn every thesis of an essay or topic sentence of a paragraph into a question. Thus,

> The free-market system in this instance proved most efficient in allocating scarce resources.

becomes

> Why in this instance did the free-market system prove most efficient in allocating scarce resources?

Then read the paragraph or paragraphs in question to see if you have supplied a clear and unequivocal answer. Are the searching questions that a critical reader might ask answered in your writing or are the questions left hanging, evaded, begged?

Still another way to "become another person" is to use a tape recorder. Read the first paragraph of your essay into the recorder. After a short interval, play back the tape. Can you identify the paragraph's topic sentence? Does the paragraph hang together well? Do the ideas flow smoothly? Which sentences sound strained and awkward and should be revised? Jot down your findings in the margins next to the appropriate sections, and repeat this process with each paragraph of the essay. Hearing someone's voice—even your own—reading your work can be an excellent means of pinpointing trouble spots.

Finally, one almost foolproof method of forcing yourself to take a cold, hard look at your work is to fill out a "checklist" on it. Your teacher may make it up for you to use or you may use the one on page 133. Having not only to hunt for but to write down your thesis state-

CHECKLIST FOR REVISION

General Structure/Organization

Thesis: _____
_____

Topic Sentences:

1. _____
_____

2. _____
_____

3. _____
_____

4. _____
_____

5. _____
_____

Can I see a logical connection between the thesis and each topic sentence? Can I see a pattern that flows from the thesis through each of the topic sentences? If not, why not? Am I going off on a tangent? Is the thesis and/or are any of the topic sentences improperly worded?

Paragraphs:
Introduction—Does my introduction introduce the subject? Limit the topic? Announce the thesis? Does it interest the reader?
   Conclusion—Does the conclusion give the reader a sense of ending, of coming to rest? Do I introduce any material that rightly belongs in the body? Do I introduce another topic?
   Are all my paragraphs unified, developed, coherent?

Content:
Is my thesis supported by proofs that form the topic sentences of the body paragraphs?
   Are the topic sentences supported by a sufficient number and variety of examples, facts, details, evidence? Do I make too many generalizations in a paragraph? Do I make generalizations that remain unsupported?
   Is the material I use as proof, given the subject and the audience, appropriate? Can I find other material in my notes that might be stronger evidence or be more persuasive?

Grammatical Problems:
Did I note any and all places in my draft that may be grammatically incorrect? Did I classify them and check the Handbook?

Common Problems:
sentence structure
sentence punctuation
proper verb tense
proper agreement
proper modification—words, phrases, clauses

word usage—wrong word, imprecise word, inappropriate word
wordiness
repetition and/or redundancy
spelling

ment and topic sentences is an almost surefire guarantee that you will have adequate ones when you finish, even if you did not have them when you started. Finding yourself faced with a list of specific questions to answer about the paper certainly lessens your chances of deceiving yourself about your work. The checklist may seem a bother at first, but the difference that it can make to your writing may be worth it.

Anything Can Be Changed

The fact that you may alter what you have originally written does not necessarily mean that you made mistakes in your first draft. Anything can be changed. A change does *not* mean a "mistake." Some changes are corrections (a misspelled word is caught, a plural verb is provided for a plural subject, etc.), but making corrections is not the essence of rewriting; it is merely proofreading. Revision means rereading what you have written, rethinking what you have written, and then rewriting anything and everything that can be improved, clarified, strengthened. Nothing is sacred; everything must measure up or be recast. Revision is more than a matter of changing a word here or inserting a comma there. The placement of punctuation or subject–verb agreement are important considerations, but undue emphasis on them, especially in the early stages of rewriting, obscures the more serious work of revision: making your written work fit what you want to say and what you want others to understand.

REVISION STRATEGIES

You should plan to read through every draft several times, concentrating on a different aspect or quality each time.

During the first reading of the draft examine the flow of the whole piece. Does your writing move logically from one step to the next? Is there a pattern to the piece? Is the pattern appropriate? On the second reading concentrate on the paragraphs and make sure that each one does what it is supposed to do—that together they make a unified whole. On your third reading, go through the draft sentence by sentence. Finally, just before you are ready to make the final copy, read the draft through again, paragraph by paragraph or sentence by sentence, but this time in reverse order. This can make clear lapses in logic or in supporting materials. You will see the need for these various readings by studying the following revision strategies, which you should use as a guide when revising your work.

Use the Probes

The inventive technique of probing that was discussed in Chapter 1 as a device for getting started on your writing assignment is equally useful as a refining and sharpening device.

1. Probe the author. Ask questions about yourself in relation to your first draft.

    Why did I write this? What is the most important thing I want to say? Am I the logical one to say this? Is this really my thought or is it something I heard from someone else? Does what I want to say sound like me? Does the work really reflect the purpose I have in writing it?
2. Probe the subject. Now that you have down on paper what you want to say, question yourself: how well does it cover the subject I'm writing on?

    Have I covered all the important aspects of the subject? Is there something in the subject matter that contradicts what I want to say? Is there other information about the subject that would make the piece stronger or clearer? Is my information (dates, names, figures) accurate and up to date?
3. Probe the audience. Recall the questions you asked yourself when you defined the nature of the audience for whom the piece was intended. Read your work as if you were a member of that audience.

    Does the piece appeal to the intended reader? Does it take into account his experience (or lack of it)? Does the piece follow through on the assumptions I make about the audience? Do I need to rethink who my audience is? Does this paragraph or that point come across clearly to the audience I'm writing for? Have I anticipated objections and questions that such an audience might raise and answered them?

Examine the Title and Lead-in

Does the title you have chosen for the piece give a real lead-in to what you are going to say? Is it catchy? If it is, good. But do not ruin the chances of your piece by striving for a clever title that ends up being strained and unconvincing. Better to use a simple straightforward title than one that is supposed to be witty but is not.

Below are three possible titles for a review of a recent Metropolitan Opera production of Wagner's *Flying Dutchman*. This production had as its major innovation the idea that the whole story of the opera takes place as the dream of the sleeping Steersman. It was a very controversial production.

The Met's New *Flying Dutchman*

This title is straightforward and serviceable, but, as it gives no hint of the author's feelings, it is not especially attention grabbing.

The Met's New *Dutchman:* Who Needs It?

This title also tells what the piece is going to be about, and it gives an idea of the writer's reaction to the subject. It has, however, an aggressive—almost surly—tone, which could alienate potential readers before they even get to read the review.

Met's *Dutchman:* Asleep at the Wheel

This title also conveys the subject of the piece, and, at the same time, makes both a statement of fact and an indirect comment on it. The Steersman *is* asleep at the wheel (fact), but the statement "Asleep at the Wheel" can also be read as an unfavorable comment on the whole production. The title is catchy, but without the harsh edge of the second example.

Examine the Thesis

Do you state the thesis or main idea of the piece in one or possibly two sentences? Put your finger on it. Is the thesis statement clear? Does the sentence before it or after it lead into it or away from it effectively?
    Let's take a look at several thesis statements taken from student papers.

The glass menagerie proves to be an escape from reality for Laura and an escape from her insecurities and feelings of shyness.

The writer here sets up the framework for his analysis of the meaning or symbolism of the actual glass menagerie in Tennessee Williams' play. The statement is clear and direct.

"The Dick Van Dyke Show" is a better program than "I Love Lucy" because "The Dick Van Dyke Show" deals with a wider range of topics, it makes a lesser use of slapstick comedy, and it more often deals with familiar day-to-day experience.

The writer here quite clearly and explicitly sets forth his reasons for preferring one show to the other. Because the criteria are clearly laid out, the reader can anticipate the writer's approach and can therefore expect to see examples of the wider range, greater emphasis on familiar experience, and lesser use of slapstick of "The Dick Van Dyke Show."

> In Browning's "Soliloquy of the Spanish Cloister," the speaker's thoughts and emotions are totally uncharacteristic of a religious person. The speaker is deceived by believing he is a good Christian when in fact he is not.

The writer's thesis statement here is weak because it is *much* too general. *What* "thoughts and emotions"? What is so un-Christian about him? Also, the structure of the last sentence is awkward. "By believing . . ." should be something like: "in that he believes that he is . . ." The writer needs specific details, quotes from the poem, to support his position.

> Allan Tate is involved in death and people's reactions to death.

The wording here is misleading. The writer, we assume, will be discussing death as a subject of Allan Tate's *poetry*, but the thesis makes it sound as if death is a central concern for Allan Tate *personally*—and we cannot automatically assume that this is true. A better thesis might be this: "In his poetry, Allan Tate writes about death and the reactions of different people to it." Ideally, the writer would then go on to name the Tate poems he will be discussing and to indicate the "reactions of different people" contained in these poems.

> I feel one of the major trends in 20th century literature was that there were few if any restrictions on what to write about, for it was more important to express what you felt.

This thesis is wordy. "I feel" is unnecesary (the whole paper should express what you feel!); "one of the major trends . . . was" is an airy phrase that tells the reader little; "there were . . ." and "it was . . ." are constructions that can be cut down with little loss of blood. The thesis can be shortened to this: "American writers in the twentieth century had more freedom than earlier ones to explore controversial subjects and to express their feelings."

Examine Opening Paragraphs

Look at the opening paragraph or paragraphs and at the thesis in particular. Do they give the reader a clear idea of the direction that you are going in? Remember, road signs can be provided by the structure of the material itself (movement from the general to the specific or from the specific to the general; cause and effect; etc.) as well as by "signaling" words. But be sure that whatever road signs you are using are clear and unequivocal to the reader.

A good introductory paragraph from a student theme is shown below:

> In *The Wild Duck,* Dr. Relling claims that the only way to make certain people happy with themselves is to create a false impression of them. Relling does this to several of the characters in the play and they all seem to enjoy this new way of seeing themselves. This life-lie theory is in striking contrast to Gregers Werle's theory that all false images must be destroyed. Relling is right, though. For some people need the motivation that this life-lie will create.

The first three sentences of the paragraph announce and limit the subject of the essay that follows. They set up the conflict between Dr. Relling's approach to life and Greger Werle's approach; this conflict is the substance of the play and the main subject of the essay. The last two sentences of the paragraph, "Relling . . . create," state the writer's attitude toward this conflict and, consequently, reveal the position the essay will take.

The pitfalls of a common device for opening paragraphs—use of a dictionary definition—are clearly shown in the following example:

> According to Webster's Dictionary, the definition of fashion is a prevailing style or mode, as in clothes. The styles are constantly changing. For one to be fashionable, he must keep up with these changing styles. From business world to the college campus, people are wearing fashionable clothes for a number of reasons. I see more people today dressing nicely than in the past. This is because the message has gotten through: dressing well is very important.

This opening paragraph begins with a dictionary definition that has no relevance to anything that follows, and, after searching for its theme, ends with a cliché. It has no particular point to make and gives the reader no idea of what the remainder of the essay will be about. The awkwardness of the paragraph probably owes much to the lack of direction of the writing.

To revise this paragraph, the writer must turn to the author and subject probes we have discussed to clarify his ideas about himself and about the subject. Opening paragraphs that are as vague and diffuse as this one often occur when the preliminary techniques of defining self, subject, and audience have been neglected. To replace the probes with a dictionary definition and to expect to write from that is a mistake frequently made by inexperienced writers. The results are generally unsatisfactory.

Another problem inexperienced writers have with opening paragraphs is the tendency to put too much into them.

> There have been many comments made about upstate university standards for admission. Many people feel that the requirements for admission are just because they have been admitted. The admission standards are in fact just, except that too much emphasis is put on the Standard Achievement Tests. For one reason these tests only measure one type of aptitude which doesn't necessarily mean you will do well in college. The classification that the scores give someone doesn't necessarily put them in the right category. Lets say a student taking one of those tests has a bad day and is then required to take the test. If the student does poorly it is pretty much a one shot deal and the one test would weigh very heavily against them.

Aside from the errors in punctuation and grammar in this paragraph, its real problem is that as an opening statement it limits the topic so narrowly that the writer will end up doing little more than repeating this paragraph for the remainder of her essay.

The use of subject probes here would give the writer a better chance to open up her theme and develop the sequence in which it should be treated. With subject probes, she could think about the whole concept of what is "just" in college admission standards and how such standards can be fairly measured. There is no lack of material in the subject matter itself, only in this writer's consideration of the subject.

Finally, some student writers, in an attempt to make their opening paragraphs sound as impressive as possible, make them far wordier and harder to understand than they need be. Consider this example:

> In the second part of this semester, most of our literature for this course surrounded writers from the South. They were twentieth-century authors, and although their styles were different, one theme was expressed in most of their writing: they were realistic about the world they were living in, but they were optimistic about the future.

The expression "most of our literature ... surrounded. ..." is not merely wordy but unidiomatic; literature *is written by* authors, it does not "surround" them. "They were twentieth-century authors" can be incorporated into the previous sentence. It is not clear, in the last part of the paragraph, why being "realistic" about their world should necessarily make their "optimism" surprising; a one- or two-word description of that world might help. The paragraph might be rewritten as follows:

> During the last half of this semester, we studied twentieth-century American writers from the South. Although their styles were different, one theme was expressed in most of the work. While they were realistic

about the imperfect world in which they lived, they were optimistic about the future.

Examine the Body Paragraphs Closely

One of the most crucial aspects of revision is the careful reading and analyzing of each of the body paragraphs in the piece.

1. Does each paragraph have one major point? You might try to outline the longest and most complex paragraph in the work just to assure yourself that it is, in fact, a single paragraph and not several thrown together.
2. Does each paragraph have a topic sentence? Locate it; put your finger on it or underline it. If you cannot find a topic sentence in a paragraph, supply one. What are you trying to say? Say it. If you cannot develop a clear topic sentence, consider eliminating the paragraph altogether. It may not belong in the piece at all. If the topic sentence is in the middle of the paragraph, make sure you feel that is the proper place for it. If it is placed at the end of the paragraph, satisfy yourself that the paragraph does logically lead up to its topic sentence. Do not just tag an awkward, out-of-place topic sentence onto the end of a paragraph that lacks one.
3. Does every sentence in the paragraph add support, clarification, expansion, or description to the topic sentences? Be careful to avoid interesting digressions that tend to make paragraphs too long and to weaken their impact by taking the reader's mind away from the main point.
4. Are the sentences in each paragraph all linked to each other? Is the paragraph coherent, or does each sentence present a new idea unrelated to the sentence before it and the one after it?
5. Does each paragraph contain adequate supporting details for the point you want it to make?
6. Is the sequence of paragraphs logical? Is it the most effective sequence in the light of what you are trying to do, your topic, and the method of organization you've chosen?
7. Do the paragraphs flow smoothly from one to the other? Are there links between paragraphs as well as within paragraphs?
8. Are the body paragraphs persuasive? Pretend to be a suspicious, hostile audience, and ask yourself whether the topic sentences of the paragraphs are proved, explained, or merely asserted. Ask yourself if the paragraphs are arranged in the most persuasive possible order.

Following are two body paragraphs from a student theme that work especially well. Note that each paragraph has it own development and, where necessary, a link with the preceding paragraph. The topic sentence of each paragraph is clearly stated. The paragraphs are taken from a student theme that discusses Catherine's education in Jane Austen's *Northanger Abbey.*

> Catherine doesn't yet know whom to trust, but she's capable of learning through her experiences, and this is basic to her maturing. After the second trip Catherine decides that she doesn't like John, even though he is her beloved brother's friend and Isabella's brother. Then, when Catherine finds out what she's missed and that she's displayed bad manners, this information reinforces the lesson she's learning. That lesson is that she must trust her own judgments when she believes she is right.
>
> *Catherine has indeed learned her lesson* by the time Isabella, James and John propose a third trip. Catherine has just made a commitment to go for a walk with the Tilneys while the three young people have decided to go on a day trip. When they inform Catherine of their plans, she refuses to go. They try every argument possible to dissuade her from taking her walk with the Tilneys, but she is adamant and won't break her engagement a second time. This is a sign of Catherine's maturity. Her lack of firmness has changed. She now sticks to what she thinks she should do, and she has an independence of mind.

In the first sentence of the first paragraph, the writer introduces a generalization that the rest of the paragraph supports with examples. The beginning sentence of the second paragraph (italicized here) provides a transition from the preceding paragraph and acts as the topic sentence of the paragraph. The rest of the paragraph is an analysis of the episode in the novel that the author uses to show how Catherine has indeed learned her lesson and matured through her experiences.

Examine Your Strategy

Look again at your opening paragraph and ask yourself if it sets up the best possible strategy you can use. Refer again to the section on ways to begin opening paragraphs (see Chapter 4). Remember, you can make a provocative or shocking statement; offer an arresting statistic; ask a question; open with a quotation or make a literary allusion; tell a joke, relevant story, or anecdote; present a description; provide a factual statement or a summary; offer an analogy or contrast; restate a personal experience; catalog relevant examples; or state a problem or popular misconception. What strategy did you use? Is it the best one for this subject? for this audience? for this occasion? What other strategies may be better?

Following are two paragraphs from student themes; each in its own way fails to develop its thesis and a strategy for dealing with it.

> The use of symbolism is very prevalent throughout Tennessee Williams' *The Glass Menagerie*. The glass menagerie is, in itself, the most evident symbol in the play. It is also the most effective.

Here the writer is so vague in his references to "symbol" and "symbolism" that the paragraph in fact does not say *anything*. What is the "glass menagerie"? In what way does Williams use it—as a symbol of what? In what way is it "most effective"? The paragraph does not begin to answer these questions. It has no strategy because it has no topic.

> There are many poems in which the speaker chooses one particular subject to talk about. But the speaker in T.S. Eliot's poem, "The Love Song of J. Alfred Prufrock," refers to people in general, as well as himself. Yes, he speaks to himself about himself. And the words that he symbolically expresses can pertain also to society. "The Love Song of J. Alfred Prufrock" reveals the weak characteristics found in an individual who has been given a chance to speak out, but he fails to do so. Such traits are in many ways typical of modern society. But in T. S. Eliot's poem one especially looks at the flaws in a specific character.

Here is a classic case of the writer's "waffling" in his search for a thesis statement. The writer here goes back and forth between saying that Eliot's poem is about the flaws of a specific character and those of modern society. It takes the writer here seven sentences to arrive at a thesis that should have been the subject of the whole paragraph. Such descriptions as "weak characteristics," "such traits," and "in many ways typical" are so vague and general that they have no real meaning.

In contrast to the two examples above, the following opening paragraph, also from a student theme, provides a strong opening presentation of the thesis. The essay addresses the question of whether Gulliver's wholly negative assessment of mankind at the end of Swift's *Gulliver's Travels* is an accurate reflection of Swift's own opinions. Note how the paragraph begins with an analysis of the process whereby Gulliver's mind is changed in the course of the book and then moves through a transition to the clear statement of the thesis or point of the essay.

> Lemuel Gulliver, the main character in Jonathan Swift's satire, *Gulliver's Travels,* is a reasonably well-educated, curious, patriotic, and truthful man who starts out innocent and as a lover of mankind. His attitude, however, changes through his experiences. After making four voyages "into several remote nations of the world," and encountering people of all shapes and sizes, physically and mentally, Gulliver comes to the conclusion that all human beings are like the vice-filled, repugnant Yahoos. The book as a whole though, does not completely uphold Gulliver's verdict. Although Swift partially agrees with Gulliver, as shown by the Lilli-

putians, pirates, Gulliver himself, and many other figures, Swift does believe that there are some truly good men, such as the Brobdingnagian king, whose example people can, and should, follow.

Clearly, the writer of this paragraph did use author and subject probes to come up with this complex but quite understandable statement. And just as clearly, the writer of the paragraph on "Prufrock" did not.

Examine the Closing Paragraphs

Do not look on the concluding paragraph as a throw-away paragraph. Your conclusion should count. It is your last chance of convincing the reader of the point of your writing. First, make sure that the reader is given enough clues to sense that the end is near. Then make use of several devices that can help you get out of the essay.

You may want to restate the thesis. You may want to evaluate the importance of the ideas that you have conveyed. Discuss some of the broader implications of your essay, or conclude with a "call to action." You may want to offer a prophesy based on your argument, but be careful of this. Some people have long memories.

You may conclude with an anecdote, quotation, or the like that effectively sums up the point of the piece. You may conclude by coming back to a figure of speech (metaphor or simile) that you introduced in the opening paragraphs. You may restate a key point you made in the opening paragraphs, or you may conclude by just using language in your last point that makes it clear that this is your *last* point ("In conclusion . . ."; "Finally . . ."; "To sum up then . . .").

Examine the Sentences

Because it may become difficult for you to avoid becoming involved again in the content of what you are saying, try here and in the two steps following to work from the end of your essay to the beginning. First read each sentence, checking to make sure that it is clear and emphatic. Then look at the sentences before and after it to make sure that the sentence is clear in its context and that it is effective in its particular place in the paragraph.

Here are some sentences that can be revised for clarity, order, grammar, logic, or wordiness:

This demonstrates the idea of the tough guy putting everything right by socking everyone else.

Clarity is a problem here: what exactly does the writer mean by "this"? Awkwardness is another; the phrase "the idea of the tough guy putting everything right" is rather jammed and strained. The sentence might be rewritten in one or two ways: "This example demonstrates the idea that the tough guy puts a situation right by socking everyone else"; "This incident demonstrates the idea that the tough guy can settle any problem by using violence."

> After the Civil War, her husband died from his wounds and Sophia Jane was left to provide for the children. This is the point when her hope for a perfect life began to crumble.

There are several problems here. It is rather awkward to have "her" coming *before* "Sophia Jane," the noun it refers to. "This is the point . . ." is not only a wordy construction but a grammatically improper one; the verb "is" is in the present tense, while the verbs in the rest of the passage are in the past tense. The passage could be rephrased as follows: "Sophia Jane's husband died after the Civil War ended, and she was left to provide for the children. At this point, her hopes for a perfect life began to crumble."

> These most popular characters, by being on the most highly rated shows, are most often tough guys: people who are strong and rugged and always the dominating personality on the show. The tough guy is a fighting leader, who always pits himself against crime.

The first part of the first sentence makes an illogical assertion: the writer suggests that popular TV characters get to be tough guys by being on the most popular shows. (If this is true, where does that leave *Charlie's Angels*?) In the second part of this sentence, the writer goes from using plural nouns to using singular ones—from "characters" and "people" to "personality." In addition, the passage is generally wordy. It might be rewritten as follows: "The most popular TV heroes on the most highly-rated shows are tough guys: men who are strong and rugged, men who have dominating personalities. The tough guys are fighting leaders; they always pit themselves against crime."

Examine the Words

Pretend that you are a camera and that you focus in on each word or expression of the draft. You have seen how expressions like "weak characteristics" give no information to the reader. Be especially hard on generalized statements or phrases. Wherever possible, replace them with specific or concrete examples. Ask yourself if any word you have used gives a false impression; that is, if the word has connotations that mean more than or the opposite of what you want it to mean.

Here are a couple of examples of sheer "deadwood"—words that can be trimmed from a sentence with no loss whatsoever:

> Married life, however, did not prove to be very fulfilling.

"Did not prove to be" here is simply a long-winded way of saying "was not." You can take four words out of this sentence with no trouble at all: "Married life, however, was not very fulfilling."

> There has been a recent trend in America towards the popularity of individual sports.

"There has been a recent trend . . ." is not only longwinded but self-important: who doesn't like to pinpoint a trend? The sentence could simply be rephrased as follows: "Individual sports have become very popular in America recently."

Check the Mechanics and Proofread

Just before you are ready to prepare the final draft, check your work for the basic mechanics of writing: grammar, punctuation, and spelling. Do not guess at the spelling of a word. If you are not absolutely sure, use the dictionary. Check the punctuation: is it clear? is it helpful? Imagine that you are the strictest English teacher you know. Question every comma. Is it the correct form of punctuation needed here, or is a colon or period needed instead? Make sure you know when you are talking about a specific person or thing (using the singular) and when you are talking about persons or things (using the plural). Identify the subject of every verb and the antecedent of every pronoun. Be sure that every sentence *is* a sentence—one that expresses a complete thought and can stand alone. Remember, at this stage it is still possible to change anything at all.

Now, proofread your final draft very carefully. Look especially for typographical errors: letters transposed, one letter substituted for another, words or even whole sentences left out, and the like. The omission of *not* in a sentence can turn your whole thesis around and leave the reader helplessly confused. (One early edition of the Bible, known as the "Wicked Bible," left out the *not* in the Seventh Commandment, printing it as: "Thou shalt commit adultery." Many eyebrows were raised on that one.) In proofreading, carelessness is your mortal enemy.

WRITING AND REWRITING AN ESSAY: A WALK-THROUGH

Imagine that your teacher assigns an essay on the possible advantages of some exotic and unlikely animal as a house pet. To get you thinking about the subject, she plays a tape of a Bill Cosby comedy routine about a rhinoceros and invites discussion. When you begin working on the assignment, you decide that you would like to present a case for the Indian cobra being a better house pet than the rhinoceros. After much thought, you set down an outline that looks something like this:

COBRA

Description: Indian carnivorous snake, 8–10′ long, poisonous.

Keep: Can sleep in basket, needs small animals to eat.

Practical use: exterminator, "watch snake."

Other uses: (1) status symbol; (2) entertainment—dances to flute music; (3) intimidation of obnoxious visitors.

RHINO

Description: large African herbivore, 15–20′ long, 1000 lbs. weight.

Keep: Needs shed to sleep in and 5–10 acres of land to support grazing (?)

Practical use: hatrack (Cosby), lawn mower.

Other uses: status symbol (Cosby).

There are some problems with the cobra, true, but on the whole the facts you have set down bear you out.

After more thought, you set to work and eventually produce the following essay:

WHY I LIKE THE COBRA

In one of his comedy routines, Bill Cosby tells about a kind of house pet that not many people would think of, the rhinoceros. The rhino, he says, can be used as a hatrack on account of its horn and you can also keep it as a status symbol because not many other people have one. I think that another animal, the cobra, makes an even better house pet than the rhino. Theres a few good things to be said for the rhino, but the advantages of the cobra outweigh these.

The rhinoceros is a large African herbivore about 15 or 20 feet long and weighing about 1000 pounds. The reason probably no one else has one is because nobody but farmers and zookeepers begin to have the room you need to keep one. Mr. Cosby is right that you can use it for a hatrack, it can also mow your lawn for you. But theres really not much you can do with it, and keeping it really is a problem for most people.

The cobra is a carnivorous snake from India, its about 8 to 10 feet long. Most Indian people who have one keep it in a big basket. It is poisonous and needs small animals to eat and a lot of people might see this as a problem. If you have a rat problem it can keep the amount of rats down, it can also scare off burglars. It can do a lot more things besides just sit there too. In India people play the flute to make the cobra come out of the basket and dance. It can also make obnoxious visiters very respectful of you for a change. All in all theres a lot to be said for the cobra.

In conclusion the cobra makes an even better house pet than the rhinoceros. People who don't like snakes or dont want a poisonous thing in the house might still like the rhinoceros, but most people will agree that the cobra for many reason is the thing to have.

You take the paper to your friend the senior English major. Her comments are these: "You can assume that your audience is prepared to go along with the idea of an odd animal as a house pet. That's implied in the assignment. But you've still got to guard against anybody saying, 'But why not just a dog?' You could do that better than you have done. What you don't do and what you have to do is convince the reader that the cobra is great and the rhino is lousy. You don't do that. You admit that the rhino has some advantages and don't say much to counter-balance that. And you admit that the cobra being poisonous and eating small animals is a problem. Nobody will want one if you don't make that look like an advantage.

"The thesis is pretty vague. What *are* the few good things you can say for the rhino? What *are* the advantages of the cobra that outweigh them? If you make all this clearer, it won't be so hard to follow what you say further on.

"Another reason the essay's so hard to follow is that you try to say everything about each animal in one paragraph. The way you had the outline organized was good because you can see there what points about the rhino you were comparing with the points about the cobra. But your paragraphs make it hard for the reader to see what you're comparing to what. In fact, after the introduction you skip over the status symbol idea altogether because you're trying so hard to get everything into two paragraphs. Make your paragraph topics the different points of comparison, not the animals themselves. And use more transitions in the paragraphs to let the reader know which way you're going. I can't always tell.

"And you need more details in the middle paragraphs to get the essay going, too. You just list the things the animals can do—such as how a cobra can frighten a burglar—and then you quit. Tell me *how* he frightens a burglar, and I might get interested.

"Another problem is that your introduction and conclusion are dull. This is not a serious topic, you know—if you make the introduction a little funnier you'll already have the reader on your side by the time you get to the evidence. And that conclusion! Not only is it dull, it's bad. The impression it leaves with the reader is that there are disadvantages to the cobra that you can't argue with. If you think you're convincing anybody that way, you'd better think again.

"Finally, the title's kind of flat. Obviously *you* like the cobra or you wouldn't be writing the essay. What the title—and the whole essay as well—has to do is give us an idea why *we* should like the cobra."

You grit your teeth, mumble, and go back to your draft. After some time and considerable struggle, you produce a second version of the essay:

EASY LIVING, SECURITY, ENTERTAINMENT, POWER, GET A COBRA TODAY

In one of his comedy routines, Bill Cosby makes an argument for a rather unlikely house pet, the rhinoceros. The lowly rhino Mr. Cosby claims is useful in several ways, its horn makes a handy hatrack and the would-be owner can be fairly sure that no one else on his block has one. As long as a person is considering getting an unusual animal though, I believe that another exotic beast, the Indian cobra makes an even better house pet than the rhino. This reptile is more practical to keep and more useful than the rhino, it also provides its owner with security, entertainment, and instant respect along with status.

One important thing for a pet owner to consider of course is the needs of the animal we wants. For most people this makes the cobra by far the best choice. The rhino is a large herbivore averaging 15 to 20 feet in length and a half ton in wieght while the cobra is a fairly small carnivore whos 8 to 10 feet long and fits easily into a basket. This means that its almost impossible for anyone except farmers and zookeepers to feed a rhino and give it a place to sleep, while even people in apartments can keep a cobra. As long as they have rats in the basement or pigeons on the roof.

The practical uses to which the rhino and the cobra can be put is another advantage for the cobra. About all the rhino can do is keep the lawn mowed and support hats, not a lot of people these days have either big lawns or a lot of hats. Almost everyone, knows at least one disgusting small animal they'd like to get rid of though and the cobra will take care of that yappy poodle next door or that squirrel who's chewing up your telephone wires in no time at all. It is also very useful as a "watch snake." The average crook is likely to mistake the dull, stupid rhino for a piece of sculpture and ignore it or try to take it away, but no theif can ignore a cobra who is spreading it's hood, swaying from side to side, and hissing furiously. Your whole neighborhood will be trouble-free before you know it.

Moving on to less practical advantages, the cobra has talents which a rhino can never develop. Both the rhino and the cobra are good status symbols because of their scarceness in this country of course but a cobra can do much more than just sit there like a rhino. For one thing it can dance in a way. Everyone knows how the Indian snake-charmers lure their cobras out of their basket with flute music, if you can play the flute even a little the cobra can be as much fun as a wide screen TV or a home computer. For another thing, the cobra can be tremendously helpful to the owner whos like Rodney Dangerfeild and "don't get no respect."

Obnoxous visitors or party guests who might just laugh at a rhino get instantly humble and respectful when they see a cobra—especially one that hasn't eaten in a few hours and wants some hors-durves!

Therefore in spite of Mr. Cosby's argument for the rhinoceros, the cobra is a much better choice than the rhino for a house pet. There is still one problem for the new cobra owner, a few cowardly people might say, "But that thing's *poisonous*. You can't keep it in the city!" Don't let a thing like that bother you. A cobra can eat a dogcatcher just as fast as it can eat a dog.

You go back to the English major with the new draft. She reads it and says: "This is a big improvement. Your case for the cobra is a lot stronger. You've turned the factor of its poisonousness and its appetite for small animals into real advantages. And you've downplayed the advantages of the rhino pretty well—calling it 'dull' and 'stupid' and so on. The organization, now, makes the argument much easier to follow. Adding some transitions also helped. And you've got some really good, snappy details helping you out there—I like the part about the yappy poodle and the one about the snake wanting the hors d'oeuvres.

"Okay, that was the good news. Now the bad news. You've got to go back through the paper again and work on all the little problems—grammar, punctuation, and spelling. You hook a lot of clauses together with commas—a mistake. Get a semicolon in there or start a new sentence. Another problem you've got, especially in the last half, is pronoun agreement. You start out in third person—'he' and 'they' and so on—and then go sliding into 'you.' Pick one or the other, but get it straight. There are a couple of subject–verb agreement problems there, too, and a dangler in the fourth paragraph. And watch out for the little things, too—spelling, and writing out numbers and putting commas around things like 'of course' and apostrophes in things like 'there's' and 'who's,' and so on. It's the little stuff that can kill you."

Before getting back to the struggle, you take a few hours off and come back a little more relaxed for a rereading. You go through the paper sentence by sentence. When you again sit down to rewrite the essay, you produce this version:

EASY LIVING, SECURITY, ENTERTAINMENT, POWER:
GET A COBRA TODAY

In one of his comedy routines, Bill Cosby makes an argument for a rather unlikely house pet: the rhinoceros. The lowly rhino, Mr. Cosby claims, is useful in several ways—its horn makes a handy hatrack, and the would-be owner can be fairly sure that no one else on his block has one. As long as a person is thinking about getting an unusual animal, though, he should consider acquiring an Indian cobra. This reptile is more practical to keep and more useful than the rhino; it also provides its owner with security, entertainment, and instant respect, as well as status.

The potential pet owner, of course, must consider the needs of the animal he wants. For most people, the cobra is much easier to maintain than the rhinoceros. The rhino is a large herbivore averaging fifteen to twenty feet in length and a half ton in weight, while the cobra is a fairly small carnivore whose eight to ten feet of length can fit easily into a basket. This means that it is almost impossible for anyone except a farmer or a zookeeper to feed and house a rhino, while even a person in an apartment can keep a cobra—as long as there is a steady supply of rats in the basement or pigeons on the roof.

The practical uses to which the cobra and the rhino can be put make up another advantage for the cobra. About all the rhino can do is keep the lawn mowed and support hats, and not that many people nowadays have either big lawns or a lot of hats. Almost everyone knows at least one disgusting small animal he would like to get rid of, though, and the cobra will take care of that squirrel who's chewing up the telephone wires or that yappy poodle next door in no time at all. The cobra is also very useful as a "watch snake." The average crook is likely to mistake the dull, stupid rhino for a piece of sculpture and ignore it or try to take it away, but no thief can ignore a cobra who is spreading its hood, swaying from side to side, and hissing furiously. The whole neighborhood will be trouble-free in a week or so.

The cobra also offers its owner some less practical benefits that a rhino can never match. Both the rhino and the cobra are good status symbols because of their scarcity in this country, of course, but a cobra can do much more than a rhino. For one thing, it can "dance," in a manner of speaking. Everyone is familiar with the Indian snake-charmers who lure their cobras out of their baskets with flute music; if the owner can play the flute even a little, the cobra can be as much fun as a wide-screen TV or a home computer, and certainly more fun than a rhino. (Has anyone ever seen a dancing rhino?) For another thing, the cobra can be tremendously helpful to the owner who, like Rodney Dangerfield, "don't get no respect." Obnoxious visitors or party guests who might just laugh at a rhino become instantly humble and respectful when they see a cobra—especially one who hasn't eaten in a few hours and wants some hors d'oeuvres!

Therefore, in spite of Mr. Cosby's argument for the rhinoceros, the cobra is a much better choice than the rhino for a house pet. There is still one potential problem for the new cobra owner: a few mealymouthed people might say, "But that thing's poisonous. They'll never let you keep it in the city!" Suggestions like this should not worry anyone for a moment. A cobra can eat a dogcatcher just as fast as it can eat a dog.

You wearily retrace your steps to the English major's room and hand her this version. She reads it, smiles, and gives up a thumbs-up.

REVISING UNDER PRESSURE

In this chapter, several strategies have been presented for you to use in revising your work. There will, however, be situations in which you cannot apply some of them. During an in-class essay exam, for example, you cannot give yourself time off between drafts or ask a friendly senior for advice; you simply have to write it then and there. This does not mean, however, that you should not even try to revise your work under these conditions; in fact, revision can be just as important when you are likely to become harried or confused as it is when you have all the time you need. You can do several things to help yourself work toward successful revision under any circumstances. One is to get so thoroughly into the habit of revising your work that it becomes second nature to you. If you judge your work as strictly as possible under relatively relaxed conditions—approaching it as objectively as you can, sharpening it, clarifying it, correcting it—you will not find revision quite so difficult under pressure. Another thing to do is to seek help when you need it. All the practice in the world will not do you much good in a vacuum; at some point or other, every writer needs advice. Reliable friends can help, and your teacher, as we have suggested, can help still more—contrary to your possible suspicions, ninety-nine teachers out of a hundred would far rather spend some extra time working with you than give you that D.

EXERCISES

1. Read this essay and analyze it by using the "Revision Strategies" on pp. 134–145, as well as the checklist form supplied on p. 133 or any other checklist your teacher may provide. Rewrite the essay or use your analysis in a class discussion.

The land in upstate New York was cleared for farming in the late seventeen hundreds to early eighteen hundreds. These farms were an important food source for a young America. The Erie canal provided transportation from farming regions to cities, especially New York. The lifestyle of these regions is looked upon as classical american rural living. Soon after the Civil war, however, began the chronic abandonment of land by the farmers.

Land abandonment occured for a variety of reasons. The less than prime farmland been depleated to the point of diminished return. Thus, the first large scale abandonment occured in the Adarondaacks and the Catskills. Most abandonment occured with the simotaneous opening of the West. The Great Plains provided a better alternative for farming than the hailly rocky land, and harsh winters of the Northeast. This idea is emphasized by the new methods and machines that resulted from the Industrial Revolution, which better applied to vast flatlands. The Depression had a signigicant impact on the remaining farmers, since few were sufficiently affluent to withstand it for so many years. Thus we see that many factors, often synergistic, caused this long term migration.

Land abandonment was the most significant factor in creating the intricate landscapes we see in upstate New York. Although todays farms are larger and more mechanized, they seem to be distributed in a random, happazard wasy interspersed with old fields and woods. In the less productive areas, like Chenango county, once declared a disaster area due to poverty, by Pres. Johnson, viable farms are few and far between. Since farmland slowly reverts to forest, in steps called seres, one sees a myriad of weedfields, grasslands, and forests. This is indicative of the differences in duration of vacency of each piece of land. The lesson to be gained from this segment of history, is that many parts of America, like southern California for example, are potentially vulnerable to decline and even abandonment.

2. Revision Exercises

a). Analyze the following argumentative essay in class—again, use the "Revision Strategies" and a checklist. Revise the essay and, in class, gather into small groups to discuss the revisions. Which are most effective and why?

BELIEFS ON ABORTION

In general most people became shocked within the late sixty and early seventy when the subject of abortion was discussed. Some of them feared the subject and other showed very little interest when the question of whether a women should have the legal right to control her body function of reproduction. But what is better to bring a unwanted child into this world or to bring into relity the information and choice of having a abortion? Therefore a woman should be allowed the freedom of choice and decision of having a abortion ornot, in all fairness to herself but in all fairness to society.

At first the subject of abortion was met with all types of objections. The forming of Anti-Abortionist groups caused varies questions to arise and intenses debates were held to discuss different aspects of whether the fetus was a living child and had the right to life regardless of the mother personal feeling. Some of Anti-Abortionist groups demonstrated and felt that it was morally wrong in the eyes of the church and all religious beliefs. But other felt that it was wrong in all standard of morality. But waht is better to conform to the rules and rights of society or to look at morality in a individual matter? By guaranteeing the legal choice of abortion and leaving the moral rights or wrongs up to the women who are involved. Then if she feels that it is morally unacceptable to her. She will not choice that alternative and will look for another solution to her problem of pregnancy.

Although pregacy is a natural and wonderful experience for most women. The problem of unwanted pregnancy can be horrible nigtmare and painful experience, without the option of legalized abortion. Just think why this option is so important to the women of this society, not only for danger to their health but also to the danger and protection, in cases of incest, rapes, and teenage pregnancy.

Therefore, this may not be the perfect solution in all cases of unwanted pregnancy but it is one of the best one for this society at this time. Just think of the over population and unwanted children in this world if the personal right of abortion is denied to the women of this society. But the most damaging and harmful effect would be to the women of this society, by forcing them back into hidden abortions, under unsanitary conditions, and unwanted children.

b). The first paragraph below is taken from Lawrence Durrell's essay "How to Buy a House"; the second was written by a student as a class exercise in revision. The class was told to use the same material and to try to convey the same general effect in their paragraphs as in the Durrell passage; however, they had to change the tone, focus, and style, and had to shift the emphasis in the paragraph.

Analyze and discuss these two paragraphs. Then compare and contrast them. Finally, choose one of the paragraphs following these two and do the same kind of revision.

> The owner swung himself almost off the ground in an effort to turn the great key in the lock which was one of the old pistol-spring type such as one sees sometimes in medieval English houses. We hung on to his shoulders and added our strength to his until it turned screeching in the lock and the great door fell open. We entered, while the owner shot the great bolts which held the other half of the door in position and propped both open with a faggot. Here his interest died, for he stayed religiously by the door, still shrouded in his sack, showing no apparent interest in our reactions. The hall was gloomy and silent—but remarkably dry considering the day. I stood for a while listening to my own heart beating and gazing about me. The four tall double doors were splendid with their old-fashioned panels and the two windows which gave internally on to the hall were fretted with wooden slats of a faintly Turkish design. The whole proportion and disposition of things here was of a thrilling promise; even Sabri glowed at the woodwork which was indeed of splendid make and in good condition.
>
> —Lawrence Durrell, "How to Buy a House"

> There was a huge, ornamental key in the old lock which looked like it was right out of the medieval English period. It was very hard to turn, but we all were so eager to get in that we helped the owner in turning the key. When the key turned and the massive doors fell open, we all rushed in, even Sabri. The owner stayed at the door propping it open with a faggot. We were all astonished by the interior, but we were especially amazed at Sabri's enthusiasm. He gasped at the tall double doors with their beautifully fretted windows and at the splendid, intricate woodwork. After seeing Sabri like this the whole place took on a thrilling promise.

> When I was a small boy, I was taken by my father, a general practitioner in Troy, New York, to St. Mary's Hospital, to wait while he made his rounds. The solarium where I sat was all sunlight and large plants. It smelled of soap and starch and clean linen. In the spring, clouds of lilac billowed from the vases; and in the fall, chrysanthemums crowded the magazine tables. At one end of the great high-ceilinged, glass-walled room was a huge cage where colored finches streaked and sang. Even from the first, I sensed the nearness of that other place, the Operating Room, knew that somewhere on these premises was that secret dreadful enclosure where surgery was at that moment happening. I sat among the cut flowers, half drunk on the

scent, listening to the robes of the nuns brush the walls of the corridor, and felt the awful presence of surgery.
—Richard Selzer, *Mortal Lessons: Notes on the Art of Surgery*

In summer, I stalk. Summer leaves obscure, heat dazzles, and creatures hide from the red-eyed sun, and me. I have to seek things out. The creatures I seek have several senses and free will; it becomes apparent that they do not wish to be seen. I can stalk them in either of two ways. The first is not what you think of as true stalking, but it is the *Via negativa,* and as fruitful as actual pursuit. When I stalk this way, I take my stand on a bridge and wait, like spring Eskimos at a seal's breathing hole. Something might come; something might go. I am Newton under the apple tree; Buddha under the bo. Stalking the other way, I forge my own passage seeking the creature. I wander the banks; what I find, I follow, doggedly, like Eskimos haunting the caribou herds. I am Wilson squinting after the traces of electrons in a cloud chamber; I am Jacob at Peniel wrestling with the angel.
—Annie Dillard, *Pilgrim at Tinker Creek*

A tall, fairly heavyset man wearing khaki trousers and a faded plum-colored sports shirt got up and walked down to the front of the auditorium. [Dr. Louis G.] MacDowell is revered from Coral Gables to Pensacola Bay as the originator of [orange juice] concentrate. From his mind came the idea that produced a seven-hundred-million dollar industry. However, as a public servant—he was, and still is, Director of Research at the Citrus Commission—he got nothing for his idea except six months of extra vacation time, which he has been using up by adding a week a year to his standard three. He has often said, with equanimity, that if he had wanted to be a rich man he wouldn't have got a Ph.D. in the first place. He hunts when he can, fishes more often, and is kept fairly busy directing the research for forty-three men. One of the commissioners leaned forward and asked MacDowell whether, in his opinion, sugar could in any way be considered a preservative. "No," MacDowell said, and, without adding a syllable, he turned around and went back into the relative darkness of the auditorium.
—John McPhee, *Oranges*

3. Revising Paragraphs

a). Analyze and revise the following introductory paragraph so it fulfills all of its functions as an introduction, reads smoothly, avoids wordiness, and is grammatically correct. Compare your revision with those done by others in the class.

Many people have voiced their opinions on what they feel is the ideal of Americans. George Orwell once stated that the American ideal was the "he-man, the tough guy, the gorilla who puts everything right by socking everyone else on the jaw." Now, many people feel that the American ideal has changed as attitudes, like beliefs in human rights, have shifted. Although this shift has occurred in America since George Orwell made this statement one can see that the American ideal has not followed the shift by looking at an indicator of public thought. Americans still like to watch someone resolve problems, especially by fighting. The image of the tough guy might be slightly modified, but he is still the idol of most Americans who regularly watch television.

b). Revise the following process paragraph:

The first step in this complicated process is preparing to hit the ball. One must first mentally prepare for the drive. The first objective is to pick the spot in the fairway where you want to place the ball, and then to visualize what this perfect shot would look like. Then, just importantly, one must relax. Think of taking a swim in the pool for a second. Now one must physically prepare for the shot. The club must be gripped properly in order to insure a proper hit on the ball. The face of the club, meaning the flat part of the club head, should be held with the left hand at the top of the club and the right hand underneath, allowing the pinky of the right hand to overlap with the index finger of the left. The next part of the preparation is the stance. You should stand with your feet about shoulder width apart, knees slightly bent, bent at the waist, back straight, and with your left side facing the target. In this position you might look like an Indian doing a war dance, but this is proper. You should be about a club's length away from the ball, and your arms should be hanging in front holding the club. Now the first step is complete, and you are ready to swing at the ball. It is now becoming apparent how complex this procedure really is.

c). Revise the following concluding paragraph. Keep all of the checkpoints for revising a concluding paragraph in mind as you consider the revision. Think about grammar, style, and wordiness, too.

How does the Grandmother compensate for the loss of a perfect life? She and Nannie make their patchwork quilts. By making the quilts they are taking select pieces of the past to make a new history. A history that tells the story the way they want to remember it, with only the goodness remaining. By doing this they have created a myth about the past. The past the Grandmother lived and the past she remembers are very different. With the myth she has built she is able to ignore the idea that her life may have been less than perfect. She is able to look back, in old age, and say life had been good to her.

4. Revise the following sentences. Consult the "Revision Strategies" on examining sentences and words, and the appropriate sections of your checklist. In class, compare your revisions. Which are most effective and why?

1. Possibly more in years past than today, it is felt that to speak a foreign language carries with it a feeling of refinement.
2. With children already knowing the alphabet and numbers, it puts the child one step ahead.
3. Hedvig also commits suicide because, her duck which was going to be sacrificed, she could not live without it.
4. If hospitals were to worry about being a business firm they might not have made the discoveries they have made.

5. A man will spend ten minutes with their child and they are ready to smack the kid.
6. But Mrs. Tow-wause's idea of Christian charity is for someone who is able to pay their bills.
7. In addition to the effect eduction and environment has on man's personality, there is the family.
8. Erving without a team behind him were helpless, just like Pacino, Hoffman, or any other movie star is helpless without other actors.
9. In Book II of *Gulliver's Travels* a different perspective is taken by Swift concerning size.
10. For in education lies the deep-seated enrichment that makes for a good society.

II

Applications

8 Writing Description, Narration, and Exposition   159

9 Argument and Persuasion   185

10 Writing About Literature   209

11 The Library Research Paper   239

12 Writing Today: For School and Work   279

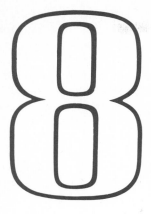

Writing Description, Narration, and Exposition

The Forms of Discourse

Applying the Forms of Discourse

Writing Description
Objective and Subjective Description
Sensory Appeals

Writing Narration
Objective and Subjective Narration
Order in Narration

Writing Exposition
Classification and Division
Definition
Process Description
Analysis
Comparison and Contrast

Exercises

Just as a mathematician develops skill by working with various forms of math such as algebra, geometry, and calculus, a writer develops skill by working with various forms of discourse: description, narration, exposition, and argumentation (discussed in Chapter 9). These four forms of discourse can be thought of as the principal ways you have of developing your prose writing.

Ideally, these forms can be used in combination. An engineer might rely on algebra to figure out the number of bricks he will need to construct a bridge, and then find he needs a geometric formula to calculate what the lengths of the steel support beams should be. A writer, assigned to write a story on the new bridge, would probably use description to relate the sights and sounds of traffic moving across it, narration to recount the day-to-day activities of the construction crew that built it, and exposition to explain why the city ordered it built in the first place.

The best way to learn about the different forms of discourse is to examine them one at a time, to see what each can contribute to a subject, and to learn to judge when a particular form applies. To that end, each form will be examined briefly before turning to an in-depth discussion of each.

THE FORMS OF DISCOURSE

DESCRIPTION.   Description is a way of making an experience come alive for readers by reproducing it in definite, sensory terms. The most effective way to do this is to appeal to the five senses, to use language that conjures sights, smells, textures, tastes, and sounds that the reader can recognize.

Often, writers concentrate on the visual aspects of what they are describing. Good description, however, uses the fact that we do more than just "see" things when we experience them. So, when we set out to reproduce these experiences for readers, we have to include the other sensory details that made it memorable.

Think about all of the senses at work when you attend a football game. You smell the crisp autumn air, and feel the heavy woolen sweater against your skin. You see the muddy red jerseys and glistening gold helmets of the players and hear the thud of blockers and the crash of cymbals on the sidelines. You taste the hot chocolate you brought with you in a Thermos. Our senses all contribute to the overall picture in front of us, and no descriptive picture can be complete without some reference to them.

At its most fundamental, description deals with objects, persons, or events that exist in space. You have a fixed object before you—a poster, a cluttered desk, a roommate's flannel shirt on the back of a chair—that can be described in terms of weight, depth, color, texture, even attitude. In other words, description fixes things in space for the reader even as it brings them to life.

NARRATION.   Narration differs from description in that it fixes events in time. It relates how things happen, how things change as time proceeds. Most novels and films employ narration to tell a story, relate events, and construct a plot. Diaries, for the most part, trace the activities of a day in chronological order, sometimes even narrating the changes in our thoughts over a day's time.

DESCRIPTION AND NARRATION.   Because space and time are often perceived together, description and narration are often used together. Writers draw concrete pictures of things and then relate how those things act in time, how they change from one moment to the next. Consider how, in the following example, physical description of objects blends with temporal narration to create a lifelike scene:

> Bert Hale, the world-famous inventor, walked into Kensington Gardens with his latest invention under his arm. It was the afternoon of Sunday, August 1st. High overhead, in a fitful easterly wind, kites were dancing, like spots before liverish eyes. From the bandstand, as if a door were being intermittently opened and closed on the music, the strains of a Gilbert and Sullivan medley blared out, then receded to a pianissimo, rose and were shut off: the scarlet and brass of the bandsmen twinkled between the low trees, as the leaves stirred nervously. A newspaper sheet wrapped itself round Bert's leg. He rubbed his eyes, into which the wind had puffed some dust, and stamping the newspaper flat, read the headlines:
>
> "Soviet Delegation Here Tomorrow. Is It Peace?"
>
> Bert's mind registered the headline as part of something that was in the air, something talked about all round him, tuning with the gay, vague, yet exasperated atmosphere of the summer afternoon, the high-flying kites, the strolling crowds, the children and dogs weaving among them—an atmosphere of suspense. But he was not concerned with it: his own private suspense was concentrated upon a single point—would the invention work?
>
> —Nicholas Blake [C. Day Lewis], *The Whisper in the Gloom*

Note how the concrete, descriptive language fixes the objects in the gardens, even as it illustrates their activities through time. (" . . . the *scarlet* and *brass* of the bandsmen *twinkled* between the *low trees*, as the leaves *stirred nervously.*") We know how the bandsmen look in the physical world, and also what the trees are doing in time.

EXPOSITION.   Exposition examines the "how" of something by answering questions of understanding. As a form of discourse it has many uses. It can explain how something can be interpreted, how one thing differs from another, how several things can be separated into categories, or even how several events can interact to bring about particular results. Exposition is the most common form of discourse, and rightly so, since the most common communication problem we face is explaining the "how" of something to someone else. Instruction manuals, essay-exam answers, business memos, and newspaper dispatches are all examples of expository writing. You can probably think of many other examples yourself.

ARGUMENTATION.   Argumentation, in one sense, means the marshaling of facts and logical thought to show that a statement is true or false, or that a proposed course of action is good or bad, effective or ineffective, useful or futile. Because of the complexity of this form of discourse, it will be the subject—along with persuasion—of Chapter 9.

APPLYING THE FORMS OF DISCOURSE

We will take a closer look at the forms of discourse by showing how each can be used to approach one object. The following photograph, which you first saw in Chapter 1, can stimulate ideas for description, narration, exposition, and even argument or persuasion.

(RUSSELL LEE: Iowa Homesteader's Wife, 1936)

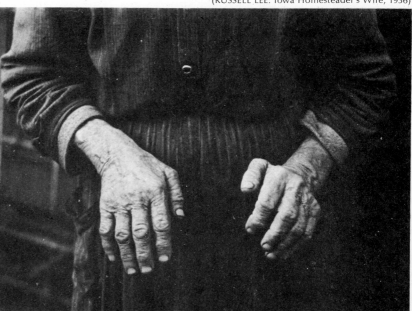

The first thing to do is to *look* at the photograph. What qualities do you see in the hands? Would you call them gnarled? Wrinkled? Blistered? All three? What about the folds of the skirt? Do they look neat and pressed? Old and worn? Faded from repeated washings? As you assemble such details into a paragraph, you will be writing a description. Perhaps, after noting the obvious physical features, you begin to interpret what you have described. What does the photograph suggest to you? Disappointment? Honor? Strength? Beauty? Do you see those hands shelling peas and scrubbing overalls? Smoothing earth in rock-strewn gardens? Gripping shaky bannisters on the way up the stairs? Such questions lead into an interpretive (or subjective) narration, where you speculate on how the hands became the way they are—that is, how time and events may have influenced their present appearance.

Taking another approach, you can use exposition to explain the composition of the photograph itself, noting how various shadings of light and dark contribute to the overall impression one gets of the woman. You could explain how its effectiveness compares to that of similar photographs or paintings you may have seen.

Next, the photograph could conceivably lead you to argumentation, to a point of view about the elderly and how they should be treated in our society after years of hard work, struggling, and suffering.

All the forms of discourse, as we have seen, can be used to approach one single object—in this case, a photograph. In your daily life, you will find that you have to communicate different things to different people, and to do so, you will need to use different kinds of writing—forms of discourse—to do the job.

Consider, now, the following daily calendar of a busy college student. Note the list of "to do" items it contains:

MONDAY, APRIL 14

A.M.—Write home. Break it to 'em gently about mid-term grades.
Go to library. Start draft of biology paper.
See Prof. Greene about extension on research project. Explain about heavy courseload.

P.M.—Write record club about overcharge. Send Debby Boone album back.
Leave note on Susan's door apologizing for behavior at party last night.
Do flyer for Sigma Chi open house. Mention refreshments, door prizes, freebies, etc.

As you can see, our student is faced with a variety of writing chores. Each piece of writing on the list has a different audience and a different aim, ranging from explanation to description to persuasion. As a result, each piece will require a different form of discourse. Let us examine three main forms as they apply to certain items on the list:

Narration, in the letter home, might help justify poor mid-term grades. The student might relate his experiences working overtime in the local pizza parlor under a cranky boss, or recount his long hours of participation in campus politics. In any case, he would explain how his time has been spent. He would focus on those activities that have drawn him away from his studies. Perhaps he would try to add a further dimension to his narrative by describing some of the new interests he has been pursuing since the start of the term—photography, drama, and ham radio. And he could always mention the added responsibilities he has had to take on since entering these new extracurricular areas. In short, his narration would attempt to give the impression of a busy, action-packed semester. Each "story" in the letter would contribute to the narrative. The cumulative effect of the narrative would be expository—explaining why poor grades resulted.

Exposition would be the proper form of discourse for our student to use in a letter to the record club. If he has been overcharged, he must explain how and where he found the error, and state what he wants the record club to do about it. "As you can see from the enclosed invoice," he might write, "your computer has blackened two purchase squares instead of one. I ordered only one record. Therefore, only one square should have been blackened for billing. Please correct this overcharge and adjust my bill accordingly." In other words, he would use basic exposition to explain how the error occurred. Sometimes expository material will be simple, other times, it will be more complex (as in the biology paper). But the job is always to communicate information as clearly and concretely as possible. When used properly, exposition gives us the explanation we need to understand something we may not have understood before. Above all, it can get things done.

Proceeding through the calendar, *description* might convince other students to attend the Sigma Chi open house. The flyer could include a tempting description of ice-cold refreshments (aimed at the reader's sense of taste), a list of door prizes, and the like. The student could even write about the house itself, describing its more appealing features: open-air porch, comfortable furniture, knotty-pine game room. Ideally, the flyer will include enough sensory details to attract those who normally do not attend such functions. The description will therefore try to work on several levels to attract the widest variety of people. In a sense, the description is also working as persuasion since it is trying to convince someone to do something. Bear in mind that much of the writing you do will involve several modes of discourse at once. Suppose that our hypothetical student, after visiting Professor Greene, is told to write a detailed explanation of why he wants an extension on the research project. The explanation could conceivably include:

1. A *narrative* recounting of the day-to-day demands of other courses (stressing trips back and forth to the library, obstacles encountered along the way, deadlines looming large, and the like)
2. An *exposition* (or explanation) of where the project presently stands in terms of completion
3. A logical *argument* for more time based on the facts already given

So far, we have looked at some of the functions of particular forms of discourse. We have seen how they can be used in everyday situations to communicate different things to different people. And we have seen that the various forms of discourse are often used in combinations. Now let us turn our attention to the range or capabilities of these forms, examining the various uses to which they can be put.

WRITING DESCRIPTION

Description attempts to translate a sensory experience into words. This means that a writer has to be aware of what his senses are perceiving, and he must find words worthy of those perceptions. For, as anyone who has ever attempted to write a description knows, language does not correspond exactly to the thing that has been perceived. Some words we use to describe are too general (see Chapter 6, "Words"), others do not convey our true impression of the thing being described. The real task is to choose words that most nearly correspond to the perception itself and that most accurately mirror your feelings about the perception—or that will render your perception most accurately to a given audience.

Descriptions fall flat when the writer expresses less than he has actually perceived and leaves a blank in the picture communicated to the reader. No writer can afford to forget the fact that virtually all readers read with an eye toward the expressive verb, adjective, or phrase that will bring the passage to life. Readers may not even be completely conscious of what they expect from a description, but they certainly feel a lack when fundamental sensory elements are not there.

Objective and Subjective Description

Imagine for a moment that you observe a robbery in a local grocery store and are asked by police to give a description of the robber. You remember that the suspect is male, white, approximately six feet two inches tall, with a jagged scar on his left cheek, a bald head, and a deep voice. With further prodding, you recall that the man wore a western-style belt buckle and brown boots. Such a recounting could be called *objective description:* the "facts" of the matter presented without personal interpretation or additional degrees of specificity.

If, however, you told the police that the man looked *nervous* and *ill-kempt,* and that his overall appearance was *disheveled,* you would be giving a *subjective description:* a personal interpretation of what you saw or thought you saw.

Most good descriptions are subjective to some degree. While the police may be interested only in objective, verifiable data, the average reader of a descriptive piece will respond to its more evocative elements. The key to effective description, then, is to write so that the reader not only sees the facts, but senses your reactions to the facts as well.

The surest way to make facts come alive is to use specific language to describe them. Always be as specific as you can. The following word list may help you see why.

LIST A	LIST B
pants	cream-colored, pleated slacks
far away	on the edge of the cloudy horizon
flowers	roses, lilies, and violets
loud	thunderous
room	motel room on Lake Erie

Each word in List B is more specific and subjective than its counterpart in List A. Needless to say, the word "flowers" is specific in that it refers to flora as opposed to milk trucks or horses, but "flowers" still prompts the question "what *kind* of flowers?" That is why List B is valuable; in each case it answers the question "what kind?"

One valuable practice tool is the ladder of specificity, where you take a general word and specify it to its most concrete form. Examine the ladder below:

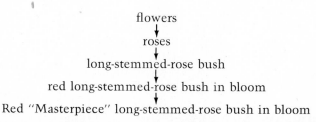

Most readers would find it easier to respond to the final rung of the ladder. It is more specific, subjective, and sensory. Yet it is often in the subtle blend of objective and subjective description that the true range of descriptive writing can be felt.

Read the passage below. Examine it for levels of objectivity and subjectivity:

Inside the house, my single goldfish, Ellery Channing, whips around and around the sides of his bowl. Can he feel a glassy vibration, a ripple out of the north that urges him to swim for deeper, warmer waters? Saint-Exupéry says that when flocks of wild geese migrate high over a barnyard, the cocks and even the dim, fatted chickens fling themselves a foot or so into the air and flap for the south. Eskimo sled dogs feed all summer on famished salmon flung to them from creeks. I have often wondered if those dogs feel a wistful downhill drift in the fall, or an upstream yank, an urge to leap ladders, in the spring. To what hail do you hark, Ellery?—what sunny bottom under chill waters, what Chinese emperor's petaled pond? Even the spiders are restless under this wind, roving about alert-eyed over their fluff in every corner.

—Annie Dillard, *Pilgrim at Tinker Creek*

The first sentence fixes the reader by describing the scene objectively: the author is watching her goldfish in its bowl. But, as the paragraph progresses, expressions such as "dim, fatted chickens," "famished salmon," and "wistful downhill drift" show subjectivity; their precision evokes a response from the senses. Consider the last sentence of the paragraph: "Even the spiders are restless under this wind, roving about alert-eyed over their fluff in every corner." The interpretive eye of the writer is evident in such words as "restless," "roving," "alert-eyed," and "fluff." And the major unifying device is the mysterious wind exerting its pull on all these things.

We can trace the overall effectiveness of the description to several elements: precision of words choice ("ripple" as opposed to "current"); concrete images ("dim, fatted chickens" instead of "barnyard fowl"); and sensory language that appeals to *all* the senses ("glassy vibration," "chill waters"). The reader can respond on several levels at once.

Sensory Appeals

The nights at Shey are rigid, under rigid stars; the fall of a wolf pad on the frozen path might be heard up and down the canyon. But a hard wind comes before the dawn to rattle the tent canvas, and this morning it is clear again, and colder. At daybreak, the White River, just below, is sheathed in ice, with scarcely a murmur from the stream beneath.

—Peter Matthiessen, *The Snow Leopard*

In the passage above, a blend of sensory appeals—cold sights, icy sounds, and frozen textures—contributes to the crystal-toned "feel" of the piece. We will now go through the paragraph and mark it for the particular sense to which each phrase appeals:

The nights at Shey are rigid (*touch*) under rigid stars (*sight*); the fall of a wolf pad (*sound*) on the frozen path (*sight and touch*) might be heard up and down the canyon (*sound*). But a hard wind comes before the dawn (*sound*) to rattle the tent canvas (*sound*), and this morning it is clear again (*sight*) and colder (*touch*). At daybreak, the White River, just below, is sheathed in ice (*sight*) with scarcely a murmur from the stream beneath (*sound*).

You might want to try for a similar blend of sensory appeals in your own writing. Make sure your word choices are precise, and that they evoke the feelings you yourself felt while viewing a particular scene.

As you grow more accustomed to descriptive writing, you might want to try unifying your description around a single idea or theme, as Matthiessen does with "cold." Instead of giving us a grab bag of unrelated sensory perceptions, he unifies the paragraph under a single wintery umbrella of whiteness and ice. Virtually every image in the paragraph revolves around the concept of cold. You can almost feel the mercury dipping as you read.

On a practical level, the Matthiessen excerpt can be used as a model for other seasonal descriptions. Try choosing a specific place during a specific season (say, a college campus during autumn) and writing a sensory paragraph based on the colors, sounds, and textures around you. One possible unifying device could be the concept of "brightness": pink and yellow leaves on the sidewalk, cider-gold sunlight filtering through the trees, and so forth. Your paragraph will be most effective if you remember to include details aimed at several senses.

WRITING NARRATION

Narration recounts a sequence of events that are either real (as in history, biography, etc.) or imaginary (as in fiction, plays, movies, etc.). Narration always involves things as they exist in time. Narration usually is arranged in sequence: "I found the gold bars, hid them in my room, and waited for Gastolph to call." Often, the purpose of narration is to draw attention to some other thing, some insight about human nature or even about a particular person that only becomes apparent as events unfold. Consider the following narrative depiction of a wild boar hunt in modern Spain:

Dismounting to kill a wounded boar is dangerous; the hunter is aided only by his dogs, which are permitted to locate and surround the boar, though they must not touch it. That is the man's job. The boar may have only a minor flesh wound, which does not impair its movements at all but can enrage it to fury. Once on a hunt I dismounted behind a hunter who had wounded a boar; I walked the other way. It was a chilly morning and I stood in high grass and lit a cigarette and lifted a wineskin, squeezing it at the base so that the warming red wine spurted in a long arc that

children, a mother overcame her hesitation about telling such "gory and threatening" stories to her son. From her conversations with him, she knew that her son already had fantasies about eating people, or people getting eaten. So she told him the tale of "Jack the Giant Killer." His response at the end of the story was: "There aren't any such things as giants, are there?" Before the mother could give her son the reassuring reply which was on her tongue—and which would have destroyed the value of the story for him—he continued, "But there are such things as grownups, and they're like giants." At the ripe old age of five, he understood the encouraging message of the story: although adults can be experienced as frightening giants, a little boy with cunning can get the better of them.

This remark reveals one source of adult reluctance to tell fairy stories: we are not comfortable with the thought that occasionally we look like threatening giants to our children, although we do. Nor do we want to accept how easy they think it is to fool us, or to make fools of us, and how delighted they are by this idea. But whether or not we tell fairy tales to them, we do—as the example of this little boy proves—appear to them as selfish giants who wish to keep to ourselves all the wonderful things which give us power. Fairy stories provide reassurance to children that they can eventually get the better of the giant—i.e. they can grow up to be like the giant and acquire the same powers. These are "the mighty hopes that make us men."

Most significantly, if we parents tell such fairy stories to our children, we can give them the most important reassurance of all: that we approve of their playing with the idea of getting the better of these giants. Here reading is not the same as being told the story, because while reading alone the child may think that only some stranger—the person who wrote the story or arranged the book—approves of out-witting and cutting down the giant. But when his parents tell him the story, a child can be sure that they approve of his retaliating in fantasy for the threat which adult dominance entails.

—Bruno Bettelheim, *The Uses of Enchantment*

The excerpt shows, in the opening line, that its purpose is to answer the question "How," in this case, how children view fairy tales. The example is detailed and then goes on to provide another perspective, that of the adult who feels uncomfortable in the role that the child has cast for her.

The thesis—that reading fairy tales aloud reassures children that they can indeed triumph over the "giant" (adults)—comes at the end of the third paragraph, and the conclusion restates the thesis.

Classification and Division

Another way exposition works is to explain by classification or division.

Classification tells us how a series of things can be separated and grouped. If you have ever looked for a job in the classified ads section, you have probably noticed that the ads are grouped according to type. Positions under the umbrella-heading "Sales" include telephone sales, door-to-door sales, retail sales, and the like. Positions under "Clerical" usually include typing positions, administrative posts, and so on. This grouping makes it easier for job seekers to locate the jobs they are interested in and to pass over those that do not apply to their particular interests or skills.

In the following excerpt from a psychology textbook, the writer discusses the grouping of various kinds of "social conflicts" into four major categories:

> What is social conflict? A good working definition is that it is any situation where two or more parties must divide the available resources so that the more one party gets, the less others get [Brickman, P., ed. *Social Conflict*. New York: Heath, 1974].
>
> There are many kinds of social conflict, and Brickman suggests that they can be divided into four major categories on a scale of social control or superimposed structure. In an *unstructured conflict,* almost anything can happen. There are virtually no social controls to regulate the action.
>
> In a *partially structured conflict,* there are some rules or expectations governing the relationship. If two people simultaneously see a bank teller opening a new window in a crowded bank, they will both walk quickly toward it, each one hoping to be first in line. Even though their competition is very real, their competitive behavior will be quite regulated. There will be no fistfights or shouting matches; in fact, neither person is even likely to break his or her calm demeanor enough to run. The competition will be carried out in the reserved, quiet manner dictated by the atmosphere of a bank.
>
> In a *fully structured* (or *normative*) *conflict,* the behavior of each participant is completely prescribed by the norms of the society or situation. The resources at stake are completely specified; so is the way these resources will be allocated. In most normative situations, the conflict is often not even recognized as a conflict. Athletic contests are ideal examples of this. Another relationship, which Brickman calls a *revolutionary conflict,* occurs when the rule structure is challenged—for example, when an army private points a gun at the sergeant instead of carrying out an order.
>
> —Charles G. Morris, *Psychology, An Introduction*

Notice the care with which the writer lays the groundwork for the classification. He begins with an explanation of the term "social conflict." After the definition has been established, the criteria for the classification is discussed ("a scale of social control or superimposed structure"). The actual categories of social conflict are then presented: unstructured conflict, partially structured conflict, fully structured conflict, and revolutionary conflict.

Definition

Definition, another expository device, often entails more than the dictionary meaning of a word. "Friend" is defined in Merriam Webster as "a favored companion; a person one knows, likes, and trusts" but to you it might mean the person who lends you her favorite cashmere sweater, drills you three nights a week in Intermediate German, and slips you the money you need to get home for your nephew's christening. As an expository device, definition helps make individual words, concepts, and abstractions easier to understand by focusing on concrete aspects of them. Consider the following definition of a sports enthusiast:

> He will wear his favorite team's uniforms—baseball caps, football shirts, or basketball shorts—call time outs during amorous moments, and speak in a language akin to ancient Greek but more commonly known as sports jargon.

For a reader, this is a much more concrete definition of a sports enthusiast than "someone who likes sports."

FORMING AN ACCURATE DEFINITION.   Whenever you choose a subject to write about, you are choosing a subject to define. Not that you "invent" a definition over and above the dictionary one; rather, you expand a one- or two-line explanation into a series of specific meanings. "God" is defined in the dictionary as the Supreme Being, but no theological writer would content himself with such a limiting label. The concept of God would probably be examined from many different angles (personal, historical, psychological, and spiritual, to name but a few) so that the writer could arrive at an individual definition of "God," a meaning he has created by examining the subject in its totality.

The same process could be used to define atheism, apathy, love, success, or honesty. The dictionary may provide a general explanation of a word, but only a thorough analysis can provide a definition.

When a writer takes on a broad, general term, the defining process becomes particularly helpful. If, for instance, you have been assigned to write an essay defining the word "teacher" and what it means to you, you could approach your definition in any number of ways. You could discuss the basic origin of the term, tracing its meaning through history, perhaps even contrasting the Socratic era of give-and-take with today's dependence on sophisticated audio-visual aids. You could talk about the teaching process itself, describing those techniques that do or do not go into the making of a good teacher.

Other methods include contrasting the personality of a good teacher with that of a less effective one, or even examining the role of the student as it relates to the role of the teacher, demonstrating how they are intertwined.

You could ask yourself questions. What is a teacher's function? Is it simply to get the material across? How and why should a teacher go about unifying a class polarized by highly motivated students and very apathetic ones? Should more be expected of students as they advance through high school and into college, or do teachers have the obligation to improve their techniques as the material becomes more difficult and the students more sophisticated?

Is it fair to expect every teacher to be ideal? If a bad teacher succeeds only in teaching you to appreciate good teachers, isn't that a form of teaching too?

As the process works to make the definition more specific, the piece being written becomes more interesting and the writer ends up taking a stand. Consider how E. B. White, writing during World War II, develops a definition of democracy by approaching the subject personally and reducing its broad nature to a series of specific, affectionate insights:

> We received a letter from the Writers' War Board the other day asking for a statement on "The Meaning of Democracy." It is presumably our duty to comply with such a request, and it is certainly our pleasure.
>
> Surely the Board knows what democracy is. It is the line that forms on the right. It is the *don't* in don't shove. It is the hole in the stuffed shirt through which the sawdust slowly trickles; it is the dent in the high hat. Democracy is the recurrent suspicion that more than half the people are right more than half the time. It is the feeling of privacy in the voting booths, the feeling of communion in the libraries, the feeling of vitality everywhere. Democracy is a letter to the editor. Democracy is the score at the beginning of the ninth. It is an idea that hasn't been disproved yet, a song the words of which have not gone bad. It's the mustard on the hot dog and the cream in the rationed coffee. Democracy is a request from a War Board, in the middle of a morning in the middle of a war, wanting to know what democracy is.
>
> —E. B. White, "Democracy"

The author, instead of trying to define an abstract concept abstractly, defines it by looking at it *concretely*. He lists those places where democracy *can be seen*. This example demonstrates how definition can control the entire shape of an essay.

Just as the many related items in a department store catalog can be said to define a store, the specific details in a catalog discourse can be said to define a subject. The main factor here is completeness. The writer defines the subject by itemizing it cause by cause, effect by effect, association by association. In the following passage, note how a catalog of an activity is created by defining the simultaneous processes that make it up:

Examples of how little we are conscious of our everyday behavior can be multiplied almost everywhere we look. Playing the piano is a really extraordinary example. Here a complex array of various tasks is accomplished all at once with scarcely any consciousness of them whatever: two different lines of hieroglyphics to be read at once, the right hand guided to one and the left to the other; ten fingers assigned to various tasks, the fingering solving various motor problems without any awareness, and the mind interpreting sharps and flats and naturals into black and white keys, obeying the timing of whole or quarter or sixteenth notes and rests and trills, one hand perhaps in three beats to a measure while the other plays four, while the feet are softening or slurring or holding various other notes. And all this time the performer, the conscious performer, is in a seventh heaven of artistic rapture at the results of all this tremendous business, or perchance lost in contemplation of the individual who turns the leaves of the music book, justly persuaded he is showing her his very soul! Of course consciousness usually has a role in the learning of such complex activities, but not necessarily in their performance, and that is the only point I am trying to make here.
—Julian Jaynes, *The Origin of Consciousness in the Breakdown of the Bicameral Mind*

What intrigues this author is our seeming lack of awareness of these processes, and to underscore his amazement he catalogs the processes in all their complexity. In fact, cataloging them simultaneously makes them seem even more intricate than they are. Notice, too, how the language reflects the activity being described.

Process Description

Another common form of exposition, *process description*, explains how certain tasks can be accomplished and how specific things can be prepared, improved, or perfected. Here you address the reader directly, almost as if he is sitting across from you. Process description usually lists the steps involved in a process ("grate cheese, add ½ cup tomato sauce, simmer over low flame"). Although the aim is to make a series of steps as clear as possible, a lively style can often transform cut-and-dried information into something much more entertaining. Consider the following introduction to a process essay:

At one time or another, practically everyone has enjoyed eating America's favorite food: pizza. There are many different kinds of pizza: thick and thin crusted, spicy and plain, even Greek and Italian. Some pizzas, however, aren't as good as others. No one likes to bite into a slice of burnt, greasy, or cold pizza, and pizzas that smell like old socks will most certainly not make your mouth water. I am going to teach the best and easiest process to make a pizza with the works . . . the perfect pizza!

Interestingly, before the writer describes the steps involved in making a pizza, he convinces us that pizza is indeed worth making. You come away with the feeling that the writer has a definite stake in whether a pizza turns out well or badly. Remember, though, that some process descriptions should remain strictly functional. Let subject matter dictate tone.

Analysis

Still another form of exposition comes into play when you analyze an entity. Here you explain the objective characteristics of something and analyze the subjective effect they have on you. Notice how completely Annie Dillard captures the essence of trees by analyzing them from several angles at once:

> I want to think about trees. Trees have a curious relationship to the subject of the present moment. There are many created things in the universe that outlive us, that outlive the sun, even, but I can't think about them. I live with trees. There are creatures under our feet, creatures that live over our heads, but trees live quite convincingly in the same filament of air we inhabit, and, in addition, they extend impressively in both directions, up and down, shearing rock and fanning air, doing their real business just out of reach. A blind man's idea of hugeness is a tree. They have their sturdy bodies and special skills; they garner fresh water; they abide. This sycamore above me, below me, by Tinker Creek, is a case in point; the sight of it crowds my brain with an assortment of diverting thoughts, all as present to me as these slivers of pressure from grass on my elbow's skin. I want to come at the subject of the present by showing how consciousness dashes and ambles around the labyrinthine tracks of the mind, returning again and again, however briefly, to the senses: "If there were but one erect and solid standing tree in the woods, all creatures would go to rub against it and make sure of their footing." But so long as I stay in my thoughts, my foot slides under trees; I fall, or I dance.
> —Annie Dillard, *Pilgrim at Tinker Creek*

The author does not merely say what trees look like or do. She analyzes the effect they have on her consciousness. Gradually we move from the objective reality of trees to her subjective responses to them. This, in turn, makes them a more complete entity, a larger presence.

Comparison and Contrast

Some expository writers find comparison and contrast an equally valuable tool. Here you analyze the differences and/or similarities between two things for the purpose of understanding both of them better. (Similarities are compared; differences are contrasted.) Journalists often use comparison and contrast to probe the stances of two political candidates, or the economic conditions of two different countries, or even the rates of return on two separate commodities. It is often easier to understand something if you see it in terms of something else.

In the following passage, a view of Disneyland at night is contrasted with the author's memory of Versailles at night. Note how he describes each place individually before drawing a final distinction between them:

> I paid one more visit to Disneyland. I asked if I could see it by night, because I wanted to see it with nobody there. Main Street was empty; only a few lights burned to guide watchmen. The skyrocket and the model of the Matterhorn were faint shapes against the sky. The woods with the Indians were full of shadows that seemed to move. The paddle-wheel boat floated on the dark waters of the lake like a ghost ship from the past. World upon world lay sleeping together, each born in the brain of the man who takes his art so seriously he worries himself to tears.
>
> My guide and I walked through the silent park, silent ourselves. I thought of another masterpiece that I had once seen at nightfall. It was the great pleasure ground of Versailles, with its statues telling Greek legends, its miniature palaces and the imitation village with its dairy where Marie Antoinette played at making butter. It was a masterpiece of its age. It was built for the amusement of kings and their women. But this one was built for my pleasure and everybody else's. Versailles was copied all over Europe. This one, I think, will be copied all over the world.
> —Aubrey Menen, "Dazzled in Disneyland"

The unifying concept of this passage is the word "masterpiece." Both Disneyland and Versailles are masterpieces in their own way, but the author draws a distinction between them by describing what each place contains and what each place means to him. Consider, too, how the expository device of comparison and contrast is blended with description, a form of discourse.

In your own writing, remember that all the forms of discourse can be mixed. Practicing with them individually will give you the skill you need to do this.

EXERCISES

1. Sensory Description

a). Refer to the picture "Iowa Homesteader's Wife" on p. 162. Look at it from the bottom up, taking careful notes on all the important details of the woman's dress and stance and the physical appearance of her hands. Using the invention exercises discussed in Chapter 1, construct a series of questions about each detail that, when answered, describes the woman in sensory terms.

Detail: What does the skirt look like? Is it limp or stiff? Old or new? How old or how new? What does its texture look like? Nubby or smooth? Open weave or closed?

Sight: Are the colors bright or subdued? Strong or faded? What is the character of this skirt? Fashionable? Out-of-date? Stylishly impractical? Or serviceable and long-wearing? When she moves does it flow like satin or float like chiffon?

Smell: What does this skirt smell like? Crisp and new off the rack? Musty from being stored away? Sweaty? Clean and threadbare? Are the odors of the kitchen caught in it? What are they?

b). Use the material you generated on the photograph to give you a sense of this woman. Use her appearance to get at her character and pick out the one trait that you think is most important. Write a three-paragraph essay that uses subjective description to convey that quality to your readers.

2. Objective Description

Make a list of details from the photograph. Pretend this photograph is one you are trying to describe to a friend in a straightforward manner. Choose a point of view and write a paragraph that describes it to convey as detailed an image as possible. Place your efforts in conveying a complete picture without guiding the reader to "see" it in a certain way.

3. Description

a). Look at the following list of adjectives and adverbs, and determine how straightforward or subjective they are in the range of description. Place each word at the point that you think is most appropriate on the scale.

red	hard
plush	elastic
brass	glossy
cuddly	walnut
succulent	teal blue
exquisite	brilliant
fundamental	rectangular

straightforward   subjective

├────────────────┼────────────────┼────────────────┤

b). Choose one of the following words: chair, coconut, coat, car. Write two descriptive paragraphs: one as straightforward and "objective" as possible, the other one rich in sensory detail.

c). Take the list below and copy it onto a sheet of paper. Fill in columns to the right of the nouns with words (nouns, adjectives, adverbs) that describe the original term more precisely. Choose words that provide a range of description from the concrete and matter-of-fact to the evocative.

Noun:

peach

scissors

hat

table

tree

d). Choose one of the words from the chart. Write a descriptive paragraph that builds upon all the words you have used to describe it in the chart. Spend some class time analyzing the paragraphs. Try to determine what makes a description lively or flat.

e). Take your descriptive paragraph, along with notes from class discussion, and write a four-paragraph descriptive essay on the word you have chosen. Try to get the reader to see the object as you see it.

4. Objective and Sensory Description: A Building

a). Spend some time looking at a building on campus that interests you, one whose design overwhelms you, looks distinctive, or dominates the space it occupies. Examine the building both objectively and subjectively, using the information discussed below.

Objective: Look at the building in a number of ways: from more than one angle, close up and far away, by going around it, by looking out from the doorway and top floor. Take notes of all the important details. Be as specific as possible.

Subjective: Look at the building. Keep the details in mind, but use them to help you get a sense of it. What makes it interesting to you? Does the building represent something or convey a specific, vivid impression? Think about the building in terms of the senses. Does it look like someone or something? Does it feel threatening, nurturing, sophisticated, humble? What do you "hear" when you look at it? Computers ticking inhumanly? Music? A booming, authoritarian voice?

b). Objective: Imagine that the administration thinks this building may be unsafe. You are an engineer who has been called in to inspect the building in order to determine its safety. Write a four-paragraph essay to the administration as a report that conveys your recommendations. This essay should describe the building in detail.

c). Imagine that the administration has decided to tear down the building. You are a graduate of the school and have many fond memories of the building. Write a four-paragraph essay as a letter to a friend in which you relate the many fine, sensory details that the building brings to mind. This essay should be subjective.

5. Formal Papers: Description

a). Write a descriptive paper about the woman in the photograph using all the information you have about her. Pretend you are her son or daughter; you have come home after many years and your life is very different from hers. Decide if you want to convey respect and love, embarrassment, resentment, or ambivalence. This essay will appear in *Parents' Magazine*. Usually, you write about being a mother or father. Now, you have reversed roles and write as a child.

b). As a staff writer for a university, you are working on a promotional brochure for the Admissions Office that describes the campus and its major buildings. One section is an essay on the building you have already been considering. Using both subjective and objective description, you want to make prospective freshmen "see" the building in order to get a positive sense of the campus.

c). If you do not like either of the topics suggested above, you might consider one of the following. Remember that you must work with the topic: figure out how it can be described, for what purpose, and to what audience.

Your favorite meal (one course)
Your favorite campus hangout
Your least favorite relative
Your favorite chair

6. Formal Papers: Narration

a). Write a narrative essay on the woman in the photograph. Choose your persona. You are submitting your piece to *Readers' Digest* as "The Most Unforgettable Character I've Met." Through your narration (of her life, a particular incident in it, etc.) you should try to convey what is unforgettable.

b). Write a narrative essay about your building. You can either "be" the building, telling a newcomer to campus about your life in relation to that of the college, or you can write to the school paper as a graduating senior. In this role, you link the "life" of the building with your life as a student.

c). Other narrative topics:
Moving into the dorm your freshman year
Your first date on campus
Returning home for the first time after being at school for a while
Your first encounter with the dining hall or cafeteria at school

7. Exposition

a). Choose three persons or objects. Using the strategies of definition, classification, process, analysis, and comparison/contrast, formulate a series of expository questions (e.g., how and what).

Example:
Shoe: How can it be defined? What can it do? What larger groups does it belong to (e.g., footwear)? What groups are contained within it (sneakers, espadrilles, etc.)? How is it made? How do I use it? If I use it, how will I feel? How is it like/unlike going barefoot?

b). Take one of the questions from the list. Spend ten minutes trying to answer the question. Then, draft a short essay. In your thesis, indicate the strategy you are using without identifying it directly. Do not pose the question; let it be implied.

c). Write a short essay (three to four paragraphs) in which you define a word used in one of the advertisements in Chapter 2. Use this advertisement, as well as any others you may know of, to provide the basis for your definition.

d). Choose something you do often (e.g., making a pizza, cleaning your room, spending an evening at a campus bar). Think of it as a process you can teach to another student. Break down the steps in the process, making them detailed or general, depending on the knowledge the student already possesses. List these steps. Review them and check those that are the most important or require the most explanation. Decide how the steps can be ordered. Can some of them be grouped together? Create an outline from this material.

e). Choose one of the following words: truck, jeans, pizza, car, beer. Try to classify the words in two ways: find two terms that place your words in broader categories and three that are more specific subcategories. Use the diagram below as a guide.
>   *Example:*   Fruit
>   Broad categories: Food, produce
>   Specific categories: Citrus fruit, orange, seed

f.) Choose one of the following: your last meal, your room, a favorite possession. Think of it as an entity, a whole. Divide it into its major parts. Look at each part and divide them into smaller units if possible.

8. Exposition: Formal Papers
Take your material on the woman in the photograph and think about it (and the photograph) in terms of things that can be explained. Choose one and write your essay on it. You might want to consider one of the following suggestions or come up with one of your own.

1. Write a paper in which you use examples from the woman's life to show that she is a strong person who has kept her dignity even though her life has been very hard. (Answer the question: what is she?)
2. Define her as a homesteader's wife, or, if you wrote a narrative paper on her, as whatever you decided she was in that paper (e.g., an Italian peasant, a sweatshop worker). This topic asks "how can I define this person?" or "what defines this person?"
3. How the photograph is put together

9. Writing Exercise: Comparison/Contrast
Go to the library and track down ads for cigarettes. Look at magazines in the 1950s, 1960s, and 1970s, and choose four or five that are representative.

a). Analyze each ad individually. How is the product promoted? What is the appeal? Who is the audience? Why?

b). Analyze each group of ads. Using exemplification, arrive at a series of generalizations about each group.

c). Compare and contrast the three groups. What do they have in common? What is different about each group? Given what you know about changing attitudes toward smoking or what you can find out (e.g., by talking to older adults, reading about smoking, etc.), try to analyze the shift in appeals over the three decades.

Argument and Persuasion

The Nature of Argument and Persuasion
Stating the Purpose
Determining the Audience
Analyzing the Subject

The "Why" of Argument/Persuasion

Beginning the Argument
Defining Terms
Hidden Value Judgments
Cultural Conditioning

Patterns of Argument
Formal Argument
Informal Argument

Exercises

My Daddy can beat up your Daddy.
No he can't. My Daddy can beat up yours.
No he can't.
Yes he can.

Perhaps you have overheard—or even once engaged in—this age-old argument. It is a classic example of an argument that can have no conclusion because neither side admits the validity of the other's arguments. Each side merely makes statements, the truth of which the other side promptly denies. The number of arguments, often on a supposedly high plane, that degenerate into this kind of a pattern is surprising. Take a quick glance at a daily newspaper, and you will discover just how much "debate" on politics, economics, or social policy ends up like a kindergarten quarrel.

Can't.
Can.

THE NATURE OF ARGUMENT AND PERSUASION

Argument and persuasion seem destined to go together; you can't have one without the other. *Argument* is that form of discourse that relies primarily upon an appeal to rationality and logic. It deals with the *why* as description/narration deals with the *what* and exposition with the *how*. *Persuasion* also relies to a great extent upon rational appeal but is buttressed with appeals to authority, to ethics, and to the emotions—in short, to nonrational concerns.

Nonrational, as used here, is not a pejorative or invidious term. Anyone who has seen that arch-rationalist of the pointy ears, Mr. Spock of *Star Trek* fame, is well aware that there are many good reasons for doing something or refraining from doing something that are not covered by logic alone. The heart has its reasons, and so does the stomach. Moral and religious concerns must also be accounted for. The nonrational is important, and it can outweigh the purely rational. It can be misused, but then so can logic. (See Chapter 2 for a review of ethical and emotional appeals.)

It may help to think of argument/persuasion as being on a sliding scale, with argument (pure rational appeal) at one end and persuasion (pure nonrational appeal) at the other. Most of your writing will move along this scale, partaking of each component but sometimes appealing more to reason and sometimes more to nonrational arguments. Good argumentative writing rests on choosing the proper mix of these different appeals to achieve the purpose of the writer. Finding the proper mix of rational and nonrational appeals depends on the writer's correctly analyzing the purpose of the piece, the makeup of the audience, and the nature of the subject.

Stating the Purpose

Before you can begin to formulate a piece of argument/persuasion, you must first have a clear, explicit view of your purpose. You cannot determine what appeals to turn to or what arguments to make until you fully understand your purpose. It might be helpful if you completed the following sentence: "When the reader finishes this I want him or her . . ."

Obviously, the sentence can be completed in an infinite number of ways:

. . . to acknowledge that triangle ABC is congruent to triangle CDE.
. . . to agree to go to the movies with me.
. . . to vote for Fred for class treasurer.
. . . to refund my $15 overcharge.
. . . to understand that property is theft.
. . . to give me the job of assistant buyer.
. . . to approach the use of nuclear power cautiously.
. . . to accept my thesis that Henry James is a frustrated dramatist.
. . . to stop playing the piano at 2 in the morning.

Just looking at some of these possible purposes gives you an idea of the kinds of argument you can write and the way you will have to range back and forth along the scale from the purely rational to the largely nonrational.

For instance, the proof of a theorem in geometry might be construed as being virtually pure logical argument. The purpose here is to show the truth of a statement by completely rigid and careful reasoning.

The reader is not asked or expected to do anything after reading the piece but acknowledge its correctness—or indicate a flaw in the argument if that is possible. The argument itself is all; there is no desire on the part of the writer to move the reader to any action whatsoever.

The style and format of the proof is absolutely rigid. The writer of such a proof is obliged to move logically from one step to the next. Each statement is accompanied by the reason for its truth directly to the right. The final statement, $\angle BOC = \angle B'O'C'$, is arrived at by pure logic and the understanding of the axioms, postulates, and definitions of Euclidean plane geometry. Proofs in many fields of mathematics and some sciences (most notably physics and chemistry) are generally of this nature, almost pure argument. They make few or no appeals to nonrational considerations.

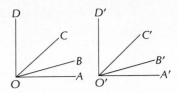

Given: *DO* ⊥ *AO*; *D'O'* ⊥ *A'O'*; ∠*AOB* = ∠*A'O'B'*; *OC* and *O'C''* the bisectors of
∠*AOD* and *A'O'D'* respectively.
Prove: ∠*BOC* = ∠*B'O'C''*.
Proof: *Statements*   *Reasons*
1. *DO* ⊥ *AO* and *D'O'* ⊥ *A'O'*.   1. Given.
2. ∡*AOD* and *A'O'D'* are rt. ∡ and   2. *Def. rt. ∡s; Post. 6.
      are equal.
3. *CO* and *C'O'* are bisectors of   3. *Given.*
      ∠*AOD* and ∠*A'O'D'* respectively.
4. ∠*AOC* = ∠*A'O'C'*.   4. Def. ∠ bisector;
                                                       Ax. 5.
5. ∠*AOB* = ∠*A'O'B'*.   5. Given.
6. ∴ ∠*BOC* = ∠*B'O'C'*.   6. Ax. 3.

SOURCE: F. Eugene Seymour et al., *Geometry for High Schools.* (New York: Macmillan, 1958), p. 45.

At the other end of the spectrum is a piece of writing whose *sole* purpose is to move the reader to some sort of action. Here nonrational arguments tend to predominate because they are more effective in rousing in the reader those emotional responses that are likely to move him or her to the desired action.

An example of this kind of appeal is the famous poster of World War II, "Uncle Sam Wants You!" The primary purpose of the poster was to encourage young people to enlist in the armed services. Its secondary purpose was to encourage the viewer to play any part in the war effort that he or she could—buy war bonds, serve as a volunteer. The argument was a direct appeal to the public's sense of patriotism—Uncle Sam (i.e., your country) Wants You.

Rational arguments could be—and were—given as to why the public should support the war effort. In this instance, however, the creators of the poster were primarily interested in moving the people to direct action. Hence, the strong appeal to the emotional values of patriotism and of belonging.

An explicit statement of your purpose, then, is the first step in determining the kind of argument/persuasion piece you are going to write. One clear indication of whether you have a clear purpose is whether you can find a concrete verb to go after the "to" in the sentence: "When the reader finishes this, I want him or her to . . ." If you can think of a good concrete verb here, you are well on your way to setting forth a clear purpose. If you find you must fall back on some version of the verb "to be," as in ". . . to be aware of the role of supply and demand in pricing policies," you will likely have trouble putting your piece together. How much better a start you would have if you rethought and rephrased the statement: ". . . to understand and appreciate the role of supply and demand in pricing policies."

Remember, if your purpose is unclear, your logic is apt to be muddied and your appeals unpersuasive. After all, who responds to an uncertain trumpet?

Determining the Audience

Now that you know what you want your reader to do or to comprehend as a result of reading your piece, you must determine who that reader is. Just stating your purpose will give you some ideas about the rational arguments and nonrational appeals you will use in your paper. Analyzing the audience in terms of what you want it to do will clarify even further the kinds of arguments and appeals that will work *with this audience.*

You are already familiar with analyzing an audience from the probes of Chapter 1. Review them and use them to determine the type of argument that is most likely to succeed in accomplishing your purpose. For instance, following is the conclusion of an article on the safety of nuclear reactors. As you read the piece, can you guess the type of audience the writer was addressing?

There is one other point on public response that needs to be mentioned. Many people responded to the Three Mile Island accident with statements such as, "They told us it couldn't happen, but it did!" In fact, no responsible person ever said that it could not happen, because the very business of quantitative risk assessment is to calculate the probability of an accident. No one will calculate a probability if he believes it is zero. What is at stake here is a widespread misunderstanding of the probability of infrequent events, a misunderstanding that is by no means confined to the nonscientific community.

Imagine, for example, a list of a million different events, each of which has a probability of one in a million of happening this year. The list might include the probability of a certain football team's going to the Super Bowl, of the OPEC cartel's deciding to lower oil prices as a goodwill gesture and so forth. If there were literally a million items on the list, and if the probability of each had been correctly calculated as one in a million, then there would be a good chance that one of those things would happen this year. When it did, one can be quite sure people would forget the other 999,999 items and would say that the probability for the event that did in fact happen had been grossly underestimated. People have a tendency to think that anything that actually occurs cannot have had a small probability of occurrence, because their view of the world is inevitably influenced by those things that do occur. Therefore even the NRC is devoting a great effort to making sure the accident at Three Mile Island will not occur again, with substantially less attention being devoted to perceiving it as a member of a large class of possible events that should not be singled out for having a high probability simply because it happened. The same comment can be made at this stage about the engine pylons on the DC-10.

All the preceding is intended to illustrate the importance to society of assessing risk in quantitative terms and of making sound interpretations of those risks. Since it is clear that we cannot live in a world without risk, the only alternative to understanding and managing the risk to which we have chosen to expose ourselves is institutional mismanagement and the squandering of resources. Examples of this abound, and it is a luxury we cannot afford.

Finally, then, any reader who has come this far will know better than to ask the meaningless question, "Are reactors safe?" The reader may want to know, however, whether I believe nuclear power is safe enough to supply a large part of our energy needs. The answer is yes, not because there are no remaining risks and uncertainties in nuclear power, nor because coal is more dangerous (although it is), but because President Carter was right when he declared that the energy crisis in which we find ourselves is "the moral equivalent of war." I see no point in not fighting that war, and nuclear power is an essential weapon in the fight.

—Harold W. Lewis, "The Safety of Fission Reactors"

The article in question was written for *Scientific American* in March of 1980. It gives a very detailed analysis of the probable-risk calculations made on nuclear reactors. The emphasis throughout is on quantifying the amount of probable risk in developing nuclear reactors and the chance of serious accident resulting from this development.

The reasoned laying out of facts and of the methods of quantifying risk probability is the kind of argument that would appeal to the readers of this magazine. Note, however, that Professor Lewis concludes his argument with one clear nonrational appeal. He appeals to the authority of the President of the United States.

On the other hand, the author of the following example, arguing against nuclear power, emphasizes the human factor as a drawback to nuclear energy.

Keeping civilian nuclear power under control requires the ultimate in technology: Essentially no errors can be permitted, no major radiation releases allowed. Nuclear technology is a "fail-safe" technology. Once a critical error is made, there can be no turning back; consequently, no errors can be made. The vital question of nuclear power development is whether or not human beings can be responsible for such an awesome task.

—Wilson Clark, *Energy for Survival*

This argument is clearly easier for a lay person to grasp than Professor Lewis's quantifying of probable risk. It puts the emphasis where the readers of Mr. Clark's book can best use their own experience to judge the safety of developing nuclear power. Clark essentially asks the reader, "On the basis of *your* knowledge of human behavior, do *you* believe that man is capable of operating a perfectly 'fail-safe' technology for any considerable length of time?" Thus Clark has shifted the point of the argument from considerations of reactor technology to considerations of human behavior—a topic most of his readers will be acquainted with firsthand.

So, too, you must adopt those arguments and use those appeals that are meaningful to your audience. Otherwise, you may end up with a perfectly crafted piece of argument/persuasion which is totally ineffective. Especially in cases where you want to persuade your audience to do something or not do something, you must show why it is in *their* best interests to act as you suggest. If your arguments do not reach your reader's personal or professional concerns, they are unlikely to get very far.

Analyzing the Subject

Keeping in mind the audience you are addressing and your purpose in writing, probe the subject of your argument, as you learned to do in Chapter 1. It may seem strange to you that examining the subject is last in this sequence of prewriting argumentation/persuasion, but it is only sensible. Until you have stated your purpose and determined your audience, you really cannot be sure which aspects of the subject are important and which are not. When you know what you want your readers to do and who your readers are, you will be ready to examine what there is in the subject that will make them do what you want them to do or understand what you want them to understand.

For instance, often a wealth of data exists about a subject. You want to choose from that data the points that will help you attain your purpose with your particular audience. In speaking about the safety of nuclear reactors, Professor Lewis emphasized one aspect of the subject and Mr. Clark another. A library full of information on nuclear power was available to the writers, and each chose to emphasize only a particular aspect of the subject. Each had to probe the subject in order to concentrate his research and writing on those aspects that would be valuable for his purpose.

Remember, do not think of data as inherently good or inherently bad. Data should only be considered relevant and irrelevant to your purposes. All data concerning your subject that is relevant to your purpose and to your audience—even if it is contrary to your thesis—is valuable to you and must be treated. On the other hand, data irrelevant to your purpose and audience—no matter how accurate it might be—is not useful to you and should be excluded. The decision to include or exclude data—or, for that matter, nonrational appeals—should be based only on the relevance of the material. That is why you must first state your purpose and determine your audience—otherwise, you will have no logical way of discriminating among the many aspects of your subject.

THE "WHY" OF ARGUMENT/PERSUASION

Once you have stated a purpose for your piece, you will immediately be confronted with the question "Why?" When you sit down to marshal your arguments and choose your appeals, you must think in terms of how well they answer the fundamental "why" question the audience asks of every argument.

The way to begin your argument is to address this "why" from the outset. Simply take the purpose statement of your proposed paper and add a "Why Should I?" after it. Play the role of your readers. Try to imagine which arguments and appeals are most likely to convince them.

In addition to beginning the organization of your paper by answering the audience's inevitable "why," you must check each statement of your piece with the same question. For instance, if you begin a paragraph by saying

> Investment in nuclear power plants at this time and with our present knowledge and technology is a risky venture.

you may be sure that the reader of that sentence has a silent "why" in mind while reading the rest of the paragraph. So should you. And you should be certain that the paragraph answers the question by giving sup-

I WANT THE READER TO . . .	WHY?
Give me a job as assistant buyer.	Because (1) I've had two years of marketing in college. (2) I've worked for two summers in the men's wear section of a department store as a salesclerk. (3) I intend to pursue a career in retailing and am majoring in business with a minor in marketing. (4) I'm dependable and anxious to succeed in this form of business. (5) I have several excellent references. (Mixture of rational argument and nonrational appeals)
Refund my $15 overcharge.	Because my credit statement showed a purchase of 2 sports shirts at $15 each, but there was a special sale that week for two for the price of one. (Include copy of sale ad and sales slip with date.) (Rational argument with supporting evidence)

porting evidence. In an argument, you can take nothing for granted. You must anticipate every "why" the audience will raise and answer it. Otherwise, your audience will remain unconvinced, and your argument will fail.

For example, you might continue the opening paragraph on investing in nuclear power plants as follows:

> . . . After the problem at Three Mile Island, we can be sure that safety measures in fission plants will be greatly expanded. New training for the operators of such plants is likely to be instituted—perhaps even mandated. Plants constructed or under construction will have to be reassessed in the light of new findings before they can be licensed to operate. All of this causes delay—and delay costs money. Nuclear plants, already hugely expensive, may well require even more costly design changes. Thus we see only the prospect of increased construction and operating costs, and it is not clear that electric rates can be increased sufficiently to recoup these new costs.

BEGINNING THE ARGUMENT

In Chapter 2, you learned about the nature of evidence and the pitfalls in dealing with facts, inferences, and opinions. The same cautions and considerations also apply to argument/persuasion. Moreover, there are additional considerations that are crucial to argument.

Defining Terms

Perhaps no single failure causes more arguments to go astray than that of failing to define one's terms at the outset of a piece. It is extremely difficult to argue about concepts like freedom, oppression, justice, equity, and the like because these terms mean different things to different people. If you have not clearly defined your terms—at least in the manner in which they will be considered in your paper—you will be arguing at cross purposes with your audience. The arguments you propose may well disprove your thesis if the audience has a different interpretation of what you are discussing than you do.

The following excerpt from James Baldwin's *Nobody Knows My Name* starts off with the thesis statement in italics. Baldwin does not wish the reader to be in doubt for a second about what he is saying.

> *Negroes want to be treated like men:* a perfectly straightforward statement, containing only seven words. People who have mastered Kant, Hegel, Shakespeare, Marx, Freud, and the Bible find this statement utterly impenetrable. The idea seems to threaten profound, barely conscious as-

sumptions. A kind of panic paralyzes their features, as though they found themselves trapped on the edge of a steep place. I once tried to describe to a very well-known American intellectual the conditions among Negroes in the South. My recital disturbed him and made him indignant; and he asked me in perfect innocence, "Why don't all the Negroes in the South move North?" I tried to explain what *has* happened, unfailingly, whenever a significant body of Negroes move North. They do not escape Jim Crow: they merely encounter another, not-less-deadly variety. They do not move to Chicago, they move to the South Side; they do not move to New York, they move to Harlem. The pressure within the ghetto causes the ghetto walls to expand, and this expansion is always violent. White people hold the line as long as they can, and in as many ways as they can, from verbal intimidation to physical violence. But inevitably the border which has divided the ghetto from the rest of the world falls into the hands of the ghetto. The white people fall back bitterly before the black horde; the landlords make a tidy profit by raising the rent, chopping up the rooms, and all but dispensing with the upkeep; and what has once been a neighborhood turns into a "turf." This is precisely what happened when the Puerto Ricans arrived in their thousands—and the bitterness thus caused is, as I write, being fought out all up and down those streets.

—James Baldwin, "Fifth Avenue Uptown: A Letter from Harlem"

Baldwin uses the simple statement almost as a definition of the problem. It is the inability of white people to understand the—to him—simple demand of the Negroes and Puerto Ricans. This inability manifests itself in the formation of ghettos, which results in a bitter social unrest. Baldwin knows that he is writing primarily for a white audience, one that does not share his convictions. So he must state—overstate some might say—his case. But he lets the reader know—right away—what his position is.

It is essential, at the outset, to set the ground rules for the argument you are going to make. This involves a careful analysis of your audience and the concepts, prejudices, and beliefs they hold. If you are aware that they differ from yours with respect to the topic of the argument, you must meet that difference head on at the beginning, as Baldwin did. Explain your position, and give your definitions. At least then everyone will know what is being talked about and in what terms.

Hidden Value Judgments

One problem related to the definition of terms comes in the assumption by the writer that his audience shares his or her set of values. Where this is the case, no problem arises, but where it is not, troubles are bound to come.

For instance, many people are thoroughly convinced that democracy—the rule of the majority—is a good thing. Holding this belief, a writer may develop an argument for a social policy on the basis that it will lead to an increase in democracy in the society. However, if the audience is not convinced of the value of democracy—and many peoples of the world are dubious about its value and efficacy—the argument will have the opposite effect from the one the writer wants. The audience will reject the argument on the very grounds on which the writer set it forth.

Cultural Conditioning

We in the Western World have set great store by our linear, causal, rational approach to data. Other peoples do not share our confidence in this approach to evaluating data. If you are trying to persuade people who have been raised in a different culture to do something, you must try to understand what their value system is and to couch your persuasive piece in terms that are meaningful to them. Again, remember that in persuasive writing the important feelings, convictions, and ways of thinking are not yours but the audience's.

Perhaps the most familiar piece of argument involving different cultural attitudes is the Declaration of Independence.

> When in the Course of human events, it becomes necessary for one people to dissolve the political bands which have connected them with another, and to assume among the Powers of the earth, the separate and equal station to which the Laws of Nature and of Nature's God entitle them, a decent respect to the opinions of mankind requires that they should declare the causes which impel them to the separation.
>
> We hold these truths to be self-evident, that all men are created equal, that they are endowed by their Creator with certain unalienable Rights, that among these are Life, Liberty and the pursuit of Happiness. That to secure these rights, Governments are instituted among Men, deriving their just powers from the consent of the governed, That whenever any Form of Government becomes destructive of these ends, it is the Right of the people to alter or to abolish it, and to institute new Government, laying its foundation on such principles and organizing its powers in such form, as to them shall seem most likely to effect their Safety and Happiness.

The words are familiar, but we often do not realize that they were written to a world that had little sympathy for rebellion and almost none for freedom or democracy. It was imperative for the framers to give their views on government, its just powers, and the rights of citizens. Note that they state that their ideas are "self-evident," which may be an example of begging the question. After all, the truths stated here were certainly not self-evident to the King of England, or to many other kings either.

Thus, it was essential for the framers to make their views of government at least plausible, so they appealed to the laws of nature—and of nature's God. Both of these concepts were accepted by most of the people they felt they were addressing. The ideas of equality and inalienable rights were, if not accepted by all, at least given some credence by thinkers in the colonies and in Europe, too. The framers, banking on their skill in enunciating these concepts in noninflammatory prose, used the ideas to put the actions of the English king in the wrong and theirs in the right.

Related to this problem of cultural conditioning is the concept of *causality*. There is a long step between seeing that two things are related to each other and saying that one thing is the cause of the other. Much of the way people view causality is part of their cultural conditioning. The West's reliance on empirical science will explain that a drought is caused by a certain shifting of the prevailing winds or of an ocean current or the like. Other cultures may explain a drought as punishment for a transgression, the breaking of a taboo, the conjunction of the stars. What seems a completely straightforward problem like establishing causality can become very complicated indeed.

This is not to imply that you can never appeal to value judgments or argue from causality. Just be sure, at the beginning of your argument/persuasion, that you have laid out all the possible problems, as the framers of the Declaration did. You must define your terms; examine any value judgments that are going to play a part in your argument, and state them clearly. Decide whether they are acceptable to your audience and, if not, that you will use them anyway, explaining them as you go. Remember, your argument has to make sense to your audience.

PATTERNS OF ARGUMENT

The paragraphs used in argument can be developed by the methods discussed in Chapter 4 (induction and deduction, definition, illustration, analogy, classification, analysis, comparison and contrast, description, and cause and effect). In short, there is no special way to develop paragraphs in an argumentative piece; you may use all the devices you know. But use them carefully and to the right effect. Be sure your analogy is an apt one, not a false one. Be sure that your cause and effect are properly related. Be sure your classification is thoroughly understood and that it is uniform. Be sure you have enough data to support a statement arrived at by induction or deduction. And so on.

Formal Argument

When writing argument/persuasion on a controversial subject, you may want to organize your arguments and appeals in a formal structure. This keeps your presentation balanced and allows you to deal with the main points of opposition to your thesis in the process of your argument. The formal structure for argument/persuasion is as follows:

1. Opening (Exordium)—give brief background of issue and supply any necessary information.
2. Thesis statement—tell readers where you stand on the issue.
3. *Confirmatio* (proof)—support your thesis with facts, judgments, analyses, and whatever else contributes to your point of view.
4. *Refutatio* (refutation)—anticipate what the other side will say in opposition to your thesis, and refute it point by point.
5. Concession—yield any points to your opponent that you know you cannot win, but try to offer an alternative solution even as you yield these points.
6. *Peroratio*—make a final, heightened appeal for support of your point of view and perhaps restate thesis.

Informal Argument

The informal structure of an argument is one that can be used on those occasions where the sides of the arguments are not so sharply drawn. The main point here is that the need for so nice a balance between conflicting points of view is not acute. You want to prove something to your reader, but instead of a body of formal opposition to your thesis there may be only objections of a general nature or a "why" to answer. In this case the following structure is the one to adopt:

1. Opening—set the background of your argument, define any terms you feel will lead to trouble later. Make clear any value judgments you will use as arguments.
2. Thesis statement—make clear to your readers where you stand and what it is you wish them to do.
3. Refute objections—here you answer objections that you anticipate will be raised against your thesis statement. Recognize in advance those objections likely to be raised and deal with them here. Disarm your opposition.
4. Proof—after countering objections to your thesis, present the evidence for your argument. Support your thesis with both rational arguments and nonrational appeals as best seem fit to persuade your audience.

5. *Peroratio*—make a final heightened appeal for support of your thesis, restating the thesis so that it now seems compelling to your audience.

Most important, do not lose sight—ever—of the interests and concerns of your audience. If the audience is primarily a hostile one (perhaps you are trying to persuade the college authorities to invite a controversial figure to give a lecture at the school), you will be best advised to use the formal structure. This takes some of the heat out of the argument and concentrates on the rational, cooler side of argumentation. Try to stay away from particularly emotional argument, as this will only inflame the hostility. Rely more on reasoned argument to make your points, thereby getting your audience at least to listen to and weigh what you are saying. Few people want to seem unfair. If you appear to be giving a fair, reasoned approach to the topic, they will feel obliged to give a fair, reasoned consideration to what you say. On the other hand, if you seem to be questioning their integrity or disregarding or ridiculing their point of view, their hostility will increase.

Following is the opening of a speech by Ben Franklin given at the Constitutional Convention of 1787.

> It is with great reluctance that I rise to express a disapprobation of any one article of the plan, for which we are so much obliged to the honorable gentleman who laid it before us. From its first reading, I have borne a good will to it, and, in general, wished it success. In this particular of salaries to the executive branch, I happen to differ; and, as my opinion may appear new and chimerical, it is only from a persuasion that it is right, and from a sense of duty, that I hazard it. The Committee will judge of my reasons when they have heard them, and their judgment may possibly change mine. I think I see inconvenience in the appointment of salaries; I see none in refusing them, but on the contrary great advantages.
> —Benjamin Franklin, Speech at Constitutional Convention

Note that Franklin is going to speak *against* the proposal. Because he does not wish to antagonize or alienate the writer of the proposal or the people who backed it, he begins by saying he is reluctant to oppose the measure. He says he has "borne a good will to it, wished it success." He explains that he is doing what he is doing "from a sense of duty."

Franklin is establishing himself here as a friend of the Convention in general and of the backers of the proposal in particular. Therefore, his arguments opposing the measure should be carefully considered because they come not from an opponent of the proceedings but from a well-wisher. Establishing the author's credentials before launching into an argument is a very effective way of forestalling later criticism. It also helps to soothe feelings that will inevitably be ruffled by the succeeding argument.

When the subject is not volatile, you can use the informal, simpler

Which Side Do You Believe?

There are two sides to the issue of nuclear power. Both sides feel strongly that their position is correct—which makes it difficult for Americans to form a responsible position on whether our country needs this source of energy.

Americans are bombarded with conflicting views and statements from numerous self-proclaimed energy experts. Some have even said that nuclear power—which currently provides 12% of the nation's electricity—should be halted altogether.

But consider the *sources* of the loudest anti-nuclear noise. Among those leading the attack on nuclear power are a host of actors and actresses, rock stars, aspiring politicians and others who think America has grown enough.

The Issue Isn't Just Nuclear

Nuclear power is not the only thing they oppose. These are often the same people who have been against development of geothermal energy in California . . . stopped new hydro-electric plants in Maine and Tennessee . . . blocked a new oil refinery for southern California . . . opposed new pipelines to deliver natural gas to the East . . . fought the building of more coal-fired plants. And they're the same people opposed to President Carter's plan for developing a synthetic fuels program. One wonders what they are *for*, and how they propose meeting America's energy needs?

For many of these people, stopping nuclear power is but one part of a political objective to slow growth across the board in America. This no-growth philosophy of the anti-nuclear leadership was clearly expressed by Amory Lovins, one of the world's leading nuclear critics, when he admitted, "If nuclear power were clean, safe, economic . . . and socially benign per se, it would still be unattractive *because of the political implications . . .*"

Support For Nuclear Widespread

On the other hand, consider the many organizations that have *endorsed* nuclear power for America's future. They include: the AFL-CIO . . . the NAACP . . . the National Governor's Conference . . . Consumer Alert . . . and many more. These groups recognize that America's need for electric power is growing at a rate of 4% each year.

Consider also that the health and safety record of nuclear power has been endorsed by a vast majority of the *scientific* community—including such organizations as the National Academy of Sciences, the World Health Organization, the American Medical Association, and the Health Physics Society.

We're not saying that nuclear power is risk free. The truth is that risks are involved in *all* energy technologies. However, the overwhelming scientific evidence is clear: nuclear power is at least as clean and safe as any other means available to generate electricity—more so than most.

Where will Americans get the electricity that is needed if not, in part, from nuclear power? That's the real question in the nuclear debate. It's the one for which the anti-nuclear leaders have no answer.

Nuclear Power. Because America Needs Energy.

(Ad created by Smith & Hanoff, Inc. on behalf of the Committee for Energy Awareness)

structure. You can rely more on nonrational appeals (only after carefully determining your audience, though). This does not mean, however, that you can abuse logic and stoop to pure emotionalism to gain your purpose. You could be unpleasantly surprised to find that your readers are not a bunch of boobies, but sensible, intelligent people just like yourself. Overestimating the gullibility of your audience is absolutely the worst mistake you can make in argument/persuasion. People resent this deeply and will not easily forgive it.

The preceding is an ad that appeared in a magazine. It is intended to persuade the reader that nuclear power is necessary for the United States. Note how unlike the earlier arguments on this subject this one is. Its main thrust is not to provide facts or a way of measuring risk. Rather it makes a central point of the character of the people who oppose nuclear power. This, you may recall from Chapter 2, is known as arguing *ad hominem*, or "against the man."

Such arguments often appeal to prejudices in the reader (hidden or open) and make the character of the opponent, not the subject itself, the main point of the argument. This is generally a dangerous tactic. It is often distasteful and, to a thinking reader, not at all persuasive. It can even be counterproductive, if the reader gets the idea that an *ad hominem* argument is being used because the writer cannot think of a stronger, more positive one.

Writing argument/persuasion is something you will be doing in school and on the job. As you have seen, it requires tact, honesty, and a lot of thought.

EXERCISES

1. Analyzing Arguments

a). The brief essay that follows was published in a magazine geared to a large urban audience. Analyze the essay, using the following questions as a starting point for the analysis.

1. What is the argumentative position taken in the essay?
2. What reasons are used to support that thesis?
3. How are the reasons developed? Are they thorough?
4. Are there any underlying assumptions of which the reader should be aware? Do they change the complexion of the argument? How?
5. Who is the "Opponent"? What is the opposing side?
6. Does the writer acknowledge this other side? How thoroughly?
7. What kinds of analytical strategies are used in the essay? Are they used properly? Effectively?

8. Are there any fallacies? What kind? Are any blocks to logical reasoning apparent?
9. Is this a good argument? A convincing one?

ECONOMIC CONTROLS VS. PERSONAL FREEDOM

There is much talk about the *potential* conflict between economic
controls and personal freedom. But the conflict is not merely potential. It
is actual. Our freedoms—of speech, press, religion—have already been
significantly curbed.

Consider freedom of speech. How many businessmen have been willing to talk publicly in opposition to governmental programs? How many
professors of medicine at major medical schools in this country would
not think three times before making a speech against socialized medicine given that their research is being financed by the National Institutes
of Health? Are professors at state universities unaware that they are
financed by legislative subsidies?

About the only people who have effective freedom of speech left are
senior professors at private universities who are nearing retirement.
Someone like me.

Thanks God for waste

It is tempting to believe that political and economic freedoms are easily distinguished, that it is possible to impose all sorts of restrictions on
economic freedom without interfering with political freedom. That is a
great fallacy. For example, is the requirement for a government license to
operate a radio station a restriction on economic or on political freedom?
We have today enormous restrictions on our freedom. The one saving
grace is the inefficiency of government. Thank God our government
wastes most of the money it spends. If it were really spending it ef-
ficiently, we wouldn't have an iota of freedom left!

Social Security is a striking example of a restriction on our freedom.
We are compelled to use part of our income in a particular way which
the government specifies and for a program that the government runs.
Social Security is presented as if it were an insurance scheme whereby individuals are paying their own money to provide their own retirement.
That's nonsense. What Social Security really is is a combination of a bad
tax system and a bad welfare program. The tax is a flat-rate tax on income
below a maximum—a regressive tax that hardly anyone would defend as
equitable. In addition, one reason why it's difficult for low-skilled people
to find employment is because the Social Security tax raises the employer's cost of hiring them. The benefit system is equally indefensible.
Does it make any sense that a person who gets a million dollars a year
from property should receive his full Social Security benefits when he re-
tires, while a person who continues to work and earns more than a limited sum does not receive a penny from Social Security between 65 and
72—yet must continue to pay the tax?

Negative income tax proposed

We should, of course, honor present obligations under Social Security
and other programs. For the future, however, we should replace the present collection of welfare programs—ADC, SSI, food stamps, housing subsidies, and Social Security—with a straightforward negative income tax.

People whose incomes are below a certain level would receive subsidies from the government, and people whose incomes are above that level would pay taxes. It's not an ideal system, but I think it would be far superior to the mess that we have now.

There's a great difference, incidentally, between the negative income tax and the minimum wage law. Those in favor of the minimum wage law have confused wage rate and wage income. It's always been a mystery to me why a young black teenager is better off unemployed at $2.60 an hour than he would be employed at $2 an hour. It doesn't do him much good to have a high wage rate if he doesn't have a job. A negative income tax, on the other hand, would provide a minimum amount of income below which nobody would have to get along.

Another aspect of governmental intervention that we've all seen is its tendency to reduce competition. There is hardly a major monopoly in the United States that doesn't derive its powers from government grants. What single law do you think would do more than any other to increase competition? The law which would have the greatest value in curbing monopoly and promoting competition would be one that would abolish all tariffs and enact free trade. International competition would be the most effective way to offset local monopoly and local power.

If we're going to establish a more favorable framework and climate for economic activity, we need to reduce the scope of government and to keep government from sitting in the back seat and hitting the driver of the car over the head every once in a while so he goes off the road.

Do you get money's worth?

Government spending in the United States has been going up now for almost 50 years. In 1928 total government spending—Federal, state and local—was about 10 percent of our national income. Two-thirds of that was at the state and local level. Now it is 40 percent of our national income, and two-thirds of that is at the Federal level. Few taxpayers, I suspect, believe that they are getting their money's worth for the 40 percent of their income which is being spent for them by government bureaucrats.

The growth of government inevitably leads to two things: financial crisis and loss of freedom. Great Britain is an excellent example of that. With government spending now reaching 60 percent of its national income, Britain is on the verge of collapse. New York City is another horrible example. Fortunately, New York, unlike Washington, does not have a printing press on which it can turn out those green pieces of paper we call money. That is the only reason why the collapse in New York City was halted as soon as it was. If they had had a printing press, if they had had a separate money, they would have pushed off the evil day by printing money and producing inflation. So, I believe that this trend toward ever-higher government spending must be stopped if this country is going to retain its freedom.

The best way to reduce government spending is across the board—a cut of 10 percent everywhere. And then the next year another 10 percent across the board.

Regulators play it safe

The drug industry is an example of an industry that has been seriously hampered by government intervention and regulation, especially since the days of Estes Kefauver in 1962. I believe that the Food and Drug Administration has, on the whole, done a great deal more harm than good. The reason is very simple—no Food and Drug administrator has ever been pilloried for *not* approving a drug which was potentially capable of saving many lives. Any Food and Drug administrator is bound to be pilloried for making the other mistake, namely, approving a drug which turned out to be harmful. As a result, the Food and Drug people have a bias in favor of holding up good drugs in order to avoid the possibility of a mistake in approving a bad one. The result is that there are many effective drugs which are available in Canada, in Britain and elsewhere which cannot be purchased by people in the United States, but which might very well save their lives.

Free enterprise is not a magic formula that can simply be uttered and become effective. It takes a certain set of social values and beliefs and attitudes for a free society to be viable.

Government cannot inculcate these habits and beliefs. They have to develop, not out of any explicit deliberative decision to inculcate them, but out of a long background. We in the United States have been extraordinarily fortunate in having been born into a society which has those beliefs. The normal state of mankind is tyranny and misery. It's been that way over the millennia in most parts of the world. It is that way today in most parts of the world. I know of no case on record in which a government has been able to inculcate ideas of the kind that are necessary to preserve a free society.

The American system originally was one where the people had close control over the government, not vice versa. We've lost that. And, unless we can regain that control—and reverse the balance—we will have lost our freedom.

—Dr. Milton Friedman

2. Argumentative Strategy

a). Discuss the argumentative strategy used in this brief, persuasive essay published by the Mobil Corporation.

1. How does Mobil diffuse hostility at the beginning?
2. How does the writer shift focus?
3. What is it about the juxtaposition of the push for solar energy and the continued need for fossil fuel and favorable policy that can convince the reader?
4. What kinds of logical strategies are being used?
5. Are there any logical fallacies?
6. Are there any underlying assumptions of which we should be aware? Any possible blocks to careful, logical argumentation? Does a recognition of them change our view of the convincing quality of the essay?
7. What kind of persuasive language is being used?

IMAGINE TOMORROW AS A RIBBON OF SUNSHINE
Brightening the night.

Solar energy won't really come of age until it's competitive in price for the *big* energy jobs, like running factories and lighting whole cities after dark.

Making the sun more cost efficient is an exciting challenge. Which is why one of our subsidiaries is spending $30 million on development and pilot production of electricity from solar cells made from silicon ribbons. The process, with no moving parts, converts the sun's rays directly into kilowatts. Not cheaply yet, but we're hopeful.

We're also realists. Which is why we keep reminding people that, despite Sun Days and other drumbeating for Ol' Sol, practical solar energy is not here *now*. Not for the *big* energy jobs. In the decades while it's being brought to economic reality, America will need all the oil, natural gas, coal, and nuclear power it can get. And a national energy policy that encourages energy producers.

So shortages can be anticipated and avoided. So America's tomorrow will be even brighter than today.

MOBIL®
Speaking out for tomorrow . . . today
© 1979 Mobil Corporation

3. Argument

a). Look at the following topics as possible suggestions for argumentation. Formulate three "why" questions for each. One should be worded so that the answer will give reasons; the next should be phrased so that the answer will provide a judgment of value; the last should provide specific examples or incidents that support the generalization contained in the question. Is each topic equally arguable? What makes some topics more subject to debate than others?

1. a required core curriculum in the liberal arts
2. teenage pregnancy
3. continued development of nuclear energy
4. the proper way to make a hamburger

b). Choose one of the topics mentioned above and two of the questions you have written. Identify the possible stands that can be taken and argued. Make a chart like the one below and list the ways in which rational arguments and persuasive appeals can be made. Do certain stands lend themselves more easily to one or the other? Why?

Question:

Stands	Argument	Persuasion
1.		
2.		
3.		

c). Examine the following argumentative theses. List three "proofs" that support the position and two proofs that oppose it.

1. Women want to be equal with men; therefore they want to be like men.
2. Fraternities and sororities are dangerous organizations and should be abolished from college and university campuses.
3. People who don't love their country should leave it.
4. By the time students have gotten to college, their minds have been rotted by television.

4. Formal Papers

a). Using all your material from your work with the photograph "Iowa

Homesteader's Wife" (see Exercises in Chapters 1 and 8), and any other information, write an argument on one of the following:

1. If you put this woman in a nursing home, she will soon give up her desire for life and die.
2. We must keep old people in our communities rather than pack them off to nursing homes, retirement communities, and other ghettoes for those over sixty-five years old.
3. The woman in this picture is proud, dignified, and courageous—or the reverse: she is demoralized, ashamed, and fearful.

b). Take a controversial campus issue over which people are evenly divided. Write an argumentative essay in which you examine the strengths and weaknesses of each and then argue for a moderate position.

5. Persuasion

Analyze the two following essays published by the Tobacco Institute.

1. What expository techniques are used?
2. What argumentative position is taken?
3. What are the strengths and weaknesses of each argument? Can you uncover any blocks to logical reasoning, any fallacies, any hidden assumptions?
4. What techniques are being used in each essay to make the argument *appeal* to a particular group? Are they successful? Why or why not?
5. Examine the language being used.
6. Who is the audience in each? What indications do we have, in the essay, that the writer is very conscious of the audience?

A WORD TO NONSMOKERS
(about working together)

Wherever you work—even if you're a billboard painter—you work with smokers, and always have.

There's nothing remarkable about that. Forty percent of the people around you are smokers, and 60% are nonsmokers. Still, we work, live, and enjoy ourselves together.

Lately, however, we've all become super-sensitive to each other and to each other's privileges and obligations. And that's not a bad thing.

We agree on many things. There are places (crowded elevators, to take the simplest example) where smoking is not appropriate. In closed and private places, the ancient courtesy of "Do you mind if I smoke?" is still the best rule. Smokers, we believe, have become more generally conscious of that courtesy. The occasional careless smoker, waving a lighted cigarette or cigar, should, in our opinion, be as quickly reminded of others' preferences by a thoughtful smoker as by a nonsmoker.

Nevertheless there *are* some people—anti-smokers rather than non-smokers—who will never be satisfied with our sensible accommodations to each other. They don't want us to work together at all. Instead they want to segregate us by law—literally to build walls between us—at considerable expense to both smokers and nonsmokers—in places where we work, shop, eat or just go to amuse ourselves.

We know that such anti-smokers do not represent the great majority of nonsmokers. And the anti-smokers know it, too. But there is a danger that others will think they do.

"When I went to the legislature," says one anti-smoking lobbyist, "they thought I had about 10,000 people behind me. That was a laugh. It was just me. I had the law passed by myself."

If it is a "laugh" for the anti-smoker, it is no joke for the rest of us for we must all, smokers and nonsmokers alike, pay the cost of such foolish laws. All of us are losers when any one of us is denied freedom of choice.

We don't think that, over the long run, that's going to happen. We think that, like our billboard painters, we'll go on working together until we get the job done.

—THE TOBACCO INSTITUTE
1776 K St. N.W., Washington, D.C. 20006
Freedom of choice is the best choice.

A WORD TO SMOKERS
(about working together)

Whether you're a billboard painter or just, as you obviously are, a reader of magazines, you've discovered that there's a difference between *non*-*smokers* and *anti*-smokers.

We all work with nonsmokers—and they work with us. Roughly 60% of the people around us are nonsmokers, and 40% of them are smokers—so we *have* to work together. And, like our sign painters, we do.

Anti-smokers are a breed apart. They don't want us to work together with nonsmokers. And they go to some extreme lengths to see that we don't.

Two examples:

1. A nationally known TV and film star was prevented from performing by a band of anti-smokers threatening violence because the star frequently smoked on stage. The occasion was a benefit to raise funds for handicapped children.

2. The executive director of one anti-smoking group announced plans to build an "army" of 2,000,000 anti-smoking militants who would go about "zapping" smokers in the face with spray from aerosol cans.

"You don't know what a rewarding feeling it is," he is quoted as saying, "the first time you spray a smoker in the face. It's hard to work yourself up to the first spray. It takes guts. But once you've broken the ice, it's easy. And you feel exhilarated."

Such people clearly do *not* represent the nonsmokers we all know and work with. They would not last long in any working environment where people must cooperate to get the job done. And we doubt very much that the "zappers" will find 2,000,000 others to go along with them. Americans just don't think that way.

Such anti-smokers are not only anti-smoking. They're giving themselves the reputation of being anti-individualism, anti-freedom of choice, anti-everything that does not agree with their special prejudices. And in that they're as much a threat to nonsmokers as they are to smokers.

—THE TOBACCO INSTITUTE
1776 K St. N.W., Washington, D.C. 20006
Freedom of choice is the best choice.

6. Persuasive Essays

a). Both of these selections are examples of persuasive writing. Analyze each one carefully. Identify the assumptions on which it is based, the different appeals it uses, the kinds of language it uses to persuade. What are its strengths and weaknesses? Compare the two. Which uses persuasive techniques more appropriately?

Fourscore and seven years ago our fathers brought forth on this continent a new nation conceived in liberty and dedicated to the proposition that all men are created equal. Now we are engaged in a great civil war testing whether that nation, or any nation so conceived and so dedicated, can long endure. We are met on a great battlefield of that war. We have come to dedicate a portion of that field as a final resting-place for those who here gave their lives that that nation might live. It is altogether fitting and proper that we should do this. But, in a larger sense, we cannot dedicate, we cannot consecrate, we cannot hallow this ground. The brave men, living and dead, who struggled here have consecrated it far above our poor power to add or detract. The world will little note nor long remember what we say here, but it can never forget what they did here. It is for us the living rather to be dedicated here to the unfinished work which they who fought here have thus far so nobly advanced. It is rather for us to be here dedicated to the great task remaining before us—that from these honored dead we take increased devotion to that cause for which they gave the last full measure of devotion—that we here highly resolve that these dead shall not have died in vain, that this nation under God shall have a new birth of freedom, and that government of the people, by the people, for the people shall not perish from the earth.

MEN FEAR WOMEN?

Throughout history, I think, most men have feared being unmanly. More specifically, I believe that they have feared women.

Current misconceptions to the contrary, men clearly have been afraid of women for centuries. Husbands intuitively knew that their wives were better in relationships and could dominate and destroy them if they get too close.

But the Industrial Revolution changed a man's role forever. Industrialization diminished the importance of physical strength. Modern machines could work equally for both sexes. In the process, man was robbed of his vital psychological defense. He became even more susceptible to a woman's emotional powers.

Over the past century, then, man has come to feel that he is unprotected, exposed and vulnerable. Understandably, he clings to an old notion—Provide well and your wife will remain happy.

The kicker, of course, is that his wife is not happy. And not only is she unhappy and dissatisfied, she has become more assertive about her dissatisfaction. She has become infinitely more independent at a much earlier age than her own grandmother.

—Dr. Pierre Mornel, M.D., "Passive Men, Wild Women,"

b). Choose a product, a position on an issue, or a position on a controversial public figure. Choose three possible audiences. What kind of appeals can be used effectively with each audience? Why?

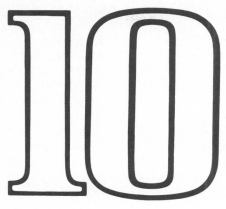

Writing About Literature

The Literary Essay

Probing

Approaches to the Literary Essay
Plot
Characterization
Setting
Point of View
Theme
Comparison/Contrast

Structure of the Literary Essay
A Note on Evidence

Choosing a Title
The Opening Paragraph
Sticking to the Thesis
The Body of the Essay
The Conclusion

Documenting the Essay
Footnotes
Quotations in the Text

Writing About Film
Guidelines for Film Analysis

Exercises

Why is it that certain books are read year after year, generation after generation, by college class after college class? To what can we attribute their staying power? What is it about these books that continues to encourage analysis?

The answer is simple. These books represent the best of American and English literature. Many instructors feel that among the benefits to be derived from exposure to literature is that students learn to recognize good writing and perhaps even to write well themselves.

Almost from the moment you come into contact with good literature, you are expected to be able to write about it, to analyze those qualities that make a literary work good or bad. In this chapter we will concentrate mainly on the fundamentals of literary analysis, stressing the structure of the literary essay and the type of evidence you should use to document your analysis. We will also look at a full-length essay, commenting on its organization and overall effectiveness.

THE LITERARY ESSAY

Writing about any aspect of a literary work requires that you bring all of your critical and analytical abilities to bear on your reading, interpretation, and judgment. An impression or "gut feeling" about a story or a poem is only a beginning. Liking or not liking a literary work is merely an impression; exploring and understanding *why* you do or do not like a particular work is the beginning of literary analysis. When you are asked to write about literature, you are being asked to respond in a formal, analytic way to a specific work, and to communicate your written response to an audience. Remember that you are not writing only for yourself, or for close friends, but for a specialized audience: your instructor and, perhaps, other students.

Writing about literature requires that you be willing to read and reread a literary work until you understand it thoroughly. Even the most accomplished professors of literature have to read and study the work until they arrive at an understanding of the chosen topic. Picking out recurring images, symbols, metaphors, and analogies is the result of careful and attentive reading. In writing about literature your aim or purpose should be to show how the various elements of literature (plot, character, setting, etc.) contribute to the overall meaning of the work. You can also write about a single element of literature, demonstrating how the author uses it to create a desired effect in a story or in a poem. A great deal of the difficulty in writing about literature originates in the development of your topic. The choice of a topic means that you must first define the scope and limits of your paper.

PROBING

Before you begin to focus on the basic elements of literary analysis, try to create ideas and material for your writing by probing. Start with an examination of your response to the work, focus on an essay topic, and then probe and question yourself how and why a topic or idea operates within a story, novel, poem, or drama. Remember that writing about literature is more than simply expressing lyrical enthusiasm about the work and more than a complaint list. You must offer textual evidence to support your thesis. In this sense, you would not answer the question, "How did you like Paris?" with a simple, "I hated it." You would say, "I hated it. It rained all the time; I caught a cold; the food was awful; and I couldn't find a decent thing to do anywhere." In other words, you would justify your feelings with illustrations and examples.

Sometimes you will be assigned a specific literary topic; other times you will have to develop one for yourself. The list of guidelines below may help you get off to a good start:

BE HONEST AND TOUGH.   Probe your responses to the work. What do you feel? Why? Ask yourself questions about the meaning of the work, and attempt to answer those questions. In short, *think* about the work and its possible meanings.

WRITE FOR A REAL AUDIENCE.   Do not concentrate on writing only for the instructor. When writing, imagine, and write for, an audience of your peers, family, and friends.

FOCUS.   Do not try to retell the whole story of a literary work. You will only confuse and bore your readers. Develop a thesis, focus on and present those details of the work that support your ideas, and show how they are important to the literary work.

USE YOUR EXPERIENCE.   Because literature deals with the problems and events that make up our lives—both on the grand scale (historically) and on the small scale (personally)—it very often treats things familiar to you personally. For instance, William Faulkner's novels, which are set in the South, may have special significance for anyone who has grown up in a small southern town, just as N. Scott Momaday's *House Made of Dawn* might carry special meaning for an American Indian. Reading and writing about literature with an eye for how the substance of a work relates to and reflects your own experiences can help you to appreciate and to write about literature better.

USE QUOTATIONS. Start with your response to the work, but don't stop there. You must back up everything you say with quotations and references to the original and, if you choose, to other critics. Be economical and use as few words as possible in a quote. Your paper is a commentary on the work, not a substitute for or a synopsis of it.

TAKE NOTES. Be an active reader or viewer. Jot down a word or phrase, an incident, a scene that affects you. Note taking helps you to reconstruct a cogent response to the work.

APPROACHES TO THE LITERARY ESSAY

Someone may have told you at one time or another that analysis of a literary work "spoils" your appreciation of it. There is no reason to suppose, however, that thinking about a piece of literature makes it less enjoyable. Actually examining the reasons why you responded so strongly to it will most likely *enhance* your enjoyment. You will be able to pinpoint which parts of it produced a strong response in you, and, in so doing, be able to appreciate the whole of the work much more.

Readers also depend on literary analyses to help them see aspects of a work they may not have seen before. The idea that analysis spoils appreciation perhaps comes from the mistaken notion that writing is like a magic show—mystifying and entertaining—but only as long as the "secrets" are kept under wraps. Certainly, some kinds of writing fall into this category (detective novels that fade into insignificance once the butler confesses) but the rewards are far greater when works of solid literary merit are examined. A literary work can offer fresh insights into the human condition and display flashes of humor, irony, and tragedy that are not contained in more "lightweight" books. A work of literary merit is not fragile. It can be excavated for several different meanings and will stand the test of time.

The works of literature you will encounter in class will probably encompass nearly every imaginable literary form: the short story, the epic, the novel, the sonnet, the fable, the drama, and even films. How are you to deal with such a bewildering array of material and forms? You do so by developing an understanding of particular approaches to literary analysis and interpretation. When you write a literary analysis, you will want to uncover how the work evokes various emotions in you, to interpret the meaning of the work, and to judge its effectiveness. In so doing, you will find that there are several basic approaches to the literary essay that will be useful time after time.

Plot

The most obvious element of a literary work is the plot. What happened? In what sequence did it happen? What significance, if any, does this organized pattern of events have on the conflict, the characters, and the theme of the work?

When you examine a literary work by analyzing its plot, you must try to determine how the pattern of events contributes to the meaning of the work. You must determine what effect each shift and turn of the plot has on the characters in the story and on the reader. The effects need not be the same. For example, in Sophocles' classic drama *Oedipus the King*, Oedipus is excited and elated as he comes closer to the truth about who murdered Laius. He is ready to ensnare the guilty person, whom he has sworn to punish to save Thebes. The audience, knowing that Oedipus himself is guilty, is anxious and fascinated as each new piece of evidence comes to light, drawing the net tighter and tighter around the unsuspecting Oedipus. This tension between how the plot affects the characters and how it affects the audience is one of the main sources of tension and interest in literary works.

Characterization

In an essay analyzing character, you are writing about how the nature of a literary character is revealed and what this revelation means to the overall meaning of the work. When you are writing an essay on character development, you must be able to pinpoint the actions and statements in the work that reveal the traits, desires, and intentions of a character. When Hamlet swears to avenge his father's death and does not, what are we to believe about him? Is Hamlet lying to his father's ghost, to us, or to himself? It is up to the reader to evaluate a character from what is said by the character himself, by the narrator, or by other characters in the story.

Be alert to the importance placed on major and minor characters, the differences between static and dynamic characters, and the primary methods of characterization. Every literary work, except perhaps poetry, has main and subordinate characters, and ascertaining a character's order of importance in a work is merely a matter of determining how much of a role he or she plays in the action of the novel, story, or play. A static character is one who stays the same throughout the work, and a dynamic character is one who changes in some important way as the story unfolds. Some of the primary ways in which an author develops a character are: (1) through physical description, (2) through a charac-

ter's actions, (3) through the comments and reactions of other characters to a particular character, and (4) through a character's thoughts and
words. Ask yourself how the characters conflict with each other, with
themselves (internal conflict), or with an outside, natural force (external conflict: the ocean, the Arctic wilderness, etc.).

Given the scope of the work, you must decide what you know about
a character. Is there a consistency in the development of a character's
traits, actions, and beliefs? Does a sudden insight at the end of the story
really seem in keeping with what you know about the character, or does
it seem more of a convenient mopping-up by the author? In all cases of
character analysis, you should focus on the traits, desires, actions, beliefs, and words set out *by the author* of the literary work. Do not judge
the characters of a book by the standards of your community or by the
standards of your friends or family. Your essay on character analysis
should examine how a character's actions, desires, and traits are developed and operate within the context of the work in which he or she
appears.

Setting

The setting of a literary work is the time, place, and mood in which the
actions or events of the work take place. Analyzing the setting is often a
matter of noticing the subtle changes in the time of day within a novel,
the underlying power that a natural force holds for the characters, or
even the style of dress which distinguishes one historical and cultural
period from another.

When you write an analysis of the setting of a literary work you
should try to relate this setting to some other aspect of the work. Do not
just describe the place in which the work is set and leave it at that. Ask
yourself what effect the author wanted to create by using a particular
setting in the first place.

For instance, you could contrast the two different settings Shakespeare uses in *Midsummer Night's Dream:* the setting of the court and
the setting of the forest. The court is very much like the real world
where dukes and duchesses rule, people fall in love and are married.
The world of the forest is a fantasy, a dream, a magic rite. Unaccount-
able changes take place in the forest, which is governed by magic, elves,
fairies, dreams, and nightmares. You could ask yourself what the relationship is between these two settings. What effect does one have on the
other, and how does the use of two contrasting settings contribute to
the overall meaning of the play?

Point of View

Another key element you can examine in an essay is the determination of the point of view in a literary work. The point of view is the vantage point from which the story is being told. It is similar to a camera lens through which you view the action before you. In a novel or short story it is not unusual for the point of view to shift. Sometimes the action will be reported by character A, other times it will be reported by character B. Two basic points of view to look for in a literary work are the *omniscient* point of view and the *personal* point of view. From an omniscient point of view, the narrator knows and reports anything and everything that is happening to any of the characters at any given time or place. In other words, the narrator knows everything that is happening to everyone. The omniscient point of view is usually told from the third person.

The personal point of view relies on eyewitness narration, using the first person ("I") to give a sense of immediacy. Here, the action reported is limited to only what the narrator (usually a character) directly observes or experiences. Remember that the two different kinds of point of view are often intermingled in a novel or short story. And again, you must try to relate the author's use of a particular point of view to the other basic elements of literary analysis to arrive at the overall meaning or theme of a given literary work.

Theme

The theme of a literary work is its main idea or basic meaning. Theme is not the same as subject. The subject of a novel may be life in the artist colony of Paris in the 1920s, but the theme may address itself to the despair and futility of life beyond the colony. The theme of a literary work is usually implicit; that is, it lies beneath the surface of the novel's action, setting, characterization, and point of view. But it is an indispensable part of the whole and should be discussed if the literary analysis is to be complete.

Comparison/Contrast

We have already mentioned writing reports and papers by using the device of comparison/contrast. In a literary essay, you should first limit the subject to something you can fit comfortably into a short paper. If you are asked to compare and contrast two writers, perhaps Robert Frost and William Butler Yeats, choose and analyze only one or two poems of each, preferably on the same or similar subjects. Make sure that your goals are clear, so that you will not fall into the trap of making broad unsupportable generalizations about the works of two writers.

If you are asked to compare and contrast two works by the same author, again limit the topic to one or two specific themes or ideas that occur in both works. You might also choose to compare two characters within a single novel, or two characters from different novels, or you might contrast the different ways in which two authors portray their characters. You could compare the ways two authors use the element of setting in their work, and you could also compare their uses of plot or of point of view. Again, the key is to think carefully about and specify the differences you are going to discuss, for example, the role of the daughter in William Yeats' "Prayer for My Daughter" and in Sylvia Plath's "Daddy."

You can compare and contrast any aspect of a literary work—imagery, figurative language, punctuation in poetry, tone, or style—with a similar aspect of another literary work, as long as you are able to gather and analyze the evidence for the comparison. And then, of course, you must express it all in clear writing.

STRUCTURE OF THE LITERARY ESSAY

When you write a literary essay, you should use the same principles of clarity and organization that you use in other forms of writing. A literary essay is an *essay*, after all. That means you should include (1) a clear thesis statement, (2) an organized group of paragraphs that supports your thesis, and (3) enough evidence from the text to support any claims you make.

Ideally, the literary essay should stand on its own and not depend on readers being intimately acquainted with the novel, story, or poem in question. You should provide enough information about the subject so that your presentation is self-contained. The reader should not have to refer to the work being discussed in order to understand your points or your textual evidence. There are really very few instances when a reader is totally familiar with a subject under discussion. A reader may never have seen the Grand Canyon, for instance, and still be able to "see" it in a good descriptive essay. A classmate of yours may never have read Fitzgerald's *The Great Gatsby* or Fielding's *Joseph Andrews* and yet find that an effective literary analysis brings these works to life. As a rule, it is much wiser to assume your audience *is not* familiar with a novel than to assume it is.

Before we discuss the structure of an effective literary essay, let us go over some of the basic guidelines for a successful presentation. Keep these in mind as you proceed through the prewriting and writing process:

1. *Avoid vague generalizations* that do not add anything to your specific interpretation of a literary work. Usually, such generalizations wander from the point. If you are analyzing a poem, discuss only that poem. Do not try to generalize about the nature of all poetry. If you are discussing a specific character in a novel, you should not wander off into vague discussions about the nature of mankind (unless you can prove from the text that the author intends this character to symbolize humanity).

2. *Use textual evidence* to support your thesis and any statements you make thereafter. Be sure that your evidence (be it a quotation, excerpt, or descriptive passage) supports a specific interpretive statement of yours. Furthermore, you have to explain what your evidence *proves*. You have to explain how it furthers your argument.

3. *Always introduce a quotation* before using it. Too often students just insert a quotation into the text of an essay without explaining why it is there, or even where it comes from. Do not be afraid to use specific references: "As Fielding notes in Chapter Two of *Joseph Andrews* . . ."

4. *Ask yourself* at every point in your essay if you are justified in saying what you are saying. "What do I mean?" "Does this quotation illuminate the point I am trying to make?" "Have I explained what my evidence demonstrates or proves?"

5. *Make sure* your thesis can be defended. If you do not find evidence in the text to support it, do not use it. Above all, do not defend an interpretation that the text contradicts.

6. *Your thesis should account* for all the important events and significant character developments in the book. Do not form a "page one" thesis that is true only up to page fifty, when the main character disavows suburbia and joins the radical underground.

7. Remember that *your personal opinion* of a literary work does not necessarily change its value. Not everyone can like every book, but you should not dismiss a well-known work without first asking yourself why so many other people like it, and why it has achieved such stature over the years. Probe a little deeper and you might like it much better. Or at least you might understand it more thoroughly.

A Note on Evidence

As we have noted throughout this chapter, a literary analysis is based on evidence: quotations, descriptive passages, imagery, dialogue, and the like. That is, it is based on words and phrases contained in the book—words and phrases that illustrate some point. You cannot consider "gut reactions" or personal opinions evidence. *They are not*. Rather, you select those portions of the text that support the thesis you have adopted as a result of reading the whole work.

The purpose of evidence is to support some idea you have about a book. In this sense, you are a literary detective, sifting through the text for strands of related information that will provide uniform evidence of your thesis. (Remember that real-life detectives use evidence only to prove something; evidence without a context is meaningless.)

Choosing a Title

The title of your essay should, of course, reflect the subject you are going to talk about. It should reveal something of the approach you intend to take. It should not, however, be so long and cumbersome that the reader expects a 50-page disquisition. Consider the following title:

An Analysis of *Moby Dick* Concentrating on Capt. Ahab's Relationship to the Whale and the Consequences of that Relationship.

The title is far too long. And it promises much more than the writer can possibly deliver in a medium-length essay. Not only does it tell us that the whole of *Moby Dick* will be anlayzed (a mammoth undertaking, as it encompasses every aspect of the novel!) but that the implications of Ahab's relationship to the whale will come under scrutiny.

A better title would narrow the focus to one literary aspect of Ahab's relationship to the whale, an aspect that can be discussed and supported with textual evidence:

Ahab and the Whale: The Imagery of Evil in *Moby Dick*.

We know from this title that the writer is going to confine himself to that imagery in *Moby Dick* which exemplifies the sinister characteristics of Ahab and the whale. Chances are that this essay would *not* include an analysis of plot, point of view, or the like unless it pertained directly to the imagery.

The title of an essay should always give some idea of what your approach will be. A heading such as *"The Red Badge of Courage,* by Stephen Crane" does not tell us anything. We know that *The Red Badge of Courage* was written by Stephen Crane, but we do not know what this writer is going to say about it. An effective title spells out, succinctly, what the essay will focus on:

The Red Badge of Courage: Heroism Redefined

From this title we can conclude that the essay will examine heroism from a different or nonconventional viewpoint, probably by focusing on the main *character*. In any case we know that the essay will not wander all over, incorporating details that have nothing to do with heroism. (For a further discussion of essay titles, see "Manuscript Format" under Principle 5 of Chapter 15, "The Conventions of Writing.")

The Opening Paragraph

The opening paragraph of your essay should elaborate on the implications of your title. Here you present your thesis statement and indicate, at least implicitly, what the structure of your essay will be.

Sometimes you will find it useful to make your thesis statement the first sentence of the opening paragraph, as in the following example:

Of the many thematic strains running through Ernest Hemingway's *The Old Man and the Sea,* perhaps the most fundamental is the idea that man can triumph over himself even as he appears to be defeated by Nature.

Immediately the reader knows that the essay is going to concentrate on "thematic strains" (or main ideas). Even someone who is not familiar with the novel—in which an old man, Santiago, battles to reverse his bad luck and regain his self-respect by catching a big fish—can tell from the thesis statement that the story is one of internal and external conflicts.

From here, the paragraph could refer to some of the major incidents of the story, demonstrating how they contribute to this main theme. In any case the paragraph would set the stage for a close chronological examination of the main ideas that Hemingway examines throughout the work—such as perseverance, determination, and eventual resignation to forces larger than yourself.

One benefit of stating your thesis right away is that it keeps you from wandering off the track or taking on more than you can handle. In the Hemingway example discussed above, there are no references to setting, tone, or mood. If these things *are* mentioned later on, they should serve a single purpose: to underscore the idea of man's ability to triumph over what he imagined were his own physical and spiritual limits.

Sticking to the Thesis

It is virtually impossible to stick to your thesis if you do not have one to begin with. In the following introductory paragraph (in which the sentences have been numbered for convenience), note how the writer waffles back and forth between ideas, contradicting himself at virtually every turn:

> (1) There are many poems in which the speaker chooses one particular subject to talk about. (2) But the speaker in T. S. Eliot's poem, "The Love Song of J. Alfred Prufrock," refers to people in general, as well as himself. (3) Yes, he speaks to himself about himself. (4) And the words that he symbolically expresses can pertain also to society. (5) "The Love Song of J. Alfred Prufrock" reveals the weak characteristics found in an individual who has been given a chance to speak out, but he fails to do so. (6) Such traits are in many ways typical of modern society. (7) But in T. S. Eliot's poem one especially looks at the flaws in a specific character.

This paragraph fails for a variety of reasons, not the least of which is its lack of a clear thesis statement. Clearly, this writer is unsure of what he wants to say, and the ensuing hodgepodge of contradictory statements makes it difficult to pinpoint what he even *means* to say.

Let us look at this introductory paragraph—sentence by sentence—and discuss each problem as it comes up:

Sentence One: "There are many poems in which the speaker chooses one particular subject to write about."

This naive statement takes obviousness to the extreme. Of course the speaker chooses something to write about. But by saying "many poems" have subjects, the writer inadvertently implies that *some* poems *do not* have subjects. Is this true? And, even if it is true, what does it mean in the context of Eliot's poem—a poem whose title alone describes a subject, namely, J. Alfred Prufrock?

Sentence Two: "But the speaker in T. S. Eliot's poem refers to people in general, as well as himself."

The word "but" is the problem here. It implies that this poem does not have a subject, while noting, in the same breath, that the poem refers to "people in general." Does this mean that "people in general" do not constitute a subject?

Sentence Three: "Yes, he speaks to himself about himself."

This sentence contradicts the previous one, where we were told that the poem deals with "people in general." It asserts the exact opposite of the statement just made!

Sentence Four: "And the words that he symbolically expresses can pertain also to society."

Here, the emphasis switches *back* to "people in general," even though Sentence Three says "he speaks to himself about himself." In just four sentences, the writer has mired himself in hopeless self-contradiction.

Sentences Five and Six: "The Love Song . . . reveals the weak characteristics found in an individual who has been given a chance to speak out, but fails to do so. Such traits are in many ways typical of modern society."

Here we see the first inkling of a topic sentence, but the writer ruins it by lapsing into vague generalities such as "weak characteristics," "in many ways typical," and so on. To compound the error, he makes a judgmental remark about society in general even though he has so far been utterly unable to distinguish it from the "himself" of the previous four sentences!

Sentence Seven: "But in T. S. Eliot's poem, one especially looks at the flaws of a specific character."

At this point one can only return, with a dumbfounded shake of the head, to Sentence Two, which explicitly states that the poem deals with "people in general."

The problems in this opening paragraph spring from one major cause: the lack of a clear thesis. If only the writer had probed himself adequately in the prewriting stage! If only he had defined his terms and settled on a point of view!

Note how the following student paragraph gets the essay off to a good start by sticking to the problem at hand, in this case an essay question asking whether Gulliver's negative assessment of mankind at the end of *Gulliver's Travels* is an accurate reflection of Jonathan Swift's own opinion:

> Lemuel Gulliver, the main character in Jonathan Swift's satire, *Gulliver's Travels,* is a reasonably well-educated, curious, patriotic, and truthful man who starts out innocent and as a lover of mankind. His attitude, however, changes through his experiences. After making four voyages "into several remote nations of the world," (title page) and encountering people of all shapes and sizes, physically and mentally, Gulliver comes to the conclusion that all human beings are like the vice-filled, repugnant Yahoos. The book as a whole, though, does not completely uphold Gulli-

ver's verdict. Although Swift partially agrees with Gulliver, as shown by the Lilliputians, pirates, Gulliver himself, and many other figures, Swift does believe that there are some truly good men, such as the Brobding-nagian king, whose example people can, and should, follow.

This is a unified, cohesive paragraph that answers the question while keeping the focus narrow. We can continue reading with a clear idea of where the essay will go, and what ground it will probably cover.

The first three sentences analyze the process that Gulliver goes through as he changes from a lover of mankind to a disillusioned specta-tor. (This analysis—aside from laying the groundwork for the thesis statement that is to come later in the paragraph—reviews the basic plot of the book for those whose memories of it may have dimmed.) Yet, be-cause the question asks for an assessment of *Swift's* attitude toward mankind, Sentence Four gives us a smooth transition from Gulliver's at-titudes to Swift's. And we are now prepared for the thesis statement that comes at the end of the paragraph: "*. . . Swift does believe that there are some truly good men . . .*" The writer has successfully distinguished between Gulliver's feelings as a character and Swift's feelings as an author—precisely what the question asked for.

Let us look at another introductory paragraph. Here the writer under-takes an analysis of the characters in Henry Fielding's *Joseph Andrews*—characters who serve as symbols for Fielding's view of the human condi-tion. The introduction sets us up for the more in-depth analysis that is to follow:

> Man's capacity for goodness and man's capacity for vanity and hy-pocrisy are explored in Henry Fielding's *Joseph Andrews,* a novel that at-tacks vices and takes a stand for moral reformation. The novel has three main characters: Parson Adams, Joeph Andrews, and Fanny. These three essentially embody the potential for good in man. Fielding also creates a series of minor characters, who, while never fully developed, serve to il-lustrate some rather unpleasant truths about mankind. In his descriptions of Lady Booby, the lawyers, and the parsons, Fielding exposes the foibles of human nature.

The above paragraph defines the area of major concern: the charac-ters in *Joseph Andrews* and what they represent on a larger scale. Already we see a deductive pattern of reasoning at work, in that the gen-eral nature of the opening paragraph indicates that more specifics are to follow: that is, specific analyses of certain characters in the book.

The Body of the Essay

The middle paragraphs of an essay provide support for the opening thesis. "Support," in this sense, can take the form of description, narration, or exposition to illuminate points in the text that support your interpretation. Here you will provide examples of *what you mean* when you say, for instance, that Fielding uses characters to make a point about human failings.

Because the middle paragraphs must bear the brunt of proving your thesis, they must be linked to each other clearly by transitional sentences and phrases that lead the reader logically from one point to the next. Each of the main body paragraphs should have an identifiable thesis statement and should, as far as possible, use the same pattern of argument as the overall pattern of the essay.

In the body paragraphs, try to focus tightly on the examples, illustrations, and references you have chosen from the work to illustrate your points. Whenever you make a statement about the work, back it up with something from the text that demonstrates it to be true.

Following is the body of the essay on "The Little People" in *Joseph Andrews*. The comments in the margin are there to provide an analysis of the strengths and weaknesses in the writer's development of the essay. Note that the whole essay is divided into two major sections: (I) a discussion of the characters of (a) Lady Booby, (b) the lawyers, and (c) the parsons, in order to develop a list of traits that characterize the "base part of human nature" and (II) an explanation of Fielding's purpose in developing the characters discussed in (I).

(Ia) A clear topic sentence, "Lady Booby exemplifies lust, dishonesty and hypocrisy," begins the paragraph. This general point must now be proved in the course of the essay.

Lady Booby is an aristocrat who exemplifies lust, dishonesty, and hypocrisy, She pretends to have respectability, while she is really lusting after Joseph in a way similar to that of the crass Slipslop, with only an added veneer of sophistication. Lady Booby even tries to use her social power to take advantage of Joseph. She thinks she is giving him a privilege by allowing him liberties, which he refuses to acknowledge.

> "How," says she, "do you think it would not disoblige me then? Do you think I would willingly suffer you?"–"I don't understand you, madam," says Joseph.–"Don't you?" said she, "then you either are a fool, or pretend to be so . . . " (page 23)

After all her attempts to seduce him have failed, her vanity and pride force her to turn Joseph out. Lady Booby is hypocritical, dishonest, and an altogether disagreeable character.

Slight digression from main flow of discussion. Why a separate paragraph just for Lady Booby's snobbery? The discourse on snobbery in the second paragraph slows the pace of the paper. Interrupts main flow. Subsequent paragraphs show a compact treatment of characters, though perhaps the discussion could have been more evenly distributed among them.

Lady Booby also epitomizes class snobbery. She is so vain and ignorant that she thinks she is above the commoners.

". . . and my lady was a woman of gaiety, who had been blest with a town-education, and never spoke of any of her country neighbors by any other appellation than that of "The Brutes." (page 18)

Use of quotation as evidence is effective here.

It is this belief that the higher the status the better the person, which not only Lady Booby and the aristocracy hold but which many others such as Slipslop and Mrs. Tow-wouse hold as well, that Fielding attacks.

This class snobbery is ridiculous because many worthy attributes such as charity, generosity, and courage are illustrated by poor people in the book. For example, it is one of the servants who lends Joseph a frock and breeches when he is fired by the callous and ungenerous Lady Booby.

(Ib) A good transition by means of summary. "Meanness" is rather vague, however.

Fielding not only attacks the class snobbery of the aristocracy; he also lashes out at the meanness of many lawyers. The first lawyer in the book, like his fellow travellers in the stagecoach, has no compassion for the suffering Joseph who has been beaten and robbed. The self-interested passengers want to leave Joseph to die.

Topic sentence

Example illustrating topic sentence.

But the lawyer, who was afraid of some mischief happening to himself if the wretch was left behind in that condition, saying no man could be too cautious in these matters [advises his fellow passengers to allow Joseph to come into the coach and to give him a ride to the next inn]. (page 43)

Interpretation of significance of example. Writer here provides a more precise definition of "meanness," which she has developed through use of an example; but she should have stated it at the beginning of the paragraph.

When the lawyer convinces the other people in the coach that they must rescue Joseph, he is only looking out for himself. Fielding is attacking the overcautiousness of lawyers and their selfishness.

(Ib) Discussion of the second lawyer moves from initial general assertion to discussion of examples and then back to general assertion of a more focused kind. Again "acts . . . despicably" is a bit vague. Use of these terms intended for connection with Ia (these were the traits characterizing Lady Booby), but they are somewhat inaccurate as a summary of the main points of Ib and should be supplemented with terms like "dishonesty," "un-scrupulousness," and "money-mindedness." Again, too, the writer should state these at *beginning* of paragraph and not force the reader to work up to the main point with her.

The second lawyer, Lawyer Scout, who isn't even Transition learned in the profession, acts equally despicably. When Lady Booby wants Joseph and Fanny to be sent away, Lawyer Scout trumps up a charge that would have them committed to Bridewell—with the help of the equally corrupt Justice Frolick. Joseph and Fanny are only saved by the interference of Squire Booby. Lawyer Scout bends the law for his own gains. He makes the law say what he wants to say. It's scoundrels like Scout and the lawyers in the stagecoach that give lawyers a bad name. Both of these men exhibit hypocrisy and snobbery: they cannot think of Joseph as a person with feelings because he belongs to the lower class and therefore cannot bring them material gains.

Writer refers to examples in order to emphasize the connection of her generalizations to the specifics on which they are based. But more specifics are needed.

(Ic) Parsons. Writer again begins with generalizations and then provides example.

Paragraph promises to discuss *several* parsons; at least one or two more should have been mentioned. Writer is starting to speed things up too much.

Another set of characters who demonstrate corruption and vice are the parsons that are interspersed throughout the book, with the exception, of course, of Parson Adams. All the other parsons are corrupt or incompetent: they tend to be ignorant, vain and ambitious. The most notable is the swinelike Parson Trulliber. Parson Trulliber is more of a merchant than a spiritual guide. He has plenty of money but refuses to lend any to Parson Adams. He is so miserly that when he offers Parson Adams a drink he "whisper(s) to his wife to draw a little of the worst ale" (page 138). Trulliber has a wonderful reputation for charity because the word "charity" is always in his mouth. However, he doesn't practice the charity he preaches. He is a true hypocrite.

Brief quotation to support this?

There are a host of other "wonderful" characters, (as well as a few truly generous people such as Betty, the postilion, and the pedlar). There's the miserly Peter Pounce, the "brave" man who runs at the first sign of danger, little, slimy Beau Didapper, crass Mrs. Slipslop, the spoiled country squire, and others. All of these characters are typical of the ugly portion of human nature. They are in sharp contrast to Joseph, Parson Adams, and Fanny who are brave, innocent, and honorable, and whose example we should follow.

For completeness' sake, the writer makes a list of the minor characters she doesn't really discuss and then focuses on a restatement of the contrast between examples and counter-examples which she finds in Joseph Andrews *and with which she began.*

Fielding also shows us how it's possible for a man to reform morally. Early in his life, without guidance, Mr. Wilson is ignorant and indulges in vanity and the pursuit of pleasure. He succumbs to many vices and squanders his inheritance until he ends up in a state of destitution and despair in debtor's prison. Fortunately, he's rescued by the charity of his future wife. Wilson learns from his experiences and adopts a way of life of simplicity and love for his family and friends. Fielding believes that men have the ability to reform if they see the ugliness of their faults.

Topic sentence

Illustration

(II) This paragraph might have been supported with a quotation, or statements more specific than these. Writer is hurrying too quickly toward conclusion—this is skimpy.

Good. Explains Fielding's purpose for the inclusion of Mr. Wilson.

Fielding has a clear purpose for creating these minor figures which he reveals to the reader:

> I declare here, once for all, I describe not men, but manners; not an individual, but a species . . . (page 159)

In this paragraph the writer shows how the points made in the preceding discussion fit into Fielding's view of mankind and into his satirical purposes.

Fielding is not condemning particular individuals, but rather the vices that are typical of people.

> . . . as in most of our particular characters we mean not to lash individuals, but all of the like sort, so, in our general descriptions, we mean not universals, but would be understood with many exceptions . . . (page 160)

In addition, even though Fielding tends to attack certain groups or classes of people, he does not intend his attack to apply to their numbers without exception.

Paragraph needs a further reference to Mr. Wilson, as he is the one who reforms.

That is, Fielding is giving his message of reformation to those people who can identify in themselves the vices of these characters. It is not meant as a universal condemnation of mankind. Fielding does realize that not all parsons are corrupt, not all the aristocracy are vain and cruel, etc. But those who fit the mold must reform.

The Conclusion

The conclusion of an essay, like its beginning, carries a great deal of natural emphasis. Take advantage of that and provide a strong ending. Make it more than just a summary of what you have already said; use it to present a genuine concluding point of your own. One way might be to express some implications of your thesis beyond the immediate context of the work. Often, writers use concluding paragraphs to speculate on the future in light of the past, as in the following example from a paper on Congreve's *Way of the World:*

> Thus Mirabell and Millamant, in contrast to the others in the play, *will* base their union on reason and mutual regard for each other's rights. But in a relationship like marriage can reason and respect play the roles these two assign to them? Have they perhaps forgotten—or not yet learned— that the heart has its reasons that reason knows not of? Their attempt is valiant—even noble. But most of us know that married life is not necessarily governed by what is valiant and noble. Is this what they both must learn—of the way of the world?

Note how the writer concludes his essay by enlarging the context of Mirabell and Millamant's marriage to include "married life" as we know it. Will they succeed?

Another way of enlarging the scope of your conclusion is to extend what you have said to similar works or other works by the same author or even to other art forms or other kinds of experience. But be careful of making vague statements about works or authors you are not thoroughly familiar with. All young writers of fiction are cautioned over and over again to "write about what they know." This admonition should not be lost on the literary essayist.

Following is the concluding statement from the paper on *Joseph Andrews.* Do you feel that it is a good and strong conclusion? Given the foregoing essay, how would you have concluded the piece?

Conclusion is essentially summary, yet it is sketchy and vague.

Fielding has created these minor characters to be essential symbols of truth. Through these figures he wishes to reveal all our "shamming." Fielding is concerned with the discrepancy between what we pretend to be and what we are as human beings. By bringing people face to face with the truth he hopes for moral reformation.

DOCUMENTING THE ESSAY

Documentation is not a form of torture invented by wicked English teachers to bedevil innocent students. It is a method by which a reader can see exactly where a quotation occurs in a work. The point of identifying quotes is ostensibly to allow the reader to check out the writer's statements for accuracy. In addition, documentation serves to focus the writer's mind. If a writer shows his statements and references can be checked, he will usually exercise care in what he says; without documentation, no such care would have to be exercised.

Footnotes

A footnote is a note of reference placed below or after the text of a printed page. It tells a reader where a quoted passage comes from. Often, instructors allow a fairly informal method of footnoting in-class assignments, but you should check with your instructor on the style of documentation he or she wants. Generally, when you first quote from the text under discussion, you should provide, in a footnote, information about the text or anthology you are using. The information required should be listed in the following order: author's name, first name and initial (if any) first; name of the story or poem (in quotations) or name of the book (underlined); the edition of the book, if any (e.g., Second Edition), the name or names of the editors, if any (for anthologies mostly); in parentheses the name of the city where the book was published (followed by a colon), the name of the publisher, and the date of publication (all this can be found on a book's title page and copyright pages); and finally the page number on which the quotation is found. The first line of a footnote takes a regular paragraph indention.

[1]Henry Fielding, *Joseph Andrews*, ed. A. R. Humphreys, (London: Everyman's Library, 1973), p. 18. All page numbers in parentheses refer to this edition.

The last sentence in this footnote is used in informal documentation to allow you to include page references in the text of your essay directly under the quotation without having to cite the source again.

MAGAZINE ARTICLES.   In quoting from a magazine article, the footnote information is as follows: author's name, first name and initial first, title of the article (in quotes), name of the magazine (underlined), the magazine's volume number in Roman numerals, the month (if given) and year of publication (within parentheses), and the page number or numbers.

The matter of footnotes can be complicated, so, to be on the safe side, check with your instructor as to the style he or she wants and follow it. (For instructions on the placement and spacing of footnotes in a formal paper, see "Manuscript Format" in Chapter 15, "The Conventions of Writing.")

Quotations in the Text

LONG QUOTATIONS.   When you are incorporating a fairly extensive quotation (more than three lines), set the quotation off by indenting it and single spacing it. After the quotation, footnote it or put the page number from which it is taken. Do not use quotation marks.

SHORT QUOTATIONS.   If you are incorporating a short prose quotation, make it part of your own text but set it off by quotation marks. The period in this instance follows the parenthetical page number, which is set outside the quotation marks.

When the quotation is part of your own text, the parenthetical page reference goes before the terminal punctuation mark. If, however, the quotation ends with an exclamation mark or a question mark, you include the marks of punctuation directly after the quotation and place a period or comma after the parenthetical page reference.

QUOTING VERSE OR VERSE DRAMA.   In quoting more than three lines of poetry or verse drama, set the lines off by themselves, indenting and single spacing with each line of verse, which would appear just as printed. Following the quotation, put the act, scene, and line number (in parentheses) for quoted material from a drama.

QUOTING BOOK-LENGTH POEMS.   For a longer poem, divided into books, or cantos, or stanzas, include this information with the line reference. For example, (*Inferno*, Canto XV, line 49) refers to Dante's *Divine Comedy*, the Inferno (Hell) Canto XV, line 49. In drama, (I. iii. 17) refers to Act I, scene three, line 17 of a play such as *Hamlet*. When you are quoting *three lines or fewer of verse*, include them in your own text and separate the printed lines by slash marks. If the quotation is in first person or in dialogue from a play or a novel and you are discussing the character speaking in the third person, you do not have to change pronouns.

Your paper is going to be easier to read if you can reduce long cumbersome block quotations to key phrases that can be woven into the structure of your sentence. This kind of reduction also emphasizes what you think is important in the quotation, and it makes your task of interpreting evidence easier.

CAPITALIZATION.   You may capitalize the first word of the quotation even if it is not capitalized in the text, if that first word begins your sentence. You can switch to lower case if the passage quoted does not begin your own sentence, but does begin a sentence in the text. Similarly, you may switch the end punctuation of the quoted passage to make it fit the punctuation of your own sentence.

TENSE AGREEMENT WHEN QUOTING.   You do not have to change tenses if you are using the present tense in the first part of your sentence, and then bring in a short quotation which is in the past tense. In other cases, you should follow the quotation exactly as it appears.

AUTHOR EMPHASIS.   If you want to emphasize a specific word in a quotation, underline it and indicate in brackets after the quotation that it is *your* emphasis and not that of the work's author. Use this device sparingly. If your typewriter does not have brackets, put them in by hand; remember not to confuse brackets with parentheses.

PRONOUN REFERENCE.   If the referent of a pronoun in a quotation is not clear, include in brackets the name or noun to which the pronoun refers. "Then he [Harold] changes his tactics . . ." If the context of the discussion makes the referent clear, do not include the name or noun.

QUOTING DIALOGUE.   When you quote dialogue, you do not need to keep using some varient of "she says." Use a comma or a colon. Avoid ending any paragraph with a quotation. Instead, explain its significance and show how it is an example of what you are discussing. If revising a paragraph, you may have to rearrange the order of the sentence in order to make the quotation the first step in the paragraph development rather than the conclusion. But the emphasis, paragraph by paragraph, should always be on your thought and your content, not upon stringing the quotations together.

WRITING ABOUT FILM

In earlier times, they were called "the movies" as in, "I went to the movies last night." Today, we refer to "film," and we are serious about it as an art form. The question "What did you think of Francis Ford Coppola's latest film?" obviously demands a more serious answer than, "How'd you like the picture?"

A common temptation is to write about film as one would write about drama. Although they have much in common, film and live drama are remarkably different in that drama relies upon the interplay between a live audience and live actors, while movies do not. With movies, only one side of the equation is live—the audience. And the composition, size, and reaction of the audience is not a factor in the effectiveness of the picture.

This difference leads to a difference in approach when writing about a film. While it is still important to analyze and write about the plot, character, and setting of a film, other aspects of a filmmaker's technique must also be considered. The visual and auditory aspects of a film dominate a viewer's impressions of it and constitute the bulk of what is written about it. Thus, writing about film involves a greater analysis of the techniques and effects which are singular to its form.

You might have noticed that a film is usually accredited to the director, that is, Stephen Spielberg's *Jaws*, William Friedkin's *The Exorcist*, John Huston's *The Treasure of the Sierra Madre*, Alfred Hitchcock's *Psycho*. The total impact of the film, its sequence of events, its camera angles, and its visual and aural details are all the result of the director's decisions. The director is sometimes spoken of as the "author" of the film.

So when you write about a film, you must be sensitive—in addition to the dialogue, the events, and the characters—to the way in which techniques are used to hold together the fast-paced action of an entire film. The plot and character development in *Star Wars* may not warrant a great deal of attention, but the imaginative use of its many special effects does. The flow of images across the screen very often takes precedence over what any of the individual scenes or performances might mean.

When writing about film, then, you may use the elements of analysis pertinent to literary forms (plot, character, setting, point of view, and comparison/contrast) but remember to relate these to the singular techniques of the film. Plot and character development may be more related to changes in color, lighting, and camera angle than to dialogue.

Much of a film's effectiveness is nonliterary. Few, very few, scenarios make good—or even decent—reading. Therefore, you must take film on its own grounds—as a visual and auditory experience.

Guidelines for Film Analysis

Only a very narrow-minded person would evaluate or analyze every film the same way. For one thing, not every film is trying to elicit the same response. Some want to make you laugh. Others want to challenge your perception of contemporary values. Still others want to overwhelm you with special effects. And there are always those films that try to do all of these things simultaneously, and more. When you see a film, you should ask yourself three basic questions:

1. What kind of film is this? (Drama, western, comedy, etc.)
2. What is it trying to accomplish?
3. How well does it succeed in accomplishing what it is trying to accomplish?

In other words, if you know you are watching a low-budgt comedy whose only aim is to make you laugh, do not judge it according to the sophisticated cinematic techniques you may have seen in other films. A low-budget comedy is not *intended* to demonstrate sophisticated techniques, any more than a serious film like Bergman's "Scenes from a Marriage" is intended to provoke gales of laughter.

The first rule of analysis, then, is to *classify* what you are looking at—to put it in the group it belongs in and evaluate it only according to the standards of that group. If a western is "bad," it is bad compared to other westerns, not compared to British drawing-room comedies where the actors all wear smoking jackets and nibble canapés.

The second rule is no less important in the process of analyzing a film. Having consigned it to its proper category, you now ask yourself what it is trying to accomplish. Suppose, in the middle of an urban drama depicting the life of a disaffected policeman, you suddenly start to feel that the director is relying too heavily on violent scenes and imagery. The thing to do at this point is ask yourself why. What point is being made? Is the director really being excessive, or is he simply trying to blast us out of our complacency by showing us a reality we may never have seen before?

The third rule is where the real work of analysis comes in. Here you ask yourself "How well does the film succeed in doing what it is trying to do?" At this point in your analysis you have to judge the end product in light of the two previous steps. But suppose you have properly classified a film as a rural drama set in 1930s Idaho, and have correctly ascertained that it is trying to make a satiric point about rural values, and *still* feel it fails as a film. If that is the case, your job is to use evidence from the film (dialogue, storyline, individual performance, etc.) to prove your point—just as you do when analyzing the merits of a particular book.

The above guidelines deal more with the theoretical aspects of film analysis. Now let us consider its practical aspects. There are some special guidelines for this kind of writing, which are as follows:

1. Do not waste time rehashing the entire plot. If possible, use only one or two sentences to do this. Calling a film "a rural drama set in 1930s Idaho" usually gives the reader an adequate frame of reference with which to understand the rest of the analysis. The purpose of analysis, after all, is to discuss a film's component parts. Plot is only one part.
2. Identify each character you speak about (with the actor's name next to it in parentheses). Remember, some of your readers will not have seen the film. State who the characters are, what function they serve, and how they relate to the other characters.
3. Be as concrete and descriptive as possible when referring to setting, lighting, cinematography, and other visual techniques. For readers who have not seen the film, you are the only camera.
4. Try to avoid hackneyed expressions such as "wonderful," "brilliant," and "masterful." They carry no more weight in a film analysis than they do in any other kind of essay. Remember, no matter how overwhelmed you may have been by a film, general words will not reproduce the experience for readers.

Whether you are writing about literature or film, your primary purpose is to aid understanding—to add another dimension to a work by focusing on some important aspect of it. Readers and viewers consult written analyses to broaden their own knowledge, just as tourists seek out guides to explain the significance of historical artifacts. Sometimes, to be sure, we can tell that a particular book is worthy of our time and attention, but we do not always know why. The job of the literary essayist, in short, is to confirm a worth that readers may only have sensed.

EXERCISES

1. Writing About Literature

a). Choose a photograph of an "unforgettable character" from a magazine or newspaper, a family collection, a library or historical society collection (something that has a story in it like the "Iowa Homesteader's Wife" in Chapter 1.) This person will be the main character of a series of literary exercises to get you acquainted with the tools a writer needs to write and a reader needs to understand and appreciate.

b). Character: 1. Spend ten minutes writing a description of the character. Begin with as much sensory detail as possible. 2. Then, analyze the photograph to judge the comment being made by the photographer. Use this to provide description and details of the person's character. 3. Finally, identify important information about the character's life: name, place of birth, etc.

c). Plot: 1. Identify the most significant events in the life of this character. 2. Decide at what point the character is when the "story" begins. 3. Given what you know about the character, come up with as many possible situations he or she might encounter. Think about the possibilities and choose one. 4. Generate as many possible events as you can. 5. Sketch out the structure of the story.

d). To develop the theme for your story, choose one of the character's most important traits: greed, sternness, loyalty. Determine how this theme can be worked out and illustrated through the plot.

e). Setting: Choose two main scenes from the story. Determine details of setting: place, time, mood, environment, dress, etc.

f). Using the information you have generated, write a story or poem about the character.

2. Thesis Statements

a). Rewrite the following theses so they are clear and precise, make assertions that must be defended, and achieve the level of generalization that can be successfully defended in a 3–5 page paper.

1. In Katherine Anne Porter's, *The Old Order,* a grandmother manipulates her sons, including the selection of their wives, until they are no longer a family unit.
2. In *Pride and Prejudice,* Jane Austen uses a variety of devices, some subtle and some blatant, to instill three attitudes toward marriage in the reader's mind.

b). Make up six titles for papers analyzing fiction and poetry with which you are familiar.

c). Write three introductory paragraphs for the same paper which introduce the thesis in different places: beginning, middle, and end. Use strategies discussed in class and in Chapter 4 to make each paragraph effective.

d). Take the story exercise you did earlier. Identify ten pieces of evidence from the characterization, plot, setting, and theme that could be used to support a thesis about the character. Write a thesis. Follow with three middle paragraphs that support the thesis. Use as much evidence as is logically possible and develop it by using techniques discussed in Chapter 4.

e). Using the same material, write three different conclusions to an essay:

one that restates the thesis
one that speaks of the larger implications
one that extends your conclusion to other works by the author, to other art forms, or to other kinds of experience.

3. Developing Papers from Theses

a). Examine the following topics. Rate them on a scale of 1 to 5—1 being very narrow and specific and 5 being broad and open. Discuss the clues each assignment gives about the nature of the analysis that the teacher requires.

1. Analyze the character of Elizabeth Bennet in Austen's *Pride and Prejudice,* focusing on the important ways in which she matures. In your analysis, include a discussion of Elizabeth's sister Jane and her friend Charlotte; show how they are used to illuminate Elizabeth's development.
2. Analyze the ways Flaubert uses setting in *Madame Bovary* to accentuate Emma's restlessness and dissatisfaction with her world.
3. Compare and contrast Lambert Shether and Chad Newsome, characters in Henry James's *The Ambassadors.*
4. Trace Mark Twain's use of the river as a symbol in *Huckleberry Finn.*

b). Once you have analyzed the topics listed above, discuss the different ways in which papers can be written on them.

c). Analyze the following titles of student papers. What are their strengths and weaknesses? How can they be improved?
1. The Effect of the Past on Child-Rearing.
2. Fowles' Use of Structure
3. The Psychological and Physical World of Madame Bovary's Fantasy World.
4. Herman Melville's Billy Budd and "Bartleby the Scrivener": An Analysis of Character

d). Analyze the following student example of an opening paragraph to determine its strengths and weaknesses and to decide how it can be revised. Rewrite the paragraph.

Ralph Waldo Emerson believes that man has the ability and knowledge to strive for a higher spiritual plateau. In concordance with the theme of Transcendentalism, Emerson feels that an understanding of reality is attained through the sensual perception of nature. The perceived objects are symbolic of a higher order. That higher order, represented by nature, is comprised of all entities of the spiritual universe. Through his use of descriptive language, Emerson, in his poem "The River," is able to produce creative images which convey his idea that there exists a strong relationship between nature and the individual.

e). Analyze the following middle paragraphs. Underline the *topic sentence* in each one and identify the *strategies* (description, quotation, comparison/contrast, definition, etc.) used in each to develop and buttress the point being used to support a thesis. After analyzing these paragraphs, make a judgment—which is the best paper? Why?

Jake Barnes is a good example of what an idealistic young American could lose in the "Great War" that might cause him to become disillusioned and therefore a member of "the lost generation." He lost not only what idealistic attitudes he may have held before the war, but in addition to that, the war made him impotent. He lost all that one could possibly lose without losing his life. He looks back with a bit of sarcasm at what the colonel said about his loss. "You . . . have given more than your life." (page 31). His desire to escape can be easily understood. He escaped to France with his fellow "lost" companions, like Brett and Mike. Their lives are not those of working for social change, but for escape. ("The Dingo. That's a great place isn't it?" "Yes. That or the new dive, The Select.") (page 36). Jake loses himself in these "dives" with his friends. He drinks, dances, jokes and gets drunk.

Catherine doesn't yet know whom to trust, but she's capable of learning through her experiences, and this is basic to her maturing. After the second trip Catherine decides that she doesn't like John, even though he is her beloved brother's friend and Isabella's brother. Then, when Catherine finds out what she's missed and that she's displayed bad manners, this information reinforces the lesson she's learning. That lesson is that she must trust her own judgments when she believes she is right.

Catherine has indeed learned her lesson by the time Isabella, James and John propose a third trip. Catherine has just made a commitment to go for a walk with the Tilney's while the three young people have decided to go on a day trip. When they inform Catherine of their plans, she refuses to go. They try every argument possible to dissuade her from taking her walk with the Tilney's, but she is adamant and won't break her engagement a second time. This is a sign of Catherine's maturity. Her lack of firmness has changed. She now sticks to what she thinks she should do, and she has an independence of mind.

f). Analyze the following concluding paragraphs. Identify the strategy used in each. Determine strengths and weaknesses. Rewrite each of the conclusions.

The belief that the world lacked order was held by many members of the lost generation. For them life was a random sequence of events, all equally important, all without meaning. Hemingway shows the random sequence by using that theory as the basis for his plot. The book is mostly chronological; however, the lack of order within that scheme is apparent. The characters drift from bar to bar, from Spain to France, from Madrid to San Sebastian, etc., with no goal or purpose in mind. One must, as Jake says, "Cruise around . . . and see what happens to you." Because the reader is deprived of the standard climax—resolution plot, he is frustrated. This repeated frustration leads to anger, tension, hopelessness, until finally the reader attains the absurdist attitude toward the book itself. Once again, the reader is experiencing the emotions of the lost generation.

"Batter My Heart" is a personal poem involving the speaker and

God. It is religious in nature and demonstrates Donne's love for God and his faith in Him. Donne is setting an example for others. Even though he has sinned he still believes that with God's help he can change and return to the Christian fold. Donne has enough faith in God to believe that he can be saved.

4. Formal Papers

a). Using any of the strategies discussed, write an essay on a piece of literature you have already read.

b). Consulting with your instructor, design a topic pertinent to the literature course you are now taking. Write an essay on that topic.

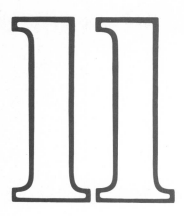

The Library Research Paper

Paper Required:
The Nature of the Quest
What a Research Paper Is
Ideas for the Paper
Brainstorming for Ideas

The Library
Coming Prepared
Using the Card Catalog
Making Bibliography Cards
On the Trail:
One Thing Leads to Another

Taking Notes:
The Raw Material of Your Paper
Integrity
Note Cards
Culling the Sources
Types of Notes

Crediting Your Sources
MLA Footnote Style
Sample Footnotes
MLA Bibliography Style
Crediting Sources in the
Social and Natural Sciences

Building the Paper

Writing and Revising the Paper

Sample Library Research Paper

Reference Sources
General Reference Sources
Specialized Reference Books,
Encyclopedias, Indexes

Exercises

Patience and Fortitude are the names of the famous lion statues that flank the steps of the New York Public Library. Every day of the school year, hundreds of college students negotiate the path between Patience and Fortitude on their way to work on assigned library research papers.

Some of the students stride purposefully and quickly up the steps, with an air of knowing where they are going and what they are about. A much larger number, however, look as though they have been sent out on a long journey to perform some poorly understood task. They approach the lions hesitantly, as if they were entering enemy territory, and they wander rather than walk through the great doors of the library.

If you recognize yourself in the first group of students described, this chapter will provide you with valuable information that you can add to your already well-stocked store of skills. If, on the other hand, you feel closer to the second group, this chapter will explain to you the nature of the quest and the methods you can use to complete it successfully.

PAPER REQUIRED: THE NATURE OF THE QUEST

On the first day of your psychology class, the instructor announces that there will be occasional quizzes, a midterm and a final exam, and a short term paper ("not too long—about 10 pages or so, with documentation; certainly no more than 20 pages"). Ever since then, you have wondered where you could ever find anything to write so much about. And what is *documentation?*

What a Research Paper Is

The assignment of a research paper will vary from course to course. Often, you will be given a general topic, which you must first narrow down to manageable proportions. Sometimes not even a general topic will be suggested. In either case, you must research the field for data on the subject about which you have decided to write. After collecting the information, which neither you nor your instructor may be at all familiar with as yet, you must organize it so that it is understandable to you and to anyone reading your paper. Finally, you must make some kind of statement about the data you have collected.

The greatest trouble most students have with research papers is not being sure what the paper is going to be about when they begin it. This, however, is no cause for alarm. The paper would not be research if you knew all answers beforehand—it would be a report. Of course, not knowing where the paper will take you or ultimately what it will say is worrisome—but it is also exciting.

Ideas for the Paper

When topics for research papers are assigned, they are generally broad and all-encompassing. They are designed that way to allow students the widest latitude in choosing what particular aspect of the topic they want to focus on. It is a rare occurrence for the subject of a research paper to be left entirely up to the student, and even if topics can be suggested by the students themselves, they will have to have some connection with the course.

When the time to begin work on the paper arrives, you should already have been thinking, as you read the text and completed other assignments for the course, about which areas you have covered would make possible topics for a research paper. You will almost always be told at the beginning of a course that a paper will be required. Be sensitive, then, to any aspects of the course that particularly interest you or pique your curiosity. Write them down, along with any comments the professor may make in his lectures or anything you may read in the newspapers or magazines or see on television that touches upon a topic you find interesting.

When you begin selecting a topic in earnest, refer to these notes and try to use them as the basis for a possible paper. You should also refer to Chapter 1 of this book and go over the invention techniques of brainstorming and probing to aid in shaping a topic for your paper.

Brainstorming for Ideas

Let us assume that your psychology class has been dealing with forms of operant conditioning—that is, changing an animal's behavior by rewarding it when it does what you want. The work you have studied has been done on mice, and there is much talk as to whether human behavior can be changed in the same way as mouse behavior can, with the same kind of reward mechanism. The term paper is to be a research paper on some aspect of animal behavior-modification. That is all you have to go on. How might you attack such a problem?

Suppose we take a typical student in your class who is a math major. She is a no-nonsense sort, eager to get ahead. She is also very interested in data processing and owns a small personal computer. How would such a student narrow down the term-paper topic to something she could handle? She can begin by brainstorming.

Let's see, some aspect of animal behavior modification. What have we done this year? Run a bunch of mice around. Do the mice really learn anything? Doubt it. Is their behavior modified? Seems so, but can't really tell. They do things they wouldn't do ordinarily. What does behavior modification mean? Are the mice really changed? Do animals change? Do humans change? Or do we all just survive? One way or another. Maybe a paper that says mice don't change, they survive? What do the mice think of the experiments? What would they say if they could talk? Crazy humans running us around like this. Paper on the mouse's-eye view of the experiment?

"Actually, I read in the newspaper last week that some people were teaching an ape—a chimpanzee—to communicate with language. Sign language, I think. Didn't read the article, only remember the headline. Porpoises, too. Program on TV about the language of porpoises. Check into teaching language to an animal. Maybe it's like learning a machine language. I know about that. That's behavior modification if the thing exists at all.

At this point, the student has a vague idea of a topic that might fill the bill. It combines a personal interest with the general subject of the paper. It is not much to go on yet, but the idea has some intriguing possibilities, which is all a student needs to begin narrowing the topic down.

This is an example of the kind of thinking you must do to arrive at a topic. It may take you several days, or even weeks, to come up with a topic. You may want to consult with the instructor about ideas that you feel might work. The point is to keep brainstorming and probing, using the work you have been doing in class and your notes as starting points. Think of anything you have read or seen on television that might be of help. It is a good idea to get into the habit of reading a good daily newspaper and at least one general weekly magazine.

After brainstorming and probing for awhile, you will get an idea for the paper, but you may not get as far as a specific topic title. It is very possible, however, to research the germ of an idea so that it can be crystallized and turned into a useful working title.

For instance, our example of the student considering a paper on teaching language to animals is one of those cases where research is needed just to nail down the topic title. "Teaching Language to Animals" is far too broad a category to serve as a topic for a paper. "Animal Language" is even worse. There is a good idea here that needs to be narrowed down, and this can only be done by investigating what is available in the field and choosing from that some specific aspect of the whole to write about. We said that the student remembered seeing something on teaching a language to monkeys in last week's newspaper. That means a trip to the library.

THE LIBRARY

Begin work at the library with two things in mind. The first is that the library is set up to make your search for information relatively easy.

This may not be obvious right away, but sooner or later you will see it. The second thing to keep in mind is that one of the key resources of any library is its staff. Never hesitate to ask a librarian for help.

Coming Prepared

One practical note: when you go to the library, take a notebook and some pens or pencils with you. You are going to be taking notes, jotting down references to other books and periodicals, and excerpting quotations that strike you as potentially valuable. Some people use 3 × 5 and 4 × 6 index cards for this purpose; these cards are useful and easy to manipulate. Or you might want to use a legal-sized pad. In any case, bring some writing materials.

You should not walk into the library and ask the librarian, "What have you got on animal behavior?" The topic is so broad that the librarian could only refer you to some general reference work, like an encyclopedia. That is why you should take time first to develop some ideas so that you will have at least one or two specific questions to ask the library staff at the outset. The more specific your questions, the more specific their answers—and the more helpful.

Our math student has put together two questions for the library staff to start her off on researching her paper.

1. "How can I locate an article I saw in last week's *Times* about teaching a language to monkeys?"
2. "Where should I look for other materials on attempts to teach languages to animals?"

In all likelihood, the library would have copies of last week's *New York Times* readily available. If the student had wanted an article that had appeared several months ago, she would be referred to *The New York Times Index*, where she could locate the date and page number of any article she thought was interesting. The material itself would probably be on microfilm, which is put into a reader and viewed on a screen somewhat similar to a TV screen.

In answer to the second question, the staff would refer the student to some general reference books such as *The Reader's Guide to Periodical Literature* and to general and/or specialized encyclopedias (page 272). These materials would tell her what has been published recently in the field she is interested in, who has done it, and what it is about. With at least one fairly specific reference to look up and some general reference sources to consult, she has a good start on finding sources for the text of her paper.

At this initial stage, it is important that you, as a researcher, note down as many places to look, authors to examine, and articles to find as you can. In the beginning of a research project, it is best to cast your net very wide. Later, as you read the literature on the subject and become familiar with it, you will be able to exclude many sources because you will know that they do not deal with what you need.

For instance, our math student, after reading the article in the *Times*, becomes intrigued with the way experiments were devised to demonstrate that apes could be taught a language—to use to communicate with humans. She decides on this topic for her psychology paper. After consulting the *Times*, she arrives at a working title: "Experiments in Teaching Language to Apes." Armed with this title, she is ready to begin the real research for her paper.

Using the Card Catalog

Your first exposure to finding books in the library will involve using the library's card catalog. This can be intimidating even in a small library. In a major one, it appears overwhelming—the card cabinets stretch out for what seem to be miles. Nevertheless, for all its size, the card catalog is basically easy to use, and it is indispensable.

The card catalog contains an alphabetical listing of every book the library has available. Each card contains the name of one book only. Each book has at least three cards: an *author card*, a *title card*, and one or more *subject cards*.

AUTHOR CARDS.   Author cards are filed alphabetically under the author's last name (*Linden, Eugene*). If a writer has more than one book in the library, the author cards are arranged, under his or her name, alphabetically by title.

TITLE CARDS.   Title cards appear alphabetically under the first word in the title, except for *The*, *A*, and *An*. In our example, you would find the card under the word *apes*. (The title card for the book *The Yearling*, though, would go under *Y* because *The*, as the first word in the title, is not counted in alphabetizing.)

SUBJECT CARDS.   A subject card has a typed or printed line across its top that briefly identifies what the book is about. Subject cards are arranged alphabetically by the first word of the heading.

The card catalog thus provides a three-way access to a book. You can use the card catalog to find out if your library owns a book whose *title* you know (look for the *title card*). Or, if you know the name of an author who has written on your topic, look under his or her name on an *author card*. Finally, you can go to the card catalog even if you have in mind only a topic. If you are hunting for books by topic, look in the

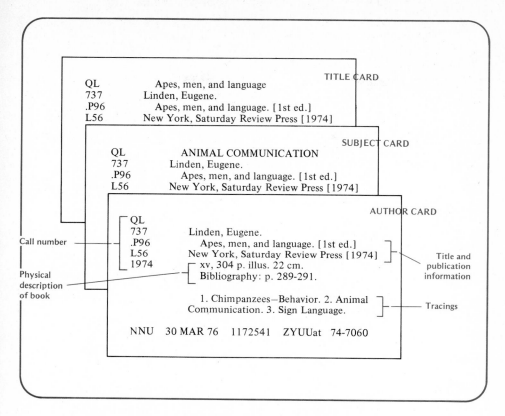

TITLE CARD

QL   Apes, men, and language
737   Linden, Eugene.
.P96   Apes, men, and language. [1st ed.]
L56   New York, Saturday Review Press [1974]

SUBJECT CARD

QL   ANIMAL COMMUNICATION
737   Linden, Eugene.
.P96   Apes, men, and language. [1st ed.]
L56   New York, Saturday Review Press [1974]

AUTHOR CARD

Call number

Physical
description
of book

QL
737
.P96   Linden, Eugene.
L56   Apes, men, and language. [1st ed.]
1974   New York, Saturday Review Press [1974]
                 xv, 304 p. illus. 22 cm.
                 Bibliography: p. 289-291.

                 1. Chimpanzees—Behavior. 2. Animal
              Communication. 3. Sign Language.

NNU   30 MAR 76   1172541   ZYUUat 74-7060

Title and
publication
information

Tracings

catalog for *subject cards* that your topic might be listed under, such as
"animal language," "communication with animals," and the like.

Catalog cards are easily understood if you take a few minutes to learn
how they are set up. See the sample cards above and the explanations
that follow.

Call Number.   The vital link between a catalog card and the book itself
is the call number, which appears in the upper-left-hand corner of all
three types of cards *and* on the spine of the book. The call number tells
you where on the shelves the book is located. Most libraries give a call
number to a book according to one of two *systems of classification.* The
Dewey Decimal system groups books according to ten major areas of
knowledge. The second, and newer, system is the *Library of Congress
system,* which is based on 20 major fields of study. The call number on
the sample cards is from the Library of Congress classification.

Author.   The author's name appears—last name first. It is sometimes
followed by the author's year of birth (and death if the author is
deceased).

Title and Publication Information. In our sample, a note following the title shows that this is the first edition of the book. The next line tells us that the book was published in 1974 by Saturday Review Press, which is located in New York.

Physical Description of Book. This entry provides some data on the book that may be useful to you. It notes, in this instance, that the book contains 15 pages of prefatory material or front matter and 304 pages of text. The book contains illustrations and is 22 centimeters high. Pages 289–291 are devoted to a bibliography.

Tracings. This is a listing of all subject headings under which the book in question can be found in the card catalog. In this case, the book can be found under three different subject headings.

It is important to note that with the advent of computerized filing systems, many libraries are phasing out their card catalogs and using book catalogs instead. *Book catalogs* are soft-cover books that are similar in appearance to telephone directories. The book catalogs are arranged the same way as the old card catalogs—three separate books, usually each of a different color, for author, title, and subject entries.

Making Bibliography Cards

Up until now, we have been talking about ways to locate the titles and the names of authors of books and articles you can use in your research. When you locate the name of a source that you think will contribute to

Sebeok, Thomas A., and Jean Umiker-Sebeok. "Performing Animals: Secrets of the Trade." Psychology Today, Nov. 1979, pp. 78–91.

QL 737
P96L56

Linden, Eugene. *Apes, Men,
and Language*. New York:
Saturday Review Press
and Dutton, 1974.

your work, you must make a written record of the author's name, the title of the work, and other relevant publishing information.

These entries are made on what are called *bibliography cards*. To prepare a bibliography card, use 3 × 5 index cards or some other suitable material. (Most student writers find the cards most convenient.) Allot one index card for each item and write on only one side of the card. Fill out the bibliography cards using one of two formats—the format for periodicals or the one for books.

BIBLIOGRAPHY CARDS FOR PERIODICAL ARTICLES.   On page 246 is a sample bibliography card completed by our student in her research on apes and language. It is a bibliography card for a magazine article. (If you are unsure exactly what information to include on a card, and in what order, see the sample bibliography entries on page 257.)

BIBLIOGRAPHY CARDS FOR BOOKS.   Above is a bibliography card for a book, also from our student's research. It contains the author's name, book title, publisher, city of publication, year of publication, and call number.

On the Trail: One Thing Leads to Another

Researchers generally find that one source leads to another, which in turn directs them to still yet another source, and so on. For example, our math student working on the paper on apes and language has already consulted one reference to the subject in last week's *Times*. At the suggestion of the librarian that there is very likely more to be found at this source, she looks up *The New York Times Index* (see page 272). Under the subject heading "Monkeys and Apes" she finds the listing "Man Talks So Oddly!" from the issue of April 20, 1967. It is by Eugene Linden.

After preparing a bibliography card for the item, she obtains the microfilm of *The New York Times* for that date and reads the article in a microfilm machine. She learns from the article that Linden is also the author of a book on apes and language. Because Linden does not give the name of the book in his newspaper article, she looks in the card catalog under *Linden* and finds an author card for the book *Apes, Men, and Language.* She makes out a bibliography card for the book and, using the call number, obtains it.

In Linden's book, she finds a bibliography of other books in the field, which in turn provide still other sources of information. (The information she derives from Linden's book and article appears on pages 263–264 of the sample research paper in this chapter.)

This is only a small example of how one source leads to another in the pursuit of a research paper. Unless you are working in an extremely esoteric or extremely new field (both unlikely in undergraduate study), you should have little trouble locating sources of information for your paper once you have a reasonably good idea of what you are looking for. One source will almost always mention another—the title of a book or an article, or the name of someone prominent in the field. Looking up that reference will lead you to other sources, and so on. Your quest now begins to resemble a hunt.

Far from finding yourself stymied by a lack of material to consult, you will generally be faced with an embarrassment of riches. This leads to the next critical step in the research aspect of your paper—taking proper notes.

TAKING NOTES: THE RAW MATERIAL OF YOUR PAPER

You have your bibliography cards and you have located the books and periodicals you discovered during your research. Now comes the heart of the matter—note taking. It is obvious that you cannot just lump all the information you have stacked in front of you into your paper and leave it at that. You must digest what you read and present it in a form your readers can understand.

Integrity

No, *integrity* is not another lion statue at the New York Public Library. It is, however, a basic ingredient in your research paper. Your work must reflect the thinking and facts of your sources, but basically it must be yours. This means that when you paraphrase and summarize (both treated later in this chapter), you must be sure that you do so in your own words. When you are using someone else's words, you must indicate that fact clearly.

Copying an article from an encyclopedia, say, and changing a few words here and there will not do. This is *plagiarism*, which means presenting as your own work the labor and creativity of someone else. Plagiarism is unethical and is against the law. Needless to say, it is a completely unacceptable practice in college work. For your own self-respect, then, if for no other reason, be sure that any work you put your name to is really your own and not that of another.

Note Cards

A common practice in note taking is to use 4 × 6 index cards. (Again, you may want to use separate sheets of paper or a pad.) In any case, it is a good idea to put only one item, from one source, on each card. If a note runs more than one card, number the cards 1, 2, 3, etc., label them with the author's name (see below), and clip or staple them together.

When you take notes, you must always indicate the exact source of the note. To do this, put the author's full last name and the page number or numbers on which the information appears in the source. If one author has written more than one of your sources, put the title after the author's name. A note card that does not fully identify its source (including page number or numbers) will be useless to you when you begin writing the paper. Do not rely on your memory in this or any other aspect of the research-paper project.

Finally, put a heading on each card that identifies the exact point of the information on the card. Keep a list of the headings you are using; try not to use too many different ones. It will be easier to assemble your cards into groups relating to the same point later on if you do not use too many different types of headings.

Culling the Sources

You now have a large stack of books and periodicals in front of you. Your first thought is that you will never be able to read them all in time, much less take notes on them and think about them. The fact is, it is not necessary to read them completely. You must learn to read selectively, that is, to find and read only those sections of the works that touch on what you are looking for. If the source is a book, turn to the table of contents or the index (or both) to find the pages that relate directly to your topic. Scan the section indicated to find out if it does indeed touch on what you are interested in, and read carefully only those passages that treat your topic specifically. Become particularly aware of the author's approach to the subject and how it differs, if at all, from the approach of others you have read. Note any new concepts or details that seem promising. In long magazine or journal articles, look for headings to indicate the location of specific topics.

Do not make the mistake of taking notes on everything you read. Be selective. You may come across a long passage, for instance, that contains more details than you need but makes a major point that is valuable to your work. In that case, pull out the key point, and maybe one or two representative details (see "Summary" below).

In all cases of note taking, accuracy is crucial. Spell correctly all names and terms pertaining to your topic. Make sure all page references are correct. Be certain you have taken down all facts, figures, dates, and concepts accurately. A mistake in your notes will be carried over into your paper and may throw into question the whole thrust of your work.

Finally, try to take all the notes you need from one source in a single sitting. For one thing, you might not be able to obtain the source again so easily. For another, you might lose your train of thought about what you have read and have to do all your work on it over again. It will be hard to maintain the accuracy needed in a research paper if you are interrupted time and again in your research. Block time out for library work and stick to it; doing this will save you time in the end.

Types of Notes

In general, researchers take three types of notes: direct quotation, paraphrase, and summary.

DIRECT QUOTATION.   When you quote directly, you are using the *exact* wording (including spelling and punctuation) of an author. To prepare a direct quotation note card, enclose the item you are quoting (even if it is just one word) in quotation marks, making sure you have quotation marks at the beginning and at the end of the quoted passage. In your paper, you will indicate to your reader the source of each quotation (see "Crediting Your Sources," pages 253–258).

However, a good research paper should not be merely a string of direct quotations held together by a series of who-said-its. Make your direct quotations count. Be sure they give information that is needed. Whenever you quote directly, try to keep the quotation short. Sometimes even a few words will do the trick; in other instances, a few sentences or a brief paragraph may be needed.

On the opposite page is a sample quotation card taken by our math student in her paper on language and apes. She chose it because she felt it could prove important to a discussion she might want to make on the

> Meaning of
> language comprehension
>
> Bronowski and
> Bellugi
>
> "The crucial activity which
> the child reaches is recon-
> struction of the language."
>
> p. 671.

learning of language by children and animals. In the final paper, a direct quotation is most useful in opening a paragraph, which will then go on to examine the meaning and implication of the quote. It is also effective at the end of a paragraph, where it serves as an authoritative source supporting the thesis of the paragraph.

PARAPHRASE.   You may be less familiar with your topic than are the writers of the sources you consult, but that does not mean that you should not explain to your readers, in your own words, some of the ideas you have learned. Explaining something in your own words—*paraphrasing*—is a useful technique for two reasons. First, it is an alternative to direct quotation, and therefore a means of avoiding overdependence on word-for-word quotation. Second, in order to use fresh wording and fresh phrasing to express accurately and clearly something that you have read, you will probably have to do a little extra thinking. You will have to digest the ideas and facts contained in the passage. Putting this understanding in your words will help make the passage all the more meaningful to you.

There are a number of points to be careful with in paraphrasing, however.

1. When you paraphrase, do not use quotation marks unless you include in your paraphrase one or more words that are distinctively the author's and should therefore not be changed. (It is legitimate to include direct quotation within a paraphrase.) Even if you have not directly quoted any of the author's words, however, you still must let your reader know the source you relied upon in writing the para-

phrase: the author, the title of the book or article, and the page number(s). Remember, the wording is your own but the arrangement of specific ideas and facts belongs to your source.

2. Be careful, in writing a paraphrase, not to substitute a word or phrase here and there and let it go at that. A paraphrase must be a *complete* restatement. Think of the matter this way: if you replace a scattering of words and phrases, the remaining language is still the author's, and therefore must appear in quotation marks. Students sometimes assume that because they have credited their source at the end of a paraphrase, it is acceptable to use some of the author's phrasing within the paraphrase, without using quotation marks to enclose the author's words. This is not correct.

To avoid any uncertainty when you paraphrase, then, consider that you have only two choices: either paraphrase the passage completely, employing your own language entirely, or paraphrase parts of the passage, and use quotation marks to enclose those words or phrases that are still the author's. No matter which method you choose, you must still credit your source.

Below is a sample of a paraphrase note card taken for the apes and language paper. (Washoe is the name of a chimpanzee that is being taught to communicate with humans.)

SUMMARY.   A summary is a very brief paraphrase. After reading a discussion that may go on for several paragraphs, or even pages, you will want to boil down—summarize—the information into perhaps a sen-

---

Brown   Psycholinguistics

Explains that a young child, looking at a picture of a dog biting a cat, might say "Dog bite" or "Bite cat" or "Dog-cat"—all three in "correct rational order". Brown argues that Washoe, looking at the picture, might produce any possible combination of "dog", "cat", and "bite", and obviously such a sequence as "cat bite" would demonstrate "no evidence that the structural meanings were understood." p. 226

> Criticisms of
> methods
>
>   Bazar,
>   "Catching Up with the
>   Ape Language Debate"
> Terrace's assertions have met
> with numerous challenges.
> His methods have been ques-
> tioned by Patterson and the
> Gardeners, who claim his
> experiment on Nim was
> poorly conducted.
>   p. 47

tence or two in your own words. Summaries are most useful when you find a passage that contains more details than you need but that makes an overall point that should be included in your paper.

Above is a summary card prepared by our student for her paper on apes and language. Note that she credits the source (giving the author's name, the title of the work, and the page number). This is crucial because even if she is not relying on the author's exact words, she is making use of the way the author has presented a group of facts and ideas.

With the note-taking part of the research project completed, the next step is the creation of an outline and the writing of a first draft. However, because the research paper requires a rather rigid form of documentation, we will examine that aspect of the paper before going on to the actual writing process.

CREDITING YOUR SOURCES

To credit your sources is simply to tell your reader where each direct quotation, paraphrase, or summary that appears in your paper comes from—that is, what book or article supplied the wording and/or the ideas. There is more than one system of documentation, as the crediting of sources is also called. We will consider two of the most frequently used systems: the Modern Language Association (MLA) style, generally employed for research papers in the humanities (English, the arts, philosophy, religion, and the like) and history, and the social science and natural science system, which is found in the *Publications Manual* of the American Psychological Association (APA). In this chapter, we will concentrate on the MLA style, since that is the one you are more likely to be using.

MLA Footnote Style

To credit a source in your paper, place a footnote numeral, or raised arabic number, at the end of a passage taken from a source (". . . at this time[1]"). In a research paper of average length (10 to 12 pages), footnotes can be numbered consecutively (1, 2, 3 . . .) throughout the paper. In longer papers that are divided into sections, footnotes are numbered consecutively within each section. Each new section begins its numbering with "1."

The actual footnote, which gives the source of the passage, carries the same raised numeral as the reference in the text and should appear in one of two places: at the bottom, or "foot," of the page or at the end of the paper. It is a good idea to ask your instructors which location they prefer. If the requirement is to place the footnotes at the end of the paper, list all the footnotes, in order, on a separate page (or pages), with the first page headed "Notes." (See the sample research paper, pages 262–270.)

If you have the choice of placing your footnotes at the bottom of the page or at the end of the paper, you might prefer to place them at the end of the paper, simply because your typing (or writing) task will be easier. You will not have to be concerned, as you type each page, about allowing enough room at the bottom of the paper for the footnote(s). (Technically, a footnote that appears at the end of a paper is called a *note*. However, the term *footnote* frequently refers to end-of-paper notes as well. In this chapter, the term *footnote* applies to both bottom-of-page and end-of-paper documentary notes.)

WHAT IS IN A FOOTNOTE?   A footnote must be accurate, and it must follow a standard form. For your reader, the standard form makes it easy to find a particular piece of information in the footnote (e.g., date or page number). For you, as researcher, a standard form will remind you to include every item of information you need.

In general, footnotes for books, for articles in magazines, and for those in scholarly journals and newspapers all vary somewhat in the specific information they contain. What follows is the standard form for the types of research materials you are most likely to use. (Some of the examples are taken from the sample paper on apes and language.) If any of the types of sources you have consulted are not included here or in the sample paper, you can find them listed in *The MLA Handbook* (New York: Modern Language Association, 1977). You can probably find a copy of the *Handbook* in the reference section of your library.

> A FEW GENERAL RULES FOR FOOTNOTES
> - Titles of books are always underlined: <u>The Yearling</u>.
> - Titles of articles in magazines, newspapers, and journals are always enclosed in quotation marks: "The Pope Comes to New York."
> - The names of newspapers, magazines, and journals are always underlined: <u>Newsweek</u>, <u>The New York Times</u>, <u>Science</u>.
> - The abbreviations <u>p.</u> stand for <u>page</u> and <u>pp.</u> for <u>pages</u>.
> - Footnotes are indented like a paragraph from the left-hand margin. The second line of the footnote then goes to the margin.
> - For more on such matters as abbreviations, punctuation of titles, and footnote placement, see Chapter 15, "The Conventions of Writing."

Sample Footnotes

- BOOKS BY ONE AUTHOR:
  [1]Eugene Linden, *Apes, Men, and Language* (New York: Saturday Review Press and Dutton, 1974), p. 14.

Note, if the book has two authors, the same style is used, except that the names of all of the authors appear at the beginning of the footnote.

- A SHORTER WORK (STORY, ESSAY, POEM, ETC.) IN A COLLECTION OF WORKS BY DIFFERENT WRITERS:
  [2]Gordon Winant Hewes, "Language Origin Theories," in *Language Learning by a Chimpanzee: The Lana Project,* ed. Duane M. Rumbaugh (New York, Academic Press, 1977), pp. 3–53.

- "UNSIGNED" ARTICLE IN A MAGAZINE:
  [3]"The Syntactical Chimp," *Newsweek,* 7 Jan. 1974, pp. 75–76.

- "SIGNED" ARTICLE IN A MAGAZINE:
  [4]Thomas A. Sebeok and Jean Umiker-Sebeok, "Performing Animals: Secrets of the Trade," *Psychology Today,* Nov. 1979, pp. 78–91.

- ARTICLE IN A NEWSPAPER:
  [5]Lee A. Daniels, "Small Claims Court: No-Frills Justice," *New York Times,* 1 May 1980, Sec. B, p. 1, cols. 1–3.

- ARTICLE IN A SCHOLARLY JOURNAL:
  [6]J. Bronowski and Ursula Bellugi, "Language, Name, and Concept," *Science,* 168 (1970), 671.

Regarding the numbers after the journal name, *Science,* 168 is the *volume number.* Volume numbers sometimes appear in Roman numerals on the journal cover. It is usual practice to "translate" the Roman numerals into arabic ones. (Many large dictionaries give Roman numeral tables, if you need help in converting.) The number in parenthesis—"(1970)"—is the year of publication. The last number, 671, is the page number. (The abbreviation *p.* is usually omitted in references to scholarly journals.)

There are some additional forms for scholarly journals. Again, consult *The MLA Handbook* for such forms, if you need them. Also, if you examine the "Notes" pages of the sample paper, you will find some standard forms we have not discussed here—a *translated work* (footnote 1), and a reprint of a previously published work (footnote 4). If you use translations or reprints, by all means follow the form in the sample paper.

SECOND (AND LATER) REFERENCES.   Sometimes a footnote for a particular book or article appears in a paper only once. However, if the book or article is credited in more than one footnote, a shortened form of the footnote may be used.

- B O O K :
    [7]Linden, p. 8.

- A   S H O R T E R   W O R K   I N   A   C O L L E C T I O N   B Y   D I F F E R E N T   A U T H O R S :
    [8]Hewes, p. 9.

- ''U N S I G N E D ''   A R T I C L E   I N   A   M A G A Z I N E :
    [9]"The Syntactical Chimp," pp. 75–76.

- ''S I G N E D ''   A R T I C L E   I N   A   M A G A Z I N E :
    [10]Sebeok and Umiker-Sebeok, p. 79.

- A R T I C L E   I N   A   N E W S P A P E R :
    [11]Daniels, p. 1.

- A R T I C L E   I N   A   S C H O L A R L Y   J O U R N A L :
    [12]Bronowski and Bellugi, p. 671.

MLA Bibliography Style

The bibliography of your paper is the listing, in alphabetical order, of the names of all the books and articles you have footnoted. In the bibliography, each item (book, article) is given only once, even if the source is cited in more than one footnote. The bibliography should be put on a separate page (see the sample research paper, below).

The standard form for entries in the bibliography differs somewhat from that for footnotes. Because the bibliography is an alphabetical listing, the authors' names appear in reverse order, with the last name first. For a two-author book or article, the second writer's name goes in normal order, with the first name first. Instead of indenting the first line, as in a footnote, indent the second (and third) line(s) of the bibliography entry. Raised numbers are not used, and there are also some minor differences in punctuation and capitalization between footnotes and bibliography entries.

The following are the standard bibliography forms for the books and articles we have been using as samples.

● B O O K :
　Linden, Eugene. *Apes, Men, and Language.* New York: Saturday Review Press and Dutton, 1974.

Note that *page numbers* are not given when a complete book is listed.

● A S H O R T E R W O R K I N A C O L L E C T I O N B Y D I F F E R E N T A U T H O R S :
　Hewes, Gordon Winant. "Language Origin Theories." In *Language Learning by a Chimpanzee: The Lana Project.* Ed. Duane M. Rumbaugh. New York: Academic Press, 1977, pp. 3–53.

The page numbers listed are the first and last ones in the shorter work.

● ''U N S I G N E D'' A R T I C L E I N A M A G A Z I N E :
　"The Syntactical Chimp." *Newsweek,* 7 Jan. 1974, pp. 75–76.

● ''S I G N E D'' A R T I C L E I N A M A G A Z I N E :
　Sebeok, Thomas A., and Jean Umiker-Sebeok. "Performing Animals: Secrets of the Trade." *Psychology Today,* Nov. 1979, pp. 78–91.

● A R T I C L E I N A N E W S P A P E R :
　Daniels, Lee A. "Small Claims Court: No-Frills Justice," *New York Times,* Late City Ed., 1 May 1980, Sec. B, p. 1, cols. 1–3.

● A R T I C L E I N A S C H O L A R L Y J O U R N A L :
　Bronowski, J., and Ursula Bellugi. "Language, Name, and Concept." *Science,* 168 (1970), 669–73.

Crediting Sources in the Social and the Natural Sciences

The system of documentation used in the social sciences and the natural sciences is more compact than the MLA footnote and bibliography system. In the social and natural sciences system, footnotes are not used at all. Instead, each quotation, paraphrase, or summary that appears in the text of the paper is followed, right in the text, by a simple indication of the source: the *last name(s) of the author(s)*, the *year of publication* and, when needed, the *page number(s)*. All three pieces of information are enclosed in one set of parentheses.

The ape was taught to indicate the name of its friend (Brown, 1976, p. 12).

If the name of the author—in this case, Brown—is referred to in the text, then include only the year and the page number in the parentheses, immediately after Brown's name.

Brown (1976, p. 12) taught the ape to indicate the name of its friend.

THE "REFERENCE" LIST.   All the sources cited in the text of the paper are then listed, usually in alphabetical order, at the end of the paper. The listing, of course, serves as a bibliography for the paper, but it goes by another name: *References*. Like a bibliography, the Reference list always begins on a page of its own.

STANDARD FORMS FOR THE REFERENCE LIST.   The social sciences and the natural sciences follow standard forms, too, which differ from the MLA standard forms. What you may find a little tricky, though, is that the standard forms in the social sciences vary somewhat from one *discipline* (area of study) to another. If you are writing a research paper in, say, psychology, or in physics, you must be sure to select the standard form that applies to research in your area. Below are some sample entries for psychology, the area that is covered by our sample paper on apes and language. See the *Publications Manual* of the APA for more information.

PSYCHOLOGY REFERENCE STYLE

- BOOK:
  Linden, E. *Apes, men, and language.* New York: Saturday Review Press and Dutton, 1974.

- JOURNAL ARTICLE:
  Bronowski, J., and Bellugi, Ursula. Language, name, and concept. *Science,* 1970, 168, 669–673.

- MAGAZINE ARTICLE:
  Sebeok, T. A., and J. Umiker-Sebeok. Performing animals: Secrets of the trade. *Psychology Today,* Nov. 1979, pp. 78–91.

BUILDING THE PAPER

At some point, you will have to conclude that the research part of the project is done and that it is time to sit down and start writing the paper. By this time, you are familiar with the problems of beginning a paper and practiced in the techniques of overcoming them. You can use many of those invention and outlining techniques you encountered in Chapters 1 and 3.

You have already written something of your research paper by virtue of having created your note cards. You have read a lot on the subject and put much of the information in your own words. Although it may not seem so, you have gone a long way toward creating the paper. The next step in the process is to get your ideas into order and write an outline of your paper.

While you were taking notes, some ideas must have occurred to you about a possible thesis for your paper. It is even more likely that several possible theses, some of them contradictory, occurred to you. This happens because as your familiarity with the field grows, your ideas will change, possibly reverse themselves. There is nothing wrong with this in a research paper. After all, you are asking questions, and learning the answers, as you go. A research project would be a real failure for you if during the course of it you learned nothing and never had to change your mind or rethink your premise.

Begin your outline by using the invention techniques of brainstorming and probing learned in Chapter 1. What you are looking for now is a thesis statement for your paper—a sentence or two that tells what the subject of your paper is and what your approach to that subject will be. Use your note cards; go through them one by one, paying special attention to the headings. Does a pattern appear in the headings? Do the cards group naturally under two or three general headings? This is a clue that there may be an underlying organization that is part of the very nature of your subject.

On the other hand, the note cards may fall into two groups that are diametrically opposed to one another. If this is the case, you may want to organize your paper by comparing and contrasting two ways of doing or interpreting something (see Chapter 8.)

Does the information on your note cards tend toward describing something? Is most of the material an analysis of something? Using the information on your note cards, try to determine what mode of development seems natural for your material. If you discover that your topic seems to call for a comparison and contrast approach, then use the probing technique to devise a thesis statement that clearly sets forth the nature of the comparison or contrast and what your approach to it will be.

Brainstorm by putting down ideas from your note cards onto a piece of paper and free associating with them. Use the knowledge you have gained in your research to test whether or not the statements you come up with are defensible. Do you have other information that contradicts this statement? If so, what does that mean? Which of your sources are you going to believe? Perhaps the paper can be organized as an argument supporting one side in a controversy, or perhaps it should be an examination of a controversy, presenting all the sides, and discussing why the controversy is important and what it may lead to.

When the invention techniques have resulted in several possible thesis statements, write them down on separate pieces of paper. Then write a simple idea outline of a possible paper supporting each thesis statement. Do not bother with the formal lettered, numbered, and indented outline yet. Just list as phrases, or even simply as words, material from your note cards that stands in support of your thesis statement.

Does a good deal of your information support, confirm, or expand your statement? Can you see why any material you have does not? Can you work around that material? Perhaps rephrasing the thesis statement will eliminate the objection to it. If that is the case, then rephrase the thesis and write another idea outline under it. Is there a better fit now between your thesis and your research material? If so, write a more expanded and detailed outline in a sentence outline this time, covering the major ideas that will become paragraphs in your paper. If the rephrased thesis still does not fit with your research material, continue the invention techniques until you arrive at a thesis statement that agrees with the facts. Then work on the outline of your paper.

The outline for a research paper will go through many changes before you finally get one that can serve as a guide for the first draft of your paper. Once you have completed the first simple idea outline, you should go on to a more detailed one that goes through each paragraph of the paper. At all times, match up what you intend to say in a paragraph with material from your research. Remember, a research paper is not a collection of your opinions; every statement you make must be supported by one or more of your sources. If you have sources that contradict what you want to say, you must cite them and show why they are not applicable in this case. (You *should* cite sources opposed to your thesis. Your instructor is likely to be aware of them and if you do not handle them in your paper, he may conclude it is because you were not able to.)

Below is the outline prepared by our math student for her paper on apes and language. Note that she found her materials falling naturally into a question of whether apes could "learn a language" in the sense that humans do. Thus, she organizes her paper as an examination of the controversy. She gives some early background on the question, then discusses the seeming breakthrough in the use of nonvocal language and treats the criticism of the breakthrough, ending with her conclusion that the experiments were valuable if inconclusive.

OUTLINE

Main idea: A controversy exists over whether ape language research
            has proven that apes can use language the way humans do.
  I. Ape language research began with the idea that apes might learn
     human speech.
     A. An eighteenth-century physician thought it would be possible to
        teach an ape to talk.
     B. Twentieth-century researchers tried to teach spoken English to
        apes on several occasions, with limited results.
 II. Ape language researchers had more success with nonvocal language
     training.
     A. The breakthrough came when researchers taught sign language
        to an ape.
     B. Chimpanzee Washoe has shown an ability to use American Sign
        Language.

C. Gorilla Koko learned sign language and then began "speaking" with the aid of a computer.
D. Chimpanzee Lana has learned a computer-controlled language called Yerkish.
III. Critics argue that apes have not shown an ability to use language the way human beings do.
A. Apes may be able to learn only the names of objects.
B. Apes cannot reconstruct what they learn in novel ways.
C. Apes cannot understand grammatical relationships.
1. They use words at random or only to gain rewards.
2. They simply imitate their teachers.
Conclusion: The ape language debate may never be settled, but the results of ape language experiments may be applied to other fields.

WRITING AND REVISING THE PAPER

With an outline prepared, you are now ready to begin writing. You know by now that you will not go through the outline one, two, three, but rather that you will have to make changes. The most important thing in the first draft is to get your ideas down in some kind of logical order. You should not expect much more than that from a first draft.

Arrange your note cards in the order you have arrived at in your outline. This will be convenient for you as you write, and will also let you know if any important items have been left out. Go through your outline, writing paragraph by paragraph. Make sure that you identify your sources for all direct quotations and for paraphrases and summaries.

In the first draft, just indicate by number the footnotes you are going to use. Do not bother writing the footnotes up at this time. You will have many changes in the following drafts and you should keep the writing of the footnotes and bibliography until the final draft.

When you have finished your first draft, review Chapter 7 of this book for revision techniques. If possible, allow some time to elapse after you have written the first draft before you go back to it. Employ the distancing techniques you learned as you reread your first draft. Remember, at this stage anything can be changed.

You should follow the revision techniques presented in Chapter 7. These are especially important in a research paper, since you must be absolutely certain that you have documented all of your statements. You must take care that your numbering of the footnotes is correct. You must be sure in the last stages of revision that you have a footnote for every reference and that the footnote is in its proper form. In addition, you must be especially careful in proofreading the final draft. Misspelled names, incorrect titles for books or articles, or incorrect page references are not acceptable in research papers. At this stage you will appreciate all the work you did in making out your bibliography cards. The more care taken then, the easier your job will be now.

Below is the paper written by our math student on apes and language. Note how she unifies her paper by explaining, in the first part of the paper, how several specific ape language phrases played a role in the teaching experiments. Then, in the second part of the paper, she shows how those same phrases were cited by critics to prove their belief that the apes in fact did not really learn the language.

The writing of a research paper is not an easy job. But once you have done it, you have really accomplished something. You have thought about a subject, focused on a certain aspect of it, compiled information about that aspect, and organized and written what you have found so that others can read and understand it. This is no mean feat.

SAMPLE LIBRARY RESEARCH PAPER

The following is a sample student library research paper. The title and the course information (immediately below) should be set up on a separate sheet of paper, as is shown on page 464 of Chapter 15.

The Ape Language Question:
Is Man Alone?

Diane Green
Psychology 101
Professor Murphy
March 11, 1981

In the seventeenth century, the French philosopher René Descartes noted that of all the species of animals only one could use language. Man and only man could speak, and Descartes believed that the gift of speech was what separated man from the other animals. He argued that "there are no men, not even the insane, so dull and stupid that they cannot put words together . . . to convey their thoughts. . . . There is no other animal . . . that can do the same."[1] Not everyone agreed that only man was capable of language, but those who thought differently lacked the evidence to support their arguments. Only recently has that situation changed. Researchers in the field of ape language study now claim that chimpanzees, orangutans, and gorillas are able to use language. These claims, however, have been challenged by other researchers and by language theoreticians.

This paper will examine the ape language controversy. A brief survey of early ape studies will be followed by a discussion of the recent experiments that have offered the strongest claims of language acquisition in apes. Then the stands taken by the critics will be presented.

Early thinking about the ape language question involved the idea that apes might actually be taught to use human speech. For example, the eighteenth-century physician Julian La Mettrie thought that a "speaking ape" was a real possibility. He saw no reason why an ape, given the proper training, could not learn to talk. La Mettrie felt that once an ape learned to speak it would be almost human. He imagined that language might change a chimpanzee, for instance, into "a perfect little gentleman."[2] The belief that an ape might be taught to speak lasted into the twentieth century.

Until the late 1960s, ape language research was dominated by efforts to teach spoken language to various nonhuman primates. In 1916 William Furness managed to get a young orangutan to say two words, papa and cup. The ape was reported to have said, "Cup, cup" when it was dying of influenza and wanted a drink.[3] In the 1930s, Winthrop and Luella Kellogg raised a young female chimpanzee with their infant son and tried to teach her English. The chimp, named Gua, never learned to speak, but she did respond correctly to a number of verbal commands. The Kelloggs list some 58 words and phrases, such as "blow the horn," "close the drawer," and so forth, that Gua apparently understood.[4] The most successful attempt to teach spoken language to a chimpanzee occurred in the early 1950s when Keith and Virginia Hayes trained a chimp named Viki to speak words that sounded much like mamma, papa, cup, and up.[5] None of these experiments proved to anyone's satisfaction that apes could be taught to use language.

A number of apparently more successful experiments took place when researchers gave up on trying to teach speech and tried another approach. They realized that speech is not the only form of language, that symbols other than spoken words can be used for communication. Robert M. Yerkes had this insight in 1925, after trying unsuccessfully to teach spoken language to a chimpanzee:

> I am inclined to conclude from the various evidences that the great apes have plenty to talk about, but no gift for the use of sounds to represent individual, as contrasted with racial, feelings or ideas. Perhaps they can be taught to use their fingers, somewhat as does the deaf and dumb person, and thus helped to acquire a simple, nonvocal "sign language."[6]

This idea, suggested by Yerkes, was not acted upon until 1966, when Beatrice and R. Allen Gardner began teaching a young female chimpanzee named Washoe to use American Sign Language (Ameslan), the language used by many deaf persons in the United States.[7] The first word that Washoe learned to sign was more, and after ten months of language training she put together her first combination of words, gimme sweet.[8] After 51 months of training she could make 152 Ameslan signs herself and respond to many others.[9] The Gardners had apparently proven that a chimpanzee could be taught a human language.

As evidence of Washoe's language skills, the Gardners point out her ability to use her vocabulary spontaneously and creatively. They believe Washoe has used some Ameslan words differently from the way she was taught to use them, and has even "made up" a few of her own words. If this is true, then Washoe may actually understand the way language works. For example, Washoe learned the sign open only in reference to doors, extended its use to containers, and then made the sign to ask the Gardners to turn on a water faucet.[10] The first time she saw a duck she invented the combination water bird, and she once called a brazil nut a rock berry.[11] According to Eugene Linden, when Washoe was taken away from her human environment and placed in a cage with other chimpanzees she referred to them as black bugs. Linden also says that Washoe might have been swearing when she signed "Dirty Jack gimme drink" to a handler who had ignored her requests for water.[12]

Another example of what might be the expression of emotion occurred when Washoe signed baby hug to her infant chimpanzee after it had been killed in a fall.[13] Later Washoe's adopted son, Loulis, was introduced to Ameslan, and the baby learned at least nine signs—from Washoe.[14]

Sign language has also been learned by a female gorilla in California. According to her trainer, Francine Patterson, the gorilla, Koko, can make over 400 Ameslan signs.[15] Like Washoe, Koko has shown that she can extend her use of language beyond what she has been taught. Some of the labels she has invented include finger bracelet for ring and white tiger for zebra. In addition to naming things, sometimes Koko seems to use her language to indicate her awareness of certain situations. Once when the gorilla had misbehaved by tearing apart a sponge, an angry Patterson shook a piece of it in front of her and asked, "What this is?" A moment later Koko signed back, Trouble.[16] Encouraged by such examples of apparently sophisticated language use, Patterson has begun to give the gorilla a new type of language training. Joan Bazar reports that Koko now takes lessons in spoken English "using a keyboard–computer linkup with a speech synthesizer. There are 46 keys available at present, each one painted with a symbol corresponding with a word. Koko can hear herself 'speak' by pushing the appropriate keys."[17]

Koko's computer, however, is not the first that has been used in ape language research. Chimpanzee Lana began using a keyboard–computer linkup in the early 1970s at the Yerkes Regional Primate Research Center in Atlanta. Part of a project headed by Duane M. Rumbaugh, Lana's language system consists of a keyboard made up of various symbols, called lexigrams, that are projected onto a screen when the keys are pressed; a computer linked to the keyboard monitors all of Lana's language activities. She uses her special language, called Yerkish, to request food, drink, music, toys, and so on. A request such as "Please machine give piece of apple" is honored by the computer only if the Yerkish lexigrams are punched in the correct order.[18] To prove that Lana had actually learned a language, and not just a procedure to get whatever treats she wanted, Rumbaugh devised this test: he punched "Please machine open" and had Lana complete the sentence. Because of the meaning of open, only the lexigram window would make sense in the sentence. When Lana made the correct choice and punched window instead of the more tempting but incorrect lexigrams candy or banana, she seemed to place meaning above appetite.[19] After conducting Yerkish conversations with Lana for as long as 39 minutes at a time,

Rumbaugh's associate Timothy Gill concluded that "Lana was operating in a domain once held exclusive to man, that of language."[20]

Critics of ape language study are not convinced that such a conclusion is appropriate. They believe that it is an overstatement to say that apes share the domain of language with man. No one doubts that the ape experimentors' reports are true. The controversy exists because ape language researchers and their critics cannot agree on a definition of language. John Limber notes that one aspect of language use is an ability to name, to use symbols to stand for things. He concedes that Washoe and other "linguistic" apes can use names or labels, but he also points out that this ability alone does not deserve to be called language.[21] The word language may be only a convenient metaphor for whatever "symbolic capacity" Washoe and Lana may have.[22] Other critics argue that ape language experiments have merely established that "apes can be taught fairly large vocabularies of symbols. . . ."[23] A vocabulary, in other words, is not a language.

Critics also argue that apes do not reconstruct what they learn in new ways, as children do when they are learning to speak.[24] Washoe's famous water bird coinage seems to prove otherwise, but that phrase may not be a reconstruction at all. The chimpanzee may not have meant water bird but simply water and bird—names for two separate, unrelated things she saw before her.[25] On the other hand, Patterson says that Koko can invent combinations "which clearly are not derived from the immediate context. These include Koko's calling a Pinocchio doll an elephant baby and a mask an eye hat."[26] But even this may not be enough to qualify Koko for entrance into the domain of human language.

In addition to the ability to learn names and use them in novel ways, there is another basic requirement of language that the apes may never be able to master: the understanding of the relationship of one word to another. The psycholinguist Roger Brown explains that a young child looking at a picture of a dog biting a cat might say "dog bite" or "bite cat" or "dog cat," but all three expressions would reveal an understanding of the subject—verb—object relationship involved. If Washoe were to look at the picture, she might sign dog, bite, and cat in any order, including cat bite, which would not show that she understood the relationship between the words.[27] Similarly, when Lana punches her lexigram symbols for "please machine give piece of apple," she may have no idea of word relationship. Some critics charge that Lana's strings of lexigrams are just "response sequences," and that all she can do is "discriminate those that terminate in reward and those that do not."[28] Ape researcher

H. S. Terrace has another explanation for what at first glance might look like evidence of grammatical understanding by an ape.

Terrace conducted sign language experiments with a young male chimpanzee named Nim. To guard against hasty conclusions, Terrace videotaped Nim's "conversations" with his teachers. After analyzing the videotapes carefully, Terrace came to this conclusion:

> I discovered that the sequences of words that looked like sentences were subtle imitations of the teacher's sequences. I could find no evidence confirming an ape's grammatical competence, either in my own data or those of others, that could not be explained by simpler processes.[29]

More sympathetic ape language researchers, including the Gardners and Patterson, have charged Terrace with misrepresenting their findings. Claiming that the Nim experiment was poorly conducted, they do not believe Terrace's conclusion should be applied to ape language research in general.[30]

The disagreement over Project Nim is only the latest evidence that the ape language controversy is far from being settled. At present, some members of the academic and scientific communities are convinced that language use is limited to human beings, while others are not. The debate may continue for some time, but many believe the implications of the recent ape experiments go beyond the argument over language.[31] Already, speech pathologists have begun to use the data provided by the Gardners, Patterson, Rumbaugh, and others to make advances in the treatment of deaf, autistic, and cerebral-palsied children.[32] This may be the direction that ape language research will take in the future, as the methods and results of language experiments with apes are applied to other fields. No one can predict just how fruitful these experiments will be, but the more we teach the apes, the more we may learn about ourselves.

NOTES

[1] <u>Discourse on Method and Meditations</u>, trans. Laurence J. Lafleur (Indianapolis: Bobbs-Merrill, 1960), p. 42.

[2] Gordon Winant Hewes, "Language Origin Theories," in Language <u>Learning by a Chimpanzee</u>, ed. Duane M. Rumbaugh (New York: Academic Press, 1977), p. 12.

[3] Eugene Linden, <u>Apes, Men, and Language</u> (New York: Saturday Review Press and Dutton, 1974), p. 14.

[4] W. N. Kellogg and L. A. Kellogg, <u>The Ape and the Child</u> (1933; rpt. New York: Hafner, 1967), pp. 287, 302–06.

[5] Keith J. Hayes and Catherine H. Nissen, "Higher Mental Functions of a Home-Raised Chimpanzee," in <u>Behavior of Nonhuman Primates</u>, ed. Allan M. Schrier and Fred Stollnitz, IV (New York: Academic Press, 1971), 106.

[6] <u>Almost Human</u> (New York: Century, 1925), p. 180.

[7] In <u>Psycholinguistics</u> (New York: Free Press, 1970), p. 213, Roger Brown gives this explanation of the type of language used by Washoe: "In signing proper, as opposed to finger-spelling, the configurations and movements produced refer directly to concepts. Some such signs are iconic, which is to say that the sign suggests its sense. The sign for <u>flower</u> in American Sign Language is created by holding the fingers of one hand extended and joined at the tips, like a closed tulip, and touching the tip first to one nostril and then another—as if sniffing a flower."

[8] Linden, <u>Apes, Men, and Language</u>, pp. 5, 27.

[9] Beatrice T. Gardner and R. Allen Gardner, "Evidence for Sentence Constituents in the Early Utterances of Child and Chimpanzee," <u>Journal of Experimental Psychology</u>: General, 104 (1975), 244.

[10] Gardner and Gardner, p. 247.

[11] Duane M. Rumbaugh, "The Emergence and State of Ape Language Research," in <u>Progress in Ape Research</u>, ed. Geoffrey H. Bourne (New York: Academic Press, 1977), p. 81.

[12] Linden, <u>Apes, Men, and Language</u>, pp. 10, 8.

[13] Harold T. P. Hayes, "The Pursuit of Reason," <u>New York Times Magazine</u>, 12 June 1977, pp. 78–79.

[14] Joan Bazar, "Catching Up with the Ape Language Debate," <u>APA Monitor</u>, Jan. 1980, p. 4.

[15] H. S. Terrace, "How Nim Chimpsky Changed My Mind," <u>Psychology Today</u>, Nov. 1979, p. 67.

[16] Hayes, "The Pursuit of Reason," pp. 77, 76.

[17] Bazar, p. 5.

[18] Duane M. Rumbaugh, Timothy V. Gill, and E. C. von Glasersfeld, "Reading and Sentence Completion by a Chimpanzee (<u>Pan</u>)," <u>Science</u>, 182 (1973), 732.

[19] "The Syntactical Chimp," Newsweek, 7 Jan. 1974, p. 76.

[20] "Conversations with Lana Chimpanzee: An Experimental Inquiry," DA, 38 (1977), 1438B (Georgia State University).

[21] John Limber, "Language in Child and Chimp?" American Psychologist, 32 (1977), 282–83.

[22] Janet L. Mistler-Lachman and Roy Lachman, "Language in Man, Monkeys, and Machines," Science, 185 (1974), 871.

[23] Thomas A. Sebeok and Jean Umiker-Sebeok, "Performing Animals: Secrets of the Trade," Psychology Today, Nov. 1979, p. 91.

[24] J. Bronowski and Ursula Bellugi, "Language, Name, and Concept," Science, 168 (1970), 671.

[25] Ann J. Premack, Why Chimps Can Read (New York: Harper & Row, 1976), p. 74.

[26] Bazar, p. 47.

[27] Brown, p. 226.

[28] Mistler-Lachman and Lachman, p. 872.

[29] Terrace, p. 67.

[30] Bazar, p. 47.

[31] In "Man Talks So Oddly!" New York Times, Late City Ed., 20 April 1976, p. 35, cols. 2–4, Eugene Linden implies that ape language research may eventually prove to be more significant than the Apollo moon missions.

[32] Bazar, p. 47.

BIBLIOGRAPHY

Bazar, Joan. "Catching Up with the Ape Language Debate." APA Monitor, Jan. 1980, pp. 4–5, 47.

Bronowski, J., and Ursula Bellugi. "Language, Name, and Concept." Science, 168 (1970), 669–73.

Brown, Roger. Psycholinguistics: Selected Papers. New York: Free Press, 1970.

Descartes, René. Discourse on Method and Meditations. Trans. Laurence J. Lafleur. Indianapolis: Bobbs-Merrill, 1960.

Gardner, Beatrice T., and R. Allen Gardner. "Evidence for Sentence Constituents in the Early Utterances of Child and Chimpanzee." Journal of Experimental Psychology: General, 104 (1975), 244–67.

Gill, Timothy Vernon. "Conversations with Lana Chimpanzee: An Experimental Inquiry." DA, 38 (1977), 1438B (Georgia State University).

Hayes, Harold, T. P. "The Pursuit of Reason." New York Times Magazine, 12 June 1977, pp. 21–23, 73–79.

Hayes, Keith J., and Catherine H. Nissen. "Higher Mental Functions of a Home-Raised Chimpanzee." In Behavior of Nonhuman Primates: Modern Research Trends. Ed. Allan M. Schrier and Fred Stollnitz. Vol. IV. New York: Academic Press, 1971, 59–115.

Hewes, Gordon Winant. "Language Origin Theories." In Language Learning by a Chimpanzee: The Lana Project. Ed. Duane M. Rumbaugh. New York: Academic Press, 1977, pp. 3–53.

Kellogg, W. N., and L. A. Kellogg. The Ape and the Child: A Study of Environmental Influence upon Early Behavior. 1933; rpt. New York: Hafner, 1967.

Limber, John. "Language in Child and Chimp?" American Psychologist, 32 (1977), 280–95.

Linden, Eugene. Apes, Men, and Language. New York: Saturday Review Press and Dutton, 1974.

————. "Man Talks So Oddly!" New York Times, Late City Ed., 20 April 1976, p. 35, cols. 2–4.

Mistler-Lachman, Janet L., and Roy Lachman. "Language in Man, Monkeys, and Machines." Science, 185 (1974), 871–72.

Premack, Ann J. Why Chimps Can Read. New York: Harper & Row, 1976.

Rumbaugh, Duane M. "The Emergence and State of Ape Language Research." In Progress in Ape Research. Ed. Geoffrey H. Bourne. New York: Academic Press, 1977, pp. 75–83.

————, Timothy V. Gill, and E. C. von Glasersfeld. "Reading and Sentence Completion by a Chimpanzee (Pan)." Science, 182 (1973), 731–33.

Sebeok, Thomas A., and Jean Umiker-Sebeok. "Performing Animals: Secrets of the Trade." Psychology Today, Nov. 1979, pp. 78–91.

"The Syntactical Chimp." Newsweek, 7 Jan. 1974, pp. 75–76.

Terrace, H. S. "How Nim Chimpsky Changed My Mind." Psychology Today, Nov. 1979, pp. 65–76.

Yerkes, Robert M. Almost Human. New York: Century, 1925.

REFERENCE SOURCES

The following listings are intended to provide you with some starting points for your library research. The first section contains the names of useful reference sources of a general nature. It is followed by a section containing the names of reference materials grouped according to subject area.

We have given you only a small sampling of the riches of resources to be found in your library. These listings will serve you well; but if you get stuck in the course of your research, or if you are unsure how to use any particular reference source, consult your librarian. He or she knows the library and will be able to guide you in your endeavor.

General Reference Sources

DICTIONARIES
UNABRIDGED
The American Heritage Dictionary of the English Language. 1969.
A Dictionary of American English on Historical Principles. 1938– .
Oxford English Dictionary [O.E.D.] Ed. J. A. Murray. 1933.
Webster's Third New International Dictionary. Ed. Merriam Company. 1961.

ABRIDGED DESK
Funk & Wagnall's Standard College Dictionary. Ed. Funk & Wagnall. 1974.
Random House Dictionary of the English Language. College ed. Ed.-in-chief, Laurence Urdang. 1968.
Webster's New Collegiate Dictionary. 8th ed. 1974.
Webster's New World Dictionary of the American Language. 2nd college ed. Ed. David B. Guralnik et al. 1976.

WORD AND USAGE GUIDES; THESAURI
The Careful Writer: A Modern Guide to English Usage. Theodore M. Bernstein. 1965.
A Dictionary of Contemporary American Usage. Bergen Evans and Cornelia Evans. 1957.
Roget's International Thesaurus. 4th ed. 1977.
Webster's New World Thesaurus. 1976.

BIOGRAPHICAL REFERENCE WORKS
American Men and Women of Science. 12th ed. 8 vols. 1971.
Chambers' Biographical Dictionary. Rev. ed. Ed. J. O. Thorne. 1969.
Current Biography. 1940– (monthly).
Dictionary of American Biography. 21 vols. Ed. Allen Johnson, Dumas Malone, et al.
Dictionary of National Biography. 22 vols. 1908–1909 and 1912–1971.
International Who's Who. 1935– (annually).
Webster's Biographical Dictionary. 1972.

Who's Who. 1849– (annually).
Who's Who in America. 1899– (biennial).
Who's Who in the World. 1st ed. 1971–1972.

PERIODICAL AND NEWSPAPER INDEXES
PERIODICALS
Humanities Index. 1974– (quarterly).
Poole's Index to Periodical Literature. 1802–1881.
Reader's Guide to Periodical Literature. 1900– (quarterly and annually).
Social Sciences and Humanities Index. 61 vols. 1907–1974.
Social Sciences Index. 1974– (quarterly).

NEWSPAPERS
Christian Science Monitor Subject Index. 1960– .
The New York Times Index. 1913– .
The Times [London] *Official Index*. 1906– .
Wall Street Journal Index.

QUICK INFORMATION SOURCES
ALMANACS AND YEARBOOKS
Information Please Almanac, Atlas and Yearbook. 1947– (annually).
The New York Times Encyclopedia Almanac. 1970. [Continued as *The Official Associated Press Almanac*. 1972– .]
The World Almanac and Book of Facts. 1868– (annually).

ATLASES
National Geographic Atlas of the World. 4th ed. 1975.
The New York Times Atlas of the World. Ed. New York Times and London Times. 1972.
The Rand McNally International Atlas. 1974.

QUOTATIONS
Dictionary of Quotations. Bergen Evans. 1968.
Familiar Quotations. 14th ed. John Bartlett. 1971.

Specialized Reference Books, Encyclopedias, Indexes

HUMANITIES
PHILOSOPHY
The Concise Encyclopedia of Western Philosophy and Philosophers. James Opie Urmson. 1960.
Encyclopedia of Philosophy. 8 vols. Ed.-in-chief, Paul Edwards. 1967.
The Philosopher's Index: An International Index to Philosophical Periodicals. 1967– (quarterly).

RELIGION
Dictionary of Comparative Religion. Ed. S. G. Brandon. 1970.
Dictionary of the Bible. James Hastings. Rev. ed. Frederick C. Grant and H. H. Rowley. 1963.

Encyclopaedia of Religion and Ethics. Ed. James Hastings et al. 1908–1927. Reprint 1971.
Exhaustive Concordance of the Bible. James Strong. 1894.
Index to Religious Periodical Literature. American Theological Library Assoc. 1953– (annually).
The Interpreter's Bible. 12 vols. 1976.
A Reader's Guide to the Great Religions. Ed. Charles J. Adams. 1965.

LITERATURE
Cassell's Encyclopedia of World Literature. Ed. J. Buchanan-Brown. 1973.
Essay and General Literature Index, 1900–1933. [Continued by supplements and periodic cumulations]. Ed. Minnie Earl Sears and Marian Shaw. 1934.
Literary History of the United States. Ed. Robert E. Spiller et al. 1974.
A Literary History of England. 2nd ed. Ed. Albert C. Baugh et al. 1967.
MLA International Bibliography of Books and Articles on the Modern Languages and Literatures. Modern Language Association of America. 1921– (annually).
Oxford Companion to American Literature. 4th ed. James D. Hart. 1965.
Oxford Companion to English Literature. 4th ed. Sir Paul Harvey. Rev. Dorothy Eagle. 1967.
Short Story Index. Dorothy Elizabeth Cook and Isabel Stevenson Monro. 1953. Supplements 1953– .

ART
Art Index: A Cumulative Author and Subject Index to a Selected List of Fine Arts Periodicals. 1929– (quarterly).
Encyclopedia of World Art. 15 vols. 1959–1968.
Guide to Art Reference Books. Mary W. Chamberlin. 1959.
How to Find Out about the Arts: A Guide to Sources of Information. Neville Carrick. 1965.
McGraw-Hill Dictionary of Art. Ed. Bernard S. Myers. 1969.
The Oxford Companion to Art. Ed. Harold Osborne. 1970.

PERFORMING ARTS (DRAMA, DANCE, FILM, MUSIC)
A Bibliography of Dancing. Cyril W. Beaumont. 1963.
The Dance Encyclopedia. Rev. ed. Ed. Anatole Chujoy and P. W. Manchester. 1967.
The Film Index: A Bibliography. Vol. I: The Film As Art. Compiled by Workers of the Writers Program of the Work Projects Administration of the City of New York. 1941.
Film Literature Index. 1974– (quarterly).
Grove's Dictionary of Music and Musicians. 6th ed. Sir George Grove. Ed. Eric Blom. 1980.
Music Reference and Research Materials: An Annotated Bibliography. 3rd ed. Vincent Harris Duckles. 1974.
Music Index. 1949– (monthly).
Film Abstracts. International Association of Music Libraries. 1967– .

MYTHOLOGY AND FOLKLORE
Funk & Wagnalls Standard Dictionary of Folklore, Mythology and Legend. Ed. Maria Leach. 1973.
Larousse World Mythology. Ed. Pierre Grimal. 1965.

HISTORY AND SOCIAL SCIENCES

HISTORY

A Bibliography of Modern History. Ed. John P. C. Roach. 1968.

An Encyclopedia of World History, Ancient, Medieval, and Modern, Chronologically Arranged. 5th ed., rev. and enl. Ed. William L. Langer. 1972.

Guide to Historical Literature. Ed. George F. Howe et al., American Historical Association. 1961.

The Oxford History of England, 2nd ed. Ed. Sir George Clark. 1937–1962.

The Oxford History of the American People. Samuel L. Morison. 1965.

SOCIOLOGY AND ANTHROPOLOGY

A Dictionary of Anthropology. Charles Winick. 1956.

A Dictionary of the Social Sciences. Ed. Julius Gould and William L. Kolb. 1964.

International Bibliography of Social and Cultural Anthropology. 1955– (annually).

International Bibliography of Sociology. 1951– (annually).

International Encyclopedia of the Social Sciences. Ed. David L. Sills. 1968.

Student Sociologist Handbook. Pauline Bart and Linda Frankel. 1976.

Social Sciences Index. 1974– (quarterly).

BUSINESS AND ECONOMICS

Dictionary of Economics. 5th ed. Ed. Howard S. Sloan and Arnold J. Zurcher. 1971.

Economic Almanac. 1940– (biennial).

Index of Economic Articles in Journals and Collective Volumes. 1961– .

International Bibliography of Economics. 1952– .

Encyclopedia of Banking and Finance. 7th ed. Glen G. Munn. Rev. and enl. by F. L. Garcia. 1973.

Business Periodicals Index. 1958– (monthly).

Encyclopedia of Business Information Sources. Managing ed., Paul Wasserman. 1970.

Sources of Business Information. Rev. ed. Edwin T. Coman. 1964.

POLITICAL SCIENCE

Congressional Record. 1873– (bound at end of each session).

Dictionary of American Politics. 2nd ed. Edward C. Smith and Arnold J. Zurcher. 1968.

Guide to Reference Materials in Political Science: A Selective Bibliography. 2 vols. Lubomyr Wynar. 1966 and 1968.

The Literature of Political Science: A Guide for Students, Librarians, and Teachers. Clifton Brock. 1969.

Political Science: A Bibliographical Guide to the Literature. Robert B. Harmon. 1965. 3rd supplement, 1974.

Public Affairs Information Service Bulletin. 1915– (quarterly).

PSYCHOLOGY

A Dictionary of Psychology. Rev. ed. Harvey Wallerstein. 1964.

The Encyclopedia of Human Behavior: Psychology, Psychiatry, and Mental Health. Robert M. Goldenson. 1970.

The Harvard List of Books in Psychology. 4th ed. 1971.

Psychological Abstracts. 1927– (monthly). See also *Psychological Index,* nos. 1–42 (1894–1935). [Later merged into *Psychological Abstracts.*]

SCIENCE AND TECHNOLOGY
  Applied Science and Technology Index. 1913– (quarterly and annually).
  The Basic Dictionary of Science. E. C. Graham. 1966.
  Harper Encyclopedia of Science. 2nd rev. ed. Ed. James R. Newman. 1967.
  McGraw-Hill Encyclopedia of Science & Technology. 4th ed. 1977.
  Van Nostrand's Scientific Encyclopedia. 5th ed. 1976.

EXERCISES

1. Find five different kinds of research sources (a general source, journal, popular magazine, specialized book, and so on) for each of the following topics:

  1. Samoan culture
  2. The Ballet Russe
  3. The difference between active and passive solar energy
  4. The Battle of Bull Run (American Civil War)
  5. Silent films

2. Take each of the following paragraphs (from articles used for the research paper on ape language) and write two paragraphs for each entry, one that incorporates a quotation from that text and one that paraphrases the information in it. Use footnotes where appropriate.

Today one can scarcely read a daily newspaper or news magazine without encountering a feature extolling the latest linguistic accomplishments of one or another ape. Contemporary introductory psychology textbooks may devote as much space to the achievements of the likes of Sarah and Washoe as they do to the language development of children. With increasing frequency, widely read journals such as *Science* publish reports of the transmutation of base primates into noble ones. It is no wonder there is a growing belief among students and scientists alike that modern behavioral science has in fact succeeded in teaching human language to apes. [page 280]
  —Limber, John. "Language in Child and Chimp?"
  American Psychologist, 32 (1977), 280–95.

The sentence and the word are the two basic features of human language that separate it from other forms of animal communication. In contrast to the fixed character of most animal sounds, the word is flexible in meaning. Many species of birds, for instance, sing one song when in distress, another when courting a mate, and still another when asserting territorial rights. It does not appear possible to teach birds to produce different songs in these situations. [page 65]
  —Terrace, H. S. "How Nim Chimpsky Changed My Mind."
  Psychology Today, Nov. 1979, pp. 65–76.

Contacted by telephone in Jerusalem where he is on sabbatical, Premack expressed amusement at the way popular opinion on ape language has swung from one extreme to another in recent years.

"Ten or so years ago when I first gave colloquia on the question, "Do chimpanzees have language?," we used to be booed and hissed. The colloquia had the character of a revival meeting. Then, after about five years, people were asking me, 'Do your chimps do so and so?' and I'd say, 'No,' and they'd say, 'Other people's do. You must be some sort of a dummy.'

"So, in a period of about five years, the chimp had emerged as kind of a hairy person. There was a complete swing away from the notion that it was virtually sinful to consider the possibility of any relation between man and any other species." [page 4]

        —Bazar, Joan. "Catching Up with the Ape Language Debate." *APA Monitor*, Jan. 1980, pp. 4–5, 47.

3. Answer the following questions. The information you will need will be found in the library.

1. From the Reader's Guide for 1953–1955, find where the article "Baptism of Faulkner" appears.
2. What is the name of an article by Dr. Charles Moorman about T. S. Eliot's *The Wasteland*?
3. Find articles dealing with the controversy over realism in fiction in British periodicals in the nineteenth century.
4. Where do you go to find the exact source of these lines from the poet Browning: "Swift as a weaver's shuttle fleet our years:/ Man goeth to the grave, and where is he?"
5. What does the word "harrow" mean and what is its history in the English language?
6. Where do you go to find out what the first edition of Gibbon's *Decline and Fall* was and when it was published?
7. Find a brief article on totemism.
8. Where would you find out if *Brave New World* is still in print? Give publisher, price, etc.
9. Find all of the following information from one book: population of Bangkok, altitude of Winston-Salem, N.C., president of Dominican Republic, and schedules of tides at various ports for a given year?
10. Find a brief biography, with picture, of Leontyne Price.
11. Where would you find a brief article on the legend of Hero and Leander?
12. What is the L.C. classification for works dealing with theory of learning?
13. What is the L.C. classification for blood chemistry?
14. What is the L.C. classification for a work dealing with the quantum theory?
15. What is the L.C. classification for a book called *Science Remaking the World*?
16. What is the L.C. number for books on barbecue cookery?
17. Where could you find a brief, authoritative account of how oil was used in the Bible?

18. How was William Golding's *Lord of the Flies* received when it was published in the U.S.? Give examples.
19. Find titles of some various *Who's Who in . . .* that your library has. Where are they?
20. Where could you find an account of Roger Maris's 1960 season?
21. Find an article about the history of wool.
22. Find an article explaining why the cow is sacred to Hindus.
23. Find a brief, authoritative account of Tony Trabert's career.
24. Find a description of St. Peter's Basilica.
25. What did a reputable U.S. newspaper have to say editorially about the selection of President John F. Kennedy's cabinet?

Writing Today: For School and Work

The Exam Essay
Read the Question
Watch the Clock
Make Your Answer's Structure Evident
Compare and Contrast
Analysis
Analysis and Evaluation

The Resume
Format and Appearance
Types of Resumes—Functional and Chronological

Writing for Business
Business Letters
Memos and Reports

Writing for School and Work
The Brief
The Précis or Abstract
The Report

Technical or Scientific Writing

The Oral Report

Exercises

This chapter presents guidelines and models for the practical course work and business writing you will face at one time or another. The most important points to keep in mind about these kinds of writing are that they are directed to specific situations (sometimes to specific individuals) and that they are designed to accomplish specific ends. You want a good grade in a history course and must write a paper to get it. You want a job that you know is open. You want to make a good impression with a verbal report you must give either in class or at a business meeting.

Five of the most common types of school and business writing are discussed here: the exam essay; business writing (resumes, letters, memos, and reports); writing briefs, précis or abstracts and course reports, technical or scientific writing; and the oral report. Store this chapter away for reference; you will be using it long after you leave college.

THE EXAM ESSAY

Few college students obtain a degree without having to sit down and, under pressure, put together a coherent essay on a midterm or final exam. The essay question tests not only what you have learned but how well you are able to select material, organize it, and inform others with it. Learning to cope with essay questions on exams is as much a part of college as football games and lectures.

Read the Question

In an essay exam begin with a careful study of each question. Ask yourself first, "What does this question want?" You have learned about probing in earlier chapters of this book. Now is the time to use that technique to its fullest.

Ask yourself questions about the way in which the question is framed. Does it put its requirements in such a way that the method of answering is suggested? Is the question looking for a cause-and-effect relationship? Does it suggest an analysis of the parts making up the subject of the question? Does it ask you to compare or contrast two entities? You have studied all these methods of developing paragraphs, so you should be familiar with them when you meet them in an essay question. Once you understand the thrust and direction of the question, you have a good start on organizing and developing your answers.

For instance, practically no exam would give such an open and non-structured question as:

Discuss the law of supply and demand.

The reason it would not is that almost any essay—even the silliest and the simplest—on the subject would have to be accepted. The essay could say *anything* about the law. On essay questions, instructors are usually looking for something specific, and they will frame their essay questions accordingly.

> Discuss the law of supply and demand in a free market system, stressing particularly its effect on maximum and minimum prices and the way in which it tends to stabilize pricing structure. Use examples.

This question provides a much more concrete set of instructions and calls for a set of specific replies. It also requires knowledge of the subject. You must establish how the law of supply and demand affects prices in a free market, and you must use examples of price changes for a particular item under various conditions of supply and demand. Your essay, therefore, will be made up of an expository section, explaining the workings of supply and demand, and an example section, showing how the law works in specific instances. The question suggests—as many questions do—the form and content of its own answer. If the question reads, "List at least five causes of the breakdown of the world monetary system in the 1930s and show how they are interrelated," you have an enumeration and analysis ahead of you. If the question reads, "Define the theory of checks and balances and explain its effect on the development of the Supreme Court," you would have to develop your essay by definition and then by example.

Understanding the question—the terms, requirements, and boundaries of the question—will also help you decide how to frame your answer. It tells you what *not* to write about. Write only *to* and *for* the question. Good well-written material is of no value if it does not answer the question.

Pay attention to restrictions on subject matter given in the wording of the question. A perfectly splendid little essay on the failures of the Grant administration to curb government corruption will not serve to answer a question that asks about official corruption in the era just *prior* to the Grant administration. Address yourself only to the elements stated or implied in the essay question. Anything else is a digression. It will not help you on the exam, and it takes away time you can spend more profitably elsewhere.

Watch the Clock

Most exams have time limitations—generally one to three hours. Learn to use the time to your best advantage. Do not get carried away in answering a single question and fail to complete the exam. Assess the contents of the exam against the time allotted. If it is an hour-long exam and it consists of three parts—one short answer and two essays—you had better divide up the hour into appropriate parts depending on the value or difficulty of each of the questions.

Suppose one of the essay questions requires a fairly straight listing of parts while the other essay involves some complex explanatory material. Give yourself 15 minutes apiece for the short answer and easy essay question, and allow a half hour for the more difficult essay. Check your watch to see that you are on schedule.

Keep in mind the relative values of each part of the exam. Do not waste half your time on a question that is worth only 20 points and end up unable to complete a question worth 40 points. Generally speaking, the more points assigned to a question, the more detailed and specific your answer must be. Make sure you give yourself the most time possible for the harder or more valuable questions.

With any essay question, regardless of the time you have left, take two to five minutes to jot down the points and organizational scheme suggested to you by the form of the question. This can be time well spent. Never write an essay off the top of your head, or you will very likely wind up digressing or leaving out some crucial part of the answer required by the question. Use the probing and brainstorming techniques discussed in the text to get a solid grip on the question and on the form you want the answer to take. The result will be a better written and much more cohesive, coherent, and comprehensive answer.

Make Your Answer's Structure Evident

Sometimes even nonsense written with a clear organizational pattern can give an impression of content. By the same token, good ideas can be misunderstood if they appear in an essay that is jumbled or that lacks an easily grasped structure. Make your transitions clear. State your topic sentences in the beginning and make them clear and straightforward.

There are three primary causes for the fall of the Roman Empire: economic, moral/religious, and political. First, the economic difficulties . . .

With this kind of beginning you have alerted the reader what will come first and what will follow. Devote one or two paragraphs to each of the causes, clearly marking the transition from one cause to the next.

Secondly, the moral climate and the religious turmoil . . .

Finally, the political morass exemplified by . . .

Make your conclusion clear, giving a summary of your thesis and of the reasons why it is true.

> In conclusion, we see that the three causes . . .

At no point should you leave the reader in doubt about what you are discussing or what you want to say about it. Remember, if the instructor is in doubt about what you are saying, he or she will conclude that you have not mastered the material. This reaction translates into a low grade, exactly the opposite of what you want.

On an exam essay, your best friend is the simple, clear declarative sentence:

> Much has been written about the cost involved in protecting the environment. I would like to discuss some of the costs of *not* doing so.

> Seating representatives of labor on the boards of directors of large corporations is an idea whose time has come—and passed.

> Marketing is that function of business that concerns itself with making things happen, with putting goods and services in circulation, with causing movement.

> Media interference with the election process results in a kind of Heisenberg "Uncertainty Principle," whereby the apparatus designed to examine something changes or destroys what it is supposed to report on.

After you have made a clear beginning, you can develop your exposition by one or more of the various methods of paragraph development discussed in Chapter 4. As mentioned earlier, if the question itself suggests a particular method, use it.

We will now examine some of the more common types of questions you may face on an exam.

Compare and Contrast

Instructors like to use comparison/contrast questions because such questions are economical. They cover the most ground in the least amount of space, and they imply an organizational pattern to aid the student.

Comparison/contrast is a little like definition in that in using such a form you want to show what something really is by exploring what it has in common with something else. (See Chapter 4.) Or you want to show what something is *not* by pointing out how it differs from something else. A comparison stresses the similarities between the things or items discussed while a contrast stresses the differences.

You must decide in the beginning whether the items in the question are basically alike, with superficial differences, or whether they are essentially different, with superficial similarities.

Often there will be a strong hint on how to proceed, either from the text for your course or from the professor's lectures. Certainly, if a professor has spent two weeks developing the basic similarities between two seemingly dissimilar things, you will be well advised to stress comparison in your answer.

Once you have decided on your approach, you must organize your essay to prove your point. In a comparison, it is a good tactic to begin by conceding that, while there are obvious differences between the two things, a closer examination will show that they are fundamentally alike.

> It is true that the political and economic structures of the world at the beginning of the 1980s are markedly different from those in 1914 on the eve of the Great War. Nevertheless, the similarities between the world geopolitical picture in 1980 and that of 1914 are remarkable both in the nature of the political rivalries involved and in the economic causes of them.

The same kind of approach is valuable for setting up a contrast.

> It has long been a conceit of literature that genius and insanity are but two sides of the same coin. However, the insights of the genius, although often startling to the so-called common-sense world, couldn't be further from the fantasies of the madman.

Usually, it is a good idea to organize your material so that—in a contrast, for example—you have two or three points of similarity followed by an acknowledged or seeming difference or contrast. This in turn can be followed by several more points of similarity, followed by a contrast. End your essay with a restatement of your thesis—acknowledging the similarities you have mentioned, but reiterating your conclusions that the differences outweigh them.

It is crucial in this type of question to avoid waffling, ping-ponging, or "on-the-one-hand-this, on-the-other-hand-that" type of writing. The reader will immediately sense that you have no thesis or point of view and that you are merely trying to fill up space. This is not the way to make a good impression on an exam.

Analysis

When the time comes for you to be tested on material you have been studying for a while, your first instinct may be to repeat certain facts and definitions word for word to prove you know the material. But your professors, by and large, will be more interested in whether or not you have grasped the material's *significance*—whether you can say what it means. That is why they will often ask you to *analyze.*

Analysis means taking one whole thing (such as a concept, theory, or even something tangible like a poem) and examining the various parts that make it up. Doing this helps you understand the subject in its entirety, and lets you see how all the parts interrelate.

One way to develop skill at analysis is to practice taking large concepts and breaking them down into their component parts. (Remember, you can analyze concrete things, abstract concepts, or processes.) If you open the door of your closet, for instance, you will see what is commonly referred to as a *wardrobe.* But what does wardrobe mean? How can it be analyzed?

First of all, you would simply take note of what you see on the hangers and shelves: slacks, winter coats, track shoes, reversible blazers, silk blouses, scarves, and so forth. You could then add depth to your analysis by describing the *function* of each thing. "The track shoes support my ankles while jogging," you might conclude. "The reversible blazers give my wardrobe some versatility, and the silk blouses make me look good when I go out." A *wardrobe,* then, consists of different items of apparel worn for different reasons. This would constitute a basic analysis of the term.

Needless to say, essay exams will rarely test your ability to analyze such simple concepts as the one discussed above. But the important thing to remember is that the system of analysis remains the same, regardless of subject matter. You always take one complete entity and break it down into parts.

If you were asked to analyze the basic structure of the United States government, you could go about it in this way:

> The United States government is composed of three basic branches: executive, legislative, and judicial. . . .

You would immediately take the whole (in this case, the U.S. government) and break it down into its component parts (the three branches that constitute its basic structure). You could then discuss the primary function of each branch, just as you noted the primary functions of the various clothes in the wardrobe.

> . . . The executive branch applies the law, the legislative branch makes the law, and the judicial branch interprets the law as it is applied.

So, when you are asked to analyze, remember that your job is twofold: to explore the component parts of something, and to discuss what each part means individually and as a member of the whole.

Analysis and Evaluation

Some essay questions will ask you to take analysis one step further into evaluation. Here you would make some sort of judgment on the thing being analyzed, explaining how it succeeds or fails.

> *Question:* *Analyze* the basic structure of the United States government and *evaluate* its ability to function as a cohesive unit.

In answering this question you would proceed through the analysis— listing the branches of government and their functions—and then try to evaluate how well each branch works. Granted, the nature of this question is much broader than any you are likely to see on an actual exam, but it does allow us to assess some of the features of a good answer.

To begin your evaluation, you would first look at each branch separately, asking yourself questions based on what you have learned in the course. Is the President too powerful, or not powerful enough? Does Congress represent actual people, or only special interest groups? Is the Supreme Court biased or objective in its interpretation of the law? How well does each branch work?

Having evaluated the success of each branch individually, you could move toward a judgment on how well the executive branch interacts with the judicial branch, the legislative with the executive, and so forth. You could discuss the pros and cons of the system of checks and balances, or weigh the ability of any single branch to succeed within it.

As we have noted, most questions will not be this general. They will focus on a specific range of material that can be analyzed and evaluated in a few hundred words. Just remember that the *system* of analysis and the *system* of evaluation remain the same, regardless of the subject matter. When you analyze, you explain a thing's components. When you evaluate, you judge how well those components work individually and in unison.

THE RESUME

The resume is an essential form of writing that you must master. Without it, you will have little chance of getting so much as a job interview, much less the job itself. Even when you feel you could explain, in a single sentence, why you are perfect for a particular job, you will almost certainly be asked to bring a resume along. It is virtually impossible to try to register with an employment agency or a company's personnel department without a resume.

The resume presents you in graphic outline form to someone who may have to choose from among 300 to 400 applicants. The resume (whether sent through the mail or handed to someone across a desk) has to present the most appealing image of yourself that can possibly be presented—an image distilled from the many interests, activities, and concerns that represent you. Just as you have to choose what to highlight about yourself on the resume, the employer has to choose which applicants to interview and/or hire on the basis of the resume he receives. With luck, the image you present and the employer's needs will coincide and you will get the job.

Format and Appearance

Before we go over how to decide what to put on a resume, let us discuss how the finished product should look:

1. First of all, remember that a resume is a sheet of paper filled with type. That means that you have to approach it visually as well as verbally. You have to consider the reader's eye. Use white space between blocks of type to break up sections or categories. Most people are put off by threatening walls of print.
2. Underline important words that describe skills. (*"Assistant Division Manager* for Kreske's department store . . ."") This focuses attention on what you have done.
3. A resume should be only one page if possible. If you are young, it is unlikely that you will have held a great many jobs. Do not feel that you have to "pad" your resume with inflated language to compensate for your youth or inexperience. Your prospective employer was young once, too. Be straight about yourself!
4. Do not go overboard with tricks or gimmicks. A resume typed in bright green ink on pastel paper may attract attention, but not the kind you want. *Never* attach a picture of yourself unless you have been specifically requested to do so.
5. If possible, have the resume typed on high-quality white bond paper. Then have it professionally printed for distribution. Photostatic copies are not always clear; carbon copies are out of the question.
6. As a rule, leave out all references to hobbies unless they pertain directly to the job you are seeking.
7. Do not write a statement of career goals unless it pertains directly to the job you are seeking.
8. Federal law states that no information about age, sex, race, or marital status need be included. Similarly, no one needs your Social Security number until you are hired, so leave it out of the resume.

Types of Resumes—Functional and Chronological

If you have a few years of corporate experience behind you, you would probably use a chronological format for your resume. That is, you would describe your most recent job first and proceed down the page, listing other positions you may have held over the years.

If, on the other hand, your experience is limited to two summer jobs at a seashore resort and one-third of a B.A. degree, you would probably want to go with a functional resume, in which you emphasize skills and interests rather than years. You can draw attention away from your youth by providing a concrete picture of your skills and work-related activities. In short, you should emphasize your potential more than your limited past.

The easiest way to start constructing a functional resume is to sit down and really *think* about what you do—what skills have you acquired, no matter how young you are. Many people tend to forget that skills need not have been acquired in formal training. For example, working with a Little League or as a summer camp counselor may have given you leadership training skills. A work–study job may have taught you something about graphics or copy editing. Did you ever work in a college cafeteria? A food marketing service might be very interested in hearing your ideas for streamlining operations.

You might sit down and inventory yourself now—and update the inventory every year. When you get to be a senior, you will find it much easier to construct a good resume. In the meantime, try to keep on defining your interests. Seek out experience on and off campus. Above all, be aware of what your experiences have taught you.

Even interests that seem minor can translate into a job. Are you the one to whom friends come for advice? Maybe you should think about counseling or personnel. Are you proud of being able to quote the earned run average of every pitcher on the San Francisco Giants? Perhaps a position in a statistical analysis firm would interest you.

As the saying goes, you have to get your foot in the door before you can go anywhere. Taking an inventory of yourself right now might help you choose which door to go through.

THE FUNCTIONAL RESUME.   The functional resume emphasizes areas of skill rather than actual, full-time experience. The first category—career objectives—in the resume on page 287 simply states what kind of job the applicant is interested in: a position as an editor or technical writer. It is open-ended, yet specific enough to give the employer an immediate idea of what the writer wants.

In the next section, notice the emphasis on the word *skills.* We are not given the names of specific companies (except for one) because the author has not had full-time business experience. Instead, she empha-

C. ELLEN RIDGEWAY

518 Harold Place   (315) 555-6539
Albany, New York 18848

CAREER OBJECTIVES

Interested in position as editor or technical writer.

RELATED AREAS OF EXPERIENCE

Writing Skills: Presently engaged in free-lance writing and research for
high school English text soon to be published by Barker & Brown; completed
Master's thesis of original publishable short stories; wrote undergraduate thesis
praised for clarity and originality by baccalaureate committee; served as
assistant editor of high school newspaper and as reporter on college newspaper.

Conceptual/Innovative Skills: Presently devising original examples and
exercises for Barker & Brown textbook; taught creative writing and women's
studies courses for students of varying levels of preparation at two institutions.

Decision-Making/Teamwork Skills: Elected to freshman English
committee as graduate student, with responsibility for choosing textbooks and
deciding on appropriate "minicourses"; served on racial grievance committee in
racially troubled Southern high school.

Other Skills: Read and write French; type and edit theses and
dissertations, guaranteeing no more than one error per fifty pages of text.

EDUCATION

M.A. in English/Creative Writing, Dec. 1979   Albany College
B.A. in Literature, June 1976   New College of the
                                                    University of South
                                                    Florida, Sarasota, FL

HONORS

National Merit Scholarship, 1973.

WORK EXPERIENCE

Jan. 1980–present   Free-lance writer, editor, researcher
Jan.–March 1979   Visiting Lecturer in Literature, New
                               College of USF
Sept. 1977–Dec. 1978   Graduate Teaching Assistant in
                               English, Albany College
1976–77 and throughout   Series of part-time jobs to earn
college   money for school

REFERENCES

Available upon request.

sizes the skills she acquired in college and explains how she has put them to use in a variety of part-time capacities. Her interest in writing is the unifying thread of the resume.

An effective device in this resume is the way the writer has divided her skills into three major areas: "writing," "conceptual/innovative," and "decision-making/teamwork." From the headings alone we get the impression of an active, innovative person who is capable of making decisions and does not mind being part of a team. In fact, we learn that she managed to develop her decision-making skills by working on *two* committees.

THE CHRONOLOGICAL RESUME. The chronological resume is the kind you will find useful when you already hold a full-time job and want to get a new one. In this type of resume (see page 289 for an example), the writer orders his qualifications in time sequence. We can see what he is doing now (analyzing the efficiency of 26 weigh stations for the Interstate Trucking Commission) as well as what he has done in the past. Normally, the category of work experience would be listed before education, but, as this job-seeker is a recent college graduate, the education category seems appropriate at the top of the list. It also gives a series of subjects (accounting, business management, etc.) that fit in well with his professional goals.

Overall, this resume gives the impression of an organized, hard-working, detail-oriented person: a self-starter. The lawn-tool repair service may not seem that glamorous or important, but it demonstrates to the reader that this applicant has initiative, and initiative is what counts.

No matter what type of resume you decide to use, it is always good to be as specific as possible and to give the most complete picture of yourself that you can (providing the information applies). For practice, you may want to try rewriting the chronological resume as a functional one. See if you can take the information and shape it according to skill categories. You may even find it useful to write sample resumes for famous people, for literary characters from novels, or even for comic book heroes. The idea is to fit their "qualifications" into a precise, appealing framework, as in the example on page 290.

WRITING FOR BUSINESS

One of the oldest clichés in business is that time is money. What does this mean in business writing? It means brevity. Most business people receive much more reading material than they can reasonably handle. So your approach to all the business writing you will come to do must

JAMES F. CAVANAGH

Through May 15, 1980:

13 Hudson Place
Ossining, New York 13166
(315) 555-7858

Permanent Address:

4250 Carter Road
Rumson, New York 07004
(201) 223-1977

PROFESSIONAL
GOAL:

A challenging career as a certified public
accountant specializing in tax work.

EDUCATION:

Ossining Business College
Degree: Bachelor of Science, May 1978
Major: Accounting C.P.A. 3.4)
Major Subjects: Accounting (financial and managerial)
     auditing, business management and organization,
     management data systems, physics, mathematics.

WORK
EXPERIENCE:

9/78—present. Transport Efficiency Analyst for
Interstate Trucking Commission (Community Internship
Program of Ossining Business College). Responsible for
analyzing efficiency of 26 interstate weigh-stations;
pinpointing overages; streamlining operations by
monitoring new inspection procedures. Worked closely
with state police and Trucking Commission Authorities.

8/77—present. Self-employed. Have organized
private lawn-tool repair service; coordinated door-to-door
distribution of promotional materials to generate sales.

Summer '76. Research Assistant. Manasquan
Veterinary Institute, Manasquan, NJ. Aided third-year
veterinary student in major research project monitoring
behavior of rabbits in heat-controlled environments;
compiled all data and statistics for report.

Summer '74. Retail Salesman. Toy Mart
Maxwell Blvd. South Orange, New Jersey. Assisted
manager with floor displays, inventory, etc.

SKILLS:

Trained in business research, bookkeeping, and FORTRAN
computer programming. Some knowledge of key-punch
procedures.

BACKGROUND &
INTERESTS:

Traveled extensively in Europe and the United
States. Member of National Skeet Shooting Association,
Chess Club, Radio Club. Part-time volunteer for "Meals on
Wheels" program in lower Ossining.

REFERENCES:

Available on request.

CLARK S. KENT

123 Reeve Street, Apt. S   (201) 555-6543
Metropolis, NY 12345

CAREER OBJECTIVES

The defense of truth, justice, and the American way.

EDUCATION

B.A. in Communications, June 19— University of Gotham GPA: 4.0/4.0
Extracurricular Activities: Reporter, The Weekly Planet; Costume
Designer, Drama Club; President, Unaided Flight Club.

WORK EXPERIENCE

July 19—to present   Reporter, The Daily Planet. Usual beats:
                            Police Department, crime prevention.

January 19—to present   Crime Controller, in close co-operation with Gotham
                            Police Department and FBI. Specialties: averting
                            and/or solving candy-store robberies, abductions,
                            dam breakings, overthrows of governments, etc.

HONORS

Four-year full tuition scholarship to University of Gotham, UFO Society; Keys to
Metropolis, April 19—; Teddy Award for distinguished coverage of "Superman"
activities, 19—; Presidential Medal of Freedom, 19—.

SPECIAL SKILLS

Faster than a speeding bullet; more powerful than a locomotive; able to leap tall
buildings in a single bound. Also capable of changing clothes quickly in small
places.

REFERENCES

Ms. Lois Lane
Reporter, The Daily Planet
Metropolis, NY 12345

Mr. Perry White
Editor, The Daily Planet
Metropolis, NY 12345

Little Old Lady
Gotham Candy Store
Metropolis, NY 12345

President, United States
The White House
1600 Pennsylvania Avenue
Washington, DC 20500

be this: write and rewrite until you are positive that not one sentence—not even a single word—is not absolutely essential. Long-windedness is never much in demand. In business it is the kiss of death.

Business Letters

Business letters generally involve asking for something or answering some kind of request. The most common types of business letters are those of application, order, inquiry, claim, or complaint. You will probably have occasion to use one or more of these forms no matter what kind of job or academic program you are in. Thus you may find the following discussion helpful.

Too often, people forget that business writing requires the same sort of precision and clarity that ordinary writing does. They think they have to use a lot of jargon, or imitate the unreadable fine print they see in insurance policies. Nothing could be further from the truth. Good writing is good writing. The writer who falls prey to the notion that he has to "sound businesslike" usually ends up sounding incomprehensible. If you remember nothing else, keep in mind that business writing is only writing that happens to take place in the context of business. It still has to be straightforward, well-organized, and concise.

What follows are a few guidelines for effective business writing. Follow them also when writing letters of application and cover letters accompanying resumes, which represent your first entrance into the business world:

1. State the purpose of your letter in the first paragraph. Do not keep your reader waiting or guessing.
2. Use natural, straightforward language. If you try to come across as something you are not, the reader will spot it right away.
3. Be specific. If you are after a particular job, name it. That way, the personnel manager will not have to wonder which of the 13 positions she advertised you are interested in.
4. Use expressive verbs. Write in the active voice whenever possible. This gives the impression of an active person behind the letter.
5. Keep it short. Do not write an autobiography.
6. Edit and re-edit. Throw out any word you do not need.
7. Neatness is vital. Always double-check for errors.
8. The tone should be assertive but courteous.
9. End your letter by telling the reader what you would like to happen now. Ask for an appointment. Tell the reader to expect a phone call next week.

The letter of application should adhere as closely as possible to the guidelines listed above. If a job is at stake, you do not want to put yourself out of the running before you even get an interview. So, use the letter to *get* an interview. Make it hard for the reader to say no. But always remember to be brief and courteous.

The letter on page 293 is effective for several reasons. First of all, the writer states in the first paragraph which position she is interested in. This leaves no room for confusion on the part of the person reading the letter; he can place it immediately and move on.

In the second paragraph, we see one of the fundamental principles of good business writing at work: *narrowing your information to the concerns of a particular audience.* This writer knows she is writing to someone in the journalism business, and she knows that journalism revolves around deadlines. So, she wastes no time establishing the fact that she has met deadlines in the past and will meet them again in the future.

Note, too, that she is not afraid to use positive, assertive words like "skill" and "capacity." This may seem an obvious thing to include in a letter of application, yet many people balk at using assertive words for fear of seeming too anxious or overbearing. Actually, employers welcome confident applicants; this writer backs up her confidence by referring the reader to her resume.

In the fourth paragraph, having provided enough data about herself to encourage a preliminary judgment, she tries to dispel any negative assumptions that her credentials may have prompted. She faces up to the stereotypes sometimes associated with creative people and teachers, and deftly disposes of them by providing specific examples of her courage under fire. Thus her conclusion—"I can cope with tough situations"—seems more a statement of fact than a subjective self-evaluation.

Memos and Reports

Business memos and reports can and do deal with nearly every subject on earth. As in all business writing, it is imperative that they be brief and clear.

MEMOS.   The *memo* is most often a brief note, generally not more than one page, rarely more than two. In general, it can be somewhat informal, allowing for the writer's personality and views to show through. Most memos are written on one or another of a wide variety of memo forms, ranging from tiny scratch pads for handwritten telephone messages to formal 8½″ × 11″ bond paper embossed with the company name.

In almost every case, the memo form will have headings that give blank spaces for:

518 Harold Place
Albany, New York 18848
February 17, 1980

Mr. Ralph Singleton
Albany Features Syndicate
P. O. Box 4815
Albany, NY 13221

Dear Mr. Singleton:

I am responding to your advertisement in today's <u>Herald-American</u> of an opening for a reporter–copy editor trainee. I believe that I possess the necessary qualifications for the position.

My resume bears testimony to my interest and achievements in writing, from my work on high school and college newspapers to my present engagement with the Barker & Brown textbook. I might add only that in almost every instance I have been working against a deadline, long-term or short-term, and that I have never yet failed to meet one. I assure you that my work for Albany Features Syndicate will be just as reliable.

My skill and capacity as an editor have come into play in my school newspaper activities and, most recently, in my private typing and editing service. The guarantee I make to my typing and editing customers (again, see my resume) is one which I can also make to you.

Finally, lest my being a "creative" writer and having been a teacher should hint that I am an overly retiring personality, I assure you that I can be as "eager and aggressive" as the next person. I have, in my time, set up a committee to investigate racial violence in my high school; crossed the country three times on a Greyhound bus; and informed husky football players without flinching that they would receive well-deserved F's in English. In short, I can cope with tough situations.

I am available at your convenience to discuss your requirements and my qualifications for the job at greater length. Thank you for your time and trouble.

Sincerely yours,

C. Ellen Ridgeway

To _____; From _____; Subject_____

When you write a memo, keep those three headings in mind. Cover what the subject requires in understandable terms; then sign off. Remember that you are conveying information or requesting it from a particular person or set of people. Generally, you know your audience in a business memo, so write to it.

One problem that comes up time and again in business writing is the use of jargon. Office memos are most often written for in-house use; that is, they are to be read only by members of the same company, frequently only by members of a particular division or department. This may tempt the writer to use jargon (terms that are specific to a certain profession, business, or trade) or bureaucratese (a euphemistic term meaning writing that is windy, pretentious, and meaningless). You should resist the temptation.

All businesses, industries, trades, crafts, government agencies, and the like have their own professional jargon. Often these technical terms, acronyms, and nicknames given to procedures and processes are useful and clear to all concerned. In such situations, the use of jargon is both appropriate and accurate. The real problem with jargon surfaces when terms that are specific and useful in one profession are used in the context of another profession where they are neither appropriate nor meaningful. See Chapter 6, "Words," for a discussion of jargon and other language inflators.

BUSINESS REPORTS.   The *business report* is usually more formal than a memo. It is normally written in the third person and the material is mostly factual and concise. The report may be written to a specific individual or it may be for general use through a division or several divisions of a company.

The business report usually serves as an introduction to a problem or as a statement of a problem or event. This is often followed by a discussion or analysis of the problem or event that presents three or four different approaches to and three or four points of view of the problem. The report ends with some kind of conclusion drawn from the preceding discussion, usually accompanied by a recommendation for some kind of action. The business report, except in the concluding portion, calls for a fairly objective kind of writing.

Because some action may be taken—or not taken—on the basis of a report, you must always be careful to double check all your facts, figures, names, dates, and places to see that they are accurate and unambiguous. Indeed, this is true of all business writing—letters, memos, reports, and anything else. Business writing is action writing; it causes shipments to be made, contracts to be sent, deals to be closed. Wrong information can be costly, not only for your company but for your career as well.

WRITING FOR SCHOOL AND WORK

In many instances in college, and frequently in business, too, you will be expected to read an article or book or court case and give a brief summary or report of it. The point of this kind of writing is to be as objective as possible and to give as full and clear an idea of the important aspects of the original as possible. The forms discussed here are the brief, the précis or abstract, and the report.

The Brief

The *brief* is a short report on a court case that identifies (1) the name of the case, the court, and date; (2) the facts of the case; (3) the issue, that is, the point of law under question; (4) the decision rendered; and (5) a summary of the reasoning of the court leading up to its decision.

Below is an outline of a brief that a law student or lawyer would be expected to write. The form of the brief is quite straightforward. The outline does not provide the facts of the case, but tells what kind of information belongs in each category.

IDENTIFICATION: Name of Case
                    Court and Date

FACTS: It is helpful to characterize the plaintiff and defendant and describe the nature of the action. Your first sentence in the statement of facts should answer the question of who is suing whom for what. For example, plaintiff-buyer sues defendant-seller for breach of contract when defendant refused to deliver goods under the contract. Then go on to elaborate on the facts . . . without being unduly lengthy. Also include the contentions of both sides in the controversy. This helps you narrow down the issue in the case.

ISSUE: This is the most important part of the brief. What is the narrow question of law that the court is deciding?

DECISION: How did this court respond to the issue?

REASONING: Briefly reiterate how the court reached the result it did. You may find that setting forth the reasoning process in numbered statements aids your study of the case.

The Précis or Abstract

The *précis* or *abstract* is not as formal as the brief but it requires just as much precision. An abstract either summarizes or describes the essential ideas in a scholarly article. It is an abbreviated version of the article and should include a statement of the thesis, the development of the argument, the nature of the proof or evidence, and the conclusion. Remember that an abstract's purpose is to explain what the article *says*, not just to review its major points. It should show the relationship between the author's ideas and arguments, and let the reader see the difference between this article and others on the same subject.

A clearly written abstract should be able to stand on its own as an independent statement. That means you have to weigh the main ideas of an article precisely and honestly, putting more emphasis on those points that were given more emphasis in the original. You cannot afford to omit important ideas or fail to distinguish major points from minor ones.

THE STYLE OF AN ABSTRACT.   The following list details the style an abstract should follow:

1. *Brevity*. An abstract should be as compact and concise as possible, including only significant details. Information already apparent from the title or obvious generalizations such as "Romanticism flourished in the nineteenth century" should be omitted. As a rule, an abstract should be about one-tenth the length of the material it condenses.
2. *Paragraphing*. Assuming that the original document is article-length, make your abstract a coherent paragraph. Avoid disjointed sentences and try not to use verbatim topic sentences from paragraphs in the article.
3. *Sentences*. Vary sentence length, just as you do in other kinds of writing. You may not have the room to develop ideas as fully as you would like, but you should not make your abstract sound like shorthand just to save space. Do not omit verbs, conjunctions, or other words you need to keep sentences smooth.
4. *Language and Quotations*. The person reading the abstract knows that you are writing from the author's point of view. So you do not have to use phrases like "The author concludes . . ." or "it is believed by Fisher . . ." Avoid direct quotations from the article. Stick to an abbreviated summary of the main points.
5. *Verbs, Voice, and Tense*. As with other types of writing, use active verbs whenever you can write in the active voice. Use one tense and one voice consistently within the abstract.

6. *Format.* Type abstracts on standard typing paper, double-spaced, with one-inch margins all around. A standard bibliographical heading should begin the abstract:

Francis, W. Nelson. "Language, Languages, and Linguistic Science." In *The Structure of American English.* New York: Ronald Press, 1958, pp. 1–50.

Single-space this heading and skip three lines between it and the body of the abstract. All abstracts should be signed at the end, and a cover sheet should be attached to a group of abstracts handed in together. On this sheet give your name, course, section number, instructor, and date.

Be sure that your bibliographical heading indicates whether you are abstracting a whole chapter, part of it, or a whole book.

The Report

The *report* may be requested in a variety of forms in a variety of courses. Like the business report, the course report consists essentially of an introduction, some kind of summary of the topic being covered, an analysis based on the information in the summary, and finally some reaction, response, or conclusion drawn by the writer.

For instance, suppose a course requires you to give a report on animal language. What the instructor is looking for is an introduction to the subject of animal language, a summary of what you have read on the subject, an analysis of what the findings have been, and then some kind of response from you. "On the basis of the foregoing, I think [do not think] that the case for animals learning speech—as humans use the term—has been proved." Still, course reports seldom entail as much research as formal research papers.

Like the business report, the course report is fairly objective in presentation. This is the question, these are the issues, these are the approaches that have been taken, this is what it all adds up to. Only then will it be possible for you to take some kind of stand or draw some kind of conclusion. Remember, the report is not an argument. It needs to be characterized by neutral language and an objective attitude on the part of the writer.

TECHNICAL OR SCIENTIFIC WRITING

Very often, technical writing involves material that the average reader is not familiar with. That is why you have to be doubly careful with your language, logic, and structure, expressing your thoughts as simply as possible and providing crystal-clear transitions from one thought to the next. The best technical writers always put themselves in the position of the layman when they write, knowing all too well that what is simple to them will not necessarily be simple to others.

If you have a specialized interest or hobby, you probably know how difficult it can be to explain its more sophisticated aspects to your friends. For all your enthusiasm, they may only respond with blank stares. "Why do you keep fooling around with this stuff?" they may ask, frowning at your trays of algae or your Petri dishes glazed with mold. You may feel a little bit frustrated by it all, because you do not know how to tell them what they are missing.

Not everyone can be interested in technical subjects, of course, but almost everyone will come in contact with them at one time or another. That friend of yours who did not understand your interest in marine biology will suddenly find herself having to absorb vast new amounts of financial data for her company training program. And whether she succeeds in absorbing it or not will depend on the quality of the technical writing she reads.

The majority of technical or scientific writing deals with tests that have been made on something and what the results prove or fail to prove. Ideally, the style of such reports is clear and even-handed, regardless of how difficult the subject matter becomes. Again, it is the writer's obligation to use every principle of clear organization at his disposal (including headings, subheadings, etc.). If he does not, the subject matter will overwhelm the audience and they will stop reading.

Often, you actually incorporate an outline right into the body of the text. For instance, a scientific report may be set up like this:

I. Describe the date, place, and elements that comprise the experiment.
II. Provide a description of the methods used and the procedures followed, including:
   A. apparatus used
   B. disposition of the equipment
   C. rationale for setting up the experiment in this way
III. Give the results of the experiment, including:
   A. any tables, graphs, charts, or other statistical matter
   B. an analysis of the results
IV. Provide conclusions you have drawn from the results, including possible further experiments to be performed or suggestions for other avenues of research.

The article on pages 301–302 is taken from the *Journal of Educational Research.* Pay attention primarily to the way the headings serve as an outline for the article and as an organizational device. All the articles in this magazine, which specializes in research reports, have the

The Effect of Male Teachers on the Academic Achievement of Father-Absent Sixth Grade Boys

LEO M. SCHELL
DAN COURTNEY
Kansas State University

ABSTRACT

Previous research has shown that as a group the reading achievement of father-absent elementary school boys is very low. It has been hypothesized that these boys might benefit from instruction by a male teacher. This study investigated whether assigning father-absent sixth grade boys to male teachers would result in higher academic achievement than that of similar boys assigned to female teachers, holding fifth grade achievement test scores and intelligence quotients statistically constant. Results indicated that male teachers had no significant effect upon the academic achievement of these boys. It is suggested that strategies other than assignment to male teachers be pursued by educators committed to helping improve the academic achievement of these boys.

BOYS WHOSE FATHERS ARE ABSENT for one reason or another (death, separation, divorce, etc.) comprise a disproportionate number of low academic achievers (3, 7, 8). One of the reasons frequently hypothesized for the relationship of father absence to poor academic achievement of the sons is the lack of an adult male figure who positively models academic activities, i.e., adult males who read in the presence of, and to, their sons and who reinforce imitative behaviors (3, 7, 8). Lacking an appropriate male model, the father-absent boy may not be motivated to achieve in these areas. The lack of an available father figure who will reward management behaviors required in school, i.e., sitting down when told, listening, following directions, etc., may indirectly contribute also to lowered academic achievement.

Blanchard and Biller (4) compared four groups of third grade boys on *Stanford Achievement Test* scores and teacher grades. The groups consisted of boys with a high amount of father interaction, those with a low amount of father interaction, early father-absent boys (before age five), and later father-absent boys (after age five). The father-absent groups scored below grade level, with the early father-absent group making lower scores than the other three groups. Santrock and Wohlford (12) found that father loss between ages six and nine had a particularly negative effect on academic achievement.

It has been argued that increasing the number of male teachers might "masculinize" the school culture and indirectly contribute to improved academic achievement of boys. This has been studied indirectly by comparing achievement of boys and girls in countries where there is a predominance of male teachers in the elementary school. In three studies, one in Germany (11), one in the United States, Canada, England, and Nigeria (10), and one in Japan (9), boys' achievement was higher where a majority of the teachers were men.

Asher and Gottman (1), however, found that the sex of the teacher was not a significant factor in the reading achievement of fifth grade students in the midwestern United States. None of these studies, however, specifically examined the achievement of father-absent boys under female and male teachers.

Brophy and Good (6), after reviewing the research, suggest that male teachers may be particularly helpful for fatherless boys.

This study investigated the effects of male teachers on the academic achievement of father-absent sixth grade boys. This grade level was chosen because it was the earliest level at which there was a large enough number of male teachers and where prior standardized achievement and intelligence test scores were available.

Method

Subjects

In a large midwestern city, 193 boys on whom there were complete data were identified from school records as being father absent. Of these, 90 had been assigned to 40 male teachers during their sixth grade year and 103 had been assigned to 46 female teachers, all in essentially self-contained classrooms.

Measure

Five total subtest scores from the *Iowa Test of Basic Skills*—Vocabulary, Reading Comprehension, Language, Work Study, and Mathematics—served as both the pretest and posttest measures, having been administered in April of the fifth and sixth grade years. Intelligence quotients were from the total score of the *Short Form Test of Academic Aptitude* (13), which had been administered in April of the boys' fifth grade year.

Table 1.—Analysis of Covariance with I.Q. and Fifth Grade *ITBS* Scores as Covariates

Source	df	Vocabulary Total		Reading Total		Language Total		Work-Study Total		Mathematics Total	
		MS	F	MS	F	MS	F	MS	F	MS	F
Covariate											
Pretests	1	65.36	.270	77.41	.168	60.98	6.17*	60.08	.280	48.33	.016
I.Q.	1										
Sex	1										
Residual	189										

*$p < .05$

Procedure

t-test comparisons between the two groups were made on the five criterion measures of the *ITBS*, intelligence quotients, and chronological age. There were no significant differences on any of the *ITBS* scores nor on the chronological ages, but there was a significant difference ($p < .01$) between the mean intelligence quotients of the groups. The mean I.Q. for the boys assigned to female teachers (Group F) was 99.1, while those assigned to male teachers (Group M) was 94.1. Also, even though none of the differences between *ITBS* scores was statistically significant, Group F had higher mean scores on all five of them. Therefore, analysis of covariance with I.Q. and fifth grade *ITBS* scores as covariates was used to analyze the data.

Results

The results of the analysis of covariance for both Group F and Group M are shown in Table 1. None of the five adjusted mean scores favored boys assigned to male teachers. However, the total Language score was significantly in favor, at the .05 level, of the boys assigned to female teachers. There was no evidence that assignment of father-absent boys to male teachers, in and of itself, was able to enhance the academic achievement of these sixth grade boys.

Discussion

The results of this study seem to make it clear that it is unrealistic to assign upper grade elementary father-absent boys to male teachers with the expectation of improving their academic achievement more than what would occur if they were assigned to female teachers. The expressed hope of many educators that these boys would somehow identify with a male teacher, see school achievement as a masculine as well a feminine trait, and thus work harder and learn more, was not borne out in this study. Assignment of these boys to male teachers, in and of itself, does not seem sufficient to attain this goal. In fact, female teachers were more successful in teaching these boys those things measured by the Language subtest of the *ITBS* than were the male teachers.

Two possibly influential factors were not considered in this study: length of father-absence and availability of male models other than the father. However, what was studied seems to be within the general parameters upon which a school or a school district would base a policy. These other factors may help in assigning individual boys to particular teachers, but they seem unlikely to be considered in creating a general policy covering most father-absent boys.

Male teachers at earlier grades might possibly have a more positive effect on these boys' academic achievement than did the sixth grade teachers in this study. However, the possibility of large numbers of male teachers entering primary grades is unlikely. Therefore, educators who are sincerely interested in the academic growth of father-absent boys will have to devise a series of more activist intervention strategies beginning as early as identification is possible. Waiting until these boys are older and then merely assigning them to a male teacher probably will not help them academically any more than will assigning them to a female teacher. Numerous active intervention strategies on helping elementary school boys in general have been suggested by Austin (2), Bradley (5), and Trela (14). Interested educators should refer to these books.

REFERENCES

1. Asher, S. R., and Gottman, H. M. "Sex of Teacher and Reading Achievement." *Journal of Educational Psychology* 65 (1973): 168-171.
2. Austin, D. E.; Clark, V.; and Fitchett, G. W. *Reading Rights for Boys.* New York: Appleton-Century-Crofts, 1971.
3. Biller, H. B. "Paternal Deprivation, Cognitive Functioning, and the Feminized Classroom." In *Child Personality and Psychopathology: Current Topics,* edited by A. Davids, pp. 11-52. New York: John Wiley, 1974.
4. Blanchard, R. W., and Biller, H. B. "Father Availability and Academic Performance Among Third-Grade Boys." *Developmental Psychology* 4 (1971): 301-305.
5. Bradley, R. C. *The Role of the School in Driving Little Boys Sane.* Wolfe City, Texas: The University Press, 1976.
6. Brophy, J. E., and Good, T. L. *Teacher-Student Relationships, Causes, and Consequences.* New York: Holt, Rinehart, and Winston, 1974.
7. Herzog, E., and Sudia, C. E. *Boys in Fatherless Families.* Washington, D. C.: U. S. Department of Health, Education and Welfare, Office of Child Development, 1970.
8. Hetherington, E. M., and Deur, J. L. "The Effects of Father Absence on Child Development." *Young Children* 26 (1971): 233-248.
9. Janis, I. L. *Personality Dynamics, Development, and Assessment.* New York: Harcourt, Brace and World, 1969.

(From the *Journal of Educational Research*, 72, no. 4 (Mar./Apr. 1979), 194–95)

same organization. They (1) begin with an abstract; (2) give an introduction to the problem investigated; (3) provide a description of and rationale for the methods employed in the experiment (including, as here, information on the subjects studied, the measures—testing devices—used, and the procedures followed in the experiment); (4) present the results of the experiment (here including a chart of statistical data); and (5) end with a discussion of the results and ways in which they might be applied. In general, technical and scientific reports take on this fairly rigid kind of organization and presentation of data.

THE ORAL REPORT

At some time or other—both in the classroom and on the job—you will be called on to give an oral report. An oral rendering of a written report is almost always a condensed version of the original. You may have only five or ten minutes to cover material that may take twenty minutes or more to read. So you must select what you will include very carefully.

Only the most important points can be covered in an oral report. A listening audience has a much shorter attention span—and much more occasion for distraction—than a solitary reader has. Make your points clear and few. And do not be afraid of repetition. Remember, the audience cannot turn back to pick up something it missed.

Generally, we speak in much shorter sentences than those we use when we write. Often you can get away with using only phrases instead of complete sentences. This is because you are able to add meaning to a word or phrase with a gesture, a facial expression, or a tone of voice that carries the meaning of a paragraph. Do not try to repeat long, involved sentences from your written work. They are very hard to read properly and even harder to comprehend.

When giving an oral report, you will find graphic aids tremendously helpful. Most people are more eye-oriented than ear-oriented and having something to look at helps an audience concentrate. A large poster or an overhead transparency that presents a phrase or sentence outline of your report is an excellent device. It gives everyone an instant overview of what you are going to talk about, and it helps you keep away from digressions. It is usually a good idea to select only those visuals that will advance or further explain the material in the longer written version.

Above all, present your main points clearly in straightforward language, with an obvious and natural organization. If possible, leave time for questions at the end. In this way, you can address anything that some members of the audience missed or want more information on. Take advantage of the fact that the audience is in front of you. This is something you cannot do with written material, so make the most of it.

EXERCISES

1. How would you organize answers to the following essay questions?

a). Discuss the emergence of the Women's Movement out of the abolition movement in nineteenth-century America.

b). What were the effects (long- and short-term) of radiation on the survivors of Nagasaki and Hiroshima?

c). Compare and contrast the economic structures of Capitalism and Marxism in pre-World War II America and Russia, respectively.

d). Identify and analyze the major components of the diesel engine.

2. Refer to the excerpts from the articles on apes in Chapter 11 (pp. 275–276). Write an abstract and a précis for each.

3. Using the material in the research paper on ape language (Chapter 11, pp. 262–270), write a topic outline for a course report and a business report. In each instance, assume a role as a particular type of speaker (for instance, a visiting science lecturer, an executive trying to convince the board of directors to approve funding for ape research) and specify your audience.

4. Write appropriate business letters for each of the following situations. Bring them to class and discuss the strategies used by different students. Are some more effective than others? Why?

a). You are a recent graduate from an unknown college applying for your first job. You have some work experience and have done very well in school. Write a letter of application for a trainee position in a company that publishes a number of different trade journals.

b). You have just spent a lot of money for a new stereo system and have discovered, after assembling it, that two small, but important, parts are missing and one of the speakers is damaged. The manager of the store at which you bought it cannot be reached and her underlings have been extremely rude. Write a letter of complaint.

c). You have heard that a position may be opening up with a company you respect in an area in which you want to settle (supply the specifics). Write a letter of inquiry in which you ask about the possible position and present yourself as a likely candidate for it.

d). As a second-semester senior also in the midst of a job hunt, you have a red-letter day: two jobs for which you have applied have come through. You must size up the immediate and long-term advantages of each and notify the companies of your decision. Write a letter of acceptance and one of rejection.

5. Create resumes for the following jobs. Bring your results to class and compare them. Which are the most effective? Why?

MARKETING REPRESENTATIVE

Major investment banking firm is seeking individual experienced in the selling of consulting services to large corporations. Technical sales and management background helpful but not necessary. Salary commensurate with experience. Large benefits package.
Send resume to:
X1003 TIMES

ASSISTANT DIRECTOR OF ADMISSIONS

SUNY College at Purchase, in Westchester County, 20 miles from New York City, has an immediate opening for an experienced Asst. Director of Admissions. The College offers a wide variety of programs including liberal arts, visual & performing arts, and Educational Opportunity. Duties to include: traveling, developing recruitment programs with high schools, alumni, and faculty. Experience with direct mailings and publications desirable. Good communication skills essential. Bachelor's Degree required; Master's Degree desirable. Salary is competitive. Send resume by July 1, 1980, to:

Personnel Office, SUNY College at Purchase, Purchase, N.Y. 10577. EEO/AA Employer.

(State University of New York, College at Purchase)

Vice President Marketing

Seasoned marketing pro needed by national service corporation. To be eligible for consideration, you must be currently directing a total-marketing function.

The position entails overall responsibility for total advertising and publications program. Emphasis of program is on leadership in marketing analysis, sales training, and business planning for growth.

Salary will be commensurate with experience. Send your resume, along with salary requirements, to:
W4331 TIMES

6. Take the course and business-report outlines you did for the ape language paper. Revise the material for an oral report, and give the oral report in class. Take turns evaluating the presentations.

7. Choose one of the classified advertisements from Exercise 5 above. You want to apply for the job but do not have the exact qualifications required. Take a sheet of paper and divide it into two columns. In the first column, list the requirements specified, and in the second, your requirements. Determine how successfully or unsuccessfully you match each one. Try to figure out how you can turn your differences into positive advantages. Make up a resume and letter of application promoting yourself, with your particular talents and skills, for the job.

III

Handbook of Grammar and Usage

13 A Review of Grammar   309

14 Glossary of Grammatical Terms   345

15 The Conventions of Writing   367

16 Glossary of Usage   471

A Review of Grammar

Subjects and Predicates
Exercises

Nouns and Pronouns
Exercises

Verbs
Tense
Mood
Exercises

Modification
Attributive Adjectives
Determiners
Adverbs
Comparison of Modifying Words
Exercises

Phrases
Prepositional Phrases
Verbals
Exercises

Clauses
Exercises

Basic Patterns for Subjects
Exercises

Basic Patterns for Predicates
Exercises

**Variations in
Basic Sentence Patterns**
Questions
There/It as Expletives
Indirect Objects
Passives
Interrupters
Exercises

Compounding
Linking Ideas at Clause Level
Exercises

Conclusion

It is important for you as a writer to know about grammar. If you understand how sentences work, you will have a better grasp of how to make sentences behave for you—just as knowing how a camera works will make you a better photographer or knowing the different strokes of tennis will improve your game. A knowledge of grammar will also aid you in understanding your teacher's instructions and criticisms. The words "dangling modifier" written in the margin of one of your papers, for example, will not mean much to you unless you know what a modifier is, how it can "dangle," and what you can do to correct the problem.

Chapter 14, "Glossary of Grammatical Terms," follows this chapter. If you should happen to encounter a term in the Review with which you are not familiar, the "Glossary of Grammatical Terms" will give you a definition for it.

SUBJECTS AND PREDICATES

The grammar you learned in high school probably defined a sentence as "a group of words containing a subject and a predicate and expressing a complete thought." Even though we may argue about what a "complete thought" is, we recognize that sentences are statements and that the statements have two parts: subject and predicate. We are aware of the noun-like quality of the subject and the verb-like quality of the predicate, whether we can explain them or not. If you are asked to divide a sentence into two parts, you will invariably divide it between "subject" and "predicate." (Try it out in the examples that follow.)

Subject and predicate are necessary when a sentence must stand alone. You will recognize the following three sentences as sentences because each contains a subject and a predicate.

- Dorothy coughed.
- The doctor shook his head.
- The girl was sick.

The subject of each sentence tells us "who" or "what," and the predicate describes the action or condition following from the "who" or "what."

In each of our sample sentences, we find the subject by finding the part of the sentence that answers the question "who?" or "what?" (in these examples, *Dorothy*, *the doctor*, and *the girl*). A subject may be a single word, as in the first example above; it may be a single word plus other words that describe or qualify it; or it may even be a group of words that may be viewed as a potential sentence in itself. See how the subjects differ in these sentences:

- *She* had mononucleosis.

The subject is a pronoun, alone.

- *Young Dorothy, of Mamaroneck, New York,* came down with mononucleosis.

The subject is *Dorothy*, modified by an adjective and a prepositional phrase.

- *What she had* was an extremely rare form of mononucleosis.

The subject is a noun clause.

The elements that describe or qualify words or that can be viewed as potential sentences in themselves will be examined later. First we will look a little more closely at those words that name things: the noun and the pronoun.

EXERCISES

a). Divide each of the following sentences into subject and predicate parts. (Draw a vertical line at the point that represents this division.)

1. Tom surprised me.
2. The gifted artist, who exhibited his paintings yesterday, was glad when all of them were sold.
3. That he was guilty was apparent to everyone in the courtroom.
4. To build a bridge over this gorge will not be an easy task.
5. Getting away from work became increasingly impossible.

b). Identify and label the subject and the predicate in each of the following sentences:

1. Bartholomew went fishing.
2. Bartholomew, who had caught more fish that he and his friends could possibly eat, went home.
3. Fishing is supposed to be a very relaxing sport or pastime.
4. Sweet little Billy threw his baseball over the high fence toward the picture window Mr. Wilson had just replaced.
5. Eating, drinking, and being merry is a good way of life as long as you are healthy, wealthy, and not too wise.

NOUNS AND PRONOUNS

Nouns name persons, places, things, or ideas. *Proper nouns* name particular persons, places, or things: Annette, William Shakespeare, San Francisco, the Washington Monument, *The Washington Post*. *Common nouns* name things: woman, playwright, city, landmark, newspaper. Nouns that identify things we can see, hear, touch, taste, or feel are called *concrete nouns:* pencil, shirt, squeak, ice, artichoke. Abstract nouns identify things that are ideas rather than objects: abuse, virtue, science, love. Some nouns refer to individuals or individual items (boys, table, steps), while others are *collective,* referring to groups (committee, troop, orchestra, mob), and others refer to items which occur in *mass* or bulk (furniture, garbage, milk).

Pronouns can take the place of nouns, and they too fall into various classes. *Personal pronouns* take the place of names of persons: he, they, me, she. Pronouns that indicate ownership are *possessive* (his, our, their), while those referring to a person who has already been named are *reflexive* (himself, myself). Other pronouns relate the person or thing already named to the use of that person or thing in a clause, and they are called *relative* pronouns: who, which, that. Still others, called *interrogatives,* ask questions: who, what, which. Pronouns that stand specifically for a person, thing, or idea being singled out are called *demonstratives:* this, these, those. Still other pronouns are *indefinite:* anyone, each, every, everyone. Like nouns, pronouns can be modified by other words; again, we will see how this works when we turn to modification below.

EXERCISES

a). Substitute common nouns referring to people or objects for the proper ones in the sentences below. Avoid using modifiers except articles and possessives. How are the meanings of the sentences changed?

1. That Oriental rug is from Turkey and has been purchased by Mr. Radke.
2. When Pam became interested in cooking, she enrolled in a course taught by James Beard.
3. When Julie was in Chicago, she and Frances got tickets to see the exhibition of artifacts from the tomb of King Tutankamen at the Museum of Natural History.
4. Carol and I are fans of the New York City Ballet; we especially enjoy watching Peter Martins perform.
5. Last April, Linda flew from London to Paris on the SST.

b). Choose the appropriate collective noun from the following list and substitute it for the italicized phrase: clergy, jury, science, family, literature.

1. The *twelve men* deliberated for three hours and returned with their verdict.
2. *My father, mother, and two sisters* came to see me graduate.
3. They were married without the benefit of a *minister, priest, or rabbi.*
4. The students studied *poems, novels, short stories, and plays.*
5. I am taking courses in *biology, anatomy and physiology, and chemistry.*

c). Identify each pronoun in the following sentences as personal, possessive, reflexive or relative.

1. This dress which you bought for yourself yesterday might also fit your sister.
2. Jimmy amuses himself by playing with the airplane which his Aunt Lilien gave him for his birthday.
3. Tell me who's at the door, so that I know what to expect.
4. Here is a cookie for every child who wants one.
5. Each rule which Danny has made makes sense after all.

d). Identify the nouns and pronouns in the following sentences and classify them according to their function (abstract nouns, possessives, reflexive pronouns, etc.)

1. Bill found my father's suitcase, which was misplaced at the airport.
2. Bob himself gave me the keys.
3. Honesty is an outdated virtue.
4. Their greatest weakness is deceiving themselves.

VERBS

In the same way that the subject can be thought of as the "what" or "who" of the sentence, the predicate can be thought of as "what happens" or "what is." The core of the predicate is the verb. Go back to the first set of sample sentences. In sentence 1, Dorothy did something—she coughed. In sentence 2, the doctor did something to something—he shook his head. In sentence 3, a quality is attributed to "she"—she was sick. Each of the verbs has a name that reflects the relationship between the subject and the predicate of which the verb is a part.

- Dorothy coughed. INTRANSITIVE VERB

- The doctor shook his head. TRANSITIVE VERB

- The girl was sick. LINKING VERB

The word "intransitive" means that the "action" of the sentence does not go across to anything else, but stops with the verb itself. We do not need an object or any other word to know what is happening in the sentence. Look again at the first sentence: "Dorothy coughed" is complete in and of itself. Suppose, however, that the verb were "caught" instead of "coughed." In this situation, the action would *not* be complete without an object; we would need to know what it was that "Dorothy caught"—"Dorothy caught the ball," "Dorothy caught mononucleosis," etc. This is the situation we have in the second sentence. In this case, as we have observed, the doctor did something *to* something—shook his head. This verb is *transitive*; the "action" of the sentence goes from the verb, "shook," across to the object, "head." In sentence 3, the verb simply *links* a noun with a description. The sentence sets up a statement of what the girl was, or was like, instead of what she did: "The girl was sick"; "She was feverish"; "She felt terrible"; "She looked awful"—all these sentences do the same thing. Linking verbs can also link nouns with nouns: "The girl was Dorothy"; "Dorothy is a student"; "Her boyfriend was Tom Peterson."

As you can see, all of these descriptions of verbs are actually descriptions of relationships between subjects and predicates. We will turn now to some other attributes of verbs that are similarly conditioned by subjects—tense; aspect and attitude; and mood.

Tense

Tense indicates time, and in English we generally think of time in a three-way division: past, present, and future. (Not all languages have a past tense or a future tense—an interesting indication of the way in which language shapes our perceptions of reality.)

We form the present tense of a verb by using the verb itself, and we alter the verb's form only in the third person singular:

SINGULAR	PLURAL
I walk	we walk
you talk	you talk
he jump*s* (note the added *s*)	they jump

Most verbs in English form their past tense by adding *-d, -ed,* or *-t* to the verb form itself. We call such verbs *regular* verbs.

- Dorothy cough*ed.*
- Tom mean*t* to bring Dorothy a bouquet.

A few verbs, however—some of the oldest words in the language among them—form their past tenses irregularly, by changing the vowel or vowels in the verb. Consult a dictionary when in doubt.

PRESENT	PAST	PAST PARTICIPLE	PRESENT	PAST	PAST PARTICIPLE
become	became	become	know	knew	known
begin	began	begun	lead	led	led
bring	brought	brought	lose	lost	lost
buy	bought	bought	ring	rang	rung
choose	chose	chosen	rise	rose	risen
come	came	come	run	ran	run
do	did	done	see	saw	seen
draw	drew	drawn	speak	spoke	spoken
eat	ate	eaten	swim	swam	swum
fall	fell	fallen	take	took	taken
get	got	gotten, got	throw	threw	thrown
give	gave	given	wear	wore	worn
keep	kept	kept	write	wrote	written

Not all changes in the forms of verbs can be made even this simply, however; furthermore, not all changes in verb forms are made merely to indicate shifts in tense. The formation of the future tense in English, for example, gives some indication of these added complexities. In some situations in which we wish to indicate the future tense, we simply use the present tense (as in "Lock the door when you *leave*"). In situations in which a future-tense form *is* used, we cannot simply alter the form of the verb itself; we must add a new word to it—"shall" or "will." And, in at least some situations, the use of "shall" or "will" indicates something more to the reader than simply the fact that the action of the verb will take place in the future. "I shall leave for England at the end of the month," for example, implies something a good deal more definite and deliberate about the fact of going to England than "I leave for England at the end of the month," although either form could be used in this instance. To find out more about the types of nuances verbs can convey, we must consider *aspect* and *attitude.*

Aspect is that attribute of a verb that conveys to us information as to whether the action of the verb is complete or in progress. A past-tense verb—"Dorothy coughed," for example—tells us not only that Dorothy coughed at some point in the past but that the action is *complete*—that Dorothy did not go on coughing or is not still coughing. Verbs that tell us when an action was or is being continued are said to be in the *progressive* aspect; these verb forms consist of some form of *to be* plus the verb itself with *-ing* added to it. "Dorothy was coughing," for example, tells us that Dorothy did not start and stop coughing at any definite point and/or that she continued to cough for some time. "Dorothy is coughing" suggests, plainly, that Dorothy is *still* coughing. "Dorothy will be coughing" tells us that Dorothy will continue to cough into some indefinite point in the future ("Dorothy will cough," like "Dorothy coughed," suggests a definite incident of coughing, although one in the future instead of one in the past).

Verb forms can convey even more information than this to us: they can, for instance, tell us a good deal about the speaker's *attitude* toward, or degree of knowledge about, the action of the verb. In putting together the verb forms that convey such information to us, we use a number of words in addition to the basic verbs themselves; we call these "helping" or *auxiliary* verbs.

In English, auxiliary verbs fall into two broad categories:
(1.) forms of "to be," "to do," and "to have." You have already seen, of course, that "to be" is used in forming the progressive. It is worth mentioning as well that each of these three auxiliaries can be used as main verbs, in which case each has a meaning of its own:

- Dorothy is a typical adolescent.
- Dorothy does her own thing entirely too much.
- Dorothy has a boyfriend named Tom.

(2.) *modal* auxiliaries: may, might, can, could, will, would, shall, should, and must. You have already seen modals—*shall* and *will*—at work in the formation of the future tense. They also indicate a speaker's or writer's perception of whether an action is possible, probable, necessary, or obligatory.

Before encountering a more complete list of the possible verb forms, you should know more about the *principal parts* of the verb—the basic forms that are used by themselves or in combination with the auxiliary verbs in the possible verb forms. The first principal part is the *present infinitive—to* plus the verb. We made use of infinitives above—"to do," "to have," and "to be"—in telling you about auxiliary verbs, and you will find later that you can also use the infinitive as a noun, an adjective, or an adverb. (See "Verbals," below.) The other principal parts are the *past tense*, which we have already discussed; the *past participle*; and the *present participle*. The past participle is usually formed by adding -*ed* or -*en* to the verb, and the present participle by adding -*ing*. Like infinitives, participles are *verbals*; that is, they can function not only as parts of verb forms but as adjectives and other parts of speech. (The section below on "Verbals" will describe these other functions in more detail.)

A list of the possible verb forms appears on page 317. Think about the various distinctions of meaning between and among them; as you can see from the discussion above and the list below, we do have quite a range of possible meanings. (The possibilities are far more difficult to explain than they are for most speakers of the language to use!) As you can note from the list, too, the usual order for elements in the verb phrase is MODAL + *have* or *do* + *be* + VERB. Though probably no native speaker of English ever stops to think about it, we automatically place the various parts of the verb phrase in this order. When you realize that this list is far from complete, you can see that our verb system is impressive.

Mood

Another attribute of verbs in English is *mood*. The mood of a verb reveals the speaker's or writer's assessment of the *type* of statement into which his own statement falls. We state most communications in the *indicative* mood. When we make requests or give commands, we use the *imperative* mood, in which the grammatical subject of the sentence is always *you* and is usually deleted: *Turn off the lights, please. Bring me a unicorn. Get out of here!* And, though it is disappearing from the language, careful speakers and writers still observe that manner of expressing wishes or statements contrary to fact, called the *subjunctive*:

Subject	MODAL	Have/Do	Be	VERB
Dorothy				coughs
Dorothy			is	coughing
Dorothy				coughed
Dorothy			was	coughing
Dorothy	will			cough
Dorothy	can			cough
Dorothy	should			cough
Dorothy	must			cough
Dorothy	might			cough
Dorothy	may			cough
Dorothy	would			cough
Dorothy	could			cough
Dorothy	will		be	coughing
Dorothy	can		be	coughing
Dorothy	should		be	coughing
Dorothy	must		be	coughing
Dorothy	might		be	coughing
Dorothy	may		be	coughing
Dorothy	would		be	coughing
Dorothy	could		be	coughing
Dorothy		has		coughed
Dorothy		had		coughed
Dorothy	will	have		coughed
Dorothy	would	have		coughed
Dorothy	could	have		coughed
Dorothy	should	have		coughed
Dorothy	must	have		coughed
Dorothy	might	have		coughed
Dorothy	may	have		coughed
Dorothy		has	been	coughing
Dorothy		had	been	coughing
Dorothy	will	have	been	coughing
Dorothy	would	have	been	coughing
Dorothy	could	have	been	coughing
Dorothy	should	have	been	coughing
Dorothy	must	have	been	coughing
Dorothy	might	have	been	coughing
Dorothy	may	have	been	coughing
Dorothy		does		cough
Dorothy		did		cough

Some *spoken* dialects of American English also include:

Subject	MODAL	Have/Do	Be	VERB
Dorothy				cough
Dorothy				coughing
Dorothy			be	coughing
Dorothy		do	be	coughing
Dorothy		done		coughed

"If Tom *were* a better boyfriend, he would have brought Dorothy a bouquet." It is also seen in certain common expressions: "*Be* that as it may. Would that I *were* a king."

EXERCISES

a). Identify the verb or verbs in each of the following sentences as transitive, intransitive, or linking.

1. Barney would play ball with his friends if it weren't raining.
2. Maribeth will spend the day sewing.
3. A small child ran across the street.
4. The oncoming car has stopped just in time.
5. The policeman is stopping all cars in order to search them.
6. These shoes will be too big for Jennifer.
7. Isidore was taking a second look at the house he intended to buy.
8. He was appalled by all the shortcomings that he had overlooked.
9. He came to the conclusion that the house was not a good buy.
10. Aunt Miriam enjoys it when the sun is so warm.

b). Identify the following verbs as transitive or intransitive and make a sentence with each.

climb	shook	kick
left	fell	empty

c). Rewrite the following sentences using each of the five forms given below. In some sentences, one or more of these forms may not be possible. Explain why.

- *Example:* The little boy *ate* the cookie.

present progressive:	The little boy is eating the cookie.
past progressive:	The little boy was eating the cookie.
present perfect:	The little boy has eaten the cookie.
past perfect:	The little boy had eaten the cookie.
Future with *may:*	The little boy may eat the cookie.

1. The ship sailed away.
2. My mother lost the tickets.
3. Mary sewed her clothes in the afternoon.
4. Your dog is noisy.

d). Generate a sentence whose verb fits each of the following patterns:

1. *have* + verb
2. *be* + verb
3. MODAL + verb
4. MODAL + *be* + verb
5. *have* + *be* + verb
6. verb alone without *have, be,* or MODAL

7. MODAL + *have* + *verb*
8. MODAL + verb
9. MODAL + *have* + *be* + *verb*
10. *have* + *be* + *verb*

MODIFICATION

English sentences consist not only of subjects and predicates, but of other words or groups of words that add meaning to the sentence by describing, quantifying, qualifying, attributing, or in some other way modifying another element of the sentence. Modifiers are of two general types: adjectives, or adjectival constructions, and determiners modify nouns or pronouns; adverbs or adverbial constructions modify verbs, adjectives, or other adverbs. Modifiers may be single words or clusters of words; words in a related group, such as prepositional phrases or verbal phrases; or even groups of words that have the potential to be sentences by themselves, such as adverbial clauses or relative clauses. We will examine the general types of modifiers here; phrase and clause modifiers in particular will be given closer attention in later sections.

Attributive Adjectives

When we try to think of adjectives as single words, we generally think of *attributive* adjectives—adjectives that attribute some quality or other to the nouns or pronouns they modify: *the educational trip, the red house, the sick girl.* The attachment of an attributive adjective to a noun, as a matter of fact, may be understood as a statement *about* the noun: *The trip was educational. The house is red. The girl is sick.*

Determiners

Determiners count, specify, or limit nouns and pronouns in some way. They don't describe, as do attributive adjectives; determiners point out or determine. There are several different types of determiners:

ARTICLES.   *Articles* include *a* or *an*, which are indefinite in nature, and *the*, which is more specific and limiting; these are referred to as *indefinite* and *definite* articles respectively. Note the difference between the use of the indefinite and definite articles in this sentence:

- Dorothy said, "*The* broom you brought me was lovely, Tom, but I would have preferred *a* bouquet and *an* ounce of perfume."

(*A*, incidentally, precedes a word that begins with a consonant sound; *an* precedes a word that begins with a vowel sound.) *"The* broom" refers to a definite broom—the one Tom brought Dorothy—and the use of *the* helps to make this clear. No *specific* bouquet or ounce of perfume is referred to, however, and so "a" and "an" are correctly used with these words.

DEMONSTRATIVES.   *Demonstratives* include such words as *this*, *that*, *these*, and *those*; as their name suggests, they are even more forcefully specific than the definite article. (Consider this example: Dorothy said, "Remove *that* broom immediately!")

POSSESSIVES.   *Possessives*, as the name indicates, make ownership clear. "Ownership" does not, of course, always indicate actual *possession*; it may designate a sense of origin (*Poe's* "The Gold-bug"), relationship (*Dorothy's* boyfriend), or some other more subtle form of attachment. Possessive pronouns include *our*, *your*, *his*, *her*, *its*, and *their* (*her* illness, *his* mistake, *their* argument); the possessives of nouns are formed by adding *-'s* to most singular nouns and an apostrophe alone to most plural nouns (the *doctor's* diagnosis, the *nurses'* station).

NUMBERS.   *Numbers* include both the *cardinal* numbers (one, two, fourteen, ninety-six, etc.) and the *ordinal* numbers (first, second, fourteenth, ninety-sixth, etc.)

Adverbs

Adverbs, as we have already noted, modify verbs, adjectives, or other adverbs. They serve many functions in the sentence: they can tell *how* action was performed (manner), *where* something happened (place), or *when* something happened (time).

- Dorothy shouted *angrily* at Tom. (manner; *angrily* modifies *shouted*)
- Tom moved *away quickly*. (place and time; *away* and *quickly* modify *moved*)

Adverbs may also tell *to what degree* something is true; adverbs of this type modify adjectives or other adverbs (not verbs) and are called *intensifiers*. Intensifiers include words such as *very, rather, extremely*—as in "Dorothy shouted *extremely* loudly" or "Tom got *rather* red in the face."

Comparison of Modifying Words

Modifying words can be *compared*—that is, they can be altered to indicate degrees of difference between or among two or more things being described. When an adjective or adverb indicates the more outstanding or unusual of two things, it is said to be in the *comparative* degree; if it indicates the most outstanding of more than two things, it is said to be in the *superlative* degree. Adjectives and adverbs of one or two syllables can usually be compared by adding the syllable *-er* for the comparative degree and *-est* for the superlative:

- pretty, prettier, prettiest
- vile, viler, vilest
- fast, faster, fastest

Some adjectives and adverbs of two syllables, and most of those of more than two syllables, are compared by means of the intensifiers *more* and *most*:

- fully, more fully, most fully
- beautiful, more beautiful, most beautiful
- serenely, more serenely, most serenely
- pious, more pious, most pious

Some adjectives and adverbs, of course, are irregular in comparison. They are literally relics in the language, left over from an earlier time.

- good, better, best
- bad, worse, worst

EXERCISES

a). Rewrite the following sentences by replacing each italicized phrase with an attributive adjective.

1. Mary did not pass because she wrote sentences *that were not clear and did not make complete sense.*
2. Bill's house, *which is painted white,* is surrounded by garish homes *painted blue and yellow.*
3. My uncle, *who hoarded his money,* became a millionaire when he was forty.
4. The boxing champion, *who defeated all his opponents,* was applauded loudly.
5. The Vietnamese people have always been victimized by powerful nations *that have a tendency to conquer and exploit.*

b). Identify all the attributive adjectives, definite articles, indefinite articles, demonstratives, possessives, cardinal numbers, ordinal numbers, and interrogatives in the following sentences.

1. The Blue Angel is the fifth restaurant that I have tried in this oversized small town.
2. Whose idea was it to share a room with those other three kids?
3. Which of the two beds do you want: the wide one with the lumpy mattress or the narrow one, which is soft and smooth?
4. These four books are not mine; I can't remember who lent them to me.

5. How are we going to celebrate the Fourth of July this year?
6. Those two girls, big Tina and tiny Tanya, are quite a pair. They have many friends, but quite a few of the kids can't stand them.

c). Generate a sentence whose subject fits each of the following patterns.

1. demonstrative + noun
2. definite article + attributive adjective + noun
3. possessive adjective + attributive adjective + noun
4. definite article + cardinal number + attributive adjective + noun
5. demonstrative adjective + attributive adjective + noun

d). Use possessive pronouns wherever possible in the following sentences.

1. Jane's paper is the best in the class.
2. Dick and Tom's vacation was very enjoyable.
3. Carry is Ann's sister.
4. That home is the Andersen's.
5. Joann, who is Katy's friend, will be visiting us for a week.

PHRASES

English sentences employ *phrases* in a variety of ways. Phrases are groups of words that cannot stand alone as sentences because they lack a subject, a predicate, or both, but that function as a single part of speech. When we talked about the *subject*, for example, we talked about its "noun-like" quality. We could similarly describe the subject of a sentence as its *noun phrase*, or the noun or noun equivalent and its modifiers (note in the diagrams on p. 328 that the subject is labeled NP, or noun phrase). Likewise, the *predicate* is the *verb phrase*, or verb plus its objects, complements, or modifiers.

Prepositional Phrases

Prepositional phrases consist of a preposition—a word like *to, in, from, of, before, after,* etc., that suggests position, direction, or time; a noun or noun equivalent; and whatever modifiers are along to contribute something to the noun. Prepositional phrases are used as adjectives to modify nouns and as adverbs to modify verbs, adjectives, or other adverbs. Here are some examples:

• The reason *for the extraterrestrials' visit* was not immediately clear.

The phrase modifies *reason* and acts as an adjective.

• The extraterrestrials filed *into Dorothy's room.*

The phrase modifies *filed* and acts as an adverb.

Verbals

As we mentioned earlier, *verbals* are verb forms that can function not only as verbs or parts of verbs but as other parts of speech. The *infinitive* (*to* + the verb), for example, can be used as a noun, an adjective, or an adverb. The past participle (the verb plus *-ed* or *-en*, in most cases) and the present participle (the verb plus *-ing*) can be used as adjectives, and the verb plus *-ing* can also be used as a noun, in which case it is called a *gerund.* Here are some examples of verbals functioning on their own as different parts of speech:

- *To wait* was not easy for Dorothy. *(infinitive as noun)*
- Tom, *exhausted,* went down to the lobby *to wait. (past participle as adjective; infinitive as adverb)*
- The *waiting* extraterrestrials looked over the infirmary. *(present participle as adjective)*
- *Waiting* is not easy for extraterrestrials, either. *(gerund)*

Verbals, however, are not always simply used by themselves. Completed by objects or amplified by modifiers, they are known in traditional grammar as *verbal phrases;* these include *infinitive phrases, participial phrases, gerund phrases.* The phrases function in sentences just as the individual words do, as these examples indicate:

- *To frighten Dorothy out of her wits* was not the extraterrestrials' intention. *(infinitive phrase as noun)*
- Dorothy, *seeing the extraterrestrials in the doorway,* jumped out of bed and screamed. *(participial phrase as adjective)*
- *Seeing the extraterrestrials in the doorway* frightened Dorothy out of her wits. *(gerund phrase)*

It may help you, in using such phrases, to realize that they are partial or potential sentences—sentences with the subjects deleted that have been worked into or embedded in other sentences. Look at the second example again:

- Dorothy, seeing the extraterrestrials in the doorway, jumped out of bed and screamed.

There are really *two* main ideas here:

- Dorothy saw the extraterrestrials in the doorway.
- Dorothy jumped out of bed and screamed.

In order to avoid unnecessary repetition, however, the first sentence has been turned into a participial phrase and embedded within the second one. With participial phrases and other verbal phrases used as modifiers, of course, you must be careful not to embed the participial phrase in the wrong place, or serious misunderstandings—the kind that generations of English teachers have labeled "danglers"—will result:

- Standing in the doorway, Dorothy saw the extraterrestrials and jumped out of bed.

This translates as—

- Dorothy was standing in the doorway.
- Dorothy saw the extraterrestrials and jumped out of bed.

—a clear impossibility. The sentence must be rewritten to indicate who was *really* standing in the doorway:

- Dorothy saw the extraterrestrials standing in the doorway and jumped out of bed.

EXERCISES

a). Label each phrase in the following sentences as prepositional, participial, gerundive, or infinitive.

1. The woman wearing the ugly dress to go to dinner is my employer.
2. To own a dog is to have trouble; to own goldfish is to have peace.
3. The youngster running across the street with the fierce dog at his heels made it into the front door just in time.
4. Knowing who is your friend makes life easier.
5. Herman has been picked to go to France with the boss.

b). Generate a sentence which contains each of the following structures.

1. a participial phrase in the subject and a prepositional phrase in the predicate
2. a gerundive phrase in the subject and a gerundive phrase in the predicate
3. an infinitive phrase in the subject and a prepositional phrase in the predicate
4. two gerundive phrases in the predicate
5. an infinitive phrase in the subject and a participial phrase in the predicate

CLAUSES

Clauses, in contrast to verbal phrases, are groups of words that have both a subject and a predicate clearly expressed; in verbal phrases, as you have just learned, the subject is deleted. An *independent clause* is one which can stand on its own as a sentence; a *dependent or subordinate clause* is one which, like a phrase, functions as a single part of speech and which cannot stand on its own as a sentence. Independent clauses have already been discussed at some length and will be discussed later on; we will concentrate here on dependent clauses and their use.

The key to recognizing the difference between dependent clauses and independent clauses is in learning to recognize the ways in which dependent clauses work in sentences. Consider the following examples:

- The extraterrestrials had come to earth *because they had discovered a cure for mononucleosis.*

The whole *because . . .* clause in this sentence serves one function: it modifies *had come* (it tells *why* the extraterrestrials had come) and therefore serves as an adverb. *Adverbial clauses* function in exactly the same manner as adverbs and other adverbial constructions: they modify verbs, adjectives, or other adverbs, giving information about the manner, the time, the place, or the degree of an action. Adverbial clauses nearly always begin with a word like *because, unless, until, since, when,* etc.

- Dorothy, *who did not read science fiction,* did not know what was going on.

In this example, the clause *who did not read science fiction* describes *Dorothy*—it attributes a quality to her—and thus acts as an adjective. *Relative clauses,* or clauses introduced by relative pronouns (*who, which, that*—*who* in this case "relates" back to *Dorothy*), often function as adjectives. As you will discover below, however, appearances in such cases can sometimes be deceiving; not every clause beginning with *who, which,* or *that* functions as an adjective (some are not even relative clauses).

- The extraterrestrials knew *who she was,* however.

Who she was looks similar to the *who* clause of the second example, but you should examine it closely: it does not serve the same function in the sentence. In fact, it is the object of *knew*—it tells us who or what the extraterrestrials knew—and therefore serves as a noun. (Take another look at the second sentence above: the clause *what was going on* serves a similar function there.) Noun clauses can begin with a fairly wide range of "wh" words—*who, what, which, whoever* are a few examples—but it is more important and, in the long run, easier simply to recognize such clauses acting as subjects or objects in sentences than it is to try to memorize the words.

- *That they might be able to help her* did not cross her mind.

This clause, as you can see, also serves as a noun—this time as the subject of the sentence (it tells us just what it was that did not cross Dorothy's mind).

Dependent clauses, then, can serve as adverbs, adjectives, or nouns. Knowing this and learning to recognize the role such a clause plays in a sentence should help you to eliminate any remaining dependent/independent confusion you may still have. It is worth repeating, too, that none of the clauses in these examples could stand alone as sentences; they all depend to some extent on the sentences they are part of for their meaning.

A final note on relative clauses as adjectives is in order. When relative clauses are used in a sentence to specify something about the noun that is important or even necessary to the meaning of the sentence, we call it a *restrictive* clause and do not punctuate it with commas to set it off from the rest of the sentence.

- The extraterrestrial *who took Dorothy's hand* was the leader of the group.

(Aside from the clause, we have no other way of distinguishing him from the rest of the extraterrestrials.)

- The broom *that Tom brought Dorothy* was made of wood. (*Which broom?*)

When, on the other hand, the relative clause adds information to the sentence that is not essential to its meaning, we call it a *nonrestrictive* clause and set it off from the sentence with commas.

- Dorothy, *who did not read science fiction,* did not know what was going on.

The name *Dorothy* is sufficient identification for her; the clause adds "extra" information.

- The extraterrestrials' spaceship, *which was covered with blinking lights,* had been left in the parking lot.

Again, we know *whose* spaceship it is; the clause adds information.

In English sentences, as you have seen in this section, meaning is determined by structures and their order, as well as by individual words. Sentences are relationships between subjects and predicates; both subjects and predicates may include additional structures that modify or contribute to the meaning. The examples that follow will give you further practice at recognizing the parts of sentences, at expanding simple sentences by adding modifying structures, and at embedding phrases and clauses.

EXERCISES

a). In each of the following sentences identify each clause as a relative clause or an adverbial clause.

1. Rodney McKenzie, whom I met yesterday, is a powerful man because he sits on three important committees.
2. When it really started to rain, Bobby, who had been playing in the park, ran home.
3. The car keys are not in the place where they should be.
4. I really don't know why you are so angry.

5. I cannot tell you where Mary went because I haven't seen her all afternoon.

b). Write a sentence which contains each of the following structures.

1. a relative clause used as an adjective modifying the subject
2. an adverbial clause specifying the time *when*
3. a relative clause used as an adjective modifying a noun in the predicate
4. a relative clause used as an adjective modifying a noun in the subject and a relative clause used as an adjective modifying a noun in the predicate
5. a relative clause used as the subject and an adverbial clause specifying the reason why

BASIC PATTERNS FOR SUBJECTS

We will now look at the subject again, this time with a view to how subjects can be (and are) expanded. Good writers do not write similarly patterned sentences all the time but make their sentences richly textured, interesting, and varied. Here are the basic patterns for subjects.

SUBJECT AS SIMPLE NOUN OR PRONOUN. The subject may be a simple noun, as we saw in our earliest sample sentences:

- *Dorothy* coughed.
- *The doctor* shook his head.
- *The girl* was sick.

It may also, of course, be a pronoun:

- *She* coughed.
- *He* shook his head.
- *Everyone* was worried.

SUBJECT AS NOUN PLUS MODIFIERS. Any of these simple nouns or pronouns can be modified by adjectives, and the adjectives in turn can be modified by adverbs:

- *Young Dorothy* coughed.
- *The first handsome doctor* shook his head.
- *The uncommonly ugly girl* was sick.

Modifiers may also be prepositional phrases:

- *Young Dorothy, of Mamaroneck, New York,* coughed.
- *The uncommonly ugly girl with the wart on her nose* was sick.

And subjects may also be modified by verbals, specifically the present or past participle or phrases beginning with these participles:

- *The handsome doctor, overworked and rushed,* shook his head.
- *Complaining of a sore throat, Dorothy* coughed.
- *The girl, having caught mononucleosis,* was sick.

Verbals, as you will recall, are really *embedded sentences*—sentences with the subjects deleted—and the diagram for this pattern indicates this:

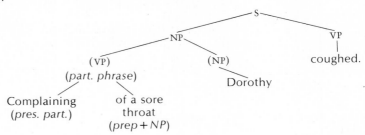

SUBJECT AS NOUN PLUS RELATIVE CLAUSE.   Besides adjectives, prepositional phrases, and verbals, a subject may also contain another modifying structure, one that contains its own subject and predicate. Relative clauses, as you saw on page 325, can modify nouns or pronouns.

- *Dorothy, who did not read science fiction,* was confused.
- *The extraterrestrial who took Dorothy's hand* was the leader.

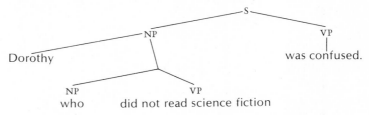

SUBJECT AS VERBAL.   Not only can the simple noun or pronoun in the subject be modified by a verbal; the subject may itself *be* a verbal. Infinitives and gerunds, that is, can function as noun equivalents.

- *To wait* was not easy for Dorothy.
- *Waiting* is not easy for extraterrestrials, either.
- *To frighten Dorothy* was not the extraterrestrials' intention.
- *Seeing the extraterrestrials* frightened Dorothy.

SUBJECT AS CLAUSE.   Finally, the subject may itself be a noun clause—a dependent clause functioning as a noun.

- *What Dorothy had* was a rare form of mononucleosis.
- *That they might be able to help her* did not cross her mind.
- *Whoever believes this story* must be extremely gullible.

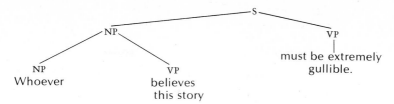

Look again at the pictures accompanying the patterns for subjects. Do you notice that the relative clause, the noun clause, and the verbal are shown as "sentences"—though in altered form? The fact that their form is altered is important, because it means that these constructions cannot stand by themselves as sentences. They would be called *sentence fragments*. We cannot say "who did not read science fiction" (except as a question) or "that they might be able to help her" or "seeing the extra-terrestrials" or "to frighten Dorothy" or "whoever believes this story." Indeed, our intuitive sense that these constructions are derived from sentences (or subject–predicate relationships) probably accounts for inexperienced writers sometimes writing fragments. However that may be, the relative clause, the noun clause, and the verbal are derived from a sentence *in meaning*, but *in form* are not sentences.

Because an English sentence is made up of subject and predicate, then, only those structures that *have* a subject and predicate are considered complete sentences. But it is true that *context* sometimes permits us to understand structures that have been deleted. Thus, while "Jody" or "will not" or "in the study" are incomplete by themselves, in the appropriate context where we understand what has been deleted (subject, verb, or even subject and predicate), we would perhaps accept the fragments, particularly in recording dialogue.

- Who's missing? / Jody *(is missing)*.
- Jody, you'll go with me tomorrow. / Will not. *(I will not go with you tomorrow.)*
- Where's that book? / In the study. *(That book is in the study.)*

For further discussion of fragments, and cautions against their use, please consult this item in Chapter 15, "The Conventions of Language."

EXERCISES

a). Identify and label the modifiers in the subject of each of the following sentences as determiners, adjectives, prepositional phrases, or present or past participles.

1. The fresh-baked bread smells wonderful.
2. Faded and torn jeans were the big fashion.

3. Which book do you want to read?
4. The budding rose in the front yard will open soon.
5. The white house with the brown shutters on Oak Street is the one I talked to you about.

b). Write a sentence whose subject is modified in each of the following ways.

1. determiner + adjective(s)
2. prepositional phrase only
3. determiner + past participle
4. present participle + prepositional phrase(s)
5. past participle + prepositional phrase(s)

c). Identify the subject in each of the following sentences as a verbal, a noun clause, or as a noun modified by a relative clause.

1. To be of help to his friend who had lost his job was Alfred's newest concern.
2. That Genevieve can never succeed if she is that sloppy is clear to me.
3. The ship that had been in the harbor for over a week has finally left.
4. Sailing his beautiful boat is Eric's favorite form of recreation.
5. To get her groceries a little cheaper, Annette took advantage of every sale.

BASIC PATTERNS FOR PREDICATES

Having taken a look at some of the potential forms for subjects, we can realize that simply by understanding the structures presented so far, we can greatly expand a short sentence. We can see similar possibilities when we turn our attention to predicates. Just as subjects may vary literally from one letter *(I)* to a potentially infinitely long series of modifiers and embedded sentences, so predicates can range from a single verb to a potentially limitless series of embedded sentences and modifiers.

PREDICATE AS INTRANSITIVE VERB AND MODIFIERS.   We saw, in looking at the verb phrase, that the verb in a sentence may itself be one or several words. In addition to the ways in which we can change nuances of meaning according to the form of the verb we use, we can add other information to the predicate by using *adverbials*. Adverbials may be simple adverbs, clusters of adverbs, phrases, or whole clauses; generally, as you have learned, they indicate the manner, the place, or the time of an action. In sentences containing *intransitive verbs*—verbs in which the "action" does not go across to any object, but stops with the verb itself—adverbials are, in fact, the *only* means of expansion. Let us see how we can use adverbials to expand the basic sentence pattern when the verb is intransitive:

- Dorothy coughed.
- Dorothy coughed *repeatedly*.
- Dorothy coughed repeatedly *yesterday*.
- Dorothy coughed repeatedly *in class* yesterday.
- Dorothy coughed repeatedly in class yesterday *until she was blue in the face*.

And, of course, as soon as we introduce a prepositional phrase with its noun or a clause with its subject and predicate, we also introduce the possibility of further modification (*history* class, *nearly* blue in the face, etc.).

PREDICATE AS TRANSITIVE VERB (PLUS MODIFIERS) AND OBJECTS (PLUS MODIFIERS).

When a verb is *transitive*—that is, when its action goes across to an object—we can expand the sentence with adverbials, just as we can with intransitive verbs:

- The doctor shook his head.
- The doctor shook his head *sadly*.
- The doctor shook his head sadly *as he read Dorothy's chart*.
- The doctor shook his head sadly *in the examining room* as he read Dorothy's chart.

But because the transitive verb has an object, we can expand the sentence greatly by realizing that, just as nouns can be modified in the subject, so they can be modified in the predicate. Thus, all the options for modification—adjectives, adverbs (intensifiers), phrases, and clauses—exist for these *direct objects* as for any noun, wherever it occurs. Thus an expansion like this is possible:

- The doctor shook *that slightly bald but still good-looking head of his* sadly in the examining room as he read Dorothy's chart.

In some cases, there is yet another possibility for expansion: some transitive verbs, such as *to give, to tell, to bring, to teach*, etc., can have an *indirect object* as well as a direct object, and the indirect object in turn can be modified. (The indirect object can be thought of as a kind of shorthand for *to* + *noun* or *for* + *noun*. In a sentence like "Dorothy gave Tom a dirty look," *look* is the direct object—*what* Dorothy gave—and *Tom* is the indirect object—the person *to whom* she gave it.

- Dorothy gave Tom a dirty look.
- Dorothy gave *poor unimaginative Tom, who had just brought her a broom instead of a bouquet,* a dirty look.

PREDICATE AS LINKING VERB (PLUS MODIFIERS) AND COMPLEMENT (PLUS MODIFIERS)

Remember our sample sentence illustrating the linking verb?

- The girl was sick.

This sentence has possibilities for expansion, too. First, we can modify the verb itself with adverbials.

- The girl was sick *today.*
- The girl was sick *in the library* today.

We can also modify the adjective to which *was* links the subject—called the *predicate adjective*—with appropriate adverbials.

- The girl was sick *to her stomach* in the library today.
- The girl was *so* sick to her stomach *from eating chocolates* in the library today *that she had to go home.*

As we noted earlier, linking verbs can link nouns with nouns, as well as adjectives with nouns. In these cases, the noun to which the subject is linked—called the *predicate nominative* or the *predicate noun*—can be modified like any other noun.

- Dorothy is a student.
- Dorothy is a *straight-A* student.
- Dorothy is a straight-A student *in English at Jefferson University.*

EXERCISES

a). Identify the adverbials in each of the following sentences as adverbs (possibly modified themselves), phrases, or clauses.

1. The ambulance responded extremely quickly to the call for help.
2. He was wandering in a leisurely fashion by the lakeside as the sun was setting.
3. Sam watched the baseball game on TV eagerly while sipping his beer.
4. The cat jumped from the top of the refrigerator to the middle of the kitchen table and landed in the pot of stew.
5. I left my pet snail outside the door yesterday; he's still there today.
6. Paula keeps her chickens under the front porch because she doesn't have room for a real chicken coop.
7. Chipmunks can cover short distances extremely quickly when they are frightened.
8. Little Billy really ruined George's surprise party when he told him all about it.
9. Klutzy Enid falls off her high-heeled sandals every time she tries to wear them.

b). Write a sentence whose predicate is modified in each of the following ways.

1. with one or more adverbs
2. with an adverbial phrase
3. with an adverbial clause
4. with an adverbial phrase and an adverbial clause
5. with one or more adverbs and an adverbial clause

VARIATIONS IN BASIC SENTENCE PATTERNS

Normal word order in modern English sentences is Subject–Verb–Object (SVO). In modern English, order indicates meaning. As a moment's reflection will make clear, the language has its ordering principles. Some arrangements of words in sentences simply do not make sense, and some variations in order change meaning:

- Around Tom chased the room Dorothy.

This sentence is nonsensical.

- Dorothy chased Tom around the room.
- Tom chased Dorothy around the room.

Both of these are permissible as sentences, but they clearly mean two different things.

We have already seen some ordering rules in action in previous sections. In the verb phrase, for example, we saw that auxiliary verbs precede the main verb; among the auxiliaries, modals come before *have* or *do*, and *have* comes before *be*. With adverbials, however, the order can be subjected to some variation, according to what you want a sentence to say and what you want to emphasize. Consider these examples:

- Dorothy coughed repeatedly in class yesterday.
- In class yesterday, Dorothy coughed repeatedly.

In the first sentence, the emphasis is on the fact that Dorothy coughed repeatedly. In the second, because the adverbials of place and time have been moved to the beginning of the sentence, the emphasis is accordingly on the place and time of the action.

The sections that follow will tell you more about possible variations of word order in English, with suggestions as to their use and cautions against their misuse.

Questions

There are several different patterns for questions in English. One pattern presents no particular difficulty: it differs from a regular statement only in the emphasis that is usually placed on one or two words—in fact, it usually echoes a statement that has just been made—and is thus known as an *echo question*.

- Dorothy came down with *mononucleosis?*
- *This* is a spaceship?

Not all questions, of course, are this simple. To form "yes–no" questions—that is, questions to which the usual answers are "yes" or "no"—we move the first of any auxiliary verbs in the verb phrase up to precede the subject. If there are no auxiliary verbs, a form of *to do* precedes the subject, unless the main verb is a form of *to be*.

- Dorothy was coughing in class yesterday.
- Was Dorothy coughing in class yesterday?

There is only one auxiliary verb in the sentence; therefore, it is moved up in front of *Dorothy*.

- Dorothy had been coughing a lot before class.
- Had Dorothy been coughing a lot before class?

There are two auxiliaries in this sentence, but only the first is moved to precede the subject.

- Dorothy coughed in class yesterday.
- Did Dorothy cough in class yesterday?

This sentence has no auxiliary verb. Accordingly, the proper form of *to do*—in this case, the past tense—is placed before the subject. *Coughed*, of course, becomes *cough* to accompany *did*.

- Dorothy is sick.
- Is Dorothy sick?

There is no auxiliary verb in this sentence either, but the main verb is a form of *to be*. In this case, the main verb itself is simply moved up to precede the subject.

Of course, not all questions can be answered with "yes" or "no," either. We form questions to which we expect more complex answers by substituting a "wh-" word—*what, which, who, whose, whom, when, where, how, why*—for some part of a statement, placing this word at the beginning of the question, and then following the rules for "yes–no" questions where these apply.

- Dorothy coughed repeatedly in class yesterday.
- *Who* coughed repeatedly in class yesterday?

Who is substituted for *Dorothy*; since Dorothy is already the first word in the sentence, no further change is necessary.

- *When* did Dorothy cough in class?

When replaces *yesterday*. It is placed at the beginning of the sentence; since *coughed* has no auxiliary, it becomes *did cough*, and did is placed in front of *Dorothy*.

- Dorothy had chased Tom around the room because he had not brought her a bouquet.
- *Whom* had Dorothy chased around the room?

Whom—the object form of *who*—replaces *Tom*, which is the direct object of this sentence. *Whom* moves to the beginning of the sentence, and the auxiliary, *had*, moves in front of *Dorothy*, the subject.

Finally, *tag questions*—two- or three-word questions—can be attached to a statement, to turn it into a question.

- Dorothy coughed in class yesterday, *didn't she?*
- Dorothy had never chased Tom before, *had she?*

There/It as Expletives

Another way of varying normal Subject–Verb–Object order in sentences is to use the words *there* or *it*—not *there* as an adverb of place (*There* is Dorothy) or *it* as a pronoun (*It* had a thorn in its paw), but there and it as *expletives*—words that do not act as nouns, verbs, or modifiers, but simply serve as fillers. We use them when we want to call attention to the *existence* of a thing, a fact, or an idea. To form sentences with *there*, we reverse the order of the subject and some form of *to be* and put *there* at the beginning of the sentence:

- A doctor was in the room.
- There was a doctor in the room.

The use of *there* lays stress on the fact that a doctor *was present*.

- Many people were coughing.
- There were many people coughing.

Again, the *fact* that many people were coughing is emphasized.

To form sentences with *it*, we put *it* and some form of *to be* before the subject and make the verb (and its object, if any) part of a relative clause modifying the subject.

- Dorothy was coughing.
- It was Dorothy who was coughing.

You will want to use *there* and *it* as expletives sparingly. For one thing, it is not always necessary to lay particular stress on a fact; if you use these constructions too often, it is like repeating a particularly loud chord in a piece of rock music—after a while, the audience will simply cease to hear it. For another, beginning writers often get mixed up about which form of the verb to use—singular or plural—in *there* constructions. You will, of course, *need* to use these constructions from time to time, but you should not overwork them.

Indirect Objects

Another variation on the strict Subject–Verb–Object sentence pattern is the use of the *indirect object*. An *indirect object* is the person or thing *to whom* or *for whom* an action expressed in a transitive verb is performed. Instead of writing out "to _____" or "for _____" as a prepositional phrase, we can simply use the noun in the blank as an indirect object, placing it between the verb and the direct object, as in these examples. (Notice, too, that it is impossible to have an indirect object without a *direct* object.)

- Dorothy gave a dirty look *to Tom.*
- Dorothy gave *Tom* a dirty look.

- The doctor wrote a note on Dorothy's case *for the nurse.*
- The doctor wrote *the nurse* a note on Dorothy's case.

Passives

Still another variation on SVO order is to put transitive verbs in the *passive voice* instead of the *active voice* (their normal form). To put a verb in the passive voice, is to change the sentence in the following way: instead of writing

- Subject + Verb + Object

we write

- Object + (a form of *to be*) + Verb (as past participle) + *by* + Subject

Study these examples of sentences in which the verbs have been changed from active to passive voice:

- Dorothy chased Tom.
- Tom was chased by Dorothy.

- The extraterrestrials had frightened Dorothy out of her wits.
- Dorothy had been frightened out of her wits by the extraterrestrials.

As you can see, the passive voice, in general, tends to make a sentence longer, wordier, and less direct. There are, however, a number of situations in which the passive is preferable to the active, or even necessary. First, if you wish to lay particular emphasis on the object of an action instead of the doer—as you might, for example, in the second example above—the passive allows you to do this by moving the object to the beginning of the sentence. Second, if the doer of an action is unknown to you, you can set up a sentence to fit the situation by putting the verb in the passive voice and deleting the *by* phrase:

- Someone towed the extraterrestrials' spaceship away.
- The extraterrestrials' spaceship was towed away.

Third, if you have some legitimate reason for not wishing to name the doer of an action—legal limitations, scientific or scholarly modesty, or simply the desire to be tactful—the passive with the *by* phrase deleted can be useful:

- Dorothy Allen beat Tom Peterson last night.
- Tom Peterson was beaten last night.

- I have discovered a cure for mononucleosis.
- A cure for mononucleosis has been discovered.

- Dorothy said, "You gave me the wrong medicine."
- Dorothy said, "I have been given the wrong medicine."

You should not, however, become so nervous about naming the doer of an action that you resort to the passive with the *by* phrase deleted in every situation. (For example, it is fairly silly, not to mention uninformative, to say "Tom was chased.") Nor, in many situations, should you use the passive voice at all; a look at almost any committee report or government publication will show you the extent to which the passive can clutter a passage of prose. The active voice is just that—more active.

Interrupters

An interrupter is just that—anything that interrupts the normal flow of a sentence. Strictly speaking, interrupters include such structures as adverbials, participial phrases, and relative clauses, when these occur in the middle of sentences. There is, however, another class of interrupters—words, phrases, and clauses that have no grammatical relation whatsoever to the sentences in which they occur. This type of interrupter is usually set off from the sentence with dashes or parentheses. Here are some examples:

- Tom decided—oh unlucky decision!—to take Dorothy a broom instead of a bouquet.
- During the time she was forced to spend in bed—six weeks, to be exact—Dorothy perfected her left hook.
- The cost of her medicines (one antibiotic was priced at $8.50 per bottle) appalled Dorothy.

As you can see, such interrupters can be a useful way of emphasizing a point. Like any unusual way of emphasizing a point, however, they should be used sparingly.

EXERCISES

a). Convert the following statements into (1) echo questions; (2) yes/no questions; (3) *wh-* questions; (4) tag questions.

1. The door opened noisily.
2. Dorothy screamed at Tom.

3. The doctor had been taking Dorothy's pulse.
4. Someone grabbed Tom by the shoulder.
5. Tom gave up with a sigh.

b). Recast the following sentences to eliminate *there* and *it*. Where you cannot eliminate *there* or *it* without changing the meaning, be prepared to justify the *it* or *there*. In some cases you may be able to shorten the sentence by eliminating words in addition to the *it* or *there*. Be prepared to discuss the effectiveness of each revision.

1. It is simply not true that Tom flipped out.
2. There are three points to keep in mind.
3. There were five nurses on the floor at the time.
4. It is the case that not one of them heard the buzzer.
5. There is no good reason to explain why.

c). In which of the following sentences can you move the indirect object without changing the meaning? In which sentences can either the indirect or the direct object be deleted without altering the meaning? Be prepared to discuss your answers.

1. His mother had to wire him money to buy a new one.
2. The orderly brought dinner in to Dorothy.
3. Tom tossed Dorothy the pillow back.
4. The nurse made her a back rest with it.
5. Dorothy asked everyone to leave.

COMPOUNDING

We have seen that a sentence is a subject and a predicate. We have also seen that the subject may be expanded by embedding other sentences or potential sentences within it, as well as by adding words and phrases that modify the simple subject. Similarly, the predicate can be expanded in the ways we have shown—by adding modifiers, and by embedding sentences or potential sentences within it.

We must realize, however, that there are still further possibilities for expansion. These are possibilities of *addition*—of yoking two similar items with a *coordinating conjunction* (words like *and, but, or, nor,* or *yet*). We can compound the subject of the sentence, the object of the verb, the verb itself, prepositional phrases and the nouns which act as the objects of the prepositions within such phrases, adjectives, adverbs—in fact, almost any item except articles and those prepositions that introduce infinitives (you would not say "the and a bouquet" or "to or for visit Dorothy").

- *The President and the Vice-President* visited Dorothy. *(compound subject)*
- The President and the Vice-President visited *Dorothy and the extra-terrestrials. (compound objects of a verb)*

- The President and the Vice-President *visited and congratulated* Dorothy and the extraterrestrials. *(compound verbs)*
- The President and the Vice-President *visited Dorothy and the extra-terrestrials, but could only congratulate the extraterrestrials through an interpreter. (compound predicates)*
- The President and the Vice-President came *in a limousine and with three Secret Service agents* to visit Dorothy and the extraterrestrials. *(compound prepositional phrases)*
- The President and the Vice-President, with *three Secret Service agents and an interpreter,* came to visit Dorothy and the extraterrestrials. *(compound objects of preposition)*
- The *slightly hesitant but enthusiastic* President and Vice-President came *promptly and willingly* in a limousine to visit Dorothy and the extraterrestrials. *(compound adjectives and adverbs)*

Not only single items can be compounded, of course. Both embedded sentences—verbals and dependent clauses—and *actual* sentences—independent clauses—can also be compounded.

- The President and the Vice-President came *to visit Dorothy and to question the extraterrestrials. (compound infinitives)*
- *Smiling broadly and carrying bouquets,* the President and the Vice-President arrived at the infirmary. *(compound participial phrases)*
- *Seeing the extraterrestrials and hearing them speak* startled the President slightly. *(compound gerund phrases)*
- The President and the Vice-President visited Dorothy and the extraterrestrials *after they had been briefed by NASA officials but before they had learned any words of Tralfamadorian. (compound adverbial clauses)*
- The President asked the extraterrestrials *who they were and where they had come from. (compound noun clauses as direct objects)*
- The President toured the extraterrestrials' spaceship, *which had been left in the parking lot but which had just been towed to the police station. (compound relative clauses)*
- The President and the Vice-President visited Dorothy and the extraterrestrials, and they all answered questions at a news conference afterwards. *(compound independent clauses)*

In compounding similar items, whether they are single words or whole independent clauses, you must be sure that the items you have joined are in fact *equal*—equal in importance and equal in structure. The fact that you are linking these items with a coordinating conjunction cues the reader to expect this equality; when the items are unequal, the reader is thrown off balance, even if the fault is minor. We speak of such lapses as faults in *parallel structure*. Here are some examples of faulty parallelism:

- The President and the Vice-President came to visit Dorothy and for questioning the extraterrestrials.

Here, an infinitive phrase, *to visit Dorothy*, is linked with a prepositional phrase, *for questioning the extraterrestrials*. The best way of correcting the problem would be to change the second phrase to an infinitive phrase—*to question* . . .—to match the first.

- During her six weeks at the infirmary, Dorothy had mononucleosis and a visit from the President.

No *grammatical* inequality is present here, but the linking of *mononucleosis* and *a visit* . . . suggests that the two phenomena are somehow equal—in effect, it suggests that the President's visit is a disease. The sentence could be restructured as follows: ". . . Dorothy had mononucleosis, but she also received a visit from the President."

You must also be careful when you compound single items to make sure that they agree in number, tense, person, and so forth, not only with each other, but also with single items with which they are grammatically associated. For further discussion of problems in parallelism, see Chapter 15, "The Conventions of Writing."

- Dorothy had mononucleosis for six weeks and has to stay in the infirmary.

The first verb is in the past tense, but the second, which clearly refers to the same time period, is in the present. *Has* should be changed to *had.*

- The extraterrestrials' spaceship and the President's limousine was towed to the parking lot.

The sentence has two subjects but a singular verb, *was.* The verb should be plural *were.* (Further discussion of agreement, shifts in verb tense, and so on, can also be found in Chapter 15, "The Conventions of Writing.")

Keep in mind, too, that you cannot take care of all your compounding needs simply by slapping everything together with *ands;* take time to consider the relationship between the items you are linking. The ordering of the items is important, for one thing. The first item you mention, in most cases, should be the more important—insofar as "equal" items vary in importance—because it receives more emphasis as a result of its position. (Notice, for example, that we say "The President and the Vice-President," not "The Vice-President and the President.") When the joining of two structures suggests a time sequence or a cause-and-effect relationship, the item that is first in time or the cause of the phenomenon should come first: "Tom opened the door and saw Dorothy," for instance, gives us to understand that Tom opened the door *before* he saw Dorothy and that he saw Dorothy *as a result* of opening the door.

But ordering alone is often not enough to suggest the exact nature of the relationship between compound elements. A knowledge of the capabilities of the other coordinating conjunctions can often keep you from overworking *and;* there are, in fact, situations in which *and* specifically will *not* do, and you need to know which conjunction to use in these cases. As we have seen, *and* indicates the simple addition of elements; it can also indicate time sequence, cause-and-effect, and sometimes intensification ("It got warmer *and* warmer"). *But* indicates quite different relationships—usually those of contrast or opposition. It can also indicate time sequence, but only in the sense of a then-and-now contrast: "The extraterrestrials' spaceship had been parked outside *but* was now under lock and key at the police station." *Or*, or *either . . . or*, expresses the idea of alternatives: "Sooner *or* later, *either* Dorothy *or* Tom must give in." *Nor*, or *neither . . . nor*, indicates alternatives which are not possible or acceptable: "*Neither* Dorothy *nor* Tom will give in." *Yet*, like *but*, indicates a contrast: "Tom loved Dorothy *yet* decided not to bring her a bouquet." Being able to use these conjunctions properly, as you can see, can lend considerable variety to your writing.

Linking Ideas at Clause Level

The ability to link ideas in a variety of ways is especially important at the level of the clause; too many beginning writers trying to take their first steps beyond the simple SVO sentence will produce sentences like:

- The President and the Vice-President came to visit Dorothy and the extraterrestrials and they asked the extraterrestrials questions and they couldn't speak Tralfamadorian and they needed an interpreter.

Fortunately, there are a number of alternatives to such loose, stringy sentences: ideas of approximately equal weight can be linked as independent clauses in several ways, and ideas of lesser importance can be subordinated to those of greater importance as adverbial clauses, relative clauses, verbals, and so on—a technique you have been studying throughout this Review.

Independent clauses can be compounded in a few more ways than lesser elements can. They can, of course, be linked by whichever of the coordinating conjunctions best fits the relationship between them.

But there are other ways of linking independent clauses as well. If, for example, you wish to indicate an even "tighter" relationship than usual between clauses you would normally link with *and*, you can substitute a semicolon for the *and*:

- The President and the Vice-President visited Dorothy and the extraterrestrials; they discussed travel in outer space and possible cures for infectious diseases.

The semicolon is, as you will notice, a good way of avoiding too many repetitions of *and* in this sentence. Furthermore, you can indicate a number of different relationships between independent clauses by using a semicolon plus one of the *conjunctive adverbs*—words like *however, moreover, therefore, consequently, nevertheless, otherwise*, and so on.

- The President greeted the extraterrestrials in the name of the American people; *however,* he was forced to do so through an interpreter.

However serves a similar function to *but* here, but it lays even greater stress on the contrast between the President's wish to greet the extra-terrestrials and his need to use an interpreter.

- The extraterrestrials spoke very little English; *consequently,* an inter-preter had to be present during the President's visit and at the news conference.

Consequently indicates that the fact explained in the second clause is the result of the fact explained in the first; it is stronger than *and* would be here.

Even with all these possibilities, however, joining two ideas as inde-pendent clauses is not the only (or always the best) solution. If the ideas you want to link are plainly not of equal weight or significance, you should not just go ahead and join them, but should stop a moment to consider *how* they are related. For example, consider the last two clauses in the "stringy" sentence at the beginning of this section as sepa-rate statements:

- They couldn't speak Tralfamadorian.
- They needed an interpreter.

"They couldn't speak Tralfamadorian," clearly, is the reason *why* "they needed an interpreter." You can therefore link the first idea to the sec-ond as an adverbial clause:

- Because they couldn't speak Tralfamadorian, they needed an interpreter.

You could also name the antecedent of "they"—"the President and the Vice-President"—and make the first idea a relative clause describing them, since being unable to speak Tralfamadorian is one of their attributes:

- The President and the Vice-President, who couldn't speak Tralfamadorian, needed an interpreter.

You could even make the first idea into a verbal—verbals, you will re-member, are embedded sentences too, although not quite as obviously so as dependent clauses:

- Being unable to speak Tralfamadorian, they needed an interpreter.

As you can see, you have several alternatives available to you in most situations where subordination is called for. You must remember, how-ever, to keep your *main* idea—the more important idea—in the *main* or independent clause. Do not move your subordinate clause too far from the item in the main clause to which it pertains. And perhaps most important, link the subordinate clause to the main clause in a way that accurately reflects the relationship between the ideas you are joining. It would not do to link the two ideas above in any of these ways:

- Because they needed an interpreter, they couldn't speak Tralfamadorian.

The main idea is not in the main clause.

- Although they needed an interpreter, they couldn't speak Tralfamadorian.

"Although" does not accurately reflect relationship between clauses.

The ability to coordinate and subordinate ideas allows you to vary your sentences effectively and is thus one key to a good, mature prose style. As we have emphasized, no writer can hold a reader's interest by repeating the same pattern sentence after sentence and paragraph after paragraph. A good writer knows the four main sentence patterns and uses them to good advantage: *simple sentences* (sentences consisting of one main clause) for simple, emphatic ideas; *compound sentences* (sentences of two or more independent clauses joined together) to link related ideas of roughly equal significance; *complex sentences* (sentences of one independent clause plus one or more subordinate clauses); and *compound-complex sentences* (sentences of two or more independent clauses plus one or more subordinate clauses) for more complicated relationships among ideas.

Yet variety is not the writer's goal in and of itself; presenting a unified set of ideas *is*. Good writers use devices such as the use of parallel constructions and the controlled repetition of key words, phrases, ideas, or even sentence structures to achieve this goal. Maintaining a balance between variety and unity is largely a matter of keeping the reader and his needs and capabilities in mind: how much does the reader need to hear at one time? How much does he want to hear? How complicated are the ideas, and how many of them can he take in at one time? Keeping these factors in mind, and not simply striving after variety or unity for its own sake, may be your best guide to good writing.

EXERCISES

a). Combine all of the following into a paragraph of two sentences.

1. Today it is rainy.
2. The tree trunks look almost black.
3. The new green leaves have begun to appear.
4. The leaves are vibrant in color.
5. They shimmer in the wet wind.

6. There are many rainy days in April.
7. Delaware does not seem dreary.
8. Everyone enjoys the rain.
9. The rain means something.
10. Life is renewing itself.

b). Now try joining each of the above with the sentence after it by embedding or conjoining.

CONCLUSION

Once you realize that sentences are hierarchical arrangements of structures, and that structure determines meaning in English, you have a good grasp of how it is possible to vary the sentences you write to achieve different effects. Most writers pay attention to the length of the sentences they write, being careful to vary sentence length within a paragraph. And sometimes you can create quite a startling effect by writing just one simple sentence for emphasis after a series of long, complicated sentences (as we discuss in the sentence chapter). The key concept is variety, whether it be variety of sentence length or sentence structure. You can learn to play the lengths, structures, and meanings of your sentences just as surely as a jazz musician plays one instrument off against another, one melody against another, one rhythm against another—now weaving two together, now juxtaposing—but always creating a texture that is rich and interesting. But in writing, remember your audience and purpose. The audience may want or need to know what you have to say—as clearly, accurately, and gracefully as you can manage to say it. And if you get too "cute" with your prose style, you may lose your audience or alienate it.

14

Glossary of Grammatical Terms

This glossary contains definitions and examples of grammatical terms that are used in this book—especially in Chapter 13, "A Review of Grammar." Consult this glossary whenever you come across a term in the book or in your classroom discussions that you do not understand.

active, passive   See *voice.*

adjective   In general, adjectives modify, or in some way change the meaning of, nouns and pronouns. Adjectives ordinarily answer the questions *What kind?* (a *blue* balloon); *Which one?* (*that* balloon); *How many?* (*six* balloons). Adjectives may be single words or a group of words, phrases, or relative clauses.

SINGLE-WORD ADJECTIVES:
- *old* woman, *young* man

WORD CLUSTER AS ADJECTIVE:
- *six inflated blue* balloons

PREPOSITIONAL PHRASES AS ADJECTIVES:
- a woman *of advanced years*
- the man *of slender means*

RELATIVE CLAUSES AS ADJECTIVES:
- a woman *who has seen many moons*
- the man *who was wet behind the ears*

See also *article; determiners; participle.*

Adjectives may be classified as *attributive, appositive,* or *predicative,* according to their position in the sentence. An *attributive adjective* names an attribute of a noun and modifies the noun directly. It usually precedes the noun (except in the case of predicate adjectives).

- *Good* witches are hard to find; *bad* ones get all the press.

Appositive adjectives usually follow the nouns they describe. (See also *appositive* for noun counterpart).

WORD CLUSTER ADJECTIVE:
- A woman, *short and dumpy,* was merrily poisoning an apple.

See also *nonrestrictive adjective; restrictive adjective.*

Predicative adjectives, which occur in the predicate of the sentence, may be of two types: subjective complement or objective complement. An *adjective subjective complement* follows a linking verb and modifies the subject of the sentence.

- The apple looked, smelled, and tasted *wonderful,* but Snow White was soon quite soundly asleep.

An adjective subjective complement is also called a *predicate adjective.*

An *adjective objective complement* modifies the direct object of verbs like *render, make, consider,* and so on. The adjective follows its noun or pronoun.

- The apple rendered Snow White *senseless.*
- We considered her *effective.*

adverb   An *adverb* (which may be a single word, a cluster of words, a phrase, or a clause), modifies, or changes the meaning of, a verb, an adjective, or another adverb. Adverbs that modify verbs answer the question *How? (manner); Where? (place); Why? (reason); When? (time);* or *How often? (frequency).*

SINGLE-WORD ADVERB:
- The mugger worked *quickly. (How?)*

PREPOSITIONAL PHRASE AS ADVERB:
- The mugger worked *in dark alleys. (Where?)*

CLAUSE AS ADVERB:
- The mugger was caught *because he accosted a policewoman. (Why?)*

Adverbs that modify adjectives may answer the question *How? (manner)* or may serve to intensify the meaning of the adjective.

SINGLE-WORD ADVERB:
- The mugger was *physically* capable of working. *(How capable?)*

PREPOSITIONAL PHRASE AS ADVERB:
- The mugger was capable *in every respect. (How capable?)*

CLAUSE AS ADVERB:
- The mugger was *as* capable of working *as I am. (How capable?)*
- The mugger wore *very* dark clothes.

The adverb *very* intensifies the adjective *dark.*

Finally, an adverb modifying another adverb may act as an intensifier.

- The mugger thought he could run *too* quickly to be caught.

Too modifies the adverb *quickly,* which modifies the verb *could run.*

Some adverbs are incorrectly used to modify whole sentences. Sentence adverbs like *hopefully* and *regretfully* should not be used in formal writing.

agreement   *Agreement* refers to the matching of sentence elements in *number* (singular or plural), *gender* (masculine, feminine, or neuter), and/or *person* (first person, second person, third person).

Subjects and verbs must agree in *number.*

INCORRECT	• The *boys is* tall.
CORRECT	• The *boys are* tall.
	• The *boy is* tall.

A pronoun and its antecedent (the noun, noun phrase, or indefinite pronoun to which the pronoun refers) must agree in *number, gender,* and *person.* The antecedent determines the number, gender, and person.

Number

INCORRECT • When a *child* goes to the dentist, *they* may be given a piece of sugarless gum.

CORRECT • When a *child* goes to the dentist, *he or she* [OR *the youngster*] may be given a piece of sugarless gum. When *children go* to the dentist, *they* may . . .

Gender

INCORRECT • The cow kicked over the milk pail beside *her*. Then *it* walked out of the barn.

CORRECT • The cow kicked over the milk pail beside *her*. Then *she* walked . . .

Person

INCORRECT • When a girl sees Travolta, *you* feel like dancing.
CORRECT • When a girl sees Travolta, *she* feels like dancing.

antecedent   The *antecedent* (from the Latin for "coming before") is the noun, noun phrase, or definite pronoun to which a pronoun refers.

NOUN PHRASE AS ANTECEDENT:
• *The pencil sharpener* chews the pencils *it* sharpens.

INDEFINITE PRONOUN AS ANTECEDENT:
• *Somebody* apparently forgot to take *his* or *her* pencil out of the sharpener.

appositive   An *appositive* is a noun or a noun phrase that follows another noun and refers to the same person, place, object, or idea as the noun does.

• Margaret Marsh, *an American historian at Stockton State College,* has published a book on feminist anarchists.

Appositives that supply information necessary to identify or specify the noun being referred to are called *restrictive appositives.* Restrictive appositives are not set off by commas.

• The writer *Joyce Carol Oates* has published a new novel.

The appositive, *Joyce Carol Oates*, identifies *writer*. Commas are not used in this example. Appositives that supply additional rather than essential information are called *nonrestrictive appositives* and are set off by commas.

• The writer of the book *Them, Joyce Carol Oates,* has published a new novel.

The appositive, again *Joyce Carol Oates*, is not essential to identify *writer*. The phrase *of the book Them* already identifies *writer*.

article   The *articles—a, an,* and *the*—are adjectives that are members of the adjective subclass *determiners.* (Determiners are adjectives that count or point out rather than actually describe their nouns.) *A* and *an* indicate that a singular noun will follow. They are called *indefinite articles* because they do not point out a specific person, place, or object.

- He bought his mother a goldfish because she wanted one.

The sentence indicates that his mother had not selected a particular goldfish. The article *the* signals that either a singular or a plural noun will follow. Unlike *a* or *an*, *the* points to a definite or specific person, place, or thing. Therefore, *the* is called the *definite article*.

- He bought his mother *the* goldfish of her choice.

The sentence indicates that his mother had selected a particular goldfish.

auxiliaries   Auxiliaries—the verbs *to be, to have*, and *to do*—combine with either the past participle form or the *-ing* form of a verb. (The *past participle* may be an *-ed* or *-d* verb form or an irregular form like *written, spoken, bought*, and so on.) Auxiliaries and the verbs used with them (called *main* verbs) create tense forms. Auxiliaries are also called *helping verbs*.

- He *is planning* a real blowout for a party. *(present progressive tense)*
- She *hasn't* jogged since she was hit by the bus. *(present perfect tense)*
- *Don't* you remember our old friend, jolly Mr. Crumpet? *(present tense)*

awkward passive   An *askward passive* occurs when a passive voice verb is used instead of a clear, more direct active voice verb. See *voice*.

AWKWARD • The movie *was seen* by me.
CORRECT • I *saw* the movie.

case   *Case* is a word derived from Latin grammar. In Latin, relationships between words are indicated primarily by the form of a word or words, not by word order. The particular form a word takes to show its use in a sentence is called its *case*. In modern English, relationships between words are indicated primarily by word order. Only English pronouns and possessive nouns have retained case forms (case forms were used more widely in Old English).

Pronouns have three different cases: the *nominative case* (for pronouns used as subjects—"*He* sits"); the *accusative* or *objective case* (for pronouns used as objects—"I saw *him* sitting beside *her*"); and the *possessive case* (to indicate ownership or origin—*his* toy, *her* mother).

Nouns do not change form for the nominative and the accusative. In the possessive case an apostrophe is used with both the singular and the plural. (See also *possessive*.)

clause   A *clause* is a group of closely related words having both a *subject* and a *predicate*. A sentence must include at least one *independent* *clause* (also called a *main, major,* or *coordinate* clause.) An independent clause can be used alone to express a grammatically complete thought. A *dependent clause* (also called a *minor* or *subordinate* clause) may form part of a sentence. If punctuated as a sentence, however, it becomes a fragment, since it does not communicate a grammatically complete thought. Dependent clauses are introduced by *subordinators*—either subordinating conjunctions (see *conjunction*) or relative pronouns (see *pronoun*).

- Jane loves Milton's *Paradise Lost. (independent clause)*
- *Although* Jane loves Milton's *Paradise Lost* . . . *(subordinating conjunction introducing a dependent clause)*

To turn the dependent clause into a sentence, add an independent clause.

- *Although* Jane loves Milton's *Paradise Lost,* she is not likely to praise his Satan.

A *noun clause* is a dependent clause that can be the subject or object of a sentence, the object of a preposition, or the indirect object, and it may also serve all the other functions of a noun.

- *Whoever sold you that dreadful hat* was a real con artist. *(subject)*
- A real con artist knows *that a sucker is born every minute. (object)*
- The salesman sold *the man who owns the bakery* a dreadful hat. *(indirect object)*
- The hat was sold to *the man who owns the bakery. (object of the preposition)*

collective noun   A *collective noun* designates a group or class of individuals—for example, *family, faculty,* or *committee.* Such nouns may be considered either singular or plural, but in American usage they are usually considered singular.

- The *jury has* made *its* decision.

comma splice   A *comma splice* occurs when two independent clauses are improperly joined by a comma. To correct a comma splice, the clauses may be joined by a semicolon or by a comma followed by a coordinating conjunction (*and, or, for, nor, but, so,* and *yet*).

INCORRECT
- The lion believes himself the king of the jungle, his mate knows otherwise.

CORRECT
- The lion believes himself the king of the jungle; his mate knows otherwise.
- The lion believes himself the king of the jungle *but* his mate knows otherwise.

See also *fused sentence; run-on.*

comparison of adjectives and adverbs   *Comparison* denotes the change in form of an adjective or an adverb to express degree. There are three degrees of comparison: (1) the *positive degree* (or the ordinary form of the adjective), which suggests no comparison; (2) the *comparative degree*, which expresses either an increase or a diminution from the *positive degree* when two elements are involved; (3) the *superlative degree*, which expresses the greatest or the least degree of the positive when three or more elements are being compared.

POSITIVE	COMPARATIVE	SUPERLATIVE
good	better	best
bad	worse	worst
ugly	uglier	ugliest

Many one- or two-syllable adjectives and adverbs are made comparative and superlative by adding -*er* and -*est*, while others, particularly adverbs of two syllables, can take *more* and *most*. Adjectives and adverbs of more than two syllables require modification by the adverbs *more* in the comparative degree and *most* in the superlative degree.

glamorous   more glamorous   most glamorous

complement A *complement* is the word or words that complete the meaning of a verb. The verb combined with its complement becomes the predicate to make a grammatically complete sentence. A *transitive verb* must have at least a direct object as its complement. An *intransitive verb* does not take a direct object but may take modifiers.

TRANSITIVE VERB:
- John Doe *assassinated* the king.

INTRANSITIVE VERB:
- John Doe *remains* in jail.

The prepositional phrase *in jail* is a modifier of the verb, *remains*.
A noun clause may also serve as the direct object of a transitive verb.

- John Doe didn't *believe that he was guilty. (noun clause as a complement)*

A linking verb (the verb *to be* and verbs like *seem, become, feel, taste*) has as its complement either a noun that remains the subject (see *predicate noun*) or an adjective that describes the subject (see *predicate adjective*). The complement of a linking verb is called a *subjective complement.*

- John Doe did not *feel guilty,* though.

The linking verb is *feel;* the predicate adjective is *guilty.*

conjunction Conjunctions are used to join sentence elements.

There are two kinds of conjunctions, *coordinating* and *subordinating*. Coordinating conjunctions (*and, or, but, nor, for, so,* and *yet*) link words, phrases, or clauses of equal rank in pairs or in series.

- apples, pears, *and* oranges *(words)*
- on earth *or* in heaven *(phrases)*
- Birds fly, *but* fish swim. *(clauses)*

A subordinating conjunction, which always comes at the beginning of the dependent clause, joins dependent clauses to independent clauses.

- Our neighbors were pleased *when we left town because they didn't like living next to our goat farm.*

Common subordinating conjunctions include *after, as, before, once, till, until, when, whenever, as soon as, if, unless, provided, provided that, even if, even though, although, in case, however, since, because, while.* See also *clause.*

conjunctive adverb   Words like *hence, thus, then, moreover, indeed, nevertheless, however,* and *consequently* are called *conjunctive adverbs.* A semicolon must be used with a conjunctive adverb if the adverb appears in the second part of a compound sentence—a sentence that contains two independent clauses.

- George despised smokers. *Nevertheless,* he fell for Esme, who smoked cigars.
- George preferred to be with nonsmokers; *therefore,* he befriended Paula, an antismoking activist.
- George worked for the antismoking campaign; his job, *consequently,* was suited to his need.

Conjunctive adverbs are used primarily as transitions.

context   *Context* refers to the parts of a sentence, paragraph, or essay surrounding a specific word or passage that help determine its exact meaning. When something is quoted "out of context," it is stripped of its full and exact meaning.

demonstratives   *Demonstratives,* which are subclasses of pronouns and adjectives, point out particular persons, places, things, or ideas. *This, these, that,* and *those* can function either as pronouns or adjectives, depending on how they are used in the sentence.

- *That* is the act of a kind heart. *(pronoun)*
- *That* man has a kind heart. *(adjective)*

dependent clause   See *clause.*

determiners   *Determiners,* a subclass of adjectives, indicate in a sentence that a noun will follow. They tend to count or to point out nouns rather than actually describe them. *A, an,* and *the* (also called *ar-*

ticles) are the most common noun determiners. The *demonstrative adjectives* (*this, these, that, those*), numbers, and words like *some, any,* and *all* also can function as determiners.

- He had stolen *those* gold earrings our mother always wore.
- He tied up *six* members of the family.
- *All* crooks deserve to go to jail.

direct and indirect questions   A *direct question* presents the exact words of the speaker. It is always enclosed in quotation marks.

- *"Who are you?"* asked the caterpillar.

An *indirect question* occurs when the speaker's words are reported rather than quoted directly. Since the speaker's *exact* words are not presented, quotation marks are not used.

- The caterpillar asked Alice *who she was.*

For the discussion of the correct sequence of tenses with indirect questions, see Chapter 15, "Principle 2."

direct object   A *direct object* receives the action of a transitive verb. The direct object is the *complement*—that is, the completer—of such a verb. In a sentence, the direct object may be a word, a phrase, or a noun clause. In most cases the direct object is not the same as the subject. Only when a reflexive direct object is used—the cat washed *itself*—does the direct object rename the subject.

- Maime liked *baths.* *(word)*
- Maime liked *bathing in milk and olive oil.* *(gerund phrase)*
- She hated *to pay for the concoction,* however. *(infinitive phrase)*
- She often lamented *that she had not been born in the age of Cleopatra.* *(noun clause)*

elliptical construction   In an *elliptical construction,* a word or some words that belong grammatically, but which may be unnecessary for the sense of the sentence, has been omitted. Common instances of elliptical constructions include

(1) omission in imperative sentences *(commands, requests)* :

- Come here! *(You is understood as the subject.)*

(2) omission in parallel constructions (see *parallelism*):

- Some like grog hot; some cold. *(Some like grog hot, some like it cold.)*

(3) omission in comparisons:

- She likes him better than me. *(. . . better than she likes me.)*

finite verb   A *finite verb* is a verb that makes an assertion and changes in form to show grammatical person (first, second, or third person) and number (singular and plural). Such a verb may be called the main verb in a sentence, in contrast to verbals (gerunds, infinitives, and participles), which do not show person and number and which are never the main verb in a sentence.

fused sentence A *fused sentence* occurs when two independent clauses are improperly run together using no punctuation or conjunction. To correct a fused sentence, the clauses may be joined by using a semicolon or by using a comma followed by a coordinating conjunction (*and, or, for, nor, but, so,* and *yet*).

INCORRECT • A mouse is beastly it's always gobbling cheese.
CORRECT • A mouse is beastly; it's always gobbling cheese.
• A mouse is beastly, *for* it's always gobbling cheese.

See also *comma splice, run-on.*

gender *Gender* is the grammatical term for sex distinction. In English grammar there are three genders: masculine, feminine, and neuter. Only some pronouns, nouns that name specific persons, and certain other nouns—like *man, woman, girl, boy, witch, warlock, actor, actress*—express gender. The pronoun *he* is masculine. *She* is feminine. *It* is neuter.

gerund A *gerund* is a verbal that takes the *-ing* form of the verb and functions as a noun. A gerund may be used wherever a noun can be used.

• *Fishing* is fun. *(subject)*
• For him, relaxation is *fishing. (subjective complement)*
• His wife gives *fishing* a rating of zero on her list of pleasures. *(indirect object)*
• In *fishing* lie all family contentions. *(object of a preposition)*

idiom Idiom denotes the peculiar grammatical structures used by native speakers of any language. Often the meaning differs from the joined words of the construction. Foreign speakers of English often use the wrong preposition and so speak and write unidiomatic English.

UNIDIOMATIC • We are going *in* town.
IDIOMATIC • We are going *into* town.

independent clause See *clause.*

indirect object In a sentence, the *indirect object* occupies a position between the transitive verb or *verbal* (gerund, infinitive, participle) and the *direct object.* The indirect object is, in effect, the recipient of the direct object.

• The bakery sent *me* the wrong birthday cake. *(indirect object after transitive verb)*
• I asked them to send *me* the right cake immediately. *(indirect object after transitive infinitive)*

The indirect object can ordinarily be converted to a prepositional phrase beginning with *to* or *for*.

- The bakery sent the wrong birthday cake *to me.*

infinitive   The *infinitive* is a *verbal* and, as such, can neither make an assertion nor change in form to show grammatical person or number, as a finite verb can. The infinitive forms of the verb are either preceded by *to* or the *to* is understood. In English, infinitives have two tenses, but in using the auxiliaries *be* and *have* and the present and past participles the writer can derive a wide number of infinitive forms.

PRESENT ACTIVE INFINITIVE:
- to show

PRESENT ACTIVE PROGRESSIVE INFINITIVE:
- to be showing

PRESENT PASSIVE INFINITIVE:
- to be shown

PERFECT INFINITIVE:
- to have shown

PERFECT PROGRESSIVE INFINITIVE:
- to have been showing

PERFECT PASSIVE INFINITIVE:
- to have been shown

intensifier   An *intensifier* belongs to the set of adverbs that modify adjectives and other adverbs (see *adverbs*). Common intensifiers include *too, so, very, rather, much,* and *pretty.*

- She is *very* good.
- You are *too* sweet.

interjections   An *interjection* is a word or group of words that shows strong or sudden emotion.

- *Eek!* It's a mouse!
- *Shoot!* You've made a mess.

interrogatives   There are three kinds of *interrogatives*—or words that change statements to questions: *interrogative pronouns, interrogative adjectives,* and *interrogative adverbs.*

The interrogative pronouns *who, whom, whose, what* and *which* can introduce direct or indirect questions. When an interrogative pronoun introduces an indirect question, the indirect question always functions as a noun in the sentence. The interrogative pronoun needs no antecedent noun or noun phrase to identify it.

DIRECT QUESTION:
- *"Who* is that boy?" asked the teacher.

INDIRECT QUESTION:
- The teacher asked *who that boy is. (noun clause)*

The interrogative adjectives *which, what,* and *whose* also introduce direct and indirect questions.

DIRECT QUESTION:
- *"Which* house does she live in?" he asked.

INDIRECT QUESTION:
- He asked *which house she lives in. (noun clause)*

Interrogative adverbs serve two functions at once: they modify verbs, adjectives, or adverbs; and they introduce direct and indirect questions.

- *How* are you?
- I'd like to know *how you are. (noun clause introduced by adverb of manner)*
- *How far* can Evil Knieval jump his motorcycle?
- The bloodthirsty wonder *how far Evil Knieval can jump his motorcycle. (noun clause introduced by adverb of degree)*

jargon   *Jargon* refers to the often specialized vocabulary of a specific group, especially one in the academic, business, professional, and governmental area.

linking verb   A *linking verb* is a nonaction verb that requires a predicate adjective or a predicate noun as its *complement*, or completer. The complement renames or describes the subject. The list of common linking verbs includes *be, seem, become, remain, appear, prove, grow, turn, get, taste, smell, feel,* and *sound.*

- Frankenstein *was* once the ultimate *monster. (linking verb followed by predicate noun)*
- People *get livid* when they contemplate the modern monster: inflation. *(linking verb followed by predicate adjective)*

misplaced modifier, dangling modifier, squinting/winking modifier   The rule for modifiers—adjectives or adverbs consisting of one word, a cluster of words, a phrase, or a clause—is that the modifier be placed as close as grammatically possible to the element it modifies. When this rule is violated, the result is a *misplaced modifier* and often a misread sentence.

MISPLACED MODIFIER:
- The flower vendor sold bouquets to the customers *covered with aphids.*
CORRECT:
- The flower vendor sold bouquets *covered with aphids* to the customers.

A *dangling modifier* most frequently occurs at the beginning of a sentence. An introductory participle or participial phrase must modify the subject of its sentence or clause.

DANGLING PARTICIPIAL PHRASE:
- Walking out of the forest, our eyes beheld a castle.

The sentence says that eyes were walking—a ludicrous image.

CORRECT • Walking out of the forest, *we* saw a castle.

A *squinting* or *winking modifier* is a type of misplaced modifier—one that seems to modify two elements in the sentence. A squinting modifier usually produces ambiguity.

SQUINTING MODIFIER:
• The dinner that you prepared quickly made me feel ill.

CORRECT:
• The dinner that you prepared *in a hurry* made me . . .
• The dinner that you prepared made me feel ill *rather quickly.*

modal auxiliaries *Modal auxiliaries* are a group of verbs that assist in the formation of mood and tense in verb phrases. Modals include *can, could, will, would, shall, should, may, might, must, had to,* and *ought to.* Modal auxiliaries, unlike other auxiliary verbs, do not change form. See also *auxiliaries.*

mood, mode *Mood* is the property of a verb that allows it to express a fact, a requirement, a desire, a supposition, or a command. There are three moods in English: *indicative, subjunctive,* and *imperative.* The indicative mood states facts and may ask questions.

• The rain in Spain *falls* mainly on the plain.
• *Did* the rain *fall* on your garden?

The subjunctive mood expresses an idea as something requested or required, desired, conditional, or contrary to fact.

• The teacher requested that the student *stay* after school.
• *Would* that I might make a strike!
• If I *were* a great bowler, maybe I could win some money on "Bowling for Dollars."

The imperative mood is used for commands or requests.

• *Be* quiet!
• *Get* out of here!
• Please *pass* the sugar.

nonrestrictive adjective The term *nonrestrictive adjective* refers to adjectival words, phrases, and clauses that supply information unnecessary to identify, limit, or specify the noun or pronoun being modified. Such words, phrases, and clauses are set off from the sentence by commas.

• The Whites' house, *which had been built in 1929,* burned down in a spectacular conflagration.

The nonrestrictive clause, *which had been built in 1929,* does not supply information necessary to identify the house but simply furnishes additional descriptive information. See also *restrictive adjectives.*

noun   A *noun* is the part of speech that signifies a person, place, thing, idea, or quality—Karyn; Pumpkin Center, California; apron; relativity; honesty. A noun may function in a sentence as a *subject*, as a *subjective complement*, as a *direct object*, as an *indirect object*, as the *subject or object of a verbal or a verbal phrase*, or as the *object of a preposition*.

- *Karyn* likes *desserts*. *(subject/direct object)*
- *Karyn* is a master *baker*. *(subject/subjective complement [predicate noun])*
- *She* sends her *grandmother pies*. *(subject/indirect object/direct object)*
- The price of sugar causes *Karyn to quiver*. *(subject of infinitive)*
- Baking *cakes*, she often forgets the *time* of *day* or *night*. *(object of participle/direct object/object of preposition)*

A noun can be either singular or plural.

SINGULAR:
- cake, dog

PLURAL:
- cakes, dogs

A noun also has two possessive forms.

SINGULAR POSSESSIVE:
- the cake's frosting *(the frosting on the cake)*

PLURAL POSSESSIVES:
- the cakes' frosting *(the frosting on the cakes)*

Phrases or whole clauses can also function as nouns. A verb form ending in *-ing* can be used as a verbal noun (gerund).

- *To be* or *not to be* is the question. *(verbal infinitive phrase as subject)*
- *What Hamlet doesn't know* disturbs him. *(noun clause as subject)*

noun phrase   A *noun phrase* consists of a noun and its modifiers—*an upside-down container, the frequently visited mailbox, mass-transit policy*.

number   *Singular number* refers to one element, *plural number* refers to two or more elements. Nouns, pronouns, and verbs show singular and plural number. Verbs agree in number with their nouns or pronouns.

objective complement   See *adjective*.

parallelism   On the sentence level, *parallelism* refers to a consistency of grammatical form in the construction of pairs or series of words, phrases, or clauses or any coordinate elements.

NOT PARALLEL:
- skiing, swimming, and to jog.

PARALLEL:
* skiing, swimming, and jogging.

particle   See *preposition; verb with particle.*

participle   A *participle* is a nonfinite verb, or verbal, that functions as an adjective. The present and the past participles are two of the four principal parts of the verb. The present participle is constructed by adding -*ing* to the base form of the verb. The past participle ends in -*ed* (or -*d*) in regular verbs and has various forms in irregular verbs (break-broken; lead-led). The past participles of irregular verbs must be memorized.

* *Playing* the piano as he sang, the young artist performed Irish lullabies. *(present participle)*
* *Taken by surprise,* I couldn't answer immediately. *(past participle)*

parts of speech   Nouns, pronouns, verbs, adjectives, adverbs, prepositions, and conjunctions, and their subclasses represent categories of words that are based on their use in sentences. All the categories together are called the *parts of speech.*

person   *Person* is a property of both verbs and pronouns that distinguishes the *speaker* (first person), the person or thing *spoken to* (second person), and the person or thing *spoken of* (third person).

* *I* am a taxpayer. *(first)*
* *You* are a taxpayer. *(second)*
* Alas, *he* is a bum. *(third)*

phrase   A *phrase* is a group of closely related words that has no subject or predicate. Most common among phrases is the *prepositional phrase;* it is headed by a preposition that is followed by a noun or noun substitute as the object of the preposition—*to the store, in the car, on her lap.* Verbal phrases include infinitive, participial, and gerund phrases.

* *to be young, beautiful, and black (infinitive phrase)*
* *Trying her best to succeed,* she danced her way to the top. *(participial phrase)*
* *Dancing one's way to the top* is never easy. *(gerund phrase)*

Phrases may function in sentences as modifiers, either adjectival or adverbial. See also *noun phrase; prepositional phrase; verb phrase.*

possessives   Nouns, pronouns, and some prepositional phrases with *of* show that persons or things are the possessions of, belong with, or are related to other persons or things.

* The *cat's* paw *(noun)*
* *its* paw *(pronoun)*
* the paw *of the cat (prepositional phrase)*

See also *case, noun, pronoun.*

Noun possessive forms take *-'s* or *-s'*. Possessive adjectives and possessive pronouns use *no* apostrophes.

POSSESSIVE ADJECTIVES:
* my, our, your, his, her, it, their

POSSESSIVE PRONOUNS:
* mine, ours, yours, his, hers, its, theirs

predicate   Every sentence can be divided into two parts: the *subject* and the *predicate*. The *predicate* expresses what is said of the *subject* and usually consists of the verb with or without objects, complements, or adverbial modifiers.

predicate adjective   The *predicate adjective* follows a linking verb (*to be, to become, to seem, to appear, to taste, to smell, to feel, to sound, to grow*, etc.) and modifies, limits, or restricts the subject of the sentence. Attributive adjectives that name attributes of nouns (and which regularly precede nouns) can become predicate adjectives when moved to the predicate.

* Pizza is both *Italian* and *wonderful*. *(predicate adjective)*
* the *fine* wine *(attributive adjective)*
* The wine tastes *fine*. *(attributive adjective turned into a predicate adjective)*

Predicate adjectives are also known as *subjective complements*. See also *adjective.*

predicate noun   The *predicate noun* follows a linking verb and renames the subject of the sentence.

* Worms are *cultivators* of the earth.
* Death is the *worm* of life.

Predicate nouns are also known as *subjective complements.*

preposition   A *preposition* indicates a relationship between a word or words and other elements in a sentence. The relationship may be of time, of position, of direction, of origin, and so on. Prepositions may be used with a noun or pronoun to form a *prepositional phrase*. The noun or noun substitute that occurs in the phrase is called the *object of the preposition.*

* from *home*
* in the dreary *afternoon*
* a mile from *here*

Prepositions may also be used with verbs, in which case they are called *particles.*

- They *ran up* quite a bill. (particle)
- They *ran* up quite a hill.

Common prepositions include *in, on, out of, into, from, by, up, over, under, along, across, near, of, since, after, between, among, through, beyond, behind, instead of,* and *because of.*

principal parts (of the verb)   The *four* *principal* *parts* of the verb are the *base,* or *infinitive,* form; the *past tense* form; the *past participle;* and the *present participle.* Verbs whose past tense and past participle forms end in *-ed* (or *-d*) are called *regular* verbs; verbs whose past tense and past participle forms do not end in *-ed* (or *-d*) are called irregular.

REGULAR VERB:
- *(to) open, opened, (have) opened, opening*

IRREGULAR VERB:
- *(to) swim, swam, (have) swum, swimming*

pronoun   A *pronoun* is a noun substantive; it is used wherever a noun may be used in a sentence. Generally, a pronoun should have a clear antecedent—that is, it should refer back directly to its noun, pronoun, or noun phrase. The antecedent determines the pronoun's agreement as to *person, number,* and *gender.*

- *Marvin* believes in fair business practices; *his* competitors don't.

His replaces *Marvin's,* the possessive form of the antecedent *Marvin;* like *Marvin's, his* is third-person, singular, and masculine.

Pronouns are divided into several subclasses, including *personal pronouns, relative pronouns, interrogative pronouns, adjectival pronouns, indefinite pronouns,* and *reflexive pronouns.*

The *personal pronouns* have forms in three *cases.*

Subject Forms

SINGULAR	PLURAL
I	we
you	you
he, she, it	they

Object Forms

SINGULAR	PLURAL
me	us
you	you
him, her, it	them

Possessive Forms

POSSESSIVE ADJECTIVES

SINGULAR	PLURAL
my	our
your	your
his, her, its	their

POSSESSIVE PRONOUNS

SINGULAR	PLURAL
mine	ours
yours	yours
his, hers, its	theirs

The *relative pronouns* include *who* (subject), *whom* (object), *whose* (possessive), *which*, and *that*. They introduce adjective clauses.

- The man *who came to dinner* stole the silver.

The relative clause *who came to dinner* modifies the noun *man*. The compound relative pronouns—*whoever, whomever, whatever*—always introduce noun clauses.

- *Whoever let the cat out* must now take care of the kittens. *(noun clause as subject)*
- The care for the kittens rests with Susan and *whomever she trusts*. *(noun clause as object)*

The *interrogative pronouns* include *who, whom, whose, what*, and *which*. These forms introduce direct and indirect questions.

- *Who* let you stay out until 3 a.m.?
- My mother asked me *which I preferred:* typing or housework.

Adjectival pronouns include *any, all, some, both, neither*, and *few*. *Indefinite pronouns* include *one, someone, no one, anyone, somebody, nobody, anybody, something, nothing, anything, each, other, another*. The *apostrophe* and *s* are used with indefinite pronouns ending in *-one* and *-body* and with forms like *another*.

- anyone's number
- somebody's phone
- another's message

Reflexive pronouns include *myself, ourselves, yourself, yourselves, himself, herself, itself, themselves*.

- Don't trouble *yourself.*
- I hurt *myself.*

proper noun   A *proper noun* is the name of a *specific* person, place, or thing. Proper nouns are always capitalized.

PERSON:
- Marvin, Mr. Moody

PLACE:
- Syracuse, New York; Brooklyn Bridge

THING:
- a Mercedes-Benz car; Brusho toothpaste

regular, irregular   See *principal parts.*

relative pronoun   See *pronoun.*

restrictive adjectives   The term *restrictive adjective* refers to words, phrases, and clauses that supply information necessary to identify, limit, or specify the noun or pronoun being modified. Restrictive adjectives are not set off from the sentence by commas.

- The small white dog that was lost last Friday was mine.

run-on   A *run-on* is a group of two or more independent clauses strung together only by coordinating conjunctions (*and, or, nor, for, but, yet,* and *so*) without any punctuation.

RUN-ON:
- I enjoy steaming myself in a hot bath and afterward I like dowsing myself in mink oil and then I don my designer jeans and pink silk shirt and then, boy! do I feel, smell, and look good.

BETTER:
- I enjoy steaming myself in a hot bath and dowsing myself afterward with mink oil. [Compound gerunds as direct objects instead of two independent clauses.] Then I don my designer jeans and pink silk shirt, and I feel, smell, and look great. [Compound sentence correctly punctuated with a comma before the coordinating conjunction.]

See also *comma splice; fused sentence.*

sentence fragment   A *sentence fragment* is any group of words punctuated like a sentence that does not communicate a grammatically complete thought.

FRAGMENTS:
- After she had been wined and dined.
- The cad who had asked her out.
- Ending up at the downtown police precinct.

CORRECT:
- After she had been wined and dined, the cad who had asked her out was so frustrated that he attempted force, ending up at the downtown police precinct, booked for indecent exposure.

shift, inappropriate   An *inappropriate shift* refers to an inconsistency in agreement or in tense sequence.

INAPPROPRIATE SHIFT:
- The river was company enough for Huck and Jim, and *he* never said anything to either.

The pronoun shifts inappropriately from the third person neuter—*river*—to the third person masculine—*him.*

CORRECT:
- The river was company enough for Huck and Jim, and *it* never said anything to either.

slang   *Slang* is neither standard, cultivated, nor appropriate to formal writing. Slang terms can be vivid and ingenious, but in using slang the writer runs the risk of being trite or of introducing a jarring informality into an otherwise formal context.

- That so-called antique was a real rip-off.

subject   Any sentence can be divided into two parts: the *subject* and the *predicate*. The *subject* usually comes before the finite verb in the sentence to tell who or what performs the action or is in the state of being or in the condition that the verb describes. Exceptions to the rule that the subject usually comes before the verb are sentences that begin with *there* or that invert the verb to ask a question.

- A *cat* is rarely skinned.
- There is *more than one way* to skin a cat. (*More than one way* exists to skin a cat.)
- Could *anyone* be as brutal as a skinner of cats?

subjective complement   See *adjective; predicate noun*.

subjunctive   See *mood*.

subordinate clause   See *clause*.

subordinate conjunction   See *conjunction*.

syntax   *Syntax* refers to the relationship of words with other words to form phrases, clauses, and sentences. When syntax is faulty, some relationship is not correct—such as subject–verb agreement, pronoun–antecedent agreement, or parallel structure.

tense   *Tense* is a property of a verb that indicates the time expressed either by the verb or by an infinitive in a sentence. In English, verbs can express six tenses: *present, past, future, present perfect, past perfect,* and *future perfect*. Each tense has several *aspects*. For example, in the past tense, time can be expressed as *progressive* (he *was doing* time at the pen) or as *emphatic* (he *did* have a rough time in the pen).

transitive and intransitive verbs   See *verbs*.

usage   *Usage* denotes the current standards of formal spoken and written language.

verb   A *verb* is a part of speech that expresses action or a state of being. Verbs have five properties: *tense, voice, person, number,* and *mood*. In addition, depending upon whether a verb takes a direct object or a subjective complement, the verb is classified as *transitive* or *intransitive*. A *transitive* verb is one that requires an object to complete its meaning, whereas an *intransitive* verb does not. A *linking* verb indicates a relationship between the subject and the noun (or pronoun) or the adjective following.

A finite verb is the core of the predicate, without which no complete sentence may be written. Nonfinite verb forms include *infinitives, participles,* and *gerunds*. These forms cannot stand alone.

verb phrase   Traditionally, the *verb phrase* in the predicate of a sentence includes the finite verb and all its auxiliaries.

verb with particle   Some verbs cannot be separated from their particles (usually prepositions) and still preserve their meaning:

- The airplane *took off.*
- He tried to *run* me *down* on his bicycle.
- I'll *look into* that tomorrow.
- He'll *head up* the project.
- You have to *read up* on your Shakespeare.

verbals   *Verbals* are nonfinite verbs; they take the forms of present and past participles, infinitives, and gerunds. A *verbal phrase* includes the verbal and any complements and modifiers.

PRESENT PARTICIPLE:
- *Sitting in the parlor,* the cat waited for its dinner.

PAST PARTICIPLE:
- *Set for midnight,* the alarm went off an hour early.

INFINITIVE:
- *Ready to go* at midnight, I dashed to the car.

GERUND:
- *Trying hard* is considered a better path to success than is crime.

voice   *Voice* is the property of a verb that indicates whether the subject of the verb performs the action or receives the action described by the verb. If the subject performs the action, we say that the verb is in the *active voice.* When the subject receives the action, we say that the verb is in the *passive voice.*

ACTIVE   •   Ellen *wrote* the prize-winning paper.
PASSIVE   •   The prize-winning paper *was written* by Ellen.

Generally, it is better style to rely on active-voice verbs, because they tend to express the action forcefully and directly.

The Conventions of Writing

PRINCIPLE 1: Make sure that each of your sentences is a conventional sentence, unless you have a sound stylistic reason for not following the conventions.

Exercises

PRINCIPLE 2: Match the parts of sentences that need matching. Make sure that the structure of each sentence is an accurate reflection of what you intend to say.

Exercises

PRINCIPLE 3: Make sure you use the right word, and generally as few words as possible, for the purpose you want to accomplish.

Exercises

PRINCIPLE 4: Keep punctuation clear and conventional.

Exercises

PRINCIPLE 5: Keep mechanics conventional.

Exercises

PRINCIPLE 1: Make sure that each of your sentences is a conventional sentence, unless you have a sound stylistic reason for not following the conventions.

A sentence in the English language is not any group of words randomly put together by a writer. The language sets standards, or conventions, for what may be called a sentence and what may not. A sentence, first of all, can be defined as a minimum of an independent clause containing a subject and a predicate and making sense by itself. (For further discussion of the terms *clause, subject, predicate,* and other grammatical expressions used here, see the "Glossary of Grammatical Terms.") A dependent clause, a participial phrase, or some other *part* of a sentence, standing alone and punctuated as a sentence, is not a sentence. It is a *fragment.* If two or more independent clauses have been joined with only a comma, a *comma splice*—not a sentence—has been created. If the two clauses are to become a sentence, they must be linked either by a semicolon or by a comma plus a coordinating conjunction. If two independent clauses have been jammed together with no punctuation or conjunction at all, the result is a *fused sentence.* Fused sentences, like fragments and comma splices, are ordinarily not acceptable as sentences. Finally, a string of two or more loosely related independent clauses, linked to each other only by coordinating conjunctions, is not an acceptable sentence either. It is a *run-on sentence.* Professional writers sometimes break the rules of sentence building, but they do so with a purpose in mind. They may feel, for instance, that in a particular context a sentence fragment carries greater impact than would a fully expressed sentence. As a beginning writer, stick to the rules of sentence formation unless you are sure that breaking a particular rule will improve a specific piece of writing. Usually, sentences that violate the rules and conventions are awkward and confusing and sound childish.

Sentence Fragments

Writers sometimes use sentence fragments to achieve certain effects. Charles Dickens, for example, began his novel *Bleak House*—a study of the chaotic and muddled legal system in Victorian England—with a paragraph containing not one complete sentence. The society upon which the Lord Chancellor passes judgment is fogbound and muddy in more than the literal sense. Dickens makes us aware of this from the start. The sentence fragments create, in the reader's mind, a sense of the disorder in the city.

> London. Michaelmas Term lately over, and the Lord Chancellor sitting in Lincoln's Inn Hall. Implacable November weather. As much mud in the streets, as if the waters had but newly retired from the face of the earth,

and it would not be wonderful to meet a Megalosaurus, forty feet long or so, waddling like an elephantine lizard up Holborn Hill. Smoke lowering down from chimney-pots, making a soft black drizzle, with flakes of soot in it as big as full-grown snowflakes—gone into mourning, one might imagine, for the death of the sun. Dogs, undistinguishable in mire. Horses, scarely better; splashed by their very blinkers. Foot passengers, jostling one another's umbrellas in a general infection of ill-temper, and losing their foot-hold at street corners, where tens of thousands of other foot passengers have been slipping and sliding since the day broken (if the day ever broke), adding new deposits to the crust upon crust of mud, sticking at those points tenaciously to the pavement, and accumulating at compound interest.

Most writers who produce fragments, unfortunately, do not do so as consciously or as skillfully as Dickens has done here. Inexperienced writers produce fragments for a variety of reasons. Perhaps as an idea occurs to them after they have written a sentence, they hurriedly jot down the afterthought as a separate sentence. They do not bother to check to see whether the addition is a complete sentence and, if it is not, to attach it to the original sentence. Or perhaps the fragment makes a certain amount of sense in the context of the sentences around it. The writer is thus lulled into believing that there is no need to make the sentence a complete one. Beginning writers may come up with a fragment out of sheer carelessness—a failure to check their work for accuracy and completeness both during and after the actual writing. Whatever the reason for their appearance in a passage, though, fragments produced accidentally will, in all likelihood, make the passage clumsy, childish-sounding, and ineffective.

> E X A M P L E   The whole neighborhood thought that Mr. Sterling was a disgrace. Coming in at all hours of the night and singing "Roll Me Over in the Clover."

Coming in at all hours of the night . . . is not a complete sentence (it lacks a subject and a finite verb); it is a participial phrase. The phrase makes sense in conjunction with the first sentence, but it makes no sense by itself: who, after all, *would* be coming in and singing? The fragment should be combined with the sentence it amplifies.

> C O R R E C T I O N   The whole neighborhood thought that Mr. Sterling was a disgrace, coming in at all hours of the night and singing "Roll Me Over in the Clover."

Here and throughout this part of the handbook, the sentence labeled "Correction" will not be the *only* possible correction of the "Example." In the example sentence above, for example, a number of revisions are possible. One revision might be this: "The whole neighborhood thought that Mr. Sterling was a disgrace, because he would come in at all hours of the night singing 'Roll Me Over in the Clover.' "

EXAMPLE   College doesn't teach students about the real world. The world of raising a family and of trying to find a well-paying job.

The world is simply a noun modified by two gerund phrases (*of raising a family* and *of trying to find a well-paying job*). It is a perfect example of an "afterthought" fragment: the writer thought of a few specific characteristics of *the real world* and tacked them on in a fragment instead of including them in the first sentence. The repetition of *the world*, fortunately, provides a close enough link between the sentence and the fragment so that not much additional revision is needed.

CORRECTION   College doesn't teach students about the real world—the world of raising a family and of trying to find a well-paying job.

EXAMPLE   We learn how his mind works. What his flaws and achievements are.

Again, *What his flaws and achievements are* is an "afterthought" fragment. The fragment differs in structure from the *real world* fragment, however: it is a dependent clause. It has a subject—*his flaws and achievements*—and a predicate—*are (what)*—but it cannot stand alone as a complete thought. In fact, the clause is really the object of *We learn*. It should be combined with the preceding sentence. Since that sentence already contains a dependent clause acting as object, the sentence combining is easy.

CORRECTION   We learn how his mind works and what his flaws and achievements are.

EXAMPLE   When Gregers tells her that one way to get back at him is to kill the duck. She takes it as the only way.

Here, the fragment is the first "sentence" in the sequence. *She takes it ...* is an independent clause, but *When Gregers tells her ...* is a dependent clause acting as an adverb. The dependent clause cannot stand alone.

CORRECTION   When Gregers tells her that one way to get back at him is to kill the duck, she takes it as the only way.

EXAMPLE   Two roommates who don't get along may just give up on each other. Which has some advantages.

Which has some advantages is another dependent clause—a relative clause that acts as an adjective. But what does the clause modify—in other words, to what does *which* refer? It is clearly not *roommates*; in fact, it is the whole preceding sentence. The sentence and the fragment must be combined and recast to eliminate the looseness of reference.

CORRECTION   Two roommates who don't get along may just give up on each other, a solution that has some advantages.

EXAMPLE   We arrived at the dinner. The master of ceremonies and
several parents, none of whom I knew.

The master of ceremonies . . . may *look* like a complete sentence at
first, but read it again: *The master of ceremonies and several parents*
did *what?* It is a fragment, for it has no predicate.

CORRECTION   We arrived at the dinner. The master of ceremonies
and several parents, none of whom I knew, were there
already.

Comma Splices

A *comma splice* is the yoking together of two or more independent
clauses with only a comma or commas. It *is* possible to join independent clauses with commas when the clauses are very short—for example, *I came, I saw, I conquered*—but clauses much longer than these
should be joined by a semicolon or by a comma *plus* a conjunction. Depending on the particular sentence in question, the clauses can also be
turned into separate sentences. Or one less-important point can be
turned into a dependent clause. Some student writers may not see any
reason to worry about comma splices—comma splices are, after all, primarily errors of punctuation—but the problem becomes clearer when
they learn to think of a comma splice as a breach of promise. The
comma, as a unit of punctuation, is a half stop, not a whole stop. The
comma is not strong enough in itself to prepare the reader for the introduction of an entire new independent clause. Like a Yield sign instead of a Stop sign at a busy intersection, a comma alone between two
independent clauses miscues the reader.

EXAMPLE   I would advise all of you to join some club, we will all benefit from your participation.

The comma here is simply not a sufficient link between the two independent clauses. They could be joined by a semicolon.

CORRECTION 1   I would advise all of you to join some club; we will
all benefit from your participation.

Since the meaning of the second clause depends in large part on that of
the first, the second clause could be turned into a dependent clause.

CORRECTION 2   I would advise all of you to join some club, because
we will all benefit from your participation.

EXAMPLE   Almost the whole family was there, her youngest son had
not been able to make it from California.

In this example, the comma is not only an inadequate link between
independent clauses but also an insufficient indicator of the shift in emphasis from *the whole family* to *her youngest son.*

CORRECTION   Almost the whole family was there, but her youngest son had not been able to make it from California.

EXAMPLE   Andrew came through the door, his broad shoulders were stooped and he looked older than his thirty-four years.

The comma here is the only link between *Andrew came through the door* and *two* other independent clauses—*his broad shoulders were stooped* and *he looked older than his thirty-four years.* Under the circumstances, the best thing to do would be to begin a new sentence where the comma is now. (Note, too, that there should be a comma before *and*. The comma–conjunction combination is needed to link the independent clauses in the new second sentence.)

CORRECTION   Andrew came through the door. His broad shoulders were stooped, and he looked older than his thirty-four years.

EXAMPLE   The house isn't like a home any more, there is so much hostility within its walls.

One of the trickier kinds of comma splices is the linking of a short, "explanatory" second clause with a longer first clause. A comma as connector may *seem* almost "natural," because the two independent clauses are closely related in sense. A semicolon could be used to link these two clauses, but subordinate clauses might work better to highlight the relationship between the clauses.

CORRECTION 1   The house isn't like a home any more because there is so much hostility within its walls.

CORRECTION 2   There is so much hostility within its walls that the house isn't like a home any more.

The *so* of the original sentence becomes part of a *so . . . that* clause in the correction.

EXAMPLE   He did not feel that he was fighting just for the survival of his state, he felt that he was fighting for the survival of the nation.

In sentences like this, in which a structure in the first clause is repeated in the second clause (*he felt that he was fighting . . .*), beginning writers often want to use a comma. If the clauses involved are very short, commas might be permissible. The length of the clauses in the example sentence, however, calls for a semicolon.

CORRECTION   He did not feel that he was fighting just for the survival of his state; he felt that he was fighting for the survival of the nation.

EXAMPLE   I told Ron what I thought, however, he still insisted on joining the rock group.

A frequent error is the comma splice that results from a failure to use a semicolon with a conjunctive adverb (*however, moreover, therefore,* and so on) that links two independent clauses. A conjunctive adverb relates more strongly to one clause or to the other; it is not, like a coordinating conjunction, a fairly neutral link. Therefore, a semicolon, and not a comma, is used with conjunctive adverbs that link two independent clauses. Because in the example sentence *however* is more firmly connected to the second clause than to the first clause, the semicolon should come before the second clause. Note, too, that *however* can be moved to other locations within the second clause. A coordinating conjunction could not be moved.

CORRECTION   I told Ron what I thought; however, he still insisted on joining the rock group.

EXAMPLE   We have not yet considered one factor, however, it is the voters' view of Senator Pellagra.

In this example, *however* is more firmly linked to the first clause. Therefore, the semicolon should follow *however.*

CORRECTION   We have not yet considered one factor, however; it is the voters' view of Senator Pellagra.

Fused Sentences

A *fused sentence* is the jamming together of two or more independent clauses with no linking words or punctuation marks at all. In a fused sentence—to continue the traffic sign analogy—the writer has failed to put up any marker whatever at a busy intersection. The confusion that results can be even more serious than the uncertainty produced by a wrong sign (the comma splice).

EXAMPLE   The Congresswoman reversed her position she was persuaded by the arguments of lobbyists.

The Congresswoman reversed her position is one clause; *she was persuaded* ... is another. The link between the two can be indicated simply by a semicolon.

CORRECTION   The Congresswoman reversed her position; she was persuaded by the arguments of lobbyists.

EXAMPLE   Scrape the old paint until all the loose particles have fallen off then sand the area until the surface is smooth.

Then provides the suggestion of a link between the two independent clauses: *scrape the old paint* and *sand the area.* (Each independent clause has a dependent clause *until* attached to it.) But the word is not enough of a connection, because *then* is only an adverb modifying *sand,* not a conjunctive adverb or a conjunction. The two clauses must be connected more clearly.

> C O R R E C T I O N   Scrape the old paint until all the loose particles have fallen off, and then sand the area until the surface is smooth.

Be sure to insert a comma before the conjunction.

> E X A M P L E   Commuting students do not have to go through all the confusion and unpleasantness of campus life they will miss a great deal in the long run.

An explicit connection between the two clauses is needed even more urgently than in the previous examples, for there is a shift in direction between the first clause and the second. The conjunction *but* can indicate the shift.

> C O R R E C T I O N   Commuting students do not have to go through all the confusion and unpleasantness of campus life, but they will miss a great deal in the long run.

Run-ons

A *run-on* is a group of two or more (usually more) independent clauses strung together by conjunctions without punctuation. Run-ons are usually not as difficult to follow as fused sentences. But run-ons are loose, slack, and often disjointed constructions that can almost always be tightened up for the good of the sentence. Consider these examples:

> E X A M P L E   I drove to Coyne Field and I watched a lacrosse game and I went to the movies with Gary and I saw *Star Wars* and I had fun.

The sentence can be revised in several ways. As you try recasting it, however, keep in mind that certain ideas should remain together or be integrated even more closely—driving to Coyne Field and watching the lacrosse game, going to the movies with Gary and seeing *Star Wars.*

> C O R R E C T I O N   I drove to Coyne Field and watched a lacrosse game; afterwards, I went to see *Star Wars* with Gary. I had fun.

> E X A M P L E   We can use this money to pay the taxes or we can buy a new house or we can get a Mercedes or we can spend the weekend in Las Vegas.

Again, there is more than one way to rework this sentence. The simplest solution might be to turn the string of clauses into a series of infinitive phrases (it is not necessary to express the *to* each time).

> C O R R E C T I O N   We can use this money to pay the taxes, buy a new house, get a Mercedes, or spend the weekend in Las Vegas.

> E X A M P L E   We have only one option and it must be carried out immediately for we have only thirty years' worth of fossil fuel left.

An effective tactic here might be to emphasize the drama of *We have only one option* by setting it off as a separate sentence. *However* can be inserted in the new second sentence to serve as a link between the two sentences.

> C O R R E C T I O N   We have only one option. It must be carried out immediately, however, for we have only thirty years' worth of fossil fuel left.

EXERCISES

a). Sentence Fragments
Each exercise item contains a sentence fragment. Eliminate the fragment either by combining it with the adjoining sentence or by creating two sentences.

1. I didn't mind being late to the party. Because I didn't want to go in the first place.
2. Large picture windows break easily. Which costs a great deal to replace.
3. The Department of Public Works had an enormous clean-up job to do. When the storm was over.
4. If all goes well. We should finish in about three hours.
5. Many people today are looking for kinds of transportation other than the car. Bicycles, buses, subways, for example.

b). Comma Splices
Eliminate the comma splices in the following sentences by using appropriate punctuation.

1. Life presents many challenges, however, the determined individual nearly always meets them.
2. Gregory made many mistakes, for one thing, he underestimated the strength of Henry's character.
3. Laura wants to start an off-campus study group, her plan is workable.
4. When we arrived, we found that we had packed all the wrong things, the weather was much colder than we had expected.
5. Peter, you must be exhausted, you've worked about twelve hours today.

c). Fused Sentences

Correct the fused sentences below. You can do so by supplying appropriate punctuation, by adding a coordinating conjunction, by turning part of the sentence into a dependent clause, or by creating two sentences out of the one.

1. Jennifer is going downtown she has to buy some books.
2. George can't use his car right now his driver's license has been revoked.
3. Peter is staying home this summer he'll be working.
4. I don't think I want to go for a walk it'll be raining soon.
5. There was a big storm the other night the lights were out for five hours.

d). Run-ons

Revise the items below to eliminate the run-ons.

1. Melissa has a bad cold and she won't go to work but she will lie in the sun to get a tan.
2. This is a beautiful house and it's just the right size and the location is good but it's too expensive.
3. Annette wants to go to the movies but Ed wants to go fishing and they may end up fighting before they decide which they will do.
4. I saw a beautiful antique chair at the auction but it was very fragile and it broke when Edmund tried to sit on it.
5. The weather will turn colder and it will snow and we'll have to put on the snow tires or we'll never get out tomorrow.

e). Comprehensive Exercise

Revise the following items to eliminate sentence fragments, comma splices, fused sentences, and run-ons. The revision of each item may take one, two, or more sentences.

1. Tom has made a complete mess of this situation and I don't know how to fix things I'm sure he thinks he did just fine, he did not and he'll soon find out. Which I'll enjoy telling him.
2. The plane should be in by now; the weather getting better; the runway cleared of snow; the lights on again.
3. Betty went to the dentist and she had a tooth extracted it did not hurt as much as she thought it would so she was glad. Which is a good thing.
4. The devastation is worse in this part of the city. Because there are no hills the force of the wind is unbroken.
5. What he found out. He could never be happy as an engineer, therefore he quit school and did nothing.
6. The experiment does not work I'm going home. In spite of its importance.
7. The meat is cooked the vegetables are done we can eat. Or don't you think so.
8. For better or for worse. I'm doing this my way. Because I know what's best for me.
9. Jack told me a story. Which I don't believe is true, he's always telling tall tales.

10. Since he was absent-minded. He forgot to release the emergency brake before he went on the highway, the car began to fume.
11. Riding a bicycle is good exercise bicycles are also a good means of transportation, more people should ride bikes instead of driving cars.
12. I have no time to talk to you I have to make breakfast and send the kids off to school and then I have to make sure I get to work on time today, I didn't the last time you called me in the morning.
13. Sarah is having a hard time. Deciding what subjects to take. If she should stay in school at all, maybe she won't.
14. There were a number of things about dorm life we weren't prepared for. The noise level. The inedible food. The leaks in the roof.
15. Although living at home may have its advantages. Students who live on campus have many advantages over the commuters. Such as the fact that on-campus students can make friends more easily, they also have easier access to campus events and activities.

PRINCIPLE 2: Match the parts of sentences that need matching. Make sure that the structure of each sentence is an accurate reflection of what you intend to say.

It may be helpful to think of the sentence as a unit made up of various parts—subject, verb, modifiers—that work together to produce a complete thought. The various elements, however, cannot be combined in a sentence haphazardly. The writer must be careful to "match up" those parts of the sentence that depend upon each other or belong together, or are linked in some way. For instance, the key parts of the sentence—the subject and the predicate—must *agree.* If the subject of a sentence is singular, the verb must also be singular; if the subject is plural, so must the verb be. Although the meaning of the sentence will be clear even if the subject and predicate do not agree, nevertheless the sentence will be incorrect and ineffective because the writer of the sentence has disregarded one of the *conventions,* or standards, of the language. In other cases, the improper "matching" of sentence elements may actually make the sentence difficult for the reader to follow. The reader may not be able to figure out, for example, just what word or words a particular modifier is supposed to be describing; or to which noun a particular pronoun is intended to refer; or to which two phrases or clauses the writing is attempting to give equal emphasis. In a few cases the sentence may be grammatically correct on the surface—all of the elements may *seem* to be correctly "matched"—but it may nevertheless be so confusingly constructed that the meaning is difficult or impossible to figure out. Study the following examples, and then make it your business not to confuse the reader either by failing to "match up" the elements in your sentence that should be matched or by writing something that means something quite different from what you had intended to say.

Subject–Verb Agreement

The subject of a sentence must *agree* in person and in number with the verb. For example, a first-person singular subject *(I)* calls for the first-person singular forms of a verb *(I go)*; a third-person singular subject *(David)* requires the third-person singular form of the verb *(David goes)*; and a third-person plural subject *(the congressmen)* calls for the third-person plural form of the verb *(the congressmen go)*.

> EXAMPLE   From here we *comes* to the traffic problem.

The subject, *we*, is first-person plural. Therefore, a first-person plural verb is called for; but the writer has used a third-person singular verb form.

> CORRECTION   From here we *come* to the traffic problem.

> EXAMPLE   She *don't* want me to go to the party.

Because the subject is third-person singular, a third-person singular verb form is needed (*does not*, or contracted, *doesn't*).

> CORRECTION   She *doesn't* want me to go to the party.

When modifying phrases or clauses come between the subject and the verb in a sentence, subject–verb agreement becomes a little more difficult.

> EXAMPLE   One major goal of the programs *are* to show how learning can be fun.

The writer has confused the subject of the sentence, *goal*, with the noun that comes just before the verb, *programs*. Since the actual subject is singular, the verb should be singular too.

> CORRECTION   One major goal of the programs *is* to show how learning can be fun.

> EXAMPLE   The soap dish, along with the sponge and the toothbrushes, *are* on the sink.

Sponge and *toothbrushes* may be near the *soap dish* on the sink, but only *soap dish* is the subject. The *along with* phrase comes between subject and verb.

> CORRECTION   The soap dish, along with the sponge and the toothbrushes, *is* on the sink.

When the subject of a sentence has a compound verb, *both* verbs must agree with the subject.

> EXAMPLE   Dr. Schaeffer's theories *give* a clear picture of the unemployment problem and *suggests* possible remedies.

The first verb in the sentence, *give,* agrees with the plural subject. But *suggests* is a third-person singular verb and must be changed to the third-person plural to agree with the subject.

> CORRECTION   Dr. Schaeffer's theories *give* a clear picture of the unemployment problem and *suggest* possible remedies.

Compound subjects present still another challenge. When the two subjects are joined by *and,* they take a plural verb.

> EXAMPLE   Sam and his brother *was* not home when Peter called.
> CORRECTION   Sam and his brother *were* not home when Peter called.

The two subjects are *Sam* and *brother.*

> EXAMPLE   In Book I of *Gulliver's Travels,* Jonathan Swift shows how corrupt England and its government *was.*
> CORRECTION   In Book I of *Gulliver's Travels,* Jonathan Swift shows how corrupt England and its government *were.*

Unlike compound subjects joined by *and,* compound subjects joined by *or* or *nor* do not always take a plural verb. The form of the verb is determined by the form of the subject *nearer* the verb. If the nearer subject is singular, the verb is also singular; if the nearer subject is plural, the verb is also plural.

> EXAMPLE   Neither Francis nor Dorothy really *act* like an adult.

Dorothy is singular; the verb must also be singular.

> CORRECTION   Neither Francis nor Dorothy really *acts* like an adult.

> EXAMPLE   Either Sam or his brother *are* responsible for unloading the vegetables.

The subject closer to the verb, *brother,* is singular; therefore, the verb must be singular as well.

> CORRECTION   Either Sam or his brother *is* responsible for unloading the vegetables.

> EXAMPLE   Either Mr. Dunlap or the Smiths *shows* the guests to their rooms.

Here the subject closer to the verb is *the Smiths;* the verb therefore, must be plural.

> CORRECTION   Either Mr. Dunlap or the Smiths *show* the guests to their rooms.

Most collective nouns (nouns that are singular in form but plural in meaning) take singular verbs in American English.

EXAMPLE   The family *plan* to spend Christmas in Peoria this year.
CORRECTION   The family *plans* to spend Christmas in Peoria this year.

EXAMPLE   The committee *have* reached a decision.
CORRECTION   The committee *has* reached a decision.

Words like *each, everybody, nobody, neither,* serving as subjects of sentences have been student bugaboos for generations. Some of the words, like *everybody,* for example, sound plural, and therefore it seems unnatural in everyday speech to match them with singular verbs. In written English, however, these subjects do indeed take singular verbs. Here are a few examples.

EXAMPLE   Each of these tribes still *hold* firmly to ancient customs and rituals.
CORRECTION   Each of these tribes still *holds* firmly to ancient customs and rituals.

Each is the subject, remember, not *tribes.*

EXAMPLE   Everyone except Clarence and Mortimer *were* taken to the police station.
CORRECTION   Everyone except Clarence and Mortimer *was* taken to the police station.

EXAMPLE   None of the other members of the committee *were* interested in Harold's proposal.
CORRECTION   None of the other members of the committee *was* interested in Harold's proposal.

Finally, *there is* and *there are* constructions have hampered beginning writers for years. The thing to remember is that *there* is never the subject of the sentence. The true subject follows the *there is (are)* construction. Always be sure you know what the subject is before deciding between *there is* and *there are.* Use *there is* with singular subjects, *there are* with plural subjects.

EXAMPLE   In our society there *is* strong prejudices against people who do not happen to be young and good-looking.

The subject is not *there* but *prejudices.*

CORRECTION   In our society there *are* strong prejudices against people who do not happen to be young and good-looking.

EXAMPLE   We recognize that there *is* not enough hospitals for the population of the city.

The subject is not *there* but *hospitals.* The verb should be in the plural.

CORRECTION   We recognize that there *are* not enough hospitals for the population of the city.

Shifts in Verb Tense

In writing sentences that contain a compound verb or two or more clauses, be careful not to shift from one verb tense to another unless you wish to indicate a difference in time between the actions the verbs describe. Unnecessary shifts in verb tense may lead your readers to believe that you are describing shifts in time when in fact you are not. Such confusion can sometimes change the meaning of a sentence and is always a hindrance.

> EXAMPLE   When Mama and Papa *have* disappeared inside the front door, Ivan, Katharina, Analisa, and I *had* to wait in the kitchen.

Is the writer describing an event that still sometimes occurs or one that definitely took place in the past? We cannot be sure. Two corrections are possible.

> CORRECTION 1   When Mama and Papa *had* disappeared . . .

This version of the sentence describes an action that happened in the past.

> CORRECTION 2   Ivan, Katharina, Analisa, and I *have* to wait in the kitchen.

This version of the sentence describes an action that still occurs. Be especially careful with verb tenses when you write about works of literature. Most teachers will ask you to use the present tense in discussing a novel, a poem, or play. After all, the events in the work "happen" again and again, for every new reader and on every rereading. Whatever tense your teacher asks you to use in writing about literature, however, you must *use it consistently*. Most difficulties with the present tense in papers on literature stem from careless slips into other tenses. Shifts, as noted earlier, should indicate actual shifts in time.

Pronoun Reference and Pronoun–Antecedent Agreement

A pronoun ordinarily has an *antecedent*—the noun to which it refers. If a pronoun has no antecedent or its antecedent is unclear, the sentence contains an error in *pronoun reference*. Pronoun-reference errors can sometimes obscure the meaning of a sentence. A pronoun may have a clear enough antecedent and yet the sentence may still be incorrect. In other words, an error in *pronoun–antecedent agreement* may exist. Just as subjects and verbs must agree in number (singular and plural), so antecedents and their pronouns must agree in number and in person. A third potential trouble spot in pronouns is *case*, which is taken up in the next section.

EXAMPLE   In his speech about the impending rise in tuition, student government president Bigman Oncampus said that they should be ashamed of themselves.

Who is *they?* The best thing to do here might be to eliminate the pronoun altogether.

CORRECTION   In his speech about the impending rise in tuition, student government president Bigman Oncampus said that the college administrators should be ashamed of themselves.

EXAMPLE   Edward lived through the war and became a medical student. Mother tells me that Ivan's death was the cause of his decision.

This example differs from the first in that *his* plainly has an antecedent. The difficulty here is that the reader is at least momentarily uncertain whether *his* refers to Edward or to Ivan. Since Ivan can hardly be deciding about anything in his present condition, the sentence must be revised to indicate that the decision is Edward's. (Some indication of the nature of the decision would also strengthen the sentence.)

CORRECTION   Edward lived through the war and became a medical student. Mother tells me that Ivan's death was the cause of Edward's decision to study medicine.

EXAMPLE   The three sisters were poor, plain, and psychologically scarred by their early losses, which kept them from dealing effectively with the outside world.

Again, more than one possibility for the antecedent of *which* exists. Is it just *losses*, or is it the combination of factors listed by the writer? If the combination is the antecedent—which seems likely—the sentence might be revised as follows:

CORRECTION   The three sisters were poor, plain, and psychologically scarred by their early losses; all of these factors kept them from dealing with the outside world.

In the following examples, the pronoun antecedents are clear enough, but they fail to agree with the antecedents in person and number.

EXAMPLE   At boot camp, the would-be soldier must rise at 6:15, dress, make *your* bed, and be on the parade ground by 6:30.

Your plainly refers to soldiers. But the pronoun is in the second person, while *soldiers*—like all nouns—is in the third person. Beginning writers, especially, find it easy to slip into *you* and *your* to avoid getting caught in the confusion of *he* and *she, his* and *her, him* and *her.* Since nowadays many would-be soldiers might well be women, the simplest solution might be to turn *soldier* into *soldiers.* The correct pronoun would then be *their* (and *bed* becomes *beds*).

C O R R E C T I O N   At boot camp, would-be soldiers must rise at 6:15, dress, make *their* beds, and be on the parade ground by 6:30.

E X A M P L E   For example, if a student is caught cheating *they* will get in trouble.

Student and *they* are both in the third person, but *student* is singular and *they* is plural. This is a case of lack of agreement in number. The error stems, in part, from another attempt to dodge the troublesome choice between *he* and *she.*

C O R R E C T I O N 1   For example, if a student is caught cheating *he* will get in trouble.
C O R R E C T I O N 2   For example, if *students* are caught cheating *they* will get in trouble.

E X A M P L E   Once again, the administration has broken *their* promise not to raise tuition.

Another temptation for the beginning writer is to use plural pronouns when the antecedent is a collective noun. We use singular verbs with such nouns in standard American English, however, and we use singular pronouns as well.

C O R R E C T I O N   Once again, the administration has broken *its* promise not to raise tuition.

Everyone, everybody, each, nobody, anyone, and so on create number problems with pronouns as well as with verbs. Just as the above words take singular verbs, so they take singular pronouns.

E X A M P L E   Everyone went to *their* own room.
C O R R E C T I O N   Everyone went to *her* [or *his*] own room.

E X A M P L E   Each of Spock's compatriots lifted *their* hand in the Vulcan salute.
C O R R E C T I O N   Each of Spock's compatriots lifted *his* [or *her*] hand in the Vulcan salute.

E X A M P L E   I picked up the pieces of glass so nobody would cut *themselves.*
C O R R E C T I O N   I picked up the pieces of glass so nobody would cut *himself.*

One final problem in pronoun–antecedent agreement, aside from problems in person and number, is the confusion of *who* or *whom* with *which* and *that.* Some beginning writers will go to such lengths to avoid the *who/whom* problem that they will use *which* and *that* when the names of persons or animals are the antecedents. Less often, they will use *who* and *whom* with collective nouns. Neither practice is correct.

EXAMPLE   It is not healthful for children to live with parents *that* constantly fight.

CORRECTION   It is not healthful for children to live with parents *who* constantly fight.

EXAMPLE   Silva plays a sane character to *which* the audience can relate.

CORRECTION   Silva plays a sane character to *whom* the audience can relate.

EXAMPLE   The greatest harm might come to the networks *who* have replaced some of their shows with educational programs.

CORRECTION   The greatest harm might come to the networks *that* have replaced . . .

Pronoun Case

Not only must pronouns agree with their antecedents in person and number, but they must be "matched" correctly in another way: in *case*. For example, pronouns used as subjects or as predicate nominatives must be in the *nominative* case (*I* for first-person singular, *he* or *she* for third-person singular). Pronouns serving as direct or indirect objects or as objects of prepositions must be in the *objective* case (*me* for first-person singular, *him* or *her* for third-person singular).

EXAMPLE   Laura screamed as if it were her who had been struck.

In conversation, we probably would say *her*. The function *her* serves in the sentence is that of a predicate nominative in the dependent clause, however. Therefore, the pronoun should, in written work, be in the nominative case, *she*.

CORRECTION   Laura screamed as if it were *she* who had been struck.

EXAMPLE   Bromley is taller than him.

In order to determine the correct pronoun case, you may find it helpful to complete the implied statement at the end of the sentence: *than . . . is*. You can then see that the pronoun is really the subject of an implied clause and should be in the nominative case.

CORRECTION   Bromley is taller than *he* [is].

Who and *whom* often confuse new writers. You can usually choose correctly between *who* and *whom* if you pay attention to the function of the pronoun in the sentence.

EXAMPLE   He has a wife, Faith, *who* he loves very much.

Who is the direct object of *love* and should therefore be in the objective case.

CORRECTION   He has a wife, Faith, *whom* he loves very much.

It is possible, of course, to *overcorrect*—to assume that if a pronoun sounds "proper" and "elegant" it must be the right one. This is by no means always true. Your guideline in determining the correct case of a pronoun must always be the function the pronoun serves in the sentence, not the sound of the sentence. Here are a few instances of overcorrection:

EXAMPLE   Everyone except Katie and *she* was injured in the wreck.
CORRECTION   Everyone except Katie and *her* was injured in the wreck.

The pronoun is the object of the preposition *except*.

EXAMPLE   Lunk showed Jim and *I* the swelling in his ankle.
CORRECTION   Lunk showed Jim and *me* the swelling in his ankle.

The pronoun is an indirect object.

EXAMPLE   *Whom* will win the Heisman Trophy this year?
CORRECTION   *Who* will win the Heisman Trophy this year?

The pronoun is the subject of the sentence.

Misplaced or "Dangling" Modifiers

Your teacher may sometimes feel compelled to ornament your papers with the fierce word "dangler!" What error does the word indicate? You have probably placed a modifying word, phrase, or clause in such a way that it appears to modify the wrong word or does not actually modify anything in the sentence. Such errors can make you look downright silly at times. More important, they can be serious hindrances to your readers.

Although misplaced words are generally not as problematic as misplaced phrases or clauses, they can still cause the reader to stop and question your meaning for a moment or two. Here are some examples:

EXAMPLE   He feels he cannot trust his wife because he suspects that even David may not be his child.

How many children does the man have? How many does he suspect are not his? The placement of *even* throws the matter into doubt. The word, therefore, should be relocated.

CORRECTION ... he suspects that David may not even be his child.

EXAMPLE For students who are not successfully able to write a composition, freshman English can be of great help.

Successfully appears to modify *able*, but such an interpretation does not make a great deal of sense. The degree of success applies not to *ability*, but to the act of *writing*. The sentence makes more sense when rephrased:

CORRECTION For students who are not able to write a composition successfully, freshman English can be of great help.

Misplaced phrases and clauses can be real troublemakers, for they can cause writers to say something quite different from and often more ridiculous than what they had meant to say.

EXAMPLE Firms are afraid to train those who may tend to quit because of retraining costs.

The placement of the phrase *because of retraining costs* makes it sound as though the costs are a reason for the resignation of *those who may tend to quit*. The statement is not very plausible.

CORRECTION Because of retraining costs, firms are afraid to train those who may tend to quit.

EXAMPLE Her skin was as soft as tiger's fur with long silky hair and dark brown eyes.

The absurdity here is fairly obvious. (Have you seen much tiger's fur with long silky hair and dark brown eyes?) In fact, the writer could best revise this by eliminating the prepositional phrase entirely.

CORRECTION Her skin was as soft as tiger's fur, and she had long silky hair and dark brown eyes.

EXAMPLE The truck hit the mailbox on the corner, crossing the intersection.

Apparently it is not safe for mailboxes to cross the streets these days. The participial phrase must be moved and *when* added.

CORRECTION When crossing the intersection, the truck hit the mailbox on the corner.

EXAMPLE In the third scene, Tom hurls his coat across the room, which hits the shelf and breaks some of the glass.

Here a whole clause has been misplaced, and it sounds as though the room is what hits the shelf.

CORRECTION In the third scene, Tom hurls his coat across the room, and it hits the shelf and breaks some of the glass.

Parallelism

Sentence elements in pairs or in a series must be made parallel—that is, they must be in the same grammatical form. Failure to pair words with words of equal weight and similar structure, phrases with similar phrases, or clauses with similar clauses can disrupt the balance and the meaning of a sentence.

> EXAMPLE   When Joe stored his furniture, he put his "goodbye" on a physical level rather than *emotional*.

The writer has paired a modified noun *(a physical level)* with a single adjective *(emotional)*. The problem is not hard to correct.

> CORRECTION   When Joe stored his furniture, he put his "goodbye" on a physical level rather than on an emotional one.

> EXAMPLE   James was *a member* of the Chamber of Commerce, *a member* of the Rotary, and *was on* the School Board.

This sentence contains two nouns followed by prepositional phrases plus one prepositional phrase without a noun *(was on the School Board)*. This problem can also be corrected fairly simply.

> CORRECTION   James was *a member* of the Chamber of Commerce, *a member* of the Rotary, and *a member* of the School Board.

A better and shorter version would be, "James was a member of the Chamber of Commerce, the Rotary, and the School Board."

> EXAMPLE   She was a good wife and mother, hard-working, level-headed, and knew how to keep Andrew happy.

Here we have a whole string of dissimilar elements; *wife* and *mother* are nouns; *hard-working* and *levelheaded* are adjectives; and *knew how to keep Andrew happy* is a verb and a noun clause. The writer would probably have to strain this sentence too much to turn all the elements into nouns, adjectives, or verbs followed by clauses. It might best to write the sentence as three separate independent clauses.

> CORRECTION   She was a good wife and mother; she was hard-working and levelheaded; and she knew how to keep Andrew happy.

> EXAMPLE   The best time to exercise is one hour before eating or two hours after you have eaten a full meal.

This sentence is a little trickier than the others. The problem is that *before eating* is a prepositional phrase and *after you have eaten a full meal* is a dependent clause.

> CORRECTION   The best time to exercise is one hour before you eat or two hours after you have eaten a full meal.

EXAMPLE   On the train to Atlanta, Nelson becomes aware of his own dependence on Mr. Head and that he would have a hard time doing without him.

In this sentence, a series of prepositional phrases *(of his own dependence on Mr. Head)* is paired with a clause *(that he would have a hard time doing without him)*. It is easier to expand the phrases than to contract the clause, so the sentence can be corrected in this way:

CORRECTION   On the train to Atlanta, Nelson becomes aware that he is dependent on Mr. Head and that he would have a hard time doing without him.

Some beginning writers produce sentences in which the paired elements are parallel, but they omit key words or phrases that make the parallelism clear.

EXAMPLE   In Brobdingnag, Gulliver is treated as a rare pet or a plaything but never a man.
CORRECTION   In Brobdingnag, Gulliver is treated *as* a rare pet or a plaything but never *as* a man.

EXAMPLE   He explains to her that their love will last forever and therefore she has nothing to worry about.
CORRECTION   He explains to her that their love will last forever and *that* therefore she has nothing to worry about.

Incomplete or Misconstructed Comparisons

Comparisons are useful, but they can present pitfalls. When you set up a comparison, be sure that the reader understands which two elements you are comparing. Cast the two elements of the comparison in the same grammatical form (*both* should be subjects or *both* should be objects, for instance) and "carry through" the second element as completely as the first. Be sure, too, that you do not *compare* (point out likenesses) when what you really mean to do is to *contrast* (show differences). Finally, be sure that your comparison is sensible—that you are not comparing two elements that simply cannot be logically compared.

EXAMPLE   Women are more patient with children than men.

Does the writer mean that men are relatively impatient with children, or that women are inclined to prefer children to men? The reader has no way of knowing. Two corrections are possible.

CORRECTION 1   Women are more patient with children than men are.

CORRECTION 2   Women are more patient with children than they are with men.

EXAMPLE "I Love Lucy" has more slapstick comedy than "The Dick Van Dyke Show."

Strictly speaking, the sentence says that "I Love Lucy" contains both slapstick comedy *and* "The Dick Van Dyke Show"—a notion that Dick Van Dyke would probably object to. The comparison must be carried through to its real conclusion.

CORRECTION "I Love Lucy" has more slapstick comedy than "The Dick Van Dyke Show" does.

Passive Voice

When an English sentence is phrased as "X does Y," we say that it is in the *active voice*. When the doer and the receiver of the action trade places in the sentence, however—that is, when the sentence is phrased "Y *is done by* X," or simply "Y *is done*"—we say that the sentence is in the *passive voice*. (For a more complete discussion of active and passive voice, see the "Glossary of Grammatical Terms.") The passive voice is useful when a writer wishes to emphasize the receiver of an action. The passive is natural, too, when an action has no particular doer or doers. In our increasingly webby-minded world, though, writers are so reluctant to link an action directly to its doer that they work the passive voice to death, with wordiness and vagueness as the result. Every time you find yourself using the passive voice in your writing, stop and ask yourself whether the active voice would not in fact be clearer and more direct.

EXAMPLE It is being realized by many that marriage isn't a thing to rush into.

Many who? There is no reason why the "realizers" should not be identified and put in their proper place in the sentence.

CORRECTION Many men and women today realize that marriage isn't a thing to rush into.

EXAMPLE The eyes of many people are made to water by smoke in the air.

Once again, what is the real focal point of this sentence—the *eyes* or the *smoke?*

CORRECTION Smoke in the air makes many people's eyes water.

EXAMPLE As one enters the building, a totally new image is conveyed.

The writer gives only the faintest hint as to what is doing the conveying. A major overhaul of the sentence is called for.

CORRECTION   The entrance of the building conveys a totally new image to the observer.

EXAMPLE   Many papers should be written by the students in this course because greater control of the English language will thereby be gained by them.

Perhaps so, but the writer might have given more convincing proof of the statement by rephrasing the sentence to eliminate both passive constructions.

CORRECTION   The students in this course should write many papers in order to gain greater control of the English language.

EXERCISES

a). Subject–Verb Agreement
Correct the following sentences by making the subjects and the verbs agree.

1. There is several reasons for obeying the speed limit.
2. Mark and David, more than any of my friends, likes to ski.
3. None of the students in this class are biology majors.
4. Susan or Carol are probably going to take one of the leading roles.
5. The lights in the hallway is going out.
6. Either Amanda or Tom are upset during much of the play.
7. The sofas that I put on either side of the mirror is an antique.
8. Everyone at the party were having a good time.
9. After three days, there were still much work left to do.
10. All of these carpets is very valuable.

b). Tense Shift
Revise the sentences to eliminate unnecessary shifts in verb tense. If a sentence can be revised in two different ways, write both revisions.

1. When Anthony came home, he finds Gina at the typewriter.
2. Mary has gone swimming; I hope the water wasn't too cold.
3. When Pamela went for a walk, she meets a friend of hers.
4. The car stops at our house and then took off very fast.
5. I am sure Frank can do it if he would only try.
6. In the novel, Philip didn't want to hurt Miranda, but he can't understand that his reckless behavior upsets her.
7. Joseph and Andrew meet on the bus trip, but they didn't travel together all the time.
8. I couldn't lose any weight, even though I run every day.
9. I had saved enough money, but I'm still not going to Europe.
10. When George parachuted into Cambodia, he is taken prisoner.

c). Pronoun Reference and Pronoun–Antecedent Agreement
Correct the following sentences by making sure that the pronouns have clear antecedents and that the pronouns agree, in person and in number, with their antecedents.

1. Each student will find out their grade shortly after the exam.
2. At Snootyhill School, the students never had to clean their rooms; we had maid service.
3. Caroline never pays attention, and it causes a number of problems.
4. A student can pass the exams easily if you don't panic.
5. Several people that we didn't know were at the meeting.
6. The board of directors, who finally makes all decisions, refused to act.
7. No one likes to admit when they're wrong.
8. Sarah told Nancy that she has to pick up Karen at 5 o'clock.
9. Christine or Samantha will bring their car.
10. Helen had the courage to do what she felt was right, and this led her to confess her wrongdoing.

d). Pronoun Case

Correct the following sentences by making sure that all pronouns are in the correct cases. Make sure, too, that no other incorrect pronoun forms are used.

1. Mr. West gave instructions to Bill and I.
2. Who should I give these books to?
3. Joe always kept to himself and never told his problems to Silvia.
4. Gina was angry with Thomas because he and Dave had gone out.
5. The man who the car hit is in critical condition.

e). Danglers

Rewrite the following sentences to eliminate misplaced or dangling modifiers. You may revise a sentence by turning it into two complete sentences.

1. She peeked into her daughter's room who wasn't home yet.
2. The dog ran across the street with the brown spots.
3. Because they are psychological, Hamlet finds his problems hard to solve.
4. He told stories by the campfire in the evening most of which weren't really true.
5. *Bleak House* may be the most important Dickens novel who was one of the greatest novelists of the nineteenth century.

f). Parallelism

Correct the following sentences for proper parallel structure.

1. I have to write papers for my history professor, English teacher, and philosophy class.
2. Charles is extremely interested in fitness and in being a good athlete.
3. The Houyhnhnms in *Gulliver's Travels* are perfectly rational creatures who resemble horses and have no concept of lying or deceit.
4. At the ceremony, Virginia received awards for her participation in the tennis tournament and being the captain of the basketball team.
5. Gregers believes his theories are accurate and, therefore, that he will be able to help Gina and Hjalmar.

g). Comparisons

Correct the faulty comparisons in the following sentences.

1. Billie loves me more than Susie.
2. Math is harder, but biology is more fun.
3. The flowers are of a brighter color than the water is green.

4. Tom was more thrilled with his success than Peter.
5. I'll meet you downtown faster than the stores will close.

h). Passive

Rewrite the following sentences in the active voice.

1. A great deal of insight can be gained by students when they take this course.
2. The causes of many infectious diseases have been discovered by twentieth-century medicine.
3. Going to college after high school is a choice made by many.
4. After much debate, the decision to proceed as planned was made by the board of directors.
5. At the recital, good performances were given by several of the children.

i). Comprehensive Exercise

Correct all errors in the following sentences. Watch for errors in subject–verb agreement, in pronoun–antecedent agreement, in pronoun reference, in pronoun case, in verb tense, in misplaced modifiers, in parallelism, and in comparisons. Watch, too, for weak passive voice sentences.

1. In each person's life, after they have done much thinking, there comes a time when you had to choose a course in life.
2. Alfred believes that Henry is honest and James trusts him which is his mistake.
3. After the storm was over during the picnic their belongings could be found by no one which had dropped large hailstones.
4. Since the report is being written now, James and him will have to be told that the editing has to be done by them.
5. Shakespeare's "dark mistress" which is the point of the poem is not your average mistress.
6. Emily never eats dessert or she drinks coke because she is trying to lose some weight when she's dieting.
7. Nancy's dog has had puppies but she will have to give them away or have too many. Either is not a good solution.
8. The freezer broke down. The food will spoil I just bought so much of and I can afford it even less.
9. Parson Jones believes in charity and being kind to your fellow humans, but many other people do not act this way.
10. One character in *Joseph Andrews* that showed generosity was Betty where it tells how she gives Joseph one of Mr. Tow-wouse's shirts to wear.
11. Each character in the book has their reasons for being in the book and being where in the book that they are; whether it's to make a particular point or for a more general purpose.
12. Parson Adams always looks out more for other people than himself, and this is a very important point made by Fielding.
13. There seems to be many other families that share the Wingfields' predicament which lived during the Depression so they suffered through hard times.
14. We hoped that everyone will come fairly early so that Mick and John has a chance to finish their magic act before it gets dark.
15. It is clear that by the end of *Gulliver's Travels* horses are preferred to people by Gulliver, and you know that can't be quite right.

PRINCIPLE 3: Make sure you use the *right* word, and generally as *few* words as possible, for the purpose you want to accomplish.

Mark Twain once said, "The difference between the right word and the almost-right word is the difference between lightning and the lightning bug." Many writers are content to get by with lightning bugs instead of lightning in their work. Even if the meaning of the sentence is clear in spite of it, a poorly chosen word or phrase is as much a hindrance to readers as an error in sentence structure would be. Readers are forced to slow down for a second or two, and they may stop reading altogether if they have to slow down too often. Furthermore, in many instances of poor word choice the meaning of the sentence is *not* clear, and readers must stop completely in order to puzzle out the writer's intentions.

Many writers, of course, do realize that they have trouble finding the right word for every purpose. Too many writers, however, think that they can get around the difficulty by throwing up smoke screens of various sorts: by falling back on worn-out phrases and expressions; by padding sentences with unnecessary words and phrases; or by using such vague and general terms as to obscure their intentions even further. Remedies like these are almost worse than the problems they are intended to solve (or to conceal). Teachers who tell you to express yourself as simply and clearly as possible are not just talking in order to hear their own voices. They are talking to you.

Wrong Part of Speech for the Purpose

Errors in parts of speech are usually simple to correct. Most standard dictionaries (aside from pocket-size editions) list, either in the word entry itself or in neighboring entries, the different parts of speech into which the word may be transformed. If you suspect you are using the wrong form of a word for its function in a sentence, look the word up in the dictionary and check the entry or entries that pertain to the word.

EXAMPLE   He never intended *to injury* his mother.

Injury is a noun, and a noun cannot follow *to* as an infinitive. A verb is needed instead.

CORRECTION   He never intended *to injure* his mother.

EXAMPLE   The *lose* of his mother distressed Joe terribly.

Here the opposite problem occurs: *lose* is a verb, and what the writer needs is a noun to serve as the subject of the sentence.

CORRECTION   The *loss* of his mother distressed Joe terribly.

EXAMPLE   Her father refused to believe in the *innocence* aspects of her relationship with Steve.

Innocence is a noun, but the word needed is an adjective to modify *aspects.*

CORRECTION   Her father refused to believe in the *innocent* aspects of her relationship with Steve.

EXAMPLE   *Logically* thinking is an important aid in communicating with other people.

The problem in this sentence is a little trickier. If *logically thinking* were a participial phrase acting as an adjective, there would be no difficulty with *Logically.* The word *thinking* is the subject of the sentence, however. Therefore, an adjective, not an adverb, is needed to modify *thinking.*

CORRECTION   *Logical* thinking is an important aid in communicating with other people.

A word may sometimes be in the appropriate parts-of-speech category but still be in the wrong form for the purpose intended.

EXAMPLE   Many teenagers and women experience discrimination in technical fields such as *engineers.*

Engineers is a noun, and a noun or a noun substitute is indeed what the sentence calls for at that point. *Engineers,* however, is not a *field.* Another form of the word must be used.

CORRECTION   Many teenagers and women experience discrimination in technical fields such as *engineering.*

Incorrect Choice of Transitive and Intransitive Verbs

A *transitive verb* is a verb that needs a noun or a noun substitute to complete its action: "The boy *threw the ball.*" An intransitive verb needs no such noun or noun substitute: "The boy *ran* away." New writers sometimes run into difficulty by using a transitive verb where an intransitive verb is needed, and vice versa. You can usually correct your error by supplying a missing object or by substituting a transitive verb for an intransitive one. (Incidentally, if you are not certain whether a verb is transitive or intransitive, the dictionary entry will give you this information. Read the entire entry, because some verbs can be transitive in some contexts and intransitive in others.)

EXAMPLE   He has to release from his past.

Release is a transitive verb. Like all transitive verbs, it must have an object. The simplest way to revise the sentence is to indicate who or what is being released.

CORRECTION   He has to release *himself* from his past.

EXAMPLE   Then he *culminated* her fantasy by giving her a kiss.

Culminated is not a transitive verb. (*To culminate* is "to come to a conclusion" or "to arrive at the highest point.") The best thing to do would be to try another word.

CORRECTION   Then he *completed* her fantasy by giving her a kiss.

Faulty Predication

The notation "faulty predication" in the margin of your paper probably indicates that either the verb itself or the whole predicate is inappropriate for the subject in structure or in meaning. Faulty predication usually calls for a replacement of the verb in question or a restructuring of the entire sentence.

EXAMPLE   In *Northanger Abbey*, Jane Austen has written into Isabella some very negative traits.

The verb phrase here is both awkward in structure and inaccurate in meaning: an author does not "write" traits "into" a character. The writer of the sentence can revise it by substituting a verb for *written into*.

CORRECTION   In *Northanger Abbey*, Jane Austen has given Isabella some very negative traits.

EXAMPLE   Bringing a gun onto the scene can cause an already dangerous criminal into desperate action.

Again, the verb phrase here simply does not fit. An act does not "cause" someone "into desperate action." More than one revision is possible here.

CORRECTION 1   Bringing a gun onto the scene can provoke an already dangerous criminal into desperate action.
CORRECTION 2   Bringing a gun onto the scene can cause an already dangerous criminal to act desperately.

The writer must be especially careful not to introduce faulty predication with forms of the verb *to be*. A sentence may have the structure: "Subject—*to be* verb—complement." The *complement* in such a sentence is either a noun (or a noun substitute) or an adjective that identifies or describes the subject ("*He* is a good *boy*"). The *to be* verb indicates an equality between the subject and the complement. Make sure that the words in the complement position are in fact on equal footing with the subject.

EXAMPLE   A good deal of his life was around that piano.

In this example, a prepositional phrase—*around that piano*—follows *was* and acts as an adverb rather than as a true complement. The sentence must be revised. Here are two possible revisions:

CORRECTION 1   A good deal of his life was spent around that piano.
CORRECTION 2   He spent a good deal of his life around that piano.

EXAMPLE   The section of I-75 between Cordele and Unadilla is where I saw the most state troopers.

Here, again, the form of *to be* is completed by an adverbial construction—this time, an adverb clause. The sentence can be revised in at least two ways.

CORRECTION 1   The section of I-75 between Cordele and Unadilla is the area in which I saw the most state troopers.
CORRECTION 2   I saw the most state troopers in the section of I-75 between Cordele and Unadilla.

Improper Idiom

An *idiom* is an expression that, over the years, has become a custom or a convention in the language. There is really no systematic way to learn idioms, because they are highly individualistic and often illogical. Beginning writers must simply have an ear and an eye for what they write and watch out for obvious violations of the conventions. One generally reliable indicator of an unidiomatic expression is that it *sounds* clumsy or "off" when it is spoken aloud. Many new writers try so hard to sound "educated" in their writing that they produce expressions no one would ever use in speech.

Here are some examples of unidiomatic expressions and their corrections:

EXAMPLE   It would have done him more harm than help.

The problem here is fairly simple: the idiomatic expression is *more harm than good*, not *more harm than help*.

CORRECTION   It would have done him more harm than good.

EXAMPLE   Alan Alda's jokes run over smoothly and effectively.

Run over is not an expression we usually apply to jokes; its associ-ation with traffic mishaps is too strong. The writer probably meant *go over.*

> CORRECTION   Alan Alda's jokes go over smoothly and effectively.

> EXAMPLE   The reader begins to sense a feel of peace and tranquillity in the poem.

The reader may begin to *"feel a sense"* but is probably not likely to *"sense a feel"* (at least not in a poem).

> CORRECTION   The reader begins to feel a sense of peace and tran-quillity in the poem.

A good many unidiomatic expressions are the result of the misuse of prepositions.

> EXAMPLE   Amanda is trying to escape the agony of the situation by re-flecting to her past.

One does not "reflect *to* one's past," but *on* it.

> CORRECTION   Amanda is trying to escape the agony of the situation by reflecting on her past.

Another fairly common idiom problem is the use of the infinitive where it is awkward or inappropriate.

> EXAMPLE   There is no law prohibiting two unmarried people to raise a family.

Here, the expression is not *prohibiting . . . to raise* but *prohibiting . . . from raising.*

> CORRECTION   There is no law prohibiting two unmarried people from raising a family.

Misuse of Words

As all writers know, it is altogether too easy to select the wrong word for the job. In order to correct a word-use error, the writer must understand exactly why the word does not belong in the sentence. A word may sim-ply not have the meaning the writer is looking for. Or the writer may have confused the needed word with a similar-sounding one (*penetrate* and *perpetrate* may look and sound alike, but their meanings are not at all related). Perhaps, on the other hand, the writer has used a word as a kind of shorthand for a relatively complex idea that needs to be ex-plained in more detail. Finally, the writer may have used a word that has the meaning he or she is looking for but has overtones (called con-notations) that are inappropriate in the context.

Writers should make themselves aware of the possibilities for errors in word use and should select their words carefully. When in doubt, they should consult a reliable dictionary.

> EXAMPLE   The disappearance of Mr. Wingfield has an *antagonistic* effect on the family.

This writer has simply used the wrong word. *Antagonistic* means "actively opposed or hostile." The family might possibly feel antagonistic toward Mr. Wingfield, but *antagonistic* cannot describe the *effect* he has on the family. Some word suggesting *deterioration* in the family structure would be better.

> CORRECTION   The disappearance of Mr. Wingfield has a *detrimental* effect on the family.

> EXAMPLE   Mr. Haines was involved in an illegal business *ordeal.*

This is an instance in which a word that *sounds* similar to the correct word has been used.

> CORRECTION   Mr. Haines was involved in an illegal business *deal.*

> EXAMPLE   Being in love gives a person a feeling of happiness and platitude.

Since *platitude* means "a banal, trite, or stale remark," the writer probably had *gratitude* in mind.

> CORRECTION   Being in love gives a person a feeling of happiness and *gratitude.*

In the next example, the writer has relied upon a word to carry more meaning than it rightfully can.

> EXAMPLE   His theory about the proper basis for marriage is an *imaginary* one.

Obviously a theory cannot be *imaginary.* But it is far from clear just what else the writer might mean. The teacher discussed the sentence with the student; it turned out that the student had intended *imaginary* to mean "not based on reality."

> CORRECTION   His theory about the proper basis for marriage is not *based on reality.*

> EXAMPLE   Being at a very *influential* age, I decided to follow my mother's advice and take guitar lessons.

Again, a word is being used as "shorthand"—and misleading shorthand at that—for a more complicated concept that it implies. What *influential* suggests is that the writer was old enough to be influencing others; as the rest of the sentence indicates, however, she herself was being influenced.

> CORRECTION   Because I was at an age at which I was *easily in-fluenced,* I decided to follow my mother's advice and take guitar lessons.

A better and less wordy version might be: "Because I was only eleven, and easily influenced, I decided . . ."

> EXAMPLE   During a battle in southern France, Anna's father was killed and her brother was *rendered legless.*

The phrase *rendered legless* is stilted and slightly comical. In fact, it almost makes the brother's plight a laughing matter, and the writer surely did not intend this.

> CORRECTION   During a battle in southern France, Anna's father was killed and her brother lost both legs.

> EXAMPLE   Henry Morgan and Alan Alda of "M*A*S*H" are very well *seasoned.*

It is possible to speak of *seasoned actors. Seasoned* by itself, however, suggests that Morgan and Alda have been flavored with satisfactory amounts of herbs and spices—a feat that not even Colonel Sanders could manage.

> CORRECTION   Henry Morgan and Alan Alda of "M*A*S*H" are both *seasoned actors.*

Invented Words

Some new writers, in their desperate search for the right word, may accidentally come up with a term that does not exist in English. There is no simple formula for avoiding word invention; you must simply develop a sense of what is an English word and what is not. Again, when you are at all in doubt, consult a dictionary.

> EXAMPLE   *Annunciating* our goals is the first step toward making them a reality.

This sentence was written by a company president who should have known better. In the excitement of *announcing* his goals, he has evidently gotten the occasion mixed up with the Catholic feast of the Annunciation.

> CORRECTION   *Announcing* our goals is the first step toward making them a reality.

EXAMPLE   When you watch an Alfred Hitchcock movie, you have a tense *unknowingness* of what is going to happen next.

The student writer, to do him justice, was looking for a word for the creepy, crawly sensation that Hitchcock loved to create in his audiences. *Unknowingness*, unfortunately, is simply not that word—or a word at all.

CORRECTION   When you watch an Alfred Hitchcock movie, you are tense because you *never know* what is going to happen next.

Inappropriate Level of Usage

Writers may sometimes use a word or phrase that is correct in meaning but is not consistent with the *level of usage* of the work—that is, the word is too informal or too formal. In the final draft of a term paper, for example, the level of usage should be relatively formal: no slang, no colloquialism, and no vulgarities (unless, of course, the paper is about slang, colloquialism, and vulgarity). This does not mean, though, that stilted, dead, or archaic language is called for; constipated prose is just as inappropriate, in its own way, as slang. (See the section that follows on "Deadwood.") In less formal contexts, of course, writers should use the language that the particular situation calls for. College students, for example, have a fairly reliable sense of appropriate language in a letter to parents, in a note to a roommate, and so forth. The sense of what is appropriate, in fact, should guide your choice of usage levels in your own work: if a word or a phrase stands out glaringly as too formal or too informal for your purpose, you should probably find a more suitable expression.

EXAMPLE   If Gus Trenor had wanted Lily all along, he should have made a pass at her earlier so that she could have understood his intentions.

This sentence comes from an English paper. If the writer had been describing, say, a singles bar scene, *made a pass at her* might have been the appropriate phrase. The phrases that appear are not appropriate, of course, in a description of fictional characters in a formal paper.

CORRECTION   If Gus Trenor had wanted Lily all along, he should have made his intentions clear earlier.

EXAMPLE   Disturbed by the amount of epidermis his daughter was revealing in her décolletage, the minister promptly enveloped her in a pelisse.

The words *epidermis*, *décolletáge*, and *pelisse* may possibly provide some insight into the way the minister thinks, but they slow down the reader. Less stilted diction is called for.

CORRECTION Disturbed by the low-cut dress his daughter was wearing, the minister promptly threw a shawl around her.

EXAMPLE Fellow citizens, this here man and this here woman want to get hitched in the legal bond of wedlock. If any galoot knows anything to block the game, let him toot his bazoo or keep his jaw shet now and forever.

This delightful passage from Mendel LeSeur's *North Star Country* is appropriate for a movie or a novel set in the West. In other contexts, the more conventional form would apply.

CORRECTION Dearly beloved, we are gathered here together in the sight of God to join this man and this woman. . . .

Deadwood

The padding of sentences with unnecessary or weak words and phrases—which some writers and teachers call *deadwood*—threatens to turn the English language into bureaucratese. Government officials and corporate executives are particularly prone to use expressions like *at this point in time, in the last instance, with respect to* (instead of *about*).

In your own writing, try not to surrender to the deadwood trend. If you have a 750-word paper due the next day and have written only 500 words, go back to your brainstorming and prewriting (see pages 11–13) and try to add another point or two of substance instead of padding the ones you have. As the following examples indicate, deadwood is not an effective way to make writing look scholarly or impressive; deadwood can obscure the meaning of any real points being made. Sometimes, too, it simply hides the fact that no points are being made at all.

EXAMPLE There have been many studies that have revealed that a significantly large amount of stimulation that contributes to a student's intellectual development occurs outside the classroom.

Windy, isn't it? Let us try going through the sentence section by section to see what can be changed or eliminated.

There have been many studies that have revealed: There is . . . , There are . . . , It is . . . , and so forth should be used only sparingly as sentence openers. *There have been* here can certainly go. *That have* can be eliminated as well; the only real information in this part of the sentence is that *many studies have revealed. . . . that a significantly large amount of stimulation: significantly large amount* is triple deadwood. In fact *that a significantly large amount of stimulation* can be abbreviated to a simple *that much stimulation . . . that contributes to a student's intellectual development:* Two *that* clauses on top of each other in a sentence are awkward and unnecessary. *That contributes to* here can be shortened to *of: stimulation of a student's intellectual development . . . occurs outside the classroom:* At last, the central point of the sentence.

We now have this sentence: "Many studies have revealed that much stimulation of a student's intellectual development occurs outside the classroom." This is better than the original, but not good enough. For one thing, the need for *Many studies have revealed that . . .* is questionable: the information given in the sentence is not difficult to understand and does not require elaborate proof. For another, *stimulation . . . occurs* is a weak and static way of describing what goes on; it would be better to omit *occurs* and turn *stimulation* into a verb. The sentence in its third form might read like this:

> A student's intellectual development is much stimulated outside the classroom.

Or, less clumsily:

> Much of a student's intellectual development is stimulated outside the classroom.

The original twenty-six-word sentence has been trimmed to ten or eleven words and this, in itself, is a vast improvement. The sentences in the examples that follow have been subjected to a similar shortening; you might want to try supplying the intermediate steps for yourself.

EXAMPLE	When one glances over these stories, they do not appear to be very similar, but if one examines them in more detail, several similarities become apparent.
CORRECTION	These stories seem quite different at first but are actually similar in several ways.
EXAMPLE	Only by a thorough and frustrating investigation can one ascertain the theme of the work; however, the very struggle necessitates identifying with a quandary not unlike that which the character in the poem also confronts.
CORRECTION	The theme of the work is difficult to determine, but the very difficulty requires the reader to identify with the character in the poem and the struggle he faces.
EXAMPLE	The main reason for the imbalance is due to the circumstances of checks being written and deducted from the checkbook balance which have not yet been received by the bank, consequently not initiating a deduction.

CORRECTION   The reason for the imbalance is that you have written checks and deducted them from your checkbook balance before the bank can receive and deduct them.

EXAMPLE   Through his senses Joe perceives different occurrences in his past life.

CORRECTION   Joe remembers events in his life.

Redundancy

Redundancy is the unintended or needless repetition of an idea. A frequent source of redundancy is a modifying word or phrase that provides no more information than the word it modifies: *a musical piano, a plane flying in the sky, to walk on foot, a round globe, a professional doctor,* and so on. Redundancies can occur in clauses too: "The foreign student, who came from abroad, enrolled in the program." Redundancies are not difficult to eliminate if you check your work with an unsparing eye. Examine the modifiers (words, phrases, and clauses) you have used to be sure that they do not merely restate the meaning of the word they modify. Make sure, in other words, that the modifiers provide additional information.

EXAMPLE   In my personal opinion, I think Senator Pellagra should resign.

Avoid prefacing statements with phrases such as *in my personal opinion* or *I think*—and certainly do not use two at once. The fact that the writer has made the statement indicates that the opinion is his. Both the "prefaces" here can be omitted.

CORRECTION   Senator Pellagra should resign.

EXAMPLE   Edgar Allan Poe is renowned for his horrifying tales, which have frightened readers for years.

If Poe's tales had *not* been *horrifying*, they would not have frightened readers for years.

CORRECTION 1   Edgar Allan Poe is renowned for his horrifying tales.

CORRECTION 2   Edgar Allan Poe's tales have frightened readers for years.

EXAMPLE   Mr. Ricketts, that stupid nincompoop, has failed to realize the true facts of the matter.

Nincompoops *are* stupid; facts *are* true.

CORRECTION   Mr. Ricketts, that nincompoop, has failed to realize the facts of the matter.

Vagueness

Writers—especially unpracticed ones—will occasionally write sentences that are so vague and unfocused that they do not mean much of anything. Sometimes such writers are puzzled as to how to begin a paragraph or an entire essay; sometimes they are aiming for a transition from one idea to the next and lose their way; sometimes they are simply concealing the fact that they have not done the necessary groundwork for their writing. It is often difficult to show "corrections" of vaguely worded sentences in isolation; the writer usually needs to supply more facts, revise the entire direction of the thought, or eliminate the offending sentence altogether. The best way to avoid writing vague, mushy sentences is to know fairly well what you plan to say and how you plan to say it before you begin writing.

EXAMPLE   There are various programs shown on television today.

A fine statement of the obvious. The writer should try a different opening gambit.

EXAMPLE   Character traits, although they may vary from individual to individual, are found in every person in a play. In most plays, however, certain characteristics are found in the main character.

An even finer statement of the obvious. Sooner or later, however, the writer will have to admit that he has not read the play he's writing about.

EXAMPLE   In our world of increasing complexity, the responsibilities of everyday life will no doubt continue to bring with them even higher levels of frustration. Being constantly challenged with novel situations, someone or something will have to give.

This introduction gives no idea whatever of the subject of the essay to follow—it could be anything from an uprising in Upper Volta to the condition of the San Andreas Fault. Perhaps the writer is not sure either what the subject is to be.

EXAMPLE   The best thing about clubs, though, is that, in all honesty, there is something for everybody.

Here, at least, the writer is prepared to elaborate on the statement. She takes too long to lead up to an idea that is not at all difficult to grasp, however; she should move directly into her discussion of the activities that clubs offer.

EXAMPLE   It seems as though we can picture Brown, and, although the story is being told with us as spectators, the narrator involves us with Young Goodman Brown.

Ideally, the assertion should be true of every story ever written. The writer has said nothing about the techniques Hawthorne uses to *achieve* these ends in "Young Goodman Brown."

Euphemisms

A *euphemism* is an expression used to avoid direct reference to some person, thing, or event considered "unmentionable"—sex, age, death, imprisonment, for example. Calling a spade a spade is not always possible or desirable, of course: it is hardly tactful, for instance, to address a person in his sixties as an "old man." Where it is possible to avoid euphemisms without wounding someone's feelings, however, do so. All too often, euphemisms are a convenient way to avoid confrontation with the facts of life; almost inevitably, they make your prose fat and sluggish.

EXAMPLE   The residents at the county correctional facility created a major disturbance this morning.

CORRECTION   The prisoners at the county jail rioted this morning.

EXAMPLE   Former Mayor Alexander passed away last week and was laid to rest in the Methodist memorial garden.

CORRECTION   Former Mayor Alexander died last week and was buried in the Methodist cemetery.

EXAMPLE   The parents protested against the new sex education course, which covers such subjects as time of the month, being in the family way, and assault.

CORRECTION   The parents protested against the new sex education course, which covers such subjects as menstruation, pregnancy, and rape.

Clichés

A *cliché* is a figure of speech which—to borrow one for a moment—is as dead as a doornail. Many of the metaphors and similes (see pages 406–407) we use in everyday speech had a life of their own at one time, but have long since been pronounced ready for the boneyard. Do not make your writing flat and stale by dragging such images into it. You can use a figure of speech to illustrate or emphasize a point, but, when you do, strive for freshness. For example, if you find the illustrations in this section unutterably tedious, do not say, "This bores me to tears." Say, "This book is as dull as a box of rocks." Do not strive so hard that you entangle yourself in absurdity, though (see "Inappropriate and 'Mixed' Metaphors," below). Precise language and specific details are often better substitutes for clichés than overstrained images.

EXAMPLE   He was so hungry that he could have eaten a horse.
CORRECTION   He was so hungry that he ate three fastburgers, two orders of french fries, and a triple-scoop ice cream cone.

EXAMPLE   Professor Swatnit is as crazy as a loon.
CORRECTION   Professor Swatnit cursed at us in classical Greek for twenty minutes yesterday.

EXAMPLE   The thought of telling my parents I wrecked the car scares me to death.
CORRECTION   If I had a choice between telling my parents I wrecked the car and jumping into an active volcano, I'd probably take the jump.

Inappropriate and "Mixed" Metaphors

Similes and metaphors can lend richness to writing, but only if they are appropriate. Writers occasionally attempt to use a figure of speech that just does not belong in the sentence. "I was getting writer's cramp, so I put my tape recorder away" is an example of a wayward figure of speech. Sometimes the contrast between the metaphor or simile and the idea in a sentence is so ludicrous as to prevent the reader from taking the writer seriously. At the very least, such a contrast is a distraction. Some writers even go so far as to "mix metaphors" in a sentence—to create two or more metaphors that have little relation to each other *or* to the idea they illustrate. Again, watch the images you use in your writing. They should be neither worn-out nor absurd.

EXAMPLE   The swing toward math and science of the educational pendulum today is having a bad effect on the student.

The idea of the educational system as a "pendulum" is farfetched, to say the least; one imagines that the "bad effect" might be a blow on the hapless student's head.

CORRECTION   The emphasis on math and science in the schools today is having a bad effect on the student.

EXAMPLE   The loss he suffered was only one branch of the tree. He had other branches to fall back on.

Not only is the idea of a loss as a *branch of a tree* peculiar, but the idea of "falling back" on another such "branch" makes this passage completely ridiculous.

CORRECTION   The loss he suffered was only a temporary setback. He had other resources to draw on.

EXAMPLE   The work of Professor Burns stands like a Rosetta stone to shed light on this previously unexplored subject.

The work is a free-standing, light-producing stone? One metaphor of the three here will do.

C O R R E C T I O N   The work of Professor Burns sheds light on this pre-viously unexplored subject.

E X A M P L E   The use of sound effects made the movie shine.

One might argue for *shining sound* as an image in its own right, but the combination of *sound* and *shine* to describe something else is unwise.

C O R R E C T I O N   The use of sound effects—especially the hero's beeps, whistles, and moans—made the movie memorable.

EXERCISES

a).   Wrong Part of Speech for Purpose
Revise the following sentences so that every word is in the appropriate parts-of-speech category and in the correct form for the sense intended.

1. He never believed in his son's honest.
2. Coherently organizing is an essential requirement for the paper.
3. Sheila's father lives in a prestige suburb.
4. The depart of my friend fills me with sadness.
5. He said he would arrive on time, but he came lately.
6. Mary certainly dances good.
7. She decorations her apartment beautifully.
8. Young people today are increasingly drawn to the medicine profession.
9. The little boy runs very quick.
10. Newton was a great inventive.

b).   Incorrect Choice of Transitive and Intransitive Verbs
Revise the following sentences so that transitive and intransitive verbs are correctly used.

1. The boy threw before leaving.
2. Chauncey lies the newspaper on the floor.
3. The tennis players conversed the weather before the game started.
4. This furnace does not emit.
5. When Lucy spilled on the rug, she ruined forever.

c).   Faulty Predication
Rewrite the following sentences to correct faulty predication.

1. Her happiness is comprised of a high-paying job and a cooperative family.
2. The failure of his son claimed Mr. Penner's death.
3. My greatest difficulty is when I have to make a decision.
4. Your first visit to a village always brings out a novel and quaint experience.
5. Quick reflexes are for learning a sport.

d). Improper Idiom
Revise the following sentences by replacing unidiomatic language with idiomatic language.

1. His visits are far but few between.
2. Jane showed no interest for the young artist.
3. James's elegant sister can carry the most bizarre fashions.
4. I would jump the ship if I were Jim.
5. All the further we went, the rockier the path became.

e). Misuse of Words
Replace the words used incorrectly with more appropriate ones.

1. Attesting her on the road, he shouted obscenities.
2. Setting on the park bench, he watched the people go by.
3. I like every feature of the first house we saw accept for the kitchen.
4. Sarah inferred that Tom had been dishonest.
5. The driver on the left had the rite of way.

f). Invented Words
Replace any invented words in the following sentences with the correct expression.

1. The innocent villager became the escapegoat of the soldiers, who killed him to scare the enemy.
2. When her children departed, she was filled with a terrible sense of nothingful.
3. He is a very cute and lovesome puppy.

g). Inappropriate Level of Usage
Rewrite the following passages, which were taken from student papers. Make the level of usage consistent throughout each passage. Be sure that the level of usage is appropriate to the context in which the passage appears.

1. So, ladies and gentlemen, I am now going to introduce you to the narrator of Chaucer's *Canterbury Tales*. He is one of the pilgrims, but he sure does make himself unobstrusive.
2. My sisters, legalized abortion can be the most effective tool for subverting the tyrannical, male sexual domination. All women should firmly unite in their fight for legalizing abortions as a first step towards the overthrow of the partricarchal government.
3. I know that the Congressman is a real groovy guy, very much in tune with the kids of today. Therefore, I'm sure that he is going to bust up the President's draft proposals.
4. My precious offspring: I shall be submerged in grief after you have departed.

h). Deadwood/Wordiness
Eliminate deadwood and wordiness from the following sentences.

1. King Arthur's court is described in the most grandiose of language as a place where the ideal of chivalry is found.
2. The slaying of his foes becomes for the knight a challenging adventure.

3. As William continues on his journey and comes across a castle, the plot is further complicated by a new twist in the story.
4. Although the soldier is not aware of it, all of his skills are to be tested.
5. It is clear that the rain will soon be pouring down.

i). Redundancies
Eliminate the redundancies in the following sentences.

1. In my opinion, I feel it is of utmost importance to have regular medical checkups.
2. Dracula is a horribly terrifying movie character, and has always frightened film audiences.
3. She visits me every day, interferes with my daily routine, and makes it impossible for me to do my everyday chores.
4. Bob was so surprised at hearing the news of her marriage that he was filled with amazement.
5. The main subject of my paper will be a topic of interest to all women who have female concerns on their minds.
6. Please repeat this song again.

j). Vagueness
Revise the following sentences to make them more specific.

1. The events of this interlude are conveyed in very general terms.
2. The choice made by each of the characters has a great deal of bearing on the rest of the play.
3. While Eloisa and Hermia are similar in certain ways, they contrast in others.
4. Although the speakers in the two poems express themselves with equal intensity, the poems differ in tone and attitude.
5. He is not secure in anything but in his desire to be close to a higher being.

k). Euphemisms
Identify the euphemisms and replace them with the direct references they are intended to disguise.

1. Bob inherited no money because his grandmother was called to her reward before she made her will.
2. When the Russians entered Hungary, they announced that they had come to liberate the country from reactionaries.
3. My grandmother is one of the many senior citizens who live in this golden-age residence.
4. His young son became so disturbed that he had to be isolated.
5. She excused herself from the assembled company and went to the ladies' room.

l). Clichés
Revise the following sentences to eliminate the clichés.

1. Seeing her parents quarrel frequently, Mary was convinced that their marriage was on the rocks.
2. During the harvest, my grandmother was busy as a bee working on her farm.

3. Since they raised the prices of oil, the Arab countries have made progress by leaps and bounds.
4. When we decorated our house for Christmas, it looked as pretty as a picture.
5. Trying to find this book is like looking for a needle in a haystack.

m). Mixed Metaphors
Underline the mixed metaphors. Revise the sentences to make the metaphors consistent.

1. He was filled with a burning anger that froze his ability to reason.
2. The cat made a bold, ferocious leap and began to crawl toward the mouse.
3. She bloomed into a beauty at the age of sixteen and became a predator of young men's hearts.
4. The strands of satire that are neatly woven through this tale are used as a tool to convey the meaning of the events.
5. She danced in smooth-flowing movements and in some of her poses she resembled a statue.

n).   Comprehensive Exercise—Sentences with Multiple Errors
Revise the following sentences to correct all errors in diction.

1. It is my firm belief that the boy's intelligent impressed the teacher so much that she recommended him.
2. Tom hit and ran away as quick as lightning and hid behind a tree.
3. The primitive types of tribal people were wiped out by the conquered soldiers.
4. Mary's ludicrousity of behavior made her friends accost with horror.
5. I firmly and strongly urge my fellow students to refrain from all kinds of undisciplined behavior, 'cause bustin' up each other's faces ain't gonna do no thing for our grades.
6. The little boy feeds regularly, but is also very cruelly toward his dogs.
7. It is a true fact that the Tate Gallery exhibits the works of many paintings and engravings.
8. The wind was sighing in the trees and the sunny stream dribbled merrily.
9. She tiptoed into the room, very quiet, very softly, and sat down as meek as a mouse.
10. These lines refer back to the various injunctions stated in the preceding paragraph, and clearly and explicitly reveal the writer's stand.
11. She did not inform to her parents that she was expecting.
12. The reason he saw *Star Wars* was because he was keenly interested in science fictional as a gender.
13. Every night, Dracula slithers along the emptiness corridors of his castle waiting to pounce ferociously on his next victim.
14. Will's misfortune was his son's death and the subsequent remarriage of his daughter-in-law.
15. Bill sat down on the side of the lake and kept on waiting for three hours for his young son who had gone for sailing.

PRINCIPLE 4: Keep punctuation clear and conventional.

Punctuation marks, contrary to popular belief, are not completely arbitrary symbols taught by English teachers for the sole purpose of confusing students. Punctuation marks are, it is true, "arbitrary" in the sense that they are an agreed-upon set of symbols. (No real attempt was made to standardize punctuation in English until the early nineteenth century; in fact, it was only then that large numbers of people began learning how to write.) Certainly, however, punctuation marks help to create order and meaning in writing. They tell the reader when an idea, a statement, or a question has been completed; they signal the major divisions within sentences and the logical and grammatical relationships among the divisions; they indicate to the reader which parts of a sentence are to be stressed and where the pauses should fall when the sentence is read aloud. Finally, they indicate possessives, contractions, direct quotations, and other matters that are not apparent in spoken language.

If you are still not convinced of the importance of punctuation, try making sense of the following unpunctuated paragraph:

> And then as quickly as it had come Christmas was over the dinner plates were piled high in the sink wrapping paper littered the living room floor and we were practically hoarse from singing carols though the bitter wind howled outside the house was warm perhaps more from the feelings of its inhabitants than from the fire that crackled around the hearth when I looked at my mother her eyes glistened reflecting the firelight she was sitting next to my father who was smoking his pipe puffing rhythmically she turned to him and said Boris we have much to thank God for

The absence of most of the capitalization that the paragraph calls for contributes to the confusion, of course. But, then, you would not know which words to capitalize unless you knew how the paragraph was to be punctuated. You would have to break the paragraph into sentences before you could capitalize.

We will begin with a discussion of the types of punctuation that indicate natural breaks in spoken language.

Commas

We are not attempting here to cover every possible use of the comma—only those points that generally prove troublesome to beginning writers. One such point has been mentioned in "Rule 1": the use of the comma with independent clauses—a comma should precede the conjunction. An exception can be made if the clauses are very short: "She set the table and he fried the eggs." Nevertheless, a comma by itself is not sufficient to link two independent clauses. Here are some examples of incorrectly and correctly punctuated independent clauses.

> EXAMPLE   I don't mind going to the roller disco but I would rather be home playing poker.

The sentence is readable without the comma, but a comma will clearly signal that a new independent clause and not, say, a second verb phrase follows the conjunction. The comma will also help mark the shift in direction from the first clause to the second.

> CORRECTION   I don't mind going to the roller disco, but I would rather be home playing poker.

> EXAMPLE   John Cleese is in charge of the Ministry of Silly Walks on "Monty Python's Flying Circus," he is also responsible for the "dead parrot" routine.

Here, two independent clauses are linked only by a comma. The comma could be replaced either by a semicolon, by a comma plus a conjunction, or by a period (which would turn the clauses into two sentences).

> CORRECTION   John Cleese is in charge of the Ministry of Silly Walks on "Monty Python's Flying Circus"; he is also responsible for the dead parrot routine.

A second frequent use of the comma is to indicate the end of an introductory element in a sentence. Place a comma after a fairly long introductory phrase or clause, or after *any* introductory element if the sentence is likely to be unclear without the comma. Consider the following examples.

> EXAMPLE   Inside Jean's houseplants were brown and withered; outside her garden looked as though an army of woodchucks had been at work in it.

The omission of commas after *inside* and *outside* makes it look as though the writer has set the action *inside Jean's houseplants* and *outside her garden.*

> CORRECTION   Inside, Jean's houseplants were brown and withered; outside, her garden looked as though an army of woodchucks had been at work in it.

> EXAMPLE   As most of the other students cheered the Deltas walked out of the Honor Council meeting.

Like the sentences above, this example lacks clarity: is *Deltas* the direct object of *cheered* or the subject of a new clause? A comma prevents any misreading.

> CORRECTION   As most of the other students cheered, the Deltas walked out of the Honor Council meeting.

> EXAMPLE   What little ambition he has he may have achieved out of respect for her.

The chances of an actual misreading here are not as great as in the previous examples, but a comma after the introductory clause helps to clear up the confusion of *he has he may have.*

> CORRECTION   What little ambition he has, he may have achieved out of respect for her.

A word, a phrase, or a clause may interrupt the flow of a sentence to contribute information that is useful but not essential. Such an interrupter should have a comma before it *and* after it. An interrupter that *is* essential to the meaning of the sentence, on the other hand, should *not* be set off by commas.

> EXAMPLE   Lessing does not however explore the thoughts of Dorothy's husband Jack.

However is a conjunctive adverb that serves as a transition from an earlier sentence but is not essential to the *meaning* of this sentence. The name of Dorothy's husband is not strictly necessary, either; we may assume that Dorothy has only one husband, or at least only one at a time. Both *however* and *Jack* should be set off by commas from the rest of the sentence.

> CORRECTION   Lessing does not, however, explore the thoughts of Dorothy's husband, Jack.

> EXAMPLE   Nelson on the other hand is a rebellious youngster.

On the other hand, like *however* in the previous sentence, is serving as a transition from an earlier idea.

> CORRECTION   Nelson, on the other hand, is a rebellious youngster.

> EXAMPLE   You can be sure that a woman, who has been married three times, knows something about men.

Here *who has been married three times* is an example of an interrupting modifier that *is* essential to the meaning of the sentence. Without the clause, we have no idea *which woman* the sentence is discussing. The commas, therefore, should be eliminated.

CORRECTION You can be sure that a woman who has been married three times knows something about men.

EXAMPLE The Red Food Store on the corner of Third Avenue and Elm Street was firebombed yesterday.

It is not always clear whether an interrupter should be set off by commas. In this case, we need to know how many Red Food Stores there are. If there is only one Red Food Store, *on the corner of Third Avenue and Elm Street* does not add necessary information and should be enclosed in commas. But if there are several Red Food Stores, the location of this particular one *is* a necessary piece of information, and commas are not needed.

CORRECTION 1 Sentence remains as is. (more than one store)
CORRECTION 2 The Red Food Store, on the corner of Third Avenue and Elm Street, was firebombed yesterday. (one store)

Some beginning writers tend to use a comma to separate a subject from a predicate, or a verb from the rest of a verb phrase. This is one use of the comma that should be avoided; a comma can lead the reader to believe that an interruption follows or precedes the comma.

EXAMPLE Teenagers in the United States, have more freedom of choice today than ever before.

Teenagers in the United States is the subject; *have more freedom . . .* is the predicate. The two should not be separated.

CORRECTION Teenagers in the United States have more freedom of choice than ever before.

EXAMPLE To reform the state legislature in one term, would be impossible for almost any governor.

To reform the state legislature in one term—an infinitive phrase—is the subject of the sentence. Deletion of the comma is essential, because the unwary reader can be fooled for a moment into thinking that the phrase is an interrupter and looking for a "subject" that is not there.

CORRECTION To reform the state legislature in one term would be impossible for almost any governor.

EXAMPLE John Lennon and Paul McCartney wrote, "Lucy in the Sky with Diamonds."

This may be a familiar way of punctuating sentences that contain titles of works, but the comma does not belong. (After all, the same student would probably not write "She wrote, a letter.")

CORRECTION   John Lennon and Paul McCartney wrote "Lucy in the Sky with Diamonds."

Although the problem of punctuating elements in pairs and elements in series is a perennial one, it is not a difficult one to solve. Words, phrases, or brief clauses in pairs should *not* be separated by a comma: *X and Y*. Words, phrases, and clauses in series, on the other hand, *should* be separated by commas: *X, Y, Z, and Q*. (The comma before *and* in a series has recently come under attack. It is probably still better to include the comma, however, for it avoids confusion in cases like this one: "Among the comedians discussed were Abbott and Costello, Laurel and Hardy, Chaplin and Fields." The last two mentioned were never a team, and a comma would make this clear: ". . . Chaplin, and Fields.") The following examples and corrections demonstrate the proper punctuation of words, phrases, and brief clauses in pairs and in series.

EXAMPLE   Esmerelda liked Desmond's good looks, and Desmond's car.
CORRECTION   Esmerelda liked Desmond's good looks and Desmond's car.
(Compound direct objects.)

EXAMPLE   In both stories we see a relationship between strong physical needs, and the confused emotions that can arise from them.
CORRECTION   In both stories we see a relationship between strong physical needs and the confused emotions that can arise from them.
(Compound objects of a preposition.)

EXAMPLE   We bought tomatoes lettuce cucumbers and kohlrabi.
CORRECTION   We bought tomatoes, lettuce, cucumbers, and kohlrabi.
(Direct objects in a series.)

EXAMPLE   The doctor has told Oscar that he must go on a diet begin taking medication and arrange for regular physicals.
CORRECTION   The doctor has told Oscar that he must go on a diet, begin taking medication, and arrange for regular physicals.
(Verb phrases in a series.)

EXAMPLE   He entered the room he saw Esmerelda and he fell in love with her.
CORRECTION   He entered the room, he saw Esmerelda, and he fell in love with her.
(Brief independent clauses in a series.)

Semicolons

You have already seen the semicolon in action. The major function of the semicolon is to link independent clauses that are not otherwise connected or are joined only by a conjunctive adverb (*however, moreover, consequently, therefore,* and so on). Here are two more examples illustrating the way semicolons work as independent-clause linkers:

> E X A M P L E   Charles Dickens was a famous novelist, he was also an actor in amateur theatrical productions, the editor of several magazines, and the father of ten children.

This sentence contains a comma splice: *Charles Dickens was a famous novelist* is one independent clause, and *he was also . . .* is another. The correct punctuation is vital here, because the combination of the comma splice and the series of predicate nominatives in the second clause produces real confusion.

> C O R R E C T I O N   Charles Dickens was a famous novelist; he was also an actor in amateur theatrical productions, the editor of several magazines, and the father of ten children.

> E X A M P L E   Karen's book was about to be published, moreover, she had just won the Irish Sweepstakes.

Moreover with a comma cannot connect two independent clauses, but a connective like *and, or,* or *but* preceded by a comma could. If this point still confuses you, remember that the sentence would be an ordinary comma splice if *moreover* were moved, as it could be: "Karen's book was about to be published, she had, moreover, just won the Irish Sweepstakes." Note, too, the clause into which *moreover* shifts—the second, not the first. The semicolon, therefore, should go before *moreover* in order to place the word in the second clause.

> C O R R E C T I O N   Karen's book was about to be published; moreover, she had just won the Irish Sweepstakes.

Some new writers, after a thorough study of the horrors of comma splices, become so overwhelmed with "comma panic" that they begin putting semicolons everywhere just to be on the safe side. You can keep yourself from giving in to "comma panic" if you remember that independent clauses, and *only* independent clauses, should be linked by semicolons. Do not use semicolons to link dependent clauses with independent clauses; do not use semicolons to join phrases to sentences. (The only other way in which the semicolon is used, in fact, is to separate items in a series that already contains commas.)

The sentences that follow contain instances of the misuse of semicolons.

EXAMPLE As Honey and Nick looked on; Martha gave George a slap in the face.

As Honey and Nick looked on is not an independent clause; it is a dependent clause acting as an adverb (it tells us *when* Martha slapped George). The clause should be linked to *Martha gave George . . .* by a comma, not by a semicolon.

CORRECTION As Honey and Nick looked on, Martha gave George a slap in the face.

EXAMPLE Grant believed that democracy was right; not because he felt that it was fair but because he was familiar with it.

This example is a little more difficult, because it contains a compound dependent clause. Even so, the semicolon is not the right connective.

CORRECTION Grant believed that democracy was right, not because he felt that it was fair but because he was familiar with it.

EXAMPLE Hjalmar allows himself to be drawn into a trap by his friend Gregers; a trap that ends in tragedy.

A trap that ends in tragedy is not an independent clause, either; it is a noun modified by a relative clause. (*That ends in tragedy* describes *trap.*) Since the writer evidently wishes to stress the fact that the trap leads to tragedy, the noun and its clause should probably be set off from the rest of the sentence by a dash. (See "Dashes" on page 421.)

CORRECTION Hjalmar allows himself to be drawn into a trap by his friend Gregers—a trap that ends in tragedy.

EXAMPLE The speaker's sense of the passage of time; however, is reflected in the imagery and diction.

The writer is responding not wisely but too well to the word *however:* having included the word in the sentence, she automatically places a semicolon before it and a comma after it. What follows *however* here, though, is not a full clause but the predicate of the sentence. Remember that conjunctive adverbs do not *always* link clauses; look before you leap.

CORRECTION The speaker's sense of the passage of time, however, is reflected in the imagery and diction.

Beginning writers occasionally use semicolons to introduce a series. Probably such writers have in mind the fact that a *colon* sometimes introduces a list. Semicolons never do, though. (For a more detailed discussion of colons, see below.)

EXAMPLE   Jane Austen wrote; *Pride and Prejudice, Emma, Mansfield Park,* and three other novels.

Pride and Prejudice and the other words are the direct objects of *wrote.* They should not be separated from the verb by a semicolon or by anything else.

CORRECTION   Jane Austen wrote *Pride and Prejudice, Emma, Mansfield Park,* and three other novels.

EXAMPLE   For the preparation of window trim, you will need the following; scrapers, sandpaper, putty, and a putty knife.

Scrapers, sandpaper, putty, and a putty knife is a list, not a clause; such lists are introduced by colons, not semicolons.

CORRECTION   For the preparation of window trim, you will need the following: scrapers, sandpaper, putty, and a putty knife.

It *is* in the listing of items in series that the only other acceptable use of the semicolon occurs. As we mentioned earlier, semicolons are used to separate items in a series if the items already contain commas.

EXAMPLE   We could not get airline tickets to Terre Haute, Indiana, Chattanooga, Tennessee, or Eugene, Oregon.

The American reader, of course, knows which of the items in this list are cities and which are states; hapless foreigners lighting on this sentence, however, would be thoroughly confused. To help them out— and to clarify matters generally—semicolons should be placed after the names of the states.

CORRECTION   We could not get airline tickets to Terre Haute, Indiana; Chattanooga, Tennessee; or Eugene, Oregon.

EXAMPLE   Also arrested in the moonshine haul were Billy Bob Busbee, 48, of Jessup, Bob Lee Pruitt, 23, of Cheatham Springs, and Jim Bob Abercrombie, 35, of Buckhorn Hollow.

Again, semicolons to indicate which pieces of information belong with which would be a courtesy to the reader.

CORRECTION   Also arrested in the moonshine haul were Billy Bob Busbee, 48, of Jessup; Bob Lee Pruitt, 23, of Cheatham Springs; and Jim Bob Abercrombie, 35, of Buckhorn Hollow.

Colons

The colon (:) introduces or separates various kinds of material within a sentence. One of its most common functions is to introduce lists. One word of caution is needed: the list, and the colon, should only follow a grammatically complete statement—an independent clause.

> EXAMPLE The courses I am taking this fall are: the Preschool Child, Intermediate Tennis, Human Sexuality, and Death and Dying.

The material that precedes the colon in this example is not a complete sentence. A colon after *are* makes no more sense than it does after *is* in a sentence like "My mother is: a Roman woman." The problem can be corrected in one of two ways.

> CORRECTION 1 The courses I am taking this year are the Preschool Child, Intermediate Tennis, Human Sexuality, and Death and Dying.
>
> CORRECTION 2 The courses I am taking this fall are these: the Preschool Child, Intermediate Tennis, Human Sexuality, and Death and Dying.

> EXAMPLE The Chieftains played several reels, including; "The Star of Munster," "Drowsy Maggie," and "The Morning Dew."

The writer has probably confused the semicolon and the colon. A colon can be used in the sentence, if *including* is dropped. And the sentence can survive without the colon if *including* remains.

> CORRECTION 1 The Chieftains played several reels: "The Star of Munster," "Drowsy Maggie," and "The Morning Dew."
>
> CORRECTION 2 The Chieftains played several reels, including "The Star of Munster," "Drowsy Maggie," and "The Morning Dew."

The colon can also be used to introduce or call the reader's attention to a word, a phrase, or a clause that sums up or explains the independent clause preceding it. Note again, however, that *only* an independent clause can precede the colon. There are no restrictions on what can follow the colon.

> EXAMPLE David returned to his old job, which he hated, for only one reason, the salary.

The *salary* serves to explain the rest of the sentence and can therefore be introduced by a colon. In fact, it should be, because there are too many commas in the sentence as it stands.

> CORRECTION David returned to his old job, which he hated, for only one reason: the salary.

> EXAMPLE The fraternities were in agreement on this demand; that the administration should put beer in the drinking fountains.

Here the material preceding the semicolon is an independent clause, but what follows the semicolon is a dependent clause. A colon should replace the semicolon, because a dependent and an independent clause cannot be linked by a semicolon. The dependent clause here serves to explain the nature of the fraternities' demand.

CORRECTION   The fraternities were in agreement on this demand: that the administration should put beer in the drinking fountains.

EXAMPLE   Mrs. Rittenhouse was wearing a designer dress and a pair of one-hundred-dollar shoes: she looked terrible, however.

The colon here is *not* appropriate. The second independent clause does not explain or sum up the first; indeed, it completely reverses the direction of the first.

CORRECTION   Mrs. Rittenhouse was wearing a designer dress and a pair of one-hundred-dollar shoes; she looked terrible, however.

Still another function of the colon is to introduce direction quotations, especially rather long and formal ones. Commas, of course, can also introduce direct quotations. If you are confused as to which symbol to use, remember that a colon must always be preceded by an independent clause, while a comma need not be.

EXAMPLE   I remembered that the old hobo had said: "A good fast run is better than a bad stand."

The colon here is inappropriate, for the material before it is not a complete clause. *Said* needs an object. A comma should replace the colon.

CORRECTION   I remembered that the old hobo had said, "A good fast run is better than a bad stand."

EXAMPLE   I remembered what the old hobo had told me, "A good fast run is better than a bad stand."

Here the comma *is* preceded by an independent clause. The comma is awkward in this sentence, though. In fact, one could argue that the sentence is actually a comma splice. In any case, the colon is the better punctuation.

CORRECTION   I remembered what the old hobo had told me: "A good fast run is better than a bad stand."

Finally, the colon serves a few miscellaneous purposes illustrated here.

GREETING OF A BUSINESS LETTER:
• Dear Ms. Abercrombie:

TIME IN NUMERALS:
- 10:14 a.m.   2:00 p.m.

BIBLICAL REFERENCES:
- Exodus 1:11   John 3:16.

SUBTITLES OF BOOKS AND ARTICLES:
- *The Uses of Enchantment: The Meaning and Importance of Fairy Tales.*
- "No Way to Go: Flying the Atlantic on a Concorde."

Dashes

The dash (—) separates elements of a sentence when such separation is needed for emphasis or for clarity. The dash can set off elements that come either at the beginning or the end of the sentence and that explain the main part of the sentence. And dashes can mark off sentence interrupters—elements that break into a sentence to provide information.

We will look first at dashes that set off explanatory elements at the beginning or end of a sentence.

EXAMPLE   "Blood, toil, tears, and sweat," these were the only things Winston Churchill could promise England when he became prime minister in 1940.

The comma that links Churchill's words to the rest of the sentence is weak. A dash instead of a comma would stress the drama of Churchill's statement, and make the sentence tighter and stronger as well.

CORRECTION   "Blood, toil, tears, and sweat"—these were the only things Winston Churchill could promise England when he became prime minister in 1940.

EXAMPLE   A mad cougar, a mad dog, a mad man, the whole story's insane.

Here, the comma linking the *mad* series to the rest of the sentence is downright confusing. The reader cannot tell where the series ends and the sentence proper begins.

CORRECTION   A mad cougar, a mad dog, a mad man—the whole story's insane.

EXAMPLE   Everything Judy owned had been put on the truck, her piano, her china cabinet, her bedroom set, her pool table, and all the rest of it.

More comma confusion! The reader might be fooled into thinking that the series of words following *truck* is intended to modify *truck;* this is certainly not the case.

CORRECTION   Everything Judy owned had been put on the truck—her piano, her china cabinet, her bedroom set, her pool table, and all the rest of it.

Be cautious in using dashes, though. Keep in mind that parts of a subject or of a predicate should never be separated from one another or from the rest of the sentence.

EXAMPLE   All he could say as the ambulance attendants carried him off was—"You've got the wrong person."

In this sentence, the dash is improperly used. *You've got the wrong person* is *not* supplementary or explanatory material. It is the predicate nominative of the sentence.

CORRECTION   All he could say as the ambulance attendants carried him off was "You've got the wrong person."

EXAMPLE   Esmerelda came home from work and put on her most alluring dress for Desmond—when he arrived for dinner, her ecstasy was complete.

The dash here separates two independent clauses (the second independent clause is introduced by a dependent clause). As you have learned, there are many acceptable ways of dealing with pairs of independent clauses, but "dashing" is not one of them.

CORRECTION   Esmerelda came home from work and put on her most alluring dress for Desmond. When he arrived for dinner, her ecstasy was complete.

Writers wishing to lay stress on an *interrupter*—any word, a phrase, or a clause that interrupts the normal flow of a sentence—can use dashes instead of commas to set it off from the rest of the sentence. Dashes should be used in particular when the interrupter contains one or more commas itself.

EXAMPLE   She said that her "pair of Excedrin headaches," her two children, would be coming home from school soon.

Dashes would be more useful than commas to set off *her two children*. The commas do not prepare the reader for the slight jolt in learning that the children are being described as Excedrin headaches. Dashes would alert the reader to the element of surprise in the sentence.

CORRECTION   She said that her "pair of Excedrin headaches"—her two children—would be coming home from school soon.

EXAMPLE   He asked the sheriff, in fact, he begged him, to see that the murderers were brought to justice.

Again, dashes should be substituted for the commas setting off *in fact, he begged him*. The fact that a comma is used *within* this interrupter creates considerable confusion in the sentence. Dashes would, moreover, emphasize the urgency of the request.

CORRECTION   He asked the sheriff—in fact, he begged him—to see that the murderers were brought to justice.

EXAMPLE   Everyone I know here—teachers, counselors, and friends—seems to think I should stay in school—but that latest D in physics makes me think—I'd be better off in a factory—or in a cornfield.

This is a rather extreme example of overuse of the dash. Having written one set of dashes that *is* correct—the pair around *teachers, counselors, and friends* explains who *everyone* is—the writer has apparently decided to put in several more. The third dash should be a comma (the comma and the *but* introduce an independent clause). The fourth and fifth dashes should be eliminated altogether. Dashes should not be made to substitute for other forms of punctuation when the other forms are called for; still less should they be inserted into a sentence at random.

CORRECTION   Everyone I know here—teachers, counselors, and friends—seems to think I should stay in school, but that latest D in physics makes me think I'd be better off in a factory or in a cornfield.

(*Note:* Whether you are writing by hand or typing, be sure not to write or type a hyphen when you mean to insert a dash, and vice versa. In longhand, a dash is a long mark and a hyphen a short one. To make a dash on the typewriter, hit the hyphen key *twice* (--) without skipping any spaces between the hyphens or between the words the dash is separating. To type a hyphen, simply hit the hyphen key *once* (-) without skipping a space between the hyphen and its preceding or following words.)

Hyphens

Hyphens are generally used to connect words with words (and sometimes with prefixes and suffixes) in order to create units of meaning for which there are no single words. (The hyphen is also used at the end of a line to show that a word goes on to the next line. See "Syllabication" on page 456.) One such "unit of meaning" created by hyphenation is the *compound adjective.*

EXAMPLE   Twelve year old Lamont Booker is the youngest person ever to compete in the hundred meter run at this meet.

Twelve year old and *hundred meter* should each convey one specific meaning to the reader. But if the phrases remain unpunctuated and positioned before the noun, they tend to drift apart in the sentence. These compound adjectives should be hyphenated.

CORRECTION Twelve-year-old Lamont Booker is the youngest person ever to compete in the hundred-meter run at this meet.

EXAMPLE Last week of the term fever hit the campus yesterday when eight long haired individuals took off their clothes in front of the administration building.

Again, it is not clear without hyphens whether the two compound adjectives in this sentence *are* compound adjectives.

CORRECTION Last-week-of-the-term fever hit the campus yesterday when eight long-haired individuals took off their clothes in front of the administration building.

Hyphens are also used to form many compound nouns. (Some compound nouns are written as separate words and some are written as one word; the conventions are less standardized for compound nouns than for compound adjectives. If you are in doubt about any compound noun, consult a dictionary.)

EXAMPLE My brother in law is editor in chief of the *Salt City Review.*
CORRECTION My brother-in-law is editor-in-chief of the *Salt City Review.*

EXAMPLE My great grandmother got mixed up in a free for all on the merry go round.
CORRECTION My great-grandmother got mixed up in a free-for-all on the merry-go-round.

In the following example, the writer has contracted "hyphen fever" and has inserted them where they should not be used.

EXAMPLE Virginia, Lester's first-cousin-once-removed, is in high-school in Oklahoma.
CORRECTION Virginia, Lester's first cousin once removed, is in high school in Oklahoma.

Numbers and fractions present a few special cases. Numbers between *twenty-one* and *ninety-nine* are hyphenated. (Numbers greater than *one hundred* are generally written as numerals; see "Numbers" on page 459).

EXAMPLE They were stranded in the desert for forty six hours.
CORRECTION They were stranded in the desert for forty-six hours.

Fractions used as adjectives are hyphenated; fractions used as nouns are not hyphenated.

EXAMPLE   The bill legalizing marijuana for cancer patients was passed with not much more than a two thirds majority.

CORRECTION   The bill legalizing marijuana for cancer patients was passed with not much more than a two-thirds majority.

EXAMPLE   Exactly two-thirds of the House—290 representatives—voted for the bill legalizing marijuana for cancer patients.

CORRECTION   Exactly two thirds of the House—290 representatives—voted for the bill legalizing marijuana for cancer.

Prefixes and suffixes are units that can alter the meaning of the words to which they are attached (called *root words*). Prefixes go at the beginning of a word, suffixes go at the end. Many prefixes and suffixes have become permanently joined to their root words (*pre*liminary, delect*able*). But some prefixes and suffixes usually or always require hyphens to link them to their root words. *Self-, ex-, all-,* and *-elect,* for example, always take hyphens.

EXAMPLE   Oil baron J. R. Ewing is a self made man. Any government official who doesn't agree with him can expect to become an ex official.

CORRECTION   Oil baron J. R. Ewing is a self-made man. Any government official who doesn't agree with him can expect to become an ex-official.

Prefixes ending in vowels are often joined to their root words with hyphens, especially if the root words begin with the same vowel.

EXAMPLE   Thoughtful people must reevaluate the preelection process in this country, for it is turning into a circus.

CORRECTION   Thoughtful people must re-evaluate the pre-election process in this country, for it is turning into a circus.

If the prefix precedes a consonant, it is not usually hyphenated.

EXAMPLE (CORRECT)   Your terms must be redefined.

If a root word is a proper noun, a hyphen is always used to join a prefix to it.

EXAMPLE   The House UnAmerican Activities Committee accused Lillian Hellman of being proCommunist.

CORRECTION   The House Un-American Activities Committee accused Lillian Hellman of being pro-Communist.

Hyphens can also indicate, in cases of doubt, which words in a sentence form compound adjectives.

EXAMPLE   Tom has opened a large men's clothing store on State Street.

CORRECTION 1   Tom has opened a large-men's clothing store on State Street.

The store might stock size 52 suits.

CORRECTION 2   Tom has opened a large men's-clothing store on State Street.

The store itself is big.

EXAMPLE   The first item to go on the block at the auction was an odd looking glass.

CORRECTION 1   The first item to go on the block at the auction was an odd-looking glass.

The container was peculiar or unusual.

CORRECTION 2   The first item to go on the block at the auction was an odd looking-glass.

It was an unusual mirror.

Question Marks

The question mark is used at the end of a sentence that poses a direct question. Be careful to distinguish between sentences that ask *direct* questions and ones that ask *indirect* questions.

EXAMPLE   Why is this man smiling.

This sentence is a direct question. The entire sentence forms the question being asked. Moreover, the sentence is in the proper inverted order for questions (verb–subject instead of subject–verb). The end punctuation, therefore, should be a question mark.

CORRECTION   Why is this man smiling?

EXAMPLE   Karen asked Don why he was smiling?

The question contained in this sentence is "why he was smiling." It is not in inverted order, but in normal subject–verb order. The main part of the sentence, furthermore, is not a question but a declarative statement: "Karen asked Don ..." (In fact, the question is the direct object of "asked.") The sentence is thus an indirect question. Indirect questions, because they are really declarative statements, should be punctuated with periods.

CORRECTION   Karen asked Don why he was smiling.

EXAMPLE   Karen asked Don, "Why are you smiling."

In this sentence, Karen's question is not repeated indirectly, but directly quoted. As a direct quotation, it should be punctuated as a question.

CORRECTION   Karen asked Don, "Why are you smiling?"

EXAMPLE   Did Karen ask Don why he was smiling.

Why he was smiling is still an indirect question. The whole sentence, however, is also a question—a question within a question. The sentence should be punctuated with a question mark, not because of Karen's question but because of the question posed by the sentence as a whole.

CORRECTION   Did Karen ask Don why he was smiling?

Question marks can also be used with statements—sparingly—to suggest scepticism or disbelief.

EXAMPLE   Beth went with Egbert to the wrestling match.

As a declarative sentence, this is perfectly correct. Should you wish to stress that Beth's date is for some reason an unusual occurrence—that Beth does not usually go out with Egbert, that Beth and Egbert do not usually go to wrestling matches, or that the whole event is strange—you can keep the declarative word order but add a question mark at the end. Some use of italics (underlining on the typewriter) is permissible here as well.

CORRECTION   Beth went with *Egbert* to the wrestling match?

A question mark should be used with an *interrupter* that is a question, even if the sentence that contains the interrupter is not a question.

EXAMPLE   My mother told the Cub Scouts—were they even listening to her—to assemble in front of the park entrance at nine o'clock.

The element enclosed in dashes is a question, but the main part of the sentence is not. The sentence is not an indirect question, however, because the parenthetical element is not a dependent clause but, rather, an interruption in the flow of the sentence. As a separate element here, it can be punctuated with a question mark if need be. The clause in dashes does need a question mark, for the reader might find the sentence confusing without it.

CORRECTION   My mother told the Cub Scouts—were they even listening to her?—to assemble in front of the park entrance at nine o'clock.

Exclamation Points

Exclamation points, as the name implies, should be reserved for genuine *exclamations*—for ideas (whether words, phrases, or clauses) to which you wish to give special emphasis. Use exclamation points one at a time and sparingly. The overuse of exclamation points can numb your readers to such an extent that they will pay no particular attention when you really do have something to exclaim about.

EXAMPLE   George! I'm going to the store for milk!

Nothing in this statement is particularly urgent. The exclamation points, therefore, should be eliminated. Ordinarily exclamation points should not be sprinkled through dialogue (conversation in a written work). People do not usually talk to each other at the top of their lungs (except in heated arguments). Even in an argument, the best weapon may be a calm voice. Calmness in dialogue is represented by the period.

CORRECTION   George, I'm going to the store for milk.

At times, of course, an exclamation point is appropriate.

EXAMPLE   George, the house is on fire.

Here the exclamation point is a permissible substitute for the comma and the period; nobody is *this* calm.

CORRECTION   George! The house is on fire!

The exclamation point can also be used at the end of a forceful imperative statement—that is, after a command.

EXAMPLE   Get your fat hands off me.
CORRECTION   Get your fat hands off me!

Parentheses and Brackets

Parentheses, like commas and dashes, are used to set off material that interrupts the flow of the sentence. Brackets have a more specialized purpose—they are used to enclose material that the writer wishes to insert in a quoted passage. There is an important difference, too, between parentheses and dashes. Parentheses do not ordinarily emphasize the interrupter. Like an interrupter in commas, an interrupter in parentheses contains information that supplements the main part of the sentence but is not essential to it. Of the two sets of marks, parentheses downplay this information more explicitly. Use parentheses when you have material that needs to be included in a sentence but absolutely does *not* need to be emphasized.

EXAMPLE   Because Holly Sue had been brought up in Mount Tabor, Ohio, population 450, her adjustment to life in New York City took some time.

The phrase *population 450* is an example of the type of information that should be put in parentheses. The phrase tells us that Holly Sue was brought up in a small town, but the reader will probably already have guessed that from the name of the town. The failure to use parentheses, in fact, makes the phrase *more* of an interrupter than it deserves to be. The interrupter becomes a distraction.

CORRECTION   Because Holly Sue had been brought up in Mount Tabor, Ohio (population 450), her adjustment to life in New York City took some time.

Note that a comma is still used after the parenthetical phrase. The comma is in no way related to the phrase, though. It simply divides the independent clause from the dependent clause in the sentence. Whenever the material in parentheses does not stand as a complex sentence by itself, commas and periods at the end go *outside* the parenthesis, not inside.

EXAMPLE   I have dealt with the issue of Medicare funds and their abuse at greater length elsewhere—see page 36, for example.

See page 36 . . . is more of an interruption here than it should be. The dash, even more than commas in the *Holly Sue* example, is a sort of red flag calling attention to what is an afterthought: the writer happened to think of one place in which the issue in question was discussed fully.

CORRECTION   I have dealt with the issue of Medicare funds and their abuse at greater length elsewhere (see page 36, for example).

Sometimes a writer will find it useful to place a complete sentence in parentheses.

EXAMPLE   Although Hank certainly had the looks and the build for the part, he was having trouble learning his lines and saying them convincingly. Some insiders on the set were cruelly recommending him for courses in "remedial gumchewing."

The second sentence is an example of a complete sentence that probably should be put in parentheses. By enclosing the sentence in parentheses, the writer is indicating that he is not giving as much weight and credibility to the insiders' comments as he is to the observable fact that Hank has trouble with his lines.

CORRECTION   Although Hank certainly had the looks and the build for the part, he was having trouble learning his lines and saying them convincingly. (Some insiders on the set were cruelly recommending him for courses in "remedial gumchewing.")

When a complete sentence is enclosed as such in parentheses, the end punctuation is enclosed in the parentheses with it.

Parentheses, like dashes and exclamation points, do not improve by an increase in number. Ration your use of parentheses.

> EXAMPLE The new dress (her mother insisted) was too expensive and sophisticated for her (and, besides, her father would surely disapprove of it).

This sentence is an example of the overuse of parentheses. The interrupter *her mother insisted* is not absolutely essential to the sentence, but the information it contributes is not so minor as to justify its being put in parentheses. It should be enclosed in commas. The *and, besides* ... clause is not an interrupter, but is an independent clause that should be joined to the rest of the sentence with the comma–conjunction combination.

> CORRECTION The new dress, her mother insisted, was too expensive and sophisticated for her, and, besides, her father would surely disapprove of it.

Brackets are used to enclose material you may want or need to add to a direct quote. (We discuss brackets here because they are often confused with parentheses.) Writers may insert bracketed material into a sentence if a word or a phrase in a quoted passage is clear in its original context but would not be clear in its new context. The bracketed insert contains a necessary word or two of explanation. Or writers may insert *transitional* material in brackets if they are omitting words or phrases from the original. And when writers quote material that contains an obvious mistake, they can make it clear that the error is not their own by putting the Latin word *sic* in brackets after the mistake. *Sic* means "thus"—that is "as it appears in the original." *Sic* is usually italicized (underlined).

Some student writers use parentheses for brackets simply because their typewriters have no bracket key. If yours lacks one, draw in brackets in ink where they are needed.

> EXAMPLE Mr. Ricketts is reported to have said, "He Senator Pellagra is a snake in the grass."

Mr. Ricketts, of course, did not say *"He Senator Pellagra ..."* The writer reporting Mr. Ricketts's remark inserted the name of the person he was talking about to make the situation clear to the reader. *Senator Pellagra* should be enclosed in brackets.

> CORRECTION Mr. Ricketts is reported to have said, "He [Senator Pellagra] is a snake in the grass."

Writers cannot simply omit some material from a quoted passage. They must indicate that they have left out some copy. They do so by using a series of spaced dots (See "Ellipses" on page 441.) And second, they may have to fill in a gap in thought with a brief explanatory note in brackets.

In the following example, a writer is quoting a passage that contains an obvious error.

> EXAMPLE   The *New York Times* reviewer wrote, "Ms. Brodsky's new book covers important ground. . . . one of the most promising young writers in America.

The writer quoting the reviewer has omitted part of the reviewer's comments but has not made an adequate transition between the sections he has chosen to use. *One* in the second section appears to refer to the book, not to Ms. Brodsky. The writer should insert a transitional phrase in brackets.

> CORRECTION   The *New York Times* reviewer wrote, "Ms. Brodsky's new book covers important ground. . . . [She is] one of the most promising young writers in America."

> EXAMPLE   The columnist noted, "One realizes that there are positive respects to television, but it is virtually impossible to stress these to teenagers who would rather watch "Charlie's Angels" than "Masterpiece Theatre."

If the writer wishes to make clear that the choice of *respects* over *aspects* here is not his but the columnist's, he should add *sic* in brackets after the offending word.

> CORRECTION   The columnist noted, "One realizes that there are positive respects [*sic*] to television, but it is virtually impossible to stress these to teenagers who would rather watch "Charlie's Angels" than "Masterpiece Theater."

Be careful to use brackets only when you are quoting. Do not use brackets in place of parentheses.

> EXAMPLE   After paying the "entrance fee" [in most cases, four pieces of fruit, a new set of underwear, and a week's pay], the candidates were admitted into the presence of the Grand Master himself.

Since there is no indication that this sentence is a quotation from some other writer, the brackets are inappropriate. Even parentheses might not be the appropriate punctuation here. If the peculiarity of the entrance fee is an important indication of the nature of the Grand Master, the writer may want to emphasize the "entrance fee" by setting off the itemization of the fee with a dash.

> CORRECTION   After paying the "entrance fee"—in most cases, four pieces of fruit, a new set of underwear, and a week's pay—the candidates were admitted into the presence of the Grand Master himself.

Apostrophes

The apostrophe is used to form possessives and contractions. *That's all.*
It is not used to form plurals or the third-person singular of present-
tense verbs. The rules governing individual possessives and contractions
are a bit more complicated, it is true. But many new writers fall into
"apostrophe panic" simply because they have never learned when the
apostrophe is called for and when it is not.

POSSESSIVES.   Form the possessives of most nouns by adding *'s* in the
singular and an apostrophe by itself in the plural.

INCORRECT	CORRECT
the monkeys uncle [one monkey]	the monkey's uncle
the monkeys uncle [several monkeys]	the monkeys' uncle
your fathers mustache	your father's mustache
your father's mustaches	your fathers' mustaches
Paul McCartneys house	Paul McCartney's house
the McCartney's house	the McCartneys' house

To form the possessives of plural nouns not ending in *s*, add *'s* to the
plural form.

INCORRECT	CORRECT
mens underwear	men's underwear
the Childrens' Crusade	the Children's Crusade
the sheeps' pasture	the sheep's pasture

There are two acceptable ways to form the possessive of singular
nouns ending in *-s.* You can add only an apostrophe, or you can add *'s.*
Be sure to stick to one method or the other consistently throughout a
paper or an essay, however. Do not use *'s* in one sentence and an apostrophe alone two sentences later.

INCORRECT	CORRECT
Henry Jame's novels	Henry James's novels or Henry James' novels
the actress agent	the actress's agent or the actress' agent
Kurt Thoma's flip	Kurt Thomas's flip or Kurt Thomas' flip

Form the possessives of compound nouns by adding *'s* to the last word of the compound.

INCORRECT	CORRECT
my father-in-laws suit the Secretary's of State proposal	my father-in-law's suit the Secretary of State's proposal

To form the possessives of two or more nouns together, add *'s* to the last noun in the group to indicate group ownership; add *'s* to each of the nouns to indicate individual ownership.

EXAMPLES (CORRECT):
● Clark Kent and Lois Lane's typewriter (joint ownership)
● Clark Kent and Lois Lane's typewriters (also joint ownership)
● Clark Kent's and Lois Lane's typewriters (individual ownership)
● Superman and Lois Lane's romance (jointly involved with each other)
● Superman's and Lois Lane's romances (individually involved with other people)

CONTRACTIONS.   A contraction, as the name implies, is the shortening, or contracting, of two words into one. Contractions in English fall into two categories: auxiliary verbs plus *not*, and nouns or pronouns plus forms of *to be* or *to have*. The general rule for the formation of contractions is to use an apostrophe in place of the letter or letters that are dropped in the contraction. Knowing the rule makes it easier to see why; for example, *arent* and *are'nt* are incorrect as contractions for *are not*. A letter is dropped in the contraction, but it is between the *n* and the *t* of *not*, not between *are* and *not*. The correct form, of course, is *aren't*. Remember, too, that there is no space either before or after an apostrophe in a contraction.

Look closely at the similar errors in the following sentences.

EXAMPLE   Your little brother should*'nt* go to Great Falls with you if he *cant* take care of himself.
CORRECTION   Your little brother should*n't* go to Great Falls with you if he *can't* take care of himself.

EXAMPLE   *Im* not voting for Smith this year; *hes* made a mess of everything.
CORRECTION   *I'm* not voting for Smith this year; *he's* made a mess of everything.

Four sets of possessives and contractions present special problems for many beginning writers: *its/it's, their/they're, whose/who's,* and *your/you're.* The key to remembering which is which is that the *apostrophe belongs in the contraction*. Pronouns generally have their own special possessive forms—*his* and *her* or *hers*, for example—and *its*, *their*, *whose*, and *your* are four of these special forms. These pronouns form contractions, of course, in the usual way: *it's* means "it is" or "it has"; *they're* means "they are"; *who's* means "who is" or "who has"; and *you're* means "you are." If you are ever in doubt about any of these forms, simply remember that *the apostrophe belongs in the contraction, not in the possessive.*

EXAMPLE   *Its* a shame that the women's group didn't express *it's* grievances more clearly.

With the first *its*, what is called for is the contraction, not the possessive: "*It is* a shame." With the second *its*, the possessive is needed: "the grievances *of it.*"

CORRECTION   *It's* a shame that the women's group didn't express *its* grievances more clearly.

EXAMPLE   *Their* going to Green Lakes with *you're* mother.

Again, try spelling out what the sentence calls for: *they are going* and *the mother of you.*

CORRECTION   *They're* going to Green Lakes with *your* mother.

EXAMPLE   *They're* going to Green Lakes was a mistake.

Because *going* is the subject of the sentence, *they're* should be replaced by the possessive.

CORRECTION   *Their* going to Green Lakes was a mistake.

PLURALS AND VERB FORMS.   Apostrophes have traditionally been used to form the plurals of individual letters, numerals, symbols, and letters used as words (for example, "Mind your *p's* and *q's*"). *No other plurals* are formed with apostrophes. Too many beginning writers write plurals *with* apostrophes and possessives *without* them, and the resulting tangle is confusing, to say the least. Consider these examples:

EXAMPLE   The Basker*villes* trip to Europe was all arranged; the younger Basker*ville's* were wildly excited.

The first *Baskervilles* should be in the possessive: what is meant is *the trip of the Baskervilles*. The second *Baskerville* should be in the plural, so the apostrophe is incorrect. (The placement of the apostrophe in the above sentence would not be correct even if the possessive were needed.)

CORRECTION   The Basker*villes'* trip to Europe was all arranged; the younger Basker*villes* were wildly excited.

EXAMPLE   The members' of the committee will meet in one of the administration building's.

Neither apostrophe here is correct. The spelling out of the possessive formula ("the _____ of the _____") does not work in either case. Both words are simple plurals.

CORRECTION   The members of the committee will meet in one of the administration buildings.

The apostrophe should also not be used to form the third-person singular of verbs in the present tense. All too many new writers, for example, will write *He run's* instead of *He runs*. When this confusion appears along with the mixup of plurals and possessives—and it usually does—the reader can be downright bewildered. Remember that apostrophes should be used *only* with possessives, contractions, and the few plurals mentioned above.

EXAMPLE   Every time someone break's a dish in the kitchen the new waitress scream's.
CORRECTION   Every time someone breaks a dish in the kitchen, the new waitress screams.

Quotation Marks

The most common function of quotation marks is to indicate that a writer is repeating someone else's *exact* written or spoken words.

EXAMPLE   He told me, sobbed Holly, that I look like John Belushi.

Holly's speech is being reported word for word. The quotation is actually in two parts, separated by the interrupter *sobbed Holly*. Quotation marks must enclose each of the two parts. Be especially careful to put a quotation mark at the *end* of a phrase or a sentence being quoted. Many student writers do not remember that the second quotation mark is as important in setting off what has been said or written as the first mark is.

CORRECTION   "He told me," sobbed Holly, "that I look like John Belushi."

EXAMPLE   Hamlet tells Ophelia in Act III to get thee to a nunnery.

Direct quotations need not always stand as complete sentences by themselves. You can enclose a quotation within a sentence of your own *as long as you indicate which part of the sentence is borrowed*. Here, the words *get thee to a nunnery* are Hamlet's (and Shakespeare's) words, not those of the writer of the sentence. They should thus be enclosed in quotation marks.

CORRECTION Hamlet tells Ophelia in Act III, "Get thee to a nunnery."

Sometimes you may report what someone else has said in your own words. You do not need to place your wording of the original statement in quotation marks.

EXAMPLE Jim told Holly that "she looks like John Belushi."

The writer is not repeating Jim's exact words to Holly. The writer's own wording should not be enclosed in quotation marks. (Jim's *exact* words would have been "You look like John Belushi.")

CORRECTION Jim told Holly that she looks like John Belushi.

The quotation of dialogue (conversation) calls for a few special conventions to be observed. In the following example, the dialogue has been correctly handled. Note especially (1) that each new speaker receives a new paragraph, and (2) that *sobbed Holly* and other material goes in the same paragraph as the piece of dialogue to which it refers or pertains.

"He told me," sobbed Holly, "that I look like John Belushi."
"And you took that from *him*?" asked Karen. "Didn't you say anything?"
"Oh, of course I did. I'm not *that* dumb."
"What was it?"
"I told him he looks like Laraine Newman when she's playing one of the Coneheads."

Single quotation marks are used to enclose quotations within quotations.

EXAMPLE "Who says to Ophelia to get thee to a nunnery in Act III?" asked Professor Howard.

The writer's failure to use single quotation marks here makes it look as though the words *get thee to a nunnery* are Professor Howard's.

CORRECTION "Who says to Ophelia to 'get thee to a nunnery' in Act III?" asked Professor Howard.

EXAMPLE The doctor sighed, "Mr. Freeman just said, I am Napolean Bonaparte crossing the Alps to me."

The omission of single marks in this sentence makes it difficult to tell where Mr. Freeman's remark leaves off and the doctor's begins.

CORRECTION The doctor sighed, "Mr. Freeman just said, 'I am Napolean Bonaparte crossing the Alps' to me."

Quotation marks also may be used to indicate that you are speaking of a word as a word—referring to it in a special or particular way. They are also used to emphasize some word or phrase for a particular reason. (Italics can also be used for both purposes; see "Italics" on page 439.) Do not overwork quotation marks for emphasis. Too many new writers do so in order to try to slide a sloppy or dull expression past the reader.

EXAMPLE The word fantastic used to be reserved for events that truly could have happened only in a fantasy or a fairy tale. Now-adays, most people use the word chiefly as a response to the news that there is filet mignon for dinner or beer in the refrigerator.

The writer is speaking of *fantastic* as a word in and of itself.

CORRECTION The word "fantastic" used to be reserved . . .

EXAMPLE In Hamlet's feigned fit of madness, he tells Ophelia to "get thee to a nunnery."

Quotation marks around *madness* would indicate that Hamlet is not genuinely insane. In fact, the word *feigned* must then be omitted.

CORRECTION In Hamlet's fit of "madness," he tells Ophelia to "get thee to a nunnery."

EXAMPLE Senator Pellagra is really "bad news" in Washington since the story about the bribery came out.

The term "bad news" is both slangy and imprecise. Instead of trying to make the expression excusable with quotation marks, the writer should say what he really means.

CORRECTION The story about the bribery has almost destroyed Senator Pellagra's reputation in Washington.

A final function of quotation marks is to enclose the titles of songs, short stories, most poems, essays, articles, and chapters of books when you are referring to them in your own writing. Use this rule for the title of any work that is not an entire book, periodical, or other work by itself. The titles of books, novellas, *long* poems, periodicals, movies, plays, operas, and record albums are put in italics (underlining on the typewriter). For further discussion, see "Italics" on page 439 and "Manuscript Format" on page 463.

EXAMPLES (CORRECT):
- "Death Be Not Proud" (poem by John Donne)
- "I Want to Hold Your Hand" (song by Lennon and McCartney)
- "The Displaced Person" (story by Flannery O'Connor)
- "Fenimore Cooper's Literary Offenses" (essay by Mark Twain)
- "Student Power 101" (article by Ralph Nader, *Change* magazine)
- *Pride and Prejudice* (novel by Jane Austen—italics, *not* quotation marks)
- "The Role of the Porter in *Macbeth*" (student paper)

QUOTATIONS WITH OTHER PUNCTUATION. The examples we have just given of the functions of quotation marks indicate some of the ways in which other punctuation marks are used with quotation marks. We will now illustrate the conventions in more detail.

Periods and commas present no particular problems: they always go *inside* closing quotation marks.

> EXAMPLE   "Although the experiment has failed", said Professor Slobova, "the principle remains the same".

Both the comma after *failed* and the period after *same* should be moved inside the quotation marks.

> CORRECTION   "Although the experiment has failed," said Professor Slobova, "the principle remains the same."

> EXAMPLE   Like Winnie-the-Pooh, Yogi Bear can be described as a "Bear of Very Little Brain".

Even when the material in quotation marks is not a complete sentence, any periods or commas setting it off go *inside* the quotation marks in American usage.

> CORRECTION   Like Winnie-the-Pooh, Yogi Bear can be described as a "Bear of Very Little Brain."

> EXAMPLE   "Gilbert and Sullivan wrote 'I'm Called Little Buttercup'," asserted the confident contestant. "They did not, however, write 'I Want to Hold Your Hand'."

The rule for periods and commas applies even to *single* quotation marks: they go within all quotation marks, single *and* double.

> CORRECTION   "Gilbert and Sullivan wrote 'I'm Called Little Buttercup,'" asserted the confident contestant. "They did not, however, write 'I Want to Hold Your Hand.'"

Colons, semicolons, and dashes always go *outside* quotation marks.

> EXAMPLE   The first story we read in English 227 this year was Poe's "The Pit and the Pendulum;" after that, we read Bierce's "An Occurrence at Owl Creek Bridge."

The semicolon after Poe's title should be moved outside the quotation marks.

> CORRECTION   The first story we read in English 227 this year was Poe's "The Pit and the Pendulum"; after that, we read Bierce's "An Occurrence at Owl Creek Bridge."

Question marks and exclamation points in combination with quotation marks present the most difficulty. When the quotation *is* a question or an exclamation, the marks go *inside* quotation marks, as do commas and periods. When the quotation is *not* a question or an exclamation in itself, the marks go *outside* the quotation marks.

E X A M P L E   Faith asked, "Will anyone be home this afternoon"?

In this example, the material within the quotation marks is a question in itself. The question mark, therefore, should go inside the quotation marks to indicate this.

C O R R E C T I O N   Faith asked, "Will anyone be home this afternoon?"

E X A M P L E   What prompted her to tell her sister, "You smell like a pigsty?"

You smell like a pigsty is not a question; the entire sentence is the question. The question mark should thus be moved outside the quotation mark.

C O R R E C T I O N   What prompted her to tell her sister, "You smell like a pigsty"?

E X A M P L E   "Lennon and McCartney wrote 'I'm Called Little Butter-cup!' " replied the overeager contestant.

This is probably the most complex situation of all: a quotation within a quotation in conjunction with an exclamation point or a question mark. The writer should first decide where the exclamation point should go. "I'm Called Little Buttercup" is a song title, not an exclamation; the *whole* sentence (including *replied the overeager contestant*) is a statement. Only the contestant's words—the ones in double quotation marks—are an exclamation. The exclamation point, therefore, should come *after* the single quotation mark but *before* the double one.

C O R R E C T I O N   "Lennon and McCartney wrote 'I'm Called Little Buttercup'!" replied the overeager contestant.

Italics

In printed material (books, magazines, newspapers, and so on), specific words, phrases, or longer passages may be set in a kind of slanted (or sometimes scriptlike) typeface in order to distinguish them from the text as a whole. In handwritten or typed papers, writers indicate the use of italics by underlining words.

E X A M P L E   Most English majors read Melville's *Moby Dick*.
Melville wanted to redefine the word *evil*.
The whale became Ahab's *bête blanche*.

Italics are most commonly used for the titles of works that are book-length or otherwise complete in themselves. Put titles of books, newspapers, novellas, long poems, periodicals, movies, television series, plays, ships, and aircraft in italics.

EXAMPLES (CORRECT):
- *Tom Jones* (a novel by Henry Fielding)
- *The Turn of the Screw* (a novella by Henry James)
- *Beowulf* (a long poem in Anglo-Saxon)
- *Time* (a magazine)
- The *New York Times* (a newspaper)
- The *Renaissance Quarterly* (a scholarly journal)
- *Jaws* (a movie)
- *Sesame Street* (a TV series)
- *Tosca* (an opera by Giacomo Puccini)
- *Bob Dylan's Greatest Hits, Volume Two* (a record)
- U.S.S. *Enterprise* (aircraft carrier and starship)

Titles that should *not* go in italics include names of short poems, songs, short stories, essays, articles, book chapters, and your own student papers. (See "Quotation Marks" on page 435 and "Manuscript Format" on page 463.)

EXAMPLES (CORRECT):
- "The Short Happy Life of Francis Macomber" (short story by Ernest Hemingway—quotation marks, *not* italics)
- The Function of Vitamin C in the Krebs Cycle (title page of a student paper—no quotation marks, no italics)

Italics may be used when words are referred to merely as words. (Quotation marks can also be used in this fashion; see "Quotation Marks" on page 435.)

EXAMPLES (CORRECT):
- I soon discovered that the word *soda pop* was not used in elite circles, where the word *soft drinks* was more fashionable.
- He used the word *boring* the way most people use *a, an,* and *the.*

Foreign words that are neither proper names nor phrases already listed as part of the language in English dictionaries should also be italicized.

EXAMPLES (CORRECT):
- One of the novels we are reading for this course could be termed a *Bildungsroman,* for it is the story of a young woman making her way to maturity.
- Jeeves, a butler, was a man who knew the ins and outs of behaving *comme il faut.*

Use italics for some scientific terminology.

EXAMPLE (CORRECT):
- She was raising a *Nephrolepsis exaltata,* a *Dracaena marginata,* and a small *Homo sapiens.*

Finally, italics can be used for emphasis (but only sparingly).

EXAMPLE (CORRECT):
- Emma was obliged to fancy what she liked; but she could never be-

lieve that in the same situation *she* should not have discovered the truth.

—Jane Austen, *Emma*

Italics for emphasis are often overused, especially in informal writing.

EXAMPLE   I *really* hope you can come to Myrtle Beach this summer. It'll be *so* great. We'll have *such* a lot of fun and get the *best* tans of anybody in our class.

The writer should omit not only the italics but most of the italicized words themselves—they only belabor the point.

CORRECTION   I hope you can come to Myrtle Beach this summer. It'll be great. We'll have a lot of fun and get the best tans of anybody in our class.

Ellipses

An *ellipsis* (the plural is *ellipses*) is a series of three spaced dots that lets the reader know that some material has been omitted from a quotation. If your paper contains quotation after quotation punched full of holes, your readers may begin to suspect that you are withholding important information from them. Especially with short quotations or quotations that are not complete sentences, you should avoid ellipses.

EXAMPLE   Like Finley Peter Dunne's character Mr. Dooley, he was ". . . not much throubled be lithrachoor . . . ," but he was ". . . not prejudiced again' books. . . ."

Because the two quotations are so short, the ellipses are bothersome; because they are obviously not complete sentences, the ellipses are not even necessary. It is clear enough to the reader that the writer is not quoting Dunne in full.

CORRECTION   Like Finley Peter Dunne's character Mr. Dooley, he was "not much throubled be lithrachoor," but he was "not prejudiced again' books."

(Working a quotation that is not too confusing into your own sentence, by the way, is one way of overcoming the need for an ellipsis at the beginning of the quotation, if you are beginning in the middle of one of the author's sentences.)

Ellipses are necessary, however, for omissions in larger quotations. In this example, ellipses have been used correctly:

As a Canadian, Margaret Atwood has little patience with the attitude toward animals implicit in some British literature. She notes in mild irritation that "as anyone who has read Kipling's Mowgli stories . . . can see, the animals in them are really . . . Englishmen in furry zippered suits, often with a layer of human clothing added on top."

Both sets of ellipses in this example indicate omissions *within* Atwood's sentence. Sometimes, of course, you will have to omit material *between* sentences. When you do, you should insert four dots—a regular period plus an ellipsis—as this writer does:

> Barbara Tuchman emphatically describes the importance of the horse to the medieval knight who rode it:
>> The horse was the seat of the noble, the mount that lifted him above other men. In every language except English, the word for knight—*chevalier* in French—meant the man on horseback. . . . In fulfilling military service, horse and knight were considered inseparable; without a mount the knight was a mere man.

Between the end of the second sentence and the beginning of the third, three other sentences have been omitted; Tuchman's main point, however, still comes through. The period plus the ellipsis should also be used when you *end* a quotation before the actual end of the sentence you are quoting. If, for example, the writer had chosen to conclude her quotation at the word *inseparable*, she should have punctuated it like this:

> In fulfilling military service, horse and knight were considered inseparable. . . .

Note that the partial sentence still makes sense by itself. You should not produce a fragment where the original writer has a complete sentence. An ellipsis is not sufficient in itself to give a sense of completion to the quotation to indicate that the writer did not end the sentence where you have ended it.

One last point on ellipses for omission: If you are omitting more than two whole lines of verse or a whole paragraph or more of prose, type an entire line of spaced dots to indicate the large omission.

> Monday's child is fair of face,
> Tuesday's child is full of grace,
> Wednesday's child is full of woe,
> . . . .
> But a child that's born on the Sabbath day
> Is fair and wise and good and gay.

Ellipses can also be used in dialogue to indicate a significant pause or a thought that trails off. Do *not*, however, use the ellipsis as a convenient way of avoiding other forms of punctuation.

> EXAMPLE Nursery school teachers aren't paid half what they're worth . . . if most of us had to think up new things for thirty four-year-olds to do every day . . . we'd go crazy.

This writer is dodging the fact that she needs a semicolon in place of the first ellipsis and a comma in place of the second.

> C O R R E C T I O N   Nursery school teachers aren't paid half what they're worth; if most of us had to think up new things for thirty four-year-olds to do every day, we'd go crazy.

Slashes

The slash (/) is coming into vogue as book editors replace *he* with *s/he*. In college writing, though, the slash is normally used to indicate the end of a line of poetry when the writer is quoting two or three lines from a poem. (A quotation of more than three lines would be set off from the text in block form.)

> E X A M P L E   Joyce Kilmer's lines "I think that I shall never see A poem lovely as a tree ..." are now out of poetic fashion.
>
> C O R R E C T I O N   Joyce Kilmer's lines "I think that I shall never see/A poem lovely as a tree ..." are now out of poetic fashion.

Avoid overuse of the slash to offer the reader alternatives; *he/she*, *either/or*, and *and/or* are common, unfortunate, and clumsy. A good alternate to the awkward *s/he* or *she/he* is to use *they* or a plural noun.

> E X A M P L E   When a student works on a take-home exam, he/she should do as much as he/she is capable of doing and then take a break and/or have a beer.
>
> C O R R E C T I O N   When students work on take-home exams, they should do as much as they are capable of doing and then take a break either with a beer or without.

EXERCISES

a). Commas
Insert commas wherever they are necessary in the following sentences.

1. Yesterday when you were still not sure whether you were coming I made the arrangements.
2. The menu included bacon and eggs omelettes and hot or cold cereal.
3. I'm reading *Tom Jones* which is my favorite book for the third time.
4. John Donne whose poetry is highly original uses many of the conventions of his times in inventive ways.
5. To work with children successfully a person must have patience.
6. Most of us however wouldn't understand the lecture.
7. Before your mother gets home you'd better clean up the mess under your bed.

8. According to Dr. Relling's theory most people cannot face the truth about their lives.
9. There was a reason unfortunately to doubt the truth of this story.
10. The chief inspector called down from Scotland Yard asked to see the local police the local minister two of the shopkeepers and the family of the deceased.

b). Semicolons
Rewrite the following sentences, placing semicolons where they belong or eliminating semicolons that should not appear in the sentences.

1. Caroline is upset; because she thinks her father does not love her anymore.
2. Lucille misjudges both her children, however her intentions are good.
3. To prepare for an exam a student should do the following; read over the important parts of the text, read his notes, and make an outline of the important points.
4. We still need mustard, olives, and mayonnaise for the potato salad, sour cream, mayonnaise, onion, bread-and-butter pickles, pickle juice, and beef bouillion for the ziti salad, and vanilla ice cream, chocolate cake, and fudge sauce for dessert.
5. The work I've mentioned must be done today; no matter how long it takes for us to finish.

c). Colons
Correct the colon usage in the following sentences.

1. Gregory always fails to remember two things when dealing with his family his brother's tendency to feel sorry for himself and his sister's great love for their father.
2. The materials we need include: seven yards of blue chiffon, thread, two zippers, and lace edging.
3. Professor Wrigley worked on his introductory paragraph all day: but he still wasn't satisfied.
4. After looking the house over carefully, the inspector said: that the entire foundation needed rebuilding, the plumbing had to be re-done, and the wiring was unsafe.
5. She included references to: Job 3, II and Luke 2, 5.

d). Dashes
Revise the following sentences if necessary. Add dashes where they are appropriate and eliminate them where they are not needed. Where a hyphen has been used in place of a dash, correct the punctuation. You may turn one sentence into two to improve the sentence.

1. Stephen regretted his rough treatment of Blanche but his regrets came too late to prevent their divorce.
2. Many reasons, simple nervousness, fatigue, preoccupation with personal problems may keep an actor from performing well.
3. In *Joseph Andrews,* we are introduced to a host of wonderful minor characters—in addition to the main characters Mr. and Mrs. Towwouse, Parson Trulliber, Lady Booby, and Betty are some examples.
4. After I got home—from shopping—because I was tired—I forgot to do

most of the things I had planned to do-I had planned to wash the dishes, walk the dog, and sort the laundry.
5. Henry, June, and Pauline, none of them can face reality.

e).   Hyphens
In the following sentences, insert hyphens where they are needed and eliminate hyphens that should not be used.

1. We wanted to reestablish and redefine our reasons for restructuring the program.
2. Sharon could not decide which of the thirty seven flavors of ice cream to choose.
3. James had never met his second-cousin Jane.
4. Fewer than one-third of the students understood the directions.
5. The houses built by that fly by night contractor are sliding off their foundations.

f).   Question Marks, Exclamation Points
Correct the following sentences. Add question marks and exclamation points where they are necessary. Eliminate any question marks or exclamation points that do not belong in the sentences.

1. Oh. You really frightened me.
2. She asked her professor why she had to take the extra comprehensive?
3. I'd love to have a hot fudge sundae!
4. I asked my teacher why I had to rewrite this paper?
5. Before the exam, the professor asked, "Do you all have #2 lead pencils."
6. By George. I'll make sure that man is fired.
7. Can I go to the beach on Sunday!
8. Who is going to help with the dishes.
9. Do you know whether Helen has completed the project.
10. Do you want to know a secret.

g).   Parentheses and Brackets
Rewrite the following sentences. Add or delete parentheses or brackets where necessary.

1. After trying to solve the jigsaw puzzle—which his grandfather had given him—Gary finally gave up.
2. The use of pesticides in many areas, the kitchen, for example, can be dangerous.
3. Gulliver's estimate of the Lilliputians changes (during the course of his stay in Lilliput).
4. We have noticed some odd, brown patches in the lawn (none of us, however, has been able to find a cause for them).
5. All of us, John in particular, were exhausted by the end of the day.
6. Frank denied having said, "He John is a lazy bum."
7. Lucille does not really understand her son Don (and cannot, therefore, help him).
8. Marie said she would meet you in the miniature shop—right next to the old laundromat.

9. For many reasons, lack of interest, for instance, students drop out of school.
10. The speaker concluded, "So don't think you're gooder *sic* than any-one else."

h). Apostrophe (Possessive)
Form the possessive case correctly in the following sentences.

1. Is Sheila planning to join the womens' softball team?
2. If I am going to continue babysitting for these kids, I am going to have to learn some childrens games.
3. All three canarie's cages need cleaning.
4. Jamess' shirt needs ironing.
5. Myrtle came home from school; she was very excited because she had just learned about the moons' phases.
6. Her class had also looked at a flowers petals under the microscope.
7. In this country, the average men height is probably close to six feet by now.
8. The childrens laughter could be heard across the playground.
9. The Garfield's new puppy is very disobedient.
10. This breads texture reminds me of old custard.

i). Apostrophe (Contraction)
Form the contractions correctly in the following sentences.

1. Its not clear to me why there is'nt a traffic light at this corner.
2. Wont you stay for dinner?
3. As soon as were through with our exams, were going camping.
4. Many of Gulliver's ideas are'nt based on a sound assessment of facts.
5. Its a good idea not to allow perennial flowers to produce seeds once theyve finished blooming.

j). Plurals
Give plural forms for the following nouns

1. child
2. fish
3. ox
4. spouse
5. house
6. box
7. goose
8. dress
9. dish
10. itch
11. louse

k). Quotation Marks
Place quotation marks where they are needed in the following sentences.

1. He said, I would like to travel in Scotland for two weeks, but I will not have that much time.
2. She asked me if I liked Coleridge's poem Kubla Khan.
3. I've been questioning the suspects all afternoon, Constable Troz told the inspector, and each has told me a different story.
4. Our teacher's favorite essay is Thoreau's Civil Disobedience.
5. Fitzgerald's story Bernice Bobs Her Hair appeared in this public tele-vision series *The American Short Story.*

l).   Italics
Use italics (underlining) where needed.

1. In the first half of this century, per diem salaries were vastly lower than they are now.
2. The roots of the word androgynous are Greek.
3. For an exercise program to be effective, one must do the exercises every single day.
4. It is arguable that To the Lighthouse is one of the most sensitive novels ever written.
5. Laura has been working at the country club in lieu of paying for her tennis lessons.

m). Comprehensive Exercises
Rewrite the following sentences. Correct all errors in punctuation.

1. One normally uses (in sewing) a five eighths inch seam, a much narrower seam, might rip, or fray.
2. Sometimes one might want to depart from this basic rule however; when working with a very heavy material, for example.
3. Un-clear instructions can create problems such as: confusion; inaccuracy; and frustration.
4. There is one major reason why Parson Adams, is a virtuous character (in spite of the fights he gets into), he never *begins* a fight.
5. (My cousin) Frank—who is a broker—makes lots of money - in his job—working.
6. The person, whom I am supposed to meet (here), has taught me one important lesson; never assume that anyone is going to be on time.
7. George after he had been combing the woods for him all morning finally, found his little brother; playing next to a small stream.
8. Narcissa took one long last look at the soon to be sold house—which she had grown up in—she sighed—and cried a little.
9. Because Antony never really figures Cleopatra out through the entire course of the play he is always several steps behind her, this is one of the causes of the tragedy.
10. In our garden we have: tulips, daffodils, and crocuses in the front yard, geraniums and petunias along the side of the house, and marigolds, lilies, and roses in the back yard.
11. By the end of the first day on skis moreover Richard had twisted both his knees, and strained his shoulder, that was enough for him.
12. To do this job (properly) you will need: three quarter inch double faced tape—carpet tape—, a straight edge, and a sharp knife.
13. At least two thirds of the homes in this area suffered considerable damage from the storm, broken windows, trees and other greenery damaged or destroyed, porch and other roofs damaged, we will therefore have to ask for federal assistance.
14. Jane hadn't seen her great aunt Mary in several years, now she wanted to reestablish a friendship with her.
15. Marie spent the whole morning telling Ann who is after all Andrea's best friend insulting things about Andrea.
16. I've always enjoyed writing—stories and poems—particularly—my ease of expression—shows my true—lyric gift.

PRINCIPLE 5: Keep mechanics conventional.

Mechanics is the term used by grammarians and English teachers to refer to conventions other than punctuation—in particular, spelling, abbreviations, and capitalization, that have little or no relation to the spoken language but do a great deal to bring order to the written language. Free spirits through the years have rebelled against the necessity of learning the rules of mechanics, but the fact remains that rules and standards *are* needed. Suppose, for example, that everyone decided to spell by ear alone; because people hear and think differently, mass confusion would shortly result. Your eighth-grade teacher's threat to hang you by your thumbs if you did not learn "*i* before *e* except after *c*" may have had little effect upon you in grade school, but it is not too late to mend matters now that you find yourself confronted with red-penciling professors. Study the rules that follow. Though you will not be able to absorb them all overnight, you can at least develop the ability to sense when you are in trouble and need to refer to them.

Spelling: General Problems

No one pretends that English spelling is always easy, always systematic, or even always logical. English is a combination of the old Anglo-Saxon tongue, Latin, French, and many other languages. Furthermore, it has undergone at least two great shifts in pronunciation in the course of its history. Despite the irregularities of English spelling, however, *we* must conform to *its* standards—not vice versa. A potential employer, for example, is more likely to think of you as an ignoramus than as an innovator if you send in a letter of application with wildly unconventional spelling.

There is comfort for poor spellers, however: it is possible to learn how to spell *better*, if not perfectly. If you are both a poor speller and a poor reader, the most important thing you can do to improve your spelling is to improve your reading. So much of spelling depends purely on visual and aural memory that, as your reading vocabulary increases, your spelling vocabulary will probably increase too. You can make *sure* that it will by taking new words seriously. Do not slide over a word you do not recognize. Stop and look at it. Try to pronounce it aloud. Check its spelling, pronunciation, and meaning in the dictionary. Write it down several times. Use it in sentences, written or spoken. Few people, even professional writers, learn spelling easily or automatically. There is no question that learning to spell takes effort. But your efforts should produce results. You will certainly find yourself making fewer errors of inaccurate reading, sloppy pronunciation, or sheer carelessness—errors like these:

INCORRECT	CORRECT
effient	efficient
methiod	method
evaulate	evaluate
hosptials	hospitals
enviroment	environment

Another way to improve your spelling that may not have occurred to you is to learn the common prefixes and suffixes used in English. A *prefix* is a unit of one or more letters that is attached to the beginning of a word (called a *root word*) to change the meaning of the root in some way. A *suffix* is a unit of one or more syllables that is attached to the end of a word and usually changes the word to another part of speech. A good deal of spelling confusion is really confusion over prefixes and suffixes and the ways in which they are connected to words and roots.

COMMON PREFIXES	MEANING	EXAMPLES
ab-, abs-	away from	absent, abscond
ad-, at-	toward	adverb, address, attract
ante-	before	antecedent, antebellum
bene-	good, well	benefit, benefactor
co-, col-, com-, con-, cor-	with	cooperate, collaborate, combine, connect, corrupt
contra-	against	contradict, contraception
de-	down, away from	demote, decompose
ex-	out of, from	external, excursion
extra-	beyond	extraordinary, extracurricular
for-	away, off	forbear, forget, forgo
fore-	before	forefathers, foretell
il-, im-, in-, ir-	not	illegal, improper, inaccurate, irregular
inter-	between	international, interscholastic
intro-	into, within	introduction, introverted
mis-	wrong, badly	misplace, mistreat
non-	not	noncombatant, nonexistent
ob-	against	obstruct, objection
para-	beside, beyond	paramedic, parapsychology
post-	after	postgraduate, postwar
pre-	before	predict, prepare
pro-	for, forth, acting for	procure, produce, pronoun
re-	again	regain, reunite
sub-	under	subway, substitute
super-	above, over	supersonic, Superman
trans-	across	transportation, transcontinental
un-	not	unable, unbelievable

	COMMON SUFFIXES	EXAMPLES
FOR VERBS	-ate	invalidate, refrigerate
	-en	straighten, tighten
	-fy	intensify, satisfy
	-ite	ignite, unite
	-ize	realize, subsidize
FOR NOUNS	-acy	accuracy, literacy
	-age	postage, marriage
	-an	an American, an Episcopalian
	-ance	clearance, vigilance
	-ancy	redundancy, hesitancy
	-ant	accountant, occupant
	-ar	burglar, scholar
	-ary	missionary, dictionary
	-ate	acetate, mandate
	-dom	kingdom, freedom
	-ee	escapee, legatee
	-eer	engineer, racketeer
	-ence	influence, permanence
	-ency	fluency, decency
	-ent	superintendent, solvent
	-er	runner, teacher
	-ery	brewery, surgery, slavery
	-ess	actress, waitress
	-ette	statuette, majorette
	-hood	fatherhood, knighthood
	-ice	justice, malice
	-ism	patriotism, criticism
	-ist	purist, violinist, druggist
	-ite	Israelite, dynamite, nitrite
	-ity	possibility, chastity
	-ment	movement, argument
	-mony	matrimony, alimony
	-ness	bitterness, goodness
	-or	actor, debtor
	-ory	laboratory, history
	-ship	citizenship, dealership
	-ster	gangster, teamster
	-tion	substitution, constitution
	-tude	fortitude, solicitude
	-ty	novelty, realty
	-ure	tenure, legislature, composure
	-y	bakery, soldiery
FOR ADJECTIVES	-able	laughable, workable
	-al	hysterical, theatrical
	-ant	defiant, radiant
	-ary	elementary, auxiliary
	-ate	collegiate, passionate
	-ent	insistent, lenient

COMMON SUFFIXES	EXAMPLES
-escent	fluorescent, opalescent
-ful	dutiful, helpful
-ial	artificial, remedial
-ible	divisible, legible
-ic	volcanic, angelic
-ile	docile, hostile
-ish	foolish, devilish, Spanish
-ive	impressive, instructive
-less	careless, hopeless
-like	childlike, homelike
-ly	lovely, monthly
-ory	contradictory, desultory
-ous	bulbous, outrageous
-some	handsome, lonesome
-y	dirty, healthy, sticky, witty
FOR ADVERBS -ly	dutifully, laughably, impressively
-ward	backward, homeward
-ways or -wise	sideways, clockwise

Inflections—changes that a word can take without losing its particular meaning, such as *-ing, -ed, -en, -er,* and *-est*—can also be considered suffixes.

Prefixes and suffixes figure largely in the spelling rules that follow. We noted at the beginning of this section that spelling rules are not ironclad; there are always exceptions. Further, we are making no attempt to cover every spelling rule ever devised. The rules given here cover points that, in the experience over the years of several teachers, have created the most trouble for student writers. If you have trouble with a word not taken up here, the dictionary should always be your first resort.

If a one-syllable word or a two-syllable word with stress (accent) on the last syllable ends in a vowel plus a consonant, the consonant is usually doubled before a suffix beginning with a vowel or *-y*.

EXAMPLES:
- get/getting
- admit/admittance
- equip/equipped
- fur/furry
- control/controller
- refer/referred

If there is no accent on the last syllable, do not double the consonant.

EXAMPLES:
- stencil/stenciling
- offer/offered
- fidget/fidgety

With suffixes beginning with *consonants*, the final consonant is not doubled.

EXAMPLES:
- commit/commitment
- offer/offertory

For most words ending in a vowel plus *c*, *-k* is added before suffixes beginning with a vowel or *-y*.

EXAMPLES:
- picnic/picnicking
- panic/panicky

When *-ly* is added to adjectives ending in *-l*, the *l* is doubled.

EXAMPLES:
- casual/casually
- financial/financially
- final/finally
- legal/legally

When the last letter of a prefix is the same as the first letter of the root word, and the letter is a consonant, both letters should be kept.

EXAMPLES:
- *mis*state
- *dis*service
- *un*natural

The same rule holds true for compound words in which the first component ends and the second begins with the same consonant: both letters should be kept.

EXAMPLES:
- bookkeeper
- roommate

Words ending in a silent *-e* usually drop the *-e* before a suffix beginning with a vowel.

EXAMPLES:
- leave/leaving
- wade/waders
- captivate/captivated
- docile/docility
- force/forcible

Some words ending in *-ce* or *-ge* retain the *-e* before suffixes beginning in *-a*, *-o*, or *-u*, in order to keep the *c* or *g* soft.

EXAMPLES:
- notice/noticeable
- outrage/outrageous
- change/changeable

Words ending in one or more consonants plus silent -*e* usually keep the -*e* when the suffix begins with a *consonant*.

EXAMPLES:
- crude/crudely
- lone/lonesome
- home/homelike

Words ending in a *vowel* plus silent -*e* usually drop the -*e* before a consonant suffix.

EXAMPLES:
- argue/argument
- true/truly

Verbs ending in -*ie* change the -*ie* to -*y* before -*ing*.

EXAMPLES:
- lie/lying
- die/dying

Some elementary school teachers still swear by the old saying "*I* before *e* except after *c*, or when sounded as *a*, as in *neighbor* and *weigh*." For the most part, the old chestnut holds true. Here are some examples:

I BEFORE *E*:
- achieve
- believe
- shield
- piece
- relieve
- yield

EXCEPT AFTER *C*:
- deceive
- ceiling
- receive
- perceive

SOUNDED AS *A*:
- neighbor
- sleigh
- veil
- weigh

A handful of words take *ei* but do not fit into either the "after *c*" rule or the "long-*a*" rule: *height, weird, foreign, seize, beige,* and so on.

The next section, "Formation of Plurals," and the section "Homonyms" in Chapter 16 cover two special types of spelling problems. If you have a question about spelling that is not covered in any of these three sections—and you will, sooner or later—we repeat our earlier advice: consult the dictionary.

Formation of Plurals

Nouns in English most often form the plural with the addition of -*s*. (Note that there is *no* apostrophe between the noun and -*s*. See "Apostrophes" on page 432.)

SINGULAR	PLURAL
girl	girls
typewriter	typewriters
plan	plans
suitcase	suitcases
problem	problems

Nouns ending in a vowel followed by -*y* take -*s* in the plural. Nouns ending in a consonant followed by -*y* change the -*y* to -*ie* before adding -*s*. (Proper names are an exception to this rule: they take -*s* in the plural even if they seem to call for -*ies*.)

SINGULAR	PLURAL
monkey	monkeys
boy	boys
play	plays
memory	memories
berry	berries
party	parties
enemy	enemies
anchovy	anchovies
Moody	Moodys
Sprayberry	Sprayberrys

Nouns ending in a vowel followed by -*o* take -*s* in the plural. Many nouns ending in a consonant followed by -*o* form the plural with -*es*. (The last rule does not always apply. Some nouns that end in a consonant and -*o* take either -*s* or -*es*, and some take simply -*s*. If you are not sure which to use in a given case, consult the dictionary.)

SINGULAR	PLURAL
studio	studios
cameo	cameos
Romeo	Romeos
hero	heroes
echo	echoes
potato	potatoes
tomato	tomatoes
piano	pianos
soprano	sopranos
domino	dominoes
	or dominos
mosquito	mosquitoes
	or mosquitos

Nouns ending in *-s, -ch, -x,* and *-sh* generally form the plural with *-es.*

SINGULAR	PLURAL
loss	losses
caress	caresses
Jones	Joneses
birch	birches
ditch	ditches
tax	taxes
hoax	hoaxes
flash	flashes

Nouns ending in *-f* and *-fe* usually change the *-f* to *-v* and form the plural thus: *-ves.* Most nouns ending in *-ief* or *-oof* take only *-s* in the plural.

SINGULAR	PLURAL
wolf	wolves
leaf	leaves
shelf	shelves
wife	wives
knife	knives
belief	beliefs
chief	chiefs
roof	roofs
hoof	hoofs

A number of words, of course, do not form the plural in the ways we have listed so far. Some nouns change letters (usually vowels) *within* the word.

SINGULAR	PLURAL
man	men
woman	women
foot	feet
mouse	mice
goose	geese

Other nouns add *-en* to the singular form to become plural.

SINGULAR	PLURAL
child	children
ox	oxen

Some nouns borrow their plural forms from Latin, Greek, or other languages.

SINGULAR	PLURAL
datum (Latin)	data
phenomenon (Greek)	phenomena

Finally, a few eccentric nouns do not change at all in the plural.

SINGULAR	PLURAL
deer	deer
sheep	sheep
series	series

Compound nouns form the plural with the addition of the correct plural ending to the most important word in the compound. In some compound words the last word is the key word and therefore the one that is made plural. But frequently the word that takes the plural ending is not the last word in the compound.

SINGULAR	PLURAL
milkman	milkmen
great-aunt	great-aunts
Ferris wheel	Ferris wheels
father-in-law	fathers-in-law

Syllabication

To maintain adequate margins in your papers (typed or handwritten), you will need to follow rules for dividing words into syllables. You may sometimes have to write part of a word at the end of a line, add a hyphen, and complete the word on the following line. Before you attempt to divide a word, though, ask two questions: Can the word be divided at all? If so, how should it be divided?

A one-syllable word can never be divided. If you are approaching the end of a line and see that there is not enough room for the word, put the word on the next line.

CORRECT DIVISIONS	INCORRECT DIVISIONS
strength	streng-th
shout	sh-out
brooks	brook-s
knife	kni-fe
clenched	clench-ed

Words of two or more syllables can be divided, but several rules apply. First, do not leave a syllable of only one or two letters at the end or at the beginning of a line.

CORRECT DIVISIONS	INCORRECT DIVISIONS
alert	a-lert
lazi-ness	la-ziness
dashes	dash-es *or* da-shes
lanky	lank-y
hibernate	hi-bernate

Second, if a word contains a prefix or a suffix of more than two letters, the prefix or suffix provides a natural division.

CORRECT DIVISIONS	INCORRECT DIVISIONS
pre-tentious *or*	pret-entious,
preten-tious	pretent-ious
unfor-givable	un-forgivable
unforgiv-able	unforgiva-ble
con-struction	cons-truction
construc-tion	construct-ion

Third, words that contain double consonants can be divided between the consonants.

CORRECT DIVISIONS	INCORRECT DIVISIONS
impres-sive	impress-ive
refer-ring	referr-ing
bril-liance	brill-iance
dis-solve	diss-olve

In other cases where you must divide a word, let the dictionary be your guide. There is one important point to keep in mind when you check the dictionary's division of a word. A dictionary will indicate *every* syllable in the word—even those of only one or two letters at the beginning or the end of a word. Consistently bungled syllabications are an annoyance to anyone who has to read written work. Your taking a few seconds to check the division of a word is a small but important courtesy. (As a reward, you may find your spelling will improve as you learn more about the ways in which words are put together.)

DICTIONARY LISTINGS	CORRECT DIVISIONS	INCORRECT DIVISIONS
mul·ti·plic·i·ty	mul-tiplicity	mult-iplicity
	multi-plicity	multipli-city
	multipli-city	multiplici-ty
e·gal·i·tar·i·an	egal-itarian	e-galitarian
	egali-tarian	egalit-arian
	egalitar-ian	egalitari-an

Abbreviations

No one will deny that abbreviations can be great time- and space- savers. Many common abbreviations, though, should not be used in formal college writing. The use of other abbreviations should be confined to footnotes or bibliography entries. The lists that follow indicate the conventions for the use of abbreviations in college writing. In general, place names; parts of street addresses; most professional titles; first names; titles of college courses; months, days of the week, and holidays; and units of time and measure should be spelled out, not abbreviated.

PLACE NAMES:
- Los Angeles (*not* L.A.)
- Hamilton County (*not* Ham. Co.)
- Illinois (*not* Ill.)
- Argentina (*not* Arg.)

PARTS OF STREET ADDRESSES:
- Street (*not* St.)
- Road (*not* Rd.)

MOST PROFESSIONAL TITLES:
- professor (*not* prof.)
- senator (*not* sen.)
- general (*not* gen.)
- the Reverend (*not* Rev.)

FIRST NAMES:
- Charles Dickens (*not* Chas. Dickens)
- Virginia Woolf (*not* Va. Woolf)
- Edgar Allan Poe (*not* E. A. Poe)

The use of initials is permissible if the person in question uses initials in his professional name: J. R. R. Tolkien, B. F. Skinner.

TITLES OF COLLEGE COURSES:
- The Modern Novel (*not* Mod. Nov.)
- German 103 (*not* Ger. 103)

MONTHS, DAYS OF WEEK, HOLIDAYS:
- November (*not* Nov.)
- Wednesday (*not* Wed.)
- Christmas (*not* Xmas)

UNITS OF TIME AND MEASURE:
- hours (*not* hrs.)
- minutes (*not* mins.)
- feet (*not* ft.)
- meters (*not* ms.)
- pounds (*not* lbs.)

The following abbreviations are permissible in formal papers, but only in footnotes, parenthetical references, and bibliographies.

ABBREVIATION	MEANING
p., pp.	page(s)
1., 11.	line(s)
f., ff.	and the following (lines or pages)
vol., vols.	volume(s)
ch., chs.	chapter(s)
no., nos.	number(s)
trans.	translator, translated by
ed.	editor(s), edited by
c., ca.	about (used with dates)
b.	born
d.	died
e.g.	for example
i.e.	that is
etc.	and so on
et al.	and others (people only)
ibid.	the same (in footnotes)

These abbreviations have come to be commonly used in formal college writing.

A FEW TITLES (USED *BEFORE* NAMES):
● Mr., Mrs., Ms., Dr., St. (Saint)

DEGREES AND SIMILAR TITLES (*AFTER* NAMES):
● M.D., B.A. or A.B., M.A., Ph.D., D.D., D.D.S., C.P.A., Jr., Sr.

Note: Do not use *M.D.* or other doctoral degrees and the title *Dr.* at the same time.

ABBREVIATIONS AND ACRONYMS FOR ORGANIZATIONS:
● FBI, CBS, NASA, NAACP, SPCA, CIA

Note: These abbreviations and acronyms do not take periods.

YEAR AND TIME LABELS:
● B.C., A.D.

(*Note:* B.C. follows the year; A.D. precedes the year: 854 B.C., A.D. 162)

● a.m. (or A.M.), p.m. (or P.M.)

(*Note:* Use *a.m.* or *p.m.* with numerals, not with words)

Numbers

The conventions regarding the use of written-out numbers (twenty-four) and figures (24) vary among different types of writing. For example, newspapers and magazines, because of their space limitations, tend to use figures most of the time. In college writing, on the other hand, the standards are more formal. You should familiarize yourself with the list that follows, to know when to use written-out numbers and when to use figures.

WRITTEN-OUT NUMBERS.

CARDINAL NUMBERS THROUGH NINETY-NINE:
- one
- eleven
- twenty-seven
- ninety-nine

ORDINAL NUMBERS THROUGH NINETY-NINTH:
- first
- eleventh
- twenty-seventh
- ninety-ninth

NUMBERS THAT CAN BE WRITTEN IN TWO WORDS:
- one hundred, one hundredth
- five thousand, five thousandth
- six million, six millionth

FRACTIONS AS ADJECTIVES AND NOUNS:
- a two-thirds majority *(adjective)*
- three fourths of the population *(noun)*

NUMBERS AT THE BEGINNING OF THE SENTENCE:
- Two hundred and twenty drivers were kept waiting for an hour when the Cutter Key drawbridge jammed yesterday.

To make such sentences less cumbersome, you can rephrase the sentence so that the number does not come first: "The Cutter Key drawbridge jammed yesterday, keeping 220 drivers waiting for an hour."

TIME OF DAY, WHEN A.M. OR P.M. IS NOT USED:
- four o'clock in the morning
- eight-thirty in the evening

FIGURES.

TIME OF DAY, WHEN A.M. OR P.M. IS USED:
- 9:00 a.m., • 4:36 p.m.

Do not use *o'clock, in the morning*, etc., with a.m. and p.m.

DATES:
- April 23, 1954
- 29 August 1955
- July 4th

PAGE NUMBERS
- page 52
- (p. 52)

NUMBERS IN ADDRESSES:
- 952 46th Street, Anytown, U.S.A. 00513

N U M B E R S C O N T A I N I N G D E C I M A L S :
- 3.14159
- 6.25 percent
- $10.95

M E A S U R E M E N T S :
- 5 feet 5 inches
- 5″ x 7″ cards

Whole units of measurement—*seven feet tall,* for instance—should be written out.

T E M P E R A T U R E
- 98.6°

N U M B E R S I N A S E R I E S W H E N A T L E A S T O N E N U M B E R
I N T H E S E R I E S M U S T B E W R I T T E N I N F I G U R E S :
- Estimates of the casualties varied widely. The highway patrol stated that at least 40 people were killed and between 80 and 125 were injured. (*Not* "forty . . . eighty . . . 125.")

Capitalization

Capitalize the first letter in the first word of every sentence. This rule applies, as well, to full sentences being quoted and to full sentences in parentheses.

My sister advised me to write my paper on a narrower topic.
My sister told me, "You can't write a 750-word essay on all the women in the twentieth century."
My sister's advice is generally good. (She did tell me to put a frog in mother's bed once, but I don't hold that against her.)

Do *not* capitalize the first letter of a quotation that is less than a full sentence (or at least an *implied* sentence, like "No!" or "Fire!") unless the letter is capitalized in the original material or the quotation begins your own sentence.

The spectator in Addison and Steele's essays of the same name is self-conscious about his "Short Face."

Short Face is capitalized in the essays.

"A miserable Yahoo"—this is what Gulliver calls himself after his sojourn with the Houyhnhnms.

A miserable Yahoo is not a full sentence in itself, but it *begins* one.

Gulliver thinks of himself after his sojourn with the Houyhnhnms as "a miserable Yahoo."

Do not capitalize the first letter of an element in parentheses that is less than a full or an implied sentence.

My sister (the one who now goes to graduate school) advised me to write my paper on a narrower topic.

Always capitalize "I" as a pronoun.

I took her advice; instead of writing about women in the twentieth century, I wrote an essay on Amelia Earhart's last flight.

Capitalize the names of persons, real and invented.

Holly Sue Smith	Robert Redford
Dr. Patricia A. Moody	Hawkeye Pierce

Capitalize the names of nationalities and races.

French	Caucasian (*white* is not capitalized)
Iranian	Afro-American (*black* is not capitalized)
American	Chicano

Capitalize the names of specific places.

Los Angeles	Mississippi River	the Ukraine
Hamilton County	Andes Mountains	Japan
Illinois	the Bahamas	Mars

Capitalize the names of specific organizations.

General Electric	Kiwanis Club
Montgomery Ward	Chi Omega

Capitalize the names of days of the week, months of the year, holidays, and historical or cultural events and movements.

Saturday	April	Christmas	the Hundred Years' War
Tuesday	December	Labor Day	the Reformation

Capitalize personal titles in conjunction with the names of the persons who bear them. Titles in isolation, however, are usually not capitalized.

General Richard Merrit spoke to the Kiwanis Club.
Richard Merrit, a four-star general in the Army, spoke to the Kiwanis Club.

Capitalize geographical directions *only* when they apply to specific regions or place names.

The Northeast	the north end of town
Southern California	south of the border
West Hills, New York	"Go west, young man."

Many common nouns are capitalized when they are parts of proper nouns, but *not* when they stand alone.

Main Street	the street where you live
Ford Motor Corporation	my father's corporation
Syracuse University	the new university

Ohio River	the big, muddy river
Grandmother Smith	my grandmother
Aunt Barbara	Kelly's aunt

Capitalize the first and last words and all the important words in the title of a book or other work. (*A, an, the,* conjunctions, and prepositions of less than five letters are capitalized in titles, *only* when they are the first word of the title or the subtitle.)

The Red Badge of Courage
The Lives of a Cell
Mortal Lessons: Notes on the Art of Surgery
"Red Fire: The Story of the Fifth Brigade"
"A Good Man Is Hard to Find"
"The Lady with the Dog"

Sacred names and the titles of sacred texts of all religions should be capitalized.

God	Jehovah	Allah	Brahma
the Bible	the Torah	the Koran	the Bhagavad-Gita

Capitalize the names of specific courses, but not those of general fields of knowledge.

Invertebrate Biology	biology
Sociology 301	sociology

Manuscript Format

The rules of *manuscript format*—that is, the rules having to do with the way a formal paper should look when you submit it for grading—may not seem at first to have much to do with the other rules covered in this section. Like the other rules, however, they do a great deal toward bringing order to the written language. Specifically, they ensure that the paper you have worked long and hard on is prepared for presentation in an orderly and attractive manner.

The title page of your paper should contain the following information: the title of the paper (which should *not* be put in italics, quotation marks, or capital letters); your own name; the name of the course for which the paper has been written; the teacher's name; and the date. A sample title page showing the proper positioning of the required information appears on page 464.

As we have noted, the title of your own paper should not be put in capital letters, quotation marks, or italics.

INCORRECT	THE ROLE OF THE PORTER IN *MACBETH*
	"The Role of the Porter in *Macbeth*"
	The Role of the Porter in MACBETH
CORRECT	The Role of the Porter in *Macbeth*

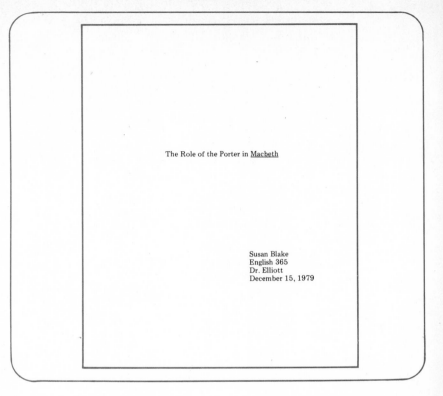

The Role of the Porter in <u>Macbeth</u>

Susan Blake
English 365
Dr. Elliott
December 15, 1979

Your title should, furthermore, give a reasonably good idea of the topic of the paper. Such titles as these do not specify the topic well enough.

One Minor Character in *Macbeth*
Knock, Knock, Knock
Macbeth

Never use as your own title the title of a work you discuss. If you do, you will confuse your reader a great deal.

Do not, on the other hand, make your title a statement of your thesis; after all, you want to leave something for the reader to discover in the paper. The following title leaves nothing to the imagination:

The Porter Is an Important Character in *Macbeth* Because He Provides a Moment of Comedy to Relieve the Tragedy of the Main Proceedings in the Play

You need not repeat the title of your paper at the top of the first page. Simply begin typing the text of the paper thirteen spaces down from the top of the page (a little over two inches); leave one-inch margins at the sides and bottom of the page; and double-space the text. A diagram appears on page 465.

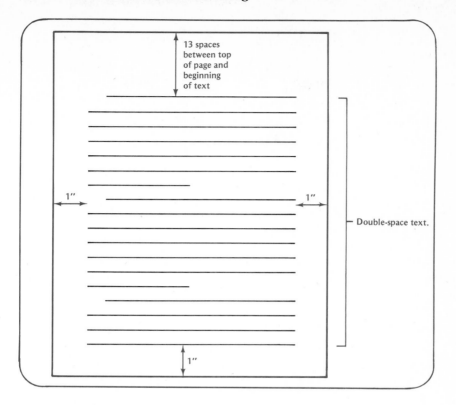

In typing the pages after the first, leave one-inch margins on all four sides. Throughout the paper, be sure to indent for new paragraphs (five spaces is the usual indentation) and to double-space the text.

Chapter 11, "The Library Research Paper," provides you with instructions on the information that you should include in footnotes. Footnotes should be typed as follows: leave four spaces between the last line of text and the first footnote on each page; indent the first line of each footnote five spaces; single-space *within* footnotes and double-space *between* them; and leave one inch at the bottom of the page after the last footnote. See the top of page 466 for a diagram.

Your teacher may ask you to use *endnotes* instead of *footnotes*. When you use endnotes, you put all your reference notes on a separate sheet or sheets at the end of your paper. To type an endnote page, skip down two inches from the top of the page and type the word "Notes"; skip another four spaces before beginning the first note; double-space both *within* notes and *between* them; and leave one-inch margins at the sides and bottom of the page. (See bottom of page 466.) If you have more than one endnote page, leave one-inch margins on all four sides of the second and subsequent pages.

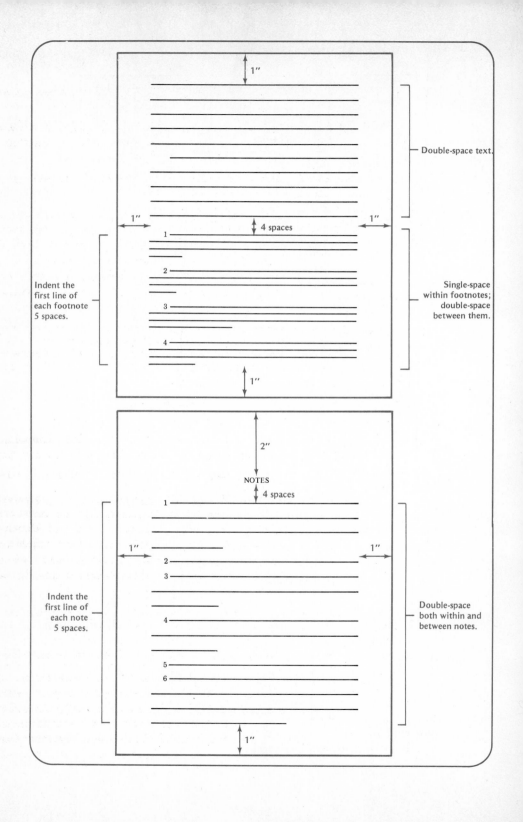

Chapter 11, "The Library Research Paper," also provides instructions on the information that should be included in bibliography entries. To type the first page of your bibliography, skip down two inches from the top of the page and type the word "Bibliography"; skip another four spaces before beginning the first entry; indent every line *except* the first one of each entry five spaces; double-space both *within* and *between* entries; and leave one-inch margins at the sides and bottom of the page. (Observe one-inch margins on all four sides of subsequent pages.) See the diagram below of a typical bibliography page.

When you type a paper, always be sure that your typewriter ribbon is *fresh* and your keys are *clean*. Having to squint at faint or blurred type rarely prepares a teacher to judge your work favorably. As a further courtesy, you should not type a paper on erasable bond or onionskin paper. Such paper will not take corrections in ink, and often even the typed material smears. Use good medium- to heavy-weight paper—twenty-pound weight is best.

If you need to make minor corrections on your final copy, by all means do so—*neatly*, in ink. You should cross out unnecessary words, without scratching a hole in the paper; a line drawn through the words

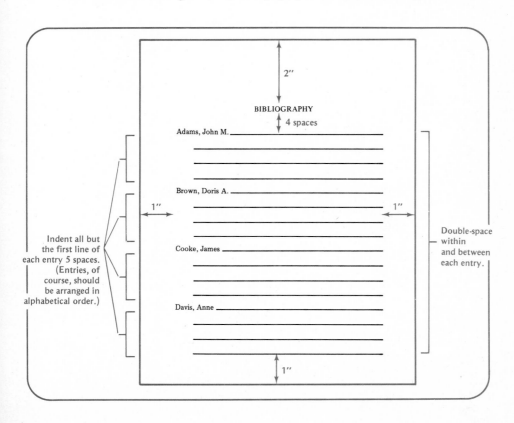

to be deleted will do. Omitted words can be added above the line like this:

George Washington $\wedge$ slept here.

If you have more than two or three words on any one line that need changing, you should probably retype the page.

EXERCISES

a). Correct the Spelling

1. backround
2. recieve
3. probly
4. nite
5. enviroment

b). Syllabication
Divide these words into syllables.

1. favorite	6. combustible
2. terribly	7. acknowledgment
3. peaked	8. eventually
4. savory	9. synonym
5. terminate	10. seasonal

c). Abbreviations
Use abbreviations wherever they are appropriate.

1. Doctor Wellborn is an excellent doctor.
2. Karen moved from London, Ontario, to London, England.
3. Professor White is not a professor of geography.
4. Sergeant Smithers is hoping he'll be promoted to lieutenant, but Lieutenant Flounder hopes he won't be.
5. Captain Beardsley is taking care of flight number 836 to Miami, Florida, because Captain Hahn is sick.

d). Abbreviations
Rewrite the following sentences. Assume they are being used in formal writing situations. Use abbreviations where they are appropriate and delete the ones used incorrectly.

1. First I visited my sister in L.A.; then I flew to Little Rock, Ark. to see my brother.
2. [14]Spiller, Thorp, Johnson, Canby, *Literary History of the United States* (N.Y.: Macmillan, 1962), page 758.
3. The Reverend Aubrey Henderson, Master of Arts, will address the

convention of the National Association for the Advancement of Colored People in New York next month.
4. Mister Smith, the pharmacist, went to Penn. State.
5. The first vol. of the gen's. memoirs is thoroughly dull. Only on p. 204, when he begins describing his military training, do his adventures begin to capture the reader's interest.

e). Numbers
Rewrite the following sentences so that the numbers and figures are used correctly.

1. 572 runners competed in the Erasmus P. Winterbottom Memorial Marathon; they began running at nine a.m. and finished at five p.m.
2. Charlotte Brontë was born on April twenty-first, eighteen hundred and sixteen, in Thornton, a small town in Yorkshire, England.
3. Jody's fever peaked last night; it reached one hundred and five degrees Fahrenheit.
4. The text of Fred's thesis is 81 pages long; the bibliography adds another 15 pages to its length.
5. I hoped to win the student government election with a ⅔ majority; I ended the race with less than ¼.

f). Capitalization
Correct the following sentences by using capital or lower case letters where they are needed.

1. Beeny's Grandfather gave him a book for his Birthday titled *A pictorial history of world war I.*
2. When the Professor asked Scott who was ruling Britain at the time of the American revolution, he said, "King Louis XVI."
3. Mike and judy spent passover in cleveland with grandmother Greenspan this year.
4. While crossing the andes on his way to the galápagos islands, Charles darwin found fossilized Sea shells at an elevation of twelve thousand feet.
5. My Father is President of the East Ridge Chapter of the rotary club, which meets every Friday at the Mount Vernon restaurant.

g). Comprehensive Exercises

1. In the first few pp. of the novel, Edith Wharton describes Lily Bart as a successful socialight of N.Y. society.
2. Shakespeares *12th Night* is one of the many play's being staged at the Stratford Thaeter this summer.
3. I will not except responsibility for your actions if somebody gets hurt with one of these knifes.
4. Doris Lessing is a famous S. Afr. novlist and one of the many womens who have displayed remarkable writing skills.
5. Bill and Sally will be living in Miami Beach for the next 2 yrs. at least.
6. Pearl Buck depicts peasant woman as bareing the burdens of child Care and manual labours.
7. *Summer* is one of edith Wharton's lesser known novel.

8. The Carrier Corporation is building a Football Stadium near Jefferson Ave.
9. When Ashenbach returned to Venice, he found conditions their really changed.
10. The Mormon Church allowed its male members to have 2 or more wifes.
11. The headmaster, Mr. Wills, enquired y the teacher had submitted her syllabi.
12. Only 6% of the population has settled hear in the Valley.
13. The zoo has many varieties of gooses, tigers, and deers.
14. henry green, in his novel *Party Going,* had depicted a modern waist land that is reminiscent of T. S. eliot's poem.
15. The Principle of this school is such a man of principal that he will not allow the students to recieve their degrees unless they dispaly good behaviors.

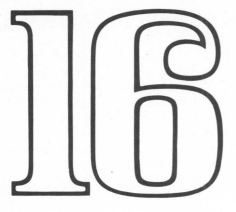

Glossary
of Usage

Introduction to Glossary of Usage
Uses of the Language
Glossary of Usage

INTRODUCTION TO GLOSSARY OF USAGE

Just as people themselves differ, so will the language they use differ. We may say "Dig it" to a friend, but "I understand" to a teacher; "y'all come" in one part of the country and "see ya" in another. The variations of American English are numerous and include both the way people speak and the way they write. Furthermore, there are differences between the way language is spoken and the way it is written. In this "Glossary of Usage," you will find labels to help you recognize the appropriate level of use for words or phrases. Using language well is not simply a matter of what is right or wrong, but rather what is appropriate for one situation, one audience, one time, one place. The labels are provided to help you to be the judge of whether a particular usage is appropriate in speech or in formal writing.

We should recognize that writing is much more conservative than speech, and that the spoken, or informal, use might not be appropriate for formal written papers. Formal situations, in speaking and writing, call for more conservative language. Thus, even though our language is moving in the direction of more liberal usages, the good speaker and writer still chooses words with care.

Uses of the Language

How can we label the various uses of the language? Imagine three overlapping circles: one is labeled *formal*, one is labeled *acceptable*, and one is labeled *informal*.

FORMAL. Some usages labeled formal are probably restricted to very careful writing situations, such as the language of legal documents or formal addresses. Some usages may be archaic, some may be on the way out of use, some may be restricted to poetic use.

INFORMAL. The informal circle includes language that is restricted to the spoken form; it may be even further restricted to usage by a particular occupational, ethnic, or geographic group. *Slang* is another label for usages that are spoken; slang usually stays in fashion for a brief period of time before either disappearing from the language or coming into wider use with altered meanings. Terms or usages that are restricted to a region of the country are labeled *dialectical*. Within what may be regarded as dialectical may be either *standard* or *nonstandard* usages. *Standard* and *nonstandard* are slippery terms and require a bit of explanation. Just as notions of what is acceptable in fashion vary from country to country, age to age, social level to social level, so notions of what is acceptable language use vary in the same ways and others. To label something as standard, then, means simply to recognize that a majority of a society would regard the use as correct.

The careful speaker and writer does not wish to give offense, to alienate an audience, simply because of verbal slips. Good advice, then, is to avoid in your papers—and probably in your speech as well—those usages labeled nonstandard. Otherwise, you may prematurely be judged negatively by your language habits.

Another issue is raised by the labels *redundant* and *incorrect*. You should aim for clear, careful, accurate speaking and writing. Sometimes the language and its speakers/writers fall into sloppy habits. We mean in this glossary to help you avoid such bad habits, and we have reserved labels such as *redundant* or *incorrect* for language that is repetitive or inaccurate, whether misplaced in the sentence or simply meaningless.

If you do not find the information you need here, where else can you go? First, to a good desk dictionary such as *Webster's New World Dictionary*. Next, for a more elaborate discussion of variations in usage, consult a guide to English usage. One excellent guide to modern usage is *The Careful Writer* by Theodore M. Bernstein. Your college library will have other recent guides to usage. Just remember that the more recent it is, the better is its chance of reflecting current attitudes about usage.

GLOSSARY OF USAGE

a, an   *A* is used before words that begin with a consonant sound (*a* book, *a* tree, *a* house). (Note the sounded *h*.) *A* is also used before words that begin with a vowel but that are spoken with a consonant sound (*a* one-way street). *An* is used before words that begin with a vowel sound (*an* elephant, *an* acorn, *an* honor, *an* honest person). (Note the silent *h*.)

a lot, alot   *Alot* is not a word, but a common misspelling of *a lot*. *A lot* is acceptable in informal writing contexts. Do not use the term in formal writing.

absolutely, absolute   *Absolutely* means "unconditionally," "completely," "perfectly." Avoid the common misuse that tones down its meaning to "yes" or "very." *Absolutely* is an adverb.

- The stormy weather made the journey *absolutely* impossible.

Absolute is an adjective.

- There was *absolute* silence in the room.

accept, except   To *accept*, a verb, means "to receive or take," to agree to.

- We *accept* your proposal.

Except, which is used most frequently as a preposition, means "other than or but."

- Everyone present *except* us liked the film.

Except is occasionally used as a verb, with the meaning "to leave out, to exclude" or "to make an exception of."

- The dean agreed to *except* the foreign student from the language requirement.

access, excess   The two words are similar in sound but different in meaning. *Access*, a noun, means "a way or means of approach, the right to enter or to use."

- We have *access* to the house while the owner is away.

Excess as a noun means "something that is of greater quantity than is usual or proper."

- He spends money in *excess* of what he earns.

Excess can also be an adjective.

- He earns *excess* profits.

ad, advertisement   *Ad* is an acceptable abbreviation for *advertisement* in informal contexts. *Advertisement* should be used in formal contexts.

adapt, adopt   To *adapt* means "to make suitable by changing or adjusting." To *adopt* means "to take up by choice and use as one's own."

- Young people in England eagerly *adopt* dress fads that London designers *adapt* from American fashions.

adverse, averse   Both words are adjectives. *Adverse*, which generally refers to conditions or events, means "unfavorable."

- *Adverse* circumstances prevented him from making the journey.

Averse, which applies to people, means "extremely reluctant or unwilling." *Averse* takes the preposition *to*.

- I am *averse* to the idea of making large profits.

advice, advise   *Advice* is a noun. *Advise* is a verb.

- You can *advise* [verb] the chairman if you wish, but he will not follow your *advice* [noun].

adviser, advisor   These are two acceptable spellings of the same word (with the meaning "one who gives advice or guidance"), but *adviser* is the preferred spelling.

affect, effect As verbs, to *affect* means "to influence" and to *effect* means "to bring about or accomplish some result."

- Excessive drinking adversely *affects* our health.
- We need to *effect* changes in the constitutional law.

Effect is more commonly used as a noun than as a verb. As a noun, *effect* means "the result of an influence" or "a desired impression or appearance."

- The adverse *effect* of malnutrition will *affect* his intellectual capability.

Affect can also be used as a verb meaning "to cultivate an effect," "to show a preference for," "to make a pretense of."

- Jane *affects* a sloppy appearance.
- He *affects* simplicity, but his BMW motorcycle cost more than your car and mine put together.

Affect is also a noun, part of the jargon of psychology, meaning "emotional response."

- He hardly responded to the bad news; in his depressed state he exhibited flattened *affect*.

again, back, refer back As adverbs, *again* indicates a repetition, while *back* means "a return to a former position."

- He was happy *again,* now that he had a new job.
- He went *back* to his hometown after he lost his job.

Refer back is a redundant expression. Use *refer* without *back*.

- Please *refer* to the list of names on page 1.

aggravate, intensify To *aggravate* is "to make (something) more troublesome or more serious; to worsen (something.)"

- Your insolence will further *aggravate* the offense.

To *aggravate* meaning "to annoy (someone)" is acceptable in informal contexts but is generally avoided in formal writing.
To *intensify* means "to increase in degree of force, vehemence, or vividness." The increase may be either favorable or adverse.

- His absence *intensified* her love for him.

agree to, agree with To *agree to* means "to consent to, to say yes to." To *agree with* means "to be of the same opinion."

- They *agreed to* accompany him to the airport.
- I *agree with* your ideas of social reform.

ain't Once a legitimate contraction for some forms of the verb *to be*, *ain't* is no longer considered to be acceptable in any context except that of very informal speech.

all ready, already   *All ready*, an adjective, means "prepared."

- She is *all ready* to take command of the meeting.

Already, an adverb, means "before or previously."

- She has *already* been given the scholarship.

all right, alright   The form *alright* is informal. In formal contexts use *all right* as two separate words.

- He does *all right* at school.
- Those shoes are *all right* for jogging.

all together, altogether   *All together* is a phrase meaning "all in one place." *Altogether* is an adverb denoting "wholly," "completely," or "entirely."

- The family were *all together* for the first time in five years.
- The idea for the dinner party was *altogether* hers.

all ways, always   The first term is a noun phrase that is rather stilted. The second is an adverb meaning "at all times" or "invariably." *All ways* is often mistakenly used when *always* is needed.

- *All ways* lead to home.
- I *always* go to the Farmer's Market on Saturday.

allude, refer   Both verbs mean "to mention." To *allude* is to mention casually, indirectly, or playfully, as by a hint or a brief reference.

- Although she never mentioned them by name, she was *alluding* to her sisters.

To *refer* is to mention directly and openly.

- She *referred* to her sisters' involvement in the tampering of the will.

allusion, illusion, delusion, elusion   An *allusion* is an indirect reference or mention.

- This passage contains an *allusion* to Milton's *Paradise Lost*.

An *illusion* is a deception or a fantasy, sometimes arising out of a false perception.

- He realized that the play was only an *illusion* of real life.

A *delusion* is a false belief, as opposed to a false perception, that results from a serious misconception or a mental disorder.

- He was suffering from the *delusion* that visitors from outer space were pursuing him.

An *elusion* is an escape or an avoidance of something. The word often has the connotation of quickness or cunning.

- His departure from home was an *elusion* of responsibility.

although, though   Both *although* and *though* can be used to introduce a dependent clause. As subordinators, the two words mean "in spite of the fact that" or "granting that."

- *Although* (or *though*) he was very ill, he insisted upon going to work.

Only *though* can be a conjunctive adverb; as such, *though* is similar in meaning to *however*.

- Alice asked James to visit her; he was busy, *though,* and could not come.

alumna, alumnus, alumnae, alumni   The first two of these Latin words are singular nouns referring to a woman *(alumna)* or to a man *(alumnus)* who has graduated from a particular school. *Alumnae* is the plural of *alumna,* while *alumni* has two uses: it is the plural of *alumnus,* and it refers to a group of both men and women graduates. In general, use the word *graduate* to refer to an individual and use *alumni* to refer to a large group of graduates.

- The university sent thousands of fund-raising letters to its *alumni*—men and women from all parts of the country.

among, between   Both words are prepositions. Use *among* to refer to three or more items. Use *between* to refer to two.

- You will find a patch of daisies *among* the rosebushes.
- I feel caught *between* two equally interesting possibilities.

amount, number   As nouns, both words refer to quantities, but of different types. *Amount* refers to a quantity that cannot be broken down into units. *Number* indicates a quantity that can be counted.

- A large *amount* of money was stolen.
- A large *number* of books were taken to the bindery.

analyzation   This term reflects the tendency of some writers to make ordinary words sound scientific or complicated. The correct form of the noun is *analysis.*

- The analysis was completed in the laboratory.

and etc.   *Etc.* is the abbreviation for the Latin term *et cetera* meaning "and other things." *And etc.* is redundant and is therefore incorrect.

and/or   This phrase is often used in business writing and legal documents as a kind of shorthand. It should not be used in other formal writing.

BUSINESS OR LEGAL CONTEXTS:
- She will purchase disability *and/or* medical insurance.

OTHER FORMAL CONTEXTS:
- She will purchase disability insurance, medical insurance, *or both.*

ante-, anti-   The two prefixes are often confused. *Ante-* means "before." *Anti-* means "against."

- The *antebellum* period refers to the years before the Civil War.
- The senator was strongly *anti-Communist.*

anxious, eager   The two words are often used interchangeably in conversation and in informal writing. In formal usage, however, *anxious* means "feeling anxiety, apprehension, or uneasiness." *Eager* means "feeling enthusiastic or impatient desire."

- I was *eager* to help my new boss.
- My parents were *anxious* about my severe headaches.

any, all   *Any* and *all* are not interchangeable. The first word is singular, and the second is plural.

INCORRECT   • He is the best of *any* student.
CORRECT   • He is the best of *all* the students.

anyone, any one   *Anyone* is an indefinite pronoun. It refers to human beings in a broad and general way. The noun phrase *any one* is more precise—it indicates "any individual person, place, or thing of a group listed."

- Can *anyone* in the world find an answer to this problem?
- *Any one* of the solutions mentioned would work.
- *Any one* of the people interviewed could do the job.

anyplace, everyplace, someplace   All of these words are indefinite pronouns and should be avoided unless the writer wishes to be vague. In formal writing use *anywhere, everywhere,* and *somewhere.*

anyway, any way   The first term is an adverb meaning "in any manner," "nevertheless," "anyhow." The second term is a noun phrase.

- *Anyway,* I can't go to Cape Cod.
- She can fix my radio in *any way* she likes, as long as it works.

anyways, anywheres   Both terms are used in colloquial speech and in writing that mimics dialect. Avoid the words otherwise.

apprehend, comprehend   *Apprehend* and *comprehend* are not synonyms, although both words are related to the process of understanding. A person *apprehends* in an instant and *comprehends* ("understands thoroughly") over a longer period of time.

as (that, whether)   *As* is not a correct substitute for *that* or *whether.*

- I am not sure *that* [not *as*] you are right.

as to, with respect to (about)   *As to* and *with respect to* may be used instead of *about,* but they often sound stilted and wordy.

WORDY • We argued *with respect to (as to)* the price.
BETTER • We argued *about* the price.

attribute, contribute   The two verbs are often improperly equated. To *attribute* (pronounced *at TRIB* ute) means "to think of something as belonging to, produced by, resulting from, or originating in." To *contribute* means "to give" or "to have a share in bringing about a result."

- The weather forecaster *attributed* the unusually cold weather to the recent volcanic eruption.
- I *contributed* to the blood bank.
- His irresponsible behavior *contributed* to her concern.

Attribute, pronounced *AT tribute*, is also a noun meaning "a trait" or "a characteristic."

- Quickness may be a desirable *attribute*.

averse, adverse   See *adverse, averse*.

awful, awfully   Both words are overused, usually with their colloquial meaning: terrible, terribly. The words should mean "full of awe." In formal writing, use the words only where they will be effective and their meaning precise.

awhile, a while   The first term is an adverb, the second a noun phrase. The two are often improperly used interchangeably. *Awhile* means "for a short period of time."

- I shall stay *awhile* and visit.

A while refers to an unspecified period of time.

- I returned from the store a *while* ago.

The length of time is not specified.

back, again   See *again, back, refer back*.

bad, badly   *Bad* is an adjective that is often used incorrectly as an adverb. *Badly* is the proper adverb form.

INCORRECT • She wanted the prize so *bad* that she cheated on the exam.
CORRECT   • She wanted the prize so *badly* that she practiced every night.
          • The child behaves *badly*.
          • The child's behavior is *bad*.

basically   This adverb is overused, especially at the beginning of sentences, where it becomes a misplaced modifier.

INCORRECT • *Basically,* the answer is correct.
CORRECT   • The answer is *basically* correct.

because   *Because* is a subordinating conjunction and is used increasingly instead of *for*. It introduces a cause-and-effect relationship, so be careful that the clause following *because* is the cause, rather than the effect. Avoid the construction "the reason is *because* ..." Semantically the expression is redundant; grammatically, the sentence requires a noun clause and *because* introduces a subordinate (adverbial) clause.

INCORRECT	• The reason he cannot go is *because* he is ill.
CORRECT	• The reason he cannot go is that he is ill.
	• He cannot go *because* he is ill.

being as, being that (because, since)   *Being as* and *being that*, when used to mean "because" or "since," are informal and are considered inappropriate in formal writing.

INFORMAL	• *Being that* John was sick, the meeting was canceled.
BETTER	• *Because* (or *since*) John was sick, the meeting was canceled.

beside, besides   *Beside* means "next to" and always has an object.

• She was sitting *beside* me.

Besides means "in addition to" and may or may not be followed by an object.

• What have you done *besides* (read a magazine)?

better, best   *Better* (the comparative form of *good*) is used to compare two people, objects, ideas, and so on.

• She is a *better* musician than her mother.

Best (the superlative form of *good*) is used to compare more than two.

• Tom is the *best* tennis player in his class.

between, among   See *among, between*.

blame on, blame for   Although *blame on* has been considered correct usage, the more appropriate and acceptable expression is *blame for*.

• He *blamed* me *for* the loss of his property.

borrow, lend, loan   To *borrow* means "to take or receive (something) with the understanding that one will return it."

• Could I *borrow* your book for a month?

To *lend* (verb) means to let someone use or have something on condition that it will be returned.

• I will *lend* you my book if you promise to return it.

Although *loan* is sometimes used as a verb in informal American English, *lend* is the acceptable form.

both ... and   An error in parallelism often occurs when the expression *both ... and* is used in a sentence.

> INCORRECT • He will advise the director to disclose the truth *both* to the secretary *and* the accountant.
>
> CORRECT • He will advise the director to disclose the truth *to* both the secretary *and* the accountant.
> • He will advise the director to disclose the truth *both* to the secretary *and to* the accountant.

bring, take, fetch   To *bring* is "to lead or carry (a person or thing) with oneself."

- I will buy the books at the store and *bring* them home.
- I will *bring* my mother home.

To take is "to get possession of, to grasp, to seize, or to carry away."

- She will *take* the newspaper away from the table.

Fetch is regional and informal.

bust, burst   *Bust*, meaning "burst," is slang and not acceptable in written language unless you are reproducing or imitating dialect.

but   For centuries *but* has been a problem for grammarians and commentators on usage. The question is whether *but* is a preposition or a conjunction. Theodore Bernstein, in *The Careful Writer*, advises that we consider *but* a preposition when the pronoun ends the sentence (Everyone went *but* me); when the pronoun appears elsewhere in the sentence, it should take the same case as the noun it appears with (No one *but* I knew where he died).

But has a negative force and should not be used before a negative statement.

> INCORRECT • The rain won't delay the game *but* a little while.
> CORRECT • The rain will delay the game only a little while.
> • The rain won't delay the game long.

but what, but that   Most good writers disapprove of *but what* and prefer *but that.*

calculate, reckon, guess   To *calculate* means "to determine by reasoning, common sense, or practical experience."

- The ship's captain *calculated* that they would reach harbor in three days.

To *reckon* in formal use means "to compute, to figure up."

- The accountant *reckoned* the total amount spent on the business trip.

To reckon is also used informally to mean "to consider, to suppose." This meaning is best avoided in formal written work.

To *guess* means "to form a notion without certain knowledge, but on the basis of some probability."

- If he has still not returned, then I *guess* he must be lost.

To *guess* used informally to mean "to suppose," or "to imagine" is also quite acceptable.

- I *guess* you are unhappy about not making the team.

can, may; could, might   *Can*, in formal use, means "to be able to" and *may* is used to show permission or suggest a possibility.

- We *can* finish cleaning in a few hours.
- You *may* stay in my house while you are in town.

Could is the past tense of *can*. *Might* is the past tense of *may*.

cannot, can not   The correct spelling is *cannot*. If you wish to emphasize the *not*, you may keep the words separate and underline *not*.

cannot help but   This phrase contains a double negative: *cannot . . . but*. Therefore, many writers consider *cannot help but* improper for formal writing. Consider your audience and writing context if you are thinking of using *cannot help but*.

INFORMAL • He *cannot help but* like her.
FORMAL   • He *cannot help* liking her.

can't hardly, can't scarcely   *Can't hardly* and *can't scarcely* are double negatives. The two phrases are colloquial and appear more often in spoken than in wirtten language. In informal writing change *can't hardly* and *can't scarcely* to *cannot* or *can't*. In formal writing only *cannot* may be used.

COLLOQUIAL • I *can't hardly* wait for vacation.
            • She *can't scarcely* find any flour.
INFORMAL   • I *can't* wait for vacation.
            • She *can't* find any flour.
FORMAL   • He *cannot* continue the study.

capital, capitol   The two words are frequently confused. In ancient Rome, a *capitol* was a temple. Today the term refers to the buildings in which the U.S. Congress and the state legislatures meet. *Capital*, which has a number of meanings, functions both as an adjective and a noun. Consult your dictionary for the various meanings of *capital*.

cause is due to   This phrase is both redundant and wordy. It adds nothing to the meaning of a sentence and sounds stilted.

INCORRECT • The *cause* of my illness *is due to* a virus.
CORRECT   • The *cause* of my illness *is* a virus.

censor, censure   The two words are often confused. *Censor* can be used as a noun or as a verb. As a noun, it denotes an official who prohibits certain kinds of behavior or who restricts the flow of information.

- The *censor* decided that no one under the age of eighteen could see the movie.

As a verb, *censor* means "to restrict."

- She *censored* her child's books until the youngster reached the age of twelve.

Censure also functions as both a noun and a verb. As a noun, it means "condemnation or disapproving judgment."

- The newspapers were united in their *censure* of the governor's new bill.

As a verb, it means to express strong disapproval.

- The newspaper editorial *censured* the governor's new bill.

center around, center on; revolve on, revolve around
The first and third terms are illogical. One *centers on* something, not *around* it.

INCORRECT	• The discussion *centered around* the problem of student apathy.
CORRECT	• The discussion *centered on* the problem of student apathy.

To *revolve* is "to move in a circular motion." One *revolves around* something, not *on* it.

INCORRECT	• The household *revolved on* the baby's needs.
CORRECT	• The household *revolved around* the baby's needs.

cite, site, sight   Problems arise with these three words because they all sound alike. To *cite*, a verb, means "to quote a written passage" or "to mention something as an example or an illustration."

- The essay *cited* Helen Keller as a woman who overcame great handicaps.

Site as a noun means "a location."

- The old Baker farm was a good *site* for the new nursing home.

Sight is used as a noun, as a verb, and as an adjective. Consult your dictionary for all its possible meanings.

coarse, course   *Coarse* is an adjective meaning "rough" or "crude." *Course* is a noun meaning "a plan of study," "a type of study," or "a way, path, or channel of movement."

- The professor distressed the students in his psychology *course* by using *coarse* language in his lectures.

commentate   This is a pseudoscientific word that expresses in ten letters what a more acceptable verb says in seven. Use *comment*, not *commentate.*

compare with/to   *Compare with* and *compare to* are not synonyms. To *compare* one item *with* another is to show how the two are alike. To *compare* one item *to* another is to compare the known *to* the less well-known.

complement, compliment   The two words sound almost the same and are often confused. *Complement* as a noun refers to someone or something that completes. As a verb, to *complement* is "to complete, especially in a satisfactory way."

- Her voice was a *complement* to her appearance.
- The light dessert *complemented* the heavy meal.

The noun *compliment* refers to words of praise. The verb to *compliment* means "to praise."

- Dr. Brown *complimented* him on his performance.
- She received the *compliments* with grace and pleasure.

comprehend, apprehend   See *apprehend, comprehend.*

consensus of opinion   The expression is redundant, since *consensus* means "an opinion held by all or by most," or "a general agreement of opinion." Use *consensus* alone.

- The *consensus* among the committee members was that the decision should be postponed.

considerable, considerably   *Considerable*, an adjective, is often used when the adverb *considerably* is needed.

INCORRECT   • It hurt *considerable.*
CORRECT   • It hurt *considerably.*

contribute, attribute   See *attribute, contribute.*

convince, persuade   The two words possess different shades of meaning. To *convince* someone is to overcome doubts and reach agreement. To *persuade* is to urge someone to *act* in some way.

- We *convinced* him that the earth is round.
- We *persuaded* her to apply for the job as forest ranger.

could, might   See *can, may; could, might.*

council, counsel, consul   The three words are confused because they sound almost the same. A *council* is "a group or body of individuals gathered to consult, discuss, advise, or make recommendations and decisions." *Counsel* as a noun involves an exchange of ideas or opinions and the advice that results from that exchange. The term also refers to lawyers who are giving legal advice and serving their clients. As a verb, to *counsel* is "to give advice." A *consul* is "an official appointed by one country to live in another country and serve the commercial needs of the home country."

- The members of the mayor's housing *council* voted not to increase rents.
- We followed our agent's *counsel* and did not buy the house.
- Our *consul* in France sent word of the new trade restrictions.

couple of, couple   Both terms refer to "a pair" of "two of a kind." In speech and informal writing, however, they may be used to indicate more than two. *Couple* used before a plural noun without *of* is considered a nonstandard usage.

INFORMAL   • Give me a *couple of* minutes to get dressed.
NONSTANDARD   • Give me a *couple* minutes to get dressed.

credible, credulous, creditable   The three words have three different meanings. *Credible* refers to persons or things that are reliable or believable.

- His story was *credible*.

Credulous refers to a person who tends to believe something too readily or who is convinced too easily.

- He was so *credulous* that he believed the murderer's alibi.

Creditable means "deserving of praise."

- The understudy made a *creditable* attempt to play the starring role.

critique, criticize   *Critique* is a noun meaning "an act of criticizing" or "a critical evaluation or judgment." Do not confuse *critique* with the verb *criticize*.

- The class listened to the teacher's *critique* of the school paper.
- The class *criticized* the school paper.

cute   This colloquial word is used so often and with so many different and frequently unspecified meanings that it has lost whatever precision it once possessed. Use *cute* sparingly in any kind of writing and avoid it in formal writing.

datum, data; phenomenon, phenomena; stratum, strata
The first word in each pair is the singular form of the word. The second in each pair is the plural. Make sure to provide a plural verb for the plural form of each word.

decent, descent   The two words vary slightly in pronunciation, and their spellings are often confused. *Decent*, pronounced *DE cent*, is an adjective meaning "proper and fitting" or "reasonably good, adequate." *Descent (de SCENT)* is a noun referring to "a coming or going down," "a lineage or ancestry," or "a sudden attack."

- The apartment, though no palace, is a *decent* place to live.
- The *descent* from the mountaintop to the valley is dangerous.

delusion, allusion, illusion, elusion   See *allusion, illusion, delusion, elusion.*

desert, dessert   *Desert* is both a verb and a noun. As a verb (pronounced *de SERT*) it means "to leave without permission," "to abandon." *Dessert*, a noun (also pronounced *de SERT*) is "the course served at the end of a meal." The noun *desert* pronounced *DES ert)* is "a dry, barren, sandy region."

device, devise   *Device* is a noun meaning "a plan," "a mechanical contrivance or invention." *Devise* is a verb meaning "to work out," "to create," "to plan."

- The *device* he created looked more like a dinosaur than a solar collector; he had even *devised* a pair of horns for it.

different from, different than   The first expression, which ends with a preposition, must be followed by a noun, a noun phrase, a pronoun, or a noun clause.

- The movie was *different from* what I had expected.

Different than, which ends with a conjunction, is followed by an adverb clause.

- Children at school often behave *differently than* they do at home.

disinterested, uninterested   Although the two words are often used interchangeably to mean "not interested," they are not actually synonyms. *Disinterested* means "impartial or objective."

- We asked John to help settle the dispute because we felt sure he would be *disinterested*—that he would not take sides.

did, done   The first verb, the past tense of *do*, is used alone: I *did*, we *did*, they *did*. Do not use *done* in place of *did*. *Done* is a past participle and always requires an auxiliary verb.

INCORRECT   • I *done* wrong.
CORRECT   • I *have done* wrong.

don't   *Don't* is the contraction of "do not" and is appropriate in informal writing. *Don't* is not the same as *doesn't*, the third person singular contraction for "does not."

INCORRECT   • She *don't like school.*
CORRECT   • She *doesn't* like school.

due to the fact that (because) *Due to the fact that* is wordy and inflated. The shorter and simpler *because* is preferred for clear and concise writing.

- Selma had to leave *because* [not *due to the fact that*] she had an appointment.

each other's, one another's The possessive is formed by adding *'s* to *other* or to *another*. Follow the possessive with a plural noun unless the noun names an abstraction that is awkward as a plural. *Each other* is used for only two, whereas *one another* is used for more than two.

- Sheila and Gail like *each other's* parents.
- The soldiers respected *one another's* courage.

economic, economical Both words are adjectives but cannot be used interchangeably. *Economic* pertains to "the management of expenses, to the production and consumption of wealth, or to the study of economics." *Economical* means "thrifty, not wasteful." *Economical* can be used in contexts that do not deal with wealth.

- The government must review its *economic* policies.
- Filling the closets with newspapers is not a very *economical* use of storage space.

effect, affect See *affect, effect*.

e.g., for example The abbreviation *e.g.*, from the Latin *exempli gratia*, means "for example." Avoid using *e.g.* in formal writing, except in footnotes and within parentheses.

either, neither *Either* and *neither* indicate "one or the other of two."

- She will have to choose *either* Radcliffe or Wellesley.
- *Neither* the book nor the movie interests me.

elicit, illicit The two words are often confused. *Elicit*, a verb, means "to draw forth" or "to cause to be revealed." *Illicit*, an adjective, means "unlawful, improper, prohibited."

- The newscaster *elicited* an angry response.
- The islanders considered holding hands in public to be *illicit* behavior.

elusion, allusion, illusion, delusion See *allusion, illusion, delusion, elusion*.

emigrate, immigrate The two words are often confused. Learn the difference by remembering the prefixes of each one. To *E migrate* is "to leave one's country or region to settle in another." *Emigrate* is usually followed by the preposition *from*. To *IM migrate*, which means "to come to or to go to a new country or region," is often followed by the preposition *to*.

- He *emigrated* from his hometown in northern Yugoslavia, traveled for two years, and finally *immigrated* to America.

eminent, imminent   The two words are pronounced differently (*EM i nent* and *IM mi nent*) and mean different things. *Eminent* means "high, lofty, prominent, noteworthy." *Imminent* means "likely to happen without delay" or "impending, threatening."

- Margaret Fuller was an *eminent* critic and feminist.
- Once they uncovered the clue, his capture seemed *imminent*.

enhance   To *enhance* is "to increase the value or attractiveness of something or someone already possessing value." The term applies to quality rather than quantity.

INCORRECT
- I *enhanced* my investments by purchasing more stocks.

CORRECT
- We *enhanced the value of our home by remodeling the kitchen.*
- She *enhanced* her usefulness to the company by taking a course in marketing.

enthuse   *Enthused* is used informally to mean "enthusiastic" or "showing enthusiasm." The word tends to sound awkward and should be used only after careful consideration of audience and writing contexts.

AWKWARD
- He was *enthused* about the architect's plans.

BETTER
- He was *enthusiastic* about the architect's plans.

etc.   *Etc.*, the abbreviation for the Latin *et cetera*. When used in English it means "and the like," "and the rest," and "and so forth." *Etc.* refers to things rather than to people and should not be used at all unless the other examples can be readily inferred: *apples, oranges, bananas, grapes, etc.* Never use the construction *and etc;* it is redundant. See *and etc.* above.

everyone, every one   *Everyone*, an indefinite pronoun, refers to people in a general way. *Every one*, a phrase, refers more specifically to "any person or thing named."

- *Everyone* in the school was invited to the party
- *Every one* of the students in that class was caught cheating.

As an indefinite pronoun, *everyone* takes a singular verb.

- *Everyone* in the stable *was* delighted to see the new colt.

everyplace, everywhere   See *anyplace, someplace, everyplace*.

except, accept   See *accept, except*.

excess, access   See *access, excess*.

factor, contributing factor   *Factor*, which refers to any of the circumstances or conditions that bring about a result, is often incorrectly used to mean "item" or "point." Since the definition of *factor* includes the idea of cause, the term *contributing factor* is redundant.

INCORRECT • Five *factors* must be covered in your essay.
CORRECT • Five *points* must be covered in your essay.
INCORRECT • The dean's insensitivity to students was a *contributing factor* in their protest.
CORRECT • In preparing a report about the firing of Dean Hurley, you must consider all the *factors* that led to it.

famous, notorious   Both adjectives refer to fame, but their connotations differ. Use *famous* when the emphasis is positive, *notorious* when it is negative.

• Lincoln's words in the Gettysburg Address are *famous*.
• Casanova was *notorious* for his seductive behavior.

fetch, bring, take   See *bring, take, fetch*.

few, little; fewer, less   *Few* and *fewer* deal with persons or objects that can be counted. *Little* and *less* refer to things that can be measured or estimated.

• A *few* of us will go to the theater.
• Most members of the group have *little* interest in drama.
• This time I'll take *fewer* books out of the library, since I'll have *less* time to read than I had before.

finalize   *Finalize* is a pseudoscientific term. It inflates diction and makes no contribution to the meaning of the sentence. Use *complete* or *finish* instead of *finalize*.

fine   The word is often used informally to mean "very well."

• I am feeling *fine* this morning.

As a description of an event—a *fine* time, a *fine* movie—it is an overworked word, like *wonderful* and *good*, and should be used with care. It has precision when one makes a *fine* point or a *fine* distinction.

foot, feet   *Foot* is singular; *feet* is plural. The singular rather than the plural form is used to qualify a noun: an eight-*foot* ladder.

formally, formerly   The two words can be confused when they are mispronounced. Form*ally* means "in a formal manner" or "with regard to form." Form*erly* means "previously."

• The company *formally* declared that it would purchase Cafex Products, Incorporated.
• Anita, who was *formerly* an announcer for WCAT radio, now works for public television.

former, latter *Former* and *latter* refer to two persons or items in proper order. *Former* refers to the first item named and *latter* to the second item named.

- In explaining the difference between cotton and wool, she noted that the *former* is a plant product, while the *latter* is of animal origin.

Use *former* and *latter* carefully. If a sentence is long and complicated, the reader may not be able to identify either the *former* or the *latter*.

forth, fourth *Forth* is an adverb meaning "out" or "forward." *Fourth* is that item in a series between the third and the fifth.

- The *fourth* petitioner to come *forth* informed the king that his daughter had eloped with the prince.

funny *Funny* (like *good, cute,* and *nice*) is such an overused word that its meaning has become vague and much of its power has been lost. Avoid *funny* unless you can use it precisely and effectively.

get, got, gotten Forms of the verb to *get* are used variously in speech and in writing. The verb may mean something other than obtain (check dictionary for basic definition), since the meaning of *get* is often vague.

INFORMAL:
- John O'Hara really *gets* me.
- Her song really *gets* [got to] the audience.

FORMAL:
- *Get* me some iced tea, please.
- I must *get* home by eleven.

good, well *Good* is an adjective that is often misused as an adverb. *Well* is the proper adverb form.

| INCORRECT | • He writes *good.* |
| CORRECT | • He writes *well.* |

hadn't ought to, ought not; had ought to, ought to have
The first and third phrases are informal and are used more in speaking than in writing. *Ought not* and *ought to have* are the formal versions.

INFORMAL	• He *hadn't ought to* have gone.
FORMAL	• He *ought not to* have gone.
INFORMAL	• Mary *had ought to* buy bread.
FORMAL	• Mary *ought to have* bought bread.

hardly See *can't hardly.*

healthful, healthy The two adjectives cannot be used interchangeably, since they have different meanings. *Healthful* means "promoting, producing, or maintaining good health." *Healthy* means "having good health" or "resulting from good health."

- Their training program, which stresses good diet, is a *healthful* one.
- The soccer players are *healthy*.

hopefully   *Hopefully* is an adverb that formally means "full of hope." It is often used at the beginning of a sentence to mean "I hope," "it is hoped," and so on. Many, however, consider this use incorrect.

QUESTIONABLE   • *Hopefully,* you'll be accepted into medical school.

CORRECT   • You'll be accepted into medical school, *I hope*.

i.e., that is   The abbreviation for the Latin *id est, i.e.* means "that is." In formal writing, spell out the phrase in English. Restrict the use of the abbreviation to footnotes and parenthetical references.

if and when, when and if   Both expressions are clichés. Use one word and choose according to the point you wish to make.

- *If* we go, we will take my mother.
- *When* we go, we will take my mother.

illicit, elicit   See *elicit, illicit.*

illusion, allusion, delusion, elusion   See *allusion, illusion, delusion, elusion.*

immigrate, emigrate   See *emigrate, immigrate.*

imminent, eminent   See *eminent, imminent.*

imply, infer   The meanings of the two words are often confused. To *imply* is "to indicate something by indirection, hint, or suggestion." To *infer* means "to conclude on the basis of what is known or generally assumed."

- What meaning is *implied* by that remark?
- What can we *infer* from the details of this photograph?

impracticable, impractical   The two words are often confused. *Impracticable* means "not able to be carried out or used in the way intended." *Impractical* means "not workable or useful" or "given to theorizing."

- Those shoes are attractive but *impracticable* for my kind of walking.
- My plans are always creative but often *impractical*.

in, into, in to   *In* as a preposition suggests location, while *into* specifies motion from one place to another.

- He sat *in* the chair until he walked *into* the den.

When using *in* as an adverb, keep it separate from the preposition *to*.

- Helen refused to give *in* to the pain.

in regard to, in regards to, as regards   These phrases are wordy and overused. *Concerning* and *regarding* are shorter and more precise.

in spite of (despite) the fact that   Both *in spite of the fact that* and *despite the fact that* are wordy and inflated subordinating conjunctions. *Although* or *though* is preferable for simple and concise writing.

- *Although* [not *in spite of the fact that*] I have a cold, I will attend the meeting.

in terms of   The expression is wordy, vague, and often redundant. Try to find reasonable, brief substitutes.

INCORRECT • We must make a decision *in terms of* John.
CORRECT   • We must make a decision *about* John.

in the case of, along the lines of   Both expressions are wordy and stilted. Shorten and simplify.

INCORRECT:
- *In the case of* my parents . . .
- *Along the lines of* our conversation yesterday . . .

CORRECT:
- *In* my parents' *case* . . .
- *In line with* our conversation yesterday . . .

incredible, incredulous   Use *incredible* to describe a person, an object, or a concept that is unbelievable or too improbable or unusual to be possible. Use *incredulous* to refer to a person who is unwilling or unable to believe, or to a response, such as a smile, that indicates disbelief.

- Columbus's contemporaries thought his ideas were *incredible*.
- Mary is an *incredible* woman: she's bright, attractive, friendly, and energetic.
- The knight was *incredulous* when he saw the dragon.
- Sarah gave Paul an *incredulous* look—she was unable to accept his excuse.

infer, imply   See *imply, infer.*

inferior than (inferior to, worse than)   *Inferior than* is not an idiom in American English. Proper forms are *inferior to* and *worse than.*

inside of (inside); outside of (outside)   *Inside of* and *outside of* are incorrect. Use *inside* or *outside.*

INCORRECT:
- He looked *inside of* the box.
- His wife looked *outside of* the house.

CORRECT:
- He looked *inside* the box.
- His wife looked *outside* the house.

intensify, aggravate   See *aggravate, intensify.*

irregardless   *Irregardless,* which is sometimes used in spoken language when *regardless* is meant, is illogical. It is inappropriate in formal writing.

it is ... that   The expression is deadwood. Avoid this construction by rephrasing.

DEADWOOD   • *It is* a job *that* we are worried about.
BETTER   • We are worried about that job.

its, it's   The two terms are often confused. *Its* is the possessive form of *it. It's* is the contraction for "it is."

- The cat licked *its* paw.
- I doubt that *it's* [it is] possible.

kind of a, kind of; sort of a, sort of   Use *kind of* and *sort of* to mean "type of," not "somewhat," and do not follow the preposition *of* with the article *a.*

INCORRECT:
- I feel *kind of* (or *sort of*) sick.
- She doesn't like that *kind of a* (or *sort of a*) movie.

CORRECT:
- I feel *somewhat* sick.
- She doesn't like that *kind of* (or *sort of*) movie.

later, latter   *Later* is an adverb meaning "after some time, subsequently." *Latter,* an adjective, means "nearer the end" or "the second of two mentioned."

- Marie will pick up her car *later.*
- She had to choose between chicken and fish; she chose the *latter.*

See also *former, latter.*

lead, led   *Lead,* when pronounced with a short *e,* is a mineral. *Led* is the past tense of the verb *to lead* (long *e*).

- Dan *led* the trapped workers out of the *lead* mine.

lend, loan   See *borrow, lend, loan.*

let's, let's us   *Let's* is the contraction for "let us" and is appropriate in informal speech and writing. *Let's us* is never correct, because *let us us* makes no sense.

level   This word is overused and wordy when worked into phrases like "*level* an attack" or "at the *literal* level." Use *level* only when you wish to indicate rank or degree.

- He reached the fourth *level* of proficiency and was unable to progress any further.

liable (to), apt (to)   See *apt (to), liable (to), prone to.*

lie, lay   *Lie* and *lay* are often confused. To *lie* means "to recline." To *lay* means "to place." The past tense of *lie* is *lay.*

INCORRECT	• *Lie* that glass on the table.
	• *Lay* on the floor and begin your exercise.
CORRECT	• *Lay* that glass on the table.
	• *Lie* on the floor and begin your exercises.

like, as   *Like* can be used as an adjective, as a verb, or as a preposition. In colloquial speech it is often used as a conjunction meaning "as," "as if," or "in the way that."

COLLOQUIAL	• My ten-year-old brother acts just *like* I did when I was his age.
FORMAL	• My ten-year-old brother acts just *as* I did when I was his age.

Remember that *like* is used with a noun or pronoun that is not followed by a verb.

- My brother looks *like* me.

little, less   See *few, little; fewer, less.*

loan, lend   See *borrow, lend, loan.*

loose, lose   The words may be confused if they are mispronounced. *Loose* rhymes with *noose* and means "unbound, slack, not tight." *Lose* rhymes with *booze* and means "misplace" or "fail to win or gain."

- A criminal is running *loose* in the county.
- This knot is *loose.*
- I often *lose* my umbrella.
- She didn't want to *lose* her chance to go to London.

lots of, a whole lot of   *Lots of* is often used to mean "many" in informal speech and writing. *Many* is preferred in formal language. *A whole lot of* is colloquial.

mad (angry, annoyed)   In colloquial language, *mad* is often used to mean "angry" or "annoyed."

- My sister was really *mad* at her fiance.

Consider your audience and writing context when choosing between *mad* and *angry* (or *annoyed*).

may, might   See *can, may; could, might.*

moral, morale   Confusion occurs in pronunciation and meaning. *Moral (MOR al)* is an adjective that means "relating to the distinction between right and wrong in behavior or character." As a noun, *moral* refers to the lesson—usually one of right and wrong—of a story or an incident. *Morale (mo RAL)*, a noun, refers to an attitude of courage, discipline, or enthusiasm in the face of hardship or difficulty.

- John is a highly *moral* person.
- The *moral* of the story is that crime does not pay.
- My *morale* was high when I began my paper; it lessened as I did the revision.
- The *morale* of the POWs remained high throughout their captivity.

most, almost   In informal usage, *most* is often used for *almost* ("Nearly"). Use *almost* in formal writing.

INFORMAL   • *Most* of us liked the movie.
FORMAL   • *Almost* all of us liked the movie.

much, many   *Much* is used with singular nouns. *Many* is used with plural nouns.

- He gives his dog *much* love.
- My daughter sent *many* kisses in the mail.

myself, I   *Myself* is a reflexive pronoun (as in I pinched *myself*) or an intensifier (I *myself* saw the judge smile). If you wonder whether *myself* is called for in a particular sentence, read the word as a single subject or object, not as a compound.

INCORRECT   • Tom and *myself* went to the lake.

We do not say, "*myself* went to the lake," but rather "Tom and *I* went to the lake." We do not say, "She played cards with *myself*," but "She played cards with *me*."

CORRECT   • She played cards with Sheila and *me*.
                • I prefer going *myself*.
                • I taught *myself* how to cook.

neither, either   See *either, neither.*

neither ... or; neither ... nor   When using *neither* as a conjunction, pair it with *nor*, not with *or*.

INCORRECT   • *Neither* the book *or* the movie was interesting.
CORRECT   • *Neither* the book *nor* the movie was interesting.

not too, not that   *Not too* or *not that* is often used informally for *not very*. Consider your audience and writing context when choosing the appropriate phrase.

INFORMAL	• The TV show was *not too* (or *not that*) enjoyable.
FORMAL	• The TV show was *not very* enjoyable.

notorious, famous   See *famous, notorious.*

nowhere near, not nearly   *Nowhere near* is sometimes used informally for *not nearly.* Consider your audience and writing context before choosing the appropriate term.

- It was *not nearly* time to depart.

number, amount   See *amount, number.*

of (have)   Careless speakers often say *of* when they mean *have,* as in *could of, should of, must of.* Auxiliary verbs must be followed by *main* verbs, not by prepositions.

INCORRECT	• I must *of* done my homework.
	• My mother would *of* punished me if she had known.
CORRECT	• I must *have* done my homework.
	• My mother would *have* punished me if she had known.

off of (off, from)   *Off of* is an incorrect coupling of prepositions. Use *off* or *from* in its place.

INCORRECT	• The bird flew *off of* the feeder.
CORRECT	• The bird flew *off* the feeder.
INCORRECT	• He threw the line *off of* the pier.
CORRECT	• He threw the line *from* the pier.

Sometimes *off* is incorrectly used for *from.*

INCORRECT	• I have to borrow a book *off* Linda.
CORRECT	• I have to borrow a book *from* Linda.

oftentimes, often   *Oftentimes* is wordy and inflated. *Often* should be used.

on account of (because, because of)   *On account of* is wordy as a preposition and should never be used to introduce a subordinate clause. Use *because of* or *because* instead of *on account of.*

INCORRECT:
- I failed *on account of* my laziness.
- Jay left *on account of* he felt sick.

CORRECT:
- I failed *because of* my laziness.
- Jay left *because* he felt sick.

on the part of   Avoid using *on the part of* when you can use *for, by,* or *among* instead.

- Protests were made *by* (not *on the part of*) the students.

one another's, each other's   See *each other's, one another's.*

orientate, orient   To *orientate* is a pseudoscientific word. To *orient* is the proper form of the verb.

- Does it take you long to *orient* (not *orientate*) yourself?

overall   *Overall* as an adjective meaning "total" or "complete" is overused and makes no sense, as in "John is an *overall* good guy." Use a substitute, like *totally* or *completely*, whenever possible.

passed, past   The two words are easy to confuse because their pronunciations are similar. *Passed* is the past tense of the verb pass (I *passed* the test). *Past* is used as a noun, as an adjective, as an adverb, or as a preposition.

- The *past* is history.
- *Past* events have much to teach us.
- The marchers trooped *past*.
- We walked *past* the shop.

peace, piece   *Peace* is a condition of "freedom from war, public disturbance, or disorder." A *piece* of something is a portion of it.

- He declared that he would not eat another *piece* of banana cream pie until there was *peace* in the house.

personal, personnel   Confusion arises over pronunciation. *Personal* (pronounced *PER sonal*) means "relating to the individual, to private concerns, to the personality." *Personnel* (pronounced *person NEL*) refers to the workforce, or staff, of an employer or to the office that hires employees.

persuade, convince   See *convince, persuade*.

phenomenon, phenomena   See *datum, data; phenomenon, phenomena; stratum, strata*.

plenty, very   *Plenty* can be used as a noun but should not be used as an adverb meaning "very."

INCORRECT	• That pie tasted *plenty* good.
CORRECT	• That pie tasted *very* good.
	• My mother made *plenty* of chicken.
	• America is the land of *plenty*.

precede, proceed   Both words are verbs, and their meanings are often confused. To *precede* means "to go before." To *proceed* means "to go on" or "to move along."

- Because John was shorter, he *preceded* Bill in line.
- After the break, we shall *proceed* with the discussion.

predominant, predominate   The two words are often confused because their pronunciations are similar. *Predominant,* is an adjective meaning "having authority or influence over others." *Predominate* is a verb meaning "to hold sway; to be the most important."

- The vice-president, though a quiet man, was a *predominant* figure in the company.
- His words *predominated* at any meeting.

premiere   *Premiere*, meaning "the first performance" is a noun and should not be used as a verb.

INCORRECT • The play *premiered* off-Broadway.
CORRECT   • The *premiere* of the play was a great success.
           • The success of the *premiere* surprised the critics.

presently, now   The two words are often confused, yet they deal with time in different ways. Use *presently* to indicate that something will happen in a little while. Use *now* to refer to something occurring at the present moment.

- Our guest will arrive *presently*—probably before I've finished dressing.
- I have no more money *now* and will have to wait until payday.

previous to, prior to (before)   While technically correct, both terms are wordy and stilted. Use *before* instead.

principal, principle   The two words are frequently confused. *Principal* as an adjective means "first in rank or importance." As a noun, *principal* refers to the head of a school. *Principle*, always a noun, means "ultimate source or cause," "fundamental truth," or "rule of conduct."

- The *principal* of the school is a forceful person.
- Pavarotti had the *principal* role in the opera.
- I gave him my *principal* reason for leaving.
- Humanitarian *principles* are important to the institution.
- What is the *principle* upon which the law is based?

proceed, precede   See *precede, proceed.*

prophecy, prophesy   Avoid confusing pronunciation and meaning. *Prophecy (PROF a see)*, a noun, is the prediction of the future or the content of the prediction. *Prophesy (PROF a si)*, the verb form, means "to predict."

- Christians believe that the *prophecies* of the Old Testament are fulfilled in the New.
- The speaker *prophesied* that death and destruction would result from the use of nuclear power.

proved, proven   Both words can be used as the past participle of the verb *to prove.*

- It has *proven* (or *proved*) to be true.

provided, provided that, providing With the meaning "on condition that," all three forms are acceptable, but *provided* is most appropriate in formal writing.

- You can play any music you like, *provided* it is not too loud.

purposeful(ly), purposely *Purposeful*, an adjective, means "having a specific goal." The adverb form is *purposefully*. The noun form is *purposefulness*.

- He approached the project *purposefully*, knowing exactly what he wished to accomplish.

Purposely, an adverb, means "deliberately, intentionally"—that is, "on purpose."

- I *purposely* left the radio on when I went out so that the house would not appear empty.

quiet, quite *Quiet* means "making no noise." *Quite* is an intensifier adverb, like *very* and *rather*.

- Little Ricky is *quite* well-behaved; in fact, it's unusual for a four-year-old to be so *quiet*.

quote, quotation *Quote*, a verb, is sometimes used as a noun. Such use, however, should be avoided in formal speech and writing. Use *quotation* instead.

INFORMAL • That *quote* is one of my favorites.
FORMAL • That *quotation* is one of my favorites.

raise, rise Distinguish between the two verbs by remembering that *raise* ("to lift," "to act as a parent to") takes an object. To *rise* ("to go higher," "to get up") does not ordinarily take an object.

- John *raises* Irish setters.
- Mother *raised* the curtain.
- I felt my spirits *rise* when I finished the paper.
- The kite will *rise* quickly.

rarely ever, seldom ever In both phrases, the *ever* is redundant. Use *rarely* or *seldom*.

reason is because, reason is that The construction "reason is ... because" is often used in informal speech for "reason is ... that."

INFORMAL • The *reason* for his departure *is because* his mother is ill.
FORMAL • The *reason* for his departure *is that* his mother is ill.

Since both phrases are redundant, the sentence can be rewritten more concisely.

- He departed *because* his mother is ill.

refer, allude   See *allude, refer.*

refer, refer back   See *again, back, refer back.*

regrettably, regretfully   The two words are often confused. Both are adverbs and share the stem word *regret.* Use *regrettably* to mean "unfortunately." Use *regretfully* to mean "remorsefully, sorrowfully."

- Brian is so sensitive to criticism that his teachers have been *regrettably* negligent in correcting him.
- *Regretfully,* my daughter told me that she could not come home for the holidays.

respectfully, respectively   *Respectfully* means "full of respect or deference." *Respectively* indicates "each one of two or more, in the order named."

- She signed the letter, "Respectfully yours."
- The book, the statue, and the plaque were given to Liz, Marvin, and Lisa, *respectively.*

revolve on, revolve around   See *center around, center on; revolve on, revolve around.*

right, rite   Do not confuse these words just because they sound alike. *Right* generally means "correct." A *rite* is "a ritual or ceremony performed according to tradition, custom, or rule."

- I chose the *right* answer.
- The initiation *rite* was difficult and terrifying.

scarcely   See *can't hardly; can't scarcely.*

seldom ever   See *rarely ever, seldom ever.*

set, sit   The two verbs are often confused. *Set* is used when its subject *places* something. *Sit* is used when its subject is, for example, in a chair—that is, is remaining seated.

- My mother *set* the vase on the sideboard.
- She *sits* at the head of the table.

Some exceptions appear in the language: the sun *sets;* liquids that become solid also *set*—concrete *sets,* gelatin *sets,* varnish *sets,* and so on.

site, sight, cite   See *cite, site, sight.*

sometime, some time   *Sometime* is generally used as an adverb meaning "at some unknown or unspecified time." *Some time,* a noun phrase, indicates a period of time.

- She told her brother that she would take him to the beach *sometime.*
- We will need *some time* to cross the desert, even in a car.

somewheres, somewhere *Somewheres,* the nonstandard version of *somewhere,* should be avoided in both informal and formal writing.

stationary, stationery The two words are easy to confuse. Station*ary* is an adjective meaning "not moving, fixed." Station*ery* is "writing material" bought from a station*er.*

- The farmer thought the barn was *stationary;* the tornado proved him wrong.
- The *stationery* was a creamy-white vellum with blue trim.

stratum, strata See *datum, data; phenomenon, phenomena; stratum, strata.*

supposed to, used to When using these phrases, be sure to include the *d* at the end of the first word.

I N C O R R E C T	• She was *suppose to* mow the lawn.
	• Tom *use to* live next door.
C O R R E C T	• Miranda was *supposed to* babysit this evening.
	• I *used to* like rock music; as I grew older, I liked it less and less.

sure (surely, certainly) In colloquial speech and writing, *sure* is often substituted for the adverbs *surely* and *certainly.* Consider your audience and writing context before using *sure* as an adverb.

I N F O R M A L	• You're *sure* right in not believing that story.
F O R M A L	• You are *surely* correct in your understanding of this poem.

take, bring, fetch See *bring, take, fetch.*

take and . . . The phrase *take and . . .* is colloquial and wordy. Avoid it in both informal and formal writing.

C O L L O Q U I A L	• Feeling ornery, he *took and* smashed the sugar bowl.
I N F O R M A L	• Feeling mean, he smashed the sugar bowl.
F O R M A L	• Enraged, he shattered the sugar bowl.

than, then The two words are often confused. Use *than* when making a comparison, *then* when referring to time.

- My stomach feels better *than* it did an hour ago.
- First, I drank some ginger ale; *then* I tried herbal tea.

that, which, who In general, use *that* to introduce restrictive clauses—clauses that provide essential identifying information.

- This is the book *that I borrowed from the library.* (The *that* clause identifies *book.*)

Use *which,* as a rule, to introduce nonrestrictive clauses—clauses that provide additional rather than essential information.

- Here is a copy of David's new book, *which I borrowed from the library.*

(The *which* is not needed to identify *book.*)

Use *who,* in both restrictive and nonrestrictive clauses, to refer to people (rather than objectives) and to pets or animals that are personified (thought of in human terms).

- The woman *who* is wearing the gray suit is my mother.
- In the story, it is the dog *who* is the hero.

their, they're, there   The three words are easily confused, since they sound alike. *Their* is a possessive adjective and always comes before a noun. (The related word *theirs* is used without the noun.) *They're* is a contraction for "they are." *There,* an adverb, indicates a place or introduces a sentence with a delayed subject.

- *Their* salad bowl is on the counter.
- The salad bowl is *theirs.*
- *They're* going home tomorrow.
- I sat *there* during the performances.
- They stopped working *there* yesterday evening and began again this morning.
- *There* are several things we have to do today.

theirselves, themselves   *Theirselves* appears in some dialects of American English. Avoid using *theirselves* in both informal and formal writing unless you are reproducing or imitating dialect.

there is, there are   Avoid beginning a sentence with *there is* or *there are* where possible; the constructions are wordy and vague. If the expressions are necessary, determine the number of the verb (singular or plural) by the subject of the sentence.

- *There is* a frog sitting on my living room carpet.
- *There are* five more in the kitchen.

this   *This* is a demonstrative pronoun and, as such, must refer to a noun. In informal speech, *this* is often used to refer to a phrase or to a whole clause. The practice leads to vagueness and, sometimes, to confusion.

this here, these here, that there, those there   Although the four phrases can be found in some dialects of American English, they do not belong in formal writing. Use these expressions only when reproducing or imitating dialect.

though, although   See *although, though.*

thusly, thus   *Thusly* is not actually a word; some writer or speaker may have created it to make *thus* sound more impressive. *Thus* is the appropriate word.

till, until; til, 'til, 'till   *Till* and *until* can be used interchangeably. *Til, 'til,* and *'till* are not appropriate in formal writing.

to, too, two   The three words are confused because they sound alike. *To* is a preposition and part of the infinitive of a verb. *Too,* an adverb, means "in addition," "besides," "more than enough." *Two* is the number between *one* and *three.*

- She drove *to* Hartford in her mother's car.
- She wants *to* help us.
- He is intelligent, handsome, and friendly, *too.*
- We own *two* cars.

to, at   In some regions of the country, *to* is used in place of *at* in constructions such as, "He's *to* camp," or "She's *to* the movies." These constructions should properly use *at.* Use *to* only if you are reproducing or imitating dialect.

try and, try to   The phrase *try and* sometimes appears in colloquial speech. In formal writing, *try to* is preferred. Consider the audience and writing context before choosing between *try and* or *try to.*

COLLOQUIAL	• Please *try and* find the book.
FORMAL	• Please *try to* find the book.

type, type of, -type   In colloquial language, the word *type* is sometimes used for the phrase *type of. Type of* is preferred in formal writing.

COLLOQUIAL	• This *type* car saves gas.
FORMAL	• This *type of* car saves gas.

The suffix *-type* also appears in contemporary writing: a *mystical-type* experience, essentially *primitive-type* behavior. The suffix rarely adds meaning to the sentence and sometimes confuses the meaning. Readers who dislike pseudoscientific jargon and buzz words will probably find *-type* offensive.

uninterested, disinterested   See *disinterested, uninterested.*

utilize, use   *Utilize,* a verb meaning "to put to use" or "to make practical use of," often appears in bureaucratic language in place of *use.*

INCORRECT	• The cat utilized the litter box.
CORRECT	• The cat used the litter box.

Distinguish between definitions and choose the appropriate word for your audience.

wait on (wait for)   *Wait on* is colloquial for *wait for.* Consider the audience and writing context, then choose the appropriate term.

well, good   See *good, well.*

when and if   See *if and when, when and if.*

where ... at, where ... to (where)   *Where ... at* and *where ... to* are often used colloquially for *where.* Use *where* in formal writing contexts.

- I don't know *where* you are [not *where* you are *at*].

which, who, that   See *that, which, who.*

whose, who's   *Whose* is a possessive pronoun often used in questions or an adjective indicating ownership. *Who's* is the contraction for "who is."

- *Whose* jacket is that?
- The girl *whose* jacket you found is from Tennessee.
- *Who's* coming to the party?

-wise   The suffix *-wise* is often used to mean "with respect to." Use of the suffix often produces a confusing construction that fails to add meaning to the sentence.

INCORRECT   • *Healthwise,* we are all fine.
CORRECT   • We are all healthy.

with respect to   See *as regards, as to, with respect to.*

your, you're   *Your* is a possessive pronoun and should modify a noun. (The related word *yours* is used without the noun.) *You're* is the contraction for "you are."

- *Your* essay was excellent.
- I've read Jane's essay but not *yours.*
- Did you say that *you're* feeling ill?

Acknowledgments

CHAPTER 1

Carroll, Lewis. *Alice in Wonderland* and *Through the Looking Glass.* New York: Grosset & Dunlap, 1957.

Cooper, Kenneth H. *The New Aerobics.* New York: M. Evans & Co., 1970.

Frank, Anne. *The Diary of Anne Frank.* New York: Modern Library, 1952.

Hawthorne, Nathaniel. *American Notebooks.* The Centenary Edition of the Works of Nathaniel Hawthorne, edited by Claude M. Simpson, vol. 8. Columbus, Ohio: Ohio University Press, 1972.

"Iowa Homesteader's Wife." Photograph by Russell Lee. 1936.

McGuire, Judith Brockenbrough. Quoted in *Heroines of Dixie: Winter of Desperation*, edited by Katherine M. Jones. New York: Ballantine Books, 1975.

Pirsig, Robert M. Excerpt from *Zen and the Art of Motorcycle Maintenance.* Copyright © 1974 by Robert M. Pirsig. By permission of William Morrow & Company.

Williams, William Carlos. "How to Write." In *New Directions in Prose and Poetry*, edited by James Laughlin. New York: New Directions Publishing Corp., 1936.

Woolf, Virginia. *A Writer's Diary: Being an Extract from the Diary of Virginia Woolf*, edited by Leonard Woolf. New York: Harcourt Brace Jovanovich, 1973.

CHAPTER 2

Carson, Rachel. *Silent Spring.* Greenwich, Conn.: Fawcett, 1962.

"Drive a Classic. Win a Classic." Advertisement. Reproduced courtesy of Jaguar Rover Triumph Inc.

Friedman, Milton. Excerpt from "Economic Controls vs. Personal Freedom." An article that appeared in Abbott Laboratories' *Commitment* magazine, Spring 1977.

Jones, Jenkin Lloyd. "A Good Case for Miniver Cheevy." Los Angeles: Los Angeles Times Syndicate, 1980.

Lebowitz, Fran. *Metropolitan Life.* New York: Fawcett, 1979.

Mornell, Pierre. *Passive Men, Wild Women.* Copyright © 1979 by Pierre Mornell, M.D. Reprinted by permission of Simon & Schuster, a Division of Gulf & Western Corporation.

Sayers, Dorothy L. *Clouds of Witness.* New York: Harper & Row, 1956.

Trippett, Frank. Excerpt from "A New Distrust of the Experts." Reprinted by permission from *Time*, The Weekly Newsmagazine; Copyright Time Inc. 1979.

"What Does a Woman Want?—Sigmund Freud." Advertisement. Reproduced courtesy of Intergold.

CHAPTER 3

Barzun, Jacques and Graff, Henry F. *The Modern Researcher.* Reprinted by permission of Harcourt Brace Jovanovich, Inc.

Norris, Frank. *McTeague.* New York: Holt Rinehart, 1950.

Sagan, Carl. "Science Fiction—A Personal View." From *Broca's Brain: Reflections on the Romance of Science.* Copyright © 1979 by Carl Sagan. Reprinted by permission of Random House, Inc.

Wolfe, Tom. Excerpt from *The Right Stuff.* Copyright © 1979 by Tom Wolfe. Reprinted by permission of Farrar, Straus & Giroux, Inc.

CHAPTER 4

Balsdon, J.P.V.D. *Romans and Aliens.* Chapel Hill, N.C.: University of North Carolina Press, 1979.

Beckett, Samuel. Excerpt from *Molloy.* Quoted in *On Being Blue: A Philosophical Inquiry*, by William Gass. Boston: Godine, 1976.

Bettelheim, Bruno. Excerpt from *The Uses of Enchantment: The Meaning and Importance of Fairy Tales.* Copyright © 1976 by Bruno Bettelheim. Reprinted by permission of Alfred A. Knopf, Inc.

Cross, Donna Woolfolk. *Word Abuse: How the Words We Use, Use Us.* New York: Coward, McCann & Geoghegan, 1979.

Dillard, Annie. Excerpt from *Pilgrim at Tinker's Creek.* Copyright © 1974 by Annie Dillard. Reprinted by permission of the author and her agent, Blanche C. Gregory, Inc.

Fothergill, Robert A. *Private Chronicles: A Study of English Diaries.* New York: Oxford University Press, 1974.

Grafton, Samuel. "Choice and Chance in Human Affairs." *Lithopinion*, vol. 3, no. 4, issue 12 (1968), p. 13.

Heilbruner, Robert L. *The Worldly Philosophers*, rev. ed. New York: Simon & Schuster, 1972.

Packard, Vance. *The Waste Makers.* New York: David McKay, 1960.

Pagels, Elaine. *The Gnostic Gospels.* New York: Random House, 1979.

Rombauer, Irma S. and Becker, Marion Rombauer. *The Joy of Cooking.* New York: Signet, 1974.

Rowling, Marjorie. *Life in Medieval Times.* New York: Paragon Book Reprint Corp., 1973.

Selzer, Richard. *Mortal Lessons: Notes on the Art of Surgery.* New York: Simon & Schuster, 1974.

Synge, J. M. Excerpt from *The Aran Islands.* In *Poems, Plays and Prose.* New York: E. P. Dutton, 1968.

Thomas, Lewis. "Ceti." From *The Lives of a Cell: Notes of a Biology Watcher.* Copyright 1972 by the Massachusetts Medical Society. These essays originally appeared in the *New England Journal of Medicine.* Reprinted by permission of Viking Penguin Inc.

Thomas, Lewis. "On Warts." From *The Medusa and the Snail: More Notes of a Biology Watcher.* New York: Viking, 1979.

Toffler, Alvin. *The Third Wave.* New York: William Morrow & Company, 1980.

Truzzi, Marcello. "On Keeping Things up in the Air." *Natural History,* December 1979, p. 45.

Winks, Robert W., ed. *The Historian as Detective: Essays on Evidence.* New York: Harper & Row, 1970.

CHAPTER 5

Aleichem, Sholom. *Adventures of Mottel, the Cantor's Son.* Trans. Tamara Kahana. New York: Collier Books, 1961.

Austen, Jane. *Emma.* Edited by Stephen Parrish. New York: Norton, 1972.

Blake, Nicholas [C. Day Lewis]. *The Whisper in the Gloom.* New York: Harper & Row, 1954.

Bowen, Elizabeth. *A World of Love.* New York: Avon Books, 1978.

Clemens, Samuel L. [Mark Twain]. *Life on the Mississippi.* New York: NAL, 1961.

Dix, Dorothea [pseudo.]. "Are Women Growing Selfish?" In the New Orleans *Daily Picayune,* 15 August 1897.

"General Confession for Morning & Evening Prayer." In *The Book of Common Prayer.* New York: Oxford University Press, 1928.

Jungk, Robert. *Brighter than a Thousand Suns: A Personal History of the Atomic Scientists.* Translated by James Cleugh. New York: Harcourt Brace Jovanovich, 1970.

Mitchell, Richard. In *The Underground Grammarian.* May 1980.

Mowat, Farley. *People of the Deer.* Boston: Little, Brown & Co., 1952.

Pirsig, Robert M. Excerpt from *Zen and the Art of Motorcycle Maintenance.* Copyright © 1974 by Robert M. Pirsig. By permission of William Morrow & Company.

Selzer, Richard. *Mortal Lessons: Notes on the Art of Surgery.* New York: Simon & Schuster, 1964.

Strachey, Lytton. "Florence Nighingale." In *Eminent Victorians.* New York: Random House, 1918.

"V-E Day." In Joseph Satin, *Reading Literature.* Boston: Houghton Mifflin, 1964.

Welty, Eudora. *Losing Battles.* New York: Random House, 1970.

Wilson, Edmund. "The Old Stone House." Quoted in *Open Form: Essays for Our Time.* New York: Harcourt, Brace & World, 1970.

CHAPTER 6

Baker, Russell. "Little Red Riding Hood Revisited." © 1980 by The New York Times Company.

Blumenthal, Michael. "Liberalism in the 1980s Must Face Basic Economic Realities." *Commitment,* an Abbott Laboratories' magazine.

Dix, Dorothea [pseudo.]. "A Strike for Liberty." In the New Orleans *Daily Picayune,* 29 October 1899.

King, Florence. *Southern Ladies and Gentlemen.* New York: Bantam, 1976.

McPhee, John. *Oranges.* New York: Farrar, Straus and Giroux, 1967.

Mattingly, Garrett, et al. "Catherine of Aragon." In *Renaissance Profiles*, ed. by J. H. Plumb. New York: Harper & Row.

Morley, Christopher. "On Unanswering Letters." In *Essays British and American.* New York: Greenwood Press, 1969.

Newman, Edwin. *Strictly Speaking: Will American be the Death of English?* Indianapolis, Ind.: Bobbs-Merrill, 1974.

Roget, Peter M. *Roget's International Thesaurus*, 4th ed. New York: Crowell, 1977.

Ross, Mario. Writing in *The Syracuse Herald-American*, 15 June 1980.

Rush, Ann Kent. *Getting Clear.* New York: Random House, 1973.

Tibbets, A. M. and Tibbets, Charlene. *What's Happening to American English?* New York: Scribner's, 1979.

U.S., Department of Transportation. *A Methodology for Determining the Role of Vehicle Handling in Accident Causation.* Washington, D.C.: Government Printing Office, 1977.

Webster's New World Dictionary, 2nd college ed. Copyright © 1980 by Simon & Schuster, Inc. Reprinted with permission.

"Word Processing Machine Operator." Classified Ad. *Syracuse Herald-American*, 23 December 1979.

CHAPTER 7

Dillard, Annie. Excerpt from *Pilgrim at Tinker Creek.* Reprinted by permission of the author and her agent, Blanche C. Gregory, Inc.

Durrell, Lawrence. "How to Buy a House." From *Bitter Lemons.* Copyright © 1957 by Lawrence Durrell. Reprinted by permission of the publisher, E. P. Dutton.

McPhee, John. *Oranges.* New York: Farrar, Straus and Giroux, 1967.

Selzer, Richard. *Notes on the Art of Surgery.* New York: Simon & Schuster, 1974.

Shaugnessy, Mina P. *Errors & Expectations: A Guide for the Teacher of Basic Writing.* New York: Oxford University Press, 1977.

CHAPTER 8

Bettelheim, Bruno. Excerpt from *The Uses of Enchantment: The Meaning and Importance of Fairy Tales.* Copyright © 1976 by Bruno Bettelheim. Reprinted by permission of Alfred A. Knopf, Inc.

Blake, Nicholas [C. Day Lewis] *The Whisper in the Gloom.* New York: Harper & Row, 1954.

Brickman, P., ed. *Social Conflict.* New York: D. C. Heath, 1971.

Dillard, Annie. Excerpts from *Pilgrim at Tinker Creek.* Reprinted by permission of the author and her agent, Blanche C. Gregory, Inc.

Feibleman, Peter S. and the Editors of Time-Life Books. *Foods of the World— The Cooking of Spain and Portugal.* © 1969 Time Inc.

"Iowa Homesteader's Wife." Photograph by Russell Lee. 1936.

Jaynes, Julian. *The Origin of Consciousness in the Breakdown of the Bicameral Mind.* Boston: Houghton Mifflin, 1977.

Matthiessen, Peter. *The Snow Leopard.* New York: Viking Press, 1978.

Menen, Aubrey. "Dazzled in Disneyland." *Holiday*, June 1963.

Morris, Charles G. *Psychology, An Introduction*, 3rd ed. Englewood Cliffs, N.J.: Prentice-Hall, 1979.

Thoreau, Henry David. *Walden* and *On the Duty of Civil Disobedience.* New York: Macmillan, 1962.

White, E. B. "Democracy." From *The Wild Flag* (Houghton Mifflin); © 1943, 1971. Originally in *The New Yorker.*

CHAPTER 9

Baldwin, James. "Fifth Avenue, Uptown: A Letter from Harlem." Excerpt from *Nobody Knows My Name.* Copyright © 1954, 1956, 1958, 1959, 1960, 1961 by James Baldwin. Reprinted by permission of The Dial Press.

Clark, Wilson. Excerpt from *Energy for Survival: The Alternative to Extinction.* Copyright © 1974 by Wilson Clark. Reprinted by permission of Doubleday & Company, Inc.

Franklin, Benjamin. "Speech in the Constitutional Convention on the Subject of Salaries, June 2, 1787." Quoted in Edward Corbett, *Classical Rhetoric for the Modern Student.* New York: Oxford University Press, 1971.

Friedman, Milton. "Economic Controls vs. Personal Freedom." An article that appeared in Abbott Laboratories' *Commitment* magazine, Spring 1977.

"Imagine Tomorrow as a Ribbon of Sunshine." Advertisement. Courtesy of Mobil Corporation.

Lewis, Harold W. "The Safety of Fission Reactors." *Scientific American,* March 1980. Reprinted by permission of W. H. Freeman and Company.

Mornell, Pierre. *Passive Men, Wild Women.* Copyright © 1979 by Pierre Mornell, M.D. Reprinted by permission of Simon & Schuster, a Division of Gulf & Western Corporation.

Seymour, F. Eugene, et al. Excerpt from *Geometry for High Schools.* © Macmillan Publishing Co., Inc. 1958. Reprinted with permission of Macmillan Publishing Co., Inc.

"Which Side Do You Believe?" Advertisement created by Smith & Harroff, Inc. on behalf of the Committee for Energy Awareness. *The Dial,* volume 1, no. 1 (September 1980), p. 29.

"A Word to Nonsmokers . . . A Word to Smokers." Advertisement. Courtesy of The Tobacco Institute.

CHAPTER 11

Bazar, Joan. "Catching Up with the Ape Language Debate." *APA Monitor,* January 1980, pp. 4–5, 27.

Limber, John. "Language in Child and Chimp?" *American Psychologist,* 32 (1977):280–295.

Terrace, H. S. "How Nim Chimpsky Changed My Mind." *Psychology Today,* November 1979, pp. 65–76.

CHAPTER 12

Schell, Leo M. and Dan Courtney. "The Effect of Male Teachers on the Academic Achievement of Father-Absent Sixth Grade Boys." *Journal of Educational Research,* vol. 72, no. 4 (March/April 1979), pp. 194-195.

State University of New York, College at Purchase. "Assistant Director of Admissions." Classified advertisement. *The New York Times,* 22 June 1980.

CHAPTER 15

Atwood, Margaret. *Survival: A Thematic Guide to Canadian Literature.* Toronto: Anansi Press, 1972.

LeSeur, Mendel. *North Star Country.* Quoted in Alan Lomax, *Folksongs of America.* New York: Doubleday, 1961.

Tuchman, Barbara. *A Distant Mirror.* New York: Knopf, 1978.

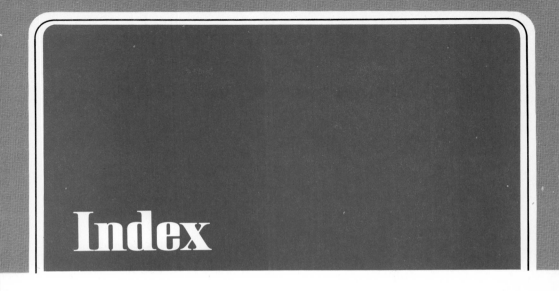

Index

INDEX OF AUTHORS AND WORKS

Note: Page numbers in **boldface** refer to entries in the Glossary of Grammatical Terms.

Adventures of Mottel, The Cantor's Son (Aleichem), 102–3
Aleichem, Sholom, 102–3
American Notebooks (Hawthorne), 12
Aran Islands, The (Synge), 79
"Are Women Growing Selfish?" (Dix), 104
Atwood, Margaret, 441–42
Austen, Jane, 106, 141

Baker, Russell, 117
Baldwin, James, 193–94
Balsdon, J. P. V. D., 73, 74
Barzun, Jacques, 59
Bazar, Joan, 276
Becker, Marion Rombauer, 76
Beckett, Samuel, 79–80
Bergman, Ingmar, 232
Bernstein, Theodore, 473, 481
Bettelheim, Bruno, 91, 172–73
Bible, 105, 145
"Birthmark, The" (Hawthorne), 12
Blake, Nicholas, 109, 161
Bleak House (Dickens), 368
Blumenthal, Michael C., 116
Book of Common Prayer, 105
Bowen, Elizabeth, 104–5
Brighter than a Thousand Suns (Jungk), 105

Broca's Brain (Sagan), 56
Burke, Kenneth, 94

Careful Writer, The (Bernstein), 473, 481
Carroll, Lewis, 4
Carson, Rachel, 41
"Catching Up with the Ape Language Debate" (Bazar), 276
Catherine of Aragon (Mattingly), 124
"Ceti" (Thomas), 89
Charlotte's Web (White), 86, 88
"Choice and Chance in Human Affairs" (Grafton), 75
Clark, Wilson, 190–91
Clouds of Witness (Sayers), 44
Collingwood, Robin, 86
Congreve, William, 227
Cooking of Spain and Portugal, The (Feibleman), 168–69
Cooper, Kenneth H., 8
Cosby, Bill, 146
Cross, Donna Woolfolk, 78

"Dazzled in Disneyland" (Menen), 179
Declaration of Independence, 8, 195–96
"Democracy" (White), 176
Dickens, Charles, 368
Didion, Joan, 86

Dillard, Annie, 82, 154, 167, 178
Dix, Dorothea, 104, 127
Durrell, Lawrence, 153

"Economic Controls vs. Personal Freedom" (Friedman), 35
Eliot, T. S., 142, 220–21
Eminent Victorians (Strachey), 103
Emma (Austen), 106
Energy for Survival (Clark), 190
Errors and Expectations: A Guide for the Teaching of Basic Writing (Shaughnessy), 130

Faulkner, William, 211
Feibleman, Peter S., 169
Fielding, Henry, 216, 222, 223
Flying Dutchman (Wagner), 135
Fothergill, Robert A., 83
Frank, Anne, 5–6
Franklin, Benjamin, 198
Friedken, William 231
Friedman, Milton, 35–36, 203

Getting Clear (Rush), 125
"Gettysburg Address" (Lincoln), 207
Glass Menagerie, The (Williams), 83, 136, 142
Gnostic Gospels, The (Pagels), 82
"Good Case for Miniver Cheevy, A" (Jones), 46
Graff, Henry F., 59
Grafton, Samuel, 75
"Great Stone Face, The" (Hawthorne), 12
Gulliver's Travels (Swift), 142, 221–22

Hawthorne, Nathaniel, 12
Heilbruner, Robert L., 77
Hemingway, Ernest, 219
Heroines of Dixie: Winter of Desperation (McGuire), 5
Historian as Detective, The (Winks), 84
Hitchcock, Alfred, 231
House Made of Dawn (Momaday), 211
"How Nim Chimpsky Changed My Mind" (Terrace), 275
"How to Write" (Williams), 11
"How to Buy a House" (Durrell), 153
Huston, John, 231

Jaynes, Julian, 177
Jones, Jenkins Lloyd, 46
Joseph Andrews (Fielding), 216, 222, 223–27
Journal of Educational Research, 300
Joy of Cooking (Rombauer and Becker), 76
Jungk, Robert, 105

King, Florence, 127

"Language in Child and Chimp" (Limber), 275
Lebowitz, Fran, 42
LeSeur, Mendel, 401
Lewis, C. Day, 109, 161
Lewis, Harold W., 190
"Liberalism in the 1980s Must Face Basic Economic Realities" (Blumenthal), 116
Life in Medieval Times (Rowling), 84
Life on the Mississippi (Twain), 98–99
Limber, John, 275
Lincoln, Abraham, 207
Linden, Eugene, 248
"Little Red Riding Hood Revisited" (Baker), 117
Losing Battles (Welty), 106
"Love Song of J. Alfred Prufrock" (Eliot), 220–21

McGuire, Judith Brockenbrough, 5
McPhee, John, 119, 154
McTeague (Norris), 59–60
Matthiessen, Peter, 167–68
Mattingly, Garrett, 124
"Medley of Mysteries, A" (Barzun and Graff), 58–59
Menen, Aubrey, 179
Methodology for Determining the Role of Vehicle Handling in Accident Causation, A, 125
Metropolitan Life (Lebowitz), 41–42
Midsummer Night's Dream (Shakespeare), 214
Mobil Corporation, 204
Molloy (Beckett), 79–80
Momaday, N. Scott, 211
Morley, Christopher, 127
Mornel, Pierre, 46, 207
Morris, Charles G., 174
Mortal Lessons: Notes on the Art of Surgery (Selzer), 75, 98, 100, 153–54
Mowat, Farley, 103

New Aerobics, The (Cooper), 8
"New Distrust of the Experts, A" (Trippett), 43
Newman, Edwin, 112
Newsweek, 116
New York Times, The 117, 143, 244, 248
Nobody Knows My Name (Baldwin), 193–94
Norris, Frank, 60
Northanger Abbey (Austen), 141
North Star Country (Le Seur), 401

Oedipus the King (Sophocles), 213
Old Man and the Sea, The (Hemingway), 219
Old Stone House, The (Wilson), 108–9

"On Keeping Things Up in the Air" (Truzzi), 85
"On Unanswering Letters: (Morley), 127
"On Warts" (Thomas), 87
Oranges (McPhee), 119, 154
Origin of Consciousness in the Breakdown of the Bicameral Mind, The, (Jaynes), 177

Packard, Vance, 81
Pagels, Elaine, 82
Parker, Dorothy, 123
"Passive Men, Wild Women" (Mornell), 46, 207
People of the Deer (Mowat), 103
Permanence and Change (Burke), 94
Pilgrim at Tinker Creek (Dillard), 82, 154, 167, 178
Pirsig, Robert, 10, 99
Plath, Sylvia, 216
Pope, Alexander, 106
Private Chronicles (Fothergill), 83
"Problem of Testimony, The" (Collingwood), 86
Psychology: An Introduction (Morris), 174

Reading Literature (Satin), 100
Right Stuff, The (Wolfe), 64–65
Roget's International Thesaurus, 114
Romans and Aliens (Balsdon), 73
Rombauer, Irma S., 76
Ross, Mario, 116
Rowling, Marjorie, 84–85
Rush, Ann Kent, 125

"Safety of Fission Reactors, The" (Lewis), 189–90
Sagan, Carl, 56–57
Satin, Joseph, 100
Sayers, Dorothy, 44
"Scenes from a Marriage" (Bergman), 232
Scientific American, 190
Selzer, Richard, 75, 98, 100, 154
Shakespeare, William, 214
Shaughnessy, Mina P., 130
Silent Spring (Carson), 41
Snow Leopard, The (Matthiessen), 167–68
Sophocles, 213
Southern Ladies and Gentlemen (King), 127
Spielberg, Stephen, 231
Strachey, Lytton, 103–4
Strictly Speaking (Newman), 112
"Strike for Liberty, A" (Dix), 127
Swift, Jonathan, 142, 221–22
Synge, J. M., 79

Tate, Alan, 137
Terrace, H. S., 275

Third Wave, The (Toffler), 74
Thomas, Lewis, 86–87, 89
Thoreau, Henry David, 171–72
Through the Looking Glass (Carroll), 4–5
Thurber, James, 86, 130
Tibbets, Arn and Charlene, 123
Time magazine, 100, 114
Tobacco Institute, 206
Toffler, Alvin, 74
Trippett, Frank, 43
Truzzi, Marcello, 85
Tuchman, Barbara, 442
Twain, Mark, 98–99, 393

Underground Grammarian, 94, 97
Uses of Enchantment, The (Bettelheim), 90–91, 172–73

Wagner, Richard, 135
Walden (Thoreau), 171–72
Waste Makers, The (Packard), 81
Way of the World, The (Congreve), 227
Welty, Eudora, 86, 88, 106
What's Happening to American English (Tibbets and Tibbets), 123
Whisper in the Gloom, The (Blake), 109, 161
White, E. B., 176
White Album, The (Didion), 86
Williams, Tennessee, 136, 142
Williams, William Carlos, 11
Wilson, Edmund, 109
Winks, Robert, 84
Wolfe, Tom, 64–65
Woolf, Virginia, 13
Worldly Philosophers, The (Heilbruner), 77
World of Love, A (Bowen), 104
Word Abuse (Cross), 77–78

Yeats, William Butler, 216

Zen and the Art of Motorcycle Maintenance (Pirsig), 10, 99

SUBJECT INDEX

a, an, 348–49, 473
abbreviations, 458–59
  acronyms, 459
  in footnotes, 255
  scholarly, 459
  of titles and degrees, 459
about, as to, with respect to, 478–79
abridged dictionaries, 271
absolutely, absolute, 473
abstract nouns, 311–12
abstracts

abstracts (*cont.*)
  in scientific reports, 303
  style, 298–99
accept, except, 473–74
access, excess, 474
accusative case, 349
acronyms, 459
active voice
  in abstracts, 298
  advantages over passive, 96, 336–37,
    389–90
  defined, 365
A.D., 459
ad, advertisement, 474
adapt, adopt, 474
ad hominem argument, 39, 200
adjectival pronouns, 362
adjective clauses, 325, 361
adjectives, **346–47**
  appositive, 346
  attributive, 319–20, 346, 360
  comparison, 320–21, **350–51**
  compound, 323–24, 425–26
  demonstrative, 320, 352, 353
  determiners, 348–49, 353
  fractions used as, 424
  interrogative, 355–56
  nonrestrictive, **357**
  possessive, 360, 361
  predicate, 332, 346, 351, 356, **360**
  restrictive, **362**
  suffixes, 450–51
addition, words for in transition
    paragraphs, 87
adverbial clauses, 325, 347
adverbials
  defined, 330
  with linking verbs, 332
  normal order, 333
adverbs
  comparison, 320–21, **350–51**
  conjunctive, **352**
  functions, 320, **347**
  intensifiers, 347, 355
  interrogative, 355–56
  suffixes, 451
adverse, averse, 474
advice, advise, 474
adviser, advisor, 474
affect, effect, 475
again, back, refer back, 475
aggravate, intensify, 475
agreement, **347–48**
  in compounding, 340
  inappropriate shift, **363**
  of pronouns with antecedent, 347, 361,
    381–84
  of subject and verb, 347, 378–80
  of verb tenses, 230, 363, 381

agree to, agree with, 475
ain't, 475
aircraft, names of, 439
all-, 425
all, any, 478
all ready, already, 476
all right, alright, 476
all together, altogether, 476
all ways, always, 476
allude, refer, 476
allusion, illusion, delusion, elusion, 476
almanacs, 272
almost, most, 495
along the lines of, 492
a lot, alot, 473
although
  vs. *in spite of the fact that*, 492
  vs. *though*, 477
alumna, alumnus, alumnae, alumni, 477
a.m., p.m.
  abbreviation, 459
  with figures, 460
  use of colon, 421
among, between, 477
amount, number, 477
analogy
  false, 38–39
  pattern of paragraph development, 75
analysis
  in exam essays, 284–86
  in expository writing, 178
  of films, 231–33
  in literary essays, 212
  pattern of paragraph development, 76–7
  of subject, for argument, 191–92
analysis, analyzation, 477
and, with *both . . .* , 481
and etc., 477
and/or
  in business writing, 477
  overuse of, 443
angry, annoyed, mad, 494
ante-, anti-, 478
antecedent, agreement of pronoun with,
    348, 361, 381–84
anthology articles, references to
  MLA bibliography style, 257
  MLA footnote style, 255, 256
antithesis, and sentence style, 104
anxious, eager, 478
any, all, 478
anyone
  vs. *any one*, 478
  pronoun agreement, 383
anyplace, everyplace, someplace, 478
anyway, any way, 478
anyways, anywheres, 478
apostrophes, 432–35
  with contractions, 433–34

with plurals, 434–35
with possessives, 432–33
appeals. *See also* argument
  emotional, 28–29
  ethical, 29
  evaluation of, 40–41
  mixed, 39–40
  against the man, 39, 200
  to numbers, 39–40
  to pity, 40
  rational, 29–30, 34–40. *See also* rational
    appeals
appearance
  of manuscripts, 463–68
  of resume, 287
appositive nouns, 348
appositive adjectives, 346
apprehend, comprehend, 478
archaic usage, 472
argument, 186–200. *See also* appeals;
    evidence
  in classical rhetoric, 39–40
  and cultural conditioning, 195–96
  defining terms, 193–94
  determining audience, 189–91
  formal, 197
  as form of discourse, 162
  hidden value judgments, 194–95
  informal, 197–200
  nature of, 186–87
  stating the purpose, 187–89
  the "why" of, 192–93
argumentum ad hominem, 39, 200
argumentum ad misericordiam, 40
argumentum ad populem, 39
articles (*a, an, the*)
  as determiners, **348–49**, 352–53
  types, 319–20
articles (in periodicals), references to
  APA reference list style, 258
  MLA bibliography style, 257
  MLA footnote style, 255, 256
as
  vs. *like*, 494
  vs. *that, whether*, 478
aspect, 315
as regards, 492
as to, with respect to, about, 478–79
at, to, 503
atlases, 272
attribute, contribute, 479
attributive adjectives
  defined, 346
  in predicate, 360
  types of, 319–20
audience
  appeals to. *See* appeals
  for argument, 189–91, 198
  for literary essay, 211

audience probes
  as preparation for writing, 15
  for revision, 135
author, film director as, 231
author cards, 244
author emphasis, in quotations, 230
authority, and ethical appeals, 29
author probes
  as preparation for writing, 14
  and revision, 135
auxiliary verbs
  categories, 315–16
  contractions, 433
  defined, **349**
  modal, **357**
  in questions, 334, 335
  in verb phrases, 364
averse, adverse, 474
awful, awfully, 479
awhile, a while, 479
awkward passive, **349**

back, refer back, again, 475
bad, badly, 479
balanced sentences, 103–4
bandwagon technique, 40
basically, 479
B.C., 459
be (to). *See also* linking verbs
  as auxiliary verb, 315
  contracted forms, 433
  faulty prediction, 395–96
  and verb aspect, 315
because, 480
  vs. *being as, being that*, 480
  vs. *due to the fact that*, 487
  vs. *on account of*, 496
  with *reason is*, 480, 499–500
before, previous to, prior to, 498
begging the question, 37
being as, being that, 480
beside, besides, 480
better, best, 480
between, among, 477
biblical references, use of colon in, 421
bibliography
  manuscript format, 467
  MLA style, 256–57
  reference list style, 258
bibliography cards, 246–47
biographical reference works, 271–72
blame on, blame for, 480
body, of literary essay, 222–27
body paragraphs
  revision, 140–41
  transitional, 86–87
books, references to
  APA reference list style, 258
  on bibliography cards, 247

books, references to (*cont.*)
  in card catalogs, 244–46
  MLA bibliography style, 257
  MLA footnote style, 255, 256
  single chapters, 437, 440
book titles
  capitalization, 463
  in italics, 437, 439
borrow, lend, loan, 480
both . . . and, 481
brackets, 428–31
  distinguished from parentheses, 428, 431
  with material inserted in quotations, 230, 430–31
brainstorming
  as preparation for writing, 12
  for research paper, 241–42, 259
  and support of thesis, 51–53
brevity
  in abstracts, 298
  in business writing, 290–93
briefs, 297
bring, take, fetch, 481
bureaucratese
  and deadwood, 401
  and fad words, 117
  in memos, 296
business writing, 290–96
  letters, 293–94, 420
  memos, 294–96
  reports, 296
  resumes, 286–90
bust, burst, 481
but, 481
but what, but that, 481
buzz words, 115–16, 117

calculate, reckon, guess, 481–82
call numbers, 245
can, may, 482
cannot, can not, 482
cannot help but, 482
can't hardly, can't scarcely, 482
capital, capitol, 482
capitalization, 461–63
  of course names, 463
  of first word in sentence, 461
  of geographical directions, 462
  with parentheses, 461–62
  of proper names, 462 –63
  of personal titles, 462
  with quotations, 230, 461
  of words in titles, 463
card catalog, 244–46
cardinal numbers
  as attributive adjectives, 320
  written out, 460
case, **349**
  of nouns, 349

  of personal pronouns, 349, 361, 384–85
causality, and cultural conditioning, 196
cause and effect
  pattern of organization, 61
  pattern of paragraph development, 80–81
  in rational appeals, 30
cause is due to, 482
censor, censure, 482–83
center around, center; revolve on, revolve around, 482
certainly, sure, surely, 501
chapter titles, 437, 440
characterization
  analysis in literary essays, 213–14
  in films, 233
checklists
  for paragraphs, 88
  for revision, 132–34
  for sentences, 107
chronological order
  in paragraphs, 79
  pattern of organization, 56–57
  in resumes, 288, 290
cite, site, sight, 483
classical rhetoric, 62–63
classification
  in exposition, 173–74
  of films, 232
  of library materials, 245
  pattern of paragraph development, 76
clauses, 324–26, **349–50**
  adjective, 325, 361
  adverb, 325, 347
  compounding, 341–43
  coordinate, 350
  independent and dependent, 324–26, 349–50. *See also* independent clauses
  noun function, 325, 328, 350, 351, 358, 362
  relative, 325, 326, 328, 346, 361–62
  restrictive and nonrestrictive, 326
  as subject, 328
"clear out and build," pattern of organization, 62
clichés, 123–24, 405–6
closing paragraph. *See* concluding paragraph
coarse, course, 483
coherence, 65–67
collections, reference to articles in
  MLA bibliography style, 257
  MLA footnote style, 255, 256
collective nouns
  defined, 312, **350**
  pronoun agreement, 383
  verb agreement, 379–80
colon, 418–21
  to emphasize summary element, 419–20
  to introduce direct quotation, 420
  to introduce list, 418–19

with quotation marks, 438
special uses, 420–21
commas, 411–15
with appositives, 348
avoiding separation of subject and
predicate, 414–15
before conjunctions, 412
with independent clauses, 412
with interrupters, 413–14
to introduce direct quotations, 420
after introductory element, 412–13
with nonrestrictive adjectives, 357
not used with restrictive adjectives, 362
with parentheses, 429
with quotation marks, 438
separating elements in a series, 415
command
with exclamation point, 427
imperative mood, 357
comma splice, **350**, 371–73
commentate, 484
common nouns
capitalization, 462–63
defined, 311
comparative degree, 321, 351
compare with, compare to, 484
comparison. *See also* metaphors
elliptical construction, 353
in exam essay, 283–84
in expository writing, 178–79
incomplete or misconstrued, 388–89
in literary essay, 215–16
of modifying words, 320–21, **350–51**
pattern of organization, 61
pattern of paragraph development, 77–78
in rational appeals, 30
complement
direct object as, 351, 353
with linking verbs, 351, 356
with *to be*, 395–96
types, **351**
complement, compliment, 484
complex sentences, 343
composition. *See also* writing
and creation, 130
process, 8–11
compound adjectives, 423–24, 425–26
compound-complex sentences, 343
compounding, 338–43
compound nouns
formed with hyphen, 423–24
possessive forms, 433
compound sentences, 339, 343
compound subjects, 379
compound verbs
agreement with subject, 340, 378–79
avoiding tense shifts, 340, 381
compound words
formation of plurals, 456

spelling, 452
comprehend, apprehend, 478
concession, in formal argument, 197
concluding paragraphs
examining for revision, 143
guidelines, 87–88
conclusion
of literary essay, 227–28
words for, in transition paragraphs, 87
concrete nouns, 311
confirmation, 63, 197
confutatio, 63
conjunctions, **351–52**
comma preceding, 412
coordinating, 338, 350, 352, 354, 363
subordinating, 350, 352
conjunctive adverbs
defined, **352**
linking independent clauses, 341–42, 352
with semicolon, 352, 416
connotation, 121–23
concensus of opinion, 484
considerable, considerably, 484
consul, council, counsel, 485
context, **352**
contractions, 433–34
contribute, attribute, 479
contributing factor, 489
contrast
in exam essay, 283–84
in expository writing, 178–79
in literary essay, 215–16
pattern of organization, 61
pattern of paragraph development, 77–78
in rational appeal, 30
convince, persuade, 484
coordinate clauses, 350
coordinating conjunctions
and compounding, 338
to correct fused sentence, 354
function, 352
to prevent comma splice, 350
in run-on sentences, 363
could, might, 482
council, counsel, consul, 484–85
couple of, couple, 485
course, coarse, 483
credible, credulous, creditable, 485
critique, criticize, 485
cultural conditioning
effect on argument, 195–96
and rational appeals, 36
cute, 485

dangling modifiers, **356–57**, 385–86
dashes, 421–23
how to type, 423
with interrupters, 422–23
with question mark, 427

dashes *(cont.)*
  with quotation marks, 438
  to set off explanatory elements, 421–22
dates, figures for, 460
datum, data, 485
days of the week
  capitalized, 462
  spelled out, 458
deadwood, 97, 145, 401–3
decent, descent, 485–86
decimals, figures for, 461
declarative sentences, with question mark, 427
deduction
  pattern of organization, 60–61
  pattern of paragraph development, 73
definite article, 319–20, 349
definition
  dictionary information, 113
  in expository writing, 175–77
  in introductory paragraph, 85, 138
  pattern of paragraph development, 74
  of terms in argument, 193–94
degrees
  of comparison, 320–21, 351
  professional, abbreviations, 459
delayed subject, 96
delusion, allusion, illusion, elusion, 476
demonstrative adjectives
  as determiners, 320, 353
  functions, 352
demonstrative pronouns, 312, 352
demonstratives, **352**
denotation, 121–23
dependent (subordinate) clauses, 324, 342–43, 350
description, 165–68
  application, 164
  as form of discourse, 160–61
  with narration, 161
  objective and subjective, 165–67
  pattern of paragraph development, 78–80
  of process, 177–78
  sensory appeals, 167–68
determiners
  articles as, 319–20, 348–49
  defined, **352–53**
  types, 319–20
desert, dessert, 486
device, devise, 486
Dewey Decimal classification system, 245
dialectical usage, 472
dialogue
  ellipses in, 442
  quoting, 230
  use of quotation marks, 436
diaries
  narration in, 161
  as preparation for writing, 12–13

dictionaries
  information in, 112–15
  reference sources, 271
did, done, 486
different from, different than, 486
directions, geographical, 462
direct object
  defined, **353**
  vs. indirect object, 354
  noun clause as, 351
direct questions. *See also* questions
  defined, **353**
  with interrogatives, 355–56
  question mark with, 426
direct quotations. *See also* quotations
  introduced with colon, 420
  in research paper, 250–51
discourse, forms of, 160–65
disinterested, uninterested, 486
distancing, 130–34
  with outside commentary, 131
  by role-playing, 132–34
  over time, 131
  value of, 130–31
division, in exposition, 173–74
do, with questions, 334, 335
documentation
  in literary essays, 228–29
  in research papers, 253–58
  on note-cards, 249
  in social and natural sciences, 257–58
don't, 486
due to, 482
due to the fact that, 487

each
  pronoun agreement, 383
  verb agreement, 380
each other's, one another's, 487
eager, anxious, 478
economic, economical, 487
economics, reference sources, 274
effect, affect, 475
effect. *See* cause and effect
e.g., for example, 487
either, neither, 487
either/or
  avoiding, 443
  verb agreement, 379
either/or thinking, 35–36
-elect, 425
elicit, illicit, 487
ellipses, 441–43
  in dialogue, 442
  for omissions, 441–42
elliptical construction, **353**
elusion, allusion, illusion, delusion, 476
emigrate, immigrate, 487–88
eminent, imminent, 488

emotional appeals
  mixed with rational appeals, 39–40
  and opinion, 33
  use of, 28–29
emotionalism, avoiding, 198, 200
emphasis
  author's, 230
  italics for, 440–41
  and positioning, 101
  with quotation marks, 436–37
  words for, in transition paragraphs, 87
endnotes, 254, 465
enhance, 488
enthuse, 488
equivocation
  confusion caused by, 37–38
  and false analogy, 39
essays
  coherence in, 65–67
  on examinations, 280–86. *See also* exam
    essays
  on films, 231–33
  literary, 210–33. *see also* literary essays
  rewriting, 146–50. *See also* revision
  titles of, in quotation marks, 437, 440
Eskimo dialects, 118
etc., 477, 488
ethical appeals, 29
etymology, dictionary information, 113
euphemisms, 405
euphony, 106
evaluation
  of evidence, 40–41
  on exam essays, 286
everybody
  pronoun agreement, 383
  verb agreement, 380
everyone, *every one*, 488
everyplace, *everywhere*, 478
evidence, 28–41
  evaluation of, 40–41
  external testimony as, 31
  facts, inferences, and opinions, 32–34
  in literary essays, 217–18
  statistics, 31–32
  and types of appeals, 28–30
ex-, 425
exam essays, 280–86
  analysis, 284–86
  comparison and contrast, 283–84
  evaluation, 286
  reading the question, 280–81
  revision, 151
  structure, 282–83
  time limits, 281–82
except, *accept*, 473–74
excess, *access*, 474
exclamation point, 427–28
  with exclamations, 426–27

with imperative, 427
  with quotation marks, 438–39
exclamations, 426–27
exordium, 62–63, 197
experience, use in literary essays, 211
expertise, and ethical appeals, 29
explanation, and exposition, 172
expletives, 335
exposition, 172–79
  analysis, 178
  application, 164
  classification and division, 173–74
  comparison and contrast, 178–79
  definition, 175–77
  as form of discourse, 161–62
  process description, 177–78
external testimony, as evidence, 31

factor, *contributing factor*, 489
facts
  insufficient, 34–37
  validating, 32–33
fad words, 116–17
false analogy, 38–39
famous, *notorious*, 489
faulty parallelism, 339–40
faulty predication, 395–96
feminist movement, 37. *See also* sexist
  language
fetch, *bring*, *take*, 481
few, *little*; *fewer*, *less*, 489
figures. *See also* numbers
  for addresses, 460
  for dates, 460
  for decimals, 461
  for measurements, 461
  for numbers in a series, 461
  for page numbers, 460
  for time of day, 460
fillers, 121
films
  essays on, 231–33
  titles of, 437, 439
  use of narration, 161
finalize, *complete*, 489
fine, 489
finite verbs
  defined, **353–54**
  in verb phrase, 364
first draft, 130, 261. *See also* revision
focus
  of literary essay, 211
  of writer, 10–11
folklore, reference sources, 273
foot, *feet*, 489
footnotes
  contents, 254
  general rules, 255
  in literary essays, 228–29

footnotes (*cont.*)
  manuscript format, 465
  MLA style, 254–56
  reference numbers and placement, 254
  samples, 255–56
  second references, 256
foreign words, in italics, 440
for example, e.g., 487
formal argument, 197
formally, formerly, 489
formal usage, 472
format
  in abstract, 298
  of manuscript, 463–68
  of resume, 287
former, latter, 490
forth, fourth, 498
fractions
  hyphenated, 424
  written out, 460
functional resumes, 288–90
funnel, of thesis, 53–54
funny, 490
fused sentences, **354**, 373–74
future tense, formation, 315

gender
  agreement in, **347–48**
  defined, **354**
  and sexist language, 117–18
generalizations, vague, 217
geographical directions, 462
gerunds
  defined, **354**
  and nonfinite form, 364
  noun function, 358
  in verbal phrase, 323, 365
get, got, gotten, 490
good, well, 490
graduate, for *alumnus*, etc., 477
graphic aids, for oral report, 303
guess, calculate, reckon, 481–82

hadn't ought to, ought not; had ought to,
  ought to have, 490
hardly, with *can't*, 482
have
  avoiding *of* for, 496
  contracted forms, 433
he/she, 443
healthful, healthy, 490–91
helping verbs. *See* auxiliary verbs
historical events, names of, 462
history, reference sources, 274
holidays, spelled out, 458
honesty, in literary essay, 211
hopefully, 95, 347, 491
hyphens, 423–26
  with compound adjectives, 423–24,
    425–26
  with compound nouns, 424
  with numbers and fractions, 424–25
  with prefixes and suffixes, 425
  in syllabication, 423, 456–57

ideas, for research paper, 241–42
idiom
  defined, **354**
  improper, 396–97
i.e., that is, 491
if and when, when and if, 491
illicit, elicit, 487
illusion, allusion, delusion, elusion, 476
illustration
  pattern of paragraph development, 74–75
  words for, in transitional paragraphs, 87
immigrate, emigrate, 487–88
imminent, eminent, 488
imperative mood, 316, 357
imperative sentences
  elliptical constructions, 353
  with exclamation point, 427
  grammatical subject, 316
imply, infer, 491
impracticable, impractical, 491
improper idiom, 396–97
in, into, in to, 491
inappropriate shift, **363**
imcomplete comparisons, 388–89
incorrect usage, 473
incredible, incredulous, 492
indefinite articles, 319–20, 349, 473
indefinite pronouns
  as antecedent, 348
  defined, 312
  possessives, 362
independent clauses
  comma spliced, 350, 412
  with conjunctive adverbs, 352
  compounding, 339
  defined, 324, 349–50
  in fused sentence, 354
  linking, 341–43
  run-on, 363
  with semicolon, 416–17
indicative mood, 316, 357
indirect object
  defined, **354–55**
  predicate patterns, 331
  sentence patterns, 335–36
indirect questions
  defined, **353**
  with interrogative pronoun, 355–56
  questions mark not used, 426, 427
induction
  pattern of organization, 60, 62
  pattern of paragraph development, 73–74
infer, imply, 491

inferences, and fact, 33
inferior than, inferior to, worse than, 492
infinitives
　forms of, **355**
　improper use, 396
　as nonfinite form, 364
　and principle parts of verb, 316, 361
　in verbal phrases, 323, 365
inflated language, 115–18
inflected forms
　dictionary information, 113
　and spelling, 451
informal argument, 197–200
informal usage, 472–73
innovation, in organization, 64–65
in regard to, in regards to, as regards, 492
inside of, inside, 492–93
in spite of (despite) the fact that, 492
integrity, in research papers, 248–49
intensifiers, **355**. *See also* adverbs
intensify, aggravate, 475
interjections, **355**
in terms of, 492
interrogative adjectives, 355–56
interrogative adverbs, 355–56
interrogative pronouns, 312, 355, 362
interrogatives, **355–56**
interrupters
　commas around, 413–14
　with dashes, 422–23
　defined, 337
　with question mark, 427
in the case of, along the lines of, 492
intransitive verbs
　complement, 351
　correct use, 394–95
　defined, 313, 364
　predicate patterns, 330–31
introductory paragraph
　guidelines, 83–86
　in literary essay, 219
　revising, 137–40
　strategy, 141
invented words, 399–400
irregular verbs, **362**
　participles, 359
　principal parts, 314, 361
irregardless, 493
it, as expletive, 335
italics, 439–41
　for emphasis, 440–41
　for foreign words, 440
　for scientific terminology, 440
　for titles, 439–40
　for words used as words, 440
　in footnotes, 255
it is . . . that, 493
it is, there are, 96, 101
its, it's 433–34, 493

jargon
　definition and use, 115, **356**
　in memos, 296
job application
　letters, 293–94
　resumes, 286–90
journal articles, references to
　APA reference list style, 258
　MLA bibliography style, 257
　MLA footnote style, 255, 256
journal keeping, 12–13

kind of a, kind of; sort of a, sort of, 493

language
　in abstracts, 298
　general vs. specific, 118–20
　guides for sharpening, 120–21
　formal and informal usage, 472–73
　inflated, 115–18
　sexist, 117–18
later, latter, 493
latter, former, 490
lay, lie, 494
lead, led, 493
lead-in, revision of, 135–36. *See also*
　　introductory paragraph
legal briefs, 297
lend, loan, borrow, 480
less, fewer, 489
letters (of alphabet), used as words, 434
letters (correspondence), 293–94
let's, let's us, 493
level, 493–94
lie, lay, 494
Library of Congress classification system,
　245
library research, 242–48. *See also* research
　papers
　card catalog, 244–46
　leads to, 247–48
　preparation for, 243–44
　reference sources, 271–75
like, as, 494
linking verbs
　defined, 313–14, **356**, 364
　predicate patterns, 331–32, 360
lists, introduced by colon, 418–19
literary essays, 210–31
　and analysis, 212
　body 222–27
　characterization analysis, 213–14
　choosing a title, 218–19
　comparison and contrast, 215
　conclusion, 227–28
　documentation, 228–29
　guidelines, 217
　opening paragraph, 219
　plot analysis, 213

literary essays *(cont.)*
  point of view analysis, 215
  probing, 211–12
  quotations, 229–30
  requirements, 210
  setting analysis, 214
  sticking to the theme, 219–22
  structure, 216
  theme analysis, 215
  use of evidence, 217–18
little, less, 489
loan, lend, borrow, 410
logic
  limitations, 186
  in rational appeals, 29–30
long poems, 229–30
  quotations from, 229–30
  titles in italics, 439, 441
loose, lose, 494
lots of, a whole lot of, 494

mad, angry, annoyed, 494
magazine articles, references to
  APA reference list style, 258
  in literary essays, 229
  MLA bibliography style, 257
  MLA footnote style, 255, 256
main (major) clause, 350. *See also*
    independent clauses
manuscript format, 463–68
  bibliography, 467
  endnotes, 465
  footnotes, 465
  margins, 464–65
  minor corrections, 467–68
  title page, 463–64
  typing paper, 467
may, can, 482
measurements
  figures for, 461
  spelled out, 458
mechanics, 448–63
  abbreviations, 468–59
  capitalization, 461–63
  checking in final draft, 145
  numbers, 459–61
  spelling, 448–53
  syllabication, 456–57
memos, 294–96
metaphors
  common problems, 123–24
  inappropriate, 406–7
  in introductory paragraph, 86
might, could, 482
minor clause, 350. *See also* subordinate
    clauses
misconstrued comparison, 388–89
misplaced modifiers, **356**, 385–86
mixed metaphors, 123–24, 406–7

MLA Handbook, 254, 256
modal auxiliaries, 316, **357**
mode. *See* mood
modifiers. *See also* adjectives; adverbs
  comparison, 320–21, 350–51
  dangling, **356–57**, 385–86
  as interrupters, 413–14
  with intransitive verb, 330–31
  misplaced, **356**, 385–86
  phrases as, 359
  of sentences, 95, 347
  squinting, **357**
  of subject, 327–28
  with transitive verb, 331
  types, 319–20
Modern Language Association (MLA) style,
    253–57
months, names of
  capitalized, 462
  spelled out, 458
mood
  defined, **357**
  grammatical features, 316–18
  as verb property, 364
moral, morale, 495
most, almost, 495
movies. *See* films
much, many, 495
myself, I, 495

names
  capitalized, 462–63
  spelled out, 458
narratio, 63
narration, 168–72
  application, 164
  and description, 161
  essential points, 169
  as form of discourse, 161
  objective and subjective, 167–71
  order in, 171–72
nationalities, names of, 462
natural sciences, documentation style,
    257–58
negatives, unnecessary, 101–2
neither, either, 487
neither . . . nor
  vs. *neither . . . or,* 495
  verb agreement, 379
newspaper articles, references to
  MLA bibliography style, 257
  MLA footnote style, 255, 256
newspapers
  indexes, 272
  titles in italics, 439
New York Times, The, 243, 244, 248
New York Times Index, 243, 248
nobody
  pronoun agreement, 383

verb agreement, 380
nominative case, 349, 384
nonfinite verbs
  types, 364
  in verbal phrases, 365
nonrestrictive adjectives, **357**
nonrestrictive clauses, 326
nonstandard usage, 472–73
not, contractions, 433
note cards
  arranging for writing, 261
  format, 249
notes. *See* footnotes; note-taking
note-taking, 248–53
  direct quotations, 250–51
  integrity in, 248–49
  for literary essay, 212
  paraphrase, 251–52
  as preparation for writing, 11–12
  summary, 252–53
  use of cards, 249
notorious, famous, 489
not too, not that, 495
noun clauses
  with compound relative pronouns, 362
  as direct object, 351
  function, 325, 350, 358
  as subject, 328
  noun phrases, **358**
nouns
  abstract, 311–12
  agreement with pronoun, 347, 348, 361, 381–84
  appositive, 348
  cases, 349
  collective, 350
  common, 311, 462–63
  compound, 423–24, 433
  concrete, 311
  fractions used as, 424
  functions, **358**
  gender, 354
  gerunds functioning as, 354
  indirect questions functioning as, 355
  to modify nouns, 94–95
  possessives, 320, 349, 358, 359–60, 432–33
  predicate, 351, 356, **360**
  pronouns for, 361. *See also* pronouns
  proper, 311, 362, 425, 462–63
  singular and plural, 358
  in subject, 327–28
  suffixes, 450
  types, 311–12
novellas, titles in italics, 437, 439
novels, narration in, 161
now, presently, 498
nowhere near, not nearly, 496
number

agreement in, **347–48**
  of collective nouns, 350
  defined, **358**
  of nouns, 358
  subject-verb agreement, 378–80
  as verb property, 364
number, amount, 477
numbers, 459–61
  appeal to, 39–40
  cardinal and ordinal, 320
  figures, 460–61
  hyphenated, 424
  in a series, 461
  written out, 460

object
  direct, 351, **353**, 354
  form of personal pronouns, **361**
  indirect, **354–55**
  noun clause as, 350
  predicate patterns, 331
  of preposition, 360
objective case, 361, 384
objective description, 165–67
objective narration, 167–71
objective process, 79–80
objectivity, lack of, 34
of, for *have*, 496
off of, off, from, 496
oftentimes, often, 496
omissions, ellipsis points for, 441–43
on account of, because, because of, 496
one another's, each other's, 487
on the part of, 496
opening paragraph. *See* introductory paragraph
operas, titles in italics, 437
opinion, consensus of, 484
opinions
  and fact, 33
  in literary essays, 217
oral reports, 303
oratory, classical, 62
ordinal numbers, 320, 460
organization, 50–57
  chronological, 56–57
  in classical rhetoric, 62
  coherence, 65–69
  deciding on, 50
  with formal outline, 54–56
  innovative patterns, 64–65
  internal patterns, 60–62
  process-based, 58
  spatial, 59–60
  the thesis, 50–54
organizations, names of, 462
orientate, orient, 497
ought not, hadn't ought to; ought to have, had ought to, 490

outline
　organizing with, 54–56
　of research paper, 258–61
　of scientific report, 300
outside commentary, and revision, 131
outside of, outside, 492–93
overall, 497

page numbers, figures for, 460
paragraphs, 72–88
　in abstract, 298
　of analogy, 75
　of analysis, 76–77
　cause-and-effect development, 80–81
　checklist for, 88
　of classification, 76
　of comparison and contrast, 77–78
　concluding, 87–88, 143
　deductive pattern, 72
　of definition, 74
　of description, 78–80
　of illustration, 74–75
　inductive pattern, 72–73
　introductory, 83–86, 137–40, 141, 219
　omitted in quotation, 442
　mixed patterns of development, 81–83
　revision, 137–43
　topic sentence, 72–73, 132, 140
　transitional, 86–87
parallelism, **358–59**
　elliptical construction, 353
　faulty, 339–40
　and sentence style, 104–5
　use of, 387–88
paraphrase, in note-taking, 251–52
parentheses, 428–31
　distinguished from brackets, 428, 431
　for entire sentence, 429
　for nonessential material, 428–29
　with other punctuation, 429
　in scientific citations, 257
　and sentence style, 105
participial phrases, 323
participles
　and auxiliary verbs, 349
　dangling, 356–57
　defined, **359**
　formation, 316
　as nonfinite form, 364
　and principal parts of verb, 361
　in verbal phrases, 365
particles, with verbs, **365**
partitio, 63
parts of speech
　avoiding wrong use, 393–94
　defined, **359**
　dictionary information, 113
passed, *past,* 497

passive voice
　avoiding overuse of, 95–96, 389–90
　awkward, **349**
　defined, 365
　and sentence patterns, 336–37
past participles, 316, 365
past tense, 316
peace, piece, 497
performing arts, reference sources, 273
periodical articles, references to
　APA reference list style, 258
　on bibliography cards, 247
　MLA bibliography style, 257
　MLA footnote style, 272
periodicals
　indexes, 272
　titles in italics, 437, 439
periodic sentences, 102–3
periods, with quotation marks, 438
peroratio, 63, 197, 198
person
　agreement in, **347–48**, 378
　defined, **359**
　as verb property, 364
personal, personnel, 497
personal pronouns, 312, 361
persons
　names of, capitalized, 462
　titles of abbreviated, 459
persuade, convince, 484
persuasion, 186–200. *See also* argument
phenomenon, phenomena, 485
phrases
　defined, **359**
　functioning as nouns, **358**
　prepositional. *See* prepositional phrases
　types, 322–24
　verb, 364
　verbal, 365
piece, peace, 497
pity, appeal to, 40
place names
　capitalized, 462
　spelled out, 458
plagiarism, 249
plays
　quotations from verse drama, 229
　titles in italics, 437, 439
plenty, very, 497
plot analysis
　of film, 233
　of literary work, 213
plurals
　formation of, 453–56
　possessive forms, 432, 434–35
poems
　quotations from, 229–30, 442, 443
　titles in italics, 439, 441
　titles in quotation marks, 437, 440

point of view, analysis of, 215
political science, reference sources, 274
positive degree, 351
positive wording, 101–2
possessive adjectives, 360, **361**
possessive case, 349
possessive nouns, **358**
  and case forms, 349
  formation, 320, 361, 432–33
  compound, 433
  two or more together, 433
possessive pronouns, 312, 320, **361**
  confused with contractions, 433–34
  no apostrophe with, 360, 434
  and pronoun cases, 349
possessives
  functions, 320, **359–60**
  apostrophe with, 432–33
precede, proceed, 497
précis, 298
predicate
  basic patterns, 330–32
  of clause, 349
  function, 310, **360**
predicate adjectives
  with linking verbs, 351, 356, **360**
  modification, 332
  two types, 346
predicate nominative, 332
predicate nouns, 351, 356, **360**
predication, faulty, 395–96
predominant, predominate, 497–98
prefixes
  hyphenated, 425
  and spelling, 449, 451
  and syllabication, 457
premiere, 498
prepositional phrases, 322, 360
  as adjectives, 346
  as adverbs, 347
  for indirect object, 355
  possessives, 359
  structure, 359
prepositions, **360–61**
  improper use, 397
  piled up, 95
  as verbal particles, 365
present infinitive, as principle part, 316
presently, now, 498
present participles, 316, 365
present tense, formation, 314
previous to, prior to, before, 498
prewriting, 11–13
principal parts of verb, 316, **361**
principle, principal, 498
probes
  for argument, 189
  example of, 15–21
  for introductory praragraph, 85–86

for literary essay, 211–12
  as preliminary to writing, 13–15
  for research paper, 242
  use in revision, 135, 139
proceed, precede, 497
process description,
  as form of exposition, 177–78
  in paragraph development, 79
  pattern of organization, 58–59
professional titles
  abbreviations, 459
  spelled out, 458
progressive aspect, 315
pronouns, **361–62**
  adjectival, 362
  agreement with antecedent, 347, 348,
    361, 381–84
  cases, 349, 384–85
  demonstrative, 352
  gender, 354
  indefinite, 348, 362
  interrogative, 355, 362
  person, 359
  personal, 361
  possessive, 320, 349, 359–60, 433–34
  in quotations, 230
  reflexive, 362
  relative, 350, 361–62
  types, 312
pronunciation, dictionary information, 113
proof, 197. *See also* evidence
proofreading
  in final draft, 145
  vs. revision, 134
proper nouns. *See also* names
  containing common nouns, 462–63
  defined, 311, **362**
  with hyphenated prefix, 425
prophecy, prophesy, 498
propositio, 63
proved, proven, 499
provided, provided that, providing, 499
psychology
  reference style, 258
publication information, in card catalog,
    246
Publications Manual of the American
    Psychological Association (APA),
    253–54, 258
punctuation, 411–43
  apostrophes, 432–35
  colons, 418–21, 438
  commas, 411–15. *See also* commas
  dashes, 421–23, 427, 438
  ellipses, 441–43
  exclamation points, 427–28, 438–39
  in footnotes, 255
  hyphens, 423–26, 456–57
  italics, 439–41

punctuation (*cont.*)
  parentheses and brackets, 428–31
  question marks, 425–26, 438–39
  quotation marks, 435–39. *See also*
    quotation marks
  of quotations, 229–30
  semicolons, 416–18. *See also* semicolons
  slashes, 230, 443
purposeful(ly), *purposely*, 499

question marks, 425–26
  with direct question, 426
  to express skepticism, 427
  with interrupters, 427
  with quotation, 426
  with quotation marks, 438–39
questions
  begging of, 37
  direct and indirect, **353**
  on essay exams, 280–81
  in imperative moood, 357
  with interrogative pronouns, 362
  interrogative words, 355–56
  in introductory paragraph, 86
  within other questions, 426
  after oral report, 303
  patterns, 333–35
quiet, *quite*, 499
quotation marks, 435–39
  in dialogue, 436
  with direct questions, 353
  with direct quotations, 435–36
  for emphasis, 436–37
  to enclose titles, 437
  in footnotes, 255
  in literary essay, 229
  with other punctuation, 437–39
  in paraphrase, 251–52
  single, 436, 438
  for words used as words, 436–37
quotations
  author's insertions, 430–31
  avoiding in abstracts, 298
  capitalization, 230, 461
  direct, 250–51, 420
  in literary essay, 212, 217, 229–30
  omissions, 441–42
  of poetry, 442, 443
  punctuation, 420, 435–39
  within quotations, 436, 439
  with questions mark, 426
  in research paper, 250–51
quote, *quotation*, 499

races, names of, 462
raise, *rise*, 499
rarely ever, *seldom ever*, 499
rational appeals
  confusing the issue, 37–39
  without enough facts, 34–37
  mixed with emotional and ethical
    appeals, 39–40
  proper use of, 29–30
Reader's Guide to Periodical Literature,
  The, 243
reason, in rational appeals, 29–30
reason is because, reason is that, 499–500
reckon, calculate, guess, 481–82
record albums, titles in italics, 437
redundancy, 403, 473
refer, allude, 476
refer back, 475
reference list, 258. *See also* bibliography
reference sources, 271–75
  almanacs and yearbooks, 272
  art, 273
  atlases, 272
  bibliographical citations, 256–58
  biographical, 271–72
  business and economics, 274
  dictionaries, 271
  footnote citations, 254–56
  history, 274
  literature, 273
  mythology and folklore, 273
  periodical and newspaper indexes, 272
  philosophy, 272
  political science, 274
  psychology, 274
  quotations, 272
  religion, 272–73
  science and technology, 275
  sociology and anthropology, 274
reflexive pronouns, 312, 353, 361
refutatio, 197
regretfully, 347
  vs. *regrettably*, 500
  sentence modifier, 347
regular verbs, 314, 359, **361**
relative clauses. *See also* subordinate
  clauses
  as adjectives, 346
  function, 325
  and relative pronouns, 361–62
  restrictive and nonrestrictive, 326
  in subject, 328
relative pronouns, 312, 350, 361–62
religion, reference sources, 272–73
reports
  for business, 296
  oral, 303
  for school, 299
requests, 357
research papers, 240–75
  defined, 240
  documentation, 253–58
  ideas for, 241
  library research, 242–48

note-taking, 248–53
outlining, 258–61
references sources, 271–75
writing and revising, 261–70
respectfully, respectively, 500
restrictive adjectives, **362**
restrictive appositives, 348
restrictive clauses, 326
resumes, 286–90
 chronological, 290
 format and appearance, 287
 functional, 288–89
revision, 130–51
 of body paragraphs, 140–41
 checklist for, 132–34
 of concluding paragraph, 143
 distancing, 130–34
 example, 146–50
 of mechanics, 145. *See also* mechanics
 of opening paragraph, 137–40
 under pressure, 150–51
 proofreading, 145
 of research paper, 261–62
 of sentences, 143–44
 of strategy, 141–42
 of thesis statement, 136–37
 of title and lead-in, 135–36
 use of probes, 134
 of words, 144–45
revolve on, revolve around, 482
rhetoric, classical, 62–63
rhythm, of sentence, 106
right, rite, 500
role-playing, and distancing, 132–34
run-on sentences, **363**, 374–75

sacred names, 463
scarcely. See *can't scarcely*
scholarly journals, references to
 APA reference list style, 258
 MLA bibliography style, 257
 MLA footnote style, 255, 256
scientific terminology, 440
scientific writing, 299–303
seldom ever, 499
self-, 425
semicolons, 416–18
 with conjunctive adverbs, 352
 to correct fused sentence, 354
 linking independent clauses, 341, 416–17
 with quotation marks, 438
 to prevent comma splice, 350
 to separate items in a series that
  contains commas, 418
sensory appeals, 167–68
sentence fragments, **363**
 clauses as, 329
 how to correct, 369–71
 skillful use, 368

sentence modifiers, 95, 347
sentences, 94–107
 in abstract, 298
 antithesis in, 104
 balanced, 103–4
 checklist for, 107
 and clauses, 349–50
 eliminating deadwood in, 401–3
 errors in construction, 368–75
 examining for revision, 143–44
 first word capitalized, 461
 four main patterns, 343
 fused, 354
 length, 99–100
 making parts agree, 377–90
 minimum requirements, 368
 normal word order, 332
 numbers at beginning of, 460
 in oral report, 303
 parallelism, 104–5, 339–40, **358–59**,
  387–88
 in parentheses, 429
 periodic, 102–3
 pitfalls in writing, 94–97
 positioning of elements, 101
 positive wording, 101
 predicate, **360**
 rhythm, 106
 run-on **363**, 374–75
 subject, **363–64**
 structure, 98–99
 style, 100–106
 topic, 72–73, 132, 140
 variations in, 97–100, 332–37
set, sit, 500
setting, literary analysis, 214
sexist language, 117–18
s/he, 443
shift, inappropriate, **363**
short poems, titles of, 437, 440
short stories, titles of, 437, 440
sic, 430
sight, site, cite, 483
simple sentences, 98, 343
single quotation marks
 with other punctuation, 438
 for quotations within quotations, 436
singular nouns, 358, 432
slang
 acceptance of, 114
 problem of, in formal writing, **363**
 usage label, 472
slashes, 230, 443
social sciences
 documentation style, 257–58
someplace, somewhere, 478
sometime, some time, 500–501
somewheres, somewhere, 501
song titles, 437, 440

sort of a, sort of, 493
sound-alike words, 121
sources. *See also* documentation; reference sources
  crediting in research paper, 253–58
  culling, 249–50
  leads between, 247–48
  scientific citation, 257
spatial organization, 59–60, 79
specificity, in description, 166
speech, parts of, 113, **359**, 393–94
spelling
  dictionary information, 113
  formation of plurals, 453–56
  general problems, 448–53
  syllabication, 456–57
squinting modifiers, **357**
standard usage, 472–73
stationary, stationery, 501
statistics, 31, 32–33
stereotyping, 36
strategy, revision of, 141–43
stratum, strata, 485
street addresses
  figures in, 460
  spelled out, 458
structure
  of literary essay, 216–28
  of sentences, 98–99
style
  of an abstract, 298–99
  of sentences, 94, 100–106
subject (grammatical)
  agreement with verb, 347, 378–80
  basic patterns, 327–29
  of clause, 349
  delayed, 96
  form of personal pronouns, **361**
  function, 310
  noun clause as, 328, 350
  of sentence, **363–64**
subject (of writing). *See also* subject probe
  analyzing for argumentation, 191–92
  discerning order in, 56–60
subject cards, 244–45
subjective complement, 351, 360
subjective description, 165–67
subjective narration, 167–71
subjective process, 79–80
subject probe
  for opening paragraph, 139
  as preparation for writing, 14–15
  for revision, 135
subjunctive mood, 316–18, 357
subordinate (dependent) clauses
  defined, 350
  positioning, 342–43
  recognizing, 324–26
  relative. *See* relative clauses

subordinating conjunctions, 350, 352
subordination, methods, 342–43
subordinators, 350
subtitles, with colon, 421
suffixes
  hyphenated, 425
  spelling, 449, 450–53
  syllabication, 457
summary, in note-taking, 252–53
superlative degree, 321, 351
supposed to, used to, 501
sure, surely, certainly, 501
syllabication, 113, 456–57
synonyms, 113–14
syntax, **364**

tag questions, 335
take, bring, fetch, 481
take and . . . , 501
tape recorder, for revision, 132
technical writing, 299–303
technology, reference sources, 275
television series, titles of, 439
tense. *See* verb tense
testimony, external, 31
textual evidence, 217–18
than, then, 501
that, which, who, 501–2
that is, i.e., 491
that there, 502
their, they're, 433–34
  distinguished from *there,* 502
theirselves, themselves, 502
then, than, 501
there
  distinguished from *their, they're, 502*
  as expletive, 335
there is , there are, 96, 101, 502
thesauri
  reference sources, 271
  use of, 112–15
theme, literary analysis, 215
thesis, 50–54
  examining for revision, 136–37
  in literary essay, 217, 219–22
  placing, 53–54
  producing, 50–51
  for research paper, 259–60
  revising, 132
  supporting, 51–53
thesis statement, 197
this, 502
this here, these here, that there, those there, 502
though, although, 477
thusly, thus, 503
till, until; til, 'til, 'till, 503
time

as distancer, 131
units of, spelled out, 458
use of colon with numerals, 421
time of day, figures for, 460
time order. *See* chronological order
title card, 244
title page, 463–64
titles
abbreviated, 459
of books and articles, 463
in card catalog, 246
choosing for literary essay, 218–19
of courses, 458
enclosed in quotation marks, 437
in footnotes, 255
in italics, 437, 439–40
of persons, 462
professional, 458, 459
revision of, 135–36
to, at, 503
to, too, two, 503
to be. See *be*
topic sentence
of body paragraph, 140
position, 72–73
revising, 132
tracings, in card catalog, 246
transitional paragraphs, 86–87
transitional words, 66, 87
transitive verbs
complement, 351
correct use, 394–95
defined, 313, 364
direct objects, 353
predicate patterns, 331
translated works, references to, 256
try and, try to, 503
type, type of, -type, 503
unabridged dictionaries, 271
uninterested, disinterested, 486
until, 503
use, utilize, 503
used to, 501
usage
defined, **364**
dictionary information, 113
inappropriate level, 400–401
labels, 472–73
reference guides, 271
utilize, use, 503

vague generalizations, 217
vagueness, 404–5
value judgments, hidden, 194–95
verbal phrases, 323–24
constituents, 365
structure, 359
as subject, 328
verbals, 316, **365**

verb phrase
constituents, 364
normal order, 333
verbs, 313–18, **364**
agreement with subject, 347, 378–80
aspect, 315
in abstracts, 298
auxiliary. *See* auxiliary verbs
complements, **351**
compound, 378–79, 381
finite, 353–54, 364
infinitives, 355
linking, 313–14, 331–32, **356**, 360, 364
mood, 316–18, **357**, 364
with particle, **365**
participles, 349, **359**, 365
person, **359**, 364
principal parts, 316, **361**
properties, 364
regular and irregular, 314, 361, **362**
strong, 120
suffixes, 450
tense. *See* verb tense
transitive and intransitive, 313, 364,
394–95
types, 313–14
voice. *See* voice
verb tense, 314–16, **364**
in abstracts, 298
agreement, 230
aspects, 364
inappropriate shifts, **363**, 381
in quotations, 230
as verb property, 364
verse drama, quoting from, 229
very, plenty, 497
voice, 95–96, 336–37, **365**, 389–90
in abstracts, 298
awkward passive, 349
as verb property, 364
volume numbers, 255

waffling, 142
wait on, wait for, 504
weasel words, 120
Webster's New World Dictionary, 112, 473
well, good, 490
winking modifiers, **357**
when and if, 491
where . . . at, where . . . to, 504
which, who, that, 501–2
who/whom, 383–85
whose, who's, 433–34, 504
-wise, 504
with respect to, about, as to, 478–79
wording, positive, 101–2
word guides, reference sources, 271
words, 112–24
appropriate use, 393–407

words *(cont.)*
  compound, 452, 456
  dictionary and thesaurus information,
    112–15
  denotation and connotation, 121–23
  examining for revision, 144–45
  general vs. specific, 118–20
  guides for selection, 120–21
  inflated, 115–17
  invented, 399–400
  letters used as, 434
  misuse, 397–99
  syllabication, 456–57
  used as words, 436–37, 440
word selection problems, 393–407
  clichés, 405–6
  deadwood, 401–3
  euphemisms, 405
  faulty predication, 395–96
  improper idiom, 396
  inappropriate and mixed metaphors,
    406–7
  inappropriate level of usage, 400–401
  invented words, 399–400
  misuse of words, 397–99
  redundancy, 403
  transitive and intransitive verbs, 394–95
  vagueness, 404–5
  wrong part of speech, 393–94
worse than, inferior than, inferior to, 492
writing
  four stages, 9–11
  mechanics, 448–53
  for oneself, 4–6, 13
  for others, 6–8
  preparation for, 11–21
  three components, 8–9

yearbooks, 272
your, you're, 433–34, 504

SUBJECT GUIDE TO
"A REVIEW OF GRAMMAR"– Chapter 13

The major sections that make up the grammar review appear in alphabetical order. They are printed in boldface color along with their page numbers. Beneath each boldface heading appears a list—also in alphabetical order—of all key terms and phrases in that section.

Clauses 324–327
Adverbial clause   325
Dependent clause   324
Independent clause   324
Nonrestrictive clause   326
Noun clause   325
Relative clause   325
Restrictive clause   326
Subordinate clause   324
Subordinating
    conjunction   325

Compounding 338–344
Complex sentences   342
Compound sentences   341
Compound-complex
    sentences   343
Conjunctive adverbs   342
Coordinating
    conjunctions   338
Parallel structure   339
Simple sentences   338

Modification 319–322
Adverbs   320
Attributive
    adjectives   319
Comparative degree   321
Definite article   319
Demonstratives   320
Determiners   319
Indefinite article   319
Intensifiers   321
Manner, place, and time   320
Numbers   320
Possessives   320
Superlative degree   321

Nouns and Pronouns 311–313
Collective nouns   312
Common nouns   311
Concrete nouns   311
Demonstrative
    pronouns   312
Indefinite pronouns   312
Interrogative
    pronouns   312
Personal pronouns   312
Proper nouns   311
Possessive pronouns   312
Reflexive pronouns   312
Relative pronouns   312

Phrases 322–324
Gerund   323
Gerund phrase   323
Infinitive phrase   323
Noun phrase   322
Participial phrase   323
Prepositional
    phrase   322
Verb phrase   322
Verbal   323
Verbal phrase   323

Predicate Patterns 330–332
Adverbial   330
Direct object   331
Indirect object   331
Intransitive verb   330
Linking verb   331
Predicate adjective   332
Predicate nominative   332
Predicate noun   332
Transitive verb   331

Sentence Patterns 332–336
Active voice   336
Indirect objects   335
Interrupters   337
Passive voice   336
Questions   333
There / it as expletives   335

**Subjects and
    Predicates 310–311**

Subject Patterns 327–330
Clause   328
Noun plus relative
    clause   328
Noun plus modifier   328
Simple noun   327
Verbal   328

Verbs 313–319
Aspect   315
Attitude   315
Auxiliary verbs   315
Imperative mood   316
Indicative mood   316
Intransitive verb   313
Irregular verbs   314
Linking verbs   313
Modal auxiliaries   316
Past participle   316
Present infinitive   316
Present participle   316
Principal parts   316
Subjunctive mood   316
Tense   314
Transitive verb   313
Verbal   323